The American South

A HISTORY

Volume I

The American South

A HISTORY

Volume I

Second Edition

❖

WILLIAM J. COOPER, JR.
Louisiana State University

THOMAS E. TERRILL
University of South Carolina

The McGraw-Hill Companies, Inc.

New York   St. Louis   San Francisco   Auckland   Bogotá   Caracas
Lisbon   London   Madrid   Mexico City   Milan   Montreal   New Delhi
San Juan   Singapore   Sydney   Tokyo   Toronto

McGraw-Hill

A Division of The **McGraw·Hill** *Companies*

THE AMERICAN SOUTH
A History
Volume I

This book is printed on acid-free paper.

1 2 3 4 5 6 7 8 9 0   DOC   DOC   9 0 9 8 7 6 5

ISBN 0-07-064438-1

This book was set in Palatino by Ruttle, Shaw & Wetherill, Inc.
The editor was Lyn Uhl;
the production supervisor was Richard A. Ausburn.
The cover was designed by Karen K. Quigley.
Project supervision was done by The Total Book.
R. R. Donnelley & Sons Company was printer and binder.

On the Cover: Slave Quarters, Sugar Cane Plantation near Donaldsonville, Louisiana. Although this photograph dates from about 1880, the scene (except for the railroad tracks) conveys the antebellum world. *Source:* The Historic New Orleans Collection, accession no. 1978.26.56.

Library of Congress Catalog Card Number: 95-81519.

About the Authors

❖

William J. Cooper, Jr. is a Boyd Professor at Louisiana State University. He received his A.B. degree from Princeton University and his Ph.D. from The Johns Hopkins University. Professor Cooper has spent his entire professional career on the faculty at Louisiana State University, where he also served as dean of the Graduate School from 1982 to 1989. He has held fellowships from the Institute of Southern History at Johns Hopkins, from the Charles Warren Center at Harvard, from the Guggenheim Foundation, and from the National Endowment for the Humanities.

He is the author of *The Conservative Regime: South Carolina, 1877–1890* (1968); *The South and the Politics of Slavery, 1828–1856* (1978); and *Liberty and Slavery: Southern Politics to 1860* (1983). He has also edited two books and written numerous articles. In addition, from 1979 to 1993, Professor Cooper was editor of the *Southern Biography Series* published by the Louisiana State University Press.

Thomas E. Terrill is Professor of History at the University of South Carolina. He received his Ph.D. from the University of Wisconsin and has been the recipient of fellowships from the National Endowment for the Humanities and from the Rockefeller Foundation. Most recently, he has been Fulbright Lecturer at the University of Genoa, Italy.

In addition to publishing several books as well as publications in periodicals and proceedings, he has helped produce a feature film for national television, a documentary, and a television course for undergraduate and graduate students. His most recent book is his co-edited *The American South Comes of Age*.

For
William Cooper and Holmes Cooper
and
Andrea Terrill and Mitchell Terrill

Contents

———— ❖ ————

Preface

———— ❖ ————

his is the second edition of *The American South: A History*. Second editions
are happy events. They mean that people liked your first edition. That is
welcome news for the authors.

Second editions, fortunately, take less time than do first editions. This one
took a good deal less than the ten years we spent on its predecessor, the first successful attempt to write a comprehensive history of the American South in forty
years. During those forty years, the South underwent sweeping changes in race
relations, in its economic system, and in its politics. At the same time, the study of
the South, how we understand the region, experienced similarly dramatic change.
No region in this country has attracted comparable attention from scholars. We
worked hard to incorporate these developments in *The American South.*

There are a number of changes in this edition. The narrative has been brought
up to 1995, and more attention has been given to several things, including the
French and Spanish colonial era, the western portion of the South, women, and
music. There is an expanded, updated bibliographical essay; some changes and
additions in the photographs, maps, and tables; and a new, revised index.

The themes and the thematic structure of the book remain unchanged, as does
the chronological framework. *The American South* reflects the basic assumption
that the South is both thoroughly American in its life and culture, yet a distinctive
region even today. The complex tension between being both like the rest of the nation but distinctive has been continuous, but how the tension was expressed varied over time from heightened expressions of superpatriotism during the War of
1812, the Spanish American War, and the Cold War to a sense of profound alien-
ation that underlay secession and the bloodiest American war, the Civil War.

The South is a joint creation of blacks and whites, so much so that we only reluctantly, for the sake of convenience, follow the convention that "southerners"
are white. We explicitly deviate from that convention in several critical instances.
The dynamics of black-white relations from slavery to the Civil Rights revolution
and thereafter are also a central theme here, as are social class and gender roles.
"Southern lady" may be a regional icon and often a reality, but women, black and
white, have been participants and catalysts throughout southern history.

Our story is set within the context of forces that recognized no national or re-

gional boundaries: European overseas empires, plantation economies and involuntary labor, the American Revolution, the western expansion of the new nation,
the revolutionary changes in life and labor in the wake of industrialization, ur-
banization and the postindustrial revolution, immigration and migration, and
new directions in cultural and intellectual currents.

We start with the colonial era, with emphasis upon British colonialism because it was so formative in the past of the American South. The first half of the
book covers the more than two and a half centuries from European colonialism in
the South to the Civil War, in which the South, as the Confederate States of America, attempted to establish its independence. The second half focuses upon recov-
ery from defeat in the Civil War to the New South and then our own time, the
Modern South.

A subtle change in the narrative requires brief discussion. There is less stress
on the South as reactive, more on the South as proactive. Dubbed "Uncle Sam's
Other Province," the South has been perceived as American, but so different as to
be an exotic dependent peopled at various times by slaves and masters, southern
ladies, shoeless dirt farmers, passive ex-slaves and their progeny, religious xeno-
phobes, and paunchy courthouse politicians. That image hardly correlates with
the dynamism of the region. Among other things, the South had a leading role in
the American Revolution, precipitated the Civil War, figured prominently in both
the populist and the progressive movements, and provided the setting and the
principal leaders for one of the most important movements in American history,
the Civil Rights revolution. Post-World War II politics in America has been profoundly shaped by developments and leaders in the South.

Throughout the book we have tried to incorporate the newer scholarship on
the South. Scholarly interest in the South has been intense. The product of that interest is remarkable and has transformed how historians understand traditional
subjects, like political leadership, plantation economics, and Reconstruction. At
the same time, historians have given previously neglected topics such as the slave
family, blacks since slavery, southern industrial workers, and women a great deal
more attention. The scope of the scholarship on the history of the South is reflected in the comprehensiveness of the bibliographical essay at the end of this
book. The essay is intended to be a guide to the major literature on the history of
the South.

Our debts to others have not changed. They have grown. That is particularly
true of our debts to our wives, Patricia and Sarah. Not once—at least within our
hearing—have they said, "Can't they talk about something else."

The extent of our debts to fellow scholars is indicated in the bibliographical
essay. Former and currently enrolled graduate students at Louisiana State University helped a great deal: Bradley Bond, Ralph Eckert, Kenneth Startup, Eric
Walther, and Keven Yeager. At the University of South Carolina, James A. Dunlap,
III, Janet Hudson, James Tidd, and Luther Faggart did likewise. Our manuscript
was reviewed by: Walter Buenger, Texas A&M University; David L. Carlton, Van-
derbilt University; Willard Gatewood, University of Arkansas; John Inscoe, The
University of Georgia; and Bertram Wyatt-Brown, University of Florida. Additional colleagues and friends who generously agreed to read portions of our manuscript and made valuable suggestions included: Robert Becker, Keen Butter-

worth, Lacy K. Ford, Jr., Gaines M. Foster, Benjamin Franklin, V, Michael F. Holt, David Katzman, Daniel Littefield, David W. Murphy, Sydney Nathans, Paul Paskoff, George Rable, Charles Royster, Allen H. Stokes, Jr., Robert M. Weir, John Scott Wilson, and R. Jackson Wilson. W. Lynn Shirley helped with maps. Several Italian colleagues and friends provided valuable perspectives: Varleria Gennaro Lerda, Fernando Fasce, and Giovanni Fabbi.

The support of fine editors was essential to the success of the first edition: Niels Aaboe, David Follmer, Jane Garrett, Christopher Rogers, and Jack Wilson. Peter Labella initiated the second edition. Lyn Uhl and Jane Vaicunas took up that effort and supervised its completion, aided by the close attention Annette Bodzin gave to the production of this edition. Working with them has been a pleasure; still, the book is ours, and we accept full responsibility for it.

William J. Cooper, Jr.
Thomas E. Terrill

$\mathcal{P}$rologue

The Enduring South

———— ❖ ————

he South, Wilbur Cash wrote in his celebrated book *The Mind of the South* (1941), is "not quite a nation within a nation but the next thing to it." The sources of that enduring distinctiveness are many and complex. As early as 1750, a generation before Americans went to war against Great Britain to secure their political independence, clear differences distinguished the southern colonies from the northeastern and middle Atlantic colonies. Those differences persisted after the American Revolution and intensified during the first half of the nineteenth century. By 1860, though the similarities among the states remained powerful, the gap between the South and the rest of the country had grown into a chasm that seemingly could not be bridged by any compromise. The American South had become synonymous, though not entirely identical, with plantations, cotton, and black slavery—with places such as Davis Bend, Mississippi.

Thirty-odd miles south of Vicksburg, Mississippi, Davis Bend was a fertile peninsula formed by a large horseshoe curve of the Mississippi River. Today, more than four generations since the flood tides of war swept over it, Davis Bend and the people who lived there in 1860 provide important clues to southern identity before that time and since. The bend got its name from Joseph Davis, a large landholder in the area and the eldest brother of Jefferson Davis, president of the Confederacy. He had prospered as a lawyer in Natchez, Mississippi, a booming cotton and commercial center that served as the capital of Mississippi until 1817, when the territory became a state. He was intensely interested in politics, and when his youngest brother, Jefferson, developed an interest in a political career, he frequently turned to Joseph for advice.

Joseph Davis bought most of the 11,000 acres of Davis Bend from the federal government in 1818 and obtained the rest from several frontier farmers who had been the first whites to settle and clear the area. Davis sold off 6,000 acres of the bend to friends. Then in 1827, when he was forty-two, he left his law practice and with his sixteen-year-old bride, three daughters from his earlier marriage, and a few slaves he had inherited from his father established a plantation at the bend.

xix

Eight years later, Jefferson Davis started a plantation of his own on 800 acres that Joseph had given him.

During the next three decades, Joseph Davis became a very wealthy man. In 1860 he was one of only nine planters in Mississippi with more than 300 slaves. He had a spacious mansion and almost a village of outbuildings, which included a cluster of slave cottages. To protect his holdings from flooding by the great river that almost encircled it, Davis and the other leading planters at Davis Bend built a mile-and-a-half-long levee that was six to eighteen feet high. Davis's twenty-five-acre flower garden was so spectacular that passengers disembarked from river steamboats to tour it. No doubt the tourists knew they were in the American South and that their host was a southerner. Neither Davis nor his plantation was typical of the South, though both were typical of what many southerners aspired to.

Davis's background did resemble that of a majority of antebellum southerners. His grandfather, son of a Welsh immigrant, was born in Philadelphia around 1730 and moved as a young man to the colonial South, first to South Carolina, then to Georgia. Joseph's father, Samuel, fought in the American Revolution, married a South Carolina woman he met while serving in the military, and took up farming near Augusta, Georgia, on land the state had given him for his military

DAVIS BEND, MISSISSIPPI (New York Public Library, Schaumberg Collection)

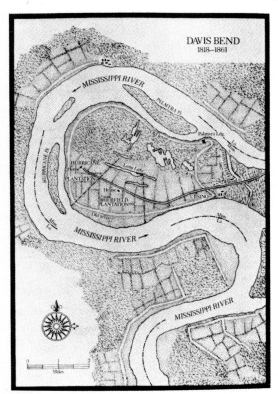

service. The family moved to Kentucky in 1793, a year after the territory had become a state, and there they produced two of that region's principal products: tobacco and horses. In 1810 the Davis family moved again, still pursuing the frontier; eventually they settled in southwestern Mississippi, an area that only nine years earlier had been ceded by the Choctaws. Settlers such as the Davises kept continual pressure on Indians to vacate western land so that whites could safely settle there. In the 1830s the Choctaws and Chickasaws gave up the last of their holdings in Mississippi and moved west beyond Arkansas to what was called Indian Territory. Whites later followed the Indians, took over most of their land, and created the state of Oklahoma; the name means "home of the Indian."

On their newly acquired land in Mississippi the Davises cultivated cotton as their major cash crop. To clear the land and plant, cultivate, and harvest the cotton, they relied on their own labor and the handful of slaves Samuel owned. Improving fortunes allowed them to build a substantial home graced by a veranda—a large step up from the four-room log cabin the family had occupied in Kentucky. The family of Samuel Davis strongly resembled the great majority of whites who populated the South from its earliest years to the Civil War: yeoman farmers who pushed south and west for more than a century and a half in search of cheap, fertile soil, frequently acquiring a few slaves, always bending their backs as they tried to improve their lot and station.

Their pursuit of the southern version of the American dream propelled such families from Virginia into the Carolinas and Georgia, southward into Florida, and westward as far as Texas before 1860. These pioneering farmers often settled in areas very different from the great plantation regions of which Davis Bend was a part. They made up the great majority of farmers in the mountains of Appalachia and the Ozarks and were predominant in the valleys and rolling hills of the piedmont and along the vast coastal plain that ran from the Chesapeake through Florida and on to the Texas gulf coast. Other southerners made their places in the cities and towns of the overwhelmingly agricultural South. Such places were sites for commercial enterprise and some manufacturing. Urban areas also afforded desired refinements for their residents and for the surrounding countryside.

Joseph Davis found Natchez a good place for an ambitious attorney, and Jefferson Davis attended a private academy near there as well as one in Kentucky. Like many ambitious Americans at the time, the youngest Davis believed that advanced education could improve his prospects. Thus, Jefferson graduated from academies to Transylvania University in Lexington, Kentucky, where he spent a year. Founded in 1780, Transylvania developed into the first center of learning west of the Appalachians and south of the Ohio River. Jefferson Davis completed his formal education at West Point. After an unexceptional academic career, he spent most of his seven-year army career at frontier posts in Wisconsin, Illinois, and Oklahoma.

Jefferson Davis briefly returned to the military in the 1840s, where he fought with distinction in the Mexican War. After 1835, however, he devoted most of his energies to his plantation and to his highly successful political career. Despite ill health, Davis drove himself to build first an impressive plantation estate and then an impressive political career. The latter pursuit required innumerable stump speeches, interminable rounds of political meetings, and mountains of correspondence with constituents and fellow politicians. Several heated disputes stopped just short of duels. Davis survived dirt roads, mud roads, carts, wagons, carriages, lurching spark-spewing trains, sailing ships, steamboats, inns, hotels, good food, bad food, and tobacco-spitting, importuning, and sometimes sweaty constituents from Mississippi to Washington and back. Davis represented his state in the United States House of Representatives and the Senate and served as a highly competent, dedicated secretary of war in the administration of President Franklin Pierce. Like other southerners in his day and later, Jefferson Davis was an American in his efforts to succeed and in his national loyalties. Indeed, Davis was convinced that as a leader first of the South in Congress and later of the Confederate States of America he was risking civil war and his life and fortune to preserve the Constitution, which he saw as the bulwark of liberty.

To Davis, the election of Abraham Lincoln posed a revolutionary threat; Lincoln's election meant the triumph of the antislavery movement—a movement dedicated to destroying southern rights. Announcing his resignation from the Senate in January 1861, Davis told his fellow senators and the nation that the southern states had been forced to secede from the Union because the Republicans who were coming to power "denie[d] us equality . . . refuse[d] to recognize our domestic institutions which preexisted the formation of the Union, our property which was guarded by the Constitution." He accused Lincoln of making "a distinct declaration of war upon our institutions." Davis asked that the states which chose to secede be allowed to do so peacefully, but if the North insisted that the South "remain as subjects to you, then, gentlemen of the North, a war is to be inaugurated the like of which men have not seen."

JOSEPH DAVIS (Eleanor S. Brockenbrough Library, Museum of the Confederacy, Richmond, Virginia)

In 1860 and 1861 the southern states seceded from the Union to prevent the federal government from intruding on their rights and abolishing slavery, the cornerstone of white southern society. To preserve the society the South took up arms against the Union. As a consequence, the Union intruded massively in the South—and with devastating impact—from 1861 until the end of Reconstruction in 1877. After the Civil War, the South erected a defense to ward off unwelcome outside intrusions in its race relations and other aspects of its life. The most concrete form of that defense was the "Solid South," or the thorough dominance of the South by the Democratic party. Fashioning itself as "the party of white supremacy," the Democratic party grounded its appeal on maintaining white unity in the South, keeping southern blacks subordinate ("in their place"), and preventing interference with that arrangement.

Erected during the 1870s and 1880s, the Solid South remained in place until after World War II. Breaches in the one-party politics of the Democratic South appeared earlier, however, under the federal government's efforts to combat the depression of the 1930s. The Solid South cracked during the 1948 presidential election, then shattered during the Civil Rights revolution of the 1950s and 1960s. Propelled by America's post-1940 economic boom and by massive federal spending in the region, a more prosperous, two-party South found a comfortable place in the Sunbelt and in national politics and became a much greater force in the nation than it had been at any previous time since the 1860s.

The South's failed attempt to reshape America by leaving the Union in 1860 defined the region and its people for all the generations that have followed. The South and southerners can be defined as the states that seceded and the people who supported secession and identified themselves then and later with what they believed was its noble cause. But defining the South and southerners only in terms of the Civil War is too narrow. Though that definition has the advantage of clarity, it seriously distorts the past and even the present. In this book, the southern states are defined as the eleven Confederate states plus Kentucky, Maryland, and, after the Civil War, Oklahoma, the creation of latter-day pioneers who erected a Dixie on the plains. Kentucky and Maryland nearly seceded. Both provided troops for the Confederacy, as did Missouri, a state deeply divided by the Civil War. This state-based definition of the South is hardly free of ambiguities. Parts of West Virginia, for instance, are more southern than west Texas, southern Florida, and parts of Kentucky and Oklahoma ever were, and substantial numbers of West Virginians served in the Confederate armed forces.

Using the Civil War as a reference point to define southerners is even more misleading. Not all southerners in the 1860s supported secession or identified with its cause, though they often suffered from the defeat of the Confederacy. Unionist sentiment was strongest in the South among mountain whites. Depredations during the war reinforced the Unionist feelings of many people, particularly in Appalachia. Black southerners celebrated the defeat of the Confederacy for obvious reasons. African-Americans lived all over the South in 1860, but usually on plantations such as those at Davis Bend, and they had interacted with whites since the seventeenth century to create much of what made the South. Without that interaction there would have been no South as the term and the region are commonly understood. Moreover, southern blacks and whites had and have striking cultural similarities and strikingly similar historical experiences. Both have experienced economic inferiority, and both have been disdained as cultural and moral inferiors. The labor, skills, and ideas of blacks have been critical to the development and evolution of the South. For the sake of convenience and clarity, however, southerners are white in this book unless we explicitly state otherwise or unless the context implies a different interpretation.

The Davises, especially Joseph Davis, certainly knew how important blacks were to them. They acknowledged the importance of blacks to their lives, in part by being lenient masters. Some local whites disparaged Joseph Davis's slaves as "Mr. Davis's free negroes." The neighbors may have had Benjamin Thornton Montgomery in mind when they said such things. Born into slavery in northern Virginia in 1819, Montgomery grew up as the companion of his young master. He moved westward involuntarily to Natchez in 1836 when, without notice or explanation, he was sold to a slave trader. The trader took Montgomery with a gang of other recently purchased slaves to the booming slave markets of Mississippi's black belt. There Joseph Davis bought Montgomery, but the young slave soon ran away. Unfamiliar with his new surroundings, Montgomery was caught almost immediately. When Davis questioned Montgomery about his attempted escape, he quickly realized Montgomery's considerable capacities and encouraged them. Montgomery, who had learned to read and write from his young master in Virginia, eventually became a mechanic, inventor, surveyor, builder, and merchant. He and his wife, Mary Lewis Montgomery, who was also literate, arranged, with Davis's approval, for the schooling of their children. Montgomery played a major role in the life of Davis Bend before and after the war reached the peninsula.

In January 1861, Jefferson Davis left Washington and returned home. In February he left Davis Bend to be inaugurated as president of the Confederacy. In April 1862, Joseph Davis took his family and about a hundred slaves and fled his river home to escape the advance of Union forces. Most of their slaves deserted them during their hasty retreat, and some of them later descended upon the mansion to pillage clothing and furniture. Union troops did even more damage when they arrived. Not long afterward, Benjamin Montgomery reasserted his leadership. Eventually, after the war, he bought the plantation from Joseph Davis, with whom he had maintained regular communication. For several years Montgomery succeeded, but forces beyond his control doomed his efforts. Eventually the community at Davis Bend dissolved. Even the river took its toll: the main channel of the Mississippi swept across the neck of the peninsula and turned Davis Bend into Davis Island.

The war destroyed the slave-based plantation society of the antebellum South: the South of planters, slaves, and highly profitable cash crops, which once was so easily identifiable, faded. Within a generation another, also easily identifiable South emerged: a region of chronic underdevelopment, poverty, one-party politics, and Jim Crow, a rigid racial caste system. Once again, to the rest of Americans the South was the deviant region. And it seemed not to change at all until World War II. That perception was wrong, however, just as was the perception that the antebellum South had been unchanging.

The South did not stand still from 1865 to 1940. The New South, a more urban, industrial South, began to appear soon after the Civil War, but it did not emerge fully until the 1920s. Still, low incomes persisted, race relations remained frozen, and one-party politics and impotence on the national scene seemed permanent conditions. But before World War II, each of these fundamental characteristics of the South after the Civil War began to change. The depression of the 1930s and the New Deal of President Roosevelt hastened change, and World War II accelerated the process by which the Sunbelt South emerged.

In the years since 1945, the economics, politics, and race relations of the South have changed so much that the South of the 1990s, the Sunbelt South, seems to have almost no connection with the South of Jefferson Davis or the South after the Civil War, even with the South of the 1930s. The South is now more prosperous than it has been at any previous time since the 1850s. Unlike the antebellum South, however, the Sunbelt South resembles the rest of the country in its politics and its race relations. Though vestiges of poverty, one-party politics, and Jim Crow remain, the picture of the poor, backward South has dissolved into an image of prosperity.

Defining southerner or southern identity is not so easy as it once was. One of the region's loyal sons and keen observers declared in 1973 that "the South is just about over as a separate . . . place." But a decade later another perceptive student of the South said that he "knows when he is in the South." The South may have lost some of its distinctiveness, but much remains. The South remains the United States' most obviously distinctive region in ways that are still very important: in culture and religion, in ethnic composition, in its sense of having a unique past, and in its sense of place. Southerners have deep attachments to their region. Those attachments have been expressed, among other ways, in the determination

BENJAMIN THORNTON
MONTGOMERY (Library of
Congress)

of southerners to remain Americans with a special regional identity even in the homogenized culture of the late twentieth century. That determination helps explain why the South has endured as the United States' most distinctive region for more than two hundred years and why the history of the South continues to fascinate so many people.

This book tries to answer two questions: What was and is the American South? What was and is a southerner? The answers to these questions depend largely on where and when they are asked. The answers are easier and clearer at some times than at others. The answer to the question about southern identity is harder and less clear now than at any time since the mid-eighteenth century. Still, the South endures. It endures in part because not even a flood of changes has washed away critical connections between the past and the present in the South.

The
American
South

A HISTORY

Volume I

Map Essay

The Geography of the South

❖

These maps delineate the major physical, geographical, and political features of the southern part of the United States. The physical characteristics of the land and the chief rivers did not change fundamentally between the seventeenth and the nineteenth centuries, though, of course, the rivers were named at different times. The political landscape of the South did change dramatically over time, however. The map on page 4 depicts the southern colonies in the middle of the eighteenth century. The following map shows the South at the end of the antebellum era. It locates the slave states in relationship to the rest of the country, marks their boundaries, and notes their dates of admission to the Union. The last map focuses on a key aspect of the colonial period by identifying the most important Indian tribes in the South and specifying their locations.

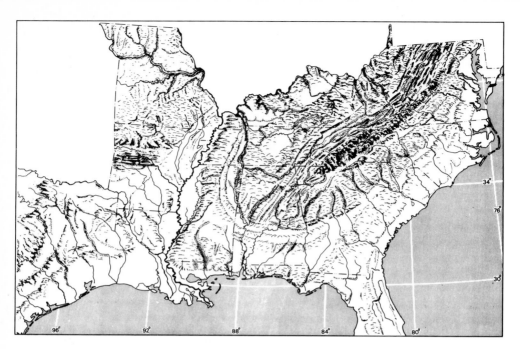

PHYSIOGRAPHIC FEATURES OF THE SOUTH (Reprinted by permission of Louisiana State University Press from *Atlas of Antebellum Southern Agriculture* by Sam Bowers Hilliard. Copyright © 1984 by Louisiana State University Press, 1984.)

GEOGRAPHIC FEATURES OF THE SOUTH

SOUTHERN RIVERS

THE SOUTHERN COLONIES IN 1750

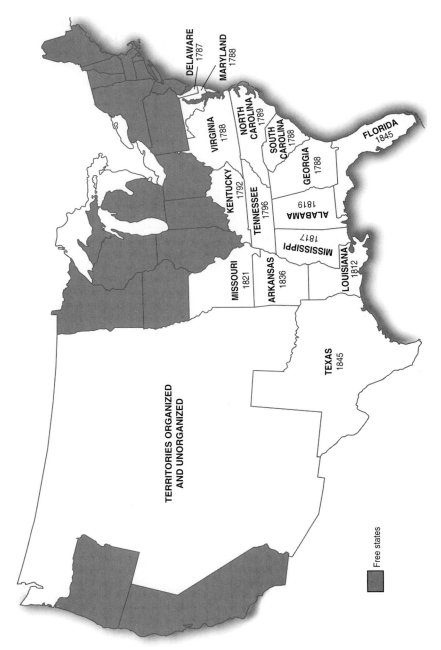

THE SLAVE STATES IN 1860

DELAWARE
1787

MARYLAND
1788

VIRGINIA
1788

NORTH
CAROLINA
1789

SOUTH
CAROLINA
1788

GEORGIA
1788

FLORIDA
1845

KENTUCKY
1792

TENNESSEE
1796

ALABAMA
1819

MISSISSIPPI
1817

MISSOURI
1821

ARKANSAS
1836

LOUISIANA
1812

TEXAS
1845

TERRITORIES ORGANIZED
AND UNORGANIZED

Free states

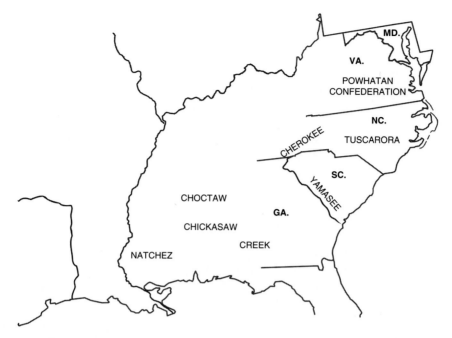

MAJOR INDIAN TRIBES ENCOUNTERED BY THE COLONISTS

1
The Beginnings

———— ❖ ————

Young George Percy landed in Virginia in May 1607. He arrived as one of 105 settlers who had sailed across the Atlantic from England in three small ships. In honor of their king, James I, they named their settlement Jamestown. A former soldier and the eighth son of an English nobleman, the twenty-six-year-old Percy and his compatriots were imbued with the notion that they were engaged in a great enterprise to benefit both England and the English.

Percy left an eyewitness account of the early months at Jamestown. His "first sight" of "faire meddowes and goodly Tall trees and such Fresh-waters running through the woods" entranced him. Abundance matched beauty. "Mussels and Oysters . . . lay upon the ground as thicke as stones." This new land also offered "fine and beautifull Strawberries, foure times bigger and better than ours in England." Exploring, Percy discovered the "most pleasant Springs" and "the goodliest Corne fields that ever was seene in any Countery." "The soile," he reported, was "good and fruitfull, with excellent good Timber." "The ground all flowing over with faire flowers of sundry colours and kindes" reminded Percy of a "Garden or Orchard in England."

Percy found that the natives could be as inviting as the land. They "entertained" the English "very kindly." "After they had feasted us," Percy wrote, "they shewed us, in welcome their manner of dancing." To Percy it seemed that he and the other settlers had landed in "Paradise."

But thorns infested Percy's garden. Relations with the natives were not always friendly. Percy recorded that one night, "when wee were going abord [our ship]," the natives appeared "creeping upon all foure . . . like Beares, with their Bowes in their mouthes." They "charged us very desperately in the faces" and wounded two Englishmen. The English fired, according to Percy, and "the sharpnesse of our shot" helped drive the natives "into the Woods." Armed conflict, in which both natives and settlers died, alternated with amity, but it never disappeared.

Other thorns tore at the English. Noting that "our men were destroyed with cruell diseases," Percy catalogued the horrors of "Swellings, Flixes, Burning Fevers." Death visited regularly, "many times three or foure in a night; in the morning, their bodies trailed out of their Cabines like Dogges to be buried."

Percy's melancholy list of the dead reads like a daily obituary, complete with cause of death. In September he cried out, "There were never Englishmen left in a foreigne Countrey in such miserie as we were in this new discovered Virginia."

Rapid, unexpected death remained a constant for many decades, but the English did not give up their colony. Percy himself rose to the governorship before he returned to England in 1612. His "Paradise" kept drawing replacements for the settlers who succumbed to the "miserie." They enabled Jamestown to survive to become the first permanent English settlement in North America. As Percy indicated, the English gazeteer of the New World located Jamestown in Virginia. Named in the 1580s in honor of Queen Elizabeth I, the Virgin Queen, Virginia was the most significant English claim in North America. Virginia became the first, and thus the oldest, English colony in what was to become the United States. It was obviously the oldest in that part of the United States that came to be called the South.

ENGLISH BACKGROUND

The English began seriously to discuss the possibilities of colonization during the reign of Elizabeth I, queen of England from 1558 to 1603. During Elizabeth's time the English were emerging from a period of turmoil and tribulation, both political and religious. Under her the English rejoiced over a newly discovered unity and sense of common purpose. Elizabeth and her advisers recognized that England lived in a precarious political world, in which powers jockeyed for position while keeping an eye on the greatest among them, Spain. Elizabeth wanted to establish England's sovereignty beyond any question; she also wanted to secure her country's place among the great powers of Europe.

England's turn toward colonization of the New World naturally followed. Among the Englishmen who determined that England's flag must be planted in the New World, Sir Walter Raleigh stood out. A favorite of Elizabeth's, Raleigh received her blessings on his attempt to colonize the land the queen authorized him to call Virginia. Raleigh took action upon the precepts laid down by the leading English thinker on colonization, Richard Hakluyt the younger. In 1584, in *A Discourse Concerning Westerne Planting*, Hakluyt eloquently pleaded for colonization. England, he piously asserted, had a duty to extend Protestantism, but his emphasis was on economics and politics: England needed to build up its trade and to supply domestic requirements from English colonies, not from foreign nations. In Hakluyt's scheme, prosperous colonies would enrich the mother country. He also saw colonies as a means to build up the royal navy and as providing critical military bases. After all, Hakluyt reminded his readers, England was involved in a great economic and political contest with Spain. Accordingly, England must act or risk disaster. Thus, for Hakluyt, colonization held out the combined promise of financial gain and political security.

While Hakluyt talked of national goals, such men as Raleigh mingled these noble ends with personal ambition. Gain and glory for England could also mean gain and glory for the Englishmen who carried out the great mission set forth by Hakluyt. Raleigh's first colonizing expedition left England in April 1585 for the outer banks of North Carolina, the finger islands that stretch along the Atlantic coast. The previous year a reconnaissance party had decided upon this location as the best place for Raleigh to begin his colonial enterprise. In the summer of 1585 the colonists, all of whom were male, went ashore on Roanoke Island, almost at the center of the outer banks. The colony did not last; after only one checkered year all the survivors returned to England. Undaunted, Raleigh prepared for another try. This time he made more complete preparations, and by including whole families he signaled to his country and his queen that he meant to succeed. Although Raleigh intended this second group of colonists to settle in the Chesapeake, they ended up in July 1587 on Roanoke Island, the site of the failed first attempt. No matter; the colonists set about the work of constructing shelter, providing food, and establishing relations with the Indians.

Raleigh intended to support and resupply his colony, but war with Spain delayed him. To confront the great Spanish Armada of 1588 all ships and sailors were needed at home. By the time a relief party reached Roanoke Island, in the summer of 1590, three years after the establishment of the second colony, it came upon one of the great mysteries of American history. No English man, woman, or child could be found, only the word *Croatoan,* the name of a nearby island, carved on a tree. A search of Croatoan turned up no trace of the colony. Precisely what became of the second Roanoke colony remains unknown. Most probably the settlers were either killed or absorbed by the local Indians. Most authorities believe that both killing and absorption took place.

OTHERS, EUROPEAN AND NATIVE

The English were not the first Europeans to set foot on the territory later known as the southern colonies. Spain, the greatest power in Europe in the sixteenth century, had led the European movement into the New World. The Spanish advance began in 1492, when Christopher Columbus, searching for a western route to the Orient, discovered America. The Spanish colonial empire, which extended from Mexico through Central America into South America and was a powerful presence in the Caribbean, had outposts in southeastern North America as well. The first Spaniard—indeed, the first European—to set foot in the region was Juan Ponce de León, who in 1513 claimed Florida for Spain. In 1539 Hernando de Soto landed on the western coast of Florida and headed inland. Over the next four years de Soto's expedition traversed an immense territory, from North Carolina to the Mississippi River. Although de Soto's journey resulted in no consequential Spanish influence, the Spanish did establish in 1565 the first permanent European settlement in North America, at St. Augustine, Florida.

Still another great European colonizing power touched the shores of the Atlantic South. Exploring for France, the Italian Giovanni Verrazzano made landfall on the North Carolina coast in 1524. Afterward he sailed along the eastern seaboard, though he did not establish a settlement. In the 1560s France did attempt settlements in southern South Carolina and in northern Florida, but the French had even less success and impact than did the Spanish, who promptly drove them out of Florida. The French, however, made their chief effort not in the

EARLY EXPLORATION IN THE SOUTH

Southeast but along the coast of the Gulf of Mexico. In 1682 the Sieur de la Salle, starting from French Canada, eventually paddled down the Mississippi River all the way to the gulf. The Mississippi Valley he claimed for his king, Louis XIV, and in his honor named it Louisiana. A few years later La Salle returned by sea with the goal of setting up a French colony. His expedition ended in his death at the hands of his own men.

The Europeans who explored and colonized the Southeast and the lower Mississippi Valley did not enter an unpopulated land. A substantial native or "Indian" population lived throughout the region, and in the Northeast as well. The designation "Indian" originated with Christopher Columbus, who gave it to the natives he encountered because he thought he had reached the Indies, off the coast of Asia.

How many Indians lived in the Americas when Columbus arrived is a vexing question. Various figures have been suggested, ranging up to 1.5 million, which is probably too high. The most-detailed investigation of the native population starts with the late seventeenth century when the data are more generally reliable. This study estimates that in 1685 about 113,000 Indians lived in the area from the Atlantic coast west to Cherokee and Choctaw country. Pushing on to the Mississippi River and into Louisiana raises the total to 190,000.

Contact with the Europeans was a demographic disaster for the Indians. By 1775 the native population had dwindled to only 35,600 in the Southeast and 55,600 including the lower Mississippi Valley. Military conflict, a constant from initial settlement, certainly contributed to the decimation, but the chief ravager was disease. Biologically unprepared for the diseases the Europeans brought with them, like smallpox, the Indians were devastated. At times entire tribes disappeared within a single generation.

The Europeans did not find a unified people. Several major tribes interacted with the English—the Powhatan Confederacy in Virginia, the Tuscarora in North Carolina, the Yamassee in South Carolina, the Cherokee in the western portions of both Carolinas, and the Creek in Georgia. The Creek also had substantial contact with Spanish Florida. Farther west the Chickasaw, the Choctaw, and the Natchez were the dominant tribes that first met the French.

These native American tribes did not live isolated from each other in some kind of sylvan paradise. They had cleared forests to build their villages and to grow their crops. They also engaged in trade as well as war with each other. As a result, a considerable transportation network traversed the South. It included pathways that served chiefly local populations like the maze permeating Cherokee country in the Appalachian highlands of western Carolina, northern Georgia, and eastern Tennessee. Hubs, where trails heading in different directions met and crossed, grew up in places that would remain transportation centers, like present-day Montgomery, Alabama, and Chattanooga, Tennessee. Then there were the connecting trails that tracked across the region like the route from St. Augustine to Mobile to Natchez, then across the Mississippi River and eventually reaching Mexico City.

The Indians were culturally unprepared to deal with the Europeans. They had difficulty coping with a people who had a written language, which permitted coordination and planning over time. Additionally the Europeans had superior weapons. Although the natives understood something about private property, they had no comprehension of accumulation or stock piling. For the Indians day-to-day subsistence along with a sense of generosity motivated trading patterns. They did not exchange for profit.

Trade first brought natives and settlers together. For the earliest European immigrants trade with the native tribes was essential for survival. It also became important for the economic development of the colonies. Initially the exchange of goods took place on the Indians' terms and within their rules of interaction. In the beginning white traders relied on Indian guides and followed Indian trails. They responded to invitations issued by the natives. Traders who failed to respect Indian customs did not succeed. At first the Indians were eager for glass beads, simple metal goods like nails, and liquor, for which they willingly bartered deerskins and slaves captured from enemy tribes.

By the eighteenth century the relationship had changed, with the colonials getting the upper hand, a process that began along the Atlantic seaboard and spread westward to the Mississippi River. Deerskins remained critical, along with slaves, on the European side, while the Indians became dependent on more sophisticated goods such as textiles, edged tools, and weapons. In fact the tribes nearer to the settlements began to act like middlemen. They concentrated on producing items like straw baskets, which they traded with more distant tribes to obtain deerskins. Then the deerskins went to the Europeans for coveted weapons. Although the dominant partner had definitely changed, the Indian-settler trade remained a key element in the economy of most colonies up to the American Revolution.

JAMESTOWN

In the beginning Jamestown provided no clue that it would be merely the first step in a process that in the next century and a half would colonize the Southeast. On the contrary, Jamestown often seemed headed toward the fate of its predecessor, Roanoke Island. Settlement at Jamestown was the project of the London Company of Virginia, also known simply as the Virginia Company, a joint-stock company authorized in 1606 by James I. Designed to permit the cost of colonization to be spread among several or several hundred investors, the joint-stock company offered a means to avoid the need for a single investor, such as Sir Walter Raleigh, to finance an expensive colonial venture without help. To attract settlers the Virginia Company offered shares to people who would invest their labor in Virginia as well as to those who would invest their money in England. The charter of the company also permitted a measure of self-government through a council that the colonists in Virginia would set up. Thus from the outset the profit motive was fundamental to the people who founded and settled Virginia.

For at least the first two decades a secure future for Jamestown was far from certain. For the voyage out 105 settlers signed on to plant the British flag in Virginia. As George Percy's narrative makes clear, these colonists soon found themselves in a desperate position. During the first winter the population dwindled to thirty-eight. Poor planning and a lack of leadership resulted in near starvation, which invited disease and brought the colony to the brink of extinction. In fact, Jamestown hung on only because of the assistance, especially the food, given by the Powhatans.

The colonists also found a leader who had the ability and conviction to drive them to save themselves. The first in a long line of Virginia notables, Captain John Smith took over leadership of the colony in 1608. Around forty years of age when he assumed responsibility for the precarious settlement on the banks of the James, Smith brought a military background to his task. He had been a soldier of fortune who had fought on the continent. A member of the Virginia Company, he arrived

JAMESTOWN: THE EARLY YEARS, A MODERN MURAL (Thomas L. Williams)

at Jamestown with the first party of settlers. Once there, he concentrated on exploration and securing food from the Indians. On an exploring venture during the first summer, Smith participated in one of the most famous episodes of early American history. By his own account—and there is no solid reason to disbelieve him—he was captured by Chief Powhatan and scheduled for execution. The chief's daughter Pocahontas, then twelve or thirteen years old, rushed forward and took Smith's head in her arms, thus preventing his executioners from clubbing him to death. After this dramatic incident, Pocahontas spent much time in Jamestown. She converted to Christianity and in 1614 married one of the settlers, John Rolfe. Two years later she and their young son accompanied him to England, where she "carried her selfe as the Daughter of a King, and was accordingly respected." Pocahontas never saw her homeland again; in 1617, just as the Rolfes were starting back to Virginia, she fell ill and died.

During Smith's year as president of the council he organized the colonists for work. He also focused their attention on developing an agriculture that would provide a consistent supply of food. When Smith left the colony, he had not guaranteed success but he had staved off disaster. In 1624 Smith published his *Generall Historie of Virginia,* in which he presented Virginia as a natural paradise that offered a bountiful future for the English. Never underestimating his own role in the brief history of the colony, John Smith believed that Virginia was destined for greatness.

Despite Smith's enormous contributions to the security of Jamestown, the settlement remained in jeopardy. Jamestown, along with the farms and homes that grew up around it, confronted three serious challenges. First, the Virginia Company never provided properly for the sustenance of the colony. For almost twenty years ruin seemed imminent. Financial problems plagued the company back in London, and the ensuing loss of interest in the enterprise afflicted the colonists in Virginia. Finally in 1624 King James I revoked the company's character, and Virginia became a royal colony. Second, the colonists had to contend with their more powerful Indian neighbors. During the initial decade, relations between colonists and Indians were reasonably good, but they deteriorated after the death of Powhatan. Then in 1622 came an attack—the colonists called it a massacre—in which at least one-fifth of the population was killed. Desultory fighting went on until the mid-1640s, when the colonists finally overpowered the Powhatan Confederacy. Their triumph was almost total. One hundred years after settlement the 200 Powhatan villages had been reduced to 12.

GROWTH AND CONFLICT IN VIRGINIA

Even more deadly than either the negligence of the company or the danger from the Indians was disease. Between 1607 and 1622 more than 4,000 men, women, and children had come to the colony. After the Indian assault only around 1,240 people remained. The Indians had killed 347 colonists; some 3,000 others had lost their lives to disease. The mortality rate that had frightened George Percy was staggering. Between 1625 and 1640 new colonists arrived at the rate of 1,000 annually, but by 1640 the population had reached only 8,000. Because there were just over 1,000 people in the colony in 1625, the total went up by some 7,000, less than half the number of new arrivals. A new disease environment multiplied by the typhus that resulted from contaminated water ravaged the immigrants. John Smith's description of Virginia as a natural paradise notwithstanding, what nature provided most colonists in Virginia was an early grave.

The easy availability of land and the hope of financial reward kept hopeful people coming to the pestilential place. Those who succeeded in this rough, dangerous world were not noted for honesty and kindness. William Tucker came to Virginia before 1620 to sell goods entrusted to him by a group back in England. Although he evidently sold what he brought, he delivered neither cash nor accounts to the people in England he represented. While he cheated his backers, he was dealing with his fellow colonists in similar fashion. Settlers objected to merchants "who have by needlesse and unprofitable Commodities . . . ingaged the inhabitants of debts of Tobacco, to the value almost of theire ensuinge croppe . . . amonge whom we have good cause to complayne of Captayne Tucker, who hath farr exceeded all other marchaunts in the [prices] of their goodes." Tucker did not outperform Abraham Peirsey, who arrived in Virginia in 1616 as manager of the company's storehouse. Though Peirsey sold his goods for two or three times more than the intended price, the business always showed a loss. Even after a decade he had never paid the company for its goods. That practice helped him leave upon his death in 1628 "the best Estate that was ever yett knowen in Virginia." Edward Blancy rose in part by marrying a widow and grabbing the estate of a man who happened to have a surname identical with that of his wife's first husband. Even a treasurer of the colony who desired more servants simply assigned sixteen tenants of the company as his own servants.

Tobacco held the key to potential wealth. Unlike the Spanish colonies in Mexico and South America, Virginia yielded no gold and no silver, but it had the golden weed, tobacco. The success of tobacco in Virginia resulted in large part from the efforts of John Rolfe. Although Rolfe is known primarily for his marriage to Pocahontas, he made a far more lasting impact on the colony, and ultimately on American history, by developing tobacco marketable in Europe. The plant was not native to Virginia. Englishmen had learned to like it from the Spanish, who had brought it to Europe from the West Indies at an early date. The Indians of Virginia did grow and smoke a kind of tobacco, but the English found it bitter. Obtaining some seed from the West Indies, Rolfe managed to produce a milder and more palatable product. Others rushed to follow his lead; tobacco grew even in the streets of Jamestown. The first shipments left for England in 1617.

Although tobacco brought wealth to colonial Virginia, even in the seventeenth century the English disagreed sharply about its use. Those who championed it described the plant as a gift from a bountiful nature. The "esteemed weed" moved one of its partisans to write:

> Earth ne're did breed
> Such a joviall weed,
> Whereof to boast so proudly.

Its enemies, however, denounced tobacco as the "chopping herbe of hell." And the opponents counted among their number King James himself. The king had no use for the chief commodity of his first North American colony. Three years before Jamestown, in a condemnation quite modern in its particulars, he castigated smoking as "a custome lothsome to the eye, hateful to the nose, harmfull to the braine, dangerous to the lungs, and in the blacke stinking fume thereof, neerest resembling the horrible Stigian smoke of the pit that is bottomelesse." James was on the losing side, however, for his own subjects as well as the continental Europeans eagerly took up the tobacco habit.

If Virginia was to realize fully the economic promise tobacco offered, changes had to be made. The introduction of fruit trees added to the vitamin supply. After mid-century the colony required ship captains to disembark new arrivals in either fall or winter so that they might become somewhat acclimatized before the rigors of summer. Although these measures did not make Virginia a healthy place, they probably helped somewhat to curb the spread of disease. Still, an increase in population depended chiefly on migration from England, which after 1640 included more women than had previously entered the colony. The additional women improved the male-female balance and contributed to the rise in the colonial birthrate. The population rose from 8,000 in 1644 to more than 14,000 in 1653, then to almost 32,000 in 1662, and to just under 45,000 in 1680. By 1700 it topped 58,000.

These years also witnessed the rise of many of the families that were to dominate the colony in the eighteenth century. Among the men who came in the 1650s and 1660s, many were younger sons of the English landed gentry; some were even members of the aristocracy. Though not of the nobility, these individuals were neither the common folk nor the riffraff. They were gentlefolk who wanted to replicate the society they had left behind. They left because their England afforded them no opportunity to rise to the wealth and influence they believed they deserved. In Virginia these gentry strove to give substance to title.

William Byrd I, progenitor of one of the most notable families in colonial Virginia, reached the colony about 1670. He came to live with an uncle, Thomas Stegg, Jr., whose father had migrated a generation earlier. Upon Stegg's death, Byrd inherited his estate, and with determination and ruthlessness he transformed his inheritance into one of the greatest of colonial fortunes. He raised tobacco, and he also moved forcefully into other endeavors. Setting up a trading station at the falls of the James River—the future site of Richmond—on the outer edge of English settlement, Byrd traded over hundreds of miles with various Indian tribes. He also dealt extensively in indentured servants and slaves. Passing up no opportunities, Byrd became an accomplished looter when times became unsettled.

Hardship, competition, the risk of failure—nothing daunted Byrd or the other immigrants. Virginia remained in large part a rude frontier where ordinary planters lived chiefly on Indian corn and water. Beef in summer, pork in fall, and game supplemented the monotonous regular diet. This open, mostly unregulated environment gave hard-driving men the chance to make their mark. And they were not always scrupulous about how they did it. Colonel Philip Ludwell, for example, used the stroke of a pen to give himself a comparative advantage. Every man who came to the colony received fifty acres of land for every person he brought with him. Ludwell had forty people, so he was entitled to 2,000 acres. But he wanted more, and with his own hand he added a zero to each number. He did not bring 400 immigrants, but he did get 20,000 acres of land. In this hurlyburly world, the likes of the first William Byrd and Philip Ludwell laid the foundations for the life of cultivation and graciousness later enjoyed by their families and by such others as the Carters, the Lees, the Randolphs—the first families of Virginia.

Social conflict pervaded this process. The conflicting interests among the older colonial elite, the hard-driving newcomers, and newly freed indentured servants—the unfree whites who formed the bulk of the labor force before 1675—made for tense, even violent times. By 1660 the peopling of the older sections of the tidewater counties made readily available acres scarce indeed. Newly freed servants and new immigrants found it more and more difficult to obtain decent land in settled areas. Their alternatives were to rent from established landowners—not their choice—or to take up land farther inland, a move that often meant trouble with the Indians. The land hungry saw the Indians as their enemies, as possessing the land they desired. Yet the royal governor and others among the elite did not want a renewed struggle with the Indians. After the triumph of the mid-1640s the colonial government designated its near neighbors, who now lived peaceably beside the whites and paid tribute in kind, as "tributary" Indians.

Governor William Berkeley in 1667 captured precisely the background of the strife rankling Virginia society: "Consider us as a people press'd at our backes with Indians, in our Bowills with our servants." This tension exploded in Bacon's Rebellion, which shook the colony between the spring and fall of 1676. At that time eager, ambitious young men, such as William Byrd I, rallied behind the leadership of thirty-year-old Nathaniel Bacon, who had been in Virginia only a year. Bacon arrived with close ties to the elite; Governor Berkeley had even placed his future foe on his council. Disagreement over Indian policy eventually led Berkeley and Bacon to armed combat. Bacon demanded a commission from the governor to attack the Indians, but Berkeley, fearful of the repercussions, refused. Despite the governor's refusal, Bacon and his followers set out.

In the ensuing conflict the upper hand seemed to belong first to one side, then to the other. In May, Berkeley branded Bacon a rebel and proceeded to capture his former associate. But once he had Bacon in his grasp, the governor imposed no punishment. Instead, hoping to end the trouble and reunite his colony, he pardoned the rebel. Bacon was not to be deterred, however. In June he brought a strong force to Jamestown and at gunpoint forced the governor to give him the commission he sought, authorizing a move against the Indians. With Bacon on the march, the governor declared the commission fraudulent and called on the people to help him stop Bacon. But it was Berkeley who was stopped. Defeated, the governor retreated to the eastern shore of the Chesapeake Bay while the victorious Bacon entered Jamestown with 400 men on foot and 120 horsemen. On September 19 he and his men torched the town—the church, public buildings, private homes, even the tavern. Outside of Jamestown homes and plantations were looted, including the governor's. William Byrd got his share.

Yet in the end Bacon's Rebellion failed. In late October Bacon died, probably of dysentery. No one else rose to replace him as leader. When Governor Berkeley returned and regained control, he had at least twenty of Bacon's lieutenants executed. The governor retained his authority, but the brutality of both sides underscored the severity of the crisis.

Bacon's Rebellion was the most violent episode in the social melee that was seventeenth-century Virginia. The future, however, was not on the side of continued turmoil. Colonists' willingness to move to new land along with the firm adoption of a new labor system worked for a more settled social order. The new century would usher in social peace and a more ordered society, though the new order commanded a heavy price.

MARYLAND

While the story in Virginia unfolded, just to the north and on the Chesapeake another colony was being established. The origins of Maryland differed from those of its older neighbor. Maryland grew out of a land grant and charter King Charles I gave in 1632 to George Calvert, Lord Baltimore, though technically they went to George's son Cecilius, the second Lord Baltimore because George died before completion of the transaction. The charter gave Calvert proprietorship of Maryland, which meant that initially he had title to all the land and that he could establish the rules for colonization. A Roman Catholic, Calvert wanted a colony in which no discrimination would be practiced against his fellow Catholics, though he never saw Maryland simply as a haven for his coreligionists. At the same time Calvert wanted to profit from his landholdings like any other English lord. To that end he envisioned a land system dominated by lords of manors who controlled immense acreages.

The first group of 200 settlers, including a cadre of Roman Catholic priests, landed in southern Maryland in 1634 and established St. Mary's City as the first colonial capital. By summer their numbers had grown to 350. Like the settlers who journeyed to Virginia, the original Marylanders all hailed from England. And in fact the social and economic course of Maryland followed a pattern quite similar to that of Virginia.

The structured, almost medieval social organization that Calvert planned for Maryland never came to pass. His system of literal lords of the manor never became important; after a decade only sixteen were in place. Instead, the almost wide-open practices common in Virginia prevailed. Without question large landowners stood at the top of Maryland's social order, but, as in Virginia, many had made their way up through ambition, drive, and good fortune. By the end of the century, again as in Virginia, the great families that would dominate affairs in the eighteenth century had emerged from the grasping pack.

On the religious front Roman Catholics retained their security throughout the century. Almost from the beginning Protestants outnumbered them, but the Catholics' association with the proprietor helped their cause. Then the Maryland Toleration Act of 1649 gave legislative sanction to nondiscriminatory practices. Although the law did not declare religious diversity a public good, it did require toleration. And toleration became the hallmark of the colony until 1691, when Protestants succeeded in obtaining a royal charter, which turned Maryland into a royal colony and ended the proprietorship of the Calvert family. Substantial changes occurred: the capital was moved from St. Mary's City, in the center of the Catholic population, to Annapolis, a Protestant stronghold; the Church of England became the established church; Roman Catholics were denied the right to vote, to hold office, and to hold religious services outside their homes.

Maryland was the only southern colony in which the royal period did not last until the Revolution. In 1715, after only a quarter century, the crown restored the proprietorship of Maryland to the fourth Lord Baltimore, who had converted to Protestantism. With the restoration the original charter of 1632 again became valid. Though the anti-Catholic statutes remained on the books, the political proscriptions were lifted from Catholics who professed allegiance to the king, and the colonial government did not rigorously enforce the prohibition against public religious services.

For the growth of Maryland it really did not matter who had basic authority. By 1650, 4,500 settlers were in the colony. In 1690, on the eve of the royalist takeover, their numbers had increased more than fivefold, to 24,000. In 1720, after the reinstatement of the proprietor, the population stood at just about 66,000. And by the eve of the Revolution it had edged above 200,000.

THE CAROLINAS

After the founding of Maryland, colonization in the Southeast subsided for almost forty years. Internal problems in the mother country, which eventually led to civil war and the execution of King Charles I in 1649, and to the temporary end of the monarchy, accounted for this considerable loss of momentum. But just as the fall of the monarchy halted colonization, its restoration under Charles II in 1660 signaled a resurgence. To reward eight of his major supporters, Charles gave them a substantial land grant in the New World. This land, which stretched southward from Virginia, was called Carolina—from Carolus, the Latin form of Charles—and its owners were known as the Lords Proprietors of Carolina.

In planning a colony for Carolina the proprietors certainly wanted to profit, and like Cecilius Calvert, they envisioned an almost medieval social organization. A document known as the Fundamental Constitutions formed their blueprint. Prepared chiefly by John Locke, the great English philosopher and political theorist, the Fundamental Constitutions blended notions advanced for the seventeenth century with an archaic social structure. The plan guaranteed religious freedom, but it authorized the establishment of the Church of England. It also provided for a stratified, hereditary nobility with such exotic titles as landgrave and cacique. Although the Fundamental Constitutions provided a master plan for the Lords Proprietors' new colony, converting theory into practice proved to be impossible.

In 1680, ten years after the proprietors established their colony, they relocated their settlement a short distance, to the present site of Charleston. The proprietors hoped to promote Carolina not only among their English compatriots but in New England and Barbados, an English-owned colony in the West Indies, which they believed overpopulated. New Englanders had no impact on South Carolina, but Barbadians had an enormous influence. During the initial decades the Barbadian immigrants became the driving force in the colony. They were willing to relocate in the new colony because Barbados's land area was not large enough to permit all of its ambitious families to establish rich plantations. The Barbadians arrived in South Carolina with the goal of creating in their new home the plantation economy they had envied back in Barbados. Despite their commitment to plantation life, the colony remained basically a wilderness until the turn of the century.

French Huguenots soon joined the Barbadians in Carolina. Driven out of France by the Catholic majority, the French Protestants had no difficulty accepting the Barbadians' vision for the colony. The career of one Huguenot immigrant testifies both to the harsh conditions in South Carolina and to the determination of its settlers. Judith Manigault and her husband left France in the mid-1680s and, after a stop in England, traveled on to South Carolina. Arriving in 1689, the Manigaults settled in the swampy country along the Santee River, approximately forty miles north of Charleston. Judith and her husband worked side by side felling trees, sawing wood, and raising crops. Their life was difficult. "I have been for six months together without tasting bread, working the ground like a slave; and I have even passed three or four years without always having it when I wanted it," she wrote a brother back in Europe. Even so, she thanked God for the good things in her life, especially the strength to bear the rigors of South Carolina. By the time of Judith's death in 1711 at age forty-two, some seventy families lived in this Santee region, where they farmed and traded with the Indians.

The early settlers struggled until the success of rice. In the beginning the South Carolina economy was based on livestock and skins, chiefly deerskins, which they traded with the Indians. A staple crop to support a growing, prosperous economy remained elusive. Although attempts to grow rice were made in the 1670s and 1680s, these efforts did not produce enough for home consumption, and certainly not enough for export. Even by 1690, when growers managed to increase their yields, they still had severe problems with the task of removing the husks from the grains of rice. But over the next twenty years Carolinians did learn to produce an economically viable crop. This success came in conjunction with the importation of slaves into the colony. Some of the slaves entering South Carolina came from areas of western Africa where rice had long been a mainstay of the diet. It seems likely that the newly arrived Africans were the key to the development of South Carolina's rice culture. They knew how to plant, cultivate, harvest, and thresh rice. The slaves surely supplied the labor in the rice fields, and it is probable that they also helped provide the knowledge critical to the successful cultivation of what became the great Carolina staple. A report to London in 1700 made the point that South Carolinians had "now found out the true way of raising and husking Rice."

The favorable outcome of the venture with rice significantly affected the growth of the colony's population. In 1680 no more than 1,000 people lived around Charleston, and by 1700 their numbers had reached only 2,260, of whom 900 were women. Then with the success of rice cultivation prosperity and confidence began to take hold. Many of the planters who prospered with rice and rose to eminent positions in the colony had Barbadian and Huguenot roots. By 1710 the population moved beyond 10,000; by 1730 it had shot up to 30,000; and by 1770 it stood at 125,000.

Although Charles II's grant to the Lords Proprietors included North Carolina, that colony had a different settlement pattern from South Carolina's. The initial settlements in the seventeenth century occurred before 1650, in the same outer banks area where the Roanoke Island colonies had foundered back in the 1580s. The colony was originally known as Albemarle, the name of one of the sounds separating the outer banks from the mainland. In 1691, North Carolina replaced Albemarle as the name of the colony. This second and permanent colonization originated in Virginia, when some settlers made the short journey from the James River region to the outer banks, and the colony of Albemarle became the colony of North Carolina. By mid-century a few hundred people were raising livestock and attempting to grow tobacco there.

When the Lords Proprietors assumed control of North Carolina, they experienced some of the same problems they confronted in South Carolina. Despite the proprietors' intentions, the Fundamental Constitutions were never enforced. They were just as impractical in North Carolina as they were in South Carolina. The in-

1660   **1775**

1700   **1790**

1750

GROWTH OF SETTLEMENT IN THE SOUTHERN COLONIES, 1660–1775

terests of the settlers in North Carolina often differed from those of the Lords Proprietors, and tension governed the relationship between the two factions. Finally in 1719 the Lords Proprietors formally surrendered their charter and North Carolina became a royal colony.

During the last twenty years of the seventeenth century settlement expanded inland. In that period and in the early years of the eighteenth century the colony greeted a variety of groups that broadened its ethnic base. French Huguenots and German and Swiss Protestants joined the colony. In the colonial era North Carolina never became as prosperous as Virginia or South Carolina, but its population steadily increased. Between 1680 and 1700 the number of North Carolinians doubled, from about 5,000 to 10,000. During the next three decades the population rose to 30,000. As in the other southern colonies, growth was enormous after 1730. By 1750 almost 73,000 people lived in the colony, and by 1770 their numbers exceeded 197,000. Some North Carolinians emulated their prosperous neighbors, growing tobacco in the Virginia border areas and rice in the southeastern corner, close to South Carolina. But most North Carolina farmers concentrated on animals, corn, and other foodstuffs. Naval stores—turpentine, pitch, rosin—obtained from the abundant pine forests formed a critical part of the colonial economy.

GEORGIA

The boundaries of Georgia, the last English colony established in the South, were initially within the area granted to the Lords Proprietors of Carolina. The first plans to settle Georgia were devised in South Carolina in an effort to create a buffer between that colony and Spanish Florida, but none of these early attempts succeeded. After both Carolinas became royal colonies, the English government took a different tack. In 1732 the crown approved a charter setting up a Board of Trustees and granting to the trustees a twenty-one-year lease on Georgia.

In colonizing Georgia the trustees had two major goals. The first was the traditional strategic aim of establishing a barrier between increasingly prosperous South Carolina and the Spanish in Florida. Then the trustees had the notion that Georgia would serve as a haven for certain social unfortunates, such as debtors, who in eighteenth-century England faced imprisonment. This philanthropic vision extended beyond the creation of a new home for people trapped by unfortunate circumstances; the trustees envisioned a new society unlike any that existed in the older colonies. They would restrict landholding to a maximum of 500 acres per person, and they banned slavery. The trustees wanted Georgians to benefit the mother country by developing crops and products not available elsewhere in the empire: instead of the veterans of colonial southern agriculture like tobacco and rice, they would cultivate mulberry trees to feed silkworms, grapes for wine, and spices.

The first settlers landed in 1733 at a place they called Savannah. Leading the 115 original settlers was James Oglethorpe, the only trustee to come to Georgia. The thirty-seven-year-old Oglethorpe became the dominant figure in early Georgia. Born in London into a prominent family, Oglethorpe served in Parliament, where his chairmanship of a committee on the condition of English jails stirred his interest in America. He made the journey to Georgia to see that the colony started off in the right direction. This original contingent included few of the social unfortunates the trustees wanted to aid. Neither did it have many who knew anything about agriculture. These new Georgians were chiefly artisans and tradespeople from small English towns. Led by Oglethorpe, who proved himself an able colonizer and leader, they set about clearing land for homes and crops, erecting a fort for defensive purposes, and laying out the town of Savannah. In the initial years the trustees sent over assistance and some 1,800 charity colonists, whose passage the trustees paid. Scottish soldiers and German Protestants supplemented the English majority. From Savannah the colony expanded inland and down the coast to the Altamaha River.

Michael Burkholder was the kind of settler the trustees hoped would immigrate to their colony. A German who still spoke his native tongue, Burkholder in the early 1740s owned about 500 acres outside Savannah. The Burkholder family farmed the land, and in addition they worked as skilled artisans. Michael Burkholder had mastered several crafts, including carpentry, millwrighting, and wheelwrighting. His oldest son and his son-in-law were shoemakers and carpenters, and his eldest daughter was a seamstress. Burkholder made sure that his five younger children learned the trades that their father and older siblings practiced.

Despite the great hopes of the trustees and the immigration of such colonists as the Burkholders, Georgia did not prosper, and many of the colonists blamed the trustees' cherished goals: restrictions on landowning, exotic crops, and the absence of slaves. After 1745 the interest of the trustees waned. Simultaneously the colonists grew more independent, and some of the inland settlements became practically autonomous. Finally in 1752, at the end of the trustees' lease, the crown assumed control of the colony. Even before Georgia became a royal colony, however, the trustees had begun to relax some of the old restrictions; the authorized size of landholdings was increased and slaveholding was permitted. The kind of determination and drive that produced the economic elite in the Chesapeake and in Carolina became evident in Georgia. These people constantly pressed for the changes that they believed would permit them to match the prosperity of the planters in South Carolina. In the two decades remaining before the Revolution, the economic fortunes of Georgia improved so strikingly that the population grew from just over 5,000 in 1750 to more than 23,000 in 1770.

FLORIDA

Spain had claimed Florida since its discovery by Ponce de León in 1513, but another half century passed before the Spanish effected a lasting settlement. In 1565 an expedition led by Pedro de Menéndez de Avilés established St. Augustine. Concerned by the arrival of the French in the northeast corner of present-day Florida in 1564, the Spanish crown acted to protect its claims as well as its land and water communication lines to the heart of the Spanish Empire in Mexico and South America. At the outset Menéndez attacked and basically annihilated the small French garrison. Then he attempted, unsuccessfully, to establish outlying settlements to the east, as near as the coast of South Carolina and as far as the Chesapeake Bay.

The ambitious plans of the Spanish monarchy for Florida failed. Unlike Mexico and South America, Florida had no precious metals to generate investment—the key for sixteenth-century Spanish colonization. Florida welcomed few colonists. In 1600 the population of St. Augustine barely exceeded 500, including men, women, and children. That about half were single men underscores the settlement's function as a military outpost. Known for poor soil, hurricanes, Indians, and pirates, St. Augustine repelled settlers instead of attracting them. In 1700 the population was only 1,500, and it stood almost alone. Not until the founding of Pensacola, 350 miles to the west on the Gulf of Mexico, in 1698 did a second consequential Spanish settlement appear.

Spanish Florida did not really grow in the eighteenth century. The goal of creating a flourishing agricultural economy never made any headway, though ranches did exist. In fact the major activity in Florida was religious. Some forty to seventy Roman Catholic priests were engaged in a missionary effort to convert Indians to Christianity. They ministered to more than 20,000 natives, though the actual number is in dispute. By the last quarter of the seventeenth century missions dotted the countryside from St. Augustine toward Pensacola.

This substantial effort did not last long. Disaster resulted when the English from their base in South Carolina attacked St. Augustine and the Spanish missions in the very early 1700s. Although the colony at St. Augustine survived, the English, with their Indian allies, literally wiped out the chain of missions that ran north and west of the town. By 1706 all had collapsed. The Spanish could count neither their economic nor their religious endeavors as successes.

The failure of the mission struggle was directly related to events on the eastern and western borders of Florida that diminished Spanish influence with the Indians and threatened Spanish control of Florida itself. Even before 1710 the English had dealt a crippling blow to the mission enterprise. Then the victory of the English over the Spanish in 1742 at the Battle of Bloody Marsh on the Georgia coast confirmed English possession of Georgia. The triumphs of the English coupled with the movement of the French into Louisiana knocked out the chief economic activity of Spanish Florida—trading with the Indians. Both the English and the French were more experienced trading partners, and they offered the Indians more abundant goods. Neither Spanish priests nor Spanish traders could compete.

When Spain surrendered Florida to England in 1763 following Britain's victory in the French and Indian War, Florida remained fundamentally what it had been two centuries before—a small military garrison. Almost every Spanish settler departed before the English took control—slightly more than 3,000 from St. Augustine, with 380 slaves and 79 free blacks; around 700 from Pensacola. The lack of economic and population growth in Spanish Florida contrasted sharply with the course of events in the English colonies to the north and east.

LOUISIANA AND
THE LOWER MISSISSIPPI VALLEY

While the Spanish struggled unsuccessfully in Florida, the French were trying with little more luck to build a colony to the west in Louisiana. Although La Salle had claimed Louisiana for France in 1682, and within two decades settlements were established on Biloxi Bay and at Mobile, no serious colonizing took place until the founding of New Orleans in 1718 by the Sieur de Bienville. The French crown saw Louisiana as the southern end of New France down the Mississippi waterway from Canada, the oldest part of the French Empire in North America.

Even after designating New Orleans as the capital of Louisiana, French colonization was sporadic and halting. By 1726 the grand total of colonists in the lower Mississippi Valley numbered only 3,784, including soldiers and slaves. Almost fifty years later, in 1763, the population had edged up to around 9,500, chiefly because of an increase in black slaves, who had outnumbered white settlers since 1730.

In the first half of the eighteenth century settlement and trade expanded slowly and in conjunction with each other. Settlers clung to the Mississippi while they moved upriver and downriver from New Orleans. A patchwork of farming, herding, hunting, gathering, trade, and transportation blended commercial and subsistence activities. Plantations raising crops for export were few, and they were not central to the colony's economy. Free Europeans and both free and enslaved

Africans interacted with the natives in a frontier environment generally without central control. The attempts by French authorities, with support from New Orleans merchants, to construct a more ordered and regulated colonial society largely failed, though they did cause tension in the colony. Like Florida, Louisiana was Roman Catholic, with priests accompanying settlers and trying to convert Indians.

This sputtering enterprise on the margin of the French Empire received a new owner in 1763. France's defeat in the French and Indian War forced its latecomer ally Spain to relinquish Florida to Great Britain. In return, France had to give Louisiana west of the Mississippi River, including New Orleans, to Spain in payment for Spain's loss of Florida. Simultaneously, that portion of Louisiana east of the Mississippi River went to Great Britain. The British designated the area as West Florida to differentiate it from old Spanish Florida, which they renamed East Florida, with the Apalachicola River as the boundary between the two Floridas.

The colonial population in Louisiana, though small, did not welcome its new rulers. Unwilling to give up their French allegiance, they forcibly rejected the first Spanish effort to take control. Not until 1769 and the arrival as governor of General Alejandro O'Reilly, with a sizable military contingent, was Spain able to secure the colony. Vigorously asserting Spanish authority, O'Reilly punished the colonial insurgents, imprisoning and executing their leaders. The Spanish takeover did not initially change the character of the colonial society and econ-

THE CABILDO, NEW ORLEANS, CONSTRUCTED IN 1799, THE GOVERNMENTAL CENTER OF SPANISH LOUISIANA AND THE SITE OF THE TRANSFER OF LOUISIANA TO THE UNITED STATES IN 1803 (Courtesy of Patricia H. Cooper)

omy. Roman Catholicism continued. The population remained small; it did not match even that of Georgia, though spread over a considerably larger area.

By the 1780s, however, Louisiana was clearly heading in a new direction, one much closer to the Southeast. After being defeated in the American Revolution, Great Britain had to return both Floridas to Spain because Spain had assisted France and the United States in the war. Spain used attractive land grants as magnets that encouraged new settlers to the lower Mississippi Valley, from Canary Islanders to loyalists from the rebellious British colonies. The black forced labor population also increased measurably, with slaves imported from the Caribbean and brought in by Anglo planters.

In the mid-1780s the colonial population in the lower Mississippi Valley had grown to 30,000—13,000 whites, 16,000 slaves, 1,000 free blacks—triple the population of twenty years earlier. At the same time a frontierlike trading economy was being replaced by a plantation economy utilizing black slaves and raising crops for export, with tobacco, indigo, and timber products leading the way.

*U*NFREE LABOR, WHITE AND RED

All of the colonies had one overpowering need: able-bodied men and women to work. The colonists faced the enormous task of converting the forests of their new domain into cultivated fields that would produce the tobacco, the rice, and the other crops necessary not merely for their survival but for the generation of the wealth they dreamed about. In the pre-machinery days of the seventeenth and eighteenth centuries, that feat required the strong backs, arms, and legs of many human beings. Those who could pay their way across the Atlantic could never achieve that goal. First, and fundamentally, this group never had the numbers to get the work done. Second, many of these people had been lured to the New World by the hope of making a fortune, and to succeed they had to have others working for them. And the pestilent environment of the seventeenth century provided few incentives to free persons of limited means. People who could exercise some choice over their destination in the New World tended to choose healthier areas, such as New England.

To fill this critical need the southern colonists looked to unfree labor. That was a familiar concept to the colonists, for English law provided for the hiring out of servants to masters, usually for a fixed term. In the seventeenth century the powerful magnet of land drew to the Chesapeake colonies a substantial number of indentured servants, English men and women who paid for their transatlantic voyage by selling their labor for a specified period, usually five to seven years. These landless, unfree laborers, chiefly young, unmarried, and unskilled men but also young, unmarried women, expected their labor to enable them in time to become landowners. Of course they expected that as landowners they would acquire servants to work for them.

In seventeenth-century Virginia and Maryland indentured servants were the mainstays of the labor force. Probably from one-half to three-fourths of all new arrivals in the Chesapeake between 1630 and 1680 came as indentured servants. Until the end of the terms specified in their contracts, these laborers were considered the chattel property of the masters who had purchased their indentures. According to the usual contract, masters had to provide clothing, food, and shelter; in return the indentured servants contributed their labor. The servants did have the basic civil rights shared by all of the king's subjects, regardless of circumstances. In the colonies a body of statute law developed to govern the master–servant relationship.

At times the system seemed to work as intended. Servants performed their required labor and subsequently became landowners themselves. John Cage was an illiterate indentured servant in Maryland in the 1640s. The owner of Cage's service evidently tried to keep him in servitude past his legal term, but Cage won a court judgment against his master. The records indicate that in 1650 Cage held title to 150 acres of land. He also served for a time as a county juror and later on apparently possessed a few servants of his own. In Virginia during the same period the Seager family made even greater strides. Oliver Seager, most likely a former servant, in 1652 had 200 acres of land in Middlesex County. After Oliver's death his son Randolph took charge of the property. Randolph Seager, too, became a county official, but a more successful one than John Cage, for in the next few years he held a variety of offices—juror, estate appraiser, constable. At his death in his early thirties he was a respected property owner.

Indentured servitude did not always lead to such careers, however. The fate that befell Elizabeth Abbott and Elias Hinton in Virginia in the 1620s indicates the horror that could await an indentured servant. Abbott and Hinton labored for the Proctors, husband and wife, who had at least four other servants. Hinton toiled chiefly in the tobacco fields; Abbott apparently worked mostly in or around the Proctor home. Both Proctors inflicted corporal punishment on their servants, and they certainly did not discriminate between the sexes. Both of them beat Abbott and Hinton unmercifully. Abbott claimed that on one occasion she was beaten with fishhooks. Hinton's final beating seems to have been with a rake. Neither Abbott nor Hinton survived their common ordeal. In October 1624 the Proctors were arrested and charged with beating both servants to death.

Most indentured servants probably did not fare so well as Cage and Seager or suffer so incredibly as Abbott and Hinton. Regardless of individual experiences, indentured servants dominated the labor force in the seventeenth century, but they practically disappeared after 1700. They never were so important in the Carolinas, Georgia, and the Gulf South as in Virginia and Maryland. This different experience of the older and younger colonies testifies to an especially momentous shift in the source and the identity of unfree laborers. Between 1650 and 1700 indentured servitude gave way to another form of unfree labor, slavery.

From an early date the colonists enslaved Indians, though the extent of Indian slavery varied widely. Indian slavery never became fundamental to the labor system of the Chesapeake. Over the course of much of the seventeenth century some Virginians tried to make slaves of Indians. Although the historical record is not absolutely clear on this issue, it is probable that few Indians in Virginia or Maryland ended up as slaves. The experience in Florida and Louisiana was similar; few Indians became slaves. But in South Carolina between 1670 and 1700, Indian slavery became widespread. Many Indians lived in and near the colony, and the various tribes traded their captives from tribal wars to the whites for enslavement.

Shortly after the beginning of the eighteenth century frontier conflicts boosted Indian slaves to their largest total, around 1,400, but by then the days of Indian slavery were almost over. The Indian population, even in South Carolina, never was large enough to provide a sufficient labor force for the whites. Moreover, the susceptibility of Indians to the whites' diseases made them unsatisfactory as slaves. Besides, the possibility always existed that Indian slaves could escape and melt back into the Indian population of the interior.

UNFREE LABOR, BLACK

By 1700 colonists from the Chesapeake to South Carolina had fixed on a much more plentiful group to furnish their slaves. Like the Indians, these people were not white, but unlike the Indians, they were not native to the New World. Neither were the whites' diseases so lethal to them, nor did they have a nearby hinterland. Black Africans became the great slave force of the colonial South. The enslavement of blacks did not begin in one location at one point in time. It developed in the Chesapeake, particularly in Virginia, over several decades. The first blacks, some possibly slaves, appeared in Jamestown in 1619; by 1660 a system of black slavery was clearly in place. Black slaves had not yet generally replaced white indentured servants as the major souce of unfree labor, but their introduction signaled the beginning of significant change. Intimate ties bound together those two complementary developments—the rise of black slavery and the decline of white indentured servitude.

Until 1650 the black population of Virginia grew very little. The first blacks who arrived in 1619 numbered around twenty; a half-dozen years later the total remained basically unchanged at twenty-three, compared to more than 1,200 whites. During the next quarter century the whites far outdistanced the blacks. In 1649 the white population stood at approximately 15,000, while the black had reached only 300.

The historical record does not make precisely clear the status of the blacks in Virginia between 1619 and 1649. The evidence does permit two generalizations, however. First, not all of these blacks were slaves; in fact, most probably were not. Some were free people; others, probably the majority, were indentured servants. Second, at times they were treated quite differently from whites. The first census, in 1629, distinguished white people from black people and often provided no personal names for blacks. In 1640 blacks were denied the right to bear arms, and they received harsher penalties than whites who had committed the same offenses. On occasion punishment for blacks was a lifetime in servitude. In 1640 three runaway servants, two white and one black, were captured. Each of the white servants was sentenced to four additional years of servitude; the black found himself bound for life. That some blacks were also being sold for life, a condition never applied to whites, also indicates that white society viewed the servant status of at least some blacks differently. Executors settling an estate in 1647 gave eight blacks to a master "to have hold occupy posesse and injoy and every one of the afforementioned Negroes forever." In addition, black servants commanded a higher price than white servants, which certainly indicates a different kind of servitude.

Although in 1650 white indentured servants still overwhelmingly supplied the unfree labor, changes taking place in the colony were setting the circumstances that would foster the massive growth of black slavery. The disparity between the costs of white and black servants dramatized that shift. In the 1640s and early 1650s a white servant with an indenture of five years or more cost around 1,000 pounds of tobacco, but a black commanded approximately 2,000 pounds of tobacco. A seasoned male or female black could bring between 2,000 and 3,000 pounds. Late in the 1650s prices rose for both blacks and whites, but a substantial differential still held. While white servants brought as much as 3,000 pounds, blacks sold for 4,000 pounds. That white masters would pay 50 percent and even 100 percent more for blacks than for whites underscores the fundamental transformation that was taking place.

Worsening relations between white servants and their masters significantly influenced the new direction. The increasing number of young men completing their servitude and clamoring for their own land led to social and political strain. This increasing tension among the whites finally erupted in 1676 in Bacon's Rebellion. The white elite had to decide whether it wanted to sustain a system that seemingly guaranteed social turmoil and strife.

To the Virginia elite, blacks offered two powerful advantages over whites as the major source of unfree labor. A black could be held in bondage for life, a condition that could never apply to an English person. A black man could also be permanently barred from the company of landowners and placed outside of political life, as no Englishman could be.

The embrace of Africans as the servant class had a further important ramification for the leaders of colonial Virginia, and for the subsequent history of the South. Whites of every social class could join together as whites vis-à-vis the black slaves. Thus racial identity became a powerful force for white unity. The growth of black slavery did help the cause of social peace among whites. The turmoil that sparked Bacon's Rebellion and racked Virginia in much of the seventeenth century did not carry over into the eighteenth.

The enslavement of blacks satisfied many needs for the white colonists. Certainly the English in Britain and in Virginia had knowledge of both blacks and slavery before the introduction of blacks into the colony. White Virginians were aware that for the bulk of the sixteenth century, blacks had been transported from Africa to work as slaves in Spanish colonies in the New World. They also knew that the English colony of Barbados had instituted slavery in the 1630s.

Critical was the black color of the Africans. To the English of the Elizabethan age, that blackness separated Africans from themselves. And just as important, it signified inferiority. In the eyes of the English the black Africans were not only different from but inferior to themselves. The reasons for that attitude were complex. In the sixteenth century no two words in the English language carried more psychological power than *black* and *white*. *White* stood for goodness and purity, *black* for sinfulness and evil. Color symbolism alone, however, did not construct racism. What the English learned about the living conditions and social activities of equatorial Africa reinforced the sharp contrast conveyed by *white* and *black*. Of course, few English people had visited tropical Africa; they formed their impressions by reading the accounts of travelers. Those reports described men and women wearing loincloths and living in straw huts. Moreover, those Africans did not worship the Christian God. To the English convinced of the superiority of their own civilization and cultural attainments the Africans appeared uncivilized, heathen, even savage. In their minds a people who wore practically no clothes, who had no grand buildings, and who were not Christian could in no way be equal to the English or to any other Europeans. That these uncivilized Africans had black skins only underscored the fundamental distinction the English perceived between themselves and the Africans. Then the actual enslavement of Africans in the New World confirmed for many English people their perception of the basic inferiority of blacks. A calculus of racial debasement and prejudice took hold.

THE SUCCESS OF SLAVERY

Thus both economics and race made essential contributions to the enslavement of blacks. Although scholars disagree as to which of the two factors had primary importance as a motivating force, all students of colonial slavery concur that both were critical ingredients in the origins of slavery. Each reinforced the other.

Between 1650 and 1700 black slavery went into the bedrock of Chesapeake society. By 1670, Virginia counted some 2,000 blacks, considerably more than the 300 of twenty years earlier. The number grew steadily through the remainder of the century until by 1700 at least 10,000 blacks lived in the colony. Maryland went from just over 1,000 blacks in 1670 to more than 3,000 in 1700. The increasing statutory recognition of slavery matched the growing numbers. As early as 1661 Virginia law recognized that some blacks served for life. During the next three decades a succession of statutes dealt in increasing detail with various aspects of slavery. Finally in 1705 the first codification of slave law took place in Virginia. In the new century the number of slaves increased massively.

South of the Chesapeake no such lengthy incubation period occurred. The Fundamental Constitutions of Carolina made provision for slavery. And coming from a society where slavery was firmly implanted, the Barbadian immigrants to South Carolina thought in terms of slavery from the beginning. Although indentured servants did come into Carolina, they never occupied a central place there. By 1700 approximately a third of South Carolina's population was black, and only ten years later outnumbered whites. Even Georgia turned to black slaves as the chief source of unfree labor within twenty years of its settlement. In Spanish Florida and French Louisiana, slavery basically accompanied settlement. Already extant in other parts of both empires, it followed the flag. The southern colonies made no more momentous decision in all of the seventeenth century than the establishment of black slavery.

2

The Economic
and Social World

❖

The availability of land had an enormous impact on the social, economic, and political structure of the colonial South. As a South Carolinian wrote in the aftermath of the Revolution, "From the first settlement in this country . . . the facility of procuring landed property gave every citizen an opportunity of becoming an independent freeholder." Land was the greatest economic asset of the colonies, in the North as in the South. Not only was land plentiful throughout the colonial period; its price remained generally reasonable. Over time land in the older, coastal regions did increase substantially in cost, but prices in newer areas remained within the financial reach of multitudes of colonists. In addition to general availability and reasonable cost, land was owned in fee simple; in other words, the overwhelming majority of landowners possessed their acres with none of the encumbrances associated with feudal land tenure.

Landownership was important for a great deal more than economic advancement. In the seventeenth and eighteenth centuries landownership provided the necessary key to respected social position and to participation in politics. Although laws generally excluded the landless from political participation, the proscription had a much broader base than statutes. A general societal attitude placed the landless outside social respectability. As a result, ownership of land became a basic requirement for both social mobility and broad political activity.

The male heads of southern colonial families surely owned land. Heading the list of landowners in the colonial South, and certainly impressing most historians, were the plantation magnates, planters who possessed enormous acreages. William Byrd I, who at one time counted 179,000 acres as his own, and Robert "King" Carter with 300,000 acres exemplify the grandees. Often these men did not simply appear and disappear within a generation, though dissipation of fortunes did occur. Many of the great families of the Revolutionary era—the Carrolls, the Lees, the Masons—benefited from the economic success of their forebears.

THE BREADTH OF LANDOWNING

Despite the grandeur of great names and plantations, the most striking feature of landownership in the colonial South was its breadth. Although social conflict over landowning had plagued Virginia for a time in the mid-seventeenth century, by the eighteenth century the great majority of white male southerners owned their own land. At the end of the colonial period no more than 30 percent of the white population in Virginia made up the landless group. In North Carolina the figure dropped to 25 percent, and in South Carolina scarcely 14 percent of the white population occupied the landless category. These figures on landownership compare favorably with those of the northern colonies, where the landless totaled approximately 25 percent of the population.

Within the landowning class a middle group occupied a prominent place. In South Carolina, 30 percent owned more than 500 acres, but fully 60 percent held between 100 and 500 acres, while 30 percent had title to between 100 and 300 acres. The landed aristocracy was less important in North Carolina, where middle-class farmers or yeomen formed a clear majority of the population.

By the middle of the eighteenth century many of these farmers were prospering, and the ongoing westward expansion that characterized the century made it entirely possible for a yeoman to become rich and even for a poor person to achieve economic independence. The geographic mobility across the broad expanse of the Southeast helped maintain a significantly high rate of social mobility. Westward expansion permitted the continuing creation of new elites—people who garnered the power and prestige accorded to the large planters. Even before 1750 this expansion spilled into the piedmont of Virginia and the Carolinas; by the close of the Revolution it crossed the Appalachians.

The creation of new elites meant a constant renewal of the upper classes. In fact, the upper class of the colonial South never became a fixed, static order. Although many of the great Virginia families, such as the Byrds, Lees, and Randolphs, could date their status back to the seventeenth century, new families constantly moved into the upper orders. Recent studies have demonstrated that families who made their mark as late as 1720 contributed to the leadership of the colony. In the younger colonies to the south the social order was even more fluid. Individuals moved into the upper class on past mid-century.

The pervasive ownership of land, along with social mobility, had enormous political and social consequences. Together they muted the potential for class conflict, though class differences and economic disparities clearly existed. But because landownership allowed participation in politics and prevented any upper class from formally stigmatizing those below as perpetually inferior or worthless, the possession of land guaranteed social and political status to most whites in the eighteenth century.

THE PLANTATION SYSTEM

The chief economic importance of land lay in the production of crops for the market. Fewer than twenty years after the settlement of Virginia commercial agriculture had become the engine driving the economy of the colony. The first tobacco shipments left Jamestown for England in 1617. During the following decade a burst of tobacco-backed prosperity created the first colonial fortunes. Those fortunes were inextricably tied to the land and to the production of a staple crop for an overseas market. Plantations and planters got an early start in the South.

The term *plantation system* aptly describes this economic activity, even though agriculturalists of all sorts engaged in it. Almost from the beginning the plantation, or large commercial farm, provided the main impetus to the southern agricultural machine. Smaller farmers often raised the same money crops, and they usually hoped to expand their farms into plantations.

The economic pattern established in Virginia formed the model for subsequent colonies. Settled in 1634, Maryland early committed itself to tobacco, just as its older neighbor had done. Although tobacco did not become the economic mainspring of the younger colonies south of the Chesapeake, staple crop agriculture surely became their economic activity. By the beginning of the eighteenth century, only thirty years after the settlement of South Carolina, its colonists were turning to the cultivation of rice, which in the new century generated an astonishing prosperity. Even in North Carolina, where the plantation system did not attain the importance it did elsewhere, the richest areas embraced the system. The youngest colony, Georgia, tried desperately to emulate its nearest neighbor, South Carolina. By mid-century, after a brief, unsuccessful effort with exotic crops and an equally unsuccessful attempt to do without the plantation system, Georgians had embraced both rice and slaves.

The system of plantation agriculture grew and flourished despite massive social and economic changes. The initial crops of tobacco and rice remained important throughout the eighteenth century and even into the nineteenth, but others appeared early, and over time an increasingly smaller proportion of southern farmers cultivated the two crops that first brought wealth to southern planters. By the middle of the eighteenth century indigo had become a major supplement to rice in South Carolina, and before the Revolution wheat had become a major money crop of the tidewater in Virginia and Maryland. Cotton, which became the monarch of nineteenth-century southern agriculture, had no economic importance during the colonial period. Afterward, however, it fit perfectly into a time-tested economic machine.

Tobacco governed the colonial Chesapeake. In 1697 the Maryland assembly recognized that "the trade of this province ebbs and flows according to the rise or fall of tobacco in the market of England." That observation held for Virginia as well as Maryland throughout the colonial era. Although little evidence is available on the size of the crop, figures on British imports provide a good sense of tobacco production because most tobacco was exported, and the bulk of it made at least its first stop in England. In Virginia the production of tobacco underwent three basic phases. From the beginning of tobacco cultivation in the first decade after Jamestown until the 1680s production soared. During the next thirty years the output leveled off at around 28 million pounds annually. Then in 1715 began another round of growth, which lasted until the Revolution. By 1740 some 50 million pounds were being produced each year; on the eve of the Revolution the poundage reached 100 million. Over the course of the colonial period tobacco

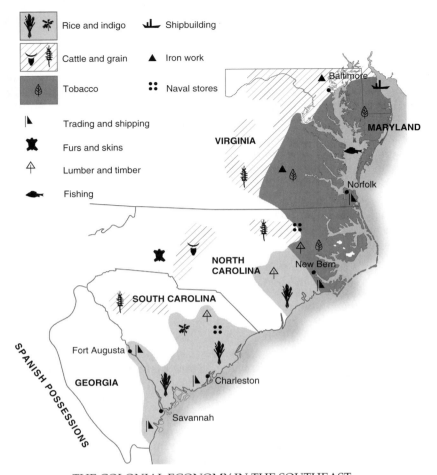

THE COLONIAL ECONOMY IN THE SOUTHEAST

prices experienced substantial movement. They fell consistently during the seventeenth-century growth, but gains in productivity maintained income for growers. Prices remained stable from the 1680s until the middle of the eighteenth century, with a slight increase early in the period. As demand increased from mid-century to the Revolution, prices moved upward.

Although tobacco dominated the Chesapeake, other crops and products contributed to the agricultural economy. Grains, chiefly wheat, became more and more important through the eighteenth century. Even in the tidewater, the birthplace of tobacco cultivation, some planters and farmers began to shift from the weed to wheat. In the Shenandoah Valley, settled in the middle of the century, grain assumed prime importance from the beginning. The production of beef and pork assisted in the diversification of Chesapeake agriculture.

Farther south rice predominated. Between 1700 and 1750 rice generated enormous wealth in South Carolina. Production expanded rapidly, from 1.5 million pounds in 1710 to 20 million pounds in 1730. The increase never ceased; by 1750 rice production rose more than two and a half times, to 50 million pounds, and during the next twenty-five years it doubled again. During this mighty surge in production the price fluctuated, but from mid-century stability prevailed, so that rice planters could count on a rise in income as production increased. After 1750 rice cultivation expanded into lower North Carolina and southward into Georgia. Still, South Carolina remained indisputably the center of rice production; in 1770, for example, South Carolina exported four and a half times more rice than did Georgia.

Rice clearly led in the southernmost colonies, but by mid-century a second crop became a notable supplement. Indigo was an important source of dye for the British textile industry. It had been grown earlier in South Carolina, but not successfully until Eliza Lucas tried her hand at it. A remarkable individual, Eliza Lucas—she later became Eliza Pinckney—at age twenty was managing her father's plantation. With indigo seed sent by her father from the West Indies and with technical help from an experienced West Indian, she made a rousing success of indigo farming. Scores of planters rushed to emulate her. With encouragement from both the colonial and British governments, production boomed. In 1748 exports from Charleston totaled just under 140,000 pounds; by 1775 more than a million pounds left the port. Indigo was also grown on a smaller scale in Georgia.

Of course not every farmer in the southern colonies raised staple crops for export. Especially in the back country, numerous farmers cared not at all about tobacco, rice, or indigo; their concern was to provide food for themselves. The chief thrust of southern agriculture, however, was indisputably commercial, and increasing numbers of back-country farmers ambitious for economic and social advancement moved toward the goal by selling grain and meat both within their colony and to other colonies. In addition, they hunted and trapped to take advantage of the vigorous market for skins, particularly deerskins. During the second quarter of the eighteenth century, when tobacco cultivation moved into the Virginia piedmont, farmers already there greeted it warmly. In sum, there was no substantial brake on the commercial engine propelling colonial southern agriculture.

OTHER ECONOMIC ACTIVITIES

Although agriculture clearly dominated the colonial economies, it did not stand alone. Probably the two most important nonagricultural economic activities were the mining and processing of iron and the extraction of pitch, tar, and other naval stores from the southern forests. Virginia, Maryland, and Pennsylvania were the major iron producers among the colonies. Mining began in Virginia as early as 1716. Furnaces, forges, and rolling mills followed, especially in the Shenandoah Valley and in western Maryland. The Virginians and Marylanders produced chiefly bar iron and pig iron, which they marketed primarily in the colonies, though exports did take place. Forest products also contributed substantially to the South's economy. Although the production of pitch, tar, and other naval stores occurred almost everywhere, the Carolinas led the way by a wide margin, with North Carolina at the top. By the eve of the Revolution the Carolinas accounted yearly for about 200,000 barrels of pitch, tar, and turpentine. Timber production also contributed to the economic development of the lower Mississippi Valley. Another, but sharply different, kind of forest product, also added to the economic health of the more southerly British colonies as well as those farther west: deerskins. Trade in deerskins thrived in South Carolina until the middle of the eighteenth century and in Louisiana even later. This trade often originated with Indian hunters who dealt with white traders. Early in the century some 53,000 skins left Charleston each year for England. By 1740 annual exports totaled between 600 and 700 hogsheads of skins. Between 1720 and 1780 Louisiana exported an average of 50,000 skins annually.

With iron, forest products, deerskins, and a host of lesser activities all supplementing agriculture, the southern colonies enjoyed a generally prosperous economy. Comparative studies of British colonial wealth underscore that conclusion; the most thorough study used data from the year 1774. The sum of private physical wealth, including land and slaves, placed the southern colonies substantially ahead of both the middle colonies and New England: southern colonies, £60.5 million; the middle colonies, £26.8 million; New England, £22.2 million. The per capita values formed a similar pattern, with the southern colonies again clearly in front. Slaves accounted for one-third of the total physical wealth of the southern colonies. When slaves are removed from consideration, however, the southern colonies were still in first place, though with a reduced margin. In nonfarm business equipment and inventory, however, New England and the middle colonies far outdistanced the South. That fact underscores the overwhelming importance of agriculture to the colonial southern economy. When all factors are considered, the evidence points clearly to a strong, productive economy.

The activities of town merchants, often also planters or at least future planters, facilitated the smooth operation of the economic system. Such towns as Annapolis and Charleston supported an enterprising, energetic merchant class. In Virginia the most important merchants were often agents of British firms; in South Carolina the merchants tended to be independent, though they worked closely with British firms. One of South Carolina's leading merchants was Henry Laurens. In 1744, at age twenty, the short, swarthy Laurens was sent to London for commercial training and to establish business contacts. Upon returning to Charleston in 1747, he received a considerable inheritance from his father, who had built up the largest saddlery business in the city. Young Henry went into the mercantile business and prospered. The export of rice and the import of African slaves dominated his affairs. In time Laurens extended the range of his activities by buying land and slaves and growing rice. By the eve of the Revolution he was primarily a planter.

In the overwhelmingly rural world of the colonial South, villages and towns were widely scattered; there were no cities in any modern sense. Yet to the colonists their towns performed vital functions as the seats of colonial government, the loci of trade, and the centers of cultural activities.

By the time of the Revolution the total population of the southeastern colonies numbered more than 1 million people, but no more than 25,000, or only 2.5 percent, lived in towns of over 1,000 inhabitants. Although population statistics for the colonial period do not permit a detailed analysis, information does exist that provides a good sense of the size of southern towns. In the seventeenth century

HENRY LAURENS,
MERCHANT AND PLANTER
(Library of Congress)

no single place had enough inhabitants to be called even a good-sized town. Throughout the eighteenth century the largest town by far was Charleston. From a population of just over 2,000 in 1700, Charleston advanced to 6,800 in 1740, to 8,000 in 1760, and to 12,000 in 1770. The fastest growing town in the late colonial era, however, was Baltimore, Maryland, which leaped from a village of about 200 in 1750 to a bustling port of 6,000 in 1775. In 1720 Williamsburg could count only 500 residents, and in 1780 just under 1,500. On the eve of the Revolution, Savannah had only 750 inhabitants; Wilmington, North Carolina, at the same time was home to only 500. Far to the west, New Orleans grew from 900 in 1726 to 5,000 in 1785.

THE PLANTERS

Great planters, located chiefly in the Chesapeake and the low country of the Carolinas and Georgia, dominated the economy and the society of the colonial South. In the eighteenth century these grandees were usually sons and grandsons of men who had made their mark or at least made a substantial beginning on the family position and fortune in the second half of the seventeenth century or very early in the eighteenth. These men ruled over thousands of acres and hundreds of slaves. Quite often they constructed impressive mansions on their plantations, and some of them also owned elegant town houses, especially in Charleston or Annapolis. Their children either went to school in England or studied at home under private tutors.

Landon Carter of Virginia, born in 1710, was one of the men at the very top of

ROBERT "KING" CARTER, GREAT COLONIAL PLANTER (Portrait by unidenti-
fied artist, The National Portrait Gallery, Smithsonian Institution)

the southern social order. The fourth son of Robert "King" Carter, whose regal
nickname signals his standing, Landon did his father proud. After an educational
sojourn in England, Landon returned to Virginia at seventeen and entered his father's planting-trading business. His determination to succeed and his careful attention to his agricultural pursuits underlay Landon's enormous success as a
planter. Starting with some 15,000 acres, he accumulated 50,000 acres and owned
some 500 slaves by the time of his death in 1778. From his plantation headquarters, Sabine Hall in Richmond County, he managed his agricultural empire. He focused his efforts on tobacco and cereals, though he also raised flax and hemp. An
avid reader as well as a committed agriculturalist, Carter read books on history,
medicine, and religion, in addition to agricultural literature. In the manner of his
class, Carter provided a governess and tutors for his children. He had clothing
and wine shipped from England. A glimpse at his wealth comes from his gift of
£800 sterling to each of his four daughters upon their marriages—at a time when
an annual living wage for a laborer was around £20 sterling.

Nothing set such grandees as Landon Carter so visibly apart from the mass of
whites or so impressed later generations as the plantation mansions they con-

WESTOVER, THE PLANTATION SEAT OF THE BYRD FAMILY (Thomas J. Waterman, photographer HAS, Library of Congress)

structed. These palaces in the wilderness represented to their builders—and still do to many people today—the ideal of a landed gentry. Mansions such as Carter's Sabine Hall, William Byrd II's Westover, and Thomas Lee's Stratford Hall, all in Virginia, and John Drayton's Drayton Hall in South Carolina are more famous than the names of the great planters who lived in them. Most of these country seats are of Georgian architecture, the classically influenced style that predominated in English public and private buildings during the eighteenth century. And without question the great planters attempted to replicate the English manor house. The first of this type erected in the colonies was the Governor's Palace in Williamsburg, completed about 1720, which set the tone for plantation mansions until the Revolution. The more impressive town houses, such as the Hammond House in Annapolis and the Miles Brewton House in Charleston, also followed the Georgian pattern. Architectural handbooks available from Britain after 1720 provided invaluable assistance to every family determined to build a palace of its own.

Plantation magnates often set their homes in rural, parklike surroundings, preferably fronting on a river. To travelers along the streams of the Virginia tidewater and the South Carolina low country, the numerous structures stretching away from an impressive mansion gave the appearance of a country village. An Englishman who traveled on the Virginia rivers in the 1730s observed "pleasant Seats on the Bank which Shew like little villages, for having Kitchins, Dayry houses, Barns, Stables, Store houses, and some of them 2 or 3 Negro Quarters all Separate from Each other but near the mansion houses. . . . Most of these have pleasant Gardens and the Prospect of the River render them very pleasant." The centrally located mansion of two or even three stories, most often brick, conveyed opulence and grandeur. The exterior image was matched by an interior that featured paneled and pilastered walls, parquet floors, molded ceilings, marble fireplaces, and a magnificent staircase.

At times wealthy planter-merchants constructed their showplaces in towns, especially in Annapolis and Charleston. One of the most impressive homes in

DRAYTON HALL, HOME OF THE DRAYTON FAMILY NEAR CHARLESTON
(South Caroliniana Library, University of South Carolina)

Charleston belonged to Miles Brewton. Like Henry Laurens, Brewton started as a merchant, prospered in the slave trade, and invested his profits in rice acreage and slaves. Around 1765 he built an exquisite town house separated from the street by a magnificent iron fence with a double gateway. Marble steps led up to a marble platform before the front door. Inside, a mahogany staircase with triple-arched window ascended to the second floor. A visitor in 1773 commented on the blue satin curtains, the blue wallpaper emblazoned with gilt, the elegant glassware, and the finely crafted goblets. Landscaped gardens and extensive servant or slave quarters dominated the grounds. Whether in countryside or town, these grand houses stood as monuments to the determined, hard-driving, wealthy individuals and families who rose to the top of the southern colonial world.

THE FARMERS OR YEOMEN AND SOCIAL MOBILITY

Of course the vast majority of southern whites possessed neither wealth, plantation manor houses, nor elegant town houses. They lived in far simpler dwellings, though the construction of their homes changed over time. In seventeenth-century Virginia the cottage predominated. Built of plaster and laths, often with a thatched roof, these cottages frequently lacked finished floors, even windows and doors. Sometimes they had a chimney of logs chinked with clay, but just as commonly the family's meals were cooked in a fire pit in the middle of a room; a hole through the roof permitted the smoke to escape. After the cottage came the simple rectangular frame house of one story; a half story could be added later as the family grew and its fortunes improved. The log cabin did not appear until after 1720, and throughout the colonial period it was found chiefly in the piedmont, where the Scots-Irish replicated the cabins they had known in Pennsylvania.

Farmers who prospered in the back country and the piedmont built their own plantation houses. Although considerably more substantial than the commonplace small frame houses and log cabins, they did not begin to match in sophistication and scale the manor houses of the tidewater and low-country magnates. Like many of the smaller houses, they were of frame construction. Private homes of brick rarely appeared in the pre-Revolutionary back country. Tall and thin, normally of two stories, these frame houses usually had roofed porches with simple wooden columns over the ground floor. A massive chimney at either end spoke of stability and substance.

Without question economic and social mobility marked the back country. The abundance of land and the relative ease of obtaining it ensured the upward movement of numerous folk. In the middle decades of the eighteenth century, Lunenburg County, Virginia, south of the James River in the area known as the Southside, offered substantial opportunity to new settlers, even to those who had been landless. Lydell Bacon, who bought 197 acres of land there in 1747, had increased his holdings to 1,060 acres by 1769. In 1748 John Hix worked for a small planter, but by 1769 he had acquired 395 acres and two slaves. Not quite so successful was George McLaughlin, who started as a laborer in 1748 and by 1769 owned 250 acres; still, those acres gave him the status of independent landowner.

The rolling, heavily forested piedmont was Scots-Irish country. Most of these people moved south from Pennsylvania in the middle third of the eighteenth century, though a smaller number arrived in southern ports directly from Northern Ireland. In the piedmont they cleared land, built cabins, and raised crops and children. Within a generation they turned a wild, rude country into farms and plantations. At the outset the new Scots-Irish differed from the established English. Socially and economically the Scots-Irish ranked below the English colonists, whose wealth and social position they could not yet match.

Many of the settlers who opened the piedmont prospered with the development of their new homeland. In the early 1730s the Calhoun family joined hundreds of their fellow Scots-Irish in emigrating from Northern Ireland to the New World. In 1733 they settled in western Pennsylvania, but a few years later they headed southward through the Shenandoah Valley to Augusta County, on the southwestern Virginia frontier. There they set about accumulating a considerable acreage. Within a decade these frontier settlers had become prosperous independent farmers. But in the mid-1750s they again looked south, this time toward piedmont South Carolina, where land had been opened by agreement between colonial officials and the Cherokees. The Calhouns became the first white family to settle in northwestern South Carolina. One of the Calhouns, Patrick, received an initial land patent of 200 acres, and through hard work and enterprise he added significantly to that total. In 1770 Patrick was elected to the colonial assembly. Twenty years later he was one of the largest slaveholders in his section of the state, with thirty-one slaves. Patrick Calhoun had traveled not only from Pennsylvania through Virginia to South Carolina but also from frontier settlement to farm to plantation. His son spent his life defending his vision of the land Patrick had pioneered; his name was John C. Calhoun.

Not everyone in the piedmont experienced the success of the Calhouns. In

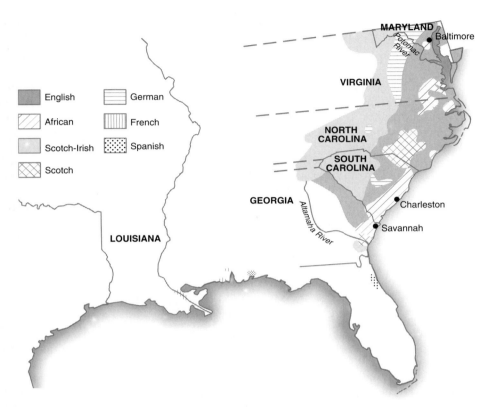

CONCENTRATIONS OF KEY IMMIGRANT GROUPS AT THE END OF THE COLONIAL PERIOD

1747 James Carter made his way down from Virginia to the Yadkin River country in North Carolina. One of the first settlers in the area, he seemed to prosper with it. Six years after arriving he bought 350 acres and became a deputy surveyor in charge of purchasing and surveying the town lands of Salisbury, soon to become the major town in Carter's county. He became a major in the militia and in 1754 went to the colonial assembly or legislature. But then Carter's creditors pressed for payment of money he had borrowed, evidently to help him get started. In 1756 he raised money by selling two slaves, but not enough to keep his creditors from taking legal action against him. The next year the sheriff sold Carter's land to pay his debts. Carter also faced charges of embezzlement, extortion, and misappropriation of state funds. The unpaid debts and the accusations cost him his reputation as well as his land. He had recovered neither when he died in 1765. Carter's sad career demonstrates that times and places of opportunity do not automatically guarantee success for everyone.

WOMEN

In the seventeenth century two critical conditions governed the lives and roles of female colonists. The first was a highly unbalanced sex ratio. Early in the century men outnumbered women by 3 or 4 to 1 in the Chesapeake. In colonies settled toward the end of the century a similar pattern prevailed. Of almost 700 settlers in South Carolina during the 1670s, only about 200 were women. Though the imbalance in the Chesapeake lessened through the century, there were always so many more men than women that every woman who wanted a husband could easily find one, whatever her financial or social position. The second critical factor was the initial status of many of the women who immigrated to the southern colonies. More than half of them arrived as indentured servants; as indentured servants women came under the same legal restraints and were subjected to the same compulsion as men. The owners of their indentures controlled their work.

Women performed a wide variety of tasks. The indentured servants, of course, had little say about what they did. Many of them worked in fields alongside men. Although promotional literature designed to attract women in Britain to sign on as indentured servants promised no fieldwork, such promises often turned out to be no more than propaganda. But many wives and daughters not bound by indentures also knew the rigors of fieldwork. In addition the chores of milking cows, making butter and bread, raising chickens, butchering and preserving meat, growing vegetables, brewing cider and beer, sewing and washing and mending clothes, and of course child care all fell to women.

Free women tended to marry between the ages of twenty and twenty-three, earlier by three years than their counterparts in England and servants in the colonies. Servants usually married quite soon after the removal of their indentures, and many of them made a significant leap upward socially by becoming the wives of substantial farmers or planters. Colonial women tended to have more children than women in England. Most families needed the labor of many children, and infant mortality was high. Mothers had responsibility for the control and rearing of children, both boys and girls. The terrible mortality rates of the seventeenth century, which affected adults as well as infants, often made for nontraditional families of complex composition. A family might include a widow, a widower, adults who had not yet married, stepchildren, and orphans along with servants.

The legal status of women in England carried over to the colonies. Women could not vote or hold public office or serve in the militia or on juries. Despite this political proscription, they did have the right to own land and to engage in business. In fact, during the seventeenth century women not uncommonly became executors of their husbands' estates. When a woman married, however, she legally surrendered all of her possessions to her husband. Any money she might earn was legally his, and he had the right to beat her so long as he used a stick no wider than his thumb. To this day we speak of a general principle based on observation rather than precise measurement as a "rule of thumb."

The increasing stability of the colonies in the eighteenth century affected women's lives in ways that were not always favorable. As the imbalance in the sex ratio declined, women had fewer opportunities to move rapidly upward through marriage. Now a woman was more likely to marry a man of her own social class, and her social mobility depended on his fortunes. With the turn to slavery and the resulting decline of indentured servants, fewer women and men entered the colonies as servants. This drop in the number of female indentured servants helped to lower the age of women at marriage. The growing distinction among classes also had an effect on women; the line separating the plantation mistress from the laborer's wife was sharper than it had been in the 1600s. In the eighteenth century labor was divided more clearly along gender lines. A far smaller proportion of women engaged in fieldwork, certainly not the plantation ladies and often not the wives and daughters of independent farmers.

With the decline in fieldwork most women spent their time in housework. The specific nature of that work varied considerably according to class. On plantations women were occupied chiefly in the supervision of the slaves who actually performed the various tasks—preserving and cooking food, cleaning the house, caring for the children, making and mending clothes for the slaves as well as for the family of the master. White women, a step down the social ladder, actually performed all the duties only supervised by the plantation mistress. Of course the arduousness of those labors depended on the family's wealth, on the geographical location of the home, and on the family's individual circumstances.

Quite a few women, however, found pursuits outside the home, out of either necessity or choice. From the Chesapeake to Georgia, all midwives were women. One of the most active and successful midwives, Catherine Blaikly of Williamsburg, had delivered some 3,000 babies by the time of her death in 1771 at seventy-six years of age. A talented woman who moved with striking success into an area usually reserved for men was Clementina Rind, whose husband owned the *Virginia Gazette* of Williamsburg. When he died in 1773, she took over the paper, and she did so well with it that she was named state printer by the Virginia assembly. In mid-century, Eliza Lucas Pinckney, by successfully cultivating indigo, made a major contribution to southern agriculture.

In the eighteenth century the legal status of women changed little, but in practice notable differences appeared. Fathers less frequently gave daughters land; ownership was concentrated more and more in male hands. More husbands wrote wills directing that their widows' inheritances were to be reduced if they remarried. And fewer and fewer wives served as executors of their husbands' estates. These shifts did not necessarily signify a substantial reduction either in the place of women in the society or in their treatment. Their primary significance lies in the evidence they provide of increasing social stability in the southern colonies and simultaneously a growing concern for the family continuity represented by the male line.

THE BREADTH OF SLAVE OWNING

Land provided the foundation for economic advancement, social status, and political activity in the colonial South, and black slavery reinforced that foundation. From the seventeenth century ownership of black slaves in addition to land identified the economically privileged. The possession of slaves became a badge of upper-class status; practically every family of the colonial aristocracy counted black bondsmen and bondswomen among its most prized possessions.

From the very beginning slave owning was associated with planting, and the large planters came to own hundreds of slaves. After all, the chief purpose of slaves was agricultural labor, and the more acres a family cultivated, the more slaves it was likely to own. Large holdings appeared early and grew over time. Robert "King" Carter owned more than 700 slaves before 1730. George Mason of Virginia, Gabriel Manigault of South Carolina, and the Marylander Charles Carroll of Carrollton also numbered their human property in the hundreds.

The breadth of slave owning was even more impressive than the size of some holdings, and this breadth equaled in importance the extent of landowning, though the number of whites who owned slaves was always smaller than the number who owned land. Slaves did not belong only to wealthy planters. In early Louisiana slave owning was largely concentrated among the small elite who ruled the colony, but with increasing slave numbers, especially after 1763, ownership became more widely distributed throughout the white population. Evidence abounds that in the eighteenth century the middle levels of white society also participated directly in slave ownership. By the 1770s nearly half of the families in the Chesapeake counties of Maryland owned slaves. Charleston's merchants and mechanics bought slaves just as eagerly and readily as did planters. Almost half of the city's mechanics who left wills between 1760 and 1785 were slave owners. Of the 190 artisans of colonial Charleston who could be identified in the 1790 census, 159 were specified as slave owners. An account of a Charleston slave sale in 1756 lists merchants, a mariner, and a widow along with planters as purchasers. Most bought fewer than five slaves.

The westward movement spurred the growth of slavery, for slavery generally accompanied colonial expansion. As white settlers pushed toward the piedmont from the older tidewater section, they carried slaves and slavery as part of their economic and cultural baggage. Most white southerners on the frontier envisioned a prosperous future for themselves, and they saw slavery as a necessary function in the equation that yielded prosperity. Exceptions did exist, however. The Germans who settled in the Shenandoah Valley of Virginia and around Salem, North Carolina, generally eschewed slaveholding.

Such deviations did not stem the westward march of slavery. When the center of tobacco cultivation in Virginia moved away from the tidal rivers to the shadow of the Appalachian Mountains, slaves still toiled in the fields. The great Charleston merchant and slave trader Henry Laurens attested to the intimate connection between geographical expansion and the growth of slavery. To associates in England, Laurens wrote in 1763, "We have now a large field for Trade opening in these colonies & a vast number of people seting [sic] down upon our frontier Lands . . . will take . . . a Cargo by one or two [slaves] in a Lot and it has been from such folks that we have always obtain'd the highest prices."

THE CASE OF GEORGIA

The best testimony to the intermixing of slavery with expansion and prosperity comes from Georgia. Georgia did not welcome its first British settlers until 1733, some 126 years after Jamestown. More to the point, the first Englishmen arrived in Georgia long after slavery had become an integral part of the society of both the Chesapeake colonies and the Carolinas. Yet the philanthropic founders of the new colony wanted to dispense with such institutions as slavery and large plantations, and the laws set up by the governing trustees outlawed both. These restrictions, however, did not last long.

Early on Georgia coveted slaves. Mired in what they viewed as poverty and backwardness, Georgians by the 1740s demanded new materials with which to build prosperity. Slaves stood high on their list. As in political matters Georgia looked for guidance to its older neighbor, South Carolina. By the 1740s slaves and rice had made South Carolina prosperous indeed. White Georgians saw the introduction of slavery as the solution to their economic problems. The agitation of the colonists prevailed, and in 1750 the trustees repealed their prohibition of slavery. Five years later the Georgia assembly enacted its first slave code, modeled on the South Carolina code of 1740.

The drive for slavery in Georgia derived from both individual and community interests. Individual Georgians believed slavery the surest means to guarantee their personal advancement. Even before the 1750 repeal, settlers had circumvented the slavery prohibition by leasing slaves from South Carolina for ninety-nine years, with the full purchase price paid as advance rent. Collectively, Georgians wanted their colony to develop and to prosper, and almost everyone saw slavery as an essential part of that development. When Georgia did in fact begin to prosper after 1750, many people pointed to slavery as the primary cause. Increasing real estate values, burgeoning production of rice, and growing personal fortunes all stemmed, in the minds of many planters and merchants, from Georgia's commitment to the peculiar institution.

THE SLAVE TRADE AND THE GROWTH OF SLAVERY

By the middle of the eighteenth century each of the southern colonies from the Chesapeake to the Mississippi had firmly committed itself to black slavery. Of course slavery was legal in all British colonies because it was legal in the British Empire, though it never became so important north of the famous Mason-Dixon line—the name given to the boundary between Maryland and Pennsylvania—as it did south of the line. By 1770 the colonies below the line had nearly nine times more slaves than the colonies above it. Across the southern colonies the percentage of slaves in the population grew substantially, but only in South Carolina did the number of blacks exceed the number of whites. That situation dated from at least 1710. By 1740 slaves numbered fully one-fourth of the southern colonial population. During the next three decades the proportion of slaves increased by more than half until on the eve of the Revolution they accounted for almost 40 percent of the population of the southern colonies.

In the seventeenth century most slaves who arrived in both the Chesapeake and Carolina came from the West Indies, but in the next century slave traders brought them directly from Africa. The slave trade was part of a larger pattern, a

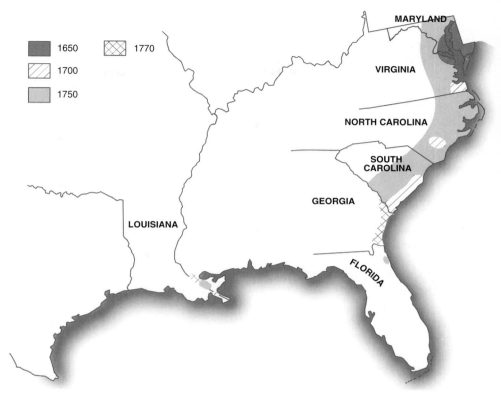

THE SPREAD OF SLAVERY, 1650–1770

three-cornered trade, often called the triangular trade. From Europe to Africa went such items as liquor, tobacco products, jewelry, firearms; to pay for these things, Africa sold slaves to the New World; and finally the products of slave plantations in the New World—chiefly sugar, tobacco, and rice—were shipped to Europe.

That the beginning of colonial empires in the New World occasioned a transatlantic slave trade surprised no one. For centuries black slaves had been brought out of central Africa, first across the northern desert, then after the middle of the fifteenth century by ship to the Iberian Peninsula. When the European Empire builders thought about filling the demand for labor in their new colonies, Africa came readily to mind. The Portuguese became the first great transporters of African slaves, but soon other competitors shouldered them aside. The Dutch and the French participated vigorously. The greatest slave traders, however, were the English, who dominated the trade at its peak in the eighteenth century.

The European traders operated along the African coast. The massive European takeover of central Africa did not commence until the mid-nineteenth century, in the waning decades of the transatlantic slave trade and after England had relinquished its place as the number one slave trader to become the staunchest opponent of the trade. On the coast the Europeans set up what they termed castles or factories—in reality trading posts. Agents of the European powers lived in them and managed the transfer of goods for human beings. The slave-trading vessels, known as slavers, anchored offshore until a full cargo of slaves was available. Once loaded, the ships headed west for the plantations of South America, the West Indies, and North America.

The Europeans could not have functioned so effectively as they did without the assistance of Africans. The arrival of seaborne European slave traders did not introduce slavery to Africans. The overland slave trade with the Mediterranean world was long established. Moreover, slavery was practiced in equatorial Africa. Africans became slaves of other Africans, usually because of defeat in battle or for the payment of debt. In certain tribes possession of slaves meant prestige for their owners. Although this kind of slavery had become a part of the African world, it had neither the motive nor the outcome of the commercially driven slavery that characterized the institution in the New World. The voracious demand created by the colonial empires had a thunderous impact on African society. Now Africans mounted expeditions designed to capture other Africans to sell to the Europeans. Sometimes the captors marched the captives over hundreds of miles to reach the coast and the slavers. The cooperation of Africans made it unnecessary for the Europeans to attempt to conquer the African interior.

The numbers of people forcibly transported across the Atlantic stagger the imagination. Although precision is impossible, the best estimates place the total number of Africans removed to the New World at around 10 million. This massive, enforced population movement occurred over more than three and a half centuries. The transatlantic slave trade began in the very early sixteenth century, grew through the seventeenth century, flourished in the eighteenth, and tapered off and finally died in the nineteenth.

The great bulk of these Africans did not, however, end up in what became the United States. Imports into British North America up to 1790 totaled around 275,000. From 1790 until the outlawing of the trade in 1808, another 70,000 came in. Then after 1808 the illegal trade probably smuggled in another 50,000 before the Civil War. Those figures add up to 395,000 slaves the trade landed in British North America. To this total, however, must be added the 28,000 brought into Louisiana during the French and Spanish periods, which ended in 1803. The sum approaches 425,000 human beings, surely a significant figure, but one that represents only 4.5 percent of all Africans brought to the New World. More than twice that many Africans—860,000—were transported to the great French sugar island of Saint-Domingue between 1681 and 1791. Yet in 1791, at the end of the slave trade to Saint-Domingue, only 480,000 slaves survived there. In contrast, despite the tiny percentage of Africans who were brought to the United States, the United States became the only major slave country in which slaves sustained and even increased their population. By 1800 the number of slaves in this country reached almost 1 million. In the next six decades the American slave population more than quadrupled, to over 4 million. During those sixty years no more than around 70,000 slaves entered the country, both legally and illegally—a number too small to affect this impressive growth.

Why the slave population reproduced itself with such success in the United States but nowhere else has no simple explanation. Several circumstances, however, undoubtedly influenced this outcome. The milder climate in the American South generally subjected the slaves to a less frightful disease environment. The more evenly balanced sex ratios that were obtained in the South were more conducive to a family structure and natural reproduction. Perhaps most important, southern planters never adopted the basic philosophy prevalent in some other slave societies, especially some of the sugar islands: that of working slaves to death and then replacing them. It seems that on the whole, slaves in the southern colonies and states received better physical care than those in bondage in the Caribbean and South America.

For the slaves bound for the New World the oceanic passage was an unspeakable horror. Men, women, and even children were crammed into narrow spaces averaging no more than four feet high. Rarely did they receive proper food and water, and the ship captains had little concern about sanitation in the slave areas. Almost unbelievable discomfort pervaded the densely packed slave deck. Seasickness and dysentery—both almost inevitable in the circumstances—resulted in frightful conditions.

Many accounts of slavers overwhelm our sensibilities. An observer described "400 wretched beings . . . crammed into a hold 12 yards in length . . . and only 3 1/2 feet in height." According to this eyewitness, "the suffocating heat of the hold" created a panic among the Africans desperate for air. Stark terror resulted. "The smoke of torment and the 54 mangled crushed bodies lifted up from the slave deck" testified to the horror.

For the captains of the slavers and for their employees, of course, slaving was an economic enterprise designed to make money. Thus they had a vested interest in landing as many Africans alive and reasonably healthy as possible. Available evidence indicates that they learned how to make the trip safer. Over the course of the eighteenth and nineteenth centuries the rate of loss among the slaves declined. Statistics from the slavers of the Royal African Company, which dominated the English trade in the eighteenth century, reveal distinct improvement in mortality rates. In the 1680s the mean loss stood at 23.4 percent; by 1791 it had dropped to 8.8 percent. Although substantial annual variations occurred over time, they did so in a lower range. The death rate among the crews of slavers, by contrast, remained around 20 percent throughout the period. The white crewmen were devastated by tropical diseases, mainly malaria and yellow fever, for which no successful treatment existed during the life of the trade.

Slaves in a New World

After the wrenching experiences of capture, sale, and ocean crossing, Africans arriving in the Chesapeake or Carolina faced adjustment to a new and different world. Much that they knew and cherished—family, tribe, religion—they had left behind in Africa. In the colonies they confronted fundamental problems. For most of them the tribe had provided a basic identity; now they had somehow to forge a new one, for any African could end up on a farm or plantation with no one from his or her own tribe. Language could pose severe difficulties. As the Africans spoke a wide variety of languages, they had to overcome substantial barriers to establish basic communication with fellow slaves as well as with the master. Many found themselves isolated in the matter of religion as well. Because the trade demanded young people, few older people such as religious leaders crossed the Atlantic. Moreover, the plants and other materials used in their native religions were seldom available in the colonies. As far as religion was concerned, then, the new slaves had been cast adrift.

In this cultural vacuum the Africans had to find their way. They did have one immediate bond: their color. Their blackness separated them from their white masters and helped them overcome lost tribal identities. In areas of extremely heavy slave population, especially when owners had purchased slaves from the same African areas and tribes, slaves were able to retain their own languages. The slaves also developed a pidgin language combining various African tongues with English, which permitted them to communicate among themselves. Probably the most famous of these pidgin languages, Gullah, the language of the sea islands of South Carolina and Georgia, survived well into the twentieth century. The old religious ways also tended to disappear, but in the colonial period no central religious experience pervaded the slave world.

During most of the seventeenth century very few slaves lived in either the Chesapeake or the Carolinas. As late as 1670 Virginia could claim no more than 2,000 slaves; that number increased to 10,000 by 1700. Considerably fewer had been brought into South Carolina before the eighteenth century. These small numbers meant that most slaves were scattered over a broad geographic area; additionally most slaveholders owned very few slaves. In Virginia the average number of slaves per holding between 1650 and 1700 was eight.

This kind of spatial pattern made it extraordinarily difficult for the newly arrived Africans to create families or even to look to each other for emotional and psychological support in the face of the incredible experience of their ocean passage and the unknown future of servitude to white masters. The sharp imbalance in the sex ratio made the establishment of any kind of family structure even more unlikely. With slaves so spread out geographically and with comparatively few women, complete slave families were not common. On a single farm or plantation they were rare indeed. Although slaves surely did establish families in the seventeenth century, especially after 1650, quite often they did not live together under a single master. Most owners, however, permitted visiting privileges so that husbands could see wives and children, and many owners tried to keep mothers and small children together. The seven children born in the 1670s and 1680s to Ann Joice, a slave of the Darnall family of Prince George's County, Maryland, either remained on the Darnall plantation or ended up with nearby planters. Life for the slave family never became easy, but never again was it so fractured as in the seventeenth century.

In the early days most black slaves worked alongside their owners to create farms out of a wilderness. Clearing forests, breaking land, erecting structures essential for living, and, of course, cultivating crops were the work and life of seventeenth-century slaves. In the Chesapeake they entered an economy already committed to tobacco, which had become the key to prosperity before slavery assumed any importance. White masters put African slaves to work on a crop unfamiliar to them. In South Carolina, however, the presence of a dominant staple did not precede the arrival of slaves. In fact, the evidence indicates that masters and slaves struggled together to find the Carolina version of tobacco. When in the 1690s the Carolina planters settled upon rice as their ticket to economic success, slaves contributed significantly to that decision. The colony would become at the same time enormously wealthy and the home of the largest percentage of slaves in the colonies.

SLAVE FAMILIES AND RELIGION

With the massive increase of the slave population during the eighteenth century, conditions for the slaves changed markedly. While the numbers of imported Africans shot up, the numbers of blacks born in the colonies also increased substantially. The presence of a significant native-born slave force provided for the transmission of tradition and culture. Slaves fresh from Africa often found themselves living among others born on this side of the ocean. This reality eased somewhat the arduous task of acculturation faced by the Africans. They were not flung utterly alone into a totally white world. Moreover, this constant mixture gave rise to a culture both African and colonial.

The expansion of the slave population did not, however, erase the sexual imbalance. Always more men than women arrived from Africa. Still, in large part because of the native-born, the ratio became less one-sided. Because men continued to outnumber women, women tended to marry young. The younger a woman marries, the greater the number of her child-bearing years and the more children she bears. The development of large plantations and the stability of independent farmers contributed to the presence of family units among the slaves belonging to one master, though the practice of marrying "away" did not end.

The evidence is clear on the existence of slave families. The Carters of Virginia, who owned hundreds of slaves and thousands of acres, certainly knew about slave families. John Carter bought a woman and her children who had been separated from their husband and father by the terms of their owner's will. A runaway carpenter, Sam, came back to his Carter master after only a week because Sam thought "it a hard case to be separated from his wife." Still another Carter wanted a seventy-one-year-old slave grandfather to live with his grandchildren. A 1761 list of fifty-five slaves belonging to a Mrs. Allen of North Carolina details family ties across generations. The list specifies that the slaves lived in six families, except for the eight who were single. It also indicates that most of the fifty-five were the children of three sets of parents. Names surely crossed generational boundaries. Some slaves were named for their fathers, and a child born in 1759 was named for her maternal grandmother. As slave families proliferated in the colonial South, a common African practice, polygamy, became a casualty. The colonies simply had too few women to permit polygamy to succeed. By 1733 only one of the 249 male slaves on Robert "King" Carter's plantation had more than one wife.

Of course the religion of the masters did not encourage polygamy. Yet in the colonial era Christianity did not penetrate the slave world as it would in the nineteenth century. Before the Great Awakening, which shook the southern colonies in the 1740s, religion did not occupy a central place in the lives of most whites, either. Even after the Great Awakening many Anglicans did not share in the fervor it aroused, and most substantial slave owners belonged to the Church of England. In any case, some slave owners feared that converting the slaves to Christianity might ultimately lead to emancipation. A major argument for slavery turned on the heathenism of the enslaved. Removal of that condition, in the minds of some masters, might lead to questions, even within the Anglican establishment, about the legitimacy of an institution that kept Christians in bondage for life. Of course, in Roman Catholic Louisiana a different situation prevailed. There from the beginning priests worked to convert African slaves as well as Indians. Although some slaves embraced Christianity, it is impossible to know precisely how many.

Because Christianity did not generally become the religion of slaves, no single religious experience predominated among them. Some slaves did profess Christianity; their conversion had been prompted by individual owners or by zealous preachers. Discovering how many were actually believing Christians is impossible, though during the colonial era the number probably remained small. Other slaves, particularly newcomers from Africa, clung to their native religion as long as they could, but maintaining the African practices in the colonies proved difficult. For the great majority of slaves religion most likely meant a combination of their African heritage, including charms and folk beliefs, and a smattering of Christian practices and teachings. But in all probability religion did not assume the importance for colonial slaves that it would for their descendants in the nineteenth century.

THE WORK AND CONTROL OF SLAVES

Whatever their religious preferences, slaves had one chief purpose: work. And work they did. Overwhelmingly slaves toiled in the fields to grow tobacco, rice, indigo, and grain. The hard physical labor essential for agricultural production before the age of mechanization was the lot of the slave. On farms and plantations slaves also engaged in a variety of other jobs, such as caring for animals, repairing buildings, and clearing new land. The routinized labor that characterized so many agricultural tasks did not confront most slaves with unfamiliar work patterns.

Many slaves had been exposed to similar activities in Africa. Consider the work of slaves in growing rice. Slaves who dropped grains of rice into a hole they had created by pressing a heel into the soft dirt and who then brushed earth over the seeds with a foot were following a pattern familiar in West Africa. Later in the season, when slaves walked in line through rice fields with hoes in hand, another African practice appeared in the colonial South. To winnow or "fan" the harvested rice the slaves made broad, flat baskets based on African designs.

Although the majority of slaves, male and female, were field hands, most engaged in several activities and some of them became skilled artisans. Especially on large plantations masters prided themselves on the abilities of the carpenters, wheelwrights, blacksmiths, brick masons, and masters of other crafts within their slave force. Some plantations boasted spinners, weavers, tanners, and even distillers. Other slaves on large estates devoted their time to caring for the manor house and for their owner's family. The tasks given Ben, a slave belonging to Landon Carter, illustrate the variety of jobs assigned even to individual slaves. Ben waited upon his master, served as a coachman, tended horses, and occasionally labored in the tobacco house. Carter, who thought that Ben "work[ed] very well," also designated him to pick up and bring to the plantation such items as oysters, salt, and wool.

But no matter their specific job assignment, from common field hand to liveried coachman, all were slaves. They or their fathers or occasionally their grandfathers had been involuntarily sold into slavery in a strange land. They had been bought and paid for along the African coast. Once they were landed in a port such as Charleston, they ended up in the hands of a slave trader who sold them for any service the new owner decreed, wherever the owner desired. Others, particularly in the Chesapeake, were hauled along the tidal rivers by the ship captain who displayed his human wares at docks and landings.

In Louisiana the small white population diffused across a large area made for a generally less tightly structured black-white world. Slaves occasionally acted as quasi-free people, setting conditions, for example, for their compliance with masters' authority. In addition, the paucity of white women and more tolerant racial attitudes and policies of the French and Spanish authorities led to more widespread interracial sexual contact. Compared to the British colonies, racial lines were not sharply defined. The designations free, slave, white, black were not always clearly perceived or enforced. By the 1790s, however, a growing population and evidence of slave unrest compelled major slave owners and government officials to redirect slave control into a path more akin to that of the Southeast.

Slave life could be brutal. As in eighteenth-century England, where the theft of a loaf of bread could lead to the gallows, punishment could be harsh. A visitor to South Carolina reported seeing a suspended cage containing a bound slave. Birds had already attacked. Blood and wounds covered his body, and his eyes had been plucked out of their sockets. A planter explained that the offending slave had killed a plantation official, and that "the laws of self-preservation rendered such execution necessary." Some planters criticized their peers' treatment of slaves. The great Virginia planter William Byrd II complained that his neighbor's "poor Negroes are a kind of Adamites, very scantily supply'd with cloaths and other necessaries." Byrd considered such lack of care a "Scandal."

Most planters, however, provided their slaves with adequate food, clothing, and shelter. To the planters, their own self-interest required no less. After all, slaves were valuable property; they represented a good portion of the wealth of the master class. While masters generally attempted to provide for the physical well-being of their bondsmen and bondswomen, they were conscious of the raw power fundamental to the master–slave relationship. And most did not hesitate to exercise their authority. Again William Byrd offers pertinent testimony. He recognized that force was an integral part of the system. "Numbers make them insolent," he observed, "& then foul means must do what fair will not . . . these base Tempers require to be rid with a tort [sic] rein, or they will be apt to throw their Rider."

3

The Intellectual, Political, and Religious World

❖

Although the political development of the southern colonies shared much with that of the other mainland colonies, particular aspects of the southern experience had a profound impact on the subsequent history of the region's political culture. Specific ideas, institutions, and practices shaped the form of southern politics even before the Revolution.

Liberty was the central political idea of the English southern colonies. Although before the 1760s southerners spent little time writing about the theoretical and philosophical dimensions of liberty, they had no doubt as to its fundamental meaning: according to the *Oxford English Dictionary*, "freedom from arbitrary, despotic rule or control." In the immediate political context of seventeenth- and eighteenth-century England, liberty meant some kind of representative government that would ensure such freedom. In England the Parliament represented the interests and protected the liberty of the king's subjects.

The distance that separated the New World from the mother country prevented any agency of the British government from performing this critical task in the colonies. An ocean voyage of 3,000 miles, requiring at least three months for the round trip, made the possibility of immediate guardianship precarious indeed. Living in a relatively small country, politically active Englishmen, both rural and urban, felt something akin to political control. Thus political liberty included connotations of geographic propinquity between the government and the governed. The colonists' intellectual defense of their assemblies clearly revealed this conjunction between liberty and local governmental control.

The Assemblies

Colonial assemblies appeared early. The House of Burgesses was founded in 1619, only a dozen years after the first settlement at Jamestown. The establishment of assemblies in the other colonies, northern as well as southern, followed the example set by Virginia, usually in even less time. These transplanted Englishmen were determined to replicate one of their most treasured institutions.

These assemblies did not come into existence simply to protect the perceived interests of a colony. Perhaps even more important, assemblies provided a vehicle for the protection of local and private rights, economic as well as political. Through the assembly, planters in various parts of a colony had a say in the governing both of the entire colony and of their own bailiwicks. To southerners liberty was never just an abstract concept. It always involved their perceptions of their self-interest. Most of them were concerned chiefly about their own liberty. Control of one's own affairs lay at the heart of liberty, of freedom from outside interference. By this definition, an individual—a tobacco planter, for example—must have his interests represented in the colonial government or risk losing his liberty. Pertinent here is the experience of the House of Burgesses. Originally the burgesses met with the Governor's Council, but by the 1650s the council was coming to be associated with the office of the governor and with executive or royal power. As a result, the burgesses felt that they must give a clear identity to their house in order to protect the interests of the local planters they represented. Thus liberty demanded a distinct House of Burgesses.

The assemblies rapidly assumed considerable authority. Even before the seventeenth century had run its course, they had successfully asserted their power and prerogative. As early as the end of the 1650s the House of Burgesses, composed of local magnates, possessed real power in Virginia. By then London could no longer effectively control affairs in the colony without the concurrence of the burgesses. When the Maryland assembly considered it appropriate to do so, it rejected legislation proposed by the proprietor, and the proprietor had to acquiesce in the assembly's decision. In South Carolina during the 1680s the Lords Proprietors sent in new people to wrest control of the colony from a group that treated proprietary instructions and directions in cavalier fashion. The colonists had disregarded directives on debts, Indian trade, and land distribution. The resulting conflict between old and new colonists only fueled the efforts of the antiproprietary faction and did nothing to undermine the growing authority of the assembly. The Glorious Revolution of 1688 in England, which rejected the doctrine and practice of supreme royal power, confirmed for the colonists the special place of their assemblies. Just as the Parliament stood in England as the protector of liberty, the colonial assemblies assumed the role of guardian against tyranny. Of course, in the eyes of the colonials that role had been the purpose of the assemblies from the beginning, but after 1688 that purpose, from the colonial perspective, fit neatly into the larger scheme of British affairs. Translated into practical terms, this theoretical role meant that the colonists were even more determined to protect their perception of their own interests by defending and by pressing the authority of their assemblies. The historian of the southern assemblies termed this great theme "the quest for power." Surely it was a quest for power—power to guarantee the liberty of the colonists by protecting their self-interest.

ASSERTION OF POWER BY THE ASSEMBLIES

Southern colonists did not wait for the Revolutionary crisis to make fundamental claims for their right to an assembly. The crown always maintained that assemblies existed only through a royal grant of privilege. Southerners rejected that position; they had more in mind than simply the political reality and the political power of their assemblies. In 1739 the South Carolina Commons House of Assembly adopted a resolution justifying its right to exist on the grounds of the basic right of Englishmen to legislative representation. "No Usage or Royal Instruction," the assembly asserted, "can take away the force of it in America." This resolution explicitly claimed for the South Carolina assembly, and by extension for all assemblies, the privileges of the House of Commons in London.

Two episodes that antedate the Revolutionary crisis reveal the determination of the assemblies and the political distance they willingly traveled to guard their sense of their liberty. The Pistole Fee Controversy in Virginia in the mid-1750s involved the power of the purse, the power to tax; the Gadsden Election Controversy, which rocked South Carolina in the early 1760s, turned on the authority of the assembly to determine its own membership.

These conflicts arose because royal governors attempted to impose their policies or their will in areas the assemblies considered their exclusive domain. In Virginia, Governor Robert Dinwiddie, who arrived in 1752, proclaimed a fee or tax of one pistole, a small Spanish coin, for use of his seal on a land patent. The House of Burgesses declared that it alone had the right to tax the people of Virginia. Addressing the governor, the burgesses asserted, "The Rights of the Subject [any of the king's subjects, even those in Virginia] are so secured by Law, that they cannot be deprived of the least part of their Property, but by their own Consent." Both sides stood their ground, the lawmakers echoing the cry made in a public toast: "Liberty and property and no pistole!" The dispute was finally settled in 1754 when the royal government in London technically upheld the governor but so restricted the imposition of the fee that the burgesses could feel vindicated.

Claiming a violation of South Carolina's election law, Governor Thomas Boone refused in 1762 to administer the oath of office to Christopher Gadsden, a recently elected member of the assembly. The assembly had perceived no problem and had seated Gadsden. The governor also maintained that the assembly existed solely at the pleasure of the crown, not by any basic right the colonists enjoyed as English subjects. Outraged by the governor's action, which it denounced as "a most precipitate, unadvised, unprecedented Procedure of the most dangerous Consequence," the assembly declared that no one else could decide its membership, and it refused to conduct any further business with the governor "until his Excellency shall have done justice to this House." This conflict also went to London for resolution. Though the decision in 1764 did criticize the assembly, it did not uphold Boone, who left the colony. With Boone gone and London making no move to challenge its claim to legitimacy, the assembly clearly had won.

Both the Pistole Fee Controversy and the Gadsden Election Controversy reveal just how tenaciously the colonists clung to their vision of their liberty. Despite the position of the governors as agents of royal power, the assemblies refused to bow or to bend. As they defined the issue, none could be more fundamental. The essence of liberty—protection against outside control, against despotic power—was at stake. The legislators saw themselves as manning the battlements at the most crucial points. They acted on the premise that "liberty and property once lost, a people have nothing left worth contending for."

REGULATION

The duty to safeguard liberty did not stop at a colony's boundaries. The colonists themselves expected their assemblies to guard them no less zealously on the issues that affected all the colonies. This function of the assembly never seriously clashed with the interests of the dominant elite, as they dominated the assemblies. For others, however, the action or the inaction of the assemblies as the guarantors of liberty could generate considerable distress.

This relationship between the colonies and their assemblies provides the most fruitful approach to an understanding of the Regulator movement, which sprang up in the back country of both North and South Carolina during the 1760s. Although the movement varied slightly in the two colonies, it had the same thrust in both. The Regulator movement did not represent a revolt of the oppressed against the privileged. In South Carolina substantial back-country men led voting, independent farmers in an attempt to gain effective expansion of the colonial legal system into their home area. They wanted courts and sheriffs close at hand to protect liberty and property from lawless bands. Small to middling planters in North Carolina led approximately 75 percent of the back-country population in an attempt to protect their local rights. The North Carolina Regulators detested the pervasive corruption in their local political and judicial institutions, a corruption at least countenanced by the assembly. The Regulators feared that sheriffs' abuse of their tax-collecting authority, with neither oversight nor correction coming from the assembly, endangered both their prosperity and their freedom. They adopted the name Regulator because "their primary goal was to gain the right to regulate their own local government."

Neither group of Regulators gained an immediate victory, but their efforts did not go for naught. In South Carolina the legal system did finally make its way into the back country, though not before the Regulation had degenerated into a vigilante movement trying to impose morality. In North Carolina, Regulation had a more fractious, even belligerent career than ended in fighting and bloodshed. Even there, however, the Articles of Settlement of 1768 left most Regulator partisans with the belief that the movement had benefited them. In neither colony did the Regulation herald any long-term divisiveness, for during the ensuing war with England the great majority of the Regulators fought for the colonial cause against the mother country.

THE ELITE AND DEFERENCE

The assemblies existed to protect and benefit their creators and constituents. In each colony the economic and social elite made up the political elite. This elite was the dominant force in the assemblies, and its members clearly envisioned the assemblies as their assemblies, organized not only to defend their interests but to advance them.

Throughout the colonial South, both in space and in time, great planters formed the keystone of the elite. From the seventeenth-century Chesapeake to eighteenth-century Georgia the men who managed the slave plantations also directed political affairs in their colonies. Although the planters surely dominated, they shared political power with two complementary groups. Everywhere the leading lawyers and the large merchants participated directly in legislative activity. Especially in South Carolina with its port of Charleston, the largest city in the colonial South, nonplanters enjoyed particular influence; in fact, the lawyers and merchants of the city usually led the assembly. The division of the southern elite into planters, lawyers, and merchants can easily be exaggerated, however, for often one man engaged in two of the three occupations. In Maryland most of the great planters were also intimately involved in commercial affairs. Many of the leading planters in Virginia were also lawyers—Thomas Jefferson, for example. The wealthy Charleston merchant Henry Laurens became a major rice planter after making his fortune in trade. Men of other influential South Carolina political families, such as the Rutledges and the Pinckneys, were lawyers first and planters second. In sum, it is unhistorical to divide the colonial southern elite into agricultural, commercial, and professional interests, as though those interests were mutually exclusive.

The elite thought of themselves and comported themselves accordingly. They treated the people they considered their social inferiors differently from the way they treated their peers, and they expected the inferiors to accept the differentiation. In the middle of the eighteenth century William Bull, Sr., lieutenant governor of South Carolina, acted on such premises. After Sunday services Bull often invited the congregation of Prince William's Parish to his plantation. Bull personally received his peers of the gentry inside his home while the other parishioners, a majority, remained outside with Bull's overseer as their immediate host. This overtly discriminatory behavior occasioned neither surprise nor antagonism. Both groups, the upper and the lower, expected the treatment they received.

The religious structure buttressed this ranking of society. In each English colony in the South, the Anglican (today the Episcopal) church was the established church: only the Anglican church had official government sanction, and public funds paid its clergy. Everywhere the Anglicans counted among their communicants the major portion of the economic, social, and political elite. Dissenting Protestant churches appealed chiefly to the lower order of society. The Roman Catholic church mattered only in Maryland, where its membership did include some of the wealthiest families, such as the Carrolls. But Catholic influence and relative strength declined in Maryland throughout the colonial era.

The vestry of the established church exercised considerable influence in the parishes, which became important units of local government. A body of prominent laymen, the vestry had responsibility for such diverse matters as relief for the poor, church construction, public education, and the hiring of ministers. The vestry was so important that notable non-Anglicans who wanted to influence local affairs sometimes got themselves elected vestrymen, even though the law specified that only Anglicans could serve. Just as the elite of a parish made up the vestry, the same elite furnished the assembly delegates. Assemblymen and vestrymen were often identical. Vestrymen and assemblymen controlled the church, local affairs, and the assemblies, and they expected their social inferiors to support their efforts.

No evidence indicates substantial chafing at this system, either at Bull's Sunday soirees or anywhere else. In the eighteenth century few of the independent or yeoman farmers, who constituted the great bulk of the southern white population, disputed this social system. Although the majority could vote and many did, practically nobody challenged the assumption of the upper class that it alone could provide proper political leadership. In the Carolina back country the yeomen normally looked to men of the higher economic and social ranks for political leadership. Even the politically active skilled artisans in Charleston and Savannah never questioned the political role of those they thought of as their betters. Many of these artisans were legally qualified to sit in the assembly, but custom awarded such seats to the elite, and before the Revolution artisans never challenged the custom. Instead they supported the individuals they perceived as helping them. The son of a Virginia farmer and carpenter spoke for his class across the South when he remembered: "We were accustomed to look upon what were called *gentle folks*, as beings of a superior order."

This political behavior is indisputably deferential politics. Not only did the gentry rule; the farmers and artisans expected them to do so and supported their exercise of authority. Important as it was, though, the politics of deference did not alone shape southern political life.

THE DEMOCRATIC CHARACTER OF POLITICS

Colonial southern politics also had a democratic configuration. The great majority of white southerners, who at any one time were of course not of the upper class, also had the right to be active politically through voting. Throughout the period each colony determined its own franchise requirements, and each restricted the franchise. Everywhere by the eighteenth century ownership of property was a prerequisite for voting, though occasionally, as in the South Carolina Electoral Act of 1721, payment of a stipulated tax sufficed. No matter the specific statutory provision at any given time, the southern colonials shared the view that only those with a tangible stake in society should have the right to vote. Although the precise number of people enfranchised and disenfranchised is impossible to ascertain, it is clear that in the eighteenth century a majority of the white males could vote in each colony. This politically relevant group probably included from 60 percent to 90 percent of the adult white males. The percentage varied over time as well as by colony. Of course, the legal right to vote does not automatically ensure the exercise of that right.

For the broad franchise to influence the political process significantly, the enfranchised must vote. Before the 1760s interest in voting and electoral activity varied. In some places and at some times interest and activity quickened; in other places and at other times they flagged. Elections in Virginia for the House of

Burgesses usually stimulated electoral enterprise, though not every contest brought an outpouring of voters. The first election for the Georgia assembly, in 1754, was fiercely contested both in the countryside and in Savannah, but in other years elections were quiet. Except in Charleston and its vicinity, South Carolinians generally showed little interest in voting before the 1760s. In the city and its environs, however, elections occasioned a flurry of activity.

The interest in elections came in no small part from the efforts of men who hungered for office. As early as 1699 the House of Burgesses lamented the excesses of office seekers and sought to restrict them, but with little success. Electioneering techniques used by successful candidates for the burgesses included meeting and speaking with prospective voters. Candidates met with church congregations; they visited in private homes and stayed overnight when campaign exertions carried them substantial distances from home. And all tried to bring joy to the voters in the way George Washington did in Frederick County in 1758. On that occasion Washington's agent supplied 160 gallons of spirits to 391 voters. Barrels of whiskey open on the courthouse green were not an unusual sight in the hurly-burly of a hot contest. Virginia probably led the way in electioneering, but such practices were certainly not unknown elsewhere. Even in young Georgia, electoral excitement in 1768 inspired two women to sally forth in a carriage to win votes for their political hero.

THE POLITICIANS

In this active electoral process the mere possession of money, social rank, and even a famous name did not guarantee political success. Conscious of their power to approve and to reject bids for office, colonial voters demanded that candidates treat them with respect. Though the candidates were not of the same class as the bulk of the voters, they had to possess characteristics that the voters approved and supported. The essential ingredient in political success, then, was not name or wealth, for many men who had both failed to achieve notable political careers. Before anything else, the aspiring political leader had to be ambitious for political place. Ambition was essential because victory usually required effort. A veteran Virginia politician who had known both victory and defeat perfectly understood the requirement, and obviously himself as well. Writing to a friend, he announced that he was "once again in a state to venture on the stormy sea of politics and public business." The requisite ambition mustered, the candidate had "to practice the arts by which [the voters'] approval could be won." Political leadership required the savvy and acumen that could transform economic and social privilege into victory at the polls.

John Robinson and Willie Jones mastered the complexities. As longtime speaker of the House of Burgesses and treasurer of the colony in the mid-eighteenth century, John Robinson gained wide popularity in Virginia. But equally important for Robinson's favorable public image was his personality. "A jewel of a man," according to one associate, Robinson possessed "a benevolence which created friends and sincerity which never lost one." Widely admired, Robinson, in the minds of politically conscious Virginians, was a man whose "opinions must be regarded."

In neighboring North Carolina just a bit later, Willie Jones proved himself an equally adept practitioner of the political art. Even those who disagreed with him marveled at his political astuteness. As one of them observed, Jones "stimulated the passions, aroused the suspicions, [and] moderated the ardor of his followers." He managed to do so because he "stole his way into [their] hearts" by "smoking his pipe, and chatting of crops, ploughs, stock, dogs, and c." Many citizens believed Jones, the sophisticated planter, the most influential public man in his state.

The qualities that blended to create the master politicians of the colonial South differed little from those that characterized leaders of subsequent generations. Most politicians, understanding that their success depended on the political culture that nourished them, vociferously defended its goodness and doggedly guarded its institutions and privileges against outside encroachment. Attacks on their own class or the deference it received were rare. Products of a system few questioned seriously, they adopted defense of it as a cardinal principle.

PARTICIPATORY POLITICS

Colonial southern politics, then, was both deferential and democratic. Without question the upper class dominated the political system, but that system was fluid and marked by constant interaction between elector and elected. Historians who emphasize either deference or democracy to the exclusion of the other oversimplify, because any valid general characterization of the system must account for both. This political process can perhaps best be described as "participatory politics."

All involved in the process, whether vote seekers or voters, recognized that popular rule underlay the liberty of their political system. Political institutions existed to guard the rights of the people, and the people's representatives worked to protect their constituents and to carry out their wishes. A former royal governor of North Carolina thoroughly understood this truth. In 1733 he described the colonials as a people "who are subtle and crafty to admiration, who could neither be outwitted nor cajoled, who always behave insolently to their governors." And ready to protect these difficult folk stood assemblymen bound to them by culture and votes. The voters of Orange County, North Carolina, instructed their assembly delegates: "Gentlemen, we have chosen you our Representatives at the next General Assembly and when we did so we expected and still do expect that you will speak our Sense in every case when we shall expressly declare it, or when you by any other means discover it." That sentiment ranged far beyond North Carolina. Failure to attempt to discern the sense of electors returned assemblymen to the ranks of electors. Without question representatives were aware that they spoke for a larger body than themselves. From at least the early 1720s the South Carolina assembly clearly responded to public opinion; thoughts of the electorate were never out of assemblymen's minds. In 1767 the Georgia assembly refused to grant a gubernatorial request because, the assemblymen explained, to grant it would violate the trust the people had placed in them.

One of the most famous political scandals in the colonial South underscored this relationship between the gentry who dominated the assemblies and the voters. Upon the death in 1766 of John Robinson, for twenty-eight years the treasurer of Virginia as well as the speaker of the House of Burgesses, the discovery was made that he had embezzled more than £100,000 of public money, which he lent to himself and close associates. Although particulars of the scandal did not become public knowledge, its general outlines appeared in the press, and rumors about its details permeated the colony. Aware that their continued power depended on the reputation they enjoyed among the electorate, the burgesses instituted legal procedures against Robinson's estate to recover the money. They also separated the offices of speaker and treasurer; never again would the same man hold both offices simultaneously. In addition they created a committee to conduct semiannual audits of the public accounts—audits that would be published.

In this instance the political elite surely acted to preserve and protect their power, but by their actions they acknowledged that such prerogatives depended on the support of social and economic inferiors who participated in the political process. In fact, the post-Robinson reforms probably strengthened the position of the elite in Virginia because the reforms demonstrated responsible leadership. They were in the best interest of all Virginians, not just of the burgesses.

CONFLICT WITH INDIANS

Through most of the colonial era the public issues with which southern politicians dealt tended to concern finance, land, and place. Often routine, they occasionally sparked heated controversy, which enlivened the political arena. Colonial assemblies and politicians also had to confront questions of defense, which usually meant relations with neighboring Indian tribes. From the moment of contact until the Revolution the Indian question remained unresolved.

The militia assumed central importance in the colonists' stance toward the Indians. Based on the principle that free men had the duty to guard and to protect their society, by fighting if necessary, the militia had a long history in England. Drawing on their English heritage, the colonists early on created militias, chiefly to contend with the presence and potential threat of the Indians. Laws made clear that white males from their late teens to middle age had a responsibility to contribute to the safety of their colony by serving in the militia. A militiaman usually had to supply his own weapon, ammunition, clothing, and provisions. Training was generally haphazard, a matter of drills and reviews on muster days scattered throughout the year. On those occasions military training tended to take second place to social festivities. The laws normally authorized the governor to name the militia officers, and he appointed them with an eye more to the prominence of their families than to their military expertise. Yet the militia understood its purpose and recognized that it could be called up in time of danger.

Though the Powhatan tribes had almost wiped out the Jamestown settlers in 1622, their strength declined rapidly in the face of white Virginians determined to beat them down. The tribes rose up one last time in 1644 and killed some 500 colonists. The Virginians retaliated vigorously and effectively, but the Indian problem did not totally disappear, for the Indians remained intimately involved with the extension of white settlements. This fact was an essential ingredient in Bacon's Rebellion. Still, after 1650 the Indians of Virginia were almost as powerless as those in Maryland, who never did have sufficient numbers to pose a serious obstacle to the settlers' advance.

No other significant difficulties with the Indians arose in Virginia before the settlement of the Shenandoah Valley in the mid-eighteenth century. At that time the Virginia frontier became embroiled in the larger Anglo-French contest for North America. Virginians in the western reaches of the colony confronted Indians backed by the French. These tribes were not descendants of the tidewater people put down a century earlier; they hailed rather from western Pennsylvania and the Ohio Valley. When the British finally defeated the French in 1763, the Virginia frontier quieted down, though the danger to exposed settlements never entirely disappeared.

The story of North Carolina reads much the same, though the events took place somewhat later. The sparseness of settlers and the small size of their scattered settlements worked against serious problems between colonists and Indians before 1700. But after 1700 a growing population resulted in a more determined expansion into the interior of the colony, which in turn led to troubles with the major local tribe, the Tuscarora. The fifteen Tuscarora villages, with a total of some 2,000 men of fighting age, were located along the chief rivers in eastern North Carolina. These people were understandably outraged when colonists captured Tuscarora women and children and sold them into slavery, and they had no higher opinion of the colonists' relentless advance to the west. Finally in 1711 hostilities erupted into a war that lasted two years. In that contest the combined militias of North and South Carolina and Virginia decisively defeated the Tuscarora forces. The Tuscarora War ended any real danger to the colonists in eastern North Carolina; nor could the Indians any longer delay the settlers' push into the central part of the colony.

South Carolina and Georgia had a different experience because they had to contend with larger numbers of Indians and also because of the Spanish presence in Florida. The Spanish were as wary of British encroachment as the Indians. From their citadel of St. Augustine, little more than 250 miles from Charleston, they recruited Indian allies to confront the British. The Creek, who lived mostly in western Georgia and what became Alabama, provided important assistance to the Spaniards.

In South Carolina the first generation of settlers engaged in an ongoing contest with various tribes, often aided by the Spanish. The critical contest came against the Yamassee, a tribe located initially in eastern Georgia. Before 1700, however, the Yamassee began to move across the Savannah River and establish towns in lower South Carolina. Relations worsened until in 1715 the Yamassee, supported by the Creek and the Spanish, assaulted the British settlements. The colonists fought back and overwhelmed their Indian opponents. The Indians' defeat in the Yamassee War ended their threat to the settlers in the low country.

Georgia was a battleground almost from the beginning. Settled in part to provide a buffer between an increasingly wealthy South Carolina and Spanish Florida, Georgia fulfilled its mission. Possible Spanish moves against either or both colonies constantly concerned officials of both, and with good reason. The Spanish viewed with dismay the British settlement of coastal Georgia, which placed British settlers no more than 100 miles from St. Augustine. But neither the Spanish nor their Indian allies could drive the British out of Georgia. The military fate of the youngest British colony was sealed in 1742 when Georgians under James Oglethorpe soundly defeated a Spanish force that had landed on the Georgia coast. This victory over the Spanish at Bloody Marsh secured South Carolina as well as Georgia. And after 1763, when Spain lost Florida to Great Britain, Spain could no longer threaten the security of the southernmost British colonies.

The success of Carolinians and Georgians along the seacoast did not guarantee a similar result in their conflict with the Cherokee in the western reaches of their colonies. From the beginning the colonists in both Carolinas and later in Georgia had traded profitably with the Cherokee, but disagreements had always arisen over proper boundaries. As settlements pushed farther and farther inland during the middle third of the eighteenth century, boundary disputes became increasingly rancorous, and almost inevitably sporadic violence broke out.

Toward the end of the 1750s the Cherokee numbering some 3,000 men were becoming increasingly unhappy with the colonial authorities. The issue of colonial intrusion into Cherokee lands could not be settled; all efforts to resolve the issue failed. Finally, fearing seemingly unending encroachments on their land, the Cherokee in 1759 attacked outlying western settlements in both Carolinas. Stung, the colonists struck back. Led by the South Carolina militia, around 1,300 men marched against the Cherokee. By 1761 a series of hard blows by the colonials had so weakened the Cherokee that they could no longer effectively resist the white onslaught. They gave up more and more of the land the colonists coveted until, by an agreement reached in 1765, they turned over most of northwestern South Carolina and retreated into the mountains. This outcome settled the Cherokee question until the Revolution.

RELIGION

Although the issue of physical security engaged the southern colonists just as it did their counterparts elsewhere, religious concerns did not assume the importance in the South that they did in New England, at least not until the mid-eighteenth century. Throughout the colonial period, for the majority of white southern colonials religion meant the Church of England, also known more popularly as the Anglican church—the established church in all the English southern colonies.

In establishing the Church of England, the assembly in every colony placed its authority behind the institution's financial and political support. Yet the established church was operating without a spiritual leader in North America. The church hierarchy in England never appointed a bishop to head the colonial church. From New England to Georgia the church had to look to London for guidance and authorization for its activities. The absence of a bishop caused serious difficulties for the colonial church. Among the most pressing problems was a shortage of clergy. With no bishop on the scene, men who felt called to the Anglican ministry had to journey to England for instruction and ordination. A paucity of Anglican ministers in the colonies was guaranteed.

During the colonial era the church did not occupy a central place in the lives or thoughts of most of its communicants. With no resident spiritual leader, with far too few clergy, with an absence of theological rigor, and with a frown on emotion, the Anglican church did not generate either fervor or excitement among its members. Its decorous formalities only rarely stirred hearts and minds. The church did, however, provide a mainstay for the social order and for the elite who dominated it. The elite were overwhelmingly of the Anglican persuasion. Their dominance of the vestry, as we have seen, complemented their dominance of the assemblies. For the elite, church and state were almost one.

All colonists not loyal to the Church of England were labeled dissenters. Dissent existed in the southern colonies from the beginning. Roman Catholics had a critical role in the founding and settling of Maryland, but the history of dissent in the southern colonies does not focus on Roman Catholics. In Maryland they quickly became a minority, though a generally tolerated one. Elsewhere they could not be found. In the colonial South, dissenters were non-Anglican Protestants.

Protestant dissent ranged across a wide spectrum. At one end stood the Huguenots, the French Calvinists who came mostly into South Carolina in the late seventeenth and early eighteenth centuries. In a relatively short time the Huguenots so thoroughly assimilated with the Anglicans that many became Anglicans themselves. By mid-century some of the leading South Carolina families, such as the Manigaults, boasted Huguenot names and Anglican loyalties. At the other end of the spectrum stood the Quakers, who had no interest in assimilation; no one else wanted to mix with them, either. In the eyes of the ascendant groups, the Quakers' pacifism, their refusal to take oaths, and later their antislavery stance made them social misfits and religious radicals. Quakers did not have an easy time, though no southern colony emulated New England and prescribed the death penalty for holding to Quaker beliefs. The Quakers never became a major social force, and their main settlement in central North Carolina remained largely isolated.

*T*HE GREAT AWAKENING

The significant impact of dissent came from the evangelicals, chiefly the Baptists, Methodists, and Presbyterians. Their influence at once generated and stemmed from a general religious movement that spanned the colonies. The Great Awakening, a series of religious revivals that originated in New England and swept through the colonies in the mid-eighteenth century, first visited the South around 1740 in the Chesapeake and then spread southward. In the southern colonies the Awakening represented in part a reaction against the formalism and lethargy of the Anglican church. Many southern colonials, eager for a more emotional and more vigorously active religious experience, looked for it beyond the established church. Widespread sentiment against public support for the church so closely tied to the colonial elite helped to propel the Great Awakening.

Revival meetings were the key features of the Great Awakening. Preachers spoke to eager crowds in buildings of every kind and in open fields. Many of these evangelists were itinerants, preachers who traveled from place to place; at each stop they called on their listeners to join the march toward salvation. The revivalists' message emphasized the necessity of an individual religious experience. Stressing the sinfulness of all, the revivalists called out that all must become aware of their sorry spiritual state. Awareness would then lead to conversion; at that point God's grace would save the believer. This was, of course, a far cry from the formalities of the established church.

Among the legion of preachers calling for repentance and renewal certain men had a tremendous influence over their audiences. Many people thought George Whitefield was the greatest orator and preacher of his day. After coming to Georgia in 1737 as an Anglican minister, Whitefield went back to England, then returned to this side of the Atlantic two years later to launch a speaking tour that took him to every southern colony. Whitefield preached the new Methodist faith, which grew out of Anglicanism, though a separate church did not appear until after the Revolution. Methodism appealed to Anglicans who believed that their church had become staid and static. It spread rapidly among the unchurched as well, especially in the poorer classes. No one was more zealous in the cause of Methodism than Whitefield. His powerful, eloquent sermons, in which he often trounced the Anglican clergy as unregenerates, attracted hearers and made converts from the Potomac to Georgia.

Samuel Davies, born in Delaware in 1723, labored with equal intensity to propagate the Presbyterian faith in the Virginia piedmont and back country. A magnificent preacher, a prolific hymnist, and a gifted organizer, he put together in 1755 the first presbytery, the governing structure of this Calvinist church, in the southern colonies. Hanover Presbytery became the mother presbytery for the Presbyterian church in the South.

The Methodists, the Presbyterians, the Baptists—all profited from the Great Awakening. In the three decades before the Revolution each of these denominations built a substantial presence in every colony. The Baptists spread into the southern colonies from New England and the middle colonies. With their emphasis on the autonomy of each congregation and their willingness, even eagerness, to accept untrained clergy, the Baptists matched the Methodists in rapid growth. During the first half of the century small groups of Presbyterians moved through such ports as Charleston into the back country. But the great Presbyterian migration came in mid-century. Moving southward from Pennsylvania into the Valley of Virginia and on down into the piedmont of both Carolinas and Georgia, Scots-Irish Presbyterians grew into a powerful force on the frontier. Although their organizational structure and their insistence on an educated clergy helped keep their numbers below those of the Baptists and Methodists, their cohesiveness and energy made their presence felt.

The Church of England simply could not match the dynamics of the evangelicals, and it watched with dismay as increasing numbers of its more enthusiastic members broke away to join the Methodists. Undoubtedly many Anglicans had no interest in competing with dissenters. Others did, but they found the going tough. One of the most dedicated was the Reverend Charles Woodmason, a native Englishman who put on the clerical collar after some ten years of various activities in South Carolina. Woodmason took as his mission the carrying of the Church of England into the back country of his own colony. Away from the low-country parishes he found considerable hostility, especially among the Presbyterians, who made every effort to undermine his missionary endeavor. Woodmason reported that to thwart his crusade the Presbyterians on one occasion provided two barrels of whiskey for the crowd gathered for his services. This tactic worked, for "the Company got drunk by 10 o'th clock and we could hear them firing, hooping, and hallowing like Indians." According to the outraged Woodmason, the nefarious Presbyterians never let up. To the mind of this harassed evangel of Anglicanism, one of their schemes was particularly diabolical: they "[took] down Advertisements for calling our People together." The offending Calvinists often altered the date and place of Woodmason's services. "When I came," a frustrated Woodmason complained, "there were no People—and on other days the People would meet and no Minister." Woodmason's tribulations underscored the extreme difficulty the established church confronted with the surge of the evangelical faiths.

The Great Awakening did not change the fact of establishment, though it did have a significant impact on the Anglican church. The Awakening provoked discussion on the issue of establishment itself; many of the evangelicals asked why their taxes should support the Church of England alone or at all. In addition the substantial anticlerical sentiment voiced by so many spokesmen of the Awakening injured the reputation and the position of the Anglican clergy. In Virginia even within the established church conflict erupted between clergy and laity over control of the ministers' salaries. This infighting hurt the ministers, who appeared overly concerned about worldly matters, and it also struck at the moral authority of the Anglican church, which could ill afford such blows. Moreover, an assault against the established church could easily become a strike at the social order in which it occupied such a conspicuous place. Without question the Great Awakening contributed to tensions in colonial society, but the social fabric remained fundamentally intact at the onset of the Revolution.

CULTURE AND EDUCATION

The southern colonies were on a cultural as well as a geographical frontier. From Jamestown to the Revolution, neither concern for education nor the life of the mind assumed major importance for most colonists. The overwhelming majority of whites spent their lives in hard physical labor to wrest a living from soil and forest. The gentry who lived in the manor houses of the Chesapeake and the Carolina low country attempted to replicate the culture of the mother country in the New World. In the colonial South, as in most of the Western world during the seventeenth and eighteenth centuries, only the upper classes had an opportunity to cultivate artistic and intellectual pursuits, even one as fundamental as reading. Those who did were so few and in general so widely separated from one another that they could not institutionalize education or the arts beyond the local level.

The educational enterprise, as understood today, simply did not exist in the southern colonies. No colony supported a public school system. In the eighteenth century the larger towns, such as Annapolis and Charleston, did have free common schools, but they reached very few young people. The upper classes tended to hire tutors to educate their children. The tutors, many of them recent graduates of northern colleges and often aspiring clergymen, introduced the scions of the gentry to the mysteries of Greek, Latin, mathematics, some history, and occasionally modern foreign languages. Some plantation families hired a tutor solely for their own children; others joined together to employ a tutor to instruct all of their children jointly. The wealthiest tobacco and rice families not uncommonly sent their sons to England for the best education the mother country offered. In this endeavor prosperous southern colonials acted differently from their counterparts in the middle colonies and New England, who rarely turned to England for the schooling of their young. Two reasons probably account for this difference: first, the richest planters had more money; second, the southern gentry were trying to emulate the English country squires in every way they could.

In the almost 170 years that elapsed between the settling of Jamestown and the outbreak of the Revolution, only one college opened its doors in the southern colonies. Chartered in 1693, the College of William and Mary at Williamsburg, Virginia, is the second oldest institution of higher learning in the United States. Only Harvard, with a 1636 birth date, has a more ancient lineage. The primary force behind the founding of William and Mary was the Reverend John Blair, a native Englishman and Anglican minister, who came to Virginia as the commissary or agent of the bishop of London. Conscious of the woeful shortage of pastors in the colony, Blair wanted a college to help provide an educated clergy for the Anglican church. The colonial William and Mary was an all-purpose institution. It had an Indian school and a grammar school as well as a collegiate course. Beset by difficulties in the beginning and quite weak early in the eighteenth century—a report in 1712, for example, indicated a total enrollment of twenty-two students—the college had become stronger by mid-century. Although William and Mary never met Commissary Blair's goal of providing the requisite number of trained ministers for the established church, it did educate many of the elite of the colony, several of whom became prominent during the Revolutionary crisis; two of its most illustrious alumni were Thomas Jefferson and James Monroe. To foster scholarship and debate, the college established the first chapter of the Phi Beta Kappa Society in 1776.

The gentry attempted to provide for themselves the cultural attractions favored by the British upper classes, and in the major towns, especially in Charleston, Annapolis, and Williamsburg, they made considerable headway. In the 1710s Williamsburg had an operating playhouse and acting company. By mid-century two professional touring troupes entertained Virginians in Williamsburg and also in smaller towns such as Fredericksburg. Beginning in those same years, acting companies performed in Annapolis. As early as 1703 visiting players entertained Charleston audiences; professional companies appeared thereafter, and before 1740 a theater had been built. The colonials preferred and attended the plays most popular in England at the time; Shakespeare was always the favorite.

Even before 1750 concerts had become as commonplace as dramatic productions. Musical groups were active throughout Maryland. Williamsburg featured chamber music concerts and by 1766 could boast of an orchestra. Charleston was the home of the most distinctive musical program in the southern colonies. Professionals from both England and the continent performed there. Concerts were presented on a subscription basis as early as 1733; the first performance of an opera in the American colonies took place in Charleston in 1735. Musical societies abounded. The most notable and the oldest in America, the St. Cecilia Society, established in 1762, sponsored an orchestra with paid musicians. Though surely not London, the largest colonial towns provided remarkable cultural offerings for their time and their location.

THE WRITTEN WORD

Southern colonials did not gain fame for their authorship. Traditionally the colonial South has been judged a literary desert in comparison with New England. More recent investigations, however, have led to the discovery that southern colonials produced writing of considerable quality and quantity. From poetry to plays to histories to sermons, the output of southerners equaled in distinction that of writers to the north. That fact has generally been established, though studies of the southern literary effort do not yet match in thoroughness and sophistication the scholarship applied to the writings of New Englanders.

Certainly histories rank among the most important of colonial southern writings, and they have received the most attention. In the southern colonies this genre originated with Captain John Smith, who brought out his *Generall Historie of Virginia* in 1624. The writing of history remained largely a Virginia enterprise. Two particularly notable eighteenth-century successors to Smith were Robert Beverley and Hugh Jones, both of whom published histories of the oldest colony. All three of these early historians had a dual purpose: not only to describe and explain events but to make Virginia attractive to new settlers. All published their works in London.

Beverley, a native Virginian, member of a notable family, and public man who served in the House of Burgesses, wrote more as a Virginian than as an Englishman. He used a wide range of sources for *The History and Present State of Virginia* (1705; a second edition appeared in 1722), which he wrote while in England. Beverley's thorough account of seventeenth-century Virginia criticized some officials and official policies (the criticism was muted in the second edition), and he argued that the "slothful Indolence" of Virginians kept them from making the most of the colony's abundant resources. At the same time, he declared Virginia "the best poor Man's country in the World" and predicted a bright future for it.

Unlike Beverley, Hugh Jones was born in England; he first arrived in Virginia as an Anglican minister, with an appointment to the faculty of William and Mary. Jones's *Present State of Virginia* (1724) focused more on the contemporary world than on the past. The laziness that worried Beverley did not bother Jones. On the contrary, Jones spoke almost admiringly of the outlook and characteristics of Virginians. Celebrating the environment, he predicted a bountiful future for the

WILLIAM BYRD II, GREAT
PLANTER AND NOTABLE
AUTHOR (Colonial Williamsburg
Collection)

colony. Even so, he advocated a more diversified economy, but admitted that the understandable commitment of Virginians to agriculture made diversification unlikely.

Undoubtedly the most noteworthy literary figure was another Virginian, William Byrd II. Born in 1674 into one of the leading families in the colony, Byrd engaged in an impressive variety of activities. With an English education and numerous long visits to the mother country—he spent half his life there—as well as experiences on the continent, Byrd was a cosmopolitan person. He wanted to recreate in Virginia the life of an English country gentleman, and with his plantation mansion, Westover, as his seat he largely succeeded. A man of business, he managed his land and his slaves so well that he not only maintained his substantial inheritance but added to it. At his death in 1744 he owned 174,000 acres. A man of public affairs, he was active in politics, both in Virginia and as a representative of various Virginia interests in London. But for William Byrd II, the life of the mind was also essential. He rose every morning at five to begin his daily reading in Greek, Hebrew, or Latin. Byrd's literary efforts ranged widely, from essays to diaries to public papers to history, though much that he wrote remained unpublished during his lifetime. His diaries, the source of much of our knowledge of his life and world, were discovered only in this century. Byrd's best-known works, *The Secret History of the Dividing Line* (about 1730) and *The History of the Dividing Line* (probably late 1730s), tell about the survey of the North Carolina–Virginia boundary conducted in 1728; Byrd had headed the Virginia party. These two books—satirical, witty, trenchantly observant of people and customs and places, marvelously written—represent a considerable literary achievement.

In a quite different area southern colonials did work of substantial intellectual merit. Colonial Americans, including southerners, moved rapidly and with respect into the best scientific circles in Europe. After all, they lived in virtually a virgin laboratory for the observation and collection of flora and fauna. The garden of William Byrd II won fame for the variety of its rare species. Dr. John Mitchell, also a Virginian, became a fellow of the British Royal Society as a result of his writings on plants and animals in his colony. Another fellow of the Royal Society, Dr. Alexander Garden of South Carolina, won fame for his work on botanical and zoological topics. In addition, the first museum in the colonies was founded in Charleston in 1773.

The southern colonies also vigorously participated in the establishment of a critical vehicle for the expression of ideas as well as for the improvement of communications. The first newspaper in the colonial South appeared in Annapolis in 1727; under several proprietors the *Maryland Gazette* carried on until the Revolution. Charleston in 1732 and Williamsburg in 1736 joined Annapolis as homes of newspapers, or gazettes, as they were invariably called. The *North Carolina Gazette* started publication in New Bern in 1751. Finally the youngest colony got its own gazette with the appearance in 1763 of the Savannah *Georgia Gazette*. In each of the other colonies, as in Maryland, these newspapers became practically permanent fixtures from their initial publication on to the Revolution. Only in North Carolina did a significant interruption occur.

The southern colonists did not live in a cultural wasteland any more than they operated in a political wilderness. Located on the western boundary of the British Empire, they, along with their fellow colonists to the north, took part in the English cultural world. Just as integrally they participated in British imperial politics. As the last third of the eighteenth century began, the attention of the colonists turned inevitably toward the increasing tension between their own view of their place in the empire and the colonial role envisioned for them by the government in London.

4

The Revolution

❖

*I*n 1763 Great Britain finally defeated France in the long struggle for domination of eastern North America. In the aftermath of this great victory, which significantly increased the size of the British Empire, the British government adopted policies that caused a profound shift in the posture of the mother country toward her North American colonies. Before 1763, London had basically followed a laissez faire policy that had given the colonies wide latitude to devise their own political institutions and develop their own ideas about their relationship with the mother country, about who had what rights and powers.

But beginning in 1763, Britain intervened more directly in colonial affairs. The Proclamation of 1763 barred settlers from crossing the Appalachians into the Ohio Valley, a major prize of the war. Never before had the British attempted to exercise such control over westward expansion. The royal government also planned to station an unprecedented 6,000 additional troops in the colonies. The administration of a large dominion, including the maintenance of a substantial army in North America, made government more expensive. That increased cost, added to the massive debt incurred during the war with France, placed an enormous burden on the British government and on British taxpayers. The government decided that the colonists should help carry the burden by contributing directly to the royal treasury.

QUESTIONS OF AUTHORITY

In every colony objections were raised. The blocking of expansion pleased few. Nobody wanted the army. The prospect of taxes imposed by Britain was anathema. Quickly the colonists' antagonism to the new empire focused on taxes, which became a reality in 1765 when Parliament passed the Stamp Act. Calling for taxes similar to those already collected in England, the Stamp Act placed a tax on all kinds of printed matter, from legal documents to newspapers.

Immediately the colonists resisted. They insisted that Parliament could not tax them, could not take their property, because they had no representatives sitting in Parliament. Nurtured on the practice of actual representation, which re-

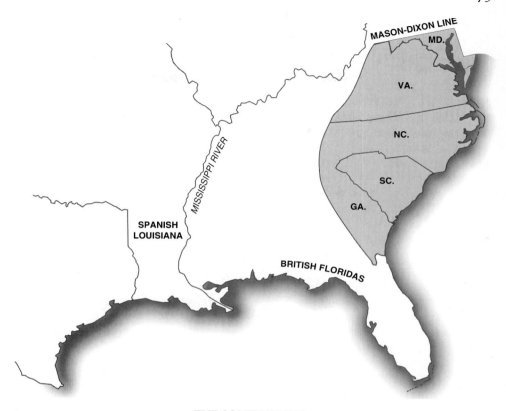

THE SOUTH IN 1775

quired assemblymen to act as the advocates and protectors of their home areas and of the constituents who elected them, the colonials rejected the contention that they were represented by every member of Parliament, who virtually represented every subject of the crown in every corner of the British Empire. From New England to Georgia colonials took up their pens to contest this new and, to them, threatening turn in British policy.

The colonials did more than write and speak—a great deal more. Direct action revealed the depth of the colonists' distress. Massachusetts called for a Stamp Act Congress, which met in New York in October 1765 with delegates from nine colonies, including three from the South. The Congress passed a series of resolutions. Protest went far beyond resolutions when mobs took to the streets. They intimidated officials, burned stamps in fact and stamp-tax collectors in effigy, looted homes, and occasionally vented their anger on anyone they happened to encounter. Finally colonists began to defy the law by using unstamped materials. In the face of such massive opposition, British officials could not carry out the provisions of the law. The Stamp Act became a dead letter.

Although Parliament attempted to defuse this explosive situation by repealing the Stamp Act in 1766, at the same time it passed the Declaratory Act, which declared that the colonies were subordinate to Parliament and that laws enacted by Parliament were binding on America. Promptly Parliament moved to translate the Declaratory Act into concrete policy. The next year it authorized the Townshend Acts, which imposed taxes on such items as glass, paper, and tea. The colonies, southern as well as northern, responded in 1769 by beginning a movement to refuse to import goods from Great Britain, and informed colonials everywhere vowed not to buy British goods. Over the next few years the situation continued to deteriorate. Several laws passed by Parliament in 1774 heightened fears and tension. Among these so-called Intolerable Acts was one that empowered the royal governor of Massachusetts to fill by appointment many offices that had been elective. Britain's determination to bring the colonists to heel was met by an equal implacability in the colonies. The Intolerable Acts, aimed chiefly at dissidents in Massachusetts, alarmed people everywhere. Legislative committees of correspondence, extralegal bodies set up first in 1773 in Virginia and then in almost every other colony to promote intercolony cooperation and solidarity, alerted all to the danger perceived in British actions. From the Virginia committee the call went out for all colonies to send delegates to a meeting in Philadelphia. The First Continental Congress, held in September and October 1774, was attended by delegates from every colony except Rhode Island. A Second Continental Congress followed in 1775; in April of that year shots were fired at Lexington and Concord. Then in 1776, with the promulgation of the Declaration of Independence, the colonies proclaimed themselves to be the United States of America, an independent nation. Through all of these cataclysmic events the southern colonies acted in concert with the northern colonies.

LIBERTY ENDANGERED

Liberty—on this concept turned the ideological conflict between England and its colonies. The idea of liberty came to the fore in the writings of certain political thinkers in seventeenth- and eighteenth-century England. These works were widely read on this side of the ocean long before 1763, and Americans took to heart their basic precept that liberty required freedom from outside control. In this view, control, beginning with interference in such areas as taxation, was a prelude to tyranny.

Taxation assumed critical importance because taxes involved property. To tax meant taking from citizens a portion of their property. And property was inextricably tied to liberty. The colonial writers clearly made the connection, and no one did so more graphically than the Virginian who declared: "Liberty and property are like those precious vessels whose soundness is destroyed by the least flaw." Thus, when Parliament taxed, it took away liberty as well as property.

In the political lexicon of the eighteenth century, the opposite of liberty was slavery. Slavery had a particular political meaning: the absence of liberty. In its political definition slavery characterized a society or a people that had lost its power to resist oppression, and that loss led inevitably to tyranny. Tyranny was seen as inevitable in such circumstances because the English writers and the colonists shared the conviction that an endemic political corruption, a greedy grasping for place and reward, hovered over every society, ready to swoop up liberty in the claws of slavery.

When colonists spoke about slavery, they were not merely employing a rhetorical device. Although the political meaning and the political use of the term were just as familiar to New Englanders as to southerners, the idea of political slavery had special force among southerners. They lived with the institution of slavery and among tens of thousands of slaves. Although not every white person owned slaves, the institution of slavery was so widespread that almost all whites, those who did not own slaves as well as those who did, the lower classes as well as the upper, knew firsthand what slavery entailed. All the characteristics associated with political slavery—dependence, tyranny, oppression, defenselessness—glowed especially brightly among people in the South, for those words described their own human institution.

Conscious of this association, white southerners directly connected their political contest against England with their domestic institution. When southerners cried out, as they so often did, "Slavery or independence!" there could be no mistaking their meaning. This conclusion is all the more inescapable because almost every prominent crier owned slaves. Their vigorous language created a powerful rhetorical weapon, a weapon grasped by conservatives as well as radicals. It mattered little where a southerner appeared along the spectrum of opposition to England, from firebrands demanding independence to moderates urging caution to conservatives anxious about the tumult. All saw and pictured the plight of the colonies and themselves in terms of the institution they knew so well. Lacerating "the oppressive and unconstitutional measures of the British government," the radical Charleston merchant Christopher Gadsden posed the alternatives for his fellow citizens. Firm resistance to British oppression, he wrote in 1769, would guarantee "the honorable rank of Freemen," but acquiescence in evil and unconstitutional taxes meant inevitable degradation. "Whatever we may think of ourselves," Gadsden warned, "we are as real slaves as those we are permitted to command, and differ only in degree. For what is a slave, but one that is at the will of his master and has no property of his own."

Gadsden did not speak in a strange dialect. A conservative lawyer from Edenton, North Carolina, James Iredell, declared that if Americans submitted to the absolute claims of Parliament, then Americans became dependent, a condition not "of free men, but of slaves." To Iredell, submission and dependence were "the very definition of slavery." Before the outbreak of hostilities George Washington had not been a major spokesman for independence, but he had no doubt that England aimed "by every piece of art and despotism to fix the shackles of slavery upon us." Washington believed that failure to establish a clear-cut American position would force all Americans to "submit to every imposition, that can be heaped upon us, until custom and use shall make us as tame and abject slaves, as the blacks we rule over with such arbitrary sway." Others echoed these sentiments: America had to stand against England or become "a sink for slaves." The connection southerners made between their own institution of slavery and their view of their conflict with England was never more sharply drawn as by a writer in the Charleston *South Carolina Gazette:* "not to be, *is better than* to be a slave."

VIEWS ON SLAVERY

This conscious and explicit juxtaposition of their political position with their institution of slavery forced white southerners to look closely at their institution for the first time. They were risking their lives and property for liberty while holding slaves. Although by 1770 slaves constituted 40 percent of the population with a value counted in the hundreds of thousands of pounds sterling, the vast majority of the white South had given neither the institution nor its growth much serious thought before the Revolutionary crisis. Now, however, thoughts about slavery flooded the consciousness of the South. Some southerners did recognize the contradiction in their position, in calling for liberty in a land of slavery. The tension created by this paradoxical stance brought forth tormented cries from some slaveholders. Yet the only concerted effort to resolve this tension by actively working for emancipation was made by the Quakers, and they were so few and occupied such a marginal position in southern society that they had little impact either on the behavior of slave owners or on the course of slavery.

The most visible antislavery spokesmen in the Revolutionary South appeared in Virginia. Many Virginia public men who called the colonies to arms against England also denounced the morality of owning slaves. To name them is to call the roll of Revolutionary heroes: Thomas Jefferson, George Mason, Richard Henry Lee—the list goes on. Some brilliant, all articulate, these men agonized over the fundamental contradiction between their deep belief in liberty and their possession of human slaves. As they saw it, their personal dilemma mirrored the predicament of their society. Despite their conviction that slavery was an unmitigated evil—a conviction one cannot doubt after absorbing the anguish that pervades their writings about slavery—they led no crusade against that special horror. Very few of them even emancipated their own slaves. Patrick Henry in 1773 spoke for this class of Virginia slaveholders when he wrote:

> Would any one believe that I am Master of Slaves of my own purchase! I am drawn along by ye general inconvenience of living without them; I will not, I cannot justify it. However culpable my conduct, I will so far pay my devoir to virtue as to own the excellence and rectitude of her precepts and to lament my want of conformity to them.

Having indicted himself, Henry mourned that "we cannot reduce this wished for Reformation to practice."

Thus the intense intellectual and spiritual antislaveryism of the great Virginians had no comparable practical dimension. During the entire span of the Revolutionary era Virginia adopted only two measures that can be counted as antislave, and neither was a direct attack on the institution. Moreover, the men with the great names can claim complete credit for neither. Opposing the international slave trade throughout the period, Virginia's public men spoke for the planters who, unlike their counterparts farther south, needed and wanted no additional slaves. Thus a substantial economic motive reinforced the ideological preference of the Jeffersons and the Henrys. They also warmly supported legislation pushed by the Quakers and passed in 1782 which permitted private manumission by individual masters. Because of this feeble antislavery record, many recent historians have challenged the depth of the antislavery sentiments voiced by Virginia's heroes. Without getting tangled in that interpretive thicket, one can draw two conclusions from the evidence. No doubt can exist about the genuineness of the intellectual and spiritual turmoil caused by the clash between slavery and liberty; and that turmoil engendered no significant alteration in slavery in Virginia.

South of Virginia antislavery sentiments were rare indeed. Those that did occur, however, were both more public and more forceful than the largely private trauma of the Virginians. The most powerful public indictment of slavery during the Revolutionary period came from the southern reaches of British settlement. At Darien, on the southern border of settled Georgia, citizens met in January 1775 to align themselves with the rebellion against Great Britain. These Georgians, some of them slave owners, promulgated a set of resolutions specifying both British evils and American goals. The fifth resolution thundered:

> To show the world that we are not influenced by any contracted or interested motives, but a general philanthropy for all mankind of whatever climate, language, or complexion, we hereby declare our disapprobation and abhorrence of the unnatural practice of slavery in America (however, the uncultivated state of our country, or other specious argument may plead for it), a practice founded in injustice and cruelty and highly dangerous to our liberties (as well as lives), debasing part of our fellow creatures below men, and corrupting the virtues and morals of the rest, and is laying the basis for the liberty we contend for (and which we pray the Almighty to continue to the latest posterity) upon a very wrong foundation.

The Darien resolution had no repercussions, absolutely none.

The Henry Laurens family carried the antislavery banner in South Carolina. Henry acted much like the Virginians he matched in wealth and social position. As early as 1763 he condemned slavery, and he often spoke about his deep wish to emancipate his slaves. But when he contemplated manumission, his self-assurance seemed to leave him. He never found the proper opportunity. Henry's son John shared his father's detestation of slavery. To a friend in 1776 he confessed, "I think we Americans at least in the Southern Colonies, cannot contend with good grace for liberty, until we have enfranchised our slaves." As well as anyone ever did, the twenty-two-year-old John Laurens illuminated the irony of the Revolutionary South: "How can we whose jealously [sic] has been claimed more at the name of oppression sometimes than at the reality, reconcile to our spirited assertions of the rights of mankind, the . . . abject slavery of our Negroes . . . ?"

Nothing had an effect. The Virginians, like Hamlet, found it easier to lament their quandary than to act to end it; the Darien resolution never had an echo; the Laurenses failed to move their state. The utter ineffectiveness of all efforts to pierce the armor of slavery testifies to the strength of the institution in the South. The reasons were many.

THE STRENGTH OF SLAVERY

The massive financial investment in slavery made successful moves against it most unlikely. Slaves were property, and the right to hold property was an inte-

gral part of liberty. No white southerner thought seriously about general emancipation without compensation because property owners had an inherent right to
their property, including human property. And for Americans the Revolutionary
struggle turned in part on their charge that England was endangering their liberty
by unconstitutionally depriving them of their property. Unless the owners of
slave property decided upon voluntary manumission, the states would have to
provide owners with huge sums in compensation. Sums of such magnitude were
simply unavailable.

The war with England revealed the close tie southerners saw between slavery
and land as congenial, even intimate, forms of property. To encourage enlistment,
several states offered a bounty of land to each man who signed up for military
service upon his honorable discharge. Georgia, South Carolina, North Carolina,
and Virginia increased that offer: every veteran who received a land bounty
would receive also at least one slave. As property, black slaves could be given by
the state to individuals, and the state recognized slaves as desirable gifts that perfectly complemented the reward of land. After all, the overwhelming majority of
the greatest fortunes in the South rested on those twin pillars, land and slaves.

Although no full-blown proslavery argument emphasizing the racial inferiority of the South's slaves appeared during the Revolutionary era, the absence of
such an argument did not indicate that white southerners took no notice of the
difference in color between themselves and their black slaves. To them that difference was a clear sign of inferiority. That belief antedated the introduction of slavery into British North America. Even that most enlightened of southerners,
Thomas Jefferson, shared the conviction that blacks stood several cultural levels
below whites. Like most of his fellow southerners, Jefferson considered that inferiority insurmountable; blacks could not be raised to equality with whites, at least
not for a long time.

This certainty about the inequality of blacks and whites added significantly to
the difficulties of emancipation. Even those white southerners who most wished
slavery gone—and Jefferson surely belonged to this group—were convinced that
emancipated slaves could not remain near their former masters. In the minds of
even sincere antislavery southerners an inundation of their society by substantial
numbers of freed black slaves meant cataclysm. To them such an eventuality
would lead to the inevitable degradation of their society and would end in the
two things they dreaded most: miscegenation and race war. This conviction that
whites and free blacks could not live together meant that emancipation would
match slavery as an evil, unless another home could be found for the newly freed
blacks. Thus, even for antislavery southerners the race problem equaled the slave
problem in horror and potential danger. The solution to the latter led to the former, for which they had no solution.

The reaction to efforts to put slaves in uniform when war came reveals how
deeply white southerners dreaded the consequences of emancipation. In 1775 the
royal governor of Virginia, Lord Dunmore, called for slaves to rally to the king's
banner in return for ultimate emancipation. Enraged, Virginia and Maryland
planters denounced Dunmore for his "diabolical schemes against good people,"
which threatened lives and property with "the *very scum* of the country." Planters

feared not only the loss of slaves who might run away to join Dunmore; more to be feared were blacks with guns in their hands, aiming at them.

Similar proposals to make slaves soldiers of the Revolution generally failed. Some 5,000 blacks did take up arms against the king, but the vast majority came from the northern states. The southern states considered the employment of black slaves to fight for the freedom of whites, but as all recognized, such a step would have to result in freedom for blacks as well, at least for those who had borne arms. Besides, if the southern states placed weapons in the hands of slaves, would the British fail to follow suit, and would racial war not then compound the horrors that the conflict had already brought? The South could accept neither possibility. Only Maryland ever authorized the enlistment of slaves. Even in the face of military disaster, which surely loomed over the South in 1780, all other states remained adamantly opposed.

THE DECISION TO REVOLT

While white southerners decided their future with slavery, they carried on their great conflict with England within the framework of southern politics. The men who led the southern colonies against Great Britain after 1763 were, for the most part, men of place and position. Although the crisis did provide an opportunity for the rise of new leaders, such as Patrick Henry, many of those who stood firm for the colonial position had been serving in assemblies or in other prominent posts. Such men as Henry Laurens had won the plaudits and respect of their fellow citizens from the Potomac to the Savannah.

These leaders of the southern colonies in revolt often did not agree on political timing and occasionally seemed to disagree even on the ultimate political goal. The particular stance taken did not depend on old or new prominence, though most recently prominent men advocated advanced positions. As firebrands of rebellion Patrick Henry and Christopher Gadsden early accepted the possibility that the colonials could secure their liberty only outside the British Empire. The cautious, careful Henry Laurens, by contrast, came slowly to a belief in political separation; he took that decisive step only after his experiences with the imperial customs system convinced him that a general corruption would indeed clamp slavery on him and his fellow colonials. In Georgia, Lachlan McIntosh, a planter and later wartime general, worried more about his financial prospects than about the question of empire until finally, in the winter of 1774–1775, British actions and the warnings of his friend Henry Laurens persuaded him that his continued liberty required participation in the rebellion. Though zealous in denouncing British threats to American liberty, Rawlins Lowndes, longtime leader in South Carolina politics, hoped against hope that the two sides could avoid a total break. In fact, not until 1776 did Lowndes back complete political independence.

Clearly, then, differences of opinion on a critical question existed among leading southerners. Emphasis on that difference and a focus on such terms as *radical* and *conservative*, however, can obscure a profound similarity among those southerners, from Henry to Lowndes. All of them spoke the same language, even with the same inflection. Each of them riveted his argument on the primary issue: liberty versus slavery. All of them agreed that the colonials must resist the Stamp Act, the Townshend duties, the Intolerable Acts; all of them insisted that the British must recognize the rights of the colonies. In sum, all concurred that the colonies and the colonists must protect themselves against what they described as the shackles of British slavery.

Southern leaders knew that no matter how mighty their effort against England, it would never succeed without widespread public support. To preserve the liberty they worshiped, they would have to arouse the public so that leaders and led shared the perception of a common danger to the freedom of all. Many of the southern elite wrote pamphlets spelling out the colonial position and castigating British machinations. Pamphlets were surely important, especially in expanding the colonial definition of liberty. Perhaps even more noteworthy in galvanizing the white masses of the South were oral appeals for the defense of precious liberty. Although this conclusion does not lend itself to ready proof, the nature of southern politics and the character of southern society strongly suggest its accuracy. The general sharing among white southerners of the liberty-slavery rhetoric bugled by speakers to their listeners certainly made simpler the task of leadership. All white southerners understood the vast chasm between freedom and slavery.

Revolutionary activity was emotional as well as practical, and the emotion injected into southern politics by spokesmen for independence had an enormous influence on those politics. It made careers. At the very beginning of his public career Patrick Henry made the elders of Virginia politics nervous. As a young member of the House of Burgesses in 1765 he startled them and aroused Virginia with a bold speech and forceful resolutions condemning the Stamp Act. Most senior burgesses agreed with Henry's position but not with his tactics. They feared that the excitement aroused by his eloquent tongue could jeopardize their control of the House as well as stimulate popular opposition to England. No matter the opinion of his elders, Henry stayed on his rhetorical course. Throughout the crisis he constantly rallied Virginians with his mighty outcries against British tyranny. And even if the story is apocryphal, his trumpet blast "Give me liberty or give me death!" dramatizes the passion of Henry's appeal. Unfortunately, only fragments of his powerful speeches have survived; most of what is known about them comes from people who heard them. Still, no doubt can exist about the power of his oratory. He stood as indisputably the greatest orator of the Revolution, and he still ranks as one of the greatest orators in all American history. Attempting to describe the magnificence of Henry's oratory, Thomas Jefferson called Henry the Homer of the spoken word. Soon the most popular political figure in Virginia, Henry was elected governor six times and enjoyed public adulation as well as public office until his death in 1799.

In Maryland the Revolutionary turmoil provided a similar political opportunity to Samuel Chase. An ambitious young lawyer, Chase had just begun his climb up the political ladder when news of the Stamp Act broke upon the colonies. Sensing the visceral opposition to the act, Chase seized the opening it provided him to win recognition as a champion of the people. Little by little he inched to the forefront of the colonial cause in Maryland. He excelled in the tumult and excitement of emotional politics. When the stamp-tax distributor for the colony arrived in Annapolis, a group of Chase's followers prevented his landing. Then Chase himself directed a mock burning and burial of the unfortunate official, who was ultimately hounded out of the colony by such tactics. From the Stamp Act forward into the Revolution, Chase solidified his position as a popular leader. He emerged not only as a chieftain of the Revolutionary cause but also as a powerful force in Maryland politics, a position he retained into the 1790s.

War Begins

When the war of words and of committees turned into a shooting war, the southern colonies joined the fight. The military conflict began in New England with a small engagement, hardly more than a skirmish. In April 1775 a British column with orders to capture or destroy munitions headed west out of Boston toward Concord, less than twenty miles away. Along the way at Lexington some seventy militiamen stood in opposition. Shots rang out; to this day who fired first is unknown. The British continued on to Concord, where they met another militia detachment, and again a brief fire-fight took place. The alarm was sounded and militiamen from the surrounding countryside gathered to strike the British. As the British returned to Boston, the militiamen harassed them all the way. War had begun—a great war that would last eight years and alter the course of history.

The next month the Second Continental Congress convened in Philadelphia. Accepting the fighting around Boston as the beginning of war, the Congress acted to protect American interests. The Congress moved in two directions. First, it created the Continental Army by authorizing the raising of troops to be sent to Boston. The Continental Army would become the mainstay of American military efforts in the long struggle against the British. Second, the Congress named a commanding general for the force it had created. It unanimously chose George Washington of Virginia, a forty-three-year-old slave owner and planter who had fought with the British in the French and Indian War. Washington promptly traveled northward to Cambridge, Massachusetts, where on July 3 he took command of American forces.

General Washington and the Continental Army, or the Continental Line, composed the national force in the Revolution. During the course of the Revolution more than 232,000 men eventually enlisted in the Continental Army, some 59,000 of them from the southern states. Of course General Washington never commanded this many men at any one time; during the last two years of the war, for example, the Continentals in service totaled just over 33,000. These units could be sent wherever the commanding general ordered and under the direction of any officer he named, subject to the agreement of Congress. Washington reported directly to the Congress. Ever conscious of the authority possessed by the Congress, Washington never attempted to substitute himself for it, though the action or inaction of the Congress often frustrated him. With Washington in command of the army there was never a hint that the military would usurp political power; he never challenged the ultimate authority of the Congress.

The Continental Line, however, could not alone stop the British. The Line could never man the far-flung battlefields of the Revolution against the much larger British force. Augmenting the Continentals and performing an essential service for the American cause were the state militias. Enlistments in the various militias numbered 145,000 throughout the eight years between 1775 and 1783; the southern states accounted for around 80,000 of that total. But far fewer were available at any one time. Each state had a militia that had been created during the colonial period. Its units owed and paid allegiance not to the Second Continental Congress but to the governor and legislature of their state. Although the militias provided essential manpower in numerous critical situations, they generally retained the right to conduct their own affairs. Usually they operated within state borders and crossed those lines only when state authorities permitted such movements. With George Washington, the Continental Army, and the several militias, the Americans prepared to face regulars of the British army supplemented by German mercenaries hired by the royal government to help put down the rebellion.

The war did not spread rapidly throughout the colonies. New England, chiefly the immediate Boston area, was the first battlefield. The major campaigns of 1776 and 1777 took place in New Jersey, New York, and Pennsylvania. The first substantial action in the South occurred in June 1776 when the British failed in an assault on Charleston Harbor. Two and a half years later, however, in December 1778, the British claimed their first significant southern triumph when they captured Savannah. Still, for the first five years of the Revolutionary War the South remained a distinctly secondary theater.

THE SOUTHERN WAR

The situation changed dramatically in 1780; now the South became the chief battleground. As early as 1778 the British began planning for a substantial southern thrust. The precise aims of their strategy remained unclear. Their initial goal, the capture of a significant seaport to serve as a supply base, made absolute sense, but after that task was accomplished the British strategists never had a clear sense of either the appropriate next step or their ultimate military aim, other than the general goal of ending the rebellion.

The British southern strategy began gloriously. In March 1780 a force of some 12,000 men commanded by Major General Sir Henry Clinton moved against Charleston, the largest city and port in the South. With the assistance of the royal navy Clinton laid siege to Charleston, defended by more than 6,500 troops under Major General Benjamin Lincoln. After two months, on May 12, 1780, Lincoln surrendered his entire command. Charleston was to remain in British hands for the duration of the war.

The fall of Charleston resulted in the greatest British victory of the war, yet the British failed to follow up their magnificent triumph. Clinton decided to divide his force and his effort. With one-third of his army, Clinton returned to New York. Behind in Charleston he left Major General Charles Lord Cornwallis with

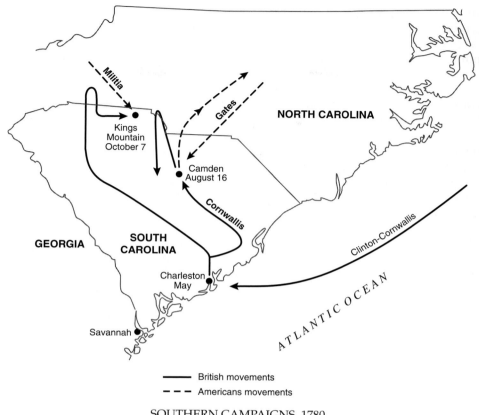

Militia

Gates

NORTH CAROLINA

Kings
Mountain
October 7

Camden
August 16

Cornwallis

SOUTH
CAROLINA

GEORGIA

Clinton-Cornwallis

Charleston
May

ATLANTIC OCEAN

Savannah

——— British movements
- - - Americans movements

SOUTHERN CAMPAIGNS, 1780

8,000 soldiers; Cornwallis had instructions to defend Charleston and to disrupt all American activities in South Carolina. He was also to render every assistance to the British loyalists in the state.

Distressed by the turn of events in the South, the Continental Congress acted to shore up the American position. To restore American fortunes the Congress chose Major General Horatio Gates, a hero of the 1777 victory at Saratoga. In North Carolina in July Gates assumed command of a reconstituted Army of the Southern Department. Immediately he headed his army into South Carolina and toward Charleston. Alerted that a new enemy was in the field, Cornwallis marched westward from Charleston to confront Gates. On August 16 just north of the village of Camden the two armies met. Although he outnumbered Cornwallis almost 2 to 1, Gates's hastily organized force, heavily dependent upon militiamen, was no match for Cornwallis's troops. When the British advanced with fixed bayonets, the militiamen panicked and fled from the field, with Gates alongside. Gates's Continentals fought well but were overwhelmed; American casualties were twice those of the British. Following so quickly upon the loss of Charleston, the disaster at Camden seemed to give the South to the British. The American side, however, did not cave in. After Camden, Cornwallis sent a detachment of almost 1,000 men to sweep the western Carolinas. Responding, around 1,000 militiamen from both Carolinas, Virginia, and Georgia met the British on October 7 at Kings Mountain, in northwestern South Carolina, and smashed them. Cornwallis's work was not yet done.

The war in the South was not restricted to organized field armies. In fact, often the most vicious and bloody contests took place between detachments of loyalists, or tories, who fought for the British, and bands of Americans, who called themselves patriots. In the Carolinas and Georgia bitter civil strife sparked a nasty guerrilla war. Tories were found in every colony, in the North as well as the South, but they were especially strong in the Carolinas and Georgia. Toryism cut across social lines. Wealthy seacoast planters and merchants in both Carolinas stood by their king. Many back-country farmers also supported the royalist cause. The reasons were undoubtedly complex; among the most vigorous tories were Scots Highlanders who had migrated to the Carolinas in the mid-eighteenth century.

Tories did more than profess loyalty to the crown; they took up arms against the rebellion. In almost every major contest in the Carolinas and Georgia, tory units accounted for a significant portion of the British army. Without them the British would have had a much more difficult task. At the same time, the tories' willingness to fight for the British pitted neighbors and friends against each other in what was almost fratricidal conflict.

At times the patriot-tory contest almost became a war of extermination. In February 1781 a group of patriots in North Carolina practically massacred some 400 tories moving to reinforce Cornwallis. The patriots, wearing uniforms similar to those of British soldiers, mounted a saber attack on the unsuspecting loyalists as they waited along a road for what they thought was the passage of a British unit. The butchery resulted in 90 dead and 150 wounded. Even prisoners were not safe; some were hacked to pieces with broadswords. The tories responded in kind. One of the most successful and brutal tory leaders, William "Bloody Bill" Cunningham, operated in mid-South Carolina. Bloody Bill supposedly developed his mighty hatred for all patriots after a band of them murdered his brother. His thirst for retaliation knew no limits. In November 1781 he and a raiding party attacked about fifteen patriots barricaded in a fortified house. After several hours of hard fighting, Cunningham set the house on fire, forcing the little garrison to surrender. Cunningham promptly hanged the leader, but the improvised gallows broke, leaving its intended victim dazed but alive. Bloody Bill reacted swiftly: he ran the fellow through with his sword. Following his lead, Bloody Bill's men killed all the other prisoners.

The viciousness of the tory-patriot war could have become even more terrible had the Indians living on the Carolina-Georgia frontier become combatants for either the British or the Americans. Certainly in 1775 neither side could predict the path the Indians might follow. After years of intrusion by whites into Indian territory, Indians had reason to distrust them all. The British were eager for the Indians' involvement, but only under their guidance and direction. They had no interest in any independent action the Indians might undertake. The Americans wanted the Indians to stay out of the conflict because they feared the physical and psychological impact of Indian war parties ranging across the back country of Georgia and the Carolinas. To keep the Indians at bay they played on tribal factionalism and distributed copious supplies of "rum and good words."

The nature of the Indian front was settled early on. In 1776 the British persuaded the Cherokee, the dominant tribe in the region, to attack the Carolina frontier. In June the Indians hit; they destroyed property, took prisoners, and killed several dozen whites. The Americans called up some 6,000 men to punish the Indians. The chief contingent, more than 1,000 men under South Carolina leadership, marched into Cherokee country and by late summer had destroyed all the Cherokee towns in their path. This offensive broke the power and the will of the Cherokee. Other tribes, aware of what had happened to the Cherokee, never became major participants. White frontier families remained alert, however; raids were always possible, and sometimes they materialized. This reality kept some of the frontier militiamen in their home districts. Still, after the Cherokee incident of 1776 the southern Indian front remained basically quiet.

THE ADVENT OF NATHANAEL GREENE

In the aftermath of Gates's disaster at Camden, Congress acted to strengthen the American cause in the South. The Congress recognized that something had to be done to revive the military effort there. In part because its past choices of commanders, including Generals Lincoln and Gates, had been so spectacularly unsuccessful, Congress asked General Washington to choose a new commander for the southern army. In October Washington picked Nathanael Greene, a Rhode Island

GENERAL NATHANAEL
GREENE, COMMANDER IN
THE SOUTH, 1781
(Independence National Historical
Park Collection)

native, then quartermaster general of his army. The thirty-eight-year-old Greene, standing just under six feet, with broad shoulders and a florid complexion, headed south. In early December, at Charlotte, North Carolina, he took over the remnant of Gates's force, no more than 1,500 men. Greene confronted a military situation that would have tested the ablest commander. His army was a wreck and supplies and morale were low. The very desperation of the situation in the Charlotte camp necessitated action. Greene divided his small army and sent one portion to eastern South Carolina, the other under Daniel Morgan to the western part of the state. Although dividing his army violated the maxims of military textbooks, Greene believed the action essential for the sustenance of his men. Moreover, the division might cause Cornwallis to split his own forces, thus making Charleston vulnerable to a quick strike.

Cornwallis had become increasingly unhappy with the restrictions placed on him by Clinton. Clinton had ordered him to disrupt American activities in South Carolina, even to pacify the state, but also to hold to his base at Charleston and guarantee its security. Cornwallis, however, came to believe that he could not quiet South Carolina until all possibility of aid from neighboring North Carolina and even Virginia had been eliminated. He proposed to eliminate it by breaking away from his base at Charleston and driving against Greene and anyone else who was out there.

Cornwallis confronted two basic problems. First, he had to decide how to contend with Greene's force, the major field army against him. Greene complicated matters when he divided his troops. Second, his forces had to march and camp in country that was home to numerous patriot bands, some of them led by superb guerrilla fighters. Such commanders as Francis Marion (the famous Swamp Fox), Thomas Sumter, and Andrew Pickens made life utterly miserable for Cornwallis and his soldiers. Dispatch riders disappeared; patrols and scouting parties were ambushed; supply trains ended up in patriot hands; cavalry detachments were routinely cut up, even slaughtered. And after rapid, brutal strikes the patriots melted away into the forests and swamps. The British could not bring these guerrillas out into the open for a conventional fight, in which their own superior numbers and weaponry could give them the advantage.

Deciding that Greene was his chief enemy, Cornwallis focused on him. He followed his opponent's lead by sending a detachment to defeat the portion of Greene's army in western South Carolina. In mid-January the Americans and British met at Cowpens, where, in a minor tactical masterpiece, combined Continental-militia units under Daniel Morgan defeated the British-tory force. At the news from Cowpens, both commanders rushed to unify their forces. Greene saw an opportunity to strike Cornwallis's main army, and Cornwallis was determined to catch and punish Morgan. Learning that a reunited British force had advanced into North Carolina, Greene retreated. Although he would have preferred to stand and fight, Greene listened to his subordinates, including Morgan, who warned him that their tired, poorly supplied troops were in no condition to face the united British army.

Across the North Carolina piedmont the two armies moved until Greene crossed into Virginia. There Greene heard that Cornwallis had rallied to his colors

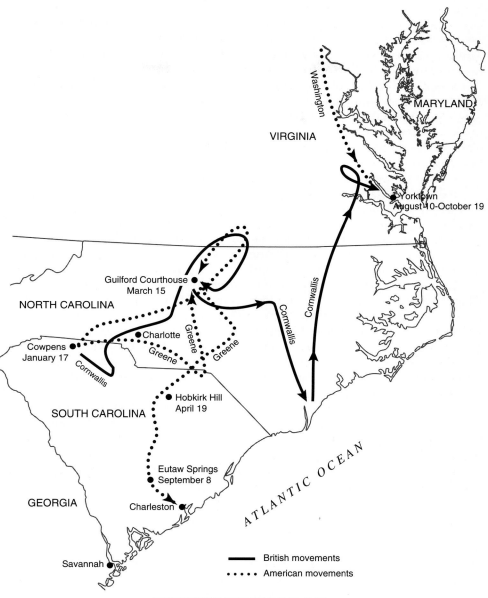

SOUTHERN CAMPAIGNS, 1781

a large number of loyalists. With these reinforcements he might be able to bring both Carolinas under tight British control. These reports were exaggerated, but Greene believed he had no choice but to head back into North Carolina. He and Cornwallis met in battle for the first time on March 15, 1781, at Guilford Courthouse, North Carolina, just north of Greensboro. The Americans had superiority in numbers but the British had the more professional and disciplined troops. After a hard, at times savage fight, Greene gave way and ordered a retreat. But Cornwallis was too bloodied to take advantage of his battlefield success. After Guilford Courthouse the two armies that had been fighting or chasing each other for four months marched away from each other.

This turnabout resulted chiefly from Cornwallis's needs and his ambitions. Even though he commanded the field after Guilford Courthouse, he was in no position to follow up his tactical victory. After weeks of marching and fighting, his army required refurbishing and resupply. In order to get that essential task done, Cornwallis had to return to the coast and a British base. Thus he headed for the nearest port: Wilmington, North Carolina. From there Cornwallis informed Clinton in New York that his campaign had been a raging success. This wildly inflated claim did not deceive Clinton. Determined to recoup his military fortunes and enhance his own fame, Cornwallis decided to take his army up into Virginia. Greene was looking in the opposite direction. With Cornwallis in Wilmington, he saw the way open to Charleston and started his troops southward. Even though Cornwallis was under orders to protect Charleston and had been informed of Greene's movements, he headed for Virginia and hoped-for glory.

Cornwallis's shift to Virginia did not leave Greene a completely open road to Charleston, for various British and loyalist units still remained in South Carolina. In April a British detachment stopped Greene at Hobkirk's Hill, just north of Camden, almost at the site of Gates's debacle. But Greene was only momentarily halted; he kept his army together and on the scene. Moreover, an aroused countryside increased problems for the British. In the summer Greene continued on and in September he struck the British again at Eutaw Springs, no more than fifty miles from Charleston. Although Eutaw Springs ended as basically a tactical draw, Greene pushed onward. By the end of 1781 the British in South Carolina found themselves confined largely to Charleston. Except for Savannah and Charleston, both Carolinas and Georgia were securely in American hands. Nathanael Greene had performed masterfully. By keeping his army together, by using the partisans, by hard fighting, and with a clear sense of his purpose, he turned disaster into triumph.

YORKTOWN

While Greene crept closer to Charleston, Cornwallis assumed command of all British forces in southern Virginia. Cornwallis finally posted his 7,000 troops at Yorktown, on the York River just up from the Chesapeake Bay. There he thought the royal navy could easily reinforce and resupply him, or if need be evacuate him to New York. Cornwallis's chief goal, however, had nothing to do with evacuation. He wanted to mount a campaign in the interior of Virginia, the state he now designated as the main theater of the war.

But George Washington, sitting in New York state, had other plans. For six years the Virginian had been fighting in the North; now he saw an opportunity to hit the British hard in his native state. The key to his hopes was the expected arrival of the French fleet in American waters. When the French had learned of the American victory at Saratoga in 1777, they had seen in an alliance with the victors a splendid opportunity to strike at their old enemy, England. They had been helping the struggling Americans since 1778. In August 1781, Washington learned that the French fleet would appear in the Chesapeake. The possibility of a Franco-American combined land-sea attack on Cornwallis excited him. Immediately he set his plans in motion. With most of his troops he headed for Virginia, though he left a small force to demonstrate against New York City and mask his primary movement.

By late September, Washington had arrived in front of Yorktown. His army, strengthened by almost 8,000 French soldiers who had accompanied the fleet, totaled some 16,000 troops, the largest he had ever led. An attempt by the royal navy to relieve Cornwallis was stopped by the French fleet. With superior numbers and artillery, Washington decided on a siege to take Yorktown. Finally on October 19, 1781, Cornwallis surrendered. Clad in new uniforms, the British troops marched to the surrender ceremony with their bands playing melancholy tunes, including one aptly titled "The World Turned Upside Down." Yorktown was the greatest American military victory of the Revolution.

Today we consider the triumph at Yorktown to mark the end of the Revolutionary War, but at the time that eventuality was not so clear. In fact, the war continued until the peace treaty was finally completed and adopted more than a year later. The great significance of Yorktown lay in its power to persuade the British government to abandon its effort to end the Revolution by force and to begin negotiations. Those negotiations took place in Europe and did not produce a final treaty until September 1783. Meanwhile, skirmishes continued in the South throughout 1782. The British presence did not end until December 1782, when the British garrison finally sailed out of Charleston Harbor.

Significant military actions also took place in the Floridas and far to the west in Louisiana. In 1779, Spain agreed to join France in the war against Great Britain, though the Spanish crown, wary of directly aiding rebellious colonies, did not make an alliance with the United States. Governor Bernardo de Gálvez of Louisiana struck quickly and kept up the attack. During the next two years Gálvez led his forces successfully against British garrisons at Baton Rouge (1779), Mobile (1780), and Pensacola (1781). The Spanish capture of those three posts ended British efforts to secure a foothold in the lower Mississippi Valley. In the treaty concluding the war Great Britain returned both East and West Florida to Spain. As a result, and immensely important for the infant United States, Great Britain retained no claims on the North American mainland south of Canada.

THE IMPACT OF THE WAR

The Treaty of Paris, ratified by Congress in April 1783, formalized the independence the United States had won on the battlefield. A new nation joined the ranks of independent states. The future development of the southern states could never

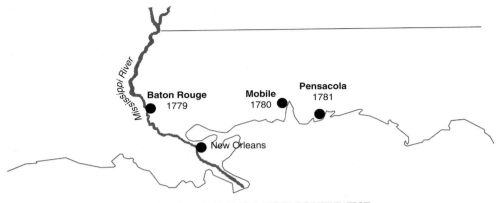

MAJOR CAMPAIGNS IN THE SOUTHWEST

be totally separated from the country they had helped create. In 1783 southerners, like all other Americans, rejoiced that they had successfully turned back Britain's effort to keep them politically dependent. After eight long years of warfare the Americans had prevailed, but the Revolution surely left its imprint on them.

The human cost cannot be tallied with any real precision. Thousands of soldiers from the southern states in both the Continental Line and militia units were killed or wounded on various battlefields. Their families had to learn to cope with their loss and make their way in the world without their dead sons, brothers, husbands, fathers. Although eighteenth-century campaigns largely spared civilians, the fury of the partisan war surely reached to noncombatants. The impossibility of obtaining precise numbers makes it extremely difficult to assess the effect of war-related casualties on the South. Certainly the human damage of the Revolution, though powerful to those directly involved, did not even begin to approach the trauma suffered by the South in 1865. The evidence does not indicate that the human price of the Revolution seriously hindered the course of the South.

The southern countryside largely escaped any substantial or long-lasting physical damage. The British army never adopted a systematic policy of destroying homes, fields, villages, or towns. Eighteenth-century armies generally did not engage in widespread destruction. The leading southern cities also emerged relatively unscathed. In Charleston, for example, some homes and buildings were destroyed during the siege, but the city remained largely intact at the end of the war. An overwhelmingly rural and agricultural area, the South did not present numerous obvious targets. Without a vigorous scorched-earth policy, which the British never adopted, little chance existed for massive destruction in the South. And it did not occur.

Even the often brutal tory-patriot conflict did not massively scar the landscape, but it did lead to harsh action against the tories. Most states banished those who had been especially active on the side of the crown. When the last British troops pulled out of the various states, many loyalists went with them. Although practices varied among the states, all of them confiscated tory property.

In Maryland alone the value of confiscated tory lands amounted to more than £500,000, Without question tories lost millions of pounds, chiefly in land, to the victors.

The British did not raze the southern countryside, but they did affect slavery. Recognizing slaves as valuable assets to their enemies, the British acted wherever they could to deprive the Americans of their slaves. Occasionally, as in the Lord Dunmore episode, the British promised freedom for slaves who left their American owners. More often the British impressed slaves to perform various tasks for the British army in areas they swept or controlled. The British were not seriously promoting emancipation; they perceived their actions as injuring their foes. Certainly thousands of slaves ended up under British control, and many never returned to their owners. When the British evacuated Charleston, they took more than 5,000 slaves with them; another 4,000 left Savannah with British troops. Many of those unfortunates ended up in slavery in the Caribbean or East Florida, though some found freedom in Canada. But for their former American owners the result was loss.

In the South, however, slavery survived. And survival, after the ideological turmoil and the military operations, underscored the importance of slavery to the South and, even more important, the widespread conviction among southerners that slavery was permanent. In the year of the Declaration of Independence, 1776, Henry Laurens declared that he could not liberate his slaves because his neighbors would identify him as "a promoter not only of strange, but of dangerous doctrines." A decade later Thomas Jefferson agreed only with great reluctance to the publication of his *Notes on Virginia,* which contained Virginia-style antislavery sentiments. Originally he had intended only a small, anonymous edition for private circulation; Jefferson feared that wider distribution of the work under his name would produce an adverse reaction that might fasten slavery even more tightly to Virginia and the South. Laurens's concerned inaction and Jefferson's troubled hesitation make it abundantly clear that the force of Revolutionary rhetoric, ideology, and even war had moved the South no closer to the abandonment of slavery. In fact, the opposite occurred. In 1784 and 1785 more than 1,200 Virginians signed petitions to the assembly protesting the private manumission act of 1782. Thus Jefferson worried needlessly; slavery was already powerfully attached to his Virginia. With slavery having withstood the cumulative force of the Revolution, the white South emerged from the experience more consciously committed to slavery than it had ever been before.

*S*LAVERY AND LIBERTY

This vigorous commitment to black slavery did not diminish the South's fervor for white liberty. White southerners had made a revolution in the name of liberty. Victorious, they had a voracious appetite for the precious commodity they had preserved. Thus southerners simultaneously loved liberty and maintained slavery. To explain this irony some historians have argued that slavery paved the way for southern faith in republicanism by eliminating the lowest class of whites, who otherwise could have threatened the stability and unity of the social order. The whites, all of whom stood above the slaves economically and socially, joined together to give thanks for the enslaved blacks, who made harmony and republicanism, and thus liberty, possible for whites. Other scholars have pointed out that the love of liberty also flourished in such places as Massachusetts, where slavery was inconsequential. They have also emphasized that numerous southerners saw slavery as a blight on the republicanism of the South even as they could envision no way to be rid of it. The critical fact, however, lies in the powerful influence slavery had on the southern attitude toward liberty. It mattered not at all whether white southerners viewed slavery as the foundation of their liberty or as a moral curse. All of them, both those who bemoaned slavery and those who supported it, saw slavery as a condition to be avoided at all hazards, no matter the cost.

Thus their acute awareness of slavery led white southerners to a highly developed sense of liberty. Noting the universality of a "high sense of personal independence" among white Virginians, Edmund Randolph, one of them, thought it derived from the "system of slavery," which nurtured a "quick and acute sense of personal liberty, a disdain for every abridgement of personal independence." White southerners embraced liberty with an all-consuming passion, a passion that had powerful political manifestations. The first great manifestation came when slave owners led the South into the Revolution. Political revolutions against legitimate authority are not normally led by the dominant economic and social class of society. Yet in the colonial South men of great wealth were revolutionaries. The names of such men as Charles Carroll of Carrollton, George Washington, James Iredell, Henry Laurens, and Lachlan McIntosh head a long list of the elite in every colony. No, these individuals and their peers did not advocate a social revolution that would destroy their privilege or their future. Still, they strode with open eyes into war against the greatest military power of their time, a war all recognized as a war of revolution. When they accepted war, they risked not only their personal safety but also their position and property in possible social upheaval and economic catastrophe. These wealthy slave owners made a revolution because they believed it essential to protect themselves from the despicable yoke of slavery. But their war for their own liberty never meant liberty for their slaves. Quite the contrary—the triumph that secured their liberty tightened the bonds on their slaves. From 1776 to 1860 the liberty white southerners celebrated always included the freedom to preserve the slavery of blacks.

THE FORM AND SUBSTANCE OF POLITICS

Just as the Revolution had a profound impact on slavery, it significantly influenced the course of southern politics. The rampant emotionalism of Revolutionary politics fundamentally affected political affairs. Throughout the years between the Revolution and the Civil War, southern politics was an emotional business. At every critical instant politicians stepped forward with historical choruses to the performances of the Patrick Henrys and the Samuel Chases. Repeatedly the appeal to emotion made careers and shaped momentous decisions.

The rhetoric of the Revolution imparted to southern politics more than emotion. Its substance also enjoyed a long, prosperous political life. Appeals to the people accenting the fragility of their liberty and emphasizing the threat of various demons to obliterate it filled southern editorials, platforms, pamphlets, and podiums right down to 1860. No political cause could hope to succeed unless it gave a clear signal that its primary goal was to guarantee the liberty of the people, a liberty that for white southerners was always entwined with slavery.

While the Revolution influenced the character of southern politics, it also modified its structure. The participatory politics that had characterized the colonial South weathered the storm of the Revolution, but not without meaningful alterations. A decade and more of emphasis on the rights of all citizens modified the equation of democracy and deference that equaled participatory politics. The experience of war added to the democratic side of the equation. This additional weight was evident in the changing attitude of the lower classes toward the upper, in the kinds of men who assumed political responsibility, and in the very basis of government.

Because of the Revolution, white southerners of the lower social orders began to question the deference they had previously shown to their social betters. When dealing with such broad societal attitudes the focus has to be on trends, not absolutes. In the colonial period some lower-class southerners had surely refused to fit neatly into their expected role; just as surely after the Revolution many others continued to feel comfortable with the old deferential ways. But the Revolution did spawn a general shift away from deference, a shift illustrated by an episode in South Carolina in 1784.

In that year the South Carolina assembly threatened to banish from the state one William Thompson, a tavernkeeper, for insulting John Rutledge, a former governor and a prominent figure in the ruling group. In a public address defending himself Thompson stood deference on its head. Acknowledging that Rutledge "conceived me his inferior," Thompson announced that he could not understand Rutledge's attitude. As a former officer in the Revolutionary army, Thompson said, he was asking for no more than the respect he deserved. Calling himself "a *wretch* of no higher rank in the Commonwealth than that of Common-Citizen" and identifying himself with "those who . . . go at this day, under the opprobrious appelation of, the *Lower Orders of Men*," Thompson pitched into "*John Rutledge*, or any of the NABOB *tribe*," who claim "to compose the grand hierachy of the State." Thompson argued that an independent people required leaders who were "*good, able, useful* and *friends to social equality*," and nothing more. Not only did Thompson fail to act deferentially, he assaulted the citadel of deferential government.

More and more men who shared William Thompson's views began to populate the assemblies, or legislatures, as they came to be called. In Virginia the number of wealthy men in the legislature declined by half after the war. In Maryland and South Carolina, too, more ordinary citizens sought and won election to the legislature. Military leadership brought to prominence such roughhewn, untutored men as Elijah Clarke of Georgia. A back-country guerrilla leader, Clarke used his wartime reputation to embark on a notable postwar career in his state. Individuals such as Clarke would probably not have become important figures before 1775. The war breached forever the old walls of political leadership as the sanctuary of the privileged.

The disestablishment of the Anglican church also contributed to the weakening of deference. Everywhere in the 1780s legislatures dismantled the legal frame-work that had given Anglicanism a special place in southern life. When the church lost its privileges, the gentry lost one of the props that elevated it above the common people. While the Anglican church lost its status as the established church, the evangelical denominations surged across the South. Led by the Baptists and the Methodists, these churches brought increasingly large numbers of southerners into their folds. Emphasizing individualism and shunning any trappings of rank or privilege, the evangelicals offered only meager assistance to a concept of deference already beleaguered by secular forces. Although most of the political leaders in the late eighteenth century still retained their Anglican ties, the increasing political influence of the evangelicals testified to the rapid growth of their congregations.

The arrival of this new kind of public man did not escape the notice of the traditional ruling class. Many of them echoed the dismay expressed by a Virginian when he saw "men not quite so well dressed, nor so politely educated, nor so highly born" take their legislative seats. Henry Laurens complained that the new legislators, knowing nothing of parliamentary procedure, thought government required "no more words than are necessary in the bargain and sale of a cow." The Henry Laurenses also feared that their new associates might not be amenable to control by the gentry.

That fear was justified, to a point. Although no social revolution took place in any southern state, the new men in the legislatures certainly made their presence felt. Largely at their behest, legislatures in every southern state but Georgia re-formed regressive tax structures. The chief reform, repealing a land tax based on acreage and substituting an ad valorem land tax, headlined a generally successful effort to base taxes more on wealth than on individuals or acreage alone.

The Revolution also modified the basis of government. A common theme ran through the state making and constitutional writing that pervaded the entire country during the war years. Southerners as well as other Americans gave all but complete power to their assemblies or legislatures. Each state had an executive that all eventually called the governor, but he had practically no authority. Basically a figurehead, the governor, though often a man of prominence and popularity, was deprived even of the veto. This political emasculation of the executive was a reaction to royal governors and to the king, executives both and, of course, integral parts of the British imperial system. Neither had absolute power, and in the colonies the royal governor shared power with the colonial assembly, which had increased its prerogatives considerably by the time of the Revolution. Still, the royal governor had power; he could terminate a legislative session and could veto legislation. In theory even more than practice, the assemblies were only a part of a large governmental machine. But during the Revolutionary crisis the cries of liberty for the people and the shouts that the people must rule merged to underwrite full authority for the legislature, the hall of the people. In the legislature sat southerners of all kinds, who as voices of the people and guardians of their liberty controlled public affairs in their states.

This democratic turn did not signify the death of deference, not at all. A great name, family, and wealth remained important. These attributes still commanded respect from multitudes of southerners, and they continued to provide the surest ticket to political advancement. The great debate in the late 1770s and 1780s over the proper relationship between the southern states and the central government of the infant United States conclusively confirmed the ongoing authority of the traditional southern ruling class.

A NATIONAL SETTING

Just as the rhetoric and ideology of the Revolution forced the South to ponder slavery, political organization for the Revolution obliged the South for the first time to consider itself as part of a larger political whole. Before the First Continental Congress in 1774, no single political group or institution devoted to making policy for all the colonies had existed in British North America. The convening of the Second Continental Congress in 1775 reinforced the new departure in colonial politics. Then with the Declaration of Independence promulgated by the Congress in 1776, the Congress asserted itself as the political voice of the new United States of America. Thus in only two years a marked transformation in governance had taken place.

Until 1774 each colony was a single polity loyal to London, whence came general political direction. Although all the colonies had shared certain patterns of development and although groupings of colonies—the southern, New England—had common institutions, each acted as an individual political entity. The colonies saw no need to adjust competing goals or to reconcile differences with one another because no common political center existed to direct the course of thirteen colonies as one political unit. But the union of all the colonies in the rebellion against England changed that long-standing political situation.

The Second Continental Congress, which assumed direction of the war effort—at first by common agreement, then under the Articles of Confederation—had to make decisions and formulate policies for a union of all the states, not for a single state or a group of states. In this new environment delegates from the thirteen states sitting in Congress had to face the political reality that the interests of the states they represented often diverged. The southern delegates certainly discovered this fact of political life, and the discovery necessarily led to the adoption of identifiable political positions.

The Second Continental Congress, which first convened in 1775, served as the government of the United States until the implementation of the Constitution almost a decade and a half later. This Congress had to wage war and simultaneously devise a plan of government that would give the country more than an ad hoc regime. To wage war it had to collect money and decide on war aims; to plan a government it had to sanction a method of taxation and fix the location of sovereignty, or ultimate authority. Although Congress began to debate the form of a permanent government in 1776, not until late in 1777 did it agree on the Articles of Confederation and transmit the document to the states for consideration. With attention focused on the war, four years passed before all thirteen states approved the Articles. During those years, the southern delegates in Congress identified the interests of their states and acted to safeguard them. As the Marylander Samuel Chase informed the Congress as early as 1776, "We [the South] shall be governed by our interests, and ought to be."

Slavery dominated those interests. To southerners, whether or not slavery continued to exist was not a fit subject for congressional debate. In July 1776—the very month independence was declared—a South Carolinian put it boldly to Congress: "If it is debated whether slaves are their property, there is an end of the confederation." While among themselves white southerners discussed their future with black slaves, albeit in generally muted fashion, they had no intention of allowing any nonsoutherners to enter their conversation. The southerners got what they demanded: the Congress never directly threatened the sanctity of slavery.

Southerners' concern with slavery, however, extended beyond the security of the institution itself. Because the Articles did not give it the power to tax, Congress had to rely on funds supplied by the states or requisitioned from them. In debating how much money should come from each state, Congress considered basing the amount on the populations of the states. The southern delegates immediately raised objections to any formula that counted slaves on an equal basis with whites. Expressing the views of his fellow southern delegates, Samuel Chase minced neither words nor sentiment. Chase told Congress that slaves were property just like any other property; as such, they should not be considered members of political society any more than livestock, because "they have no more interest in it." No matter the importance of slavery to the South, southerners had no intention of permitting their slaves to become a national asset, available to pay the costs of Congress and country. Congress finally had to abandon the attempt to include slaves in any requisition plan. Just as adamantly the southern delegates refused to consider slaves as part of their population for purposes of troop assessments.

This congressional discussion about the position of slavery dramatized the new world that the southern states and southerners had entered. With the Revolution won and the United States established, the shaping of the new nation assumed paramount importance.

5

The South in the New Nation

❖

M any historians of the South have argued over the beginnings of southern distinctiveness, over when the South began to exhibit the unique
features and common attitudes that by the mid-nineteenth century set
it apart from the rest of the country. Various scholars have located this allegedly
momentous occurrence at various points in time. This issue, however, is misleading. Distinct characteristics of the South, such as plantation agriculture and black
slavery, began in the seventeenth century. The conscious commitment to slavery
made by the South during the Revolutionary crisis simply confirmed the powerful place slavery had come to occupy in the preceding century. The suggestion
that in one year or at one time a particular southern distinctiveness appeared is
misguided. Yet in the 1770s and the 1780s southerners did begin to speak of themselves as southerners.

No one articulated this view of southernness more clearly than the Virginian
Thomas Jefferson. For the benefit of a French writer, Jefferson in 1785 spelled out
what he called "my idea of the character of the several states." He sharply separated northern and southern characteristics. Northerners he described as "cool,
sober, laborious, . . . jealous of their own liberties, and just to others." Southerners,
by contrast, were "fiery, Voluptuary, indolent, . . . zealous for their own liberties,
but trampling on those of others." Whether or not Jefferson's assessment was correct is less important than his conviction that he could identify distinctions between North and South.

Southerners also began to think in terms of specific southern interests. This
development was part of a general process that was unfolding everywhere under
the influence of the Continental Congress and the war. During this period observers elsewhere began to speak of the South as a distinctive region. Even so,
nothing fundamental had changed in the southern states; southern economic and
social institutions remained basically what they had been. Change had taken
place, but beyond the borders of the southern states. With the Continental Congress and the Articles of Confederation representing a union of American states,

southerners found themselves in a new arena that demanded a new assessment of themselves and their interests.

SELF-INTEREST

In the immediate postwar period southerners identified interests other than slavery and taxation. Tobacco, rice, and other commodities found their greatest market beyond the South. With the British Empire no longer governing trade, new patterns had to appear. Southerners knew they would not be transporting their own goods, for shipping was not one of the South's strengths. The mercantile community in the North, with its vigorous shipping industry, wanted Congress empowered to regulate external and internal commerce, the latter known as the coasting trade—the movement of goods between American ports. Many southerners objected because they feared Congress might exclude foreign ships from the coasting trade, leaving southern trade and prosperity at the mercy of northern merchants. Southerners pressed for competition among shippers, whom they expected to be eager for their business. Western trade issues also concerned southerners. The ongoing drive to the West made the South acutely aware of the Mississippi River, which was absolutely critical to the prosperity of Kentucky and Tennessee. People on both sides of the Appalachians recognized that central truth. Almost all southerners considered access to the Mississippi essential.

This belief in the intimate relationship between southern destiny and the Mississippi explains southerners' fierce opposition to the proposed Jay-Gardoqui Treaty of 1786. The treaty grew out of discussions between John Jay of New York, the American foreign secretary, and Diego de Gardoqui, the Spanish minister to the United States. Jay wanted to boost American commerce while Gardoqui wanted to arrest American expansion. In possession of Florida and Louisiana, Spain feared encroachment on its empire by the vigorous young nation to the north. The two diplomats reached an agreement that had the Mississippi as its fulcrum. In return for the United States' renunciation of claims to navigate the Mississippi for twenty-five years, Spain would open its markets to American commerce. The South was stunned. The government seemed to have no regard for southern interests. United southern opposition guaranteed that Jay and the proponents of the treaty could never muster the nine votes they needed for congressional ratification. To southerners the episode said that the North was ready to sacrifice southern concerns on the altar of its commercial desires.

Perceiving clearly their common interests, southerners also understood that they often clashed with those of the North. A southerner in Congress in 1782 referred to "these great struggles between Northern and Southern interests." In the same year the nationally minded Virginian James Madison noted that southern congressmen exhibited "an habitual jealously [sic] of a predominance of Eastern interests."

The recognition of particular southern concerns extended beyond the political leadership to southern voters, who expected their leaders to protect their interests. Although under the Articles the actual voters for congressional delegates were legislators, they spoke for the citizens who had placed them in the legislatures. Challengers for public office were quick to charge incumbents with negligence in safeguarding the South. No politician, no matter his name, experience, or reputation, could exempt himself from the requirement that he stand as a sentinel for the South. The enemies of Richard Henry Lee, who in 1776 had introduced in Congress the resolution for independence, charged in the Virginia legislature that he "favored New England to the injury of Virginia." Lee thought this accusation "so contemptibly wicked" that he did not want to take the time to refute it. But he did, and his defense was offense. To his political enemies he cried, "I defy the poisonous tongue of slander to produce a single instance in which I have preferred the interest of N.E. to that of Virg." Despite this challenge, the charge that Lee was less than zealous in safeguarding southern interests almost cost him his seat in Congress. If the southern issue could threaten a leader as notable as Lee, it could surely have an enormous impact on men with lesser reputations.

A distinct sectional consciousness can be seen in the voting patterns of southern congressmen. Students of the Continental Congress have identified a southern voting alignment that became increasingly evident as the 1770s gave way to the 1780s. By the mid-1780s southern congressmen had achieved such cohesion in their voting that the South was able to dominate the Congress. New England and the middle states also tended to vote in concert, but they did not match the South in solidarity. In sum, southerners identified their special interests in a larger arena and acted vigorously to uphold their position.

*U*NITY AND DISUNITY

The congressional consensus on areas of critical concern to the South did not mean that southerners knew no political disunity. Southerners, like all other Americans, disagreed over a variety of issues in the 1780s, and they split most markedly over financial matters. Such disputes pervaded the country. Although the disputes focused on state finances, the financial question ultimately had national implications.

Though the particulars of financial politics varied from state to state, an underlying cause provided thematic unity to the arguments over money. Rampant inflation fueled by the issuing of paper money during the Revolution had been replaced by vigorous deflation after the war. As the amount of paper currency in circulation declined, the importance of specie, or "hard money," increased. Specie was scarce in the South. The shortage of money led to hard times and anger and tough legislative fights. Almost everywhere the general financial issue assumed a political shape of two dimensions: taxes and debts.

The debate over taxation focused on two issues: the tax structure—on what basis should taxes be assessed?—and whether or not taxes should be high enough to meet the levies requested by Congress. Though southern legislatures engaged in some restructuring of state taxes, they generally refused to meet requests from Congress. State officials knew that their economies would suffer under the pressure of additional taxes. These officials also knew that they would personally suffer the wrath of hard-pressed constituents if voters were saddled with higher taxes to pay for a central government that was enthusiastically supported by very few.

In their financial distress many southerners clamored for legislative relief from debt payment as well as from tax increases. They demanded "stay laws" that would postpone the collection of legally contracted debts; and planters who still owed prewar debts to British merchants wanted those merchants barred from initiating action in state courts, despite the provision of the peace treaty upholding the right of creditors to collect such debts. Legislators heard these cries and acted in response to them, but not without opposition, for any proposal to delay or obstruct payment of legitimate debts outraged domestic creditors and others who believed that the integrity of an individual and of a society depended on the honoring of all obligations.

The clash did not simply line up poor debtors against rich creditors. The opposing sides had a more complex membership, in part because some southerners, especially planters, fell into both camps. They were lenders, but they also borrowed—from fellow planters, from American merchants, and before the Revolution from British merchants. To complicate matters further, those who believed that the treaty with England took precedence over the policy of individual states argued that one state could not undercut the treaty rights of British merchants. Despite these complications, legislators responded to the shouts for relief. The elected representatives of an aroused people who expected action could hardly do otherwise. After hard legislative fights the efforts to shackle local lenders and to thwart British creditors largely succeeded.

Recent students of this period have found the beginnings of political parties in the division over financial issues. State financial politics became connected with large national concerns because the partisan lineup in the southern states brought the local conflict into national focus. The political sides on the financial issues did not form solely or chiefly along economic lines. Partisanship depended more on general outlook or world view than on financial status or occupation. On one side, the men who opposed meeting the needs of Congress, who supported stay laws and restrictions on British merchants, insisted that the state and the desires of its citizens must come first. On the other side of the financial issues were men whose education, business and social activities, and wartime experiences had given them a broader, more nationalist outlook. They denounced their states' unwillingness to support the Congress. They foresaw a drifting, ineffective Congress that would make for a feckless nation.

NATIONALISM

These more nationalist-oriented southerners believed that the Congress and the Articles of Confederation needed an injection of strength and purpose. If these essentials were to be found, the central government had to have the power to raise its own revenue. But, in the view of these nationalists, money alone would not suffice to give pride and momentum to the nation. They were convinced that some way had to be found to make the relationship between the central government and the citizens more intimate. To these men the nation created by the Revolution was not yet secure in the dangerous world of nations. Like-minded men sounded the same warnings north of the Mason-Dixon line. Nationalists everywhere worried that national goals and the common good would be overpowered by the localist orientation of the state legislatures. They feared that the division over financial issues might undermine social and political stability. And they dreaded even more the possibility that the United States would disintegrate into several parts, most likely into the sections so clearly revealed in congressional voting. This political subdivision would create a series of little Americas that could never fend off the preying empires of Great Britain and Spain. Such a horrendous outcome would inevitably conclude with the destruction of republicanism. In short, the Revolution would fail.

Southerners were surely not the only Americans thinking this way. The stronger national government the nationalists wanted was a government republican in both form and substance. A popular base and elected representatives were essential. Men in the rest of the country shared this opinion, but the nationalist viewpoint had especially prominent advocates in the South. No American was a more forceful advocate of radical change than James Madison, who fought the political and ideological battles of the 1780s in both the Congress and the Virginia legislature.

James Madison was a bright star in the galaxy of political leaders who directed American affairs in the first generation of national life. Born in Virginia in 1751, Madison graduated from Princeton in 1771 and with the onset of the Revolution began a political career that would span forty years. His physical presence contrasted sharply with his political eminence. A short, frail man—he was only five feet four inches tall and weighed but a hundred pounds—he occasionally had difficulty making himself seen. But he never had any trouble getting his contemporaries to pay attention to what he wrote or said. Madison displayed a remarkable combination of political abilities. A close student of politics, he was thoroughly grounded in the thought of the classical and continental political theorists, and no American of his time surpassed him in ability to wrestle with the most fundamental questions of government. And Madison was as successful a politician as he was a theorist. He was an effective legislator; in Philadelphia he was a major force in shaping the Constitution. With good reason historians have called him the father of the Constitution. In the ratification debate he assumed a critical role both in Virginia and in the nation. During the early 1790s, in conjunction with his personal and political confidant Thomas Jefferson, he founded a major political party. In 1801 he became secretary of state and in 1809 the fourth president of the United States. Whether Americans agreed with him or not; most of them respected his learning, his determination, and his political skills.

Many southerners shared Madison's conviction that the Articles of Confederation had to be fundamentally altered, but many others predicted that any central government with power to raise its own revenue would run roughshod over both the states and liberty. When the Articles had been drafted in the 1770s, southerners had been among the most insistent that the states must keep more power than they gave to the central government. As Madison noted, "a jealousy of congressional usurpations" preoccupied many southerners. A surrender of power by the states, they argued, could turn liberty into despotism. The nationalist thrust of Madison and his allies seemed to be opening up the same kind of outside threat to local control that had sparked the Revolution. From this political vantage point, the specter of a powerful American central government appeared to be as great a menace as the government of George III.

DRAFTING THE CONSTITUTION

Under the Articles of Confederation disputes between and among states were not easily solved. In an attempt to deal with commercial problems that had arisen, Virginia in 1786 called for a conference to meet in Annapolis, Maryland. Attendance was poor and little could be accomplished. The delegates, under James Madison's urging, pressed the Congress to call a convention with power broad enough to consider changes in the Articles. Congress issued such a call, and delegates from twelve states (Rhode Island sent none) convened in Philadelphia in May 1787.

The delegates went far beyond their mandate. Rather than alter or amend the Articles, they fashioned a totally new governmental plan, the Constitution. They were generally convinced that radical action was essential. The delegations, including those from the southern states, consisted overwhelmingly of men who shared James Madison's commitment to the necessity of a stronger central government. Although each member of this extraordinarily able group had his eyes fixed on a secure future for the United States of America, not all agreed on the means to ensure that security. Those from large states clashed with those from small states on apportionment of power; delegates who pushed for an especially strong executive debated with colleagues who feared what they called undue concentration of power. Through all the debates, votes, and compromises, the southern delegates never forgot the special interests of the South. Madison was on target when he declared that the differences among states derived "principally from the effects of their having or not having slaves"; the fundamental division of interests "lay between the Northern and Southern."

The deliberations of the Constitutional Convention underscored the direct connection between the South's perception of southern interests and slavery. Southerners made clear their refusal to tolerate any discussion of the future of slavery, and they insisted that their slaves must be no liability to them; indeed, they expected their slaves to benefit them politically. Some southern delegates urged that slaves be counted fully for representation, while certain delegates from outside the South did not want them counted at all. After discussion an agreement was reached that fractional counting would be appropriate. Even before the convention resolved to base representation in the lower house of Congress on population alone, it decided to count a slave as three-fifths of a white person. On this critical issue the slave states won a major victory without having to give any substantial concession. When the convention made the decision to base representation on the lower house solely on population, it simply applied the already agreed upon three-fifths clause. Southerners had spoken forcefully. Observing that some delegates intended "to deprive the Southern States of any show of Representation for their blacks," a North Carolina member pronounced the verdict of the South. The South, he declared, "would never confederate on any terms that did not rate [slaves] at least as 3/5. If the Eastern States meant therefore to exclude them altogether the business was at an end." Later the convention also applied the three-fifths clause to the direct taxation provision.

From 1775 to 1787 the South repeatedly insisted that the national government keep its hands off slavery. Southerners also demanded that any national government must agree that slavery could benefit the South in any new political arena. The obverse also held: slavery must never penalize the South. As the Constitution took shape, the South won its fundamental demands on slavery.

Though southerners stood united on the institution of slavery as in their interest, they strongly disagreed on the international slave trade. Opposition to the continuation of the trade centered in the upper South, especially in Virginia. Although the Virginians who worried about the morality of slavery were either unwilling or unable—and usually both—to do anything about the institution itself, they could assault the slave trade. An attack on the trade neither damaged slavery in Virginia nor threatened slaveholders. By the 1770s many white Virginians believed their black population large enough; moreover, any restriction on the importation of slaves could only increase the value of those already in Virginia. Thus opposition to the slave trade posed no economic menace to Virginia or to Virginia slaveholders. In this instance ideological inclination and economic self-interest meshed perfectly.

South of Virginia planters wanted more slaves. In the Carolinas and Georgia the plantation system was spreading. Seacoast and back country alike were undergoing considerable economic growth, and planters believed they needed more slaves to fuel that growth. Politicians in the lower South never joined the Virginia-led chorus against the slave trade. The disunity on this issue broke wide open when the Constitutional Convention considered halting the trade. Prodded by the Virginia delegation, the convention seemed prepared to outlaw the trade in the Constitution. Reacting vigorously, delegates from the three southernmost states based their agreement to the Constitution squarely on their right to import slaves. Without that right, as a South Carolinian put it, "the expectation is in vain." In the face of such adamant opposition, the convention compromised: the Constitution would not outlaw the trade, but it would empower the new federal Congress to decide the matter twenty years after ratification. Although neither the Virginians nor the Carolinians rejoiced over this solution, both accepted it as a reasonable way out of a vexing situation.

THE RATIFICATION CONTEST

Because the Philadelphia convention, which met from May to September, conducted its affairs in secret, no debate on the Constitution took place in the South until the contest over ratification. The debate raged for a year, until the autumn of 1788. During that year the opponents of the Constitution challenged the proposed form of government vigorously. The structure and substance of this discussion illuminate just what the South saw as its basic political values and goals. The major battle in the South was fought in conventions called by each state to approve or reject the Constitution. The division over ratification basically continued the localist-nationalist contest that had marked southern politics in the 1780s.

As advocates of both sides articulated their perceptions of the critical issues, the constitutional fight underscored the South's participatory politics. Throughout the months of decision the Federalists (who advocated ratification of the Constitution) and the Anti-Federalists (who opposed it) constantly appealed to the people for support. Both sides insisted that the course they advocated would benefit "the people." Such rhetoric had a long history in the region between the Potomac and the Savannah. These polemics cannot be dismissed as cynical and meaningless rhetoric. During and after the Revolutionary crisis, southerners, along with most other Americans, had given extraordinary power to the concept of the sovereignty of the people. Committees, conventions, elections, instructions to delegates and representatives, unending appeals to the people—all gave significant weight to what may seem an empty phrase: sovereignty of the people. All the contestants in the South took seriously the voice and role of the people.

At the same time that the people received plaudits aplenty, the men with the great names massively influenced the fate of the Constitution. They propelled the Constitution forward, and often men who had served in Philadelphia stood in the front rank of the Federalist charge. James Madison, Charles Pinckney of South Carolina, James Iredell of North Carolina—such men led the forces that pushed for the Constitution. Those forces represented the planter-lawyer-merchant upper class that had directed the course of southern politics from the colonial era through the Revolution. The great majority of this traditional leadership class championed ratification, but just enough of them called for rejection to limit the inclusiveness of the upper-class constitutional club.

The Constitution did not get the same reception from all the southern ratifying conventions. It found its warmest welcome in Georgia, where it won quick and almost unanimous approval, probably because of the desire for military assistance to protect a frontier exposed to both Spanish and Indians. Its coldest response came in North Carolina, which initially rejected it. Maryland and South Carolina approved of the new plan by substantial margins, though not without strenuous objections. The deepest division, the hardest fight, and the closest margin of victory came in Virginia.

OPPOSITION

Enemies of the Constitution charged that it would weaken liberty in the South and in the United States at large by establishing "most clearly a consolidated government." For Anti-Federalists this consolidated government was "extremely pernicious, impolitic, and dangerous" because it resulted from what they termed an enormous transfer of power from the states to the central government. As they saw it, states would lose control over such critically important areas as governmental expenditures because the power to tax provided the central government with its own source of revenue. In addition, the revised basis for apportionment and the new voting procedure in a radically different Congress reduced both the image and the reality of state power. Whereas the Articles based both apportionment and voting on the states alone, each state having one vote, the Constitution added a second chamber to Congress, brought population into the apportionment formula, and required each member of Congress to vote as an individual. The size of a delegation in the House of Representatives would depend solely on the population of its state; and though each state would send two people to the Senate, the senators, just like the members of the House, would cast their ballots as individuals. Southern Anti-Federalists never used "consolidation" as a synonym for "union." They carefully separated the two; they wanted the latter but not the former. These southerners followed the traditional political dictum that liberty depended on the power to control one's own affairs, one's own destiny. One of them shouted, "Liberty! What is liberty? The power of governing yourselves. If you adopt this Constitution, have you this power? No!"

This was not the only argument advanced by the southern Anti-Federalists against the Constitution. A friend of George Washington voiced an anxiety shared by many southerners when he wrote, "If the Constitution is carried into effect, the States south of the potowmac [sic], will be little more than appendages to those to the northward of it." No other single question preoccupied the southern Anti-Federalists so much as the security of slavery. To the Virginia convention Patrick Henry repeated his lament about the evil of slavery and the impossibility of doing anything about it, but he went on to declare that "in clear, unequivocal terms" the Constitution gave the North the power to abolish slavery. Farther south no qualms about slavery accompanied fear for its health under the proposed Constitution. Rawlins Lowndes painted a melancholy scene in somber colors: "When this new Constitution should be adopted, the sun of the Southern States would set, never to rise."

SUPPORT

The Federalists met their opponents directly on every point. Emphasizing that the Constitution "takes its rise, where it ought, from the people," the old South Carolina Revolutionary Christopher Gadsden pronounced in a public letter that "all essentials to a republican government, are, in my opinion, well secured." The individual most responsible for the Constitution found perplexing as well as wrongheaded the argument that it organized a consolidated government. Before the Virginia convention James Madison countered such assertions by dwelling on the continuing importance of states in the new nation, which to his mind proved the error of all talk about consolidation. Madison maintained that a consolidated government would eliminate the power of the states, but that the Constitution did no such thing.

On one vitally important interest, slavery, southern Federalists never squirmed. Madison expressed amazement that any southerner could think that ratification of the Constitution signaled abolition. Madison, who certainly should have known, assured Virginians that "there is no power to warrant it in the [Constitution]." A South Carolinian proclaimed, "We have a security that the general government can never emancipate [slaves], for no such authority is granted." In an attempt to end all talk about the insecurity of slavery under the Constitution, a delegate to the Virginia convention who had also served in Philadelphia spoke authoritatively: "*The Southern States, even South Carolina herself, conceived this property to be secure by* [the Constitution]." No one "*had the smallest suspicion of the abolition of slavery.*"

The most striking feature of the rhetoric employed in the ratification struggle was the common theme articulated by Federalists and Anti-Federalists alike. Both sides underscored liberty—specifically, whether or not the Constitution protected it. Everyone agreed on its absolute primacy. Moreover, all concurred that preservation of liberty required protection of the South's special interests, paramount among them slavery. At the close of the Revolutionary and Constitution-making epoch all white southerners conceded that slavery was embedded in their society. They did not believe that their society could withstand any fundamental alteration of the system because such a transformation meant inevitable disorder, even upheaval. The white South did not agree on the virtue or vice of its marriage to black slavery, but it cried in unison that slavery must remain its partner, and that it was strictly a southern concern. Without control of slavery, white southerners agreed, they could not possess their own liberty. Thus on the morning of the ratification of the Constitution, just as during the Revolution, slavery and liberty were inextricably intertwined in the southern mind.

UNDER THE CONSTITUTION

The ratification of the Constitution and the creation of a different national political arena did not bury local interests under an avalanche of nationalist fervor. Although all Americans desired success for the fledgling nation, they also anticipated success for themselves and for their particular interests. From the outset southerners in Congress recognized that their northern colleagues did not take a disinterested view of public affairs. Commenting on the first session of the First Congress, a South Carolina senator observed, "Here I find men scrambling for partial advantage, State interests, and in short, a train of these narrow, impolitic measures that must, after a while shake the Union to its very foundation." Even James Madison, the ardent evangelist of the new government, admitted that congressional votes during the initial session indicated that northerners were looking out for themselves. And all the while they criticized the self-interest of the northerners, southerners maneuvered to advance their own interests.

An attempt in the First Congress to give Congress power over slavery clearly demonstrated the determination of the southerners. In February 1790 various antislavery groups petitioned Congress to assert itself on the slavery issue. In response the House of Representatives set up a special committee to specify the power of Congress over slavery. The committee, with only one southern member, reported that before 1808 Congress could interfere with neither the international slave trade nor slavery; the clear implication was that Congress could interfere at will after 1808. Southerners on both sides of the slave-trade question joined to emasculate the report. They united behind an amendment proposed by Madison: "That Congress have no authority to interfere in the emancipation of slaves, or in the treatment of them within any of the States; it remaining with the several states alone to provide any regulation therein." The passage of Madison's amendment meant congressional adoption of the southern view that the Constitution did not permit Congress to act against slavery. This policy settled upon during the second session of the First Congress, remained intact for seventy years, until the Union itself broke apart.

The debate on Congress's jurisdiction over slavery did nothing to alter the South's perception that an assault on slavery was the primary threat to its liberty. For most southerners that threat materialized in the first great struggle over the basic course the new nation would follow.

HAMILTON'S VISION

At the center of the great contest stood Alexander Hamilton of New York, secretary of the treasury in President George Washington's cabinet. Hamilton envisioned a country growing powerful and wealthy through the active agency of the central government, which would promote economic and political measures to support American commercial and financial endeavors. Hamilton had no intention of guarding local interests; in his mind they all paled beside the overriding necessity of giving life to the United States of America—one nation, not its constituent parts.

Hamilton wanted to bind the self-interest of American citizens to the nation so that the prosperity of the citizenry would be dependent on the success of the nation. The means would come through public credit: the federal government would assume all the remaining Revolutionary debts of the states, combine them with the federal debt, and fund the total as a new public debt. To facilitate this citizen-nation financial relationship he advocated a national bank chartered by Congress and capitalized with both public and private funds. Believing that the growth of manufacturing was essential for the nation's strength, he also proposed direct government subsidies to manufacturers and a tariff that would keep out cheaper foreign goods and at the same time provide revenue to operate the federal government. This grand design had a foreign policy component—good relations with Great Britain, our chief trading partner, even if to secure them the United States had to acquiesce in Britain's control of the seas. Anglo-American trade provided the tariff revenue to run the government, and Hamilton saw Britain as a source of capital for American economic growth. The South did not occupy a large place in Hamilton's national vision. Merchants, shippers, financiers, and manufacturers were much more numerous and important in the North. Thus his program had sectional favoritism built into it, though Hamilton did not think in such terms.

THE SOUTH OPPOSES

Not surprisingly, the South led the opposition to Hamilton's plans. Directed chiefly by the indefatigable James Madison, the opposition spanned the South. Of the southern states only South Carolina, with the largest city and major commercial center in the South, Charleston, offered Hamilton much support, and that support was to diminish significantly through the 1790s. Southern self-interest was surely involved. All southern states except South Carolina had already paid a substantial portion of their Revolutionary debts; thus in their eyes, Hamilton's funding scheme would require them to help others when no one had helped them. Concluding that Hamilton's program would favor commercial and financial interests in the North, southerners could see no good reason to back it.

But more than self-interest was involved. Southerners argued that Hamilton exhibited entirely too little concern for the words and intentions of the Constitution. As Madison pointed out, the Constitution made no provision for a national bank. He and his colleagues feared that such a broad interpretation would undermine the Constitution, to the public's jeopardy. And when Congress passed the bank bill in February 1791, southerners cast almost all the nay votes.

Most southerners saw no reason to interfere in an economy that permitted their agrarian society to flourish. Although many northerners agreed on the virtues of an agrarian society, its advocates and defenders were concentrated in the South. All were appalled by Hamilton's desire for structural changes in the American economy. The idea of turning the United States into a manufacturing country with a monetary system based on a funded debt and a national bank clashed with their fundamental view of society. To most southerners the agrarian society of large and small freeholders which had produced them was the best of all possible worlds. They wanted the nation to grow and prosper, but not to change in any significant sense. That this growth necessitated territorial expansion southerners recognized and approved, but this kind of expansion did not necessitate structural change. In a basic sense, Hamilton wanted to make a social and economic revolution, and the southerners did not. To be sure, their vision of society meshed with their self-interest in the 1790s, but it was not simply a function of self-interest. The public and private utterances of southerners during these years leave no doubt that their fervent commitment to their world was grounded in idealism. At the same time, the reality of their world did not always coincide with their vision of it.

This world view explains why Madison and his supporters opposed Hamilton's foreign policy. Their image of Great Britain in the 1790s remained what it had been two decades earlier—a corrupt society in which public debt and manufacturing had led to extremes of wealth and poverty that had destroyed liberty. Believing, basically correctly, that Hamilton wanted to refashion the United States after the British pattern and that such a transformation would mortally wound the Revolution by destroying the republic, they wanted no friendship with Great Britain. Madison countered Hamilton's program by proposing a policy of commercial discrimination that would force Britain, according to Madison in dire need of American products, to end restrictions on American trade.

To his opposition Alexander Hamilton seemed bent on tearing apart what the Revolution had won. Aware that they were setting the foundation stones of a new nation, all the builders understood that the emplacement would have a profound influence on the completed structure. Only this understanding explains the bitterness and viciousness of politics in the 1790s. The Virginia legislature pointed directly to the terrible danger southerners saw when it warned in 1790 that Hamilton's program entailed "a change in the present form of federal government fatal to the existence of American liberty."

When Congress enacted most of Hamilton's proposals, partisanship sharpened and led to the formation of competing parties. In the South national issues generated the private and public activity that resulted in political parties. The administration party, with President Washington as its chief luminary and Hamilton's program as its platform, called itself the Federalist party.

*F*EDERALISTS AND THE SOUTH

The Federalists appeared to have distinct advantages in their efforts to cultivate the South. George Washington headed the list. The first great national hero, Washington occupied a special place in the South. A son of Virginia, Washington proudly identified himself with his native state. As a slave-owning planter he was a member of the group that had long dominated southern politics. When Washington traveled through the South in 1791, celebration marked his tour—for himself, for the young nation, and for the local leaders who made his cause their own. And because the Federalists controlled the national administration, they could employ patronage in their own interest. Although patronage in the 1790s did not begin to match that of later years, it still provided an opportunity to reward friends and win political loyalty. Washington placed prominent southerners in the cabinet and in responsible diplomatic and judicial posts. At the local level, the

GEORGE WASHINGTON, VIRGINIAN, REVOLUTIONARY COMMANDER-IN-CHIEF, FIRST PRESIDENT (Portrait by Rembrandt Peale, The National Portrait Gallery, Smithsonian Institution, Gift of an anonymous donor)

Treasury Department and the Post Office provided numerous jobs that the administration used to build political loyalty in the states.

With the great hero at their head, local luminaries in strategic posts, and patronage to dispense, the Federalists seemed prepared to dominate southern politics; they needed only an issue or program to promote in the South. But, aside from calling for allegiance to Washington, they had none. This liability was quickly apparent when Hamilton's policies became the cornerstone of the Federalist program. Few southern Federalists publicly supported Hamiltonianism, and practically none was enthusiastic about it. The proposal to cultivate Great Britain was particularly difficult to accept. In 1795 President Washington set off a political conflagration when he submitted to the Senate a treaty that had been negotiated by John Jay. Republicans denounced the Jay Treaty for prohibiting any American commercial discrimination against Great Britain for ten years, and southerners especially condemned the provisions that aided British merchants in recovering sums they had advanced to Americans before the Revolution. From the Potomac to the Savannah public meetings railed against Jay's handiwork; in the Federalist stronghold of Charleston a mob burned the diplomat in effigy. The treaty was ratified by the Senate with no votes to spare, and in the House the motion to appropriate funds to finance the treaty's provisions was carried by only three votes.

Southern Federalists had still another massive problem. Washington excepted, no southerner who publicly identified himself with the administration's policies enjoyed broad appeal and respect in the South. Of course given the onerous problems that the major issues posed for southern Federalism, the emergence of such a man would have required the possession of almost magical political talents. The lack of a southern junior partner for Washington was of special concern in view of the dominance of the national leadership by northerners, particularly Alexander Hamilton of New York and Vice President John Adams of Massachusetts.

Without easily salable issues to take before southern voters and with no prominent national leaders rising from their ranks, southern Federalists had to rely on the prestige of George Washington. Reliance on Washington, however, was at best a short-term strategy. He would not tower over the political scene forever. Southern Federalists would find themselves in a desperate political situation if they should have to face a determined, organized opposition with both southern leaders and southern-oriented issues.

THE REPUBLICAN PARTY

Even after Congress approved Hamilton's program, its opponents kept working to build a political party that would have a chance to take power by winning elections. Although scholars do not agree on the precise date of the party's formation, a great majority of them agree that by 1793 a political party did exist—a party in the sense that a group of men armed with policy goals and a commitment to use the political process had come together to win control of the national government. These men began to call themselves Republicans.

James Madison and Thomas Jefferson were the two most important leaders of

THOMAS JEFFERSON
(The White House Collection)

this new body, and the designation Republican fit precisely their conception of the party. To them the Revolution had secured American liberty by overthrowing a monarchy and instituting a republic. What they interpreted as Hamilton's attempt to impose the British system on the United States placed republicanism and liberty in mortal danger. When Madison and Jefferson constantly attacked the "monarchists" who wanted to destroy liberty, they were aiming at the Federalists. The question was not whether an American king would actually be placed on an American throne but whether a republican America would survive.

Denouncing the British system, Madison and Jefferson insisted that America must retain its agrarian character. To the Virginians an agrarian society needed no national bank, no subsidies, no funded debt; in their view, these were plagues that destroyed liberty. Moreover, an agrarian country did not require a powerful central government because such a country did not need the fearful economic functions envisioned by Hamilton. The Republicans preached states' rights to emphasize that only local control guaranteed liberty.

For Madison this attitude marked a turnabout since the 1780s, when he had called for a stronger central government. Then Madison had believed that the Revolution and Americans' liberty were threatened by the weakness of the central government. Now, facing Hamilton's program, he saw the greatest danger to liberty in the consolidation of the national government. "Let it be the patriotic study of all," Madison wrote, "to maintain the various authorities established by our complicated system, each in its respective sphere." Strict construction and states' rights became the rallying cry of republicanism.

This rhetoric fit easily with the South's long-standing concern about outside authority. Articulated Republican fears in the 1790s harked back to worry about

JAMES MADISON
(Courtesy of The New-York Historical
Society, New York City)

British oppression, to concern about the North's domination of the government under the Articles of Confederation, to the misgivings expressed by the Anti-Federalists in 1787 and 1788. Although Madison had changed, many southerners could adopt his new stance without changing at all. That outside or northern forces were engineering this new consolidation compounded the distress of Madison and his followers. Not only were the consolidationists outsiders; they wanted to implement policies disadvantageous to the South, at least as most southerners perceived them. In sum, political heritage, local prejudice, and self-interest coalesced to give the Republicans a powerful hold on the South.

To eliminate the Federalist threat, Madison, Jefferson, and other Republican leaders chose the electoral process as the highway for their political offensive. Two basic facts dictated that choice. First, the Republicans vigorously proclaimed their devotion to the Constitution; their mission was to rescue it from the Federalists. Second, because they believed in the right thinking of the people, the electoral process had to give them power. The Republicans worked to ensure that their message reached voters. Republican leaders established newspapers that gave a Republican hue to their political coverage. These newspapers also served as an outlet for public letters and essays, which gave the leadership an opportunity to reach a wide audience and to set the tone of public debate. Complementing the public press, the leaders' private correspondence pressed their views and urged active participation. They set up committees, selected and put before voters faithful Republican candidates, and worked for their election. By mid-decade the caucus of loyal Republicans at both national and local levels had become a key feature of party organization and discipline.

Republicans hoped to transform the nation. Jefferson and Madison did not think of their political handiwork as designed only for the South. Any attempt to label the Republican party only a southern movement is simply unhistorical, but the special relationship between the Republican party and the South cannot be denied. The South and southerners played a critical role in the creation of the party, in the formulation of its ideology, and in its electoral success.

THE SOUTH AS REPUBLICAN

Southerners certainly heeded the Republicans' call. In both the First Congress (January 1790-March 1791) and the Second Congress (March 1791–March 1793) southerners made up the bulk of the opposition to Hamilton's program. The admission to the Union of Kentucky in 1792 and Tennessee in 1796 added to Republican ranks, for Federalism never prospered west of the Appalachians. Only Maryland and tiny Delaware seemed to be Federalist havens among the slave states, but even in Maryland the Republicans challenged the Federalists vigorously. The presidential election of 1796 clearly indicates the dominance of republicanism in the South. For southerners the presidential candidates—Jefferson of Virginia and John Adams of Massachusetts—personified the relative orientations of the two parties. Some Federalist leaders hoped to confuse the southern scene by manipulating the electoral process mandated by the Constitution, which specified that each presidential elector would vote for two candidates without stipulating between presidential and vice-presidential choices and without regard for party. (This process was changed to the present system, in which electors must distinguish between presidential and vice-presidential choices, by the Twelfth Amendment, adopted in 1804.) In this scheme the name of Thomas Pinckney of South Carolina was injected on the Federalist side as either vice president or possibly even president. Despite this stratagem, the Republicans scored a lopsided victory. From Maryland southward Jefferson won 54 electoral votes, whereas Adams garnered but 9, 7 in Maryland. Despite Adams's miserable showing in the South, he won the election by three electoral votes, 71 to Jefferson's 68. Adams won because he trounced Jefferson in the free states, where Jefferson could claim only Pennsylvania.

Without question the South was the most strongly Republican part of the nation. For southerners the great political contest was fought over national issues; from the birth of the nation southerners had taken a special interest in national politics. Their determination to maintain absolute control over their peculiar institution of slavery gave southerners good reason to be acutely aware of national events. And the debate in 1790 over congressional power and slavery did nothing to diminish that interest. When Alexander Hamilton proceeded to move the nation down a path most southerners believed inimical to their interests and dangerous to their liberty, national affairs became even more salient. To guard their interests, their institutions, themselves—their liberty—southerners banded together in a party they perceived as carrying their flag, with a southerner as commander in chief and southerners as important subordinates. To most southerners

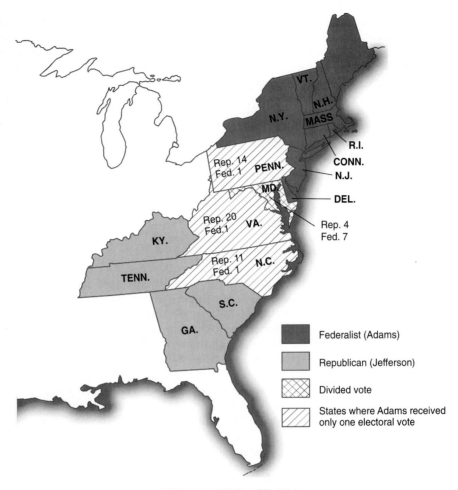

Rep. 14
Fed. 1

Rep. 20
Fed.1

Rep. 11
Fed. 1

Rep. 4
Fed. 7

■ Federalist (Adams)

▨ Republican (Jefferson)

▨ Divided vote

▨ States where Adams received only one electoral vote

THE ELECTION OF 1796

the Republican party manned the political frontier as the great army protecting southern interests and southern liberty.

THE FEDERALIST SURGE

After John Adams took the oath of office as the second president on March 4, 1797, the Federalist party had little reason to expect its status in the South to improve noticeably. Adams's inauguration signaled the retirement of George Washington, and there was no one to replace him.

Yet the relationship between the Adams administration and the South did not follow the expected path. Deterioration in the nation's relations with France unexpectedly revived southern Federalists' fortunes. Facing the possibility of war, the administration began to build up the army. George Washington was named commanding general; the great leader returned to face a new crisis. All this rejuvenated the southern Federalists. In 1798 and 1799 southerners elected more Federalists to Congress than they ever had done before or would do in the future. They even breached the Republican citadel in Virginia, which in 1799 sent eight Federalists along with eleven Republicans to Congress.

For southern Federalists it was a heady time; they seemed on the verge of breaking out of their minority mold. But their success in 1798 and 1799 lacked a secure foundation. War and Washington had served as a crutch for a lame party. Without that crutch the southern Federalists would once again stumble.

While President Adams worked to avoid war with France, he also moved to secure the position of his administration by stifling dissent. In 1798 Congress passed a series of acts designed to achieve that goal. The Naturalization Act extended the time required for immigrants—who the Federalists believed filled Republican ranks— to become citizens from five to fourteen years, and the Alien Act empowered the president to deport aliens regarded as dangerous. The Sedition Act, which made it a federal crime to attack government officials, struck directly at Republican critics of the Adams administration. The Sedition Act was no empty gesture; it was enforced. Government lawyers prosecuted Republicans, especially editors, and Federalist judges sent them to jail.

To protect their party and their understanding of American liberty, the Republican chieftains counterattacked. The tactics they employed fastened the Republican party ever more tightly to the South. When Jefferson confided to an associate, "It is true that we are completely under the saddle of Massachusetts and Connecticut, and that they ride us very hard, cruelly insulting our feelings as well as exhausting our strength and subsistence," he entwined sectionalism with politics. Still, for Jefferson ideological commitment to liberty outweighed sectional loyalty. Even so, the sectional dimension clearly in his mind reinforced the intimate bond between the Republican party and the South.

THE REPUBLICAN RESPONSE

Underscoring the traditional southern and Republican emphasis on the rights of the states and on local control, Jefferson and Madison used state legislatures as their forums. Each man wrote a set of resolutions proclaiming the unconstitutionality of the Alien and Sedition acts and denouncing the federal government's violation of the rights of the states. Madison's resolutions went to the legislature of Virginia, Jefferson's across the mountains to Kentucky. Both men stressed that the central government possessed only those powers strictly delegated to it by the Constitution. All other powers remained with the states, the contracting parties that had created the Constitution.

Although both men had the same intention, they differed in one important respect. Madison contented himself with denouncing the administration's behavior in formal fashion and urged other states to follow Virginia's lead; he provided no precise remedy for the evil he defined. Jefferson, in contrast, boldly advanced the idea that because the Constitution did not specify an ultimate arbiter of disputes, each state had "an equal right to judge for itself, as well of the infractions as the mode and measure of redress." This extreme conclusion—the seed of nullification and secession—was further than Madison and the Kentucky Republicans were willing to go. That Jefferson had broached the idea of secession remained secret for decades. Though Kentucky's resolutions were milder than Virginia's, both documents were strong. In asserting the legitimacy of states' rights and condemning the broad use of federal power, they expressed attitudes that would enjoy a long, prosperous life in the South.

A head-on collision between Federalists and Republicans—between the central government and the states—was averted when John Adams secured a diplomatic settlement with France. With the relaxation of tension between France and the United States, the parties turned to the voters to settle their differences.

THE ELECTION OF 1800

Primed for political combat, Federalists and Republicans prepared to battle for southern votes under their tested commanders, Adams and Jefferson. Partisan feelings were even stronger in 1800 than they had been in 1796 because of the passion and anger generated by the war scare. Federalists castigated Republicans as anarchists, atheists, and regicides; Republicans condemned Federalists for "delug-[ing] the world with crimes and blood." The immense organizational and publicity effort mounted by both sides only intensified the partisanship. Newspapers, committees, electoral tickets, pamphlets, broadsides—all combined to make the presidential election of 1800 a foretaste of those that would come a generation later.

The outlook for southern Federalists appeared simultaneously bright and somber. In view of their performance in 1798 and 1799, many Federalist leaders hoped that 1800 would reveal a solid Federalist base in the South, at least from Maryland to South Carolina. In Georgia and the trans-Appalachian states of Tennessee and Kentucky the Federalists made little effort and expected little return. At the same time there were problems. The passing of the war scare not only eliminated their most emotional issue; it also left them as authors of an unpopular tax measure. To finance the military buildup Congress in 1798 had passed a direct tax on land, slaves, and houses. Southerners bore a heavy portion of this tax load, and by 1800 they had grown weary of the burden. In addition, the death of George Washington in December 1799 deprived southern Federalists of the one man who had given many southerners cause for loyalty to the Federalist party. Sectional strife also plagued the party. In the month of Washington's death, southern and northern Federalists fought over the speakership of the House of Representatives; the northern majority refused to accept a southern speaker. Once again a scheme was hatched to defeat Adams in the electoral college by making the South Carolinian Charles Cotesworth Pinckney a contender for president or vice president.

The Republicans, in contrast, were united, and they enjoyed a strong southern base. Their leaders believed a strong showing in the South was essential for national victory because of Federalist strength in the North, especially in New England. With their candidate a southerner and their party attuned to southern issues, the Republicans bugled their call to southern voters: they protected southern interests, whereas the Federalists endangered them.

The election confirmed the overwhelming dominance of the Republicans in the South and left the Federalists once again with no more than political crumbs. Among the slave states only in tiny Delaware, which Adams carried, and in Maryland, which he divided evenly with Jefferson, did the Federalists do well. Overall Jefferson won 53 of the 65 southern electoral votes. In the country as a whole Jefferson defeated Adams by only 8 electoral votes, a narrow turnabout from 1796, when Adams had won by 3. But in the South neither election had been at all close; each had produced a Republican landslide. In 1800 Republicans had more to cheer about than their huge victory in the presidential race. State and local elections generally followed a similar pattern, so the Republicans erased the gains the Federalists had made during the war scare.

Although the Republican party was indisputably dominant in the South, it was not simply a southern party. Through the 1790s Jefferson and Madison wooed northerners; the results of 1800 could only have pleased them. The party won all 12 electoral votes in New York and 8 of 15 in Pennsylvania, and without them Jefferson would have lost. The Virginia–New York connection was to remain crucial to the success of the Jeffersonian Republican party. The appearance of Aaron Burr of New York on the ballot demonstrated the Republicans' determination to bridge the sectional gap. To cement a North-South alliance the Republicans nominated Burr, Hamilton's political archenemy, with the expectation that he would run second to Jefferson and so would become Jefferson's vice president. In 1800 presidential electors still did not cast votes for a vice president; each elector voted for two candidates. But the Burr candidacy proved almost too successful. As all Republican electors named both Jefferson and Burr, each man received the same number of electoral votes, though Jefferson was the undoubted Republican choice for president. Because of the tie, under the Constitution the House of Representatives had to choose a winner, and it did so on February 17, 1801, when it selected Jefferson as president. The Jefferson-Burr deadlock led directly to the Twelfth Amendment.

Tangled electoral voting notwithstanding, the Republican party controlled the southern political world. The Federalists could not match them. The Republicans possessed the leadership and the issues that best fit southern interests.

THE MARCH WESTWARD

While the political wars raged, the South was in motion. Since colonists first moved up the tidal rivers away from the seacoast in the late seventeenth century, the West, the land beyond settlement, had attracted southerners like a bright rainbow. Surely riches awaited the hardy folk who ventured there. The prosperity that followed each successive advance stirred dreams of bountiful streams, rich valleys, fertile bottomlands.

In the 1780s and 1790s the march westward led chiefly to Tennessee and Kentucky. Before the Revolution these areas—claimed by North Carolina and Virginia, respectively—had known only explorers and hunters. The most famous of

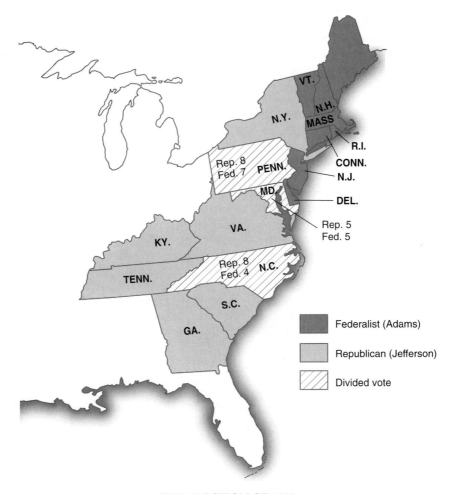

Rep. 8
Fed. 7

Rep. 5
Fed. 5

Rep. 8
Fed. 4

Federalist (Adams)

Republican (Jefferson)

Divided vote

THE ELECTION OF 1800

them was Daniel Boone, who first explored Kentucky in 1769 and in 1775 established Boonesboro on the Kentucky River. By 1780 fewer than 10,000 whites had settled in either territory, but by 1790 their numbers reached almost 32,000 in Tennessee and beyond 61,000 in Kentucky. Kentucky became the fifteenth state in 1792; Tennessee became the sixteenth in 1796. Mississippi Territory, formerly controlled by Spain but organized by Congress in 1798, also witnessed settlement around its capital, Natchez. This horizontal expansion of the South occasioned no basic change in southern institutions, which traveled west with settlers.

The conviction that opportunity abounded was the chief motive for migration. Seeing Kentucky for the first time, a new settler could not contain himself. He had never before seen "So Rich a Soil, Covered in Clover in full Bloom, the Woods alive in wild game." To his dazzled eyes "it appeared that nature in the profusion of her Bounties had spread a feast for all that lives." The "Sight so delightful to our View and grateful to our feelings almost Induced us . . . to Kiss the Soil of Kentucky." All classes joined the westward trek, though the majority were probably yeomen. The land bounties offered by North Carolina and Virginia to veterans of the Revolution provided considerable incentive. All ranks were eligible for these free allotments of western land. North Carolina's bounties were based on rank, from 600 acres for a private to more than 7,000 acres for a colonel.

The family of Mary Dewees joined the migration. After starting from Philadelphia, Mary, her husband, her children, and her brother found themselves in western Virginia in late 1788. From there they pushed on to Kentucky, where, to Mary's dismay, her brother left the Dewees and headed away alone. For Mary the trek was at the same time wondrous and dangerous. She recorded that the early winter chill and the howls of wolves made the evening fires especially inviting. Much of the food came from the abundance of game—deer, turkeys, ducks, and geese. Finally in early 1789 the Dewees decided where they would plant their roots in the new land. Mary described a spot with plentiful trees, near a spring and a beautiful pond. Once her home was established, Mary wrote that she had not been happier in years. Though not all shared Mary's final enthusiasm, thousands of individuals and families duplicated the Dewees' journey from east to west.

Edward Tyler and his family also enlisted in the trek. Between 1750 and 1780, Tyler, a native Marylander, and his wife moved about in southwestern Pennsylvania and western Virginia while he engaged chiefly in trading. During those years ten children arrived to increase the Tyler brood. In 1780 the sixty-year-old Tyler, attracted by the availability of land and favorable land laws, headed across the mountains to Kentucky with his wife and unmarried children. By 1783 he had opened a tavern in Louisville and had patented more than 1,000 acres out from the town in Jefferson County. Three of his sons along with a nephew established farms in the area, and Tyler moved to join them in 1793, forming a family enclave known as Tyler's Settlement.

Land speculators also played a role in the opening of the trans-Appalachian South. The buying up of vast western tracts in the hope of reaping financial rewards was an honorable tradition in the South. Some of the most respected southerners, George Washington and James Madison among them, invested eagerly in the proposition that western land would bring them wealth. Many speculators in the 1780s and 1790s bought up cheaply the land claims of veterans who had no intention of moving west. One of the most successful was William Blount of North Carolina, who parlayed western land grants into a fortune. By 1791 Blount and his associates had acquired almost 165,000 acres of land in Tennessee. Probably the most famous of the speculators were the four companies engaged in what became known as the Yazoo land frauds. In 1795 they bribed the Georgia legislature to grant them 35 million acres of Georgia's southwestern land claims for only $500,000. This blatantly corrupt action caused such a public uproar in Georgia that the next legislature repealed the act authorizing the grants. Ultimately the legal wrangle over the Yazoo speculation led to a major decision by the United States Supreme Court. Its ruling in *Fletcher* v. *Peck* in 1807 extended the obligation of contracts from private persons to states and defined Georgia's 1795 statute as a contract protected by the Constitution. Therefore, the Court ruled, the repeal of the statute was unconstitutional. For the first time the United States Supreme Court invalidated a state law.

THE WEST AND SLAVERY

The mountains formed no barrier to slavery. Although early figures are unreliable, slaves surely accompanied whites in their westward trek. The initial federal

THE NORTHWEST ORDINANCE, 1787

census in 1790 placed 3,417 slaves in Tennessee and 12,430 in Kentucky. The constitutions written by both in preparation for statehood protected the institution of slavery. When Kentucky revised its constitution in 1799, an effort was made to plan for gradual emancipation. The move failed, however. The first census taken after both states entered the Union, in 1800, clearly demonstrated that slavery had become woven into the social fabric. In ten years the number of slaves in Kentucky had more than tripled, to over 40,000 (18 percent of the population), while in Tennessee the count had increased more than fourfold, to 13,584 (13 percent of all Tennesseans). Throughout the slave era the two states stood as staunch slave states.

The question of slavery in the West led to one of the most notable legislative acts in American history, the Northwest Ordinance of 1787—almost the only act passed by the Articles government that is remembered. The Northwest Ordinance forbade slavery in the Northwest Territory, the area north of the Ohio River and east of the Mississippi. This massive domain had been claimed by Virginia, but in 1781 Virginia ceded it to the nation. Supported by southern votes in Congress, the ordinance is often pointed to as an enlightened action against slavery by southerners of the Revolutionary generation. That stance is then favorably contrasted with the stern advocacy of slavery in the territories by a later generation of southerners. The southern position, however, was not so clear-cut. Few southerners questioned the legitimacy of slavery in Tennessee and Kentucky, which were slave areas before they became states. In fact, white southerners were taking black slaves across the Appalachians at the very time Congress enacted the ordinance. Moreover, when the Mississippi Territory was organized in 1798, Congress did not prohibit slavery within its boundaries.

Southern congressmen supported the Northwest Ordinance for several reasons. Possibly most important was that in the 1780s southerners did not think of themselves as representing a minority position. On the contrary, many were convinced that the South would become dominant over the North. When the Northwest was populated by southerners, as they were convinced it would be, their orientation would prevail. At the same time, it is probable that others viewed the Ohio River as the western extension of the Mason-Dixon line, the border between Maryland and Pennsylvania, which separated slavery from freedom. Evidence suggests, too, that some southerners supported the exclusion of slavery from the Northwest to preclude possible competition for southern tobacco interests.

In 1800 a vibrant, confident South looked toward the new century. Southern citizens and southern culture had passed beyond the old colonial borders. A political organization embraced enthusiastically by the South prepared to take control of the national administration. From the southern perspective, all was secure.

6
Republican Ascendancy

❖

The victory of Thomas Jefferson in 1800 delighted most southerners. In the eyes of the overwhelming majority, the bitter battles of the 1790s had been struggles over the fundamental definition of the national identity and the basic orientation of the new nation. Most southerners, then, felt vindicated by the triumph of the leader and party they identified as their own. The South had surely been essential to Jefferson's triumph; without the electoral votes he won in the slave states, he would have been thrashed by his Federalist opponent, John Adams. Particularly important, southerners could interpret the results as proof positive that the nation and the South were aimed in the same direction, that they shared the same values and goals. The South and the nation were one.

When the fifty-eight-year-old Thomas Jefferson entered the White House in 1801, he had been a famous public man for twenty-five years; and through all that time he remained a Virginia planter and slave owner with an abiding commitment to his state and to his occupation. Jefferson combined intellectual and political talents in a manner matched by no other president. Truly a Renaissance man, an eighteenth-century intellectual equally at home in political philosophy and in science, an architect who created monuments to the art, Jefferson was also a skilled politician. He was a major builder of the Republican party, and in little more than half a decade he led the party to national victory. Neither his intellectual achievement nor his political success diminished his conviction that the agrarian world that produced him was the best of all possible worlds. All his life he had owned slaves, eventually more than 200 of them; they worked his lands and built his cherished home, Monticello. And he could never reconcile the institution of slavery with his devotion to freedom. Yet it was his dedication to liberty—a liberty that required local control by local citizens and local government—that, in combination with his belief in the racial inferiority of blacks, kept him from any move against slavery. Not only was Jefferson united with the chief southern economic and social institutions; his view of politics meshed nicely with the general southern view. And nothing Jefferson did in the 1790s threatened anything white southerners held dear. On the contrary, he advocated principles and practices that would secure those values and interests. Although Jefferson could never be called a sectional provincial, southerners identified overwhelmingly with him and his political cause.

Jefferson did not stand alone as a victor. In the Congress and across the South, Republicans assumed office. Jefferson would have a Republican Congress to help him redirect the future of the country, and southerners made possible that executive-legislative unity. To the Seventh Congress, which first convened in December 1801, the states below the Potomac sent fifty-nine Republicans, and but eight Federalists. By the time the Tenth Congress met, even that paltry Federalist contingent had been halved. Federalists began to disappear from the slave states. The Republican surge signaled to southerners that the nation had become reoriented in the direction toward which the South had pointed: agrarianism, not commercialism; local control, not central control. Thus, for southerners, sectional concerns were national concerns.

THE LOUISIANA PURCHASE

The two major initiatives of Jefferson's presidency took the Republicans down a different road, one that forced the South to consider quite carefully the fit between power and ideology. The Louisiana Purchase was the crucial event of Jefferson's first administration. In the president's mind the acquisition of Louisiana would give an enormous boost to his fledgling nation. The addition of the 828,000 square miles of Louisiana enabled Jefferson and his supporters to dream of a boundless agrarian empire. The idea of boundlessness was compelling because Americans had taken 150 years to cross the Appalachians, only a few hundred miles from the Atlantic Ocean. Based on that experience, settlers would not reach the western edge of Louisiana or the Rocky Mountains, 2,000 miles from the Appalachians, for centuries. The acquisition of Louisiana enabled southerners to envision their domain as expanding indefinitely. Their society had unlimited space for growth, for white farmers and black slaves. Kentucky and Tennessee, the extension of the seaboard South which joined the Union in the 1790s, came in as slave states. The treaty that transferred Louisiana from France to the United States specifically protected property rights in slaves. And the congressional legislation that organized the territory under American jurisdiction did not prohibit the introduction of additional slaves.

The Louisiana Purchase represented the first acquisition of territory that had not been part of or claimed by the United States in 1787, when the Constitution was written. And nowhere did the Constitution specifically authorize additions to the national domain. For a president who had boasted about allegiance to the letter of the Constitution, this lack of authorization was troublesome. Jefferson wanted Louisiana desperately, but he considered a constitutional amendment necessary. It would not have to precede the transfer of money for land, but Jefferson believed that constitutional sanction should be given after the fact.

Not all of the president's advisers shared his concern. Most congressional and administrative leaders, southerners included, had no doubts about the constitutionality of the purchase. Furthermore, they argued that raising the constitutional question would provide an additional weapon to the Federalists, who opposed adding Louisiana. Jefferson disagreed on the basic issue, but he did agree not to publicize his reservations. He stated clearly the reason for his doubt: "Our pecu-

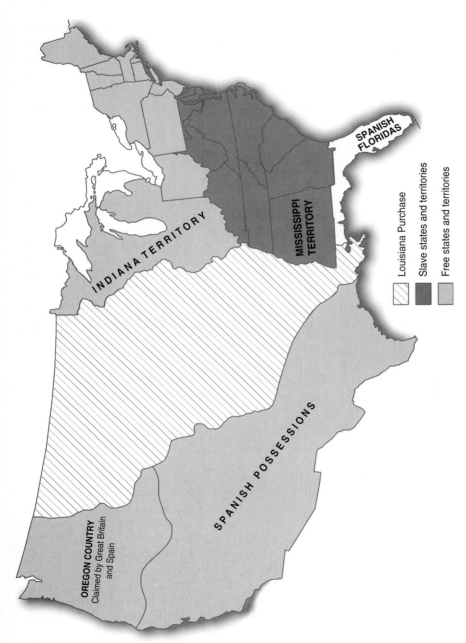

THE LOUISIANA PURCHASE

liar security is in the possession of a written Constitution. Let us not make it a blank paper by construction." But he would not risk giving up his great prize, political as well as ideological. He ultimately satisfied himself with the observation that "the good sense of the country will correct the evil of construction when it shall produce ill effects." When Jefferson forwarded the treaty to the Senate, he did not mention his uncertainty about its constitutionality. With opposition localized among the Federalists, the Senate accepted the Louisiana Purchase on October 20, 1803, by a vote of 26 to 6. Southerners and most other Americans applauded.

THE EMBARGO

In contrast to Jefferson's effort to buy Louisiana, the most important event of his second administration turned into dismal failure. From its beginning the Jefferson presidency had been caught up in the great Anglo-French conflict raging in Europe. Claiming neutrality and the right to trade with belligerents, Jefferson and his secretary of state, James Madison, had pressed both Britain and France to recognize and accept the American position. Because the powerful royal navy gave Britain control of the sea, conflict occurred most often with the former mother country. America demanded unfettered trade; Britain exercised the prerogative of power and refused to permit any commerce that would aid France, its great enemy.

Perceiving no alternative except war and rejecting that possibility, Jefferson decided to shut down American trade completely. In 1807 he submitted to Congress a bill that banned from American ports any ship seeking to enter from a foreign port or to depart for one. It authorized collectors of customs to search and detain vessels, even those in the coasting trade. Never before had a president embarked on such an ambitious program to compel obedience to national legislation. Despite this about-face from Republican teaching about the proper character of the central government, Republicans did not hold up the bill's passage. It raced through Congress—one day in the Senate, three in the House—and won the overwhelming majority of Republican votes, including those of southerners. On the state level Republicans also indicated that they stood squarely behind their president.

The embargo brought American commerce to a standstill. The economic impact on the country was devastating. The embargo strangled mercantile and shipping interests in every seaport, but especially in New England, the center of American shipping. Neither did the embargo exempt southern agriculturalists. After all, southern planters raised staple crops for an export market, a market now closed. Palpable distress gripped South and North. Republicans had inflicted a severe economic blow on the heartland of the party. The value of rice exports fell from $2.4 million in 1807 to a paltry $221,000 in 1808, a decline of 90 percent in one year. During the same year Virginia's exports dropped from $4.8 million to just over $0.5 million. Exports from Georgia in 1808 reached less than 1 percent of the 1807 total.

No matter the depths of their distress, most southern Republicans did not take to open opposition. The South Carolina House of Representatives vowed complete support for the embargo; the governor of Georgia proposed strong laws to relieve debtors unable to pay creditors because of the halt in trade. By 64 to 1 the Kentucky legislature announced its continuing adherence to the embargo. Attempts both by dissident Republicans and by Federalists to turn economic disadvantage into political advantage failed miserably.

The South's steadfastness illuminates the southern view of politics, ideology, and power. Had the Adams administration or even the second Washington administration done what Jefferson did, the Republican party, with its southern contingent in the vanguard, would have cried out against executive usurpation, tyranny, and oppression. This kind of attack on Jefferson and his policies rarely occurred. Although a coterie of southern Republicans did launch such an assault, they persuaded few of their fellows. For most southerners the identity of the men holding power was far more important than the niceties of constitutional theory or political philosophy. Southerners trusted themselves and their own leadership not to endanger fundamentally either southern interests or southern liberty. After all, most southerners perceived the Republican party as the guardian of liberty and of the South in the nation.

This view does not relegate ideology to the scrap heap. Ideology remained crucial because the South and its chosen political emissary would not always control the national government. They had not done so in the 1790s, and the time would come again when southerners would doubt that they had an emissary. Then the distinct southern ideological bent would guide the reaction to political reality as the South perceived it.

THE TERTIUM QUIDS

Not every southerner supported Jefferson's major policies, but the character of dissent emphasized the South's general allegiance to the party. Although individuals both in and out of Congress opposed specific measures for various reasons, the only serious continuous opposition appeared in 1805. Led by Virginia Congressman John Randolph of Roanoke and his North Carolina colleague Nathaniel Macon, these southern Republicans attacked Jefferson and the Republican majority for undermining "republican principles." Calling themselves Tertium Quids (a third way) to emphasize their separateness both from the administration and from the Federalist party, these southerners demanded strict adherence to the pristine Republican doctrine of the 1790s. They considered themselves guardians of the sacred text of the Virginia and Kentucky resolutions, which, to their way of thinking, Jefferson had violated. On the national level Quids were strongest in the House of Representatives, where they numbered approximately a dozen.

John Randolph, the most vigorous Quid and the most fiercely individualistic politician of his time, refused to be bound by party loyalty or commonly accepted behavior. He sometimes appeared in the House, booted, spurred, and flicking his riding crop, with a slave boy trailing behind. Then in his high-pitched voice, with a flagon of porter occasionally providing sustenance, he lacerated opponents.

"Meddling fools and designing knaves are governing the country," slashed Randolph. National affairs had been "committed to Tom, Dick, and Harry, the refuse of the retail trade of politics." The Quids called on the Republicans never to desert principles that had given birth to the party: local power, small government, and a just fear of the executive. A small band, the Quids were never able to control the legislative process, but their abilities and efforts served to remind all Republicans of their political birthright.

The Quids spoke the language of the Republican tradition and made every effort to alert their fellow southerners to the administration's apostasy, but they enjoyed few legislative triumphs and persuaded few southerners to rally round their flag. Possibly Randolph was right when he claimed that many congressional Republicans expressed Quid principles in private but voted the administration line. But purists such as Randolph and his associates could never attract much support in the South so long as governmental power was being exercised by a party that southerners identified as their own. John Randolph would not be the last notable southern political ideologue to discover that fact about his fellow southerners. Mainstream southern Republicans attacked the Quids for endangering the party and for "tend[ing] to invigorate the declining spirit of federalism." Even the economic pain inflicted on the South by the Embargo Act failed to strengthen the Quid force.

THE FEDERALISTS

No one turned to the Federalist party. The care the Quids took to distance themselves from it revealed the sorry political reputation of southern Federalists. To the Quids the Federalists stood for everything that was wrong and dangerous about the American government. And the Quids were not the only southerners who had no use for the Federalist party. After the defeat of John Adams in 1800, southern Federalists rushed toward political extinction. A brief look at election figures underscores the serious political disease debilitating southern Federalism. Charles Cotesworth Pinckney of South Carolina headed the Federalist ticket in the elections of 1804 and 1808, but he had little success in the slave states: he won only two electoral votes the first time and five the second. After the congressional elections of 1807 and 1808 the Federalists held but seven seats south of the Potomac, whereas in 1800 they had had twice that many. In 1800 the South Carolina legislature had been almost half Federalist; by 1808 the Federalists held only one-seventh of the seats. That same precipitous decline halved Federalist legislators in both North Carolina and Virginia.

A tale told by a Republican editor in North Carolina was clearly on the mark. It seems two Federalists were passing the time of day. One exclaimed, "Federalism begins to look up!" His more realistic comrade replied, "Very true, being on its back now, it can look no other way." Not only did Federalists lose most of the races they ran, they ran fewer and fewer. By 1806 and 1807 Federalist candidates appeared in only 8 percent of congressional races in the southeastern states. When the party held a nominating caucus in New York in the summer of 1808 to choose a presidential ticket, only one southerner attended. The exuberant, energetic young leaders who guided the Federalist party to resurgence in the North had no counterparts in the South. Despite the two presidential candidacies of Charles Cotesworth Pinckney, southern Federalists never matched the influence of southern Republicans at the national level. Southern Federalism did hold the loyalty of a few substantial men, at least along the Atlantic seaboard north of Georgia, but in time their numbers declined, and they never invigorated their party.

Several reasons underlay the Federalist debacle. Southerners supported the Republicans in the 1790s because Republicans dealt with the issues in ways that most southerners approved, and in power the Republicans moved on those fronts. They let the Alien and Sedition acts languish and finally die. They repealed the direct tax and cut the federal budget. Then the entire South cheered the Louisiana Purchase. Division on state issues remained unimportant; Federalists rarely tried to use them to advance the Federalist cause. The hardship caused by the embargo seemingly should have given Federalists an entrée to southern voters, yet it did not.

A more fundamental disability plagued southern Federalists: the Federalist party never succeeded in identifying itself with the hopes and fears of most southerners. In the 1790s Republicans had tarred Federalists with the brush of antisouthernism. The stain remained, and after 1800 it seemed ineradicable. In 1812 Charles Cotesworth Pinckney urged the Federalist caucus not to run a southerner for president because he did not believe the party could win a single electoral vote in the South.

In direct contrast, a common identity bound together the South and the Republican party. The South accepted the party as its representative and protector. Not even the Quids, good southerners all and with a striking southern political accent, could loosen the bonds between southerners and the party they cherished as their own. Before any serious political restiveness could threaten the Republicans' authority in the South, the general perception of the party as advocate and guardian of the South would have to change. As Jefferson's presidency demonstrated, such a momentous shift would require a thunderous shock.

THE COMING OF WAR

Although the Republican party in the South turned back the Quids with ease and faced but feeble opposition from Federalists, the administration of James Madison, who succeeded Jefferson in the White House in 1809, found itself in a difficult situation. The predicament of the administration was caused chiefly by the failure of its economic diplomacy. Although the embargo caused economic devastation at home, it had absolutely no impact on British policy. Despite the embargo and other measures passed by Congress to take its place, the British government would not agree that as a neutral nation the United States could trade with any nation it pleased, and certainly not with Britain's great foe, France. Through Madison's first term the British maintained in force the orders-in-council that forbade all ships to enter continental ports unless they had first passed through a British port and secured new clearances. In addition, the British navy continued the practice of impressment—British naval officers forcibly removed American citizens from American ships and pressed them into service in the royal navy. Between 1803 and 1812 more than 5,000 American sailors were thus forced into the king's uniform. Like Jefferson, Madison found himself in a diplomatic box. And by 1812, after five years in this untenable position, Madison and many of his countrymen had had enough.

Southerners joined in the demand that the administration and country stand up to what they termed British intimidation. Sure about their own power in the nation and about the course of the nation, southerners entered the second decade of the nineteenth century with a viewpoint that contrasted sharply with the attitude they had brought into the new century. The maturing of a second generation of Republican politicians reinforced their altered outlook. When the first session of the Twelfth Congress convened in November 1811, new names populated the roster of southern Republican congressmen. Half were in their first or second term, and many of them had only faint memories of the 1790s. They had reached political maturity after the great victory of 1800.

Moving quickly to the prominence and influence that were to characterize them during the next four decades, Henry Clay of Kentucky and John C. Calhoun of South Carolina heralded the arrival of this new generation. These two dynamic young congressmen—Clay was thirty-four, Calhoun only twenty-nine—embodied the basic forces shaping southern society and politics. They spoke for those who saw no threat from national power. Calhoun was a product of the great Scots-Irish tide that flowed into the Carolina piedmont before the Revolution.

HENRY CLAY
(Brady Collection, National Archives)

JOHN C. CALHOUN (Portrait by George P. A. Healy, Greenville County Museum of Art)

After Calhoun graduated from Yale in 1804, he returned to his native state, where he practiced law, planted, and politicked. In 1811 he married Floride Bonneau Colhoun, a tidewater heiress who was also a distant cousin. His marriage intimately involved him in the great confluence of two major groups in the white South, the upland Scots-Irish and the tidewater plantation magnates. And southern unity would become the watchword of his politics.

Henry Clay of Kentucky was the first man from west of the Appalachians to become a major force in American politics. Born in Virginia in 1777, he emigrated to Kentucky as a lad. At twenty he was admitted to the bar. He married into a prominent family and accumulated land and black slaves while he acquired an enviable reputation for charm and eloquence. A tall, lanky fellow with a captivating personality, Clay quickly became a political leader. His presence and vitality helped him achieve what today would be impossible—he was elected speaker of the House of Representatives in his first term.

With no break in the diplomatic impasse in sight, the United States drifted toward war with Great Britain. Southern politicians stood among those most eager for war. Sounding the war tocsin loudest were young southerners who had come to Congress after Madison's election to the presidency. Youthful Republican stalwarts such as Calhoun and Clay had seen firsthand the failure of the embargo. They were supremely conscious of what seemed like the impotence of their country. Through these southern eyes the nation seemed dangerously close to losing independence and sliding back into slavery under Great Britain. To these southerners the fruits of the Revolution were at stake.

Most historians today believe that the United States went to war in 1812 to salvage national honor and to preserve the liberty of the country. This conclusion meshes perfectly both with the major ideological tenets of Republicanism and with the attitude of southerners. To be sure, some southerners, chiefly westerners, did worry about Indian depredations on the frontier, and some also coveted Spanish Florida. Most, however, shared a grave concern about what they saw as the growing weakness of the country. In the eyes of many southerners, their country seemed cowed, appeared unwilling or unable to defend its most precious possession, liberty. Far from enjoying the independence it had fought for, it was once again dependent on the arbitrary whim of Great Britain. Independence required determination to preserve liberty, even if violence were required. A generally united South urged military action on the Madison administration.

PARTY AND SECTION AND WAR

Many other Republicans opposed war just as vigorously as the War Hawks—the name given to the major congressional spokesmen for conflict—advocated it. Antiwar forces were centered in the Northeast, especially in New England. Many of the opponents argued that the United States had no just cause to oppose Great Britain on the battlefield. Moreover, they thought war would be ruinous, for the country was not prepared to fight a great power.

Faced with a diplomatic policy that was not working and a divided party, the most prominent southern Republican saw no easy solutions. President Madison had been a key architect of the commercial diplomacy that had characterized Republican policy since the 1790s. In a 1792 pamphlet he had even denounced war while urging and pointing the way toward universal peace. But Madison was a dedicated nationalist, and by 1812 he had concluded that the United States could not protect its sovereignty and its independence without standing firm against the British. Moreover, many of his strongest political supporters were clamoring for war. Thus recognition that his commercial diplomacy was not working, political pressure, and fear that the country could again become subservient to Great Britain all pushed the president on June 1, 1812, to ask that Congress declare war.

By June 18 Congress had acceded to the president's request and declared war on Great Britain. Although the United States never went to war more divided than in 1812, the South stood united behind the president. The Senate voted for war by the narrow margin of 19 to 13; no southern senator joined the minority. In the House the final tally gave a 79–49 margin for a declaration of war; only three southern Republicans cast negative ballots. The war vote was partisan—Republicans voted for war, Federalists against. But the overwhelming dominance of Republicans in the South gave to a partisan vote a distinctly sectional dimension. The defection of almost twenty northern Republicans on the war question emphasized the South's commitment both to the party and to its decision for war.

The government conducted the War of 1812 according to traditional Republican dogma. The Republican party had long denounced both standing (or professional) armies and taxes; in the Republican lexicon both were mortal threats to liberty. Volunteers, Republicans believed, would always rush forth and turn back any enemies the nation might face. This war would surely provide the ultimate test for these theories. The opponent was a great power, and it had the most powerful navy in the world.

The Republican leadership did not envision major fighting anywhere within the national borders. The great goal of the war effort was to capture Canada and so to drive Great Britain off the North American mainland. Though Canada was far from the South, southern War Hawks eagerly joined the clamor to bring Canada under the American flag. In the House, John C. Calhoun cried, "In four weeks from the time that a declaration of war is heard on our frontier the whole Upper and a part of Lower Canada will be in our possession." Henry Clay bragged that "the militia of Kentucky are alone competent to place Montreal and Upper Canada at [our] feet." But rhetoric far outdistanced action; when Congress authorized building up the army by 25,000 men, only 400 enlistments came from Clay's hotbed of martial ardor.

THE RISE OF ANDREW JACKSON

While southerners were chorusing their eagerness to annex Canada, attention was also being given to the southwest frontier, particularly by those who lived near it. Their concern focused on Spanish Florida; they worried that the Spanish, with British support, would urge the Creek, known as Red Sticks, to attack whites in southwestern Georgia and in what would become Alabama. That fear became reality in the summer of 1813, when the Creek attacked Fort Mims, just above Mobile, and killed some 60 percent of its 550 defenders and occupants.

Alarmed, the governor of Tennessee called out his militia to put down the uprising. In charge of the troops ordered to deal with the Creek was Andrew Jackson, major general of the Tennessee militia. A man of ferocious energy, almost demonic determination, and incredible toughness, Jackson was a superb warrior.

In late 1813 he led his force across the Tennessee River into the heart of Alabama. He promptly engaged the Creek and won a victory at Talladega, but then in winter combat his troops suffered repulses and heavy casualties. A budding mutiny among some of the volunteers endangered Jackson's authority and the campaign. Facing the challenge directly and with loyal soldiers prepared to do his bidding, Jackson threatened to shoot any man who left the army for Tennessee. The belief that the fearsome Jackson would carry out his threat kept the army in the field. With the approach of spring, Jackson once again advanced toward his enemy. On March 27, 1814, Jackson with 3,000 men attacked a main Creek camp on the Tallapoosa River. The resulting Battle of Horseshoe Bend was a disaster for the Creek. The Tennesseans killed all but about 500 of an estimated

ANDREW JACKSON, THE GREAT HERO (Portrait by Ralph
E. W. Earl, National Museum of American Art, Smithsonian Institution, Transfer from U.S. District Court for the District of Columbia)

9,000 Creek fighting men and took prisoner 500 women and children. In August
the Creek finally signed the Treaty of Fort Jackson, dictated by General Jackson,
by which they turned over to the United States some 20 million acres of land in
southern Georgia and Alabama. The man the Indians called Sharp Knife had broken the power of the Creek forever. Now the way was open for white settlement
of the Southwest.

At the other end of the South, the Chesapeake, southerners experienced firsthand the military woes that were the American norm during the war. Just as Jackson was wrenching the Southwest away from the Creek, a major British expedition of 4,000 veterans and a supporting fleet entered Chesapeake Bay. In August
the British landed in Maryland and marched toward Washington. At Bladens-
burg, on the outskirts of the capital, they encountered a militia force that outnumbered them. But no Andrew Jackson commanded these Americans; facing British
veterans, and with President Madison watching, they turned and ran almost
without firing a shot. The British overran Washington and burned most public

buildings, including the Capitol and the White House. They found Baltimore more difficult. There both land and naval attacks failed. From a British ship where he had been detained, an American civilian watched the naval bombardment of Fort McHenry. When at dawn he detected the American flag still flying over the fort, Francis Scott Key wrote on an old letter a poem that later was set to music and widely admired. He called it "The Star-Spangled Banner."

New orleans and the end of the war

After Baltimore and Fort McHenry the southern theater of war shifted back to the Southwest. Upon leaving Baltimore, the British went to Jamaica, where they joined a major force aimed at New Orleans. Preparing to face the expected British onslaught was Andrew Jackson, who had been promoted to major general in the regular United States Army and put in command of all troops in the Southwest. Although the Americans anticipated a British strike, they did not know precisely where the enemy would land. Initially Jackson considered Mobile the most likely

THE WAR OF 1812 IN THE SOUTH

spot, but by December 1814 he had arrived in the city the British had chosen as their target, New Orleans.

Once in New Orleans, Jackson prepared energetically to meet the British threat. He threw his forceful personality directly into the fray. Determined that he alone, not city officials, would make all the crucial decisions concerning the civilian population as well as the army, he declared martial law in the city. The American troops required someone with a hand as strong as Jackson's. His force consisted of almost 900 U.S. Army regulars, 6,000 to 7,000 militiamen from Kentucky, Louisiana, and Tennessee, and a few hundred free blacks organized in a separate battalion; he even had a band of pirates. Immediately Jackson began work on the neglected defenses of the city. When he learned that the British had disembarked and moved units to within seven miles of New Orleans, he reacted swiftly. With 5,000 men he made a night attack, which checked the British advance.

After that engagement Jackson worked strenuously to build a defensive line at Chalmette's plantation, some five miles east of the city. While Jackson's men threw up breastworks, the British commander, Sir Edward Pakenham, a veteran of the Napoleonic campaigns, waited for reinforcements. Finally in early January Pakenham was ready. His tactics were unimaginative. Convinced that British soldiers who had faced the mighty French armies could easily overpower Jackson's unprofessional Americans, Pakenham decided to send his troops straight at the Americans. This decision forced the British troops to march across a narrow front, with the Mississippi on their left and a cypress swamp on their right, directly toward the American cannon and rifles.

In the foggy dawn of January 8, 1815, the Redcoats advanced with bayonets fixed. Under orders to hold their fire until the British came within easy range, the Americans watched their foe moving toward them. Finally the command rang out. American artillery raked the British lines as Jackson's infantrymen flung a sheet of lead at the Redcoats. The British made two direct assaults in the face of this withering fire before their line splintered. No soldiers could forever withstand the deadly fusillade, and they had nowhere to turn. General Pakenham, urging his men forward, was hit twice. As he was calling up his reserves, he was killed by a shell fragment.

Jackson won a great victory. Failing to break Jackson's line, the British retreated to their transports. They paid a fearful price on that January morning. Of some 5,300 men in the attacking force, almost 2,100 were killed and wounded, including three generals. The Americans, in stark contrast, suffered fewer than 20 killed, around 60 wounded and missing. General Pakenham had expected to return to England a great hero; instead his body went home in a cask of rum. The hero was Jackson, who directed the greatest American victory of the war.

Jackson's triumph had far-reaching consequences. Back in the summer of 1814 peace negotiations between American and British commissioners had begun in Ghent, Belgium. By late fall the two sides had settled on an agreement that stipulated the *status quo ante bellum.* In other words, the United States would come out of the war with its territory intact while the British made no concessions on neutral rights or impressment. On Christmas Eve, 1814, the Treaty of Ghent was signed. Thus the Battle of New Orleans was fought after a peace treaty had been completed. But New Orleans represented considerably more than an empty victory. A victorious British army sitting in New Orleans would have mocked American claims to the republic's 1812 boundaries. At New Orleans, no matter what took place in Ghent, the future of the Southwest was at stake. Jackson's battlefield victory guaranteed American control of both the Mississippi Valley and the Southwest.

Jackson's defeat of the British coupled with his destruction of the Creek as a fighting force pointed up the vulnerability of Spanish Florida. With the Indians crushed and the British turned back, Spain could not hope to hold Florida very long against an expanding United States. The weakness, even the impossibility, of Spain's position was dramatized in 1818, when General Jackson marched into Florida in pursuit of marauding Indians and runaway slaves. He drove the Indians southward and seized the Spanish garrisons at St. Marks and Pensacola. Although Jackson did not remain in Florida, the administration of James Monroe used Jackson's foray to press Spain. Secretary of State John Quincy Adams told the Spanish that if the United States had to send another expedition against Indians into Florida, American troops would remain. Accepting the inevitable, Spain in 1819 agreed to a treaty that transferred Florida to the United States.

All of these notable events between 1814 and 1819—the destruction of the Creek, the defeat of the British, the acquisition of Florida—came about in no small part because of one man, Andrew Jackson. Jackson became something Americans had not seen since George Washington: a genuine national hero. Though indisputably a national hero, Jackson had a special identity in the South. His great exploits had come in the South, and most of the officers and men who fought with him were southern. He had been born in South Carolina and as a young man had moved to Tennessee, where he began to accumulate the two possessions most prized by white southerners, land and black slaves. Southerners would not soon forget Andrew Jackson.

A NATIONALIST COURSE

Though the war had ended triumphantly at New Orleans and with the United States intact, leaders in the administration and in the Congress knew that the country had had quite a close call. Huzzahs aroused by the news from New Orleans swelled to grandiloquent expressions of national pride, but the men who made policy realized that the United States was utterly unprepared for a war with a major power. Britain's preoccupation with Europe had been as instrumental as Jackson's victory in preserving the United States. Next time the country might not be so fortunate. That knowledge had a powerful effect on the Republican party and on the South. The party, with its southern cohort in agreement, decided that the power and authority of the central government would have to be strengthened.

Even before the war was over, President Madison acted to increase the federal government's power. In his annual message to Congress in December 1814, presented as Jackson prepared to meet the British attack on New Orleans, the president called for a protective tariff, a national bank, and a system of internal improvements. Southerners not only supported this new direction, they led the way. After all, Madison was a Virginian. In the Congress every southern state provided votes for the bills pushed by the administration and directed through the legislative process by such southern Republicans as John C. Calhoun and Henry Clay.

As these measures made their way through Congress in 1816 and 1817, not every southern Republican supported every one of them. Southerners in the House voted more than 2 to 1 in favor of a national bank but by a small majority opposed the tariff of 1816. More voted against than for internal improvements, but a substantial number did support such expenditures. A Quid-like opposition that based its objections solely on doctrinal purity had little importance. The irrelevance of traditional Republican doctrine was eloquently expressed by Nathaniel Macon, the old Quid from North Carolina. Lamenting the passage of the bank bill, Macon seemingly eulogized the Republicanism he cherished when he said, "I am at a loss to account for the fact that I seem to be the only person of those who were formerly in Congress, that still cannot find the authority for a bank in the constitution of the U.S."

For southern Republicans the voting pattern in Congress was instructive. The pattern had a double weave. One thread indicated that for many southerners the old ideology, which focused on a small government with limited powers and honored agrarianism as the essence of republican society, had been suppressed or had disappeared. Those who strove to keep it alive, like the Virginia political theorist John Taylor of Caroline, spoke to an ever-shrinking audience. A second thread carried the legacy of tradition. By voting chiefly for measures that would help their localities, southerners could salve their political consciences. Unlike Calhoun and Clay, most had not become dedicated nationalists. President Madison provides a superb illustration of this divided mind. He accepted a bank and the tariff, but in the end he vetoed the internal improvements bill because the Constitution did not specifically authorize the central government to build roads and canals. Neither, of course, did it specifically authorize a national bank or a protective tariff.

SOUTHERNERS AND THE NEW NATIONALISM

Madison along with others of his generation had moved a considerable distance from their position of the 1790s. Of that generation only John Randolph, Nathaniel Macon, and their small congregation held fast to the gospel preached by Republicans in an earlier time. Adjusters such as Madison believed that the responsibilities of power at times overrode ideology. Jefferson himself had demonstrated that conviction with both Louisiana and the embargo. Then the war seared the president and the colleagues who shared his responsibility and witnessed the same unnerving events. Frightened by the weakness of the government which the war had exposed, they believed that an increase in strength was essential. Thus they consciously traveled down a new political road.

This assessment, however, does not account for the behavior of Calhoun, Clay, and others of the younger generation in every southern state. Generally these men had not participated directly in the politics of the 1790s. They had come of political age when their party was in the ascendancy. To them the exercise of power meant the Republicans' exercise of power. And because of the South's position in the party, it necessarily meant the South's exercise of power. These young southerners did not distrust either their party or themselves. They demanded war in 1812 to prevent Great Britain from crippling their country. The war persuaded them that the energetic spirit they had fostered required additional bone and muscle. Without hesitation they moved to add substance to spirit. National power had never endangered them. Always they had seen it exercised by their own elders, even by themselves. They had never seen it turned against the South or against southern interests as they perceived them.

Peace and the spectacular triumph at New Orleans confirmed the exuberant southerners in their nationalism. Building a nation, they were caught up in swirling events. They had met Great Britain a second time and survived, even prevailed. They had also finally done away with their old political enemies. The Virginian James Monroe swept the nation in 1816 to become the third successive southern Republican president. The Federalist candidate, Rufus King of New York, carried only Delaware, Connecticut, and Massachusetts. In the South the Federalist party became politically extinct. It was a heady time.

THE MARCH WESTWARD CONTINUES

The South did not expend its energy solely on legislation and elections. Southerners participated vigorously in the westward drive that between 1815 and 1820 significantly expanded the nation's settled borders. In those five years organized states for the first time reached the Mississippi. In the old Northwest Territory, beyond the Ohio River, both Indiana and Illinois joined the Union. In the Southwest settlers also pushed toward the great river. Mississippi became a state in 1817, followed by Alabama in 1819. Those two, along with Louisiana, which had entered the Union in 1812, expanded the South considerably.

This expansion contributed to the political strength of the South. From the time of the Constitutional Convention southerners had expected expansion to help them dominate the new nation. The ascendancy of the Republican party indicated that they indeed dominated it, and expansion had surely helped. The first fruits, Tennessee and Kentucky, had lengthened the Republican column. Then Jefferson purchased Louisiana, which seemed to give permanence to southern political as well as economic and ideological aspirations. Alabama and Mississippi buttressed the South's political power. As southern states were added to the Union, the three-fifths clause of the Constitution, which permitted 60 percent of the slave population to be counted for the purposes of apportioning congressmen in a state, continuously added to the number of presidential electors claimed by the South and increased the region's national political strength. After the admission of Alabama in 1819 the Union had eleven slave and eleven free states.

The South had long cast covetous eyes on Spanish Florida. Andrew Jackson's exploits there in 1818 captured the South's attention and won the plaudits of western southerners, though some seaboard southerners were alarmed by Jackson's direct action. When the United States acquired Florida in 1819, southerners

SPREAD OF SETTLEMENT IN THE SOUTH, 1800–1820

certainly expected it to end up under their influence. And when President Monroe named General Jackson as the first governor of the Florida Territory, southerners were sure that it had done so.

In 1819 the South had no reason to change its mind about the ultimate result of expansion. New southern states reinforced the political legions of the Republican party, the party southerners viewed as their own. With the remainder of vast Louisiana and nearby Florida on the horizon, the future of expansion seemed equally hospitable to southern interests.

THE DISSENTERS

Although nationalist fervor did dominate the South, a minority of southerners stood in opposition to the new faith. This opposition centered on Virginia, but not all Virginia Republicans belonged to it. The dissenters held fast to the doctrines of the 1790s and repeated Quid rhetoric against what had become mainstream Republicanism. Old Quids such as John Randolph of Roanoke continued to emphasize pure Republicanism as they had done before the War of 1812, but they were seldom called Quids now, and they were not among the chief spokesmen for this new opposition; that honor went to powerful Virginia Republicans who had opposed the Quids a decade earlier. The most important opponents were leaders of the Richmond Junto, a loosely knit organization that dominated Republican (and later Democratic) politics in Virginia for a generation. Thomas Ritchie, editor of the Richmond *Enquirer*, the best-known Republican newspaper in the South—according to the aged Jefferson, it was the only paper in the nation worth reading—warned his readers that the nationalist course undermined the hallowed truths of the 1790s.

Not only did the policies of the Madison and Monroe administrations concern the Richmond Junto and its followers; decisions of the United States Supreme Court distressed them mightily. Ironically, the author of many of the opinions that so rankled the Virginians was one of their own, with a difference. John Marshall was just as Virginian as Ritchie or anyone else, but he was a Federalist. Appointed chief justice by President Adams in 1801, Marshall remained loyal to Federalist concepts of power and authority throughout the Republican ascendancy. In the postwar years two major Court decisions gave legal sanction to the nationalist course. In 1816 in *Martin* v. *Hunter's Lessee* the Supreme Court affirmed on broad grounds that it could review and reverse, if it thought proper, all cases under the laws, treaties, or Constitution of the United States, whether they originated in federal or state courts. In effect this decision reduced state courts to inferior tribunals. Then in *McCulloch* v. *Maryland* in 1819 the Supreme Court gave powerful sanction to the broad, or classically Federalist, interpretation of the Constitution. Affirming the constitutionality of the Bank of the United States, Chief Justice Marshall announced that the Congress could pass any law that was necessary and proper to conduct national business, the only exceptions being measures expressly prohibited by the Constitution. The old strict-construction argument that the Constitution had to authorize specifically any particular measure before it could be considered constitutional made no headway before Marshall's court.

The southerners troubled by congressional laws and Supreme Court decisions wrote, spoke, and voted in a distinct minority until 1819. In that year two cataclysmic events rocked the South and the Republican party: the onset of the Missouri crisis and a financial panic. The shock waves from these massive upheavals caused fundamental shifts that altered the southern landscape and turned a minority into a majority.

THE ONSET OF THE MISSOURI CRISIS

The Missouri crisis struck at the vitals of the South. No one was surprised when Congress in 1819 considered a bill to admit Missouri as a slave state. Slavery had been legal in Missouri under both the French and the Spanish, and because the treaty by which the United States acquired Louisiana guaranteed the preservation of slavery, it had been a legitimate part of an American Missouri since 1803. And Congress had certainly admitted new slave states. Between 1792 and 1817 Kentucky, Tennessee, Louisiana, and Mississippi had all come in with little fanfare. Nor did Alabama experience any difficulty in that same year, 1819.

Missouri, however, became a great battleground when Congressman James Tallmadge of New York offered a two-part amendment to the statehood bill. First, no more slaves would be allowed to enter Missouri; second, all slave children born after statehood would become free at age twenty-five. Tallmadge proposed a gradual emancipation plan, for he advocated no change in the status of the 10,000 slaves already in Missouri. Thus Missouri would remain a slave state for decades, though not forever.

The origins of the Tallmadge Amendment remain unclear. In the years preceding 1819 antislavery activity had not been significant in either Congress or the country at large. The evidence suggests that both moral and political motives prompted Tallmadge's proposal. Many northerners were unhappy with the Constitution's three-fifths clause, which added notably to southern strength in the House of Representatives and in the electoral college. To these northerners the three-fifths clause underlay the South's domination of the national government, and they wanted that domination ended. Refusal to permit the three-fifths advantage to cross the Mississippi seemed to be a way to keep the South's power from expanding. Too, many northerners were morally offended by slavery; they believed it mocked the Declaration of Independence and blemished American liberty. Moreover, much of Missouri lay directly west of Illinois, a free state. To some northerners the admission of a slave Missouri would take slavery beyond its traditional bounds, north even more than west.

The Tallmadge Amendment ignited a political firestorm. Southerners united in denouncing it. As a result, sectional lines drew taut and Republican unity broke down. With free-state congressmen considerably outnumbering those from the slave states, a sectional vote would mean passage for the amendment. On February 17, 1819, that is exactly what happened. But later in the month the Senate rejected the amendment. When the Fifteenth Congress adjourned on March 3, the issue of Missouri's statehood had not been decided. The convening of the new Sixteenth Congress in December 1819 brought no agreement; the same split between the two chambers blocked any action.

THE SOUTH'S REACTION

Southern unity rested on three pillars. First, southerners refused to permit what they called outside interference with slavery. Since the Constitutional Convention southerners had declared that slavery was their institution and that only they could decide its future. Now the Tallmadge Amendment sought to restrict southern expansion into the Louisiana Purchase. But southerners wanted no barriers to expansion, which had always been central to their economic and political strength. Finally, the thrust of the Tallmadge Amendment undermined the South's conception of the country. The supporters of the amendment denounced slavery as an aberration in the United States, a nation dedicated to freedom and liberty. The time had come, they insisted, for Congress to put on the road to extinction the nefarious, un-American institution of slavery. The argument that liberty and slavery could not coexist fundamentally challenged the southern view of liberty and slavery. At least since the Revolution most white southerners had equated their own liberty with their right to decide the fate of their black slaves. In southern eyes a threat to their control of their slaves automatically jeopardized their liberty.

In the congressional debates that stretched through the winter of 1819–1820 southerners emphasized themes that would dominate southern political rhetoric and thinking for the remainder of the antebellum era. They emphatically reaffirmed that they would tolerate no outside interference with slavery. Southern speakers took two different tacks to make this fundamental point. The Virginians especially repeated their time-honored laments about the evil of slavery, but as always, they simultaneously insisted that slavery was solely a southern concern. At the same time a bold new southern voice staunchly defended slavery. For the first time in the national legislature southerners defended slavery as a positive good. Some southerners proclaimed that "Christ himself gave a sanction to slavery." Others painted warm, bucolic pictures of plantation life and the human affection that bound masters and slaves in friendship and harmony. Of course these apostles of bondage joined their less committed southern brothers in refusing totally to permit any outside involvement with slavery.

Although such an audacious defense had never before been heard in Congress, this language did not mean that the white South had reached some kind of historic crossroads in its attitude toward slavery. The defense clearly spelled out the South's contention that slavery was a permanent institution, but no evidence exists to indicate that the Missouri crisis prompted a hardening of attitudes on the subject. During both the Revolutionary era and the ratification of the Constitution, the South had made clear its commitment to slavery. Changes had occurred by 1819, but outside, not inside, the South. A new antislavery mood had surfaced in the North, and for the first time the South faced a sustained public attack on slavery; it responded with a public defense. Missouri did demonstrate that the South was willing to take such a stance, but the basic commitment had been consciously powerful since the Revolution.

In attacking the Tallmadge Amendment southerners for the first time made an extended connection between states rights and slavery. Previously they had often appealed to states rights to justify a broad definition of their interests; now they fused states rights with slavery. Southerners argued that the Constitution made no provision for placing conditions or restrictions on a new state such as those proposed by the Tallmadge Amendment. When advocates of restriction countered calls for states rights with assertions that the Tallmadge Amendment was needed to guarantee republican government, southerners recoiled in horror. Carried to its logical extreme, that doctrine could impose conditions not just on new states but on old ones. In the southern interpretation of the northern argument, slavery could be endangered everywhere. Constitutionally speaking, the Missouri crisis propelled the South's reaction against postwar nationalism into a headlong rush back to the 1790s, to the Virginia and Kentucky resolutions. As in that earlier time, self-interest and ideology meshed perfectly. During the lengthy debates southerners talked about more than slavery and states rights; they raised the ominous specter of disunion. One senator cried that the North's determination to interfere with slavery could end only in "a brother's sword crimsoned with brother's blood."

THE MISSOURI COMPROMISE

The Missouri crisis never became a secession crisis because Congress found a solution. The Missouri Compromise of 1820 had three elements: (1) the admission of Missouri as a slave state, (2) the admission of Maine as a free state, and (3) a slavery-freedom boundary line drawn through the Louisiana Purchase along 36°30' westward from the Mississippi River; it marked the southern border of Missouri.

Not all senators and representatives were happy about the compromise. When the three parts were presented to the Senate as a package, the vote revealed deep sectional differences. Slave-state senators supported it 20 to 2; free-state senators voted against it 18 to 4. It seems obvious that southerners saw the package as their victory. A 10-to-1 margin could not be interpreted as anything less than a perceived triumph. In the House the three parts of the compromise were presented separately, and southerners voted overwhelmingly for two parts and rejected one—the 36°30' line.

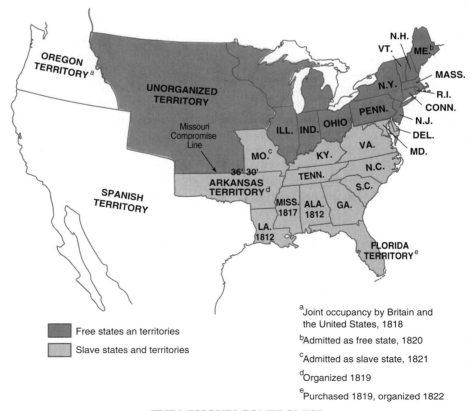

[a] Joint occupancy by Britain and the United States, 1818

[b] Admitted as free state, 1820

[c] Admitted as slave state, 1821

[d] Organized 1819

[e] Purchased 1819, organized 1822

THE MISSOURI COMPROMISE

Thirty-seven southern congressmen voted against the territorial line, considering it too great a concession. They agreed with Nathaniel Macon that "to compromise is to acknowledge the right of Congress to interfere and to legislate on the subject. This would be acknowledging too much." The major Republican editor, Thomas Ritchie, warned that acceptance of the territorial division would set a dangerous precedent by inviting the North to disregard southern interests. "If we yield now, beware," he cried, "[the North] will ride us forever." But despite their pleadings and warnings, Macon, Ritchie, and their colleagues failed to undo the compromise, which finally passed the Congress in March 1820. The crisis had passed.

The vantage point of hindsight causes wonder why the South gave in on the territorial point, which would later become the critical issue. In 1820 the southerners obviously considered paramount the admission of Missouri as a slave state. They wanted a slave state west of the Mississippi, in the Louisiana Purchase, and to get what they wanted many of them willingly gave up their right to take slaves into much of the rest of the Purchase. That the proposal for the 36°30' line originated within the proslavery camp demonstrates conclusively that in 1820 they viewed the slave state they could get now as considerably more important than other slave states they might get later. To southerners the admission of Missouri proved that the expansion of their peculiar institution, which had been so important in the first generation of the new nation, had a beachhead on the far shore of the future.

Although a few southerners objected to the territorial restriction on constitutional grounds, most did not. The virtual absence of such opposition from a major discussion of constitutional powers and slavery clearly indicates that in 1820 most southerners who thought about the subject believed that Congress had the power to act on slavery in the territories. After all, precedent had been set with the Northwest Ordinance of 1787, which prohibited slavery north of the Ohio River. Likewise, Congress legislated on slavery in the Mississippi Territory in 1798, and again in 1804 in the Louisiana Purchase, and once more in 1819 in the Arkansas Territory. Congress's refusal to prohibit slavery in each of those cases certainly did not imply limits on congressional power or opposition to the exercise of that power by southerners as well as northerners.

THE PANIC OF 1819

At the same time the Missouri crisis wracked the Congress, the Panic of 1819, the first great economic depression in American history, assaulted the American economy. The South was not spared. The panic brought an abrupt halt to the postwar prosperity that had helped create a widespread economic nationalism. That prosperity had been based in large part on agricultural exports, and cotton was the most important item on the list. The explosion in the price of cotton led to a sharp demand for the two commodities essential for its production, land and slaves. The cotton boom focused on the Southwest—the new states of Alabama and Mississippi, and to a lesser extent Louisiana, Georgia, and Tennessee. The purchase of land and slaves required more capital than most families had. Thus credit became absolutely essential to fuel the boiler that generated prosperity.

To thousands of southerners—on plantations, on farms, in the stores that supplied them and the banks that lent them money and the trading offices that speculated on them—the financial feast came to an abrupt end long before all the anticipated courses had been served. At the beginning of 1819 cotton sold for 33 cents a pound; by fall it brought less than half that amount. The utter collapse of cotton prices, caused in large part by overproduction, signaled a precipitous decline of the entire economy. The prices of other agricultural products followed cotton downward. Slave prices also tumbled. Early in 1819 the cost of a prime field hand reached $800 in Richmond and $1,100 in New Orleans; the dollar value had doubled since the war. But by 1821 the price in Richmond fell to less than $600 and in New Orleans it plummeted to $800. Bank shares, rents, real estate all collapsed after the wreck of agriculture. Bankruptcy seemed at worst imminent, at best only inevitable. Sudden, totally unexpected, the panic had a massive impact on the South, political as well as economic.

Its fury certainly jolted William T. Palfrey, a planter in St. Mary Parish, Louisiana. Noting that land prices were rising and that his slave force was increasing, Palfrey greeted the spring of 1819 with optimism, but by autumn his outlook had changed. Though his cotton had "never looked as well as it does now," the price was "so unfavorable" that even the value of slaves was collapsing. Palfrey described a "depression in price that will make a melancholy elimination in the amount of Dollars." By the spring of 1820 his situation had worsened. Despite an abundant crop, he had to keep borrowing. The notes piled up, and William Palfrey feared for his financial survival. Though he managed to hold on, many others who faced similar difficulties went under.

POLITICAL REPERCUSSIONS

On the state level the panic led to a return of financial politics, especially in the Southwest, where the aftermath of the panic seemed to replay the 1780s. Talk of stay laws, debates about circulating currency, disputes between creditors and debtors, and arguments about the proper role of banks pervaded the political arena. Both Tennessee and Kentucky enacted stay laws. Tennessee also created the Bank of Tennessee, with the power to issue $1 million in paper money and to make loans not exceeding $1,000 to a single borrower. Georgia and Alabama organized comparable institutions with similar stipulations on loan ceilings and distribution. Factions within the dominant Republican party coalesced on opposite sides of these financial issues.

This political warring brought to state politics a bitterness not seen since the 1780s. In the furor of depression politics, financial issues such as the role of banks and the rights of creditors and debtors became entangled with the most precious of all southern commodities, liberty. Debtors and opponents of banks charged that the power of banks gave them an unnatural privilege that imperiled both the independence of the community and the control individuals had over their own affairs. Many southerners viewed the banks and the paper money they issued as qualitatively different from the traditional land and slaves. The cries against this kind of privilege echoed the Republican assault on Hamilton's financial policy. In turn, politicians who considered banks and creditors as performing valuable services denounced their opponents as demagogues who denied property rights and strained the social fabric, thus endangering liberty.

The panic also had major repercussions on the relationship between the South and the rest of the nation. Facing financial ruin, many southerners searched for villains, and banks served as easily identifiable ones. Banks had provided much of the credit that underwrote the cost of land and slaves, and many banks had seriously overextended themselves. When the financial crunch came, banks retrenched and called in loans. And the financial pincers were being applied not only by local banks. The second Bank of the United States, with headquarters in Philadelphia and branches throughout the country, including ten in the slave states, had opened its doors in 1817. Both individuals and local banks did business with the national bank, which exercised no more fiscal judgment than most southern banks did. Like them, it became overextended and found itself in a precarious financial position. By the summer of 1818 the bank had almost a 10-to-1 imbalance between its specie reserve (gold and silver coins on deposit) and its immediate liabilities. And without the government-backed insurance guarantees that protect bank depositors today, a prudent balance between specie reserves and liabilities offered the only protection to depositors. To save itself, the bank retrenched with ferocity, and its southern branches were forced to do so as well.

The Bank of the United States survived, but at the partial expense of hard-pressed southerners, who cried that "the Bank was saved and the people were ruined." Though devastated southerners condemned their own banks as "horse-leeches [that] drained every drop of blood they could from a suffering community," they identified the Bank of the United States as playing an especially evil role. In the graphic image of one antibank enthusiast, southerners discovered themselves "in the jaws of the monster! a lump of butter in the mouth of a dog! one gulp, one swallow, and all is gone."

With the bank indicted as the chief villain, it took but a step to include in the indictment as accessories the nationalism and broad construction of the Constitution which had spawned the bank. Because energetic government sanctioned by an elastic view of the Constitution had permitted the creation of the bank, they became the real menaces. Most southerners found such an interpretation particularly compelling because it enabled them to speak in the congenial language they had spoken so powerfully during the Revolution and on through the 1790s. Fear of an oppressive central authority and the necessity for local control to protect liberty—once again this twin message became the cry of the South.

Antipathy toward the Bank of the United States not only brought back the old fears of national power; it also rekindled sectional animosity. Although the bank was certainly active in the South, its main office was in Philadelphia, after all. Its southern enemies had no difficulty in branding it a northern institution that benefited mainly northern financial interests.

The rejuvenated antagonism to a broad view of the Constitution and an active federal government also revealed itself when Congress considered another tariff bill in 1820. Southerners led the opposition to this measure, which called for an increase in the duties imposed by the 1816 law. They argued that an increased tariff would give a favored status to manufacturers, and that Congress should not provide an artificial stimulus to manufacturing. Southerners also asserted that a protective tariff would benefit a special interest against the people, or a nonsouthern interest against the South. The vote was more sectional than it had been in 1816. Only a tiny southern group, mostly from Kentucky and Maryland, voted aye. The votes of southern senators were crucial when by one vote the Senate indefinitely postponed the bill.

In response to the panic and to the Missouri Compromise, southerners united in rejecting nationalism, but this unity disintegrated as financial politics splintered the states. Yet the unity as well as the divisiveness rested on a widely shared perception that liberty was threatened. That perception would have enormous import in southern politics in general and in the relationship between the South and the Republican party in particular.

7

A New
Political Structure

❖

The pressures generated by the Missouri crisis and the Panic of 1819 broke the Jeffersonian Republican party apart. The tension between the advocates of national power and the guardians of local authority proved greater than the old party's ability to contain them. For southerners the struggle was especially momentous because of the intimate ties between the party and the South. For southerners the events of 1819 revived and reinforced the lesson of the 1790s— power exercised by the national government could menace the vital interests of the South.

During the Missouri controversy, the panic, and the debate over an increased protective tariff in 1820 and in 1824, southern leaders once again warned of the dangers of a strong national government buttressed by a broad interpretation of the Constitution. For the first time in Congress southerners in 1823 declared the protective tariff unconstitutional. Asserting correctly that the Constitution nowhere explicitly endorsed protection, they concluded that Congress had no authority to protect domestic manufacturing. The passage of the new tariff in 1824, despite overwhelming southern opposition, confirmed the lessons of Missouri. The South could no longer count on the Republican party to do its bidding.

The constitutional retrenchment so evident in debates over protection reached into the most sensitive areas. Southerners began to see broad construction as a potential threat to more than their economic interests and the unrestricted expansion of slavery. Nathaniel Macon confided to a friend, "If Congress can make banks, roads, and canals under the Constitution they can free any slave in the United States." John Randolph of Roanoke expanded on Macon's fearful theme in a speech to the House in 1824; in opposition to a bill that merely authorized widespread federal surveys for roads and canals, Randolph exposed the core of the South's apprehension about national power.

> If congress possess the power to do what is proposed by this bill, they may emancipate every slave in the United States. . . . And where will they find the power? They may . . .

hook the power upon the first loop they find in the Constitution; they might take the preamble—perhaps the war making power—or they might take a greater sweep, and say, with some gentlemen, that it is not to be found in this or that of the granted powers, but results from all of them—which is not only a dangerous but the *most dangerous* doctrine.

BACKGROUND TO 1824

The debate over the future orientation of the Republican party focused on the contest to choose a successor to James Monroe in the White House. The third member of the Virginia dynasty, Monroe was reelected in 1820 without opposition. For Monroe reelection brought the best of all possible political worlds—the disappearance of the Federalist party as a national entity. That no Federalist opposed Monroe in 1820 signified to him the victorious conclusion of the great political war begun in the 1790s. The serious issues facing his party and the internal conflicts raging within it held little interest for him. With his powdered wig and buckled breeches, Monroe was an artifact in fashion as well as in politics. Although Monroe seemed oblivious of the swirl around him, forceful men in his cabinet and in the Congress figured prominently in it. That southerners dominated this group pointed up the special relationship between the South and the party.

Only Monroe's secretary of state, John Quincy Adams of Massachusetts, carried northern colors in the great political parade of 1824. Both Secretary of the Treasury William H. Crawford of Georgia and Secretary of War John C. Calhoun of South Carolina ardently desired the presidency. The Kentuckian Henry Clay, as speaker, the most influential man in the House of Representatives and the most popular as well, eagerly hoped for the top prize. Each of these four brought impressive legislative or administrative credentials to the presidential race. The fifth candidate also had a notable public record, but one of a different sort. Although he had served in both House and Senate, in fact was a sitting United States senator in 1824, Andrew Jackson had never been a major figure in the national legislature. None of his competitors, however, could match his public visibility and fame. His military exploits had made him the most widely known American of his time, save possibly for the Revolutionary patriarchs Jefferson and John Adams. Never in American history has a stronger group vied for the presidency.

Although four southerners dominated the field, they neither stood together ideologically nor agreed on the future direction of the party. Calhoun, Clay, and Crawford had all been part of the new nationalism after the War of 1812. Calhoun and Clay had been especially energetic in advancing the postwar Republican doctrine of vigorous government. Crawford was not quite so outspokenly in favor of the new orthodoxy, though he never took serious issue with it. Despite his vote for the Tariff of 1824, Jackson escaped identification with any particular ideology. His heroic public image was grounded in his military exploits, not in his stand on public policy or in his political philosophy.

The traditional Republican leaders in the seaboard states adopted Crawford as the man who could ensure the demise of the unholy "Federalism" that in their view had seeped into the party. Why these men settled upon Crawford is unclear; perhaps because he was less tainted with the new nationalism than any other major figure. Although William H. Crawford is a forgotten man today, his contemporaries considered him a political leader of the first rank. The Crawford backers had no intention of remaining a local interest group. In a conscious effort to replicate the old Virginia–New York alliance, they joined with Martin Van Buren, the politically astute manager of the dominant faction in the New York Republican party. Called Radicals because in their mind they advocated a radical return to the old ways and thoughts, these men believed they would purify the party.

Though clearly distinguishable from Crawford, Calhoun and Clay did not stand together. At this time Calhoun was in transit between an ardent nationalism that could not imagine the interest of the South "to be opposed to the rest of the Union" and a zealous sectionalism that saw a growing Union threatening the security of the South. In making this momentous shift Calhoun was following his state, which was rapidly deserting postwar nationalism, and also his own conviction that increasing federal power could endanger the South. Even though he was actively participating in the southern shift, Calhoun failed to generate significant support outside South Carolina. For many southern Republicans he had been too able on the other side for too long. Clay, on the other hand, remained a stalwart behind the nationalist program he had helped to shape. He even talked about an American System in which the national bank, the protective tariff, and internal improvements would all work together for the benefit of the nation. Although enormously popular with his fellow politicians, he could not translate that goodwill into general southern support. In the South he was on the wrong side of the crucial issue.

A NEW POLITICS

With Calhoun and Clay severely circumscribed and Adams shackled by his New England identity, Crawford appeared well on his way to securing the leadership of a new generation of southern Republicans. But just as triumph seemed within his grasp, he collided with the formidable presence of Andrew Jackson. They never met in a face-to-face debate. Their direct competition occurred within the structure of southern politics, and the collision permanently altered the structure. Crawford's managers wanted to win in the old-fashioned Republican way, with the caucus of congressional Republicans awarding Crawford its presidential nomination. The caucus held an honored place in Republican tradition; Jefferson, Madison, and Monroe had all received its blessings and its nomination. In 1824 Crawford's managers saw their man as next in line.

But in the states and the nation a new politics overpowered Crawford. Though ideologically the southern Republicans were reverting to a familiar, secure position, in practice they were rushing toward the future. Denouncing Crawford's campaign as "the few political managers against the body of the people," his opponents called on the voters to defend their right of choice by crushing Crawford and the caucus. In North Carolina, Crawford's opponents organized a

People's party to discredit his campaign. The Tennessee legislature announced that the election should be left "to the *people themselves.*" Of course, the anti-Crawfordites expected to win practical political gains by freeing the selection process from the caucus.

They did succeed in destroying the caucus by defining its destruction as a practical manifestation of democracy and the preservation of liberty. The caucus became a dead letter. When it met in February 1824, duly called by Crawford leaders, only 66 Republicans attended while almost 200 stayed away. Although Crawford won the caucus's endorsement, the victory was hollow. To the multitude of southern Republicans the caucus meant nothing.

With the caucus slain and a rowdier, more popular politics victorious, appeals to the mass of voters became essential for political triumph. Managers could certainly still plot and plan; after all, such planning had brought down the caucus. Still, the result meant more direct contact with voters. In this kind of context no one in the race could match Jackson. As one of his opponents put it, "It is very difficult to electioneer successfully against General Jackson—his character and services are of the kind which *alone* the people can appreciate and feel." In fact, Jackson's strength caused Calhoun to reassess his position. Finding his candidacy overwhelmed by Jackson's surge, Calhoun opted for the vice presidency, a post for which he was unopposed.

The election demonstrated Jackson's power. He won all the electoral votes in five states along with a majority in Maryland and Louisiana. His total was 55, only one less than that of all of his opponents combined. In 1824, for the first time in a presidential election, a notable popular vote was cast. Here Jackson's dominance was unmistakably clear. Winning more than 78,000 popular votes, Jackson outdistanced his nearest rival, Crawford, by more than $2^1/_2$ to 1. Moreover, his vote exceeded the combined votes of all other candidates. Even the sainted Jefferson might not have been Jackson's match among southern voters.

Although Jackson trounced his opponents in the South, the national outcome was not so clear-cut. As none of the candidates won a majority of electoral votes, the job of electing the president fell to the House of Representatives, where the Constitution accorded each state one vote. In the House the southern vote did not follow precisely the pattern of the general election. Emphasizing his close ties to the leadership of the seaboard states, Crawford not only held Virginia and Georgia but also gained North Carolina, which had gone for Jackson. The border South went solidly for John Quincy Adams, largely because Clay brought the states of Kentucky and Missouri into the Adams camp. Clay's influence in the House helped Adams get Louisiana and Maryland, where Jackson had won a majority of the electoral votes. Although these four slave states provided votes essential for Adams's victory in the House, they were congressional votes only, based on little or no popular support.

A NEW ALIGNMENT

For the South the most important result of Adams's election came in the almost immediate coalescence of the several Republican factions into two, pro- and anti-

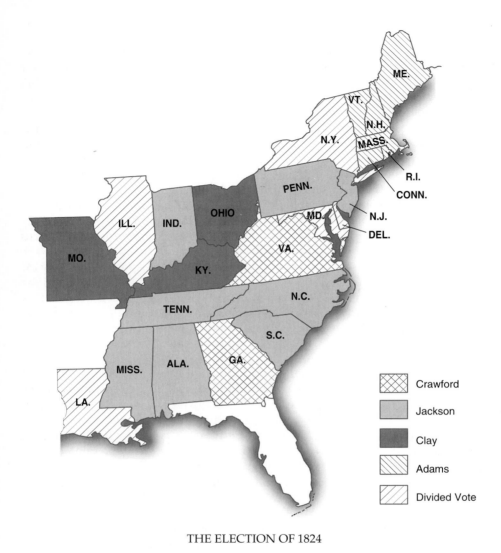

THE ELECTION OF 1824

Legend:
- Crawford
- Jackson
- Clay
- Adams
- Divided Vote

administration. President John Quincy Adams and Henry Clay, who became his secretary of state, led the pro-administration forces. Alignment with Adams was the logical move for Clay, ideologically as well as politically. Both Adams and Clay were confirmed nationalists; moreover, Clay saw Jackson as his great rival in the West. Andrew Jackson took command of the forces against the administration. In Jackson's view, the people's choice had been subverted because Adams and Clay had made a corrupt bargain—the presidency for Adams and the secretary-ship of state for Clay. The State Department was looked upon as a special prize because Madison, Monroe, and Adams had stepped directly from there to the White House. In the Jacksonian interpretation, the House would surely have ratified the popular choice and selected Jackson but for the intrigue masterminded by

Clay. No reliable evidence supports the case for an unsavory deal between Adams and Clay, but the Jackson men made effective use of the charge. Standing with the Jacksonians was Vice President Calhoun, who recognized Clay as Adams's political heir. Besides, Calhoun's move away from his strong nationalist orientation was rapidly gaining momentum.

The events of 1824 provided the springboard for a new political force that to southerners descended directly from the original Republican party. This new force had a visible, heroic leader, Andrew Jackson. It also had numerous southerners in significant positions. Calhoun was perhaps the most notable, but he had colleagues in every state. The party also laid claim to ideological purity with the accession of Thomas Ritchie and his old Republican confederates in Virginia, who joined only after overcoming their anxiety about Jackson's military background. Despite that reservation, they saw no other way to defeat the revived Federalism of another Adams. Quite aside from leaders and ideology, powerful ties formed between southern voters and Jackson, a kinship clearly shown in 1824. The Jackson party also replicated Jefferson's tie with the North. With Ritchie and Van Buren making the connection, even the same states led the way. A final similarity with the early Republicans made clear the southern idiom of the Jackson party. John Quincy Adams was the first northern president in two and a half decades, since the administration of his father, John Adams. That coincidence underscored the South's perception of a reprise of the Republican-Federalist rivalry.

As president, John Quincy Adams fueled the fires of southern opposition. The most nationally minded of any president up to his time, Adams envisioned an active central government energetically carrying out a vigorous nationalist program. In pushing for specific measures, Adams antagonized southerners in particular. No issue proved more divisive than the effort to drive Indians from their lands. When Georgia, in violation of a treaty between the United States and the Cherokee, acted to survey the Indian lands in preparation for forcing the Cherokee to relinquish them to white settlers, President Adams opposed the state's action. But to no avail—he could find little support in Congress for a firm policy in the face of an intransigent Georgia. Georgia won; the Cherokee and Adams lost; the white South cheered. For southerners, who eagerly desired Indian lands in Alabama and Mississippi as well as in Georgia, self-interest and ideology meshed. States rights protected their interests. Southerners were also appalled when Adams wanted to send an American delegation to a conference of Latin American and Caribbean nations in Panama. Because American diplomats would mingle there with black delegates from Haiti, a country founded by a slave rebellion, southerners greeted Adams's announcement with a barrage of criticism. In Congress southerners delayed passage of the appropriations bill so long that the conference adjourned before the American delegation arrived.

President Adams also fought the southerners on what was rapidly becoming the most pressing economic issue. Long a protectionist, he supported an increase in duties proposed in 1828. Although the Tariff of 1828 was in no way the complete responsibility of John Quincy Adams, it did go through Congress during his administration, and he did sign into law the highest tariff enacted before the Civil War. Its enemies, chiefly southerners, called the Tariff of 1828 an "abomination"

both because of its record rates and because of the labyrinthine politics of its passage. In their efforts to stop it, southerners tried to drive a wedge between northern and western farmers, who wanted higher duties on such products as raw
wool, and manufacturers, who advocated protection of finished goods, not raw
materials. The southern effort failed under the combined weight of the protection-
ists. Although some Jackson supporters from the North and West voted aye to so-
lidify support for their candidate in such states as Pennsylvania, where protection
was a major concern, southerners identified the measure with the Adams camp.
Jackson himself had not publicly supported it, and most southerners believed he
would work to lower the tariff if he could be installed in the White House.

In the presidential election of 1828 the South made its preference absolutely
clear. Adams and his supporters, known as National Republicans, were literally
buried under a Jackson avalanche. Below the border Jackson took every electoral
vote; along the border only Maryland, which split its vote, provided Adams with
any electoral votes. More southerners voted than in any previous presidential
election, and in many states the popular margins for Jackson were astounding. He
won in Alabama by more than 8 to 1, in Tennessee by 20 to 1; and in Georgia he
garnered 100 percent of the popular votes.

With the election of 1828 a new political age dawned. In the South the political sun shone with special brightness. Southerners overwhelmingly perceived
Andrew Jackson as their political savior, who would deliver them from the threat
of a powerful central government with all its evils. The overwhelming belief in
Jackson is a telling commentary on the South's perceptions of policy and power.
Most southerners never doubted that Jackson was with them on the great question of national versus local power. Yet Jackson had never taken a strong public
stand on the most salient question. Because of his southern identity and his heroic
image, southerners simply assumed that he stood where they did. He was the
new Jefferson. When Jefferson was in power he had moved in unexpected directions, but southerners had generally remained steadfast behind him and his party.
If Jackson followed that pattern, would he, like Jefferson, still hold the loyalty of
most southerners?

Swept into power on a flood tide of southern support, Andrew Jackson in his
first administration confronted three issues critical to the South—the tariff, the
second Bank of the United States, and Indians. His actions brought forth both
praise and blame from a South that had backed him solidly.

NULLIFICATION

In the late 1820s nothing so distressed the majority of southerners as did the tariff.
And most expected Jackson to get the high rates of 1828 lowered. The most vigorous antitariff sentiment was found in Virginia and South Carolina, where ideological sensitivity matched financial concern. To the purists a protective tariff violated the Constitution. They insisted that Jackson remove this blotch from the
holy constitutional writ. Jackson, however, did not move so directly as the southern antitariff zealots demanded. He had never adopted a doctrinaire antitariff

position. Besides, Jackson recognized that a protective tariff helped his party in critical northern states.

Jackson's dilatoriness in moving against the Tariff of 1828 led to a major national and constitutional crisis. This crisis was precipitated by South Carolina, which by 1830 had replaced Virginia as the self-proclaimed guardian of the southern ideological birthright. Living as they did in the only state with a population more than half slave, many white South Carolinians had become hypersensitive about the potential danger posed by national power to the institution of slavery. South Carolina proclaimed the faith of the newly baptized, for the state had undergone a conversion. No other southern state had been more enthusiastic about the postwar nationalism of the Republican party. But during the 1820s South Carolina began a political and ideological trek that would place the state in the vanguard of states-rights extremists.

As South Carolina moved toward intransigence, its most notable political son, John C. Calhoun, took his post as captain of the guard that watched over southern interests. Calhoun provided the theoretical framework as well as political leadership for the unhappy South Carolinians. In 1828 the South Carolina legislature published Calhoun's *South Carolina Exposition and Protest,* but his authorship was kept secret until 1831. In this work, after describing in detail what he saw as the unfairness of the tariff, Calhoun spelled out his theory of constitution making and the Union. Claiming with justification that he drew upon the Virginia and Kentucky resolutions, Calhoun insisted that the Union was a compact of states. In Calhoun's view, the individual states had created the Union, and as creators they were sovereign.

Moreover, he argued, the states gave the federal government only the particular powers enumerated in the Constitution, and no more. Thus a measure such as the protective tariff, which did not have specific constitutional sanction, was patently unconstitutional and a clear usurpation of power. As a remedy for such an abuse Calhoun spoke of a state veto. Because the individual states retained their sovereignty, Calhoun maintained, a state could interpose its will between its citizens and the federal government. Thus an individual state could veto or nullify any federal law it defined as unconstitutional. This veto could be exercised by the people of a state acting through a state constitutional convention, in Calhoun's theory the ultimate constitutional power. In Calhoun's scheme, this state veto also protected a minority from the unconstitutional acts of a majority. But Calhoun's minority rights were those of interest groups, such as southern planters and states, not of individuals. In fact, in 1832, when South Carolina nullified the tariff, the opponents of nullification were forced to conform or face the loss of their political rights. Calhoun did provide a legal way to overturn nullification: an amendment to the Constitution approved by the required three-fourths of the states would make any policy legitimate.

While Calhoun penned probing essays on the nature of the Constitution and American federalism, others in his state acted—and without Calhoun's public support. As early as the fall of 1830 they attempted to call a convention so that South Carolina could nullify the Tariff of 1828. Facing stiff opposition from Jackson supporters who claimed that the president should be given more time and

from others who considered that the basic idea behind nullification was prepos-
terous, they failed.

Undaunted, the nullifiers mounted a forceful, energetic effort to awaken the
state to the dangers they saw. Even the lowered tariff enacted in 1832 failed to sat-
isfy them, for it retained the hated principle of protection. After its passage the
nullifiers again tried for a state constitutional convention in a campaign that
forced Calhoun to take sides publicly. This time the nullifiers persuaded a sufficient number of their fellow South Carolinians that the action of the national government threatened their well-being as well as the sovereignty of their state. In
November 1832 the convention met and solemnly nullified the tariffs of 1828 and
1832. After March 1, 1833, the convention declared, both tariffs would be null and
void in South Carolina. It also stipulated that any attempt by the national government to use force would bring disunion. Later, the effective date of nullification
was postponed until after Congress adjourned in order to allow national lawmakers a final chance to give up protection.

The reaction was instantaneous, and not to the nullifiers' liking. Andrew Jackson denounced nullification as treason. In a public proclamation, known as the
Nullification Proclamation, he announced that any attempt to enforce nullification would by definition be an attack on the Union. Deeds accompanied words
when the president poured troops into the Charleston forts and asked Congress to
go on record in support of any action that might be required to suppress nullification.

The other southern states offered South Carolina no tangible assistance.
Although most of them continuously railed against the tariff, none joined South
Carolina in nullification. Nullification was both too radical and too arcane.
Though southerners almost universally agreed that the tariff was hurtful, few believed that it mortally endangered vital interests. The theory itself perplexed
many. In Calhoun's construct a state could be simultaneously inside and outside
the Union. To many southerners South Carolina was behaving rashly.

With the nullifiers and President Jackson seemingly headed for collision, the
president maneuvered to avoid a head-on crash. In his annual message in December 1832 he advocated that Congress lower the tariff rates even further. That
month Calhoun, who had resigned the vice presidency, returned to Washington as
a United States senator. Even as Calhoun vigorously defended his state before the
Senate, he sought some way to avert a confrontation between state and nation. He
pressed forward on two fronts: he urged caution and delay upon his hotheaded
comrades back home, and he cooperated even with his ideological enemy Clay to
get a compromise tariff.

Finally in March 1833, with Calhoun and Clay in league, Congress passed a
compromise tariff that lowered rates in slow stages to the 20-percent level by
1842. At the same time Congress overwhelmingly approved Jackson's Force Bill,
which reaffirmed the president's right to use force if South Carolina in any way
interfered with the enforcement of federal laws. President Jackson signed both
bills. Reconvening, the nullifiers claimed victory. The convention rescinded its
nullification of the tariff laws, and in a final meaningless act nullified the Force
Bill.

The legacy of the nullification crisis was not at all clear-cut. At first glance

Jackson's firmness seemed to leave no doubt that the federal government would be supreme over state governments. But among the nullifiers the conviction prevailed that they had stood up to the central government, and it had come to terms with them. Thus confrontation could lead to success. At the same time, Jackson's ringing pronouncements about the authority of the federal government frightened some of his southern partisans, people who gave no support to nullification. To these stalwart states-righters, Jackson's view of federal prerogatives was every bit as disturbing as nullification. They began to wonder whether they had misplaced their political faith.

*T*HE BANK

Even while the stormclouds of nullification gathered, still another whirlwind swirled around the president. The second Bank of the United States had not played a significant part in Andrew Jackson's first campaign for the White House, but as president he quickly thrust the bank to the center of the political arena. Almost from the beginning the president questioned the bank's value to the country as well as its constitutionality. But he did not put the bank at the top of his agenda; after all, its charter ran until 1836. Believing—in a massive political miscalculation—that the bank could overpower all opposition, the congressional faction headed by Henry Clay obtained a recharter in 1832, four years in advance. If Jackson vetoed the recharter, they thought, he would be driven out of office in 1832. So whether he signed it or not, they would win. They were wrong. In a ringing veto message, Jackson denounced the bank as unconstitutional and castigated it as a parasite feeding off the people. Southerners generally supported the president's stand. Most southern congressmen did not vote for recharter, and few supported the unsuccessful effort to override the veto. The mass of states-rights, strict-construction southerners viewed the bank as a "reptile," a "sin against the Constitution." To most southerners the very purpose of the Jackson movement was to halt and, if possible, to do away with everything connected with the abhorrent postwar nationalism. They cheered the veto.

Jackson, however, did not want the bank to have even the four years of life left to it. After his reelection he moved in the autumn of 1833 to withdraw all federal deposits from the bank. The law permitted withdrawal only if dereliction or mismanagement could be demonstrated. There was no such demonstration, but Jackson ordered the federal funds removed anyway. To southerners, ever alert for unwarranted assumptions of power, Jackson's course seemed just as dangerous as the bank had been. "It is certainly," wrote one in language as vigorous as the president's, "the most atrocious, high handed despotick measure that ever was before assumed by the most absolute monarch." That was surely an exaggeration, but just as surely Jackson had moved beyond a strict reading of the law. And coming just after his claims for federal and executive authority in the nullification crisis, his removal of the deposits reinforced those earlier concerns that Andrew Jackson had become a power-mad president who could not be trusted to protect the sacred truths of strict construction and limited federal power.

INDIAN POLICY

Although Andrew Jackson claimed and exercised considerable federal power, his Indian policy closely followed states-rights precepts and delighted most southern Jacksonians. Jackson, of course, had gained much of his fame as an Indian fighter, and he surely believed that whites were destined to own and farm the land possessed by Indians all the way from Georgia to the Mississippi River.

Like most other southern whites, Jackson took a paternalistic view of the Indians. Though he did not agree that the only good Indian was a dead Indian, he believed that whites were better guardians of the Indians' welfare than the Indians themselves. He did think that the Indians could survive either with their traditional customs or by adopting the civilized ways of the whites, but he was convinced that they must do so beyond the Mississippi, beyond both the mercenary influence of the whites and the competing authority of the states.

Andrew Jackson knew firsthand the southern whites' lust for the Indians' land. When Jackson announced his position in his first annual message to Congress in December 1829, he did not equivocate: the federal government must stand by Georgia in its contest with the Cherokee. Otherwise, "the objects of this Government are reversed, and . . . it has become a part of its duty to aid in destroying the States which it was established to protect." No states-rights zealot could have put the case more forcefully.

Jackson's actions matched his words. Not only the Cherokee but the Choctaw and Chickasaw felt the full force of Jackson's determination. Jackson saw only one possibility: the Cherokee must move west, and he pressed that course upon them. Finally in 1835 the Cherokee yielded. By the Treaty of New Echota they agreed to accept $5 million and land in the Indian Territory (Oklahoma) in exchange for their land in Georgia. The majority of the Cherokee did go west—most of them removed by force—but a thousand or so fled into the mountains of North Carolina, where eventually they were provided a reservation.

Even before the Cherokee treaty, Jackson had secured for white settlement the lands of the Choctaw and Chickasaw in Alabama and Mississippi. Those tribes were given stark alternatives: move or be exterminated. By 1832 they bowed to the inevitable and agreed to cross the Mississippi. They, too, received land in the Indian Territory.

In pushing the Indians out of the old Southwest, Andrew Jackson had wielded the power of the federal government to do just what those states wanted. Now millions of acres of land in Georgia, Alabama, and Mississippi were opened to white settlers, and they poured in. No white person in the South forgot who had made those lands available to whites. Thus the distress occasioned among many southerners by Jackson's stance on nullification and withdrawal was tempered by his acquisition of Indian land.

JACKSON AND ABOLITION

President Andrew Jackson had to contend with a new, and to southerners frightening, development concerning slavery. When William Lloyd Garrison began publication of his *Liberator* in Boston in 1831, the antislavery movement took on a new, uncompromising tone. Concern about the morality of slavery had been around a long time; some southerners had even shared it. But before 1830 the overwhelming majority of antislavery Americans, northerners as well as southerners, saw slavery as a vexing dilemma, one that history had presented to the country. They certainly did not include slaveholders as an essential part of the problem. And they believed that slavery could be eliminated only gradually and over a long period. Garrison and his abolitionist colleagues hurtled into gradualism and bowled it over. They demanded immediate and uncompensated emancipation of all slaves. Moreover, they condemned slave owners as corrupt, both as a group and as individuals. To them a slavemaster was by definition immoral. Though these abolitionists were not numerous, they had a substantial political impact. To southerners it seemed that a herd of wild bulls was preparing to trample over them.

Abolitionists moved on two major political fronts. First, they mailed pamphlets and other publications into the South as well as across the North. Southerners were outraged to find these "incendiary publications," as southerners termed them, on their doorsteps. In Charleston in July 1835, citizens removed the materials from the post office and burned them in a public bonfire. The president, a slave owner himself, shared their anger, and in his forthright manner he moved against the abolitionists. His postmaster general directed that no abolitionist tract could be delivered unless the addressee had requested it. That order eliminated the incendiary publications in slave country, because few southerners wanted to receive them and those who did certainly did not want to be publicly identified as being on the mailing list of Garrison and his friends.

On another front, the abolitionists focused directly on the people who were expected to respond to the pleas of citizens—United States congressmen. To the House of Representatives came a multitude of petitions requesting the abolition of slavery in the District of Columbia, over which Congress had complete authority. The reception of these petitions and their presentation to the House enraged southern congressmen. To solve this problem, the Democratic party, with Jackson's agreement, supported a proposition known as the gag rule, which declared that all petitions would be immediately put on the table without formal presentation to the House.

*T*HE RISE OF THE WHIGS

In the contest to succeed Jackson, victory went to a northerner, Martin Van Buren of New York. Even before the nullification crisis he had bested Calhoun, the early contender for Jackson's favor. When Jackson installed Van Buren as vice president in 1832, Van Buren clearly became the heir apparent. Even though Jackson had blessed him, most southern Jacksonians had serious reservations about a northern president. After all, the only previous two northern presidents—the Adamses, John and John Quincy—had been largely responsible for the success of new, southern-dominated parties. Adding the highly flammable issue of abolition to that natural liability could surely alienate southerners, no matter how devoted they might be to Andrew Jackson. As most southerners saw it, Jackson could be trusted, but they were not at all sure about Van Buren. By the time the Democratic party gave Van Buren its presidential nomination in May 1835, a surging opposition challenged the Democrats' supremacy in the South.

The Democrats had good reason to worry. The halcyon days of 1828 and 1832, when Andrew Jackson had run roughshod over the token opposition put up by the National Republicans were long gone; the presidential election of 1836 promised to be a donnybrook. The National Republican party, burdened by the Adams administration and a platform urging a vigorous national government, never made any headway in the South.

Andrew Jackson's overwhelming strength had more than a little to do with the growth of an effective opposition to his party. So many people expected so much that some were sure to be disappointed. The first were the antitariff zealots, who were dismayed when Jackson did not obliterate the principle of protection. Then many people who distrusted a powerful executive were frightened by Jackson's Nullification Proclamation and his actions in the withdrawal affair. Joining these more ideologically inclined southerners were those politicians who lost out in the race for place and reward within the Democratic party. By 1834 these dissidents, added to the National Republicans, formed a sizable group. But they certainly were a variegated crew, ranging from nullifiers to American System men, from ideologues to opportunists. The politically astute, however, recognized that only one formula afforded any chance for political health and victory in the South. Success could be attained, as a former Jacksonian editor noted, only "by the Nationals coming down to our standard of strict Construction of the Constitution and by no other means." This new party bore no ideological resemblance to the defunct National Republican party.

These southerners, along with other Americans opposed to Jackson, created the Whig party. The term *Whig*, borrowed from the British tradition, denoted someone opposed to executive authority, and Andrew Jackson certainly represented such authority. Only opposition to Jackson glued the Whigs together. Between 1834 and 1836 the national Whig party did not present anything resembling a united political front. Nothing so dramatized early Whig disunity as the election of 1836, in which the party presented three sectional candidates for the presidency: Daniel Webster of Massachusetts, William Henry Harrison of Ohio, and Hugh L. White of Tennessee. The choice of White is instructive about early southern Whiggery. A former Jacksonian—in fact, a close friend of Jackson—White stood for those who believed that Jackson had deserted time-honored principles and had turned over the party to time-serving politicians.

Although southern Whiggery between 1834 and 1836 was in a large sense a part of the states-rights renewal that had been building for more than a decade, the excitement it helped to create derived from something at once more fundamental and more emotional. The abolitionists' all-out assault on slavery and slave owners frightened and angered the South. Their tactics demanded constant vigilance and unyielding defense. In such a time, southern Whigs argued, only tried native sons could be trusted with leadership.

"The cause of Judge White is the cause of the South," shouted the enthusiastic Whigs. The Democrats, Whigs charged, had tainted credentials: Martin Van Buren was a political chameleon, and he even had abolitionist friends. In the face of this onslaught, the Democrats found it impossible to make 1836 a referendum on the old National Republican–Jacksonian economic issues. The universal complaint of southern Democrats, "Judge White is cutting into our ranks," forced a direct response to the Whigs. Southern Democrats defended Van Buren while they paraded the prosouthern actions of the Jackson administration—the ouster of the Indians, the destruction of the Bank of the United States, the hampering of the abolitionists. White could never win, they insisted, because the race was not just between White and Van Buren. Pointing out that three Whig candidates were running, the southern Democrats claimed that a large vote for White could send the election to the House of Representatives, where chicanery and dealmaking would prevail. With 1824 and Adams's triumph over Jackson fresh in memory, the Democrats had a responsive audience.

The southern Jacksonians stemmed the Whig surge, but the challenging party made a good showing. Although Van Buren won, the Whigs below the border took two states and won 49 percent of the popular vote. Such a showing by a second party was unprecedented in the South. Neither the Federalists nor the National Republicans had ever come close to this kind of performance. Along the border the Whigs also did well, carrying Kentucky and Maryland, but even the National Republicans had never been feeble there. The result on the border was another sign of the difference between those states and the slave states farther south, for the successful Whig candidate in the border states was William Henry Harrison, not Hugh White.

THE POLITICAL ARENA

The presidential election of 1836 took place in a political arena with wide-open doors. Although those doors had never been fully closed, after 1830 the democratization of southern politics intensified, in law as well as in practice. By the mid-1830s white male suffrage prevailed everywhere except in Louisiana, which embraced it in 1845, and Virginia, which did so in 1851. By 1830 the voters, not the legislature, chose presidential electors in every state but South Carolina, where legislators retained that prerogative through the Confederacy. After Maryland went to a popularly elected governor in 1837, every state did so but Virginia, where the voters took on that responsibility in 1851, and South Carolina, where they never did. After 1835 only four states maintained property qualifications for the holding of some offices, and only the two Carolinas retained them in the 1850s. In every state except South Carolina, most local offices were thrown open to popular elections.

Political campaigns after 1830 expanded upon the lively, even boisterous practices that had marked southern politics since the colonial era. The young John A. Quitman expended every effort to attain a seat in Mississippi's legislature. At a large gathering just before the election, Quitman astonished and wooed the crowd with his feats of running, jumping, boxing, and wrestling. He capped an impressive performance by outshooting the area's leading marksman. Then with a sure political touch he offered his prize, a fat ox, to the dejected loser and won the cheers and political support of the onlookers.

One of the greatest extravaganzas took place in Georgia during the heated presidential contest in 1848. In late August the Democrats staged a massive two-

THESE PAINTINGS BY GEORGE C. BINGHAM CONVEY A SENSE OF THE
POLITICAL CULTURE IN THE JACKSONIAN ERA
Top: *Stump Speaking* (Collection of Boatmen's National Bank of St. Louis)
Bottom: *Election Day* (St. Louis Art Museum Purchase)

day rally just outside Atlanta. The trains as well as the roads were jammed with political pilgrims. Thousands crowded the grounds, and "as the shades of night set in, the whole surrounding county was illuminated by fires enkindled at the numerous encampments, and every house, out-house, barn and shed in the vicinity, which could afford a shelter, was filled to overflowing." Speakers, bands, barbecues, and more speakers entertained the throng. The speeches went on almost nonstop; beginning on Monday afternoon, they continued into the night, started up again Tuesday morning, and stopped only at midnight. Special cheers went to the group that brought "a six pounder [cannon], and to the whole-souled Democrats, who took charge of it, the loud thunder of whose artillery was in unison with the enthusiasm that pervaded the whole mass." The faithful enjoyed themselves immensely while party orators urged them on to even greater exertions for the Democratic party.

In this intensified campaign activity the canvass assumed a pivotal role. Canvassing—or making a political speaking tour through a congressional district or a state—began in the 1830s and soon became commonplace. Often the canvass originated with one candidate, but two or more competing contestants quickly joined to make it a procession. The arduousness of some of these tours staggers the modern imagination. Possibly the most Herculean canvasses marked the tight gubernatorial battles fought in Tennessee between James K. Polk and his Whig opponents. During his first and only successful race, in 1839, Polk rode more than 1,300 miles in a little more than two months to make forty-three scheduled speeches and numerous impromptu ones in thirty-seven of his state's sixty-four counties. In 1843, he and his Whig opponent crisscrossed Tennessee for some 2,300 miles and spoke for five or six hours each day. It took these knights of the hustings four months to complete their strenuous crusade.

Southern voters certainly responded to these massive efforts. One-half of those eligible voted in 1836; that percentage reached beyond 75 in 1840 and 1844. In 1860 some 70 percent of southern voters cast ballots. Hotly contested state and congressional races brought out voters in equal and even greater numbers. These turnouts clearly prove that southern politicians did not have passive constituents. Keen observers of southern politics noted that southern voters were particularly well informed about political issues. It seemed that in the South "everybody talked politics everywhere," even the "illiterate and shoeless." This political sophistication impressed Daniel R. Hundley, an Alabamian with a Harvard law degree who lived in Chicago. Hundley thought the average southerner "on the whole much better versed in the lore of politics and the provisions of our Federal and State Constitutions" than his northern counterpart. Hundley attributed this awareness, which extended all the way to the "poor men in the South," to the political discussions that pervaded the "public barbecues, court-house-day gatherings, and other holiday occasions."

*A*NOTHER PANIC

Martin Van Buren hardly had time to move into the White House before the Panic of 1837 struck. For the second time in less than twenty years massive tremors shook the economy. Falling prices and wages, increasing unemployment, business failures, and foreclosures wracked the entire nation. The South was hit just as hard as it had been in 1819. In one sense, 1837 replicated 1819: the collapse of cotton prices heralded general depression. The weighted annual price in New Orleans tumbled from just over 15 cents a pound in 1835 to just over 13 cents in 1836, then plunged all the way to 9 cents in 1837—a drop of 40 percent in only two years. Slave prices followed the downward movement of cotton. In major markets they declined by as much as one-third in three years. This plunge in the prices of cotton and slaves wreaked havoc throughout the southern economy. The booming Southwest was especially hard hit. Planters and farmers retrenched and struggled to survive; some pulled through, others did not. Merchants, factors, and bankers found themselves playing the same desperate game.

The troubles that befell the Georgia planter John A. Cobb underscore the personal devastation caused by the panic. Owner of 150 slaves on his Jefferson County plantation and of an imposing mansion in Athens, John Cobb also invested in Georgia gold mines, banks, and railroads. During the panic his bank and railroad stock depreciated rapidly, and his gold mine produced virtually nothing. By 1840 Cobb's debts totaled almost $75,000 and his creditors were demanding payment. Unable to meet his obligations, Cobb suffered a mental collapse. His son Howell tried to help and most of his slaves were sold, but the hard times made it impossible to find a buyer for the plantation. Bright hopes had been dashed and a proud man defeated. This sad story was repeated countless times across the South.

The panic also had profound political repercussions for parties in the South. Simply put, economic depression helped the southern Whigs. Voters blamed the party in power for hard times, just as they do now, and the Whigs benefited. After 1837 the Whigs generally gained in state elections, and they looked forward optimistically to 1840.

President Van Buren's response to the panic also had a significant political impact. To remedy the economic ills besetting his country the president proposed the Independent Treasury, or the Subtreasury, which would divorce the government and banks. Instead of making use of various state banks to hold government deposits—Jackson's alternative to the Bank of the United States—Van Buren proposed that the federal government become its own banker. This approach appealed to John C. Calhoun, who had never been altogether comfortable with the Whigs, though he had been loosely associated with them since 1834. Moreover, Calhoun was especially pleased by Van Buren's ringing affirmation of states rights and his forthright stand against abolition. As a result, Calhoun announced his return to the Democratic party. His shift had immediate political fallout because the partisan allegiance of his followers could influence the orientation of state politics. In Mississippi, for example, the shift of the Calhounites gave the Democrats the upper hand.

THE ELECTION OF 1840

The Democrats were hard-pressed as the presidential election approached. Van Buren had numerous southern friends along with the loyal support of the party, but he generated no enthusiasm among southern voters, even among Democrats. No matter how vehement his declaration of friendship for the South or how vigorous his denunciation of abolition, most southerners could not overlook Van Buren's origins or his unsavory political reputation.

The Whigs were united behind one candidate: Henry Clay. No, the southern Whigs had not turned into National Republicans; rather Henry Clay presented a new political face. Jettisoning his American System, his economic nationalism, he wooed the South with advocacy of states rights and condemnation of abolitionists. As they embraced Clay, most southern Whigs also prepared to become part of a truly national party. The Whigs scheduled their first national convention for December 1839 in Harrisburg, Pennsylvania. Organizationally the southern Whigs were moving forward while ideologically they remained firmly in place.

Although most slave states sent delegates to Harrisburg and to a man voted for Clay on the first ballot, the convention turned elsewhere for its candidate. To southerners, however, the nomination of William Henry Harrison of Ohio posed no problem: Harrison was a native Virginian and a member of a prominent family. As a congressman he had voted with the South in the Missouri crisis, and in the 1830s he denounced abolition. The convention also helped the southerners in two other ways. John Tyler, a stalwart states-rights Whig from Virginia, was named vice president. And when the delegates, unable to agree on a platform, decided not to adopt one, the southerners were left free to run their campaign as they saw fit.

In the South the campaign of 1840 replayed that of 1836. Economic issues did not dominate the campaign. Even though the hard times surely made Whigs more attractive and Democrats less so, the parties did not emphasize specific economic programs, except for the Independent Treasury. Each party stressed its claim to be the protector of southern interests and accused the other of infidelity to those interests. The Whigs condemned Van Buren as unsavory and untrustworthy, and promoted Harrison as a true son and friend of the South. The Democrats, in turn, praised Van Buren's firm stance against abolition and his unswerving friendship for the South. Harrison they pictured as unprincipled and tainted with abolitionism.

The campaign of 1840 had a momentous impact on the South. Harrison carried seven slave states; even more impressive, he won more than half the popular vote below the border. Two-party politics had definitely arrived in the South. Although the South's allegiance had shifted since the 1790s, it had shifted en bloc. First the Jeffersonian Republicans and then the Jacksonian Democrats dominated southern politics. The Federalist party in the South had controlled only local pockets; the National Republicans were even weaker. But after 1840 two vigorous parties, each claiming to be the champion of the South, competed on an almost equal footing across the slave states.

THE POLITICS OF SLAVERY

The political war that began between Democrats and Whigs in the mid-1830s brought a special character to southern politics. This uniqueness is best described as the politics of slavery. The politics of slavery encompasses the interchange

among the major forces that influenced antebellum southern politics: the institution of slavery, parties and politicians, the political structure, and the fundamental
values of southern white society.

These basic forces did not suddenly spring up full-blown in the 1830s, yet before the competition between Democrats and Whigs, southern politics could not
properly be called a politics of slavery. The existence of two competing parties, the
increased democratization of politics, the volatility of the antislavery issue—
together they simultaneously caused and demanded a more intense effort by
politicians to reach a larger number of voters. To succeed in a two-party world,
southern politicians had to beat not only opponents in their own organization but
those in another as well. That competition increased the intensity of electoral politics.

The existence of a second competitive party was crucial. For the first time in
the South, parties seriously competed with each other to defend southern interests. From the beginning of parties in the 1790s southerners had looked upon the
political party as an advocate for the South in the nation. Because southerners understood that they had a special stake in the direction of national policy, no party
could flourish in the South unless it had an identity as such an advocate. A party's
prosperity in the South depended on the conviction of southern voters that it gave
first place to its duty to protect southern liberty in the nation. The rise of abolitionism compounded that political truth.

If a party was to prosper in the politics of slavery, it had to have a northern
connection that, at the least, accepted the southern interpretation and use of slavery-related issues. Because in the southern view the chief purpose of a political
party was to protect southern interests in the nation, a national party was essential. But southern partisans had to have the support or at least the acquiescence of
their northern comrades on slavery-related issues. If the northerners opposed the
position of their southern brethren, then the basis for a national party in the South
was undermined. Besides, southern politicians in that party would become vulnerable to the charge that they held to party alliance only for place and reward,
not to guard the South. Unchecked, that onslaught could endanger the attacked
with political extinction.

The faithfulness of northern associates was a requirement not only for success
at the polls but for the personal honor of the individual southern politician. His
party's defense of southern liberty allowed a southern politician to blend his ambition for power and place with the holy mission of defending the South. His lust
for the perquisites of office could be ennobled by his stated desire to protect
southern liberty. But if his party refused to stand with the southerners on slavery-
related questions, then his opponents in the South could castigate him as a grab-
ber for place and, even worse, as uncaring about special southern concerns. Such
a charge carried with it the stain of dishonor, and no southern politician could afford such a stigma. Unless he could demonstrate the lie of such stigmatizing, then
he stood dishonored as an individual and before his community. Both this vilify-
ing and the essential defenses against it remained unceasing.

Southern politicians, both Democratic and Whig, shared the belief that a national party provided the best protection for southern interests. Representing a
minority section, the southern party men grounded their strategy for guarding

special southern concerns on cooperating with northerners to gain national power. Such a national party precluded a sectional assault on the South because the North was politically tied to the South. To northerners, southerners offered the prize of national political power and the rewards stemming from it. To southerners, an alliance with the North offered the surest means of protecting their liberty.

THE SPECIAL PLACE OF CALHOUN

This party solution to the problem of protecting the South in the nation dominated the South to 1860. Before the 1850s only one major political force rejected the party solution. John C. Calhoun pronounced the fundamental premise of the party men fraught with peril. To his mind they wrote a fatal prescription for the South because they failed to appreciate both the numerical superiority of the North and the potential political power of antislavery ideology. In view of the minority position of the South in the nation, Calhoun feared the time would come when the more powerful North would feel "an obligation of conscience to abolish [slavery]." Thus he viewed as a slow-acting poison the political strategy so vigorously touted by the party men.

Calhoun's political force had an unsettling effect on southern politics because he rejected the rules followed by the party men. He and they approached the politics of southern safety from opposite directions. The politics of slavery that captured Democrats and Whigs came out of southern culture and produced a rhetoric designed for the South and southern voters. Most southern politicians were concerned about the success of their party, both in their home states and in the nation. Rhetoric spotlighting slavery was a political weapon designed to best the opposing party in the southern political arena. Accordingly, the politicians aimed it at southern, not northern, audiences. Calhoun, on the other hand, cared most about maintaining the parity of the South as a section in the nation. Although Calhoun surely wanted support from southern voters, his major goal was to confront the North with demands.

Distrusting the unwritten party compact, Calhoun wanted an open, public declaration from the North that southern liberty would never be endangered. He envisioned a declaration coming from Congress which would abide by his and the South's theory of the Constitution, the protection it gave to slavery and to southern liberty. Although Calhoun believed that the Constitution protected the South in 1840 just as it had done in 1789, he believed also that the rise of abolition necessitated a reaffirmation of that protection.

While the party men were preaching the politics of accommodation, Calhoun was crying out for a politics of confrontation. To ensure southern success when the confrontation occurred, he worked to unify the South. Urging southerners to turn away from partisan loyalties, Calhoun insisted that "the South should overlook all minor differences and unite as one man in defense of liberty."

Despite his attacks on parties, Calhoun did act with them at times, always on his own terms. After rapprochement with the Democrats in 1837, much of his political influence grew out of the close association of many of his followers with

that party. Calhoun made a mighty effort to win the Democratic presidential nomination for 1844. When he lost, he did not accept defeat as a good party loyalist.
Though Calhoun could look with disdain upon parties and keep his distance
from them when it suited him to do so, he could neither convert nor defeat them.

Calhoun never attained the southern unity he so desperately wanted. Wherever he turned, from the 1830s to his death in 1850, he met the implacable force of
party. Despite his dire warnings, he was never able to baptize the mass of southerners in his antiparty church. The major southern party leaders condemned Calhoun as a man consumed by ambition and as a fomentor of political difficulties.
They called him "John Crisis Calhoun."

PARTISANSHIP AND ECONOMICS

The politics of slavery formed the fundamental boundary lines within which parties in the South had to function. A party that crossed those lines risked political
extinction, but within them parties could differ sharply on substantive questions.
And parties surely did. Within the states and at the national level Democrats and
Whigs fought bitterly over concrete issues. Democrats praised their party for rest-
ing on "the sovereignty of the people" and condemned the Whigs as aristocrats
wedded to "odious distinction"—in southern politics a death sentence if allowed
to stand. A newly elected governor of Tennessee compared the Democratic party
with "the Church Militant: both fight against error—one in the moral, the other in
the political field." Turning aside Democratic accusations, Whigs cried that they
guarded "popular liberty" from the Democratic "political wireworkers" who
threatened "the subversion of civil liberty." Whigs proclaimed that only their
party guaranteed "the Liberties of the People."

The first Democratic-Whig division over economic questions took place after
the Panic of 1837. Just as in the 1780s and after 1819, the aftermath of the panic
saw deep division within the South over economic and financial policy. Politicians took divergent approaches to the problems of the times, and the like-
minded coalesced under party banners. Such differences had not been instrumental in the formation of the southern Whig party or in the origins of two-party
politics in the South; in the late 1830s, however, partisan loyalties sharpened re-
sponses to the depression.

Banking became the focal point of concern. The panic that devastated planters
and farmers also hammered banks. Banks had become an important part of the
growing southern economy, and they enjoyed bipartisan support. In discussing
the formation of banks, a Democratic editor in Arkansas observed, "No party
question was raised; it was deemed indispensable that we should have institutions of the kind." Banks furnished much of the credit that financed economic expansion, chiefly the purchase of land and slaves. When the panic struck, it not
only delivered banks a heavy blow, it also obliterated the general public support
that banks had enjoyed.

From the panic on into the 1840s, attitudes toward banks and banking separated Democrats from Whigs. Although events and issues were not identical in
every state, a general political pattern did emerge. Whigs generally favored

banks, and Democrats usually opposed them. The use of banknotes (or paper money) in addition to coins (hard money or specie); the suspension by banks of specie payments—that is, the refusal of banks to redeem paper money for coins; even the need for banks at all—these issues dominated public debate. Taking an almost classic Jeffersonian stance, Democrats attacked banks with their paper money and credit as harmful to the economic health and independence of southern agriculturalists. Whigs, on the other hand, pictured banks in partnership with agriculture in a common quest for prosperity. Whigs argued that states ought to encourage banking because it was essential for economic development. Democrats countered that states should not become involved in such matters; in their view, the economic future depended on individual initiative and effort. Across the slave states newspapers and election platforms were filled with discussion about banks and banking policy. In state after state bitter legislative battles over financial questions sharply divided Democrats and Whigs.

Economics and National Politics

The division over financial policy in the states received powerful reinforcement at the national level. President Van Buren's proposal of the Independent or Subtreasury, which would divorce government revenue and banks, divided Whigs and Democrats from its introduction in 1837 until its passage in 1840. Whigs insisted that banks and the government should cooperate while Democrats argued for separation. The division over the Independent Treasury did not, however, indicate any basic shift in partisan approaches to national economic policy. Southern Whigs and southern Democrats alike remained faithful to their common credo of limited government. Economic nationalism captured neither party. The strict constructionism of Henry Clay in the late 1830s and the campaign of 1840 testified to the hold that the traditional southern approach to national power had on the Whigs as well as the Democrats.

But in the early 1840s southern Whigs broke from the southern consensus and adopted economic nationalism. This sudden transformation grew out of the political turmoil following the death of President William Henry Harrison after only one month in office. Henry Clay in the United States Senate was determined to dominate the party through his influence in Congress. And a Clay Whig party would be dedicated to Clay's traditional program—economic nationalism or the American System, including a national bank and a protective tariff. After his short, unhappy fling with strict construction in the late 1830s, which had failed to gain him the presidency, Clay returned to his long-held views on energetic government and national economic policy. In a special session of Congress beginning in May 1841, Clay moved to repeal the Independent Treasury and create a new national bank.

Opposing him stood President John Tyler. The first vice president to assume the highest office upon the death of a sitting president, Tyler was a states-rights Virginian who had broken with the Democrats over nullification. Just because he had moved into the White House, Tyler had no intention of giving up his political heritage. The creation of a national bank struck at the core of his constitutionalism. Twice in the summer of 1841 Tyler vetoed Clay-sponsored bank bills. Those vetoes broke the unity of the newly victorious Whig party.

Southern Whigs could not hope to remain neutral in this controversy. They clung to Clay. This marked transformation, which placed southern Whiggery foursquare behind Clay's American System, had both political and economic roots. Clay had become the voice of the party; Tyler was branded as an apostate. Loyalty to the party, built up in two presidential elections and countless state contests, dictated that southern Whigs remain with an organization that promised opportunities and rewards. Besides, with the South still mired in depression, they thought a new economic approach just might turn into a political tonic. When a Tennessee Whig editor in 1843 called his state "A WHIG STATE—A NATIONAL BANK STATE—A TARIFF STATE—A CLAY STATE," he defined the southern Whig party.

The political distance traveled by United States Senator Willie P. Mangum of North Carolina illustrates the dramatic shift in southern Whiggery. Mangum had been a Jacksonian who had supported Jackson's veto of the bill rechartering the second Bank of the United States. After Jackson's withdrawal of deposits, however, he turned toward the Whigs and campaigned vigorously for Hugh L. White. Then he backed the states-rights version of Henry Clay for the Whig presidential nomination in 1839. But in 1841 Mangum became the ally of the real Henry Clay. When the congressional Whigs read President John Tyler out of the Whig party, Mangum chaired the party meeting. In his journey Mangum was joined by tens of thousands of Whigs below the Potomac.

OTHER PARTISAN ISSUES

Financial politics did not furnish the only evidence of partisanship in the states. Consider the dispute in Alabama over state support for public education. Alabama was so overwhelmingly Democratic that it never voted for a Whig presidential candidate, nor did the Whigs ever control the legislature. Thus the Democratic position that the state should basically stay out of education was never really threatened during the Democratic-Whig years. Yet Alabama Whigs never gave up trying to change state policy. They maintained that a strong educational system was necessary to improve the people and the state. To increase the visibility and political liability of the Whigs' position on this question, the Democrats who dominated the legislature often put Whigs in charge of the education committee. Invariably the committee brought in reform bills, which the Democrats proceeded to kill on the floor. Then they gleefully took to the public the message that the Whigs accused Alabama farmers and voters of "ignorance, poverty, filthiness, vulgarity and indecency." An exaggeration, to be sure, but the Democrats were convinced that such charges helped keep the Whigs in a minority position.

Not all local issues revolved around the proper activities of a state government. In the North Carolina gubernatorial election of 1848 the Democratic candidate, David Reid, proposed the elimination of the provision that only property-holders were eligible to vote for state senators. White manhood suffrage obtained in elections for president, for governor, for congressmen, and for the state House of Representatives, but the state constitution limited the right to vote for state senators to white men who owned at least fifty acres. The Democrats, who had been generally whipped by the Whigs throughout the 1840s, hoped they had found an issue that would turn North Carolina politics around. Applying to their proposal the magnetic term "equal suffrage," the Democrats proclaimed, "Equality in the exercise of suffrage among free white men who are citizens of our State, is one of the first principles of Democracy." This assault put the confident Whigs on the defensive, but they quickly rallied. Reverting to the rhetoric of an earlier time, they took the Democrats to task for trying to "humbug" the people with "newfangled clap-trap." Whigs mocked the Democrats' discovery that the voters had been "laboring under a tyranny and oppression" that they had not known they were experiencing. In the end Reid lost, but by fewer than 1,000 votes; the Democrats had never done so well in a North Carolina gubernatorial contest. "Equal suffrage" remained a partisan issue until the 1850s, when the fifty-acre requirement was finally removed from the North Carolina constitution.

Possibly the clearest illustration of bitter partisan division can be seen in Tennessee, a state almost evenly divided between Democrats and Whigs. In 1841 both of Tennessee's seats in the United States Senate had to be filled. Of course, the United States Constitution directed that state legislatures select United States senators. (The Seventeenth Amendment, which transferred that right to the people, was not adopted until 1913.) Traditionally in Tennessee a joint session of House and Senate had chosen senators. If that practice were to be followed in 1841, the Whigs would win, because more Whigs than Democrats sat in the House, though the Democrats did control the Senate. But it was not to be. In the Senate a group of thirteen ferociously committed Democrats refused to go into a joint session to elect senators. Their absence prevented a quorum, so no election could take place. For two years, between 1841 and 1843, Tennessee had no representation in the United States Senate. These principled or stubborn Democrats became known as the "Immortal Thirteen," who saved Tennessee from the evil policies of "this motley crew" of Whigs. A leader of the Immortal Thirteen, the future president Andrew Johnson, defended his and his colleagues' actions as protecting the fundamental interests of Tennesseans from the "vile wretch[es]" and the "heterogeneous mass" that composed the Whig party. The Whigs, appalled, spoke of democracy ruined and tyranny triumphant. This fight was surely a struggle over place and power, but it also occurred over the meaning of place and power, not only for political advantage but also for public policy.

Other local issues transcended party lines. The most fundamental of these issues rested on geography or state sectionalism, and they often caused internal divisions within the parties. Western Virginia and western North Carolina chafed over apportionment plans that gave more power in the state legislature to the older, eastern areas. Stretching back to the colonial era, these provisions clearly discriminated against the westerners, and the fights over them pitted west against east more than Whig against Democrat. Yet more Whigs than Democrats supported western aims because the east in both states tended to be Democratic. In eastern Tennessee, however, Democrats and Whigs usually joined to advocate state aid for projects that would improve transportation in their rugged land. Another source of friction lay in the three-fifths clause of the United States Constitution. Several states, among them Alabama and North Carolina, followed that example in apportioning legislative seats. Opponents, most of whom represented areas with few slaves, demanded what they called the white-basis plan of apportionment, which would completely exclude slaves from consideration. In North Carolina the white-basis plan tended to be associated with Whigs, in Alabama with Democrats, but before 1860 neither state adopted it. These sectional differences strained party lines because a party that forcefully adopted one position on a geographical issue alienated its own loyalists on the other side. Statewide parties found no easy solution to this problem.

Local political differences, those strictly partisan as well as those enmeshed with state sectionalism, existed for the life of the Democratic-Whig competition in the South. Some of the arguments antedated those parties; some outlasted them. The disagreements could be identified with the Democrats and Whigs only so long as those parties retained their political vitality, and that life span depended on their allegiance to the politics of slavery.

DEMOCRATS AND WHIGS

Divided over economic and other issues, the two parties carried their message to southern voters, most of whom were allied with one or the other. Pinpointing the distinctions between Democratic and Whig constituencies is a vexing task. Detailed investigations have generally failed to reveal dramatic differences between Democrats and Whigs on the basis of wealth, social class, or slave ownership. The best evidence suggests that Whigs, whatever their class or occupation, were more commercially oriented and lived in more commercially oriented towns and counties. This conclusion certainly fits with the divergent positions on financial issues taken by the two parties in the 1840s. Because of the overwhelming homogeneity of the southern white population, such ethnocultural forces as antagonism between Roman Catholics and Protestants, between native-born Americans and immigrants, were not at all central in southern party differences. Those forces did have a substantial impact in the North, but not in the South. Whatever the motivation for party affiliation, the identifications became intense and were reinforced by partisan rivalry in constant electoral battles.

Though the party preferences of various political subdivisions within states may be identified, patterns of partisan loyalty are difficult to establish with any certainty. Motivation in the political population depended in large part on family, neighborhood, friendship, local magnates, and similar forces—forces basically immeasurable and extraordinarily difficult for the historian to uncover, except in individual cases. Both parties, however, drew the bulk of their voting strength from planters and farmers. That was guaranteed by the dominance of agriculture in the South.

8
Plantations and Farms

———— ❖ ————

During the first six decades of the nineteenth century, just as in the years before 1800, the South was overwhelmingly agricultural. And the major thrust of this agricultural economy remained unchanged—the production of staple crops for market, often an export market. The plantation, the large agricultural enterprise, continued to occupy a central position in southern agriculture. In the antebellum era four crops, two traditional and two new, dominated commercial agriculture, but these crops were not grown across the entire region. Significant regional differences underscored the variety in southern agriculture.

Tobacco

The oldest major crop in the South, tobacco, which first brought wealth to Virginia in the 1620s, was still a major money crop two centuries later. Although tobacco retained its importance for many farmers and planters, its chief growing areas shifted. Tobacco culture spread from the Virginia and Maryland tidewater to the Virginia piedmont by the second half of the eighteenth century. In the nineteenth century tobacco largely disappeared from the tidewater. By mid-century the center of tobacco farming in the eastern South had moved below the James River to south-central Virginia, the area known as the Southside, and to the adjacent counties of north-central North Carolina. In Maryland the counties along the western shore of the Chesapeake continued to raise the ancient crop, but it was all but absent from the eastern shore. Tobacco had also assumed importance across the mountains in Kentucky and Tennessee, which by 1860 produced more tobacco than any other state except Virginia.

Tobacco country was not necessarily prosperous country. Prices were fairly good until 1807, but the Embargo Act hurt tobacco producers, and so did the War of 1812. When agricultural prices rose after the war, prosperous seasons returned for tobacco growers. But the Panic of 1819 put an end to the first good times in a decade. Favorable prices returned briefly in the 1830s, only to be swallowed up in the Panic of 1837. Finally the general prosperity of the 1850s brought a decade of strong prices. The table below shows what happened. In the five major tobacco states production fell by over 34 million pounds between 1839 and 1849. But between 1849 and 1859 poundage shot up nearly 181 million pounds, a 109 percent increase during the decade and a 73 percent increase over the 1839 total.

TOBACCO PRODUCTION (MILLIONS OF POUNDS)

	1839	1849	1859
Virginia	75.3	56.9	124.0
North Carolina	16.9	12.0	32.9
Maryland	24.9	21.4	38.4
Kentucky	53.4	55.5	108.1
Tennessee	29.6	20.1	43.4
Total	200.1	165.9	346.8

The rejuvenation of tobacco in the 1850s was based on more than a general upturn in agricultural prices. Around 1850 the Slade brothers, Eli and Elisha, of Caswell County, North Carolina, developed a new variety of tobacco that had a brighter color. A new curing process preserved the yellow color. Termed Bright Yellow, this variety of tobacco brought considerably more per pound than did the traditional dark variety. During the 1850s techniques for cultivating Bright Yellow were publicized. Initially Bright Yellow served as the wrapper for plug tobacco, but after the Civil War it became the basic ingredient in cigarettes. Bright Yellow clearly helped the price, but even more important for tobacco growers, the price held firm during the explosion in production.

Although Bright Yellow transformed price and use, cultivation practices change little from those of the colonial era. Early in the spring workers burned the vegetation on small, carefully selected parcels of land to sterilize the soil and destroy weeds. Then on these seedbeds the tiny tobacco seeds were sown. In late spring the young tobacco plants were transplanted to the fields where they would grow to maturity. But transplanting did not signal the end of careful attention. Plowing and hoeing were necessary to control grass and weeds, and the growing tobacco plant required suckering and topping. Suckering—the pulling off of subordinate leaves—encouraged the growth of the large leaves that brought good prices. In addition the main stem of the plant had to be broken off, or topped, to prevent the plant from going to seed. Both of these time-consuming tasks had to be performed by hand, as did the onerous and continuous job of picking green tobacco worms off the leaves. At maturity the plants were cut and hung in log tobacco houses or barns, where slow fires and smoke cured the leaves. The cured tobacco was packed in hogsheads, large barrels that in the antebellum years contained almost 1,500 pounds of the weed, and transported to market.

Because of the intensive hand labor involved in growing tobacco, a single worker, free or slave, could care for only two or three acres. Tobacco did not require expensive equipment. Careful attention to the many details of planting, cultivation, and harvesting held the key to a successful crop. Tobacco could provide quite a decent return per acre. In 1850 the gross value of the average yield was about five times that of wheat.

Tobacco

Rice

Hemp

Sugar cane

MISSOURI

MARYLAND

VIRGINIA

KENTUCKY

NORTH CAROLINA

TENNESSEE

ARKANSAS

SOUTH CAROLINA

GEORGIA

ALABAMA

TEXAS

MISSISSIPPI

LOUISIANA

FLORIDA

MAJOR HEMP, TOBACCO, RICE, AND SUGAR CANE REGIONS, 1860

Tobacco was a suitable crop for both large planters and small farmers, and both grew it. Fully 90 percent of the farmers in the Roanoke River valley, the center of Virginia's tobacco culture, raised the weed. The average tobacco acreage per farm in these seven counties was between eight and nine, far from massive. The larger growers cultivated the bulk of the crop. In Charlotte County, for example, 17 percent of the growers produced 57 percent of the crop. One of the greatest tobacco planters was Samuel Hairston of Pittsylvania County, who owned more than 1,500 slaves. In 1855 his plantations were worth $600,000 and his total wealth was placed at more than $3 million.

The potentially high rate of return for tobacco did cause one serious problem: it often caused farmers and planters to forget that the crop severely depleted the resources in the soil. Three or four years of tobacco could destroy the fertility of any piece of land. Agricultural reformers urged the rotation of crops and some growers managed to maintain the fertility of their acres by this means, but many more simply shifted tobacco to another portion of their holdings. Because most growers, even substantial ones, raised relatively few acres of tobacco, they found it simpler and more profitable to abandon a depleted parcel and plant their seedlings somewhere else.

In the colonial period most tobacco was exported, but in the nineteenth century an increasingly large share of the crop went to American manufacturers, who processed it for a domestic market. Although the amount of unprocessed tobacco exported grew to an all-time high of 198,846 hogsheads in 1859, by that time almost half of the crop remained in the United States. Much of it went to the nearby Virginia towns of Danville, Lynchburg, Petersburg, and especially Richmond, where in 1860 more than 10,000 workers labored to manufacture snuff, cigars, and the massively popular plug (or chewing) tobacco. The tobacco enterprise epitomized the old ways and the new directions that marked the South of the mid-nineteenth century. The oldest staple, which had been critical in Virginia for more than two centuries, provided the raw material for an increasingly important industry, the manufacture of tobacco products. And in the last decade before the Civil War both were prospering. In 1860 tobacco occupied a central place in a thriving agricultural and industrial economy.

RICE

Rice, the crop that had first brought wealth to South Carolina, continued to be a major staple in the nineteenth century. In the 1800s rice had not moved far from its domain centered in South Carolina—along the coast between Georgetown and the Savannah River, with a slight northern extension along the Cape Fear River in North Carolina and a more substantial thrust along the Georgia coast down to the Altamaha River. The rice area expanded so little because cultivation depended on the tidal flow of rivers, and even on restricted portions of the rivers. The acres devoted to rice had to be above the level where salt water intruded but still within the powerful influence of tides.

Along the tidal rivers of lower South Carolina and Georgia—the Waccamaw, the Pee Dee, the Santee, the Cooper, the Ashley, the Combahee, the Savannah, the Altamaha—stood the heaviest concentration of great slave plantations in the South. Slaves accounted for 90 percent of the total population, and their owners were among the wealthiest and most baronial of all the slavemasters. On James H. Couper's Hopeton Plantation, on the Altamaha, some 500 blacks toiled in the rice fields. Robert F. W. Allston, of Georgetown District, possessed 590 slaves, who worked his seven rice plantations totaling 4,000 acres. The prince of the rice planters was Nathaniel Heyward, whose plantations on the Combahee River he called "gold mines." When Heyward died in 1851, his estate included more than 2,000 slaves, 5,000 acres of riceland, and a larger acreage of timber. The value of the estate exceeded $2 million.

These enormously wealthy planters presided over an enterprise that combined a paradoxical mix of modern technology and primitive cultivation practices. Considerable engineering sense and skill were essential to a successful rice operation. To protect the crop from overflowing rivers and simultaneously to permit the regulated use of the tidal flow required an elaborate system of dikes, levees, canals, and sluice gates. All that building and maintenance necessitated an immense amount of labor; hence the huge slave gangs. Unlike tobacco, rice could not be produced by small operators. The massive investment required for slaves, construction, and milling shut out all but the wealthy.

The actual preparation of the land and the cultivation and harvesting of the crop differed little from practices of ancient times. The key implement was the hoe. Slaves with hoes in hand broke the land and prepared it for planting. Slaves, again with hoes, worked through the young rice several times to keep out grasses and weeds. Then when harvest time came, hoes were replaced by sickles, which the slaves used to cut the rice. Experiments were made with reapers, but they simply did not work well in the boggy ground.

The milling of rice—the removal of the kernel from the husk with as little breakage of the grain as possible—took place at three locations. Initially most large plantations had their own mills, but advancing technology so increased the size and sophistication of the machinery that plantation mills gave way to commercial mills. By mid-century commercial mills in Georgetown, Charleston, and Savannah handled the bulk of the crop milled in this country. But by 1850 most of the rice was shipped to Europe for milling as well as for sale.

Rice production did not match the sharp advances posted by the other major staples in the nineteenth century. In the decade before the Civil War it declined by some 13 percent. Exports showed no appreciable increase between the 1790s and 1860. Though South Carolina's share of the crop shrank from 74 percent to 63 percent between 1849 and 1859, the state retained its traditional position as the first state of rice. In the same period, Georgia's share of the total rice crop more than doubled, to 28 percent. North Carolina, which had a small gain in production, remained a distant third. Even when production declined, the price, which had reached its antebellum high in 1816 at 6.1 cents a pound, failed to remain strong. Between 1840 and 1860 it generally hovered around 3 cents a pound. Because rice planters were large operators, they could make money despite low prices. But in contrast to the rest of southern agriculture, rice was static. Rice certainly did not hold the key to either the prosperity or the economic future of the South.

*S*UGAR *CANE*

Like rice, sugar cane faced geographical constraints. Because it needed a growing season of at least eight months and plentiful rainfall, successful commercial cultivation was impossible above 31° latitude. In antebellum America this climatic requirement restricted sugar cane to southern Louisiana and sparsely settled Texas and Florida. As late as 1860, Louisiana produced 96 percent of the American crop.

Sugar cane came relatively late to Louisiana. It had no significance during French domination, which ended in 1763. Not until the Spanish period was nearing its close, in the mid-1790s, did commercial production of sugar cane take hold. The efforts of one man had a great effect on the development of the crop in Louisiana. In the 1770s Etienne de Boré emigrated from France to Louisiana, to a plantation some six miles above New Orleans, currently the site of Audubon Park. In the early 1790s Boré, desperately searching for a profitable crop, turned to sugar cane. Success, however, required more than the harvesting of a crop; it also necessitated transformation of the juice of the cane into sugar—the process of granulation. With determination and the assistance of an experienced sugar maker who had emigrated from Saint-Domingue after the great slave rebellion, Boré prevailed. In 1795 he made a profit of $5,000 on a crop that he sold for $12,000. Boré's pathbreaking effort led other planters to see sugar cane as their economic future.

In the nineteenth century sugar cane became the leading crop of southern Louisiana. As early as 1802 some seventy-five plantations produced around 6 million pounds of sugar. By the mid-1820s production had climbed to 30 million pounds annually. Substantial growth continued through the antebellum years. In 1860 the total was 221,840 hogsheads, each containing about 1,100 pounds of sugar.

Making a profitable cane crop was complicated and difficult. The anticipated arrival of the first killing frost, which would ruin the cane, controlled the growing season. Unlike the West Indies, Louisiana did have frosts, and the first usually arrived in early November. The cane had to come out of the fields before then even if it was not fully ripe. Some cane was cut before it was completely mature, but the fertility of the rich delta soil compensated for the lack of maturity. Frost also influenced planting practices. In the frostfree West Indies, the cane was replanted only once in every ten or twelve years, because new cane sprouted from the roots of the previous crop. Louisiana's frost shrank the twelve years to three; thus one-third of the crop had to be replanted each year. Stalks were placed in a furrow and covered with earth by a field hand wielding a plow or a hoe.

The low, fertile land of the cane region made for special requirements. Because most cane was planted along the lower Mississippi or its appendages on land basically at sea level, levees became absolutely essential to prevent flooding. The low elevation in conjunction with the high rainfall—almost 60 inches annually—required an extensive network of ditches to facilitate draining and bridges to make possible movement on and across plantations. A visitor to one plantation of 1,360 acres estimated that it contained 100 miles of ditches and 200 bridges within its boundaries. In the days before the internal combustion engine, building and maintaining these structures entailed an immense amount of labor. A planter had to have lots of people around. Obviously sugar cane did not attract many small operators. In the major sugar parish of Ascension in 1859, only six cane farmers had fewer than 900 improved acres.

The milling process further stacked the odds against all but substantial planters. The mill turned cane juice into sugar, with molasses the chief by-product. Initially, crude mills were driven by oxen or horses, but the introduction of steam power in 1822 transformed their operations. By 1854 over 75 percent of the mills in Louisiana were operated by steam. Throughout the antebellum era various technical improvements, such as vacuum pans for more efficient granulation, made sugar mills even more complex and required considerable technical knowledge and ability to run. To construct an up-to-date mill or to revamp an old one a planter could expect to spend a minimum of $12,000.

Not surprisingly, wealthy planters dominated sugar production. In 1860 John Burnside of New Orleans owned five cane plantations totaling 7,600 acres of improved land valued at more than $1.5 million. His sugar mills and other equipment were worth $250,000, and his slaves more than $500,000. His 1859 crop amounted to 3,060 hogsheads, which had a value of at least $250,000. Magnolia Plantation in Plaquemines Parish had over 2,200 acres, with 950 in cultivation; it fronted the Mississippi for more than two miles and had a massive levee system to prevent flooding. In 1861 Magnolia produced a gross income of $148,000 from the sale of sugar and molasses. William J. Minor, of Natchez, Mississippi, owned three cane plantations and 400 slaves, together worth approximately $1 million. As a group the sugar barons of the 1850s outdid in opulence their fellow slave owners across the South.

The marketing of sugar differed from that of the other major staples. The domestic market absorbed nearly all the sugar produced. Before the Louisiana Purchase, in fact, the United States had imported sugar from Louisiana. Now that Louisiana was a state and the American population was growing, markets never became a major preoccupation for cane planters. They spent their time striving to maintain a tariff that would give them an advantage over lower-priced West Indian sugar. And they succeeded for the entire period, but after the Tariff of 1846 at a considerably lower rate.

Sugar cane growers faced the same fluctuations in prices and weather that plagued all farmers and planters. Still, sugar was a vigorous and prosperous part of the economy. From 1840 to 1860 the price remained generally good, and in the 1850s it was excellent. The general sugar economy certainly shared in the prosperity of the last antebellum decade. No decline or fall was in sight.

COTTON

Although tobacco, rice, and sugar cane were important staples, none matched the undisputed monarch of nineteenth-century agriculture. Cotton was king. A visitor who journeyed through the region in 1827 noted that he never lost sight of cotton in one form or another. In Charleston he found the wharves "piled up with mountains of Cotton, and all your stores, ships, steam and canal boats crammed with and groaning under the weight of Cotton." On the main streets of the city pedestrians had to "dodg[e] from side to side to steer clear of the cotton waggons." When he moved inland to Augusta, he found cotton boats crowding the Savannah River and cotton warehouses covering entire blocks. As he traveled westward toward Montgomery, cotton fields, cotton bales, and cotton gins seemed omnipresent. Montgomery, he discovered, was "overstocked with cotton, and no boats to take it away." Finally the visitor reached New Orleans, where on his first night he attended a play put on in "a steam cotton-press house." A fitting end to this cotton pilgrimage came when he asked for directions to a gambling emporium. He would find it "at the Louisiana Coffe-house, just below the cotton-press, opposite to a cotton ware-house." This thousand-mile journey from the Atlantic to the Gulf of Mexico had been one long odyssey of "Cotton! Cotton!! Cotton!!!"

This trip from South Carolina to Louisiana did not encompass the whole of the area that was to become the antebellum cotton kingdom. By 1860 cotton fields stretched from North Carolina in the east to Texas in the west and from Tennessee down to Florida. Before the Civil War the cotton kingdom was never static. It was established in the late 1790s and early 1800s in South Carolina and Georgia, where its center remained until the 1820s. After the War of 1812 and the opening of the Southwest, cotton moved west rapidly until by mid-century the Gulf states dominated production.

The alluvial lands along the lower Mississippi River, including portions of Arkansas, Louisiana, and Mississippi, were the richest cotton country in the South. Enriched by the periodic flooding of the Mississippi and its tributaries, this soil provided a magnificent home for cotton. Not far behind was the Alabama black belt, which stretched across the center of the state and angled toward the northwest as it approached the Mississippi line, where it spilled over into a few counties. The black belt was named not for the thousands of slaves who toiled on its farms and plantations but for the heavy black clay that produced the bountiful crops of white gold. Other notable cotton areas were the Tennessee River valley in northern Alabama and the river valleys of eastern Texas.

This massive geographical expansion required fertile land and a labor supply, which the Southwest and slaves provided, but it rested in large part on a major technological advance, the invention of the cotton gin. In the early years the future of cotton was clouded by the difficulty of separating the cotton fiber, or lint, from the cotton seed. Cotton cloth came from the lint, not the seed, and until the two were separated, the process of making cotton cloth could not begin. Accomplishing this separation by hand was slow and tedious work, and basically uneconomical. Improvement was essential before the growing of cotton could become a major enterprise.

The key step was taken by a Yankee inventor during a sojourn on a Georgia plantation. Upon graduation from Yale in 1792, the New Englander Eli Whitney headed south to be a tutor and ended up on a plantation owned by the widow of General Nathanael Greene. Here he began to work on a mechanical cotton gin, a machine that would pull the lint from the seed. In 1793 he built a machine that had a cylinder with wire teeth which rotated against a hopper filled with cotton and tore the lint from the seed. He added another cylinder with brushes revolving in the opposite direction to remove the lint from the wire teeth. The cotton gin was born. Improvements would be made—circular saws eventually replaced the wire teeth, for example—but the basic idea was in place, and it worked. Before the end of the decade cotton gins dotted the southern countryside. The birth of the cotton gin heralded the coming of the cotton revolution.

The revolution involved short-staple (or upland) cotton, not long-staple (or sea island) cotton. Long-staple cotton—the designation came from the length of the lint after it was separated from the seed—came into Georgia from the Bahama Islands in the mid-1780s. The name sea island became common because this variety of cotton was grown only on the sea islands of South Carolina and Georgia, where it was a near neighbor of rice. And like rice, sea island cotton supported a few extremely wealthy planters. Production, like the growing area, remained largely stable: 11.6 million pounds were exported in 1820, 15.6 million pounds in 1860. The longer staple gave this cotton a silky texture, and the cloth made from it commanded a high price. Sea island cotton cost several times more than its upland cousin (so named because it was grown away from the coast). Between 1820 and 1860 the annual average price in Charleston, the central market, never dropped below 16.6 cents a pound and often reached 30 cents and more, all the way to a high of 47 cents in 1860. The corresponding prices for upland cotton in New Orleans ranged between 5.5 and 17.9 cents and rarely exceeded 11 cents.

The rapid geographical expansion of upland cotton was matched by an explosion in production. At the beginning of the century just over 73,000 bales were produced; by 1820 that number had almost quintupled, to just over 335,000 bales. The same kind of jump occurred during the next two decades: the number of bales topped 1 million in 1835 and reached 1.35 million in 1840; by 1860 the cotton states raised and ginned 4.5 million bales of cotton. The price farmers and planters received for their cotton was never fixed or certain. It boomed early, but collapsed after the Panic of 1819; in New Orleans the average annual price fell from 21.5 cents in 1818 to 11.5 cents in 1822. Through the remainder of the 1820s and on into the 1830s the price fluctuated, but by the mid-1830s it seemed to stabilize at a reasonable level. The Panic of 1837 ravaged the price, which plummeted from 13.3 cents in 1836 to 7.9 cents in 1839 and kept on falling to a low of 5.5 cents in 1844. Throughout the 1840s, difficult years for most cotton planters, cotton prices remained generally depressed. But the 1850s were quite another story. Expanding production, which more than doubled in the decade, did not undermine prices. Cotton brought a profitable 11.1 cents in 1860, about one-half cent less than in 1850. The Panic of 1857, unlike its predecessors of 1819 and 1837, had no adverse effect on cotton prices. This was a farmer's dream: price stability at a profitable level and production rising sharply. In the final antebellum decade cotton led the way to a general agricultural prosperity. Southerners could reasonably believe that cotton was indeed king.

The particulars of cotton cultivation enabled both large planters and small farmers to grow it successfully. The seed was planted in the spring, then hoed and cultivated until the cotton plants were large enough to be out of danger from grass and weeds. To make a crop one needed only one's labor, a plow, and a draft animal to pull it. Of course, the greater the acreage planted, the more labor, plows, and animals that were needed. Normally horses or mules were used on cotton farms—mostly mules in the chief cotton regions. The amount of cotton planted depended on the size of the labor force available to pick the crop. When cotton bolls ripened and opened in the fall, people had to go into the fields and pick them, and picking a given acreage required more people than cultivating did. Depending on acreage and weather, the picking season could extend over several months, even into winter. Unpicked cotton had no value, so growers had no incentive to raise more than they could harvest. A reasonable estimate is that for each laborer, free or slave, six to nine acres would be planted.

Once picked, the cotton had to be ginned and packed into bales before shipment to market. Although by mid-century considerable improvements had been made on Whitney's gin, the antebellum gins never became the technological equals of rice or sugar mills. Most substantial plantations had their own gins to process their cotton and that of neighbors as well. Few small operators ran their own gins; they generally used the facilities on nearby plantations. In areas of few plantations, a farmer or group of farmers would operate a gin that serviced numerous small farmers.

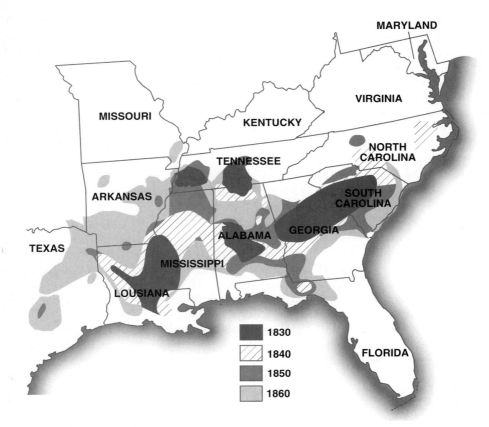

THE SPREAD OF COTTON, 1830–1860

Although small farmers did raise cotton, economies of scale favored the large planters. Most recent studies make clear that larger growers made more use of fertilizer, improved varieties of seed, and progressive cultivation practices than did small operators. Moreover, the substantial planters usually possessed the best land, produced the bulk of the crop, and made the greatest profit. In 1860, for example, in the richest cotton area, the alluvial river bottoms of the lower Mississippi Valley, the top 10 percent of the planters controlled 50 percent of the improved acreage and produced just over 50 percent of the cotton. This group of large planters also possessed 55 percent of the total agricultural wealth—the sum of real and personal property owned by all farmers and planters.

Cotton certainly formed the foundation for some of the greatest plantation fortunes. From 1801, when Wade Hampton I of Columbia, South Carolina, received $90,000 for a 600-bale crop, cotton provided wealth and power. Hampton went on to amass an agricultural empire with massive cotton estates in South Carolina and Mississippi along with a huge sugar cane plantation in Louisiana. At his death in 1859, Frederick Stanton of Natchez, Mississippi, owned plantations in Louisiana and Mississippi totaling over 15,000 acres. In that same year his three major plantations turned out 3,054 bales of cotton valued at $122,000. In the mid-1840s the former slave trader Isaac Franklin owned almost 11,000 acres in Tennessee and Louisiana. Between 1847 and 1849 his plantations produced on the average more than 1,100 bales annually. Farther to the east the fields of Joseph Bond of Macon, Georgia, yielded 2,100 bales of cotton in 1858.

General prosperity and expansion in the cotton economy depended on markets. And the textile mills of the Industrial Revolution had a voracious appetite for southern cotton. The Industrial Revolution came first to Great Britain, which remained the largest buyer of southern cotton all the way down to 1860. But the spread of the textile industry to the continent and its rapid growth in the United States created new consumers avid for the fleecy staple. In fact, as the table below shows, during the final two antebellum decades the continental and American markets for cotton were growing at a more rapid rate than the British, though it, too, expanded sharply.

COTTON CONSUMPTION

	1839–1840 (bales)	1859–1860 (bales)	Percent increase
Great Britain	1,022,000	2,344,000	130
Continental Europe	453,000	1,069,000	136
United States	336,000	953,000	184

Those numbers make it easy to understand why most cotton growers in the 1850s thought their market inexhaustible and their crop indispensable.

OTHER CROPS AND LIVESTOCK

Although southern agriculture came to seem synonymous with its major money crops—tobacco, rice, sugar cane, cotton—they were not grown on every farm or plantation. In some areas, mostly in the upper and border South, other crops predominated. In the bluegrass region of Kentucky and in the counties along the Missouri River in Missouri, farmers and planters depended on hemp, used chiefly as bagging and rope for cotton bales. Hemp first gained importance in Kentucky in 1790, and Kentucky remained its major producer. In the 1850s hemp production declined there, though it increased in Missouri. By the 1860s those two states raised 75 percent of the American crop. American hemp, however, never captured what seemed to be its most likely market, the United States Navy. The navy preferred the water-rotted hemp imported from Russia rather than the dew-rotted native variety. And down to 1860, despite political pressure, the navy and the growers never got together.

By 1860 wheat was grown in every slave state except Louisiana and Florida, but production centered in the upper South and in the border states. In the South per capita production of wheat increased in the last antebellum decade, though the South's share of the national crop declined because of the surge of middle western wheat. In the tidewater and the Shenandoah Valley of Virginia, in eastern Tennessee, and in Kentucky and Maryland wheat was a significant crop. Much of the wheat grown in these areas remained in the South, where it supplemented the food supply.

Of all the crops in the antebellum South, corn was the most widely grown. Every slave state raised corn. The leaders were Missouri, Kentucky, and Tennessee. Southern production went up continually, to more than 436 million bushels in 1859. At the same time the South's share of the national crop declined from almost two-thirds in 1839 to just over one-half twenty years later. As with wheat, the burgeoning Middle West outpaced the South in production of corn. Although as a commercial source of corn the South did not compete with the Middle West, southern corn production was essential to meet food and forage requirements throughout the plantation South.

The South also had a sizable livestock population. Cattle were found in every state. As early as the eighteenth century, the people who lived in the forests and back country of the Southeast kept herds of cattle. In the nineteenth century, herders joined the westward trek, but the continued growth of farms and plantations reduced their numbers and importance. Although cattle pervaded the South, by 1860 the westernmost southern state, Texas, was already emerging as dominant in cattle, and that dominance was to become pronounced in the postwar decades.

Hogs provided the basic meat in the southern diet. Pork was a dietary mainstay for blacks and most whites. Few people of either race passed many days without pork in some form—fried, roasted, or boiled, alone or mixed with vegetables. Almost every family with any land at all kept some hogs, but even so, a commercial market for hogs did exist, chiefly to feed the cities and the larger plantations. So pork became a cash crop for some southerners, especially in Tennessee and Kentucky, which between 1840 and 1860 had the greatest concentration of hogs. Much of this pork went southward to sugar cane and cotton plantations.

Not surprisingly, the South had a huge number of work animals. In a largely nonmechanized agricultural economy, draft animals were essential. Least numerous were oxen, though they were evenly distributed through the region. Horses abounded. From the sturdiest workers to the sleekest racers, horses formed a natural part of the southern world. Most southerners, whether they favored carriages, wagons, or saddles, could not contemplate transport for business or pleasure apart from horses.

The animal most closely identified with southern agriculture enjoyed little of the favored image often bestowed upon horses. The mule was singularly a southern animal; in 1860 southerners owned almost 90 percent of the nation's mule supply. Mules had infrequent encounters with carriages and races; they spent their lives in plow harnesses. Though horses outnumbered them, mules spanned the southern region. The major plantation areas, such as the Alabama black belt and the alluvial lands along the lower Mississippi, had a substantial mule population that worked in the cotton and cane fields. The large number of mules in Kentucky, Tennessee, and Missouri was accounted for by the raising of stock for sale to the plantations and farms of the Deep South.

ECONOMIC TRENDS

Across the southern countryside and in the towns and cities as well, prosperity depended on the health of agriculture. In view of the diversity of crops planted in the region, one economic condition did not always prevail throughout the slave states. With the rise of cotton, however, its fate had an enormous impact on the economic well-being of the South.

Although the volumes and prices of crops fluctuated from year to year and localities experienced their economic ups and downs, it is possible to generalize about sectionwide trends. At the same time, the existence of local variations must never be forgotten. Between the last years of the eighteenth century and the end of the antebellum era, the southern agricultural economy underwent five general periods:

1. Before the War of 1812: The introduction of cotton into South Carolina and Georgia along with reasonable prices for rice made for prosperity. Though not so dynamic as the rice country, the Chesapeake area knew generally good prices for tobacco. But the Embargo Act of 1807 caused abrupt change; trade stopped and economic stagnation pervaded the region.

2. The War of 1812 to the Panic of 1819: The war years were difficult but peace brought a return of good times, even a boom in cotton country. The boom was brief, however.

3. The Panic of 1819 to the Panic of 1837: Although the Panic of 1819 delivered a crushing blow, a slow comeback took place in the 1820s. Rice remained stable and sugar cane did well. By the 1830s a new enthusiasm stirred the South; once again times were flush in the Southwest. Many people became excited at the prospect of railroads that would connect the South with the Midwest.

4. The Panic of 1837 to the late 1840s: The panic struck ferociously; this period represented the deepest and most prolonged depression in the antebellum period. In some places cotton prices plunged to less than 5 cents a pound. Tobacco and rice also suffered, though sugar cane held on. As hard times wore on, optimism all but disappeared in bitter political fights over financial policy.

5. The late 1840s to 1861: Prosperity returned; the depression was a rapidly fading memory. Across the South the 1850s was the most prosperous single decade thus far in the nineteenth century—and it would not be matched until the twentieth. Everything went the southern way. Substantial increases in the production of most staples did not depress prices, which either rose or at least remained stable. The Panic of 1857, unlike its two predecessors, had little effect on the boisterous southern economy.

These five periods describe the general direction of the southern economy at specific times. That framework does not at all mean that within a particular period everyone prospered or suffered. At all times some individuals were making fortunes while others were going broke, and some managed to do both. Nor were economic conditions identical across the section in every year or in every decade. The Panic of 1837, for example, did not hammer sugar cane so hard as cotton. Other factors entered into the equation as well. The western cotton belt, especially the alluvial land along the lower Mississippi, was more fertile and productive than the eastern. Thus when prices were good, western planters tended to be more prosperous than their eastern counterparts; and when prices dropped, the easterners usually experienced greater hardships.

FINANCE AND A MARKET ECONOMY

In the South the size of farms exceeded the national average, and economies of scale did exist. Larger farms and plantations were generally more efficient and more prosperous than smaller ones. Of course there were exceptions, but large operators had a clear advantage, especially in the major staple regions. That southern farms and plantations averaged more acres than those elsewhere in the country was not accidental. In a time before much mechanization, the most serious drawback to expansion in agriculture was the need for large numbers of hands to do the work. Most American farm families had to depend solely on their own efforts because hired help was scarce. Throughout the antebellum years land remained available and cheap in the newer states and the less settled regions. Families that wanted to make their own way, and most did, could relatively easily buy farms of their own. Thus a substantial population of permanent agricultural laborers never developed. In the South, however, slaves provided the labor needed to build huge agricultural operations. Thus slavery gave to southern agriculturalists with ambition, determination, and good fortune the opportunity to move far beyond the limits imposed by a restricted labor supply in other regions.

Like most other businesses, southern agriculture required capital. Some agriculturalists—small farmers bent on self-sufficiency and the very wealthiest—might rarely need credit, but for most of them credit was just as essential as sunshine and rain. The cost of planting a crop, marketing it, and supplying the physical needs of a slave force, to say nothing of acquiring more acres or slaves, required larger expenditures of money at one time than most agriculturalists had readily available. Thus, like most other business operators, southern farmers borrowed. They borrowed from family members and friends but chiefly from banks and factors. From 1820 onward banks operated in most slave states, though their character, number, and wealth varied enormously. By 1860 Virginia counted sixty-five banks and neighboring North Carolina had fifty; Arkansas and Florida, by contrast, had fewer than five. As far as banking was concerned, the South was in general a poor relation to the rest of the country. In 1860 the bank capital of New York City exceeded $100 million, a figure greater than any southern state could claim and more than the combined total of all the banks in Baltimore, Louisville, St. Louis, New Orleans, Mobile, Charleston, and Richmond.

Most planters, however, did not deal directly with banks to finance their crops. Instead they worked with factors, middlemen who performed an indispensable economic function in the antebellum South. Factors operated between the grower and purchaser of staple crops. But a factor was more than a broker—a person who merely brings together seller and buyer. Factors conducted business in their own names, and they often made advance payments to planters against the money they expected to receive when their crops were sold. Quite often the factor became a planter's major source of credit. And if the factor did not provide credit himself, he arranged a line of credit for the planter. Factors supplied planters with a variety of critical information and services. To provide market information in both the United States and Europe was an essential duty of a factor. With that information and their factors' advice, planters decided when to sell their crops and in what market. Many factors served as purchasing agents for their planter clients. In this role factors bought goods and supplies ranging from slave provisions to clothes and furniture for the planter family. Thus the factor was at the same time a supply merchant, a crop broker, a fount of financial information, and a source of financing. For these services planters paid factors a commission, usually 2.5 percent of the gross proceeds from the sale of a crop.

Every major market center, especially the seaports, had numerous factors. In New Orleans, Maunsel White's career spanned the first half of the nineteenth century. White arrived in Spanish Louisiana from Ireland in 1801. Early on he became active in the factoring business, and for decades he was one of the leading factors in the greatest southern seaport. White of course arranged for the sale of crops, chiefly cotton and sugar cane, and advanced money to planters. In the supply part of his business White purchased and sent to his planter clients an enormous variety of goods, including skins, lace caps, bonnets, cordage, meat, and lard. White did business with an impressive list of planters, including Zachary Taylor and Andrew Jackson, whose affairs White handled from 1826 until Jackson's death in 1845.

White's successful career as a factor led him to other activities. He became a large property owner in New Orleans and a substantial sugar cane planter. His major plantation, Deer Range, downriver from New Orleans, was valued at $200,000. Committed to his city and state, he contributed generously to the infant University of Louisiana (renamed Tulane University in 1884). When White died at Deer Range in 1863, he had been witness to massive transformations in the economics and politics of Louisiana and the South. Such men as White were integral parts in the antebellum agricultural system.

Most farmers and small planters, however, did not deal with factors. They sold their crops to local merchants or to neighboring larger planters, often for cash. Credit could be involved; merchants or planters might provide various supplies, which would be paid for from the proceeds of the crop sale. For the smaller operators, then, the market tended to be local. They had only an indirect connection with the larger financial world of New Orleans, New York, and England, though that world had considerable influence on local prices. Farmers across the South had to make a decision about the market, about whether or not to participate in it. As landowners—and the overwhelming majority of all southern agriculturalists owned their land—they could determine their own course. In the eighteenth century many farm families shunned the market in favor of self-sufficiency; they focused on providing the food and clothing they needed. But in the nineteenth century, especially with the spread of cotton, more and more families became involved in growing crops for the market. The decision to participate in the market economy did not necessarily mean a shift to slave labor. Half of the farms in the cotton states had no slaves, but only one-quarter grew no cotton.

This movement from self-sufficiency to participation in the market was an on-going process. Not all farm families made the shift at the same time; some made it, then changed their minds; others never made it. Despite the diversity, the trend was unmistakable. More and more southern farm families joined the ranks of those enmeshed in the market; they produced a crop to sell. For most farmers going with the market was a major decision. A way of life was at stake. To say yes meant that providing food and clothing for the family took second place to the production of a money crop, usually cotton. But to say no could mean being left behind. When new areas came into the market, everyone tended to push for rail-roads and other improvements in transportation. A family with a crop to sell had to be concerned about marketing, about the availability of an efficient, inexpensive means to transport that crop to market. And wagons crammed with a few bales of cotton and pulled by a team of mules over miserable roads for considerable distances simply were not good enough.

THE FOOD SUPPLY

With so many southerners committed to growing crops for the market, the question of feeding family and slaves had to be faced. Concentration on a staple crop and the market could lead to bare cupboards and an empty pantry. Even so, individual insufficiency did not necessarily mean any widespread shortage of food. The South produced ample food to feed its population, white and black.

Regional differences and variations did exist, however. Major plantation regions with large slave populations and a massive commitment to staple crops tended to import foodstuffs from other areas. Cities, too, had to obtain food supplies elsewhere. Generally speaking, these needs were supplied within the region. The commodity most in demand was meat, chiefly pork. From commercial hog farms in the upper and border South, especially in Tennessee and Kentucky, drovers brought hogs down into the great cotton belt and the cane country. Cattle often followed the same routes. Coastal areas were serviced from New Orleans with animals first brought downriver to the Crescent City. Seaports along the Gulf of Mexico and the South Atlantic not only received cargos from New Orleans for distribution in their hinterlands; they also sent seafood inland.

The internal southern grain trade differed from the pattern established for meat. The major grain in the southern diet, corn, was so abundant that it never had to be transported over any great distance. Most cities' shipments came from nearby growers. Wheat was less plentiful and often had to be brought from other states. Charleston, for example, in 1850 brought wheat in by rail from northern Georgia, North Carolina, and even Tennessee. In the same year Mississippi and Louisiana received shipments that originated in the upper and border states and even in the Midwest.

*T*HE FORMATION OF PLANTATION DISTRICTS

In some parts of the South, such as the rice districts, plantations were dominant and farms were few. Other areas, such as northeastern Alabama, had many farms but few plantations and slaves. But in most of the South plantations and farms co-existed. In the major staple regions plantations were surely more important economically but they did not drive out farms. Away from those counties farms often had more significance, yet plantations could be found in substantial numbers.

Plantations had been a part of the Chesapeake and the South Carolina coast since the eighteenth and in some cases even the seventeenth centuries. By the mid-nineteenth century plantations were still characteristic of those two colonial bastions. In most of the South, however, plantations appeared only after 1800, and in the burgeoning Southwest usually not until after the War of 1812, when settlement began in earnest.

In the Southwest much of the best land that eventually supported plantation agriculture had initially been public land. In the 1820s numerous speculators and even squatters led in the creation of rich plantation districts. In 1818 John Brahan, the receiver of the public land office in Huntsville, Alabama, bought for $317,622 more than 44,000 acres in the rich Tennessee River valley. Much of that land, sold and resold, became prime cotton plantations. John Coffee of Tennessee, a friend as well as a military and business colleague of Andrew Jackson, used his position as government surveyor to purchase for himself and some friends almost 23,000 acres, many of which became the cores of thriving plantations.

In the 1820s and 1830s the Alabama black belt became a magnet both for men looking to make their first mark and for established families in the seaboard states seeking to renew or increase their wealth. All saw the magnificent black soil as the fount of riches. The purchase in Perry County alone of more than 90,000 acres in only five years, between 1830 and 1835, underscores the furious pace of settlement. Elisha King came to the black belt in 1819 as an obscure settler from Georgia. In 1820 he acquired 1,028 acres in Perry County and planted cotton. By his death in 1852 he was master of almost 8,000 acres and 186 slaves. In 1835 sixty-five-year-old James Lide, a substantial planter, left his home in Darlington District, South Carolina, for Dallas County in search of a secure source of wealth. With him came his wife, six children, one daughter-in-law, and six grandchildren.

But the Southwest had no monopoly on the creation of plantation districts, even after the War of 1812. In the older states plantations found their way into areas that had not previously known them. In upcountry South Carolina the development of plantation agriculture went on continuously between 1820 and 1860, albeit at an uneven pace. In some counties plantations took hold early; in others it never did; and in most there was a lengthy transition period. Thus throughout the antebellum era the upcountry knew change. By 1850 the upcountry produced over half of the cotton grown in South Carolina but it had only 36 percent of the slave population, which totaled over 50 percent for the state as a whole.

Hancock County, Georgia, in the lower piedmont between Augusta and Milledgeville, made its transformation only in the 1850s. During the decade the

THE PLANTATION BELT, 1860 (Areas Where Farms Averaged 600 Acres or More)

more affluent planters bought up land that previously had belonged to small farmers. That process diminished the number of landowners in Hancock by 16 percent. As a result, the white population declined from 4,201 in 1850 to 3,871 in 1860. At the same time the slave population rose from 7,306 to 8,137. With the multiplication of plantations, land values in the county shot up by 47 percent. The number of holdings valued at $10,000 or more quadrupled. Such property accounted for only 4 percent of all holdings in 1850 but in 1860 represented fully 15 percent.

Families pushed out by the growth of plantations usually followed one of two possible courses. Many of them joined the never-ending westward migration. This move might be to the adjoining county, to the next state, or to a location hundreds of miles away. In fact, many of these migrants left voluntarily; they were not really forced away. Responding to the call of newer lands and greater wealth in the West, tens of thousands of Virginians, Carolinians, and even Georgians traveled west during the last antebellum generation. These people happily sold out and headed toward the sunset in the hope of becoming rich or richer. When the Lide family left South Carolina for the Alabama black belt, several other families from the neighborhood moved with them. Practically an entire community went west at one time.

Others moved only because they had no choice. In the race for wealth they finished out of the running, their poor showing caused by bad luck, lack of ambition, or simply no interest in becoming enmeshed in the burgeoning market economy. These families generally tried to find a spot in advance of the plantation frontier where they could farm and live in their traditional manner. It was a hard living, though, and when the spread of plantations gave them an opportunity to sell their land and pay their debts, they sold out and moved on. Many moved often.

Although many families left the newly created plantation districts, either voluntarily or involuntarily, others remained and slid down into landlessness. White tenant farmers and farm laborers did exist in the South before 1860, though their numbers did not begin to match the post–Civil War figures. In Hancock County, Georgia, for example, the census of 1860 listed 198 farm laborers. Among them was David Ware, who migrated there from North Carolina around 1840. Toward the end of the decade he became a tenant on a plantation owned by Andrew J. Lane. Ware worked hard and prospered. By 1850 he owned 5 horses, 100 hogs, and two dozen cows; he also produced 650 bushels of corn, 100 bushels of peas and beans, 400 bushels of sweet potatoes, 3 tons of hay, and 3 bales of cotton. Ware seemed on his way up the social and economic ladder, but disaster struck. In 1852 his home burned, and he was forced, apparently evicted, from Lane's plantation. The record is unclear as to whether Lane wanted Ware gone, but that is a distinct probability. The result for Ware is clear, though we do not know the reason: his fortunes hurried downward. According to his former landlord, Ware's holdings "dwindled down to nothing." The census of 1860 carried David Ware as a farm laborer.

In 1860, as during the previous two centuries, the prosperity of the South and of southerners depended on the land. And as southerners contemplated the last four decades of the nineteenth century, they had every reason for confidence and optimism.

9
The Institution of Slavery

❖

When people talk about slavery, they are usually talking about the slavery of the 1840s and 1850s. They seem to assume that the institution always had the form it did then. But slavery changed over time. Though the institution of 1850 inherited many features of the slavery of a hundred years earlier, it was not an exact replica. Slavery responded to and shared in the continuities and changes that marked all other facets of southern life between the colonial era and Civil War.

CHANGE AND CONTINUITY

Major similarities spanned the decades. None was more important or more obvious than the place of work. In 1860 just as in the seventeenth century, the overwhelming majority of slaves worked as agricultural laborers. For two centuries they had provided the muscle power of southern agriculture. Two aspects of ownership also followed the colonial pattern—concentration and distribution. Although precise figures for the colonial period are not available, in all probability the planters owned most of the slaves. Certainly they did in 1860. But many other people owned slaves too, among them artisans and small farmers. Even before the Revolution slaveholding had been broadly democratic, and it still was in the 1840s and 1850s.

In still another important way the late antebellum institution resembled its youthful predecessor. As white settlers pushed inland to the piedmont and toward the mountains, black slaves moved along with them. This westward advance did not slow in the nineteenth century. When white southerners reached the Mississippi, when they arrived in Texas, their black slaves stood beside them.

Although similarities were powerful, sharp differences separated colonial slavery from its nineteenth-century descendant. Perhaps the most obvious distinction was the absence of slaves freshly arrived from Africa. Under the authority of the Constitution, Congress prohibited the international slave trade as of January 1, 1808. Despite the legal ban on importation, slaves were smuggled into the South down to 1860, but the numbers were not large. The best modern studies put the figure at around 50,000 over more than fifty years. This small group had no significant impact on the culture or demography of a slave population that increased from just under 1 million in 1800 to 4 million in 1860.

Though an outlawed international trade largely disappeared, a thriving internal slave trade assumed major importance. During the colonial period slaves were certainly sold in colonial seaports for employment in the back country. These slaves, however, moved relatively short distances, and the continued importation of Africans precluded the growth of an intercolonial slave trade. But the rush west after 1815 necessitated the movement of slaves from the eastern South to the western South. When it was no longer possible to bring in substantial numbers of slaves from Africa or elsewhere in the New World, the interstate slave trade burgeoned. It played an instrumental role in the westward movement of the slave population.

In a quite different sphere, and paradoxically, momentous change took place in the slaves' religion and probably in their family life. Before the Revolution, Christianity had made little headway among slaves, as whites showed little interest in intruding into their slaves' religious life. That situation changed with the massive growth of the evangelical denominations in the nineteenth century. Christianity became a major influence in the slave world. Whites pushed it and slaves willingly accepted it, though not without placing their own distinctive imprint on their masters' religion. At the same time, family life became more important in the slave community. Studies of the colonial period are few and evidence is scarce, but recent scholarship has underscored the primary role of the slave family in the last antebellum generation.

The increasing importance of Christianity and family point not only to change in the life of the slaves but also to a change in whites' perception of their bondsmen and bondswomen. In the nineteenth century whites began to speak of their slaves as part of their own family, a practice not common before the Revolution. This shift, so critical for whites as well as blacks, has been aptly characterized as "the domestication of African slavery."

THE DISTRIBUTION AND CONCENTRATION OF SLAVES

During the 1840s slavery spread across the South, all the way to the Rio Grande. After Texas and Florida became states in 1845, slavery was legally protected and constitutionally sanctioned in fifteen states plus the District of Colombia. The institution, however, was not evenly distributed throughout the thousands of square miles covered by those states. By 1860 the proportion of the population accounted for by slaves ranged from almost zero in some areas to 90 percent in others.

Slavery did not flourish in regions where the topography and the soil failed to support plantation agriculture. The great Appalachian heartland, reaching from western Virginia down to northeastern Alabama and encompassing western North Carolina, eastern Tennessee, and northern Georgia, provided a home for few slaves. This part of the South was generally inhospitable to plantations and plantation culture. When the Civil War came, much of western Virginia broke away and in 1863 joined the Union as West Virginia. Simultaneously eastern Tennessee furnished military units to the United States Army and was arguably home to more Union sympathizers than any other part of the Confederacy. Slaves were also exceedingly scarce in the piney woods of southeastern Mississippi, the mountains of northwestern Arkansas, and the vast barrenness of western Texas.

At the other end of the distribution scale came the sea islands that stretched along the South Carolina–Georgia coast from north of Charleston to the Florida line. There rice and sea island cotton plantations teemed with slaves; this is one of the regions where slaves constituted 90 percent of the population. Whites were equally outnumbered along both banks of the Mississippi River above and below Vicksburg, where rich alluvial soil supported enormous cotton plantations.

Most of the South fell between these two extremes. Over the South the slave population totaled 33 percent of the entire population. In every state slaves congregated in the sections of richest soil and most prosperous agriculture—Alabama's black belt, the cotton belt of central Georgia, the sugar parishes in southern Louisiana, the tobacco counties of Southside Virginia. The institution pervaded the whole of only one state, South Carolina. In 1860 South Carolina retained the position it had held since the early eighteenth century as the blackest of southern colonies or states, with a slave population of 55 percent. Elsewhere, only in Mississippi did the percentage of slaves reach 50 percent.

From the oldest settled area along the Chesapeake Bay to the newest in Texas, slavery was firmly implanted and growing. In the last antebellum decades all signs pointed to the continued growth of the institution that in the South was already two centuries old. The number of slaves in every state except Maryland and Delaware grew between 1840 and 1860, though the impact of the interstate slave trade moderated the increase in the older eastern states. With a slave population in 1860 of only 1.4 percent, Delaware was a slave state in name only. State law still protected the institution, but economically, ideologically, and politically its influence was rapidly declining. Maryland remained a slave state but it was unmistakably following Delaware's lead. The sharp decline in the percentages of both slaves and slave owners distinguished Maryland from the states below the Potomac. Far to the west in Missouri, where a battle over slavery had sparked a national crisis in 1820, a similar pattern prevailed. Only Kentucky retained a percentage of slaves and owners that still marked it as a thriving slave state. The border states, then, marked more than a geographic border; by 1860 they also marked a social, economic, ideological, and political border.

Just as slaves were not distributed evenly across the South, their concentration varied. In 1860, 393,967 southerners owned slaves, an increase of 13.8 percent over the number of owners in 1850. Still, only 4.9 percent of the white population in the slave states owned even one slave. But the owners of record were certainly not the only white southerners directly involved with slavery. According to census figures, a family in 1860 averaged five members. Thus, to obtain a more accurate count of the southerners intimately involved with slavery requires multiplying the number of titular owners by the average family size. The result, almost 2 million people, represented fully one-quarter of the white population, and in the eleven states that made up the Confederacy the number equaled 30 percent. With such a substantial proportion of white southerners having a direct stake in slavery, the powerful influence of the institution is easily understandable.

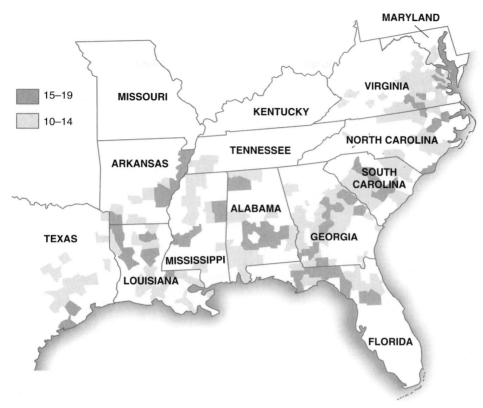

AREAS WHERE NUMBER OF SLAVES AVERAGED 10–19 PER HOLDING, 1860

Just as the ownership of slaves plunged deep into southern white society, it also spread across a broad economic spectrum. Slave ownership in the mid-nineteenth century followed the pattern established during the colonial period. It was a democratic enterprise. In 1860, 72 percent of the owners possessed fewer than ten slaves and more than half owned fewer than five. In 1850 those percentages had been 73 and 50. In both years the largest category of owners barely made it into the slave-owning class with only one slave. In 1850 owners of one slave totaled 68,820; a decade later that number reached 77,324. These masters were obviously not great planters living in manor houses or riverfront palaces. Most were small farmers or artisans who worked alongside the slave who made them legally part of the master class.

Historians usually consider that planter status required the possession of at least twenty slaves. Though the categories often employed are somewhat arbitrary, they are helpful: small planters were those who owned between 20 and 50 slaves; large planters, from 50 to 100; great planters, more than 100. Though the owners in none of these three categories was very numerous, they were still consequential. The substantial planters accounted for only 11 percent of all slavehold-

AREAS WHERE NUMBER OF SLAVES AVERAGED 20 OR MORE PER
HOLDING, 1860

ers in 1850 and 12 percent in 1860, but they and their plantations gave a special identity to the antebellum South.

The slave owners who dominated the southern economy and stood at the social summit of southern society could not match in splendor some of their labor-owning colleagues elsewhere in the world. Until 1861, Russia also had a social and economic system based on human bondage. The institution of serfdom was fully established in the seventeenth century. By the nineteenth century the great nobles of Russia had accumulated massive numbers of serfs. Prince Iusupov counted 54,703; Count Vorontsov had 54,703; Count N. P. Sheremetev's serfs reached the staggering total of 185,610. In 1858 more than 2,400 landlords owned between 500 and 1,000 serfs and 1,382 had more than 1,000. No slave owner could match those serf owners. According to the 1860 census, only fourteen southerners owned more than 500 slaves and of them only one possessed more than 1,000. Thus, while wealthy and powerful in their own domain, southern slave owners were neither the greatest nor the richest masters.

From the slaves' perspective, the pattern of ownership was the exact opposite of the one the masters saw. Most whites who possessed slaves had very few, but most slaves were members of considerably larger holdings. In 1860 planters with more than twenty slaves accounted for only 12 percent of all slave owners, but they owned 48 percent of all the slaves. In contrast, 71 percent of the masters with fewer than ten slaves held only 32 percent of the slaves. These numbers show clearly that almost half of the slave population labored for the planter class.

Like so much else in southern history, slave ownership did not make up a neat, tidy package. Slave owning was certainly not uncommon in the South. Without a doubt the wide extent of ownership over more than a century was of critical importance in securely fastening slavery on the society. Simultaneously, the skewed ownership pattern underscored the special position of the landed planter class.

SLAVE CODES

All southern states grouped laws governing slaves in "slave codes." The first codification of statutes pertaining to slaves occurred in Virginia in 1705; in the nineteenth century such codes governed the master-slave relationship across the South. In describing the condition of servitude the codes were invariably harsh. The codes had a simple basic thrust—the total submission of all slaves to their masters, and by extension to all whites. The Louisiana Code of 1806 did not mince words:

> The condition of the slave being merely a passive one, his subordination to his master and to all who represent him is not susceptible of modification or restriction . . . he owes to his master, and to all his [master's] family, a respect without bounds, and an absolute obedience, and he is consequently to execute all orders which he receives from him, his said master or from them.

The codes specified restrictions on slaves' activities. Slaves were forbidden to play drums or horns. They had no legal standing in court; no court accepted their testimony. Laws directed slaves to step aside when whites passed. Other statutes forbade the teaching of reading or writing to slaves, even by their masters. Slave marriages were not recognized by the law. Slaves were forbidden to gamble or trade with whites, free blacks, or other slaves. They were not permitted to possess guns. Limitations on the sale of slaves, even the taking away of children from mothers, barely existed. The slave was property, or chattel, and so could be freely bought or sold. In 1861 the Alabama Supreme Court cogently described the inevitable effect of slavery as "a complete annihilation of the will." The slave "ha[d] no legal mind, no will which the law [could] recognize."

The codes sharply circumscribed the lives of slaves. The Alabama Code of 1852 was forceful and direct: "No slave must go beyond the limits of the plantation on which he resides, without a pass, or some letter or token from his master or overseer, giving him authority to go and return from a certain place." Slaves who violated this law were to be "apprehended and punished."

The racial character of slavery underlay the enforcement of restrictions on slaves' movements. Any white could halt and demand identification from any black. Blacks out on the road had to be prepared to prove either that they were free persons or that they had permission to be away from their home plantation. From the Red River valley of central Louisiana, Solomon Northup reported that fear of the omnipresent whites served as a massive deterrent to unauthorized movement. Northup, a free black from New York who had been kidnapped and sold into slavery, confessed that apprehension about scrutiny by whites along the roads helped keep in check his great desire to escape his bonds. Although the entire white community acted as a brake on the free movement of slaves, one group had the specific responsibility of enforcing the laws governing their movements— the slave patrol.

Across the rural South the slave patrol provided a visible sign of white authority. Officially sanctioned by law, the patrol had enormous powers vested in it by the state or the white community. In view of the Anglo-American judicial tradition, the legal conception of the patrol and the functions assigned to it were extraordinary. The patrols possessed both judicial and executive power. The Alabama slave code of 1852 charged patrols "to enter in a peaceable manner, upon any plantation; to enter by force, if necessary, all negro cabins or quarters, kitchens and outhouses, and to apprehend all slaves who may there be found, not belonging to the plantation or household, without a pass from their owner or overseer; or strolling from place to place without authority." The patrols in Avoyelles Parish, Louisiana, were authorized to "take up and punish slaves that they [found] away from their Masters' premises without a permit." Thus patrols acted as sheriff, judge, and jury. And without any question slaves feared the patrols. Reminiscences of former slaves are filled with that fear.

Although the slave patrol was a formidable force for the preservation of white authority, it must not be equated with a totalitarian police force. Patrols were not the enforcement arm of an omnipotent state. Despite statutes calling for service by the great majority of the white male population and specifying a regular schedule of patrolling, men shunned such duty and the patrols operated sporadically, unless rumors circulated that a slave had killed a white person or that the slaves in the region were fomenting rebellion; then patrol activity increased sharply. A patrol was like a group of deputy sheriffs on call. When the white community felt the need for its services, the patrol could respond quickly.

PATTERNS OF MANAGEMENT

Slave owners had to manage their slaves. Because 95 percent of all slaves worked on farms or plantations, the overwhelming majority of owners were engaged in agricultural management. Because of the great variety both in the classes of owners and among individuals within those classes, however, it is not possible to describe precisely the practices followed by all owners. Still, a general pattern can be discerned.

Small farm families who owned few slaves usually combined their managerial responsibilities with their own physical labor. These families, the largest group of slaveholders, normally worked in the fields beside their slaves. Together they prepared the ground, planted seeds, cultivated the growing crop, and harvested it at maturity. In the off-season they joined in such tasks as repairing fences, refurbishing buildings, and clearing land. Though the master might assign his slaves a specific duty, such as caring for livestock, in which his own family did not participate, the white farm family and their black slaves labored together in a common enterprise.

The large farmers and the small planters were really interchangeable; the distinction between them is largely semantic. Although in our time the word *planter* connotes a wealthy operator of a large agricultural enterprise, in the antebellum South *planter* and *farmer* were synonymous. This person owned from ten to twenty or more slaves. These slaves were usually managed in one of two ways, but in neither instance did the master or his family engage in physical labor with their chattels. Instead, the master devoted his time to giving orders and managing the agricultural enterprise.

The first type of organization was quite simple. The planter or farmer personally directed the activities of the slaves. No other white person came between master and slaves. The master usually chose one slave to act as foreman of the group, or, in antebellum terms, the driver—the slave who drove the other slaves to work. With the help of the driver the master directly oversaw the labor of the slave force.

The second type of organization introduced another white person, a second figure of white authority over black slaves: the overseer. On farms and plantations of this sort the overseer occupied a central place, and on larger estates he was absolutely critical. The master issued orders to the overseer, who transmitted them to the slaves. At times the overseer would also work with drivers, who were responsible to the overseer just as the overseer was to the master. But with or without drivers, the overseer had responsibility for the daily labor performed by the slaves. Master and slaves might still have direct and frequent contact, but the presence of an overseer altered the relationship between owner and owned. To the slaves the overseer became the most visible, almost omnipresent symbol of white authority.

Large estates—the sort of plantations most people have in mind when they think of the antebellum South—had complex hierarchical organizations. No master of such an enterprise could possibly manage alone all of the wide variety of day-to-day activities of the many slaves the plantation needed—at least 50, often more than 100. The successful owner of a large plantation had to be an able manager of financial operations and of personnel. Market conditions, crop prices, interest rates, shipping costs all had to be carefully considered and weighed when critical decisions were to be made—how many acres to plant, when to sell the crop, whether to borrow money for expansion. The planter had to be able to cope with poor harvests as well as good ones, with low prices as well as high. Unless he managed his finances well, he had little chance to succeed at anything else. Of course, reasonably content, hard-working, productive slaves were indispensable to the financial success and stability of the plantation.

*O*VERSEERS

To ensure that he had just such a slave force on his estate, the large planter needed assistance. The large plantation could not function without an overseer; he was the key subaltern. The overseer carried out the general policy set by the master. He translated the wishes, goals, and orders of the master to the slaves. *They* may be a more accurate term than *he*, for a large plantation where more than 100 slaves labored over thousands of acres often employed more than one overseer. With no automobiles, radios, or telephones, one person could effectively oversee only a limited area of activity. Whether he worked alone or as one of several, the overseer regularly made decisions in regard to the planting, cultivating, and harvesting of the crops as well as the disciplining of the slaves.

Overseers were generally assisted by slave drivers. White assistant overseers were rare. If more than one overseer was employed, each usually had assigned tasks and a corps of slaves to supervise. The slave drivers performed the same essential functions on the large estates as on the small ones. The larger the plantation, the more drivers.

Without overseers the slave plantation could not have functioned as it did. In the antebellum South *overseer* had a very specific meaning: a white man who managed slave labor on a plantation. The overseer was the man in the middle; he stood between the owner and the slave. To the former he was the employee who made sure that the slaves worked to make crops and produce wealth. To the slaves he was the embodiment of white authority, of the power vested by the state in the owner.

Overseeing was at best a difficult job. It required a technical knowledge of agriculture—about preparing the land, about planting, about cultivation, about harvesting. An overseer had to be well versed in the particularities of the major money crop grown in his region—cotton, tobacco, rice, or sugar cane—and of the crops produced for food and forage, especially corn. In a time before government-supported agricultural colleges and agricultural extension services, the overseer's expertise was essential for a productive and profitable plantation. Many owners were also agricultural experts, but some of them spent little time on their plantations. The overseer was always on the scene.

Overseers also had to be expert at what today would be called labor relations. Sometimes the tasks assigned the overseer seemed impossible. His fundamental mission had twin goals that often conflicted. On the one hand, owners demanded the largest possible crop; on the other, they usually directed their overseers not to work the slaves too hard, not to overtax them, and certainly not to impose such harsh working conditions as to cause unrest. Plowden Weston, a large rice planter in Georgetown District, South Carolina, told his overseers that he would judge their performance by "the general well being of the negroes; their cleanly appearance, respectful manners, active and vigorous obedience; their completion of their tasks well and early; the small amount of punishment; the excess of births over deaths; the small number of people in hospital, and the health of the children." Failure in either respect—a poor crop or dissatisfied slaves—often led to dismissal. Thus overseers had to find and then hold to a middle way, but that way proved to be elusive. The overseer had to concern himself with more than his employer's guidelines. The slaves under his charge were not simply passive pawns who blindly followed his commands. Slaves often complained directly to their owners about mistreatment by the overseers. Whether or not an overseer had actually mistreated the slaves, such charges could never be cavalierly dismissed.

Slaves were valuable. And most owners viewed job security for overseers as considerably less important than a seemingly satisfied slave force. As a result, the successful overseer had to strike a balance between the concerns of the master and those of the slaves.

The difficulty of the overseer's position is seen in the turnover of overseers on most plantations. Many planters hired a new overseer every year. Trouble with overseers occupies a large place in the letters of planters. Time and time again planters complained to friends and relatives that their overseers were unsatisfactory. Dismissals of overseers and searches for new ones were constant topics. And always the complaint was either that the overseer failed to make a crop or that he mishandled the slaves. In the minds of most planters, mismanagement of slaves could fall into any of three categories. Most often it meant harsh treatment, but at times it signified just the opposite, loss of control. Occasionally owners intervened because of what they termed familiarity—the sexual involvement of male overseers with female slaves.

The problems faced in 1856 by Martin Phillips, a planter in Hinds County, Mississippi, illustrate the tension between owners and overseers. Less than one month after hiring an overseer named Champion, Phillips became dissatisfied. He let Champion go for laxness in enforcing plantation rules, but the two reconciled their differences and Phillips gave Champion a reprieve. More problems quickly arose, however, and in the middle of the growing season Phillips fired Champion again, this time permanently. Before 1856 was over, the harried Phillips tried two more overseers, with equally unsatisfactory results.

Most overseers worked for resident planters, but absentee ownership was not uncommon. James K. Polk, the eleventh president of the United States, lived in central Tennessee, south of Nashville; he also owned a cotton plantation in Yalobusha County, in the northern part of Mississippi. Living on and running Polk's plantation was a series of overseers, none of whom seemed to stay there very long. Polk tried to visit this plantation at least once a year, but he really managed it through correspondence with his various overseers and with a neighboring planter, who kept him posted on activities at his Mississippi property. The friend assured Polk that despite many difficulties, the plantation was not facing ruin. In an era when transportation and communications were slow, Polk's overseers seemingly had far greater freedom of action than many others. Yet Polk's experience mirrored that of most planters who resided on their plantations with their overseers. Neither distance nor the lack of it made simple the owner-overseer relationship.

This vexing part in the slave regime carried few social pluses. An overseer stood much lower on the social ladder than a planter, and it mattered not at all if the plantation was less than prosperous. An occasional overseer was a younger son of a small planter, but most overseers were young men who had grown up on farms, with and without slaves. Some of these people hoped to use overseeing as a stepping-stone to landownership and even slaveholding. In short, they wanted to become planters. Some did make the transition, and in that sense the role of overseer assisted social mobility in white society. One who did was Jordan Myrick. A native of Brunswick County, Virginia, he moved in 1803 at age seventeen to the South Carolina rice country, where he went to work as an overseer on a

Cooper River plantation. After twenty-five years of employment with the same planter, Myrick was able to buy a small rice estate and thirty-three slaves. There is no way of knowing how many men repeated Myrick's experience, but the record clearly indicates that the number was not large.

An overseer's salary varied with crop and region. On average, wages were higher on sugar cane and rice plantations than in cotton and tobacco country. Three reasons account for this disparity. First, cane and rice plantations tended to be larger operations and to have more slaves in residence. Second, cane and rice were more complicated crops to raise and so required more technical expertise. Third, the sugar and rice mills of the antebellum era were considerably more advanced technologically than the cotton gins. Overseers generally had to be knowledgeable about the critical first step that turned raw agricultural produce into a marketable commodity. Overseers' salaries ranged from $700 to $2,000 a year on cane and rice plantations, from $200 to $1,000 on cotton and tobacco plantations. In an emergency a cotton planter could hire an overseer for $20 to $25 a month. An overseer was also provided with a house and usually with land and labor for a vegetable garden. Inflation over the years makes the purchasing power of antebellum wages very difficult to estimate, but the vast majority of overseers did not find the job a springboard to wealth.

The difficulty of succeeding in every aspect of the job underlay both the widespread dissatisfaction expressed by planters and the high turnover among overseers. A few planters dispensed with overseers and took on the work themselves, with the aid of slave drivers. Bennett Barrow, a large cotton planter in West Feliciana Parish, Louisiana, denounced overseers as "good for nothing" and "a perfect nuisance." They made no positive contribution to southern society, Barrow complained; "I hope the time will come when every overseer in the country will be compelled to adopt some other mode of making a living." With the assistance of slave drivers, he kept a tight grip on the more than 200 slaves who tilled his acres. But Barrow was an exception. The overseer occupied such a central place in the plantation South that the structure of the plantation and even of the regime could not survive without him.

SLAVE DRIVERS

Overseers could not function effectively without slave drivers. Except for the handful of slave overseers, drivers were the slaves most important for the smooth operation of a plantation. Drivers held positions of responsibility. For this post, owners and overseers chose the men they considered the most loyal and dependable of their slaves. On some plantations the position became associated with a particular family and was passed on from father to son.

Drivers were usually placed in charge of a gang of fellow slaves. The number of slaves in a gang varied, but it usually was about ten. An overseer charged a driver to see that his gang effectively carried out its assigned task of the moment—planting, plowing, harvesting, repairing fences, clearing land, or any of the countless other jobs necessary to make a crop and keep a plantation going. The driver, in turn, was responsible to the overseer for the work of his gang.

Although he had genuine responsibility, the driver was still a slave. Though the members of his gang recognized the driver as a subordinate of overseer and master, and thus an extension of white authority, they also saw him as one of themselves. And just as the driver made sure that the slaves worked, he also represented them to the overseer. He attempted to protect his gang from impossible work assignments, from infringements on what slaves saw as their rights—the length of the noon break, for example, or the number of rest periods.

Planters acknowledged the special position of the driver. The driver often lived in a more spacious cabin than the field hands and other slaves. He might also enjoy a larger vegetable garden, better clothes, a more varied diet, extra privileges, such as more time off or special niches for his wife and children. Planters wanted all slaves to understand clearly that drivers were distinctive.

Drivers had an exceedingly difficult role to play, if they played it well. They were direct extensions of white authority into the slave community; at the same time, they spoke for that community to white authority. Like his overseer, the driver found himself in the middle—between black and white, slave and free—but he viewed the middle position from a different perspective. He faced a conflict that the overseer escaped because he was white. Some drivers tried to resolve the conflict by identifying their interests with those of the whites. The most responsible drivers acted to maintain harmony and order on the plantation. Though they never forgot the interests of the white people for whom they worked, they also worked for their fellow blacks by articulating their interests and desires to their masters.

WESTWARD MOVEMENT AND THE INTERSTATE SLAVE TRADE

When southern whites moved westward, so did black slaves. White southerners had become so dependent on slave labor that they considered it essential for their prosperity. Many slaves accompanied masters who migrated from the Southeast to the Southwest. Others went with kinsmen or agents of planters who invested in southwestern lands but sent others to manage the new plantations. In both instances slaves remained with their old owners or at least with people closely associated with them. Although the slaves did experience a sharp and usually permanent separation from their original homes, they were not wrenched totally away from familiar whites or even from their own kin and friends, unless the master had left older slaves with his relatives or friends, or had sold some slaves to finance his own move. The slaves who journeyed with relatives or agents of their master experienced a more pronounced separation from the old familiar ways. On the journey and in the West their ultimate authority would be not the old master but someone else in his family or his employ. That change might be for better or for worse. They also left behind friends and kin whom the master retained on the home plantation.

There is no way to know precisely how many slaves went west along either of those two roads. Travelers reported numerous caravans of masters and slaves

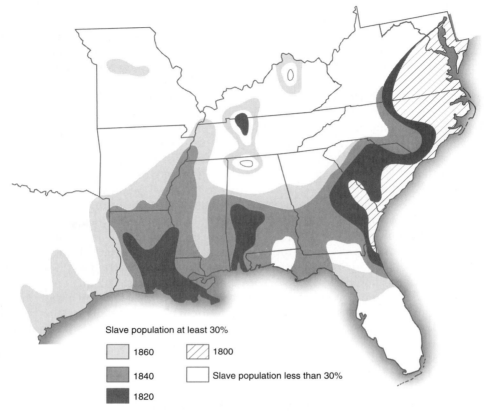

Slave population at least 30%

☐ 1860   ▨ 1800

■ 1840   ☐ Slave population less than 30%

■ 1820

THE EXPANSION OF SLAVERY, 1800–1860

traveling west together, especially in the 1820s and 1830s. Not all of the whites they saw accompanied by slaves were planning to settle in the West, however; some were slave traders.

The interstate slave trade was a thriving business that grew with westward expansion. It commenced in serious fashion in the 1820s and became a major operation between 1830 and 1860. The traders, who moved scores of thousands of slaves between 1,000 and 2,000 miles, were the latter-day counterparts of the great merchants of colonial seaports who funneled slaves to tidewater plantations and back-country farms. But the colonial merchants, no matter their wealth, never operated on the geographical scale of the nineteenth-century traders.

These traders bought slaves in the eastern states, initially Virginia and Maryland, later the Carolinas and Kentucky as well. The newly purchased slaves were then shipped west (or south in the case of Kentucky) either by the purchasing company or by other traders. Although nearly every town of any size had a slave market, two in the West became the key distribution points at the western end of the slave trade: New Orleans and Natchez.

Those cities represented the ends of the two great trade routes, by sea and by

SLAVE COFFLE, SLAVES HEADED WEST IN THE INTERSTATE SLAVE TRADE

land. Slaves shipped from the Chesapeake and from ports to the south and west—Wilmington, Charleston, Louisville—were destined for New Orleans. The ships that carried them were specially fitted for the trade. Slaves bound for the West went overland in what were called slave coffles—groups of slaves, sometimes 100 or more, moving under the watchful eyes of professional traders. It is impossible to ascertain precisely the number of slaves going west by ship or on foot. Each method was important, and each was widely used.

One of the largest and best-known slave-trading firms was Franklin & Armfield, from 1828 until 1841 a major force in the interstate slave trade. The senior partner, Isaac Franklin, a Tennessean born in 1784, began to trade in slaves as early as 1819. In 1828 he formed a partnership with a nephew, John Armfield, to purchase slaves and transport them from Virginia to the Southwest. The two partners handled separate ends of the business. Headquartered in Alexandria, just across the Potomac from Washington, Armfield was the buyer; his assignment was to obtain slaves to meet the demands of planters and farmers in the Southwest. To accomplish his mission Armfield certainly did not operate in secret. Washington newspapers carried notices under the Franklin & Armfield banner: "Cash for any number of likely Negroes, of both sexes, from 12 to 25 years of age." The company advertised for "field hands" and "mechanics of every description." And for them, Armfield told prospective sellers, "we will give higher prices, in cash, than any other purchaser who is now, or may hereafter come into the market."

Armfield bought slaves either through his own agents or from local traders and held them temporarily at the company's headquarters in Alexandria, to which he welcomed visitors, even abolitionists. By all accounts, Armfield presided over a well-run establishment. One abolitionist visitor reported surprise at finding the slave quarters clean and the slaves well cared for. He made the establishment sound almost like a hotel. But of course the guests could not check out. Eventually they would be transferred to the Southwest.

Franklin waited in the West, where he supervised the selling end of the business. Armfield sent slaves west both by water and by land. Most left Alexandria in ships, either owned or leased by the firm, headed for New Orleans. Many of the slaves were sold there, but some were transshipped to points farther up the Mississippi or even up the Red River. A substantially smaller segment of this human traffic marched overland to Natchez. An observer reported in 1833 that Franklin & Armfield's annual shipments numbered between 1,000 and 1,200 men, women, and children.

THE DIMENSIONS OF THE SLAVE TRADE

The slave trade, so well represented by Franklin & Armfield, was critical to the economic health of the South. After the international slave trade closed in 1808, southerners had no other way to populate the growing West with slaves. Some traders smuggled slaves into the country, but evidence indicates that the number of slaves smuggled between 1808 and 1860 totaled only around 50,000, far fewer than were needed to meet the demand generated by the expanding southwestern frontier. It has been estimated that between 1800 and 1860 more than 800,000 slaves moved by all routes from east to west. By the 1850s the annual total had reached 25,000. At this level the traffic had a value of some $20 million a year.

The slaves shipped west were chiefly under thirty years of age and came from the natural population growth of the eastern slave states. As Franklin & Armfield's advertisements indicate, traders preferred young slaves, both male and female. Young, vigorous slaves could better withstand the rigors of the journey to the lower Mississippi Valley. Besides, they brought the highest prices from planters, who wanted strong bodies to labor on cotton and sugar cane plantations. The impressive ability of southern slaves to reproduce themselves accounts for almost all the human cargo of the interstate slave trade. In the older eastern states, slave populations in general did not decline between 1820 and 1860, but their rate of increase was not comparable to the rate for the entire South. Too many of their sons and daughters took the involuntary westward trip.

The enormous size of the interstate trade often prompts questions about slave breeding. From the days of the abolitionists to our own time some people have talked of slave-breeding farms and plantations, presumably conducted just like an animal-breeding operation. Whether commercial slave breeding was practiced is a vexing problem. Massive literary evidence lends no credence to any argument for sizable breeding establishments. Recently more quantitative-oriented historians, known as cliometricians or econometricians, have attempted to throw light on this issue. After studying a computer sample of cotton plantations and incorporating statistics on the ages and sexes of slaves, they conclude that less than 1 percent of the more than 5,200 farms and plantations in the sample could have been slave-breeding centers—that is, farms or plantations with three times as many women as men between the ages of fifteen and forty-four plus an unusually large percentage of children under age fourteen. The tiny percentage in this instance along with the absence of literary evidence leads to only one logical conclusion. Although it is reasonable to assume that in a society as large and diverse as the antebellum South some entrepreneurs may have bred slaves in the expectation of making a profit by selling their offspring at some time in the indefinite future, such operations were rare. Slave breeding never assumed any commercial importance in the South.

Southerners clearly recognized the centrality of the trade. They knew that their economic health and political power depended on the movement of slaves from east to west. And they acted on that knowledge. As early as 1807, when Congress outlawed the international trade, southerners made sure that no prohibitory laws touched any other aspect of slavery, including the interstate trade. Southerners in Congress continued to fend off all attempts to tamper with their slave trade. An important weapon in the southern arsenal against the Republican party in the late 1850s was the charge that Republicans intended to interfere with the trade through the interstate commerce clause of the Constitution. The potential of such interference southerners depicted as dangerous.

Most southerners were not hypocrites about the trade—almost every community of any size had its slave market—though some were clearly troubled by it. Perhaps the most vigorous denunciation of the men who traded in human beings came from the pen of Daniel R. Hundley, an Alabama native and ardent defender of the South. In 1860 Hundley described the typical trader as "a coarse, ill-bred person, provincial in speech and manners, with a cross-looking phiz, a whiskey-tinctured nose, cold, hard-looking eyes, a dirty tobacco-stained mouth, and shabby dress."

Yet traders were by no means social pariahs. The trade made Isaac Franklin a wealthy, respected planter. At his death his estate was valued at $750,000. It included Angola, a large plantation fronting the Mississippi River in Louisiana; Angola is now the name and site of the Louisiana State Penitentiary. In Charleston, Louis de Saussure and Thomas Gadsden, holders of aristocratic names and prominent social positions, were major slave traders. These men followed in the path of the great eighteenth-century merchant Henry Laurens, whose dealing in slaves helped make him rich and powerful. In neither the eighteenth nor the nineteenth century did the occupation of buying and selling slaves do anything to lower one's social standing, if one had such standing to begin with, or to prevent one from acquiring high status, if one were successful.

THE PROFITABILITY OF SLAVEHOLDING

Slave owning was itself a commercial enterprise. Although at times masters and slaves developed a deep, caring reciprocal relationship, the slave plantation or farm had to return a profit on the capital invested in it. Unless he made some money, the master would not forever remain an owner of slaves and acres. The profitability of slaveholding had two separate but related dimensions: the individual slave owner and the South as a whole.

Slavery as a labor system was financially rewarding for masters. Of course, over the years individual slave owners prospered and went bankrupt, just as businessmen of all sorts have always done, but masters could expect to make money. This conclusion is generally accepted by historians. Current scholarly investigations of profitability differ considerably in methodology from earlier approaches. Historians used to look only at account books and ledgers of individual planters, then use accounting procedures to decide whether or not that individual planter made or lost money. That approach remains useful for study of people who left full financial records. But in the late 1950s scholars began to employ economic theory and economic models in an effort to generalize about profitability. Using this new methodology, the cliometricians or econometricians have made a powerful case for the profitability of slavery. They are convinced that slavery returned a profit for masters across the South. This view has swept the field; now most historians of slavery and the South accept the proposition that in general masters who invested in a slave plantation could anticipate a return that matched investments in business enterprises in the North.

This generalization about profit is subject to two qualifications, First, there were economies of scale; larger plantations tended to generate a better return than smaller plantations and farms. Second, sectional variations within the South determined the formula by which profit was calculated. In the Southwest, enormously fertile land produced tremendous crops and profits. But back in the older, eastern states, the income from slave sales made up a critical component of the equation that yielded return on investment. In these areas agriculture alone could not normally guarantee a rate of return that meant prosperity. Thus the interstate slave trade was essential for the maintenance of prosperity in the Southeast as well as for the source of labor in the Southwest.

The economic prosperity of the South matched the financial success of slave owners. Slave labor underlay an economy that performed impressively during the last antebellum generation. Although the Panic of 1837 struck the South and the nation a severe blow, the slave states began to recover in the mid-1840s and went on to sustained growth and prosperity. Between 1840 and 1860 the value of slaves increased from just under $3 billion to more than $6 billion. Cotton gave the South a comparative advantage that supported an explosion in production which did not splinter prices. The number of bales produced from 1840 to 1860 shot up from 1.35 million to 4.5 million while the price moved upward from around 9 cents to about 11 cents a pound. Although historians do not agree about either the short-term or the long-term effects of slavery on industrial growth, capital invested in manufacturing in the South leaped from just over $53 million in 1840 to $163.7 million in 1860. In the two decades between 1840 and 1860, per capita income in the South advanced by 39 percent, above the national average. In the middle of the nineteenth century a growing economy and general prosperity gave the slave South every reason for optimism.

10

The World of the Slaves

❖

*I*n 1860 some 4 million black slaves lived in the South, a fourfold increase since
the beginning of the nineteenth century. The influence of slavery was felt in
every aspect of the white South. External events had a tremendous impact on
the course of slave society. The technological developments that modernized the
textile industry, first in Britain and later in the United States, stimulated a seemingly insatiable demand for cotton. The invention of the cotton gin made it economically feasible to grow enough cotton to meet a good part of that demand.
And the opening of the old Southwest following the War of 1812 ensured the massive horizontal expansion of cotton agriculture.

Two other events affected the cultural values that shaped the slave world. The
rise of evangelical Christianity in the late eighteenth and early nineteenth centuries paved the way for the Christianization of the slaves. The almost simultaneous closing of the international slave trade precluded any substantial infusion of
newly enslaved Africans into the American slave population. And in the absence
of large numbers of imported slaves, no major challenge was offered to the direction taken by an increasingly American slave community.

WORK

The agricultural work performed by most slaves had a seasonal and rhythmic
pace that depended on the crop. Slaves were involved in every phase of agricultural production—preparing the ground, cultivating the crop, harvesting it, and
doing the curing, ginning, or milling necessary to prepare it for market.

Few slaves were exempt. Masters generally permitted only the very young,
the very old, and the infirm to escape work. On plantations children generally
started out as one-quarter hands, progressed as young teenagers to one-half
hands, and finally became full or prime hands. When age at last slowed their
work, they moved back down the slope from full to one-quarter hands. This rat-
ing system was applied to both men and women. Many women worked in the

fields beside the men, though on large plantations some served as household workers and nurses.

On plantations two basic schemes of work prevailed, the task system and the gang system. As the gang system pervaded the cotton kingdom, it became the dominant mode in the slave South. This was the system of slave gangs supervised by drivers, and ultimately by overseers. A traveler in Mississippi in the 1850s saw the gang system in action. He "found in the field thirty ploughs, moving together, turning the earth from the cotton plants, and from thirty to forty hoers, the latter mainly women, with a black driver walking among them with a whip, which he often cracked at them. . . . All worked very steadily." The gangs usually worked from sun to sun. An overseer reported that he rarely started his gangs "fore daylight." A field hand in South Carolina spoke of long hours. "I was always obliged to be in the field by sunrise," he remembered, "and I labored till dark." From sunrise to sunset—that was the norm.

The task system was prevalent in the rice country and was widely used in the cultivation of hemp, but it found few adherents elsewhere. This system, too, organized slaves in small work groups under drivers and overseers, but the basic work assignment differed. Instead of keeping at a job every working hour, each slave had a specific task or tasks to accomplish. On his rice plantations in Georgetown District, South Carolina, Robert F. W. Allston expected an able-bodied man with a spade to break 1,500 square feet (one-thirtieth of an acre) of riceland in a day, after it had been turned by a plow. On Allston's plantations the overseers set the daily tasks and the drivers saw to their completion. On Oxmoor, the plantation seat of the Bullitt family near Louisville, Kentucky, a slave was required to break 100 pounds of hemp a day. Slaves had to finish the task or tasks assigned to them, which might or might not take up all the daylight hours.

The work of slaves was not always directly connected with crops. Some jobs, such as feeding and caring for livestock, had to be done every day; other duties occupied slaves during the slack times in the cycle of crop production. Slaves did the work essential to keep the plantation or farm in good running order. They built new fences and buildings, maintained and repaired old ones, cleaned ditches, cleared new ground, and engaged in a multitude of other activities so that the chief enterprise, the production of a staple crop, could succeed.

On large estates some slaves became specialists, the skilled artisans of the plantation world. Though they were never so numerous as the field hands, these experts were a critical part of the work force. Neither the farming nor the household operations of a plantation could function smoothly without their skills. The northern traveler Frederick Law Olmsted found a variety of specialized jobs on a cotton plantation outside Natchez. Here the work of 135 slaves was dedicated to raising cotton. The sixty-seven field hands and their drivers were supported by a specialist group that included a blacksmith, a carpenter, a wheelwright, a teamster, a keeper of the stable, a hog tender, a cattle tender, two seamstresses, a midwife, a nurse, and a cook for the overseer. The manor house on the typical plantation required at least cooks, butlers, maids, nurses for the children, and gardeners. Obviously not every plantation slave was a common field laborer. Slaves filled numerous skilled and even managerial positions.

WORK STRATEGIES

To motivate their slaves to work, most masters employed two basic strategies—incentive and force, the proverbial carrot and stick. Incentive had two dimensions. The first was a general demonstration that the master cared about the slaves. He demonstrated his concern by treating them fairly, providing decent housing and ample food, and keeping families together. An owner who made clear to the slaves that their welfare was important to him won their loyalty, occasionally even praise. Solomon Northup described his master, William Ford, as a "kind, noble, candid, Christian man." As long as he belonged to Ford, Northup did his very best. Northup acted upon his conviction that "fortunate was the slave who came to [Ford's] possession."

Masters also developed a variety of incentives designed to cultivate loyalty and reward specific acts. Permitting slaves, at least favored slaves, to have their own gardens was not uncommon. The Florida planter George Jones allowed the head of each slave cabin a quarter-acre allotment or "garden patch" behind the cabin. That patch enriched the slaves' diet with a variety of vegetables, such as tomatoes, corn, yams, okra, and collards. Others went even further and permitted slaves to sell surplus vegetables, even cotton. On his Hill of Howth plantation in Greene County, Alabama, William Gould permitted his slaves to grow their own cotton. In 1840 his cotton book recorded the pounds of cotton produced by his slaves: "David 1140, Jordan 730, Phil 850, Bill 1000, Bob 947, Peter 1050, Augustus 500 and Squire 475."

Many provided rewards for faithful and superior service. A Tennessee planter noted in his diary that he had "given the servants a Dinner on Saturday in commemoration of their faithful working." Thomas Dabney of Hinds County, Mississippi, provided small cash prizes—just a few cents—for his best cotton pickers. Hugh Davis of Alabama was one of many planters who divided slaves into rival teams that competed for prizes, which ranged from cash to food supplements to extra time off.

This incentive system was not a one-way street. Evidence abounds that slaves influenced their own situations. By custom and often by law, Sunday was the slaves' day. Except for punishment and essential duties, masters left the slaves to their own activities. When slaves did labor for their masters on Sunday, payment of a wage underscored the unusual circumstances. Payment for work on Sunday was so widespread that the practice was seemingly institutionalized. In 1836 the Supreme Court of Louisiana declared that "slaves are entitled to the produce of their labor of Sunday; even the master is bound to remunerate them, if he employs them." In the face of such a deep-seated tradition—which the slaves, of course, considered a right—only a reckless master would fail to honor it.

Direct communication with owners provided an opportunity for slaves to protect their interests, especially against overseers. A planter wrote to his overseer in 1858 that the slaves were to be permitted "to come to [him] with their complaints and grievances and in no instance shall they be punished for so doing." The slaves of such masters had a direct influence on their treatment, for those masters responded to their slaves' opinions. "I found so much dissatisfaction among the negroes that I placed under [my overseer's] charge," wrote an Alabama planter, "that I could not feel satisfied to continue him in my employment." Slaves' reports of an overseer's abuse of pregnant women relayed by the plantation physician brought a prompt and firm response from the Georgia planter-politician Howell Cobb. Although the slaves' situation was certainly not enviable, they were not totally helpless. They could act, and they did act to defend their interests.

At the same time, the use of force was an omnipresent reality in the slave South. Almost all well-run plantations had rules that stipulated specific punishments for violations: extra work, cancellation of a scheduled Saturday-night dance, solitary confinement or the stocks, and a multiplicity of other deprivations and restrictions. But eventually all had to rely on force, especially the whip, which became the symbol of white authority. The use and abuse of the whip varied widely. While the whip cracked rarely on some plantations and on others often, it was never absent. Bennett Barrow of Louisiana, a hard master, did not hesitate to use his; some of his slaves averaged a whipping a month. On some Sea Island plantations every slave's back was scarred. Whipping offenses included running away (the most serious), stealing, and poor work. Every slave realized that he or she might feel the sting of the lash. And the accounts of former slaves indicate their acknowledgment of its power. The universal application of physical force by white upon black had a profound impact on both. Its meaning has never been more acutely discerned than by a conscientious North Carolina slaveholder: "It is a pity that agreeable to the nature of things Slavery and Tyranny must go together and that there is no such thing as having an obedient and useful Slave, without the painful exercise of undue and tyrannical authority."

INDUSTRIAL SLAVES AND SLAVE HIRING

Some 5 percent of slaves worked in industrial enterprises, ranging from lumbering operations to city factories. The number of such slaves increased over time as the southern industrial economy expanded, though the figures remained small throughout the slave era. Almost every kind of industrial endeavor relied on the labor of slaves.

Three of the most important southern industries made widespread use of slaves. Efforts to bring cotton mills to the cotton fields took slaves from the fields to the factories. By 1860 more than 5,000 slaves labored in textile mills. Edward McGehee's mill in Mississippi and the Saluda factory in South Carolina each employed more than 100 slaves in their operations. The southern iron industry depended on slave labor. Slaves made up the bulk of the labor force at most upper-South ironworks. These works ranged from small companies with only a few slaves to large, sophisticated establishments that owned hundreds of them. The ironworks controlled by Senator John Bell in the Cumberland River region of Tennessee owned 365 slaves. The most famous of all southern iron manufacturers, the Tredegar Iron Company of Richmond, Virginia, used more than 100 slaves during the 1850s. Southern tobacco factories used slave labor almost exclusively. Centered in Virginia, this industry provided the workplaces for thousands of slaves. In the 1850s fifty-two tobacco plants employed 3,400 slaves in Richmond alone.

A slave named Tooler operated the chafery and refining forges at Buffalo Forge, an ironworks in the Shenandoah Valley near Lexington, Virginia. The position demanded considerable skill. Tooler worked iron before it was wrought into bars. The master assigned work quotas to his slaves, and encouraged additional effort by setting up a credit system that rewarded slaves who exceeded their quotas. When slaves had amassed credit they could draw on their accounts for such goods as sugar, tobacco, coffee, clothes, and even cash. Because of the responsibility of his position, Tooler could earn between $3 and $5 a ton for extra work. Occasionally he withdrew cash from his account for trips to Lynchburg, Virginia, possibly to see his wife. Tooler remained a slave at Buffalo Forge until 1865.

Other industries also used slaves extensively. The transportation industry, chiefly railroads and steamboats, was completely dependent on slaves. Almost all southern railroads were constructed with slave labor, and slaves performed myriad tasks on steamboats. Skilled slave machinists worked in Daniel Pratt's famous cotton gin factory in Alabama. The 153 slaves who worked at a brick plant in Biloxi Bay, Mississippi, produced 10 million bricks annually. Slaves drove the printing press of the *Charleston Courier.* They mined coal in Virginia and Kentucky and gold in North Carolina. They staffed saltworks and operated tanneries. In short, slaves could be found in almost every industry in the South.

Although most slaves worked directly for their owners, whether in field or factory, some owners hired out their slaves to other whites. A widespread practice in both agricultural and nonagricultural areas, slave hiring increased the flexibility of the system and occasionally of the slaves' lives. Many planters hired slaves from each other at harvest time. Some manufacturing enterprises, especially in the upper South, routinely hired surplus slaves from the countryside. Railroads often hired slaves for construction crews from slave owners along the routes. Many city families hired rather than bought domestic servants.

The contracts that governed such arrangements specified the fee to be paid to the slave's owner, the term of the hire (usually from January to Christmas), and the kind of work to be performed. The hirer agreed to provide proper clothing, food, and general care. On January 1, 1832, C. W. Thurston of Louisville "promised to pay James Brown Ninety dollars for the hire of Negro Phill until 25 Dec. next. And we agree to pay taxes and doctor bills. Clothe him during said time and return him . . . with good substantial cloth or . . . shoes and socks and a blanket."

A small number of slaves were permitted to hire their own time, though the practice was illegal nearly everywhere. This system was generally restricted to cities, and chiefly to those in the upper South. These people, usually artisans, had considerably more freedom of movement than other slaves. This device permitted masters to escape the cost of feeding, clothing, and housing the artisan while reaping financial rewards from the slave's skill. Allowed to find work for themselves, these slaves had only two obligations: to stay out of trouble and to make payments to their masters at regular intervals. In describing the terms by which he hired his time to work in the Baltimore shipyards, Frederick Douglass spelled out the guidelines that governed such arrangements: "I was to be allowed all my time; to make all bargains for work; to find my own employment, and to collect my own wages; and, in return for this liberty, I was required, or obliged, to pay . . . three dollars at the end of each week, and to board and clothe myself." Masters expected prompt and regular payment. The account books of James Rudd of Louisville show the system at work. Rudd permitted his slave Yellow Jim to hire out his own time for $5 a week. In eight years Rudd collected nearly $1,900 from him. Of course, this flexibility could have drawbacks for a master. Rudd noted the most serious in his ledger: "December 11, 1853, Ranaway."

DIET AND DRESS

Work requires energy, and for human beings food provides the energy. Thus if slaves were to work at all productively, they had to have sufficient food. The evidence indicates that the vast majority of slaves had ample food. In a system as large and diverse as southern slavery, surely some slaves did not have enough to eat, but they were few and not characteristic of the system. Although most historians agree on the quantity of food provided to slaves, they tend to differ on its quality. The question of quality can never be answered authoritatively because the enormous variety of individual circumstances makes it impossible to establish precise diets for the bulk of the slave population.

The foundation of the slave diet consisted of pork and corn. At times sweet potatoes and, in the coastal region, rice were substituted for corn. Molasses was also quite commonly part of the basic menu. The standard plantation ration was a peck of cornmeal and three to four pounds of pork for every slave, distributed weekly. The pork ration usually consisted of bacon and fatback, not hams and chops. An unrelenting diet of pork and corn was surely monotonous, but fresh vegetables and fruits in season, grown either in the slaves' plots or in the owner's gardens and orchards, provided variety and essential minerals as well. Slaves and masters raised chickens, too, and some slaves supplemented their provisions by trapping and fishing. It is impossible to know the complete range of these supplemental foods or the frequency with which slaves enjoyed them. Some slaves always had many of them available; others rarely saw anything but corn and pork.

Though slaves' diets varied widely, some generalizations can be made. Despite the variations, the quantity and quality of the slave diet enabled the vast majority of slaves to live productive lives. Malnutrition was not common. The diets of slaves and of most whites were quite similar. The average white family in the countryside ate almost exactly what the slaves ate. Wealthy families on plantations and in the cities surely ate better than slaves, but they also ate better than most other whites. Corn, pork, and molasses were the staple foods of the rural South, for both black slave and free white.

Slaves probably enjoyed more variety in their diets than they did in their clothing. Most masters were not generous with their allotments of clothes. Masters typically made two allotments a year: a set of lightweight clothes for each slave at the beginning of summer, a heavier outfit for winter. Both were coarse and plain. The issue often included a hat or cap for the man and a kerchief for the woman. A slave usually had only one pair of shoes, brogans, for in warm weather no one wore shoes, and young children usually went naked. The paucity of clothes along with the absence of socks could bring suffering in cold weather.

Hand-me-downs from whites, chiefly to house servants and other favorites, enabled those so favored to add individuality to their clothing. Others might spruce up their drab attire by boiling it with dye extracted from local plants. Some augmented their meager allotments with items purchased in rural stores with money they received as rewards or from the sale of produce.

Most slaves displayed considerable ingenuity in their dress. They used strips of discarded material and clothing and anything else available to turn their slave garb into distinctive outfits. In a real sense they created their own wardrobe, limited though it surely was. Travelers constantly commented on the incredible variety in slaves' clothing. Masters also testified to their slaves' determination to individualize their dress. Notices of runaway slaves printed in newspapers often carried careful descriptions of the clothing the runaways were wearing when they were last seen.

HOUSING

The term *slave quarters* has a double meaning. It can refer to an individual structure or dwelling in which slaves lived, or to a group of slave dwellings. And on plantations most masters preferred that the dwelling places of their slaves be grouped together.

In both meanings slave quarters had tremendous variety. A family that owned only one or two slaves, or perhaps a single slave family, might provide quarters for them in their own house, or in a shed attached to the house or to a barn, or in a small cabin close to the house. Such a cabin was usually a clapboard

SLAVE QUARTERS, SUGAR CANE PLANTATION NEAR DONALDSONVILLE, LOUISIANA. Although this photograph dates from about 1880, the scene (except for the railroad tracks) conveys the antebellum world. (Historic New Orleans Collection)

(a)

(b)
VARIOUS TYPES OF SLAVE CABINS
(a) Ruins of tabby cabins, Kingsley Plantation, Florida (Courtesy of Kingsley Plantation State Historical Site, Fla.)
(b) Brick cabins, Boone Hall Plantation, South Carolina (Courtesy of Bradley Bond)

structure, small and rectangular, commonly twelve feet by ten. The floor was usually of trampled earth. If the cabin had a window, it was provided with wooden
shutters but not with windowpanes. If it had a chimney, it was commonly made
of sticks and clay.

Masters on large farms and plantations employed a greater variety of building materials, though the simple wooden shack or cabin was pervasive. Some
masters embellished them, though. Whitewash improved the appearance of
crude cabins. Wooden floors, glass windowpanes, and brick hearths made for
warmer, more comfortable living. Brick chimneys increased safety. Some prosperous masters, chiefly in the upper South, even built their whole quarters of brick.
Sturdy brick quarters remain today on the grounds of Boone Hall Plantation, near

(c)

(c) Wooden slave "apartments," Horton Grove, North Carolina (Courtesy of Kenneth M. McFarland and the Stagville Center, Durham, N.C.)

Charleston. Along the Atlantic coast from Carolina to Florida, tabby was widely used for slave cabins. Made from sand, oyster shells, and water, tabby made for solid, secure structures. At Kingsley Plantation, in northeast Florida, a row of tabby cabins still stands. They testify to the strength of tabby and to the organization of the quarters.

Whatever the basic construction material they favored, masters grouped their cabins together. Most plantations had a single grouping, but some had several quarters of a few cabins each. James Couper, for example, at his Cannon's Point Plantation on St. Simon's Island, Georgia, constructed his slave cabins in groups of four. Most cabins in a plantation's slave quarters were identical or very similar. Sometimes larger cabins were provided for drivers and other outstanding slaves. Some cabins at Kingsley Plantation have two rooms, the larger with a tabby floor. With around 455 square feet of living space, they were intended for slave notables.

Masters with a mind to both their own profits and the welfare of their slave force planned thoughtfully for their slave quarters. The description provided by a planter along the Big Black River in Mississippi indicates the care taken by concerned masters.

There being upward of 150 negroes on the plantation, I provide for them 24 houses made of hewn post oak, covered with cypress, 16 by 18, with close plank floors and good chimneys, and elevated two feet from the ground. The ground *under* and around the houses is swept every month, and the houses, both inside and out, white-washed twice a year. The houses are situated in a double row from north to south, about 200 feet apart, the doors facing inwards, and the houses being in line, about 50 feet apart. At one end of the street stands the overseer's house, workshops, tool house, and wagon sheds; at the other, the grist and saw-mill, with good cisterns at each end, providing an ample supply of pure water.

Toward the end of the antebellum era many major planters had slave quarters on their minds. They were planning for the future. A glimpse into the future they envisioned can still be had at Horton Grove, in Durham County, North Carolina. In the late 1850s this area belonged to Paul Cameron. Among the largest and wealthiest planters in the South, Cameron owned almost 800 slaves and 30,000 acres in North Carolina, Alabama, and Mississippi. In 1851 Paul's father, Duncan Cameron, designed and built at Horton Grove what today would be called four-plexes. Each building had two stories and contained four wood-floored rooms, two on the first floor and two on the second, each almost seventeen feet square. A hallway four feet wide separated the rooms, providing space for a stairway leading from the first floor to the second. The houses sat well above the ground on high pilings. The brick walls were faced with board-and-batten siding; the inside walls were whitewashed. A brick chimney at either end of the building provided a fireplace for each of the rooms. A tin roof reduced the possibility of fire.

DISEASE

Shelter, food, and clothing all had an influence on the health of slaves. Their health depended basically on genetics, the practices of their owners, and the state of medical knowledge before 1860.

A genetic trait limited mainly to black people has to do with blood cells—misshapen blood cells known as the sickling trait. This trait had both a positive and a negative impact on the health of slaves. It helped make them highly immune to the more virulent forms of malaria, a fact noticed both by planters and by medical authorities in the antebellum South. To them it meant that blacks were naturally suited to labor in hot climates where malaria and other fevers were common. This relative genetic immunity had evolved in Africa, where malaria was a constant threat. While it was helpful in warding off malaria, hemoglobin abnormalities may very well have made slaves susceptible to miscarriage, aching joints, and leg ulcers, all often noted as health problems among slaves. Slaves were also particularly susceptible to respiratory diseases. Although the specifics of their blood-cell makeup affected their susceptibility, their historical experience also contributed to it. Africans had little experience with pulmonary infection before they were brought to the cooler climate of North America, and it wreaked havoc on them. Epidemiological research has proved that even mild "domesticated" diseases can devastate previously unexposed populations. Thus Europeans coped more successfully with respiratory illnesses than with fevers while Africans had the opposite experience.

The attitude of masters was also a force in the health of slaves. Most slave owners showed real concern for their slaves, for two reasons. The first was self-interest. Slaves were valuable, and it made enormous sense to maintain their health. A sick and physically incapacitated slave could not work so productively as an able-bodied one, and a dead slave represented a total financial loss. Thus the economics of slave owning instructed masters to do everything possible to keep their slave force healthy. Self-interest had still another dimension. With whites and blacks living and working in close contact, disease within the slave population could quickly spread to the families of the master and the overseer. No one understood the dynamics of contagion but everyone knew it occurred. The second reason was humanitarian. Most slave owners professed a sincere interest in the well-being of their slaves. The same Christian culture and morality that underlay masters' respect for slaves' marriages and their families prompted a deep concern for their physical health. This motive did not, of course, influence every master, but it was generally pervasive throughout the South.

The records testify to the planters' provision of medical care. Many masters and mistresses acted as doctors and nurses on their plantations. A former slave remembered his mistress: "She was with all the slave women every time a baby was born. Or, when a plague of misery hit the folks she knew what to do and what kind of medicine to ease off the aches and pains." Between 1842 and 1847 the Alabama planter James Tait paid a yearly average of $160 for doctors' services. In 1847 the overseer on John A. Quitman's plantation in Terrebonne Parish, Louisiana, arranged for a physician to visit the place twice a week through the year. Between 1850 and 1856 William P. Gould paid one doctor $2,667.49 for visits to his fifty slaves.

Although most masters tried to aid their sick slaves, the slaves often spurned that assistance and turned to their own folk remedies. In every locale, if not on every plantation, an herb doctor or conjurer practiced a folk medicine that relied on herbs and roots. This was one means by which slaves retained strong ties with their African past. A former slave from South Carolina recalled, "Oh, de people never didn' put much faith to de doctors in dem days. Mostly, dey would use de herbs in de fields for dey medicine." These remedies may or may not have relieved physical distress, but they certainly helped give the slaves a sense of self-worth. They had a medicine just as the masters did, and both were ineffective. The pervasive bleeding practiced by white doctors for almost every possible ailment had no more restorative power than the green figs and salt that the herb doctors prescribed for cholera.

Neither white nor slave medicine helped very much because no one really understood the germ theory of disease. In the eighteenth century and the first half of the nineteenth, medical knowledge was still quite primitive. Cholera, which felled white and black alike, is caused by bacteria and is contracted chiefly through contaminated water. No one understood the connection, and no one developed any effective counter to it. Four times between 1830 and 1860 cholera epidemics ravaged parts of the South. Whites and blacks suffered together, but because of their almost universal poverty and poor living conditions, blacks were hit harder.

Despite less than ideal living conditions, the slave population multiplied. Between 1800 and 1860 the number of slaves more than quadrupled, from just under 1 million to 4 million. As only around 70,000 new slaves entered the country during the period, this impressive growth cannot be attributed to the international slave trade.

MASTERS AND SLAVE FAMILIES

The natural increase in the slave population raises the question of slave families. Did slaves form families? The answer is both yes and no. The negative comes directly from the law; no slave code gave legal sanction to a slave's marriage or to the resulting family. The much more important response, however, is positive. In practice slave families flourished, with the strong support of masters. Although slave families had no legal standing, they rested on the firm foundation of custom, morality, and self-interest.

Morality and self-interest motivated the commitment of slave owners to their slave families. In a Christian culture the family is sacred, and even if not every master was a practicing Christian, the South was surely a Christian culture. Masters continually spoke of their slaves as part of their extended family. The privileged position held by the concept of family easily encompassed the slaves. Most masters encouraged their slaves to live in families. They not only permitted slave marriages, they often performed them. And slave cabins were usually allocated to families. As the Virginian William Massie explained, keeping his family, free and slave, together "would be as near that thing happiness as I ever expect to get."

Self-interest also formed a part of the master's profamily stance. Slaves committed to each other formed a mighty force for obedience and work. With a family structure the slave cabin became a place of solace, warmth, and love. Slaves' attachment to their spouses, their children, and their parents provided a source of comfort that owners believed, justifiably, would enhance their slaves' overt loyalty to the person who permitted their unions—the master. Masters understood this reality; there can be no other explanation for their willingness to permit their slaves to marry other masters' slaves. A male slave whose wife lived on another plantation customarily was permitted time off each week to spend with her, and their children added to the wealth of the neighbor, not to the husband's master.

Whites and blacks testified to the importance of slave marriages. Masters involved themselves in the slaves' ceremonies, from the simplest to the most lavish. The customary slave wedding was simple: the couple jumped over a broomstick, to the applause of their families and friends. One marriage took place in a field, bride and groom standing between the handles of a plow. Masters occasionally hosted the broomstick ceremony in their homes. Mistresses often provided wedding finery for favored slaves (especially house servants), filled the house with flowers, and invited their neighbors to witness the ceremony and toast the newlyweds at a sumptuous feast. Of course there was an element of sham in these costume affairs, and some slaves surely chafed at the role written for them by master and mistress. Still, for most of the participants, white and black, those festivities symbolized the commitment of free and slave to family. Just as the kind of ceremony varied, so did the person who performed it. Masters often officiated; so did ministers, both white and black. All recognized the seriousness of what was happening.

For the slaves the wedding, extralegal though it was, was a time for joy, but joy tempered by the realization that the master who permitted the marriage could also control its duration. A former slave from Virginia commented: "We slaves knowed that them words wasn't bindin'. Din't mean nothin' lessen you say, 'What God has joined, caint no man pull asunder.' But dey never would say dat. Jus' say, 'Now you married.' " No slave wedding included the words "till death do you part." A black preacher pronounced his own version of the familiar pledge: "Till death or buckra [whites] part you."

For masters the breakup of slave families by sale drove a wedge between the mutually supporting motives of morality and self-interest underlying support of those families. Most slave owners anguished over the choice between financial loss and the separation of family members. Although most planters chose business over sentiment, even a cursory glance at the manuscript record makes clear the intensity of the ordeal. Facing massive debts, Thomas B. Chapin, who grew sea island cotton on St. Helena Island, South Carolina, had to make this choice. "Nothing can be more mortifying and grieving to man," he recorded in his journal, "than to select out some of his Negroes to be sold. You know not to whom, or how they will be treated by their new owners. And Negroes you find no fault with—to separate families, mothers & daughters, brothers & sisters. . . ." Most masters who confronted Chapin's dilemma acted as he did, though many suffered considerable losses to keep families together or at least to sell members within visiting distance. Nothing else about slavery so troubled southern whites as the separation of families, and reformers called for legal restrictions against it. In his 1860 book *Social Relations in Our Southern States*, Daniel R. Hundley, a stalwart defender of the institution, advocated that it be placed "upon a more humane basis than it rests upon at present" by legislation disallowing "families to be broken up and sold to separate masters." Hundley's appeal, like others before it, went unheeded. In 1860 slave codes had not been changed. Slaves' marriages and the security of their families were in the hands of their masters.

*S*LAVES AND THEIR FAMILIES

Recent scholarship had demonstrated conclusively that slaves lived in families and took their family life seriously. Slaves were generally monogamous after marriage, though their mores attached no stigma to premarital sex. The reality of slave life, however, caused quite a few men and women to have more than one spouse before they finally were widowed. The sale of either husband or wife often led both to form a new union.

Slaves' commitment to the concept of family was not destroyed by separation. In 1828 the Pettigrews of North Carolina acquired a four-year-old girl named Patience. Separated from her family of origin Patience grew up in the community of Pettigrew slaves. At seventeen she had a daughter by Dick Buck. The couple married two years later. Dick's father, William, died the following year, and they named their first son for him. Living a conventional family life, Patience and Dick became the parents of seven children in all.

The behavior of emancipated slaves during and immediately after the Civil War makes clear the meaning of family in the slave community. Across the South roads were filled with slaves traveling toward hoped-for reunions with loved ones from whom they had become separated. Ben and Betty Dodson had been apart for twenty years. When they met in a refugee camp, Ben was overcome with joy. "Glory, glory, hallelujah!" he shouted. Embrace alternated with disbelief, then finally reassurance: "Dis is my Betty, shuah. I foun' you at las'. I's hunted an' hunted till I track you up here. I's boun' to hunt till I fin' you if you's alive." It is impossible to know how many former slaves shared the good fortune of Ben and

Betty Dodson, but surely William Carter of Georgia, whose father had been purchased by a Virginia planter, spoke for many when he said that the best thing
about being free was that "he could come back to us."

Slaves' names also indicated the strength of their families. Masters knew
slaves only by their first names; a master's recognition of a slave's surname was
rare indeed. Yet slave families often adopted surnames, which other slaves knew
and respected. When the daughter of a Mississippi planter asked her nurse,
"Mammy, what makes you call Henry Mr. Ferguson?" the nurse's response spoke
volumes about the slaves' sense of family and self-worth. "Do you think 'cause
we are black that we cayn't have no names?" The prevalence of family surnames
became quickly apparent upon emancipation, when slaves used them openly.

Not all families had surnames, but those that did not promptly adopted one
when they became free. The new surnames came from a variety of sources. Some
adopted the name of their most recent master; some opted for that of an earlier,
more fondly remembered owner. Other families chose to identify with their
emancipator; Lincolns and Abrahams were not uncommon. Still others selected
the names of people they admired or simply chose a name they liked. Whatever
the source, the publicly announced surname helped give concreteness to a sense
of family that had survived the rigors of servitude.

The slave family had great strength, and both black and white knew its
power. This truth was never more dramatically described than by the great political orator John Randolph of Roanoke, who was also a large slaveholder. Randolph
was asked to identify the person whom he ranked as the very best speaker he had
heard. "The greatest orator I ever heard," he responded, "was a woman. She was
a slave and a mother and her rostrum was an auction block."

SLAVES AS CHRISTIANS

Only religion matched family in importance to most slaves. Family and religion
reinforced each other. The Christian religion emphasized the value of the family
and the family embodied the earthly representation of God's love. Both provided
a powerful moral sensibility to the life of the slaves.

White southerners showed little interest in Christianizing their slaves before
the rise of evangelical Christianity in the last quarter of the eighteenth century.
The Great Revival, however, made religion a much more vital part of the white
community than it had been earlier, and the newly converted lost no time in seeking to convert other people, both white and black. The uses of Christianity in the
ongoing effort to control a large and growing slave population soon became apparent to them. To most white southerners, a Christian slave was somehow less
threatening to them and their society than a heathen.

Whites certainly tried to evangelize the slaves. Individual planters urged
Christianity on their own slave family. The major denominations mounted substantial home mission campaigns aimed at slaves. White ministers, in sermons delivered to both whites and blacks, preached the efficacy of the Gospel for slaves.
Ministers especially dedicated to slave conversion wrote pamphlets and books
advising their ministerial brethren on the proper approach to win the souls of

slaves. A number of white churches even welcomed blacks as members, though most provided a separate seating area for the slave congregation. Many masters also encouraged slaves to have separate services on plantations. These sponsored events, however, usually had white preachers, or at least a white presence if a black were preaching. In many urban areas blacks—both slave and free—had their own churches, presided over by a black minister, almost always a free man.

The message that whites preached to blacks focused exclusively on individual salvation. The white clerics and lay people did preach that one God watched over and loved all, that Jesus Christ died for all and was lord of all; on those fundamental questions blacks and whites received identical messages. But one theme dominated the sermons delivered to the slaves by the whites: servants, obey your masters. Just as all must obey their heavenly master, so slaves must obey their earthly master. The reward for faithful service to both masters was heaven.

Slaves responded enthusiastically to Christianity, but not precisely as whites either wanted or believed. Slaves accepted Christianity for several reasons. Many were committed Christians; for them the Christian message was the key to life. But more mundane considerations also made Christianity attractive. Particular events, such as funerals, provided opportunities for legitimate emotional release that might otherwise make whites uneasy. Finally, the role permitted and assumed by black preachers gave both them and their congregations a sense of pride.

The substance of slave Christianity did not coincide precisely with the message preached by whites. Slaves took the Christian message and molded it into a living, vital religion that spoke meaningfully to them as individuals and to their condition. The theology of the slaves affirmed life and love, certainly central themes in their spirituals. Rejecting the notion that their bondage stemmed from some fault in themselves, slaves rejected also the doctrine of original sin. The theology of the slaves emphasized deliverance, and that message dominated their spirituals. In one of them slaves sang:

> But some ob dese days my time will come,
> I'll year dat bugle, I'll year dat drum,
> I'll see dem armies, marchin' along,
> I'll lif' my head an jine der song.

Moses, who led God's chosen people out of bondage, was a hero almost equal to Jesus. In fact, Jesus and Moses often seemed forged into one deliverer.

Slaves grasped at one major tenet of their masters' theology—the concept of heaven. The slaves accepted St. Paul's message that equality would reign in heaven (so did many whites, for that matter). In God's kingdom there would be neither bond nor free, for all would be one in Jesus Christ. To slaves this vision of heaven diminished the whites' claim of superiority on earth. The prospect of equality in heaven undermined the pretensions of the earthly powerful.

To slaves no one expounded their Christianity so forcefully as the black preacher. And it is almost impossible to overestimate his importance in the slave community. Many slave preachers could read the Bible, despite laws forbidding the teaching of reading to slaves. Many more had memorized huge sections of Scripture. To most slaves and not a few whites, black preachers were more power-ful proclaimers of the Gospel than whites. The evidence is indisputable that even in the mid-nineteenth century, blacks ministered to whites as well as to their own. Slave preachers helped lead the slave community in extraordinarily difficult cir-cumstances to forge an identity founded on self-worth.

Though slave Christianity had immense emotional and psychological value for the slaves, it had no political strength. Slave Christianity sounded no call to revolution and inspired no armed prophets. Without a belief in original sin and bearing no responsibility for their enslavement, slaves felt no compulsion to prove or to improve themselves. There was no millennialism, no specified time when all wrongs would be righted. Slaves took this world as it was and struggled in it. The widespread adoption of Christianity by the slaves also precluded any re-ligiously charged cultural clash between blacks and whites. Though they prayed for different things, both worshiped the same God.

REJECTION OF BONDAGE

The absence of a revolutionary thrust in the slaves' religion did not at all mean that slaves accepted enslavement as their proper station in life. It is impossible to know precisely what every slave thought, and undoubtedly there were some who internalized the white view of them as slaves. The evidence is overwhelming, however, that the vast majority of slaves rejected the whites' perception of them. Though by the mid-nineteenth century practically no slave had ever known any other condition, slaves were well aware of the sharp difference between slavery and freedom. And they opted for freedom. When Frederick Law Olmsted asked a Louisiana slave what he would do if he were free, the answer made clear that freedom meant options.

> If I was free, massa; if I was free (with great animation), I would—well sar, de fus thing I would do, if I was free, I would go to work for a year, and get some money for my-self,—den—den—den, massa, dis is what I do—I buy me, fus place, a little house, and little lot land, and den—no; den—den—I would go to old Virginny, and see my mud-der. Yes, sar, I would like to do dat fus thing; den, when I com back, de fus thing I'd do, I'd get me a wife; den, I'd take her to my house, and I would live with her dar; and I would raise things in my garden, and take 'em to New Orleans, and see 'em dar, in de market. Dat's de way I would live, if I was free.

During the war years, the approach of Union armies signaled the dawning of a new day. Across the South slaves left farms, plantations, and their masters to be-come refugees. A few remained on the home place with their owners and became the source of the postwar scenario that depicted loyal servants standing firmly with their white people in the face of Yankee invasion. Although those few pro-vided a factual basis for a story enmeshed in white tradition, they were a small minority. Time and again whites were astonished to see the slaves they accounted as faithful, loyal, and contented march off to the armies in blue.

Before that day came, many bondsmen and bondswomen made known their unhappiness. Overt rejection of bondage took many forms. Minor acts of sabotage occurred regularly. A slave with a hoe could chop young cotton plants as well as grass. Buildings burned, equipment ruined, food stolen—all could indicate the slaves' rejection of their oppression. These acts, however, could become a double-edged sword. Masters could and did retaliate with repressive measures that affected all the slaves on a plantation or farm, not just those who had acted. Thus pressure from within the slave community could curtail such activities.

Possibly the most common expression of dissatisfaction was running away. Slaves ran away from their owners for many reasons, but principally to escape anticipated punishment or to see family members on other farms and plantations. Some also slipped away simply because they could not take their bondage any longer. Most runaways either returned of their own accord or were soon caught, usually within a week. It was extremely difficult for slaves to lose themselves in the population. Whites could identify neighborhood blacks, and if they saw one they did not recognize, they could demand to see a travel permit. Some runaways managed to stay away as long as they did only because other slaves provided them with food and occasionally even shelter at night.

While hunting in Louisiana in the 1820s, the famous artist John James Audubon encountered a runaway. This fugitive (he is not named) had found a precarious sanctuary for himself and his family in one of the swamps in the southern portion of the state. The slave told Audubon that he had run away because he and his family had been split up on the auction block. Escaping from his new home on a stormy night, he had made his way into the swamp. Then he spirited his wife away from her plantation and even managed to secure some of their children. In these circumstances survival was doubtful, and even a runaway as enterprising as this one needed assistance. Only supplies provided by house servants at their original plantation had enabled this daring family to survive as long as they had. Audubon returned with the slave family to their original master and persuaded him to reunite them by buying them back. Unfortunately, the stories of most runaways did not have such a happy, if bittersweet, ending.

The historical record indicates that the overwhelming majority of slaves formed their identity in psychological and emotional terms that generated a positive view of their worth within the boundaries of enslavement. Slaves could and did stand for their perception of their worth. As best they could, slave husbands and fathers provided for and protected wives and children. Slave wives and mothers loved, served, and comforted husbands and children. All the while these bondsmen and bondswomen were convinced both that God had not created them to be slaves and that someday they would be delivered from slavery. They awaited their day of jubilee.

Some slaves, however, simply could not remain in the pattern, even a pattern broad enough to encompass minor sabotage. Chronic troublemakers, the whites called them. They were constantly disrespectful of whites; they continually disregarded plantation rules; they ran away time and time again; some even dared to raise a hand against overseer or master. When a slave was seen to fit this category, whites moved promptly. When punishment failed, the usual reaction was to sell the troublemaking slave—and the sale normally meant the transfer of the slave a substantial distance away.

*R*EBELLION

These individual acts, however, only rarely coalesced into a direct challenge to the slave system, and the few slave revolts that did occur paled in comparison with the cataclysms that rocked the Caribbean and South America. In 1823, for example, thousands of slaves rose in Demerara, British Guiana, and 2,000 took part in a major battle. The South experienced nothing remotely like the massive rebellion on Saint-Domingue led by Toussaint L'Ouverture, which began in 1794 and resulted a decade later in the overthrow of French authority and the creation of a black state, Haiti.

Tangible reasons account for this difference between the South and most other New World slave societies. In the South whites were numerically dominant. Although by 1860 the slave population totaled over 4 million, 8 million whites were living in the slave states. Slaves did have a substantial majority in a few areas, such as the sea islands of South Carolina and Georgia, but they were too isolated to have any hope of success in a land where the whites controlled both weapons and police power. The whites could confront any rebellion with militia units and even elements of the regular United States Army in addition to hastily organized but well-armed planters and farmers.

Neither sanctuaries nor friendly groups that could harbor or aid slave rebels existed. The only sparsely settled areas—such as the mountains of western North Carolina and the swamps of southern Louisiana—were remote, and to reach them rebellious slaves would have to travel significant distances through thickly settled countryside. And almost every southern white agreed that slave rebellion was the greatest disaster that could strike their society. Mutinous slaves would have to confront this phalanx of whites without any hope of allies. No group in the South would aid them. By 1860 the Indians had been subjugated, but even earlier, when numerous independent Indian tribes lived in the South, they failed to provide either sympathizers or a haven for slaves seeking escape from the system. From colonial times most Indian tribes owned slaves themselves and were on the lookout for runaways. The Seminoles of Florida would harbor runaways, but they lived on the periphery of the slave South. No tribe constituted even a minor threat to the social stability of slavery.

In addition to the adverse calculus of power, emotional and psychological forces in the southern slave community worked against revolt. Religion and family gave a meaning to life, even within a harsh and cruel system. As a result, most slaves developed neither the ideology nor the desperation that open rebellion required.

Throughout the centuries of slavery in the American South, only six major conspiracies or revolts can be documented. Three occurred before statehood, one in colonial South Carolina in 1739, the other two in Louisiana, the first in 1795 during the Spanish dominion and the second in 1811 after the American takeover. The earliest, the Stono Rebellion, took place near Charleston, South Carolina, in September 1739. Of central importance in this uprising were the differences between England and Spain. Spanish authorities in St. Augustine, Florida, promised freedom to any slave who escaped to Spanish territory, and over time some South

Carolina slaves had managed to get there. When war was declared between England and Spain, some twenty slaves, led by a man named Jemmy, seized the opportunity to make a break for Florida. As a first step they broke into a store, decapitated the two owners, and made off with small arms and powder. As they headed southward they acquired reinforcements until they numbered between sixty and one hundred. Almost as soon as the uprising began, the alarm was sounded. Late that same day between twenty and one hundred local planters and farmers banded together and attacked the rebels. With this attack the rebellion disintegrated, though it took the whites the better part of a month to track down all the participants. Casualties included about twenty-five whites and thirty-five slaves killed.

The conspiracy that took place in Pointe Coupee, Louisiana, during the spring of 1795 also had connections to conflict between European powers. Because of the French Revolution, Spain and France were at war. In the mid-1790s, with the greatest slave rebellion of all under way in Saint-Domingue, France executed its monarchs and abolished slavery in all its colonies. News of these events spread through Spanish Louisiana, certainly reaching the slave population. In Pointe Coupee, more than 100 miles above New Orleans, slaves outnumbered whites by 3 to 1. The slave Antoine Sarrasin took the lead in a plot aimed at killing whites and capturing weapons. He traveled through the countryside enlisting followers, mostly other slaves, but also a few whites. Some of the rebels undoubtedly hoped for a French invasion that would make Louisiana part of revolutionary France. Although the conspirators planned carefully, the conspiracy never became a rebellion. Aware of an imminent strike, certain slaves informed their masters. The authorities moved in quickly, arresting Sarrasin and numerous others. In promptly held trials fifty-seven slaves and three whites were convicted. The punishments were brutal; twenty-three slaves were hung, then beheaded, and their heads were nailed to posts along the Mississippi River between Pointe Coupee and New Orleans.

In January 1811 slaves in St. John the Baptist and St. Charles parishes, up the Mississippi River from New Orleans, assaulted the system. Evidently without any planning, the slaves on one plantation attacked the planter and killed his son. Armed with cane knives, axes, and clubs, they started downriver toward New Orleans, killed another white, and steadily gained recruits until their force included at least 200 men and perhaps as many as 500. Armed planters in the area immediately sounded the alarm and took to the field. When word reached Brigadier General Wade Hampton, in command of the United States Army forces in New Orleans, he rushed upriver with both regular troops and militiamen. Within two days the combination of local and official forces crushed the rebellion, which left more than sixty slaves killed or executed. To demonstrate to the slave population the fate that awaited rebels, the victors, like their Spanish predecessors a decade and a half earlier, displayed the heads of decapitated rebels on poles along the Mississippi from the plantation of origin all the way to New Orleans.

The two most elaborately planned rebellions also never went beyond the conspiracy stage. Discovery of the plots by whites prevented either from developing into an open revolt. During the summer of 1800 a group of slave artisans led by Gabriel, a literate blacksmith, planned an attack on Richmond, Virginia. Like the

Pointe Coupee affair, Gabriel's design had its genesis in widespread talk of the French Revolution and the overthrow of tyranny, which in Virginia followed hard on the American Revolution with its rhetoric of liberty. It also seems that the bitter partisan differences between Jeffersonian Republicans and Federalists in Richmond, in which the Republicans praised France, led Gabriel and other slaves erroneously to believe that some whites, especially artisans, would stand with black advocates of freedom and egalitarianism. The evidence also suggests that two white Frenchmen conspired with Gabriel.

Gabriel and his chief lieutenants were slaves whose owners permitted them considerable latitude to travel about the countryside and talk with other slaves. Gabriel and his associates recruited around Richmond for months, with the intention of capturing the arsenal for arms and then kidnapping the governor. Their success was to signal a general rising in the countryside, but the ultimate goal of the rebellion remains unclear. Approximately 200 men were scheduled to enter Richmond on the night of August 30, 1800. Gabriel's hopes were undone by his widespread recruiting efforts. Slaves aware of the plot informed their masters, who took their warnings seriously. The governor, the future president James Monroe, called out the militia to patrol suspected rendezvous areas. Almost simultaneously a violent thunderstorm disrupted the conspirators' attempts to unite. Although no attack ever occurred and no whites died, white authorities investigated, held trials, and executed about twenty of the plotters, including Gabriel.

The uncovering of a plot by slaves and free blacks to take over their city terrified white Charlestonians in the summer of 1822. This plan was conceived by a remarkable man, Denmark Vesey, a literate carpenter who had purchased his own freedom. Chafing at the continuing enslavement of others in his family, Vesey sought to strike at the system. As associates Vesey enlisted other skilled artisans, both slave and free. In his preparations he was influenced by the Bible, by antislavery speeches made in Congress during the Missouri Compromise debates, and, through his most important lieutenant, Gullah Jack, by African religion. Vesey's scheme involved at least eighty conspirators organized into teams with specific targets. Vesey assigned the key points of the municipal guardhouse and the arsenal to his own team. With those posts captured and weapons secured, the rebels hoped to command the city. What they planned to do then is uncertain, but Vesey seems to have contemplated sailing to Haiti. But it was not to be. When several slaves privy to the plot became frightened and informed their masters, whites at first listened in disbelief, then became convinced and moved swiftly into action. On June 16 the militia squelched the conspiracy before it became a revolt and before any white person could be killed. Immediately investigations were mounted and trials held. In the next two months thirty-five rebels, including Vesey, were executed, and thirty-seven more were banished from the state.

The bloodiest and most famous of all southern slave revolts took place in Southampton County, Virginia, in 1831. Between August 21 and 23 of that year the slave Nat Turner led between sixty and seventy slaves in a rebellion that cost more than sixty white and numerous black lives. In critical ways this revolt differed from the conspiracies formulated by Gabriel and Denmark Vesey. Its setting was a rural county, not a city. Although its chieftain could read and write, he was a field hand, not an artisan. Also no evidence indicates that Turner planned his assault over as long a period as Gabriel and Vesey had done or with the care that marked their efforts. That was probably a major reason Turner actually attacked the white community. Turner acted so precipitously that no one had time to inform on him.

Turner was a formidable figure. In his call to rebellion he relied chiefly on the Bible. Something of a mystic, Turner exhorted his listeners to follow him as an instrument of the Lord. Convinced that God had chosen him to lead, Turner emerged as a Christian prophet who inspired others to follow.

Turner made final plans on Sunday afternoon, August 21; that night, armed with axes, he and his band struck. Although Turner's revolt began in his own neighborhood, his immediate goal lay some ten miles distant: the county seat and the arms stored there. The name of the village was, ironically, Jerusalem. Beyond that initial goal it is not at all clear precisely what Turner intended to do. Turner never reached Jerusalem. Late in the afternoon of August 22, whites engaged Turner's forces in a pitched battle and dispersed them. The next morning another group of whites, aided by slaves, broke up the remnants of Turner's party. Most of the rebels were killed or captured, but Turner escaped and remained at large for nine weeks. While the search for him continued, his followers were tried and twenty were executed; ten others were transported out of the state. Finally, on October 30, Turner was captured. He was tried at the Southampton County Court on November 5 and hanged six days later.

These six incidents left a powerful legacy. The possibility of a slave revolt was seldom far from whites' minds. In the aftermath of each revolt some slaves met violent deaths at the hands of whites uncertain about the extent of the conspiracy and determined to demonstrate their control. A white Virginian drove home the point in the wake of Nat Turner's revolt. Whites reacted so vigorously, he explained, because of "the suspicion eternally attached to the slave himself—the suspicion that a Nat Turner might be in every family; that the same bloody deed might be acted over at any time and in any place; that the materials for it were spread through the land, and were always ready for a like explosion." Whites had always to be prepared for revolt.

11

Learning, Letters, and Religion

❖

The life of the mind occupied an important place in southern history from the Revolution to the Civil War. At the same time, the South could not be called an intellectual society, nor did it offer great rewards for intellectual endeavors. In those respects, however, the South differed little from the rest of the country. In a fundamental sense, an intellectual act created the United States. Much of the modern thought of Europe in the eighteenth century surrounded and permeated the coming, the conduct, and the outcome of the American Revolution. The conviction that through human reason humans can determine their fate underlay this intellectual ferment. The southern Revolutionaries were in the mainstream of this movement, even at the forefront; emphatically they were not outsiders. The basic documents of the Revolution, chiefly the Declaration of Independence and the Constitution, embody this faith in human reason, and southerners heavily influenced both documents. Thomas Jefferson of Virginia wrote the Declaration; although the Constitution did not have a single author, several southerners, led by the Virginian James Madison, greatly influenced its final form. Thus just as the South was instrumental in building the nation, southern intellectuals were among the leaders who charted its direction.

INTELLECTUALS AND THE SOUTH

These men did not fit the common view of alienated intellectuals; they were men of action. Although such men did not disappear after the Revolution, their influence in politics declined during the nineteenth century. Only John C. Calhoun matched the Founding Fathers in power of intellect and public influence, and the role he played differed from theirs. That difference is instructive about antebellum southern history. Jefferson and Madison devoted their efforts to building a nation of which the South was a part. Calhoun began in the same vein, but became famous for his attempt to protect the South against the nation. Whereas initially the South was part of a whole, by the 1820s many southerners began to view nation and section as divisible. After Calhoun, southern intellectuals concerned about politics—such men as Nathaniel Beverly Tucker of Virginia and William Gilmore Simms of South Carolina—found their political homes within southern sectional radicalism, a movement to destroy the nation.

Southern public men were not uniquely intellectual, but intellectuals did play active and important roles in southern politics. A certain irony was at work here. Between 1775 and 1860 intellectuals as public men were intimately a part of southern political life, yet politics had no appeal for them; public life in its broadest sense can be said to have co-opted them. In the modern world intellectuals have become known chiefly as critics of their society, as outsiders; in the antebellum South intellectuals were concerned with the support and defense of the South and its institutions, not the criticism of them.

Many southern intellectuals, like their counterparts elsewhere, identified themselves as members of a particular group and gave themselves a special mission. "Sacred circle," the term Simms used to describe himself and the other men who shared his work and goals, tells much about the perspective of southern intellectuals. They had a sacred duty to the South—to understand it, to explain it, even to defend it, but not to criticize it or question its fundamental organization.

In the Revolutionary generation southern intellectuals found their chief occupation in defending the colonies against a perceived British tyranny and in creating a new polity. The next great intellectual movement, which came more than a half century later, emphasized defense of the South against a perceived northern tyranny. These later intellectuals did not advocate change, however. On the contrary, they warned of the danger of change. Rather than work to create something new, they stressed the need to protect what had been built. This fervent activity focused on and revolved around the institution of slavery.

Southern intellectuals never got away from slavery. In the Revolutionary era they struggled to reconcile the institution with their ideology. Although they did not put forth an overt defense of slavery, neither did they mount a direct assault on it. To emphasize the joy of liberty and the horror of bondage while holding tens of thousands of human beings in slavery troubled many intellectuals. In private, most of them wished slavery gone. Wishing was their major activity, for they simply could not devise any practical plan that they believed could work. They recognized that persuading the white South to give up slavery now would be incredibly difficult, probably impossible, no matter what plan they might propose. When the time was right, slavery would fall of its own weight. Thus they satisfied themselves that somehow progress would eventually destroy slavery. As late as 1814 the most eloquent of the Revolutionaries, Thomas Jefferson, left the end of slavery to "the younger generation."

That generation, however, moved in exactly the opposite direction. It created an intellectual defense of slavery unprecedented in the South and unique in the New World. Slavery had of course produced defenders before the second quarter of the nineteenth century. As early as the 1780s the Reverend William Graham, rector and principal instructor at Liberty Hall Academy (now Washington and Lee University), defended slavery in a lecture that he gave annually to the senior class. Drawing on both the Bible and the ideology of race, Graham anticipated the proslavery ministers of a later time. Christianity, he maintained, sanctioned slavery, and to his mind slavery was the proper status for inferior blacks. During congressional debates on Missouri in 1820 and 1821 several southerners found no difficulty in reconciling slavery with the Bible. Some of them described slavery as a patriarchal system based on reciprocal loyalty between kind masters and faithful slaves. Later in the 1820s similar arguments flowed from the pens of other southern stalwarts. Still, before 1830 no full-blown systematic defense of slavery had appeared.

THOMAS R. DEW AND THE CLERGY

The first major text in the proslavery canon came from the pen of Thomas R. Dew, a professor at the College of William and Mary. In 1832, when Dew was thirty years old, he published his *Review of the Debates in the Virginia Legislature of 1831 and 1832*, a commentary on wide-ranging debates in the legislature on the future of slavery of Virginia. In rejecting the arguments of Virginia antislavery spokesmen and making the case for slavery, Dew laid the foundation that would hold up the mature proslavery argument over the next three decades. Professor Dew discussed slavery in practical, historical, and philosophical terms. He stressed the nature of slaves as property and underscored the massive financial investment—tens of millions of dollars—that Virginians had in their slaves. In a society that honored and protected private property, Dew insisted, the rights of propertyholders had to be guarded. It had been proposed that the state purchase slaves from their owners and set them free; Dew considered that suggestion impractical. The financial burden would be unbearable; moreover, finding a home outside Virginia for the emancipated slaves would be impossible. With that point Dew underscored the powerful issue of race. No whites in Virginia, even the most vigorous opponents of slavery, envisioned free blacks remaining in the state. Thus by showing the impossibility of removing the freed slaves, Dew undermined the argument for emancipation.

But Dew did not rest his case solely on practical grounds. He went on to place southern slavery in the mainstream of Western history. Pointing to the great civilizations of the past—the Greek, the Hebrew, the Roman—Dew stressed that the institution of slavery flourished in each. He drew upon both secular and religious texts to demonstrate the legitimacy of slavery. On the basis of his study of Aristotle, who had considered Greek slavery justified by the manifest inequality among peoples, Dew found slavery perfectly suited for blacks and for the South. In the history of the children of Israel, as recorded in the Old Testament, Dew found divine sanction for slavery—a sanction upheld by the New Testament, for Jesus Christ made no attack on slavery. Thus, according to Dew, the slaveholding South was the legitimate descendant of both classical civilization and the Judeo-Christian tradition. Slavery, in sum, was a worthy part of the good society. After Dew, the intellectual defenders of slavery focused on three major areas: religion, history and social organization, and science.

Protestant Christianity, with its reliance on the unerring accuracy of Holy Scripture, was the bedrock of southern society. In this society a Bible-centered argument for slavery assumed central importance. If white slave owners could not believe that the Bible sanctioned slavery, they would face a terrible moral and psychological dilemma.

The southern clergy took the lead in defending slavery as divinely inspired and biblically sanctioned. That had not always been the case. In the late eighteenth and early nineteenth centuries a number of southern ministers questioned the morality of slavery, but those doubts faded as the white South began to articulate its commitment to the institution. Standing foursquare behind slavery, the preachers pointed to the Old Testament patriarchs, instruments of God and slave owners to a man. Never, they correctly maintained, did the laws of Israel condemn slavery; on the contrary, those laws protected servitude. Turning to the New Testament, they depicted both Jesus and Paul as supporters, if not champions, of slavery. They emphasized that the Son of God had lived in a slave society and had never attacked the institution of slavery. If he did not attack it, he must have supported it. Southern clerics took as their chief text Paul's letter to Philemon, by which he returned the runaway slave Onesimus to his lawful owner. In the southern view, if the great apostle acted in such fashion, how could anyone in the nineteenth century dare to question the legitimacy or morality of slavery?

The blackness of southern slaves buttressed the clerical position. Believing totally, as did almost every other white American, that blacks were an inferior race, the proslavery clergy searched for the scriptural origins of that inferiority. They found it in Genesis, where Noah cursed his grandson Canaan. According to the King James version—the Bible of the pre–Civil War South—Canaan would be "a servant of servants"; God would bless and "enlarge" Noah's favored sons, and Canaan would be their servant. For southerners, who regularly used *servant* to stand for *slave*, the meaning could not be doubted. And in fact they interpreted the language correctly; both the Revised Standard Version and the New English Bible use the word *slave*. To the southern clergy the issue could not have been clearer. Were not their own people blessed and enlarged? In their minds, God himself had favored them and chosen the descendants of Canaan for bondage; since the time of Genesis blacks had been fulfilling the role specially assigned to them. Thus for the religious defenders of slavery, the blackness of southern slaves only confirmed their scriptural argument.

The ministerial guardians of slavery stood at the front rank of their profession. It was not only the less educated, the less able, the less recognized who took up the cause. Eminent Episcopalians, Presbyterians, Baptists, and Methodists across the South proclaimed that the "master who rules his slaves and provides for them, according to Christian principles, [can] rest satisfied, that he is not in holding them, chargeable with moral evil, nor with acting in this respect, contrary to the genius of Christianity." In fact, the ministers saw the evangelization of the slaves as one of their great callings. The Reverend James H. Thornwell of South Carolina explained, "We feel that the souls of our slaves are a solemn trust and we shall strive to present them faultless and complete before the presence of God." To that end each of the major Protestant denominations launched a mission campaign to the slaves during the final antebellum generation. Conferences were held, instructional pamphlets and books were published, and missionaries were sent to preach to the slaves, all carrying the message that Christianity could save

their souls, but on earth their Christian duty required loyalty and obedience to
their masters.

HISTORY AND SOCIETY

Appeals to the authority of history and emphasis on the proper social organization matched the religious defense in importance. On these points southerners extended and developed themes that Dew had touched upon. Southern intellectuals
who participated in this endeavor covered a wide range—such public men as
John C. Calhoun and James H. Hammond; literary figures such as the leading
writer of the region, William Gilmore Simms; academics such as Nathaniel Beverly Tucker of the College of William and Mary and George Frederick Holmes,
who settled in 1857 at the University of Virginia; publicists and journalists such as
James D. B. De Bow, editor of *De Bow's Review*. These men and their colleagues
built their case for slavery with four major building blocks: history, the racial inferiority of blacks, the equality of whites, and the physical well-being of slaves in
comparison with that of free laborers.

The proslavery spokesmen emphasized that slavery was an integral and a legitimate part of Western history. Constantly they pointed out that the cherished and
admired products of Greece and Rome—the poetry, the philosophy, the art, the
political theory—all sprang from a slave-based society. The conclusion seemed inescapable: slavery represented not barbarism but high culture and virtue.

Although they placed their institution in a broad historical context, the southern apologists also focused on its particular identity. Slavery was especially appropriate to the South, they held, because of its racial character. Southerners
argued that slavery provided the best—indeed, the only—way for two such dis-
similar races to live in the same place. To southerners the racial inferiority of
blacks—on which most northern and European contemporaries agreed—made
any other social arrangement impossible. Advocates of slavery asserted that the
inferior blacks were especially well suited to be slaves. As slaves, they had their
physical needs met by their owners; an all-encompassing social welfare system
protected them from the vagaries of a world they were not equipped to face un-
aided. To the southerners, moreover, the inferiority of blacks provided a great opportunity for the superior whites. According to this script, southern whites were
engaged in a massive civilizing effort, which in time could lift up the slaves from
ignorance and social savagery. This secular civilizing mission would match in
value and efficacy the conversion efforts of the churches. In this scheme slavery
became a highway to Christian civilization for blacks. Its end, of course, was not
in sight.

To the defenders of slavery no benefit surpassed in importance the aristocracy
of color made possible by the institution. In their view slavery underlay a real
equality among whites. Southerners insisted that every society had its degraded
class, its poverty-stricken menials, or, in the arresting phrase of the South Carolina
planter-intellectual James H. Hammond, its "mudsills." That reality, in the southern argument, necessitated a harsh division among whites based on economics. In
the South, however, race, not economics, marked the fundamental dividing line in

society. "The poor white laborer at the North is at the bottom of the social ladder," read the southern brief, "whilst his brother here has ascended several steps and can look down upon those who are beneath him, at an infinite remove." In the proslavery text, the presence of black slaves rather than white workers in the mudsill class guaranteed equality among southern whites and thus a political democracy unmatched elsewhere in the civilized world.

And under slavery even the black mudsills in the South fared better than their white counterparts elsewhere. Southern defenders maintained that the Industrial Revolution was responsible for terrible human carnage. Pointing to the desperate condition of many factory workers in the North and in England, southerners described those laborers as far worse off than slaves. Those "wage slaves," they charged, were "free but in name." The South Carolinian William J. Grayson published in 1856 a long poem in heroic couplets, *The Hireling and the Slave*. To Grayson and his compatriots the caring master provided for the physical wants of the slave while industrial employers left their workers to fend for themselves. As Grayson put it, "The slave escapes the perils of the poor." The moral dimension of free versus slave the southerners rejected as distorting the true situation of the slave and the laborer.

A NEW THRUST

In the mid-1850s the defenders of slavery advanced in a new direction that took them from the particular to the general. This thrust drew upon the mainstream arguments about the care of the master and wage slavery, but it moved beyond the peculiar institution of black slavery to a more theoretical advocacy of slavery as a superior social system regardless of racial characteristics. In an attempt to underscore its objectivity, this argument clothed itself in the garments of the new science of society that was beginning to capture the interest of Western intellectuals. In 1854 Henry Hughes of Mississippi published his *Treatise on Sociology: Theoretical and Practical*. In the same year the Virginian George Fitzhugh wrote *Sociology for the South; or the Failure of Free Society*, and three years later he followed it with *Cannibals All! or Slaves without Masters*.

Hughes and Fitzhugh argued that slavery served both masters and slaves so well that it should govern social relations in all societies, not just in the South. In their view, slavery should not be restricted to biracial situations; the value of slavery was so enormous that white laborers would fare much better as true slaves than they did as wage slaves. Though Hughes shunned the word *slavery* in favor of the more scientific-sounding *warranteeism*, his argument was clearly based on southern slavery. Fitzhugh pictured the social reality of the industrial world as a vicious system in which capital cruelly exploited labor. To his mind, only slavery, by combining capital and labor, could inject humane values into industrial society. Then justice and decency would prevail. Without the introduction of slavery, Fitzhugh predicted class warfare, even revolution.

Among scholars Hughes and especially Fitzhugh have known a popularity they never knew in their own time. Scholars have found them fascinating chiefly for two reasons: first, they attacked perceptively and forcefully the evils of the Industrial Revolution; second, they took the proslavery argument to its logical conclusion. In the South of the 1850s, however, talk of enslaving white workers, or even of making them warrantees, did not get far at all. By that time all adult white males had the right to vote in an essentially democratic political process. Neither white voters nor the politicians who courted their votes had any interest in pushing slavery across the racial boundary. Quite to the contrary, they stressed black slavery as the cornerstone of white equality. When ardent southerners compiled proslavery writings with a view to spreading their message, they omitted Hughes and Fitzhugh. The first of these compendiums, *The Pro-Slavery Argument as Maintained by the Most Distinguished Writers of the Southern States,* came out in Charleston in 1852, before the major work of either Hughes or Fitzhugh. But the considerably heftier *Cotton is King and Pro-Slavery Arguments,* published in Augusta, Georgia, in 1860, also excluded the self-proclaimed sociologists of slavery.

A SECOND NEW DIRECTION

Southerners turned to still another of the new sciences to bolster their institution of slavery. This one focused exclusively on race. Numerous men of science on both sides of the Atlantic embraced ethnology, the science of racial differences, during the mid-nineteenth century. Racial origins and types were the consuming interest of ethnologists, who then believed that human beings had multiple origins. According to the early ethnologists, different human races originated at different times. This position was anathema to the clerics, who insisted that all human beings were literally descended from Adam and Eve. The foremost southern proponent of ethnology was Dr. Josiah Nott of Mobile, Alabama. A native of South Carolina and graduate of South Carolina College, Nott had studied medicine at the college of Physicians and Surgeons in New York City and received his medical degree from the University of Pennsylvania before settling in Mobile in the 1830s. A widely respected clinician and surgeon, Nott also worked hard to improve medical education and to professionalize the practice of medicine.

Nott was also a scholar who became an active and respected member of the transatlantic community of ethnologists. Totally committed to his society and believing that the truths of science should govern social and moral relationships, Nott worked to put science behind slavery. To his mind, ethnology provided indisputable evidence in support of slavery. He and his fellow ethnologists believed that different races had not only different origins but different capabilities. In an attempt to demonstrate that blacks were inferior to whites and that they constituted a separate and distinct species, Nott took cranial measurements, compiled statistical data, and investigated the position of black people in ancient civilizations, such as the Egyptian. In 1854 he published with George Gliddon of Philadelphia, another leading American ethnologist, his major work, *Types of Mankind: or Ethnological Researches, Based upon the Ancient Monuments, Paintings, Sculptures, and Crania of Races, and upon Their Natural, Geographical, Philological and Biblical History.*

Nott realized that the religious orthodoxy of the South would cause problems for him and his argument. Most southerners, after all, accepted the biblical account of creation. To blunt the criticism he anticipated, Nott tried to present his scientific investigation as a Christian duty, but his effort availed him little. Though he thought of himself as fighting the battle of scientific truth against ignorance, his "science" was seriously flawed, and the biology of Charles Darwin soon replaced the ethnological explanation for the origin of species. In the South ethnology was never widely accepted. Because Nott and his doctrine were so vigorously assailed, most proslavery theorists tried to avoid both Nott and the question of racial origins. Yet Nott's work is one more demonstration that thoughts of slavery preoccupied southern intellectuals.

The reason for the burgeoning and ramification of the proslavery argument lends itself to no single, final answer. At the same time the historical record does permit reasonable certainty about the primary motives that prompted southerners to take up the proslavery cudgels. One possibility can be quickly eliminated; the defenders of slavery never really believed that their efforts could change prevailing opinion in the North. In their view, most of the North had already made up its mind, and any positive impact proslavery writings might have would be incidental.

The evidence points to three basic causes underlying the birth and maturation of the proslavery argument. Self-defense was significant. It is not accidental that the growth of the proslavery argument paralleled the growth of an articulate anti-slavery and antisouthern opinion in the North. In the face of what they saw as unfair and unwarranted condemnation of themselves and their institutions, southerners felt compelled to strike back. To them silence would signal either acquiesence or agreement. Rejecting both, southerners turned to a positive defense of slavery. In doing so they provided a buttress for the white South. Any wavering or defensive or doubting southerners could turn to the proslavery canon and find extensive arguments for the worth and rightness of slavery. That the proslavery argument helped weld a basic southern unity on the issue of slavery cannot be doubted. Finally, the southern intellectuals who built the defense of slavery also had a part in its development. Searching for a way to be of use to the society that needed them, these men committed a substantial portion of their intellectual talent to erecting an edifice designed to emphasize the legitimacy and value of their society. By that act these southern intellectuals joined their counterparts in the North and Europe.

SCIENCE

Intellectual activity in the antebellum South was not confined to the formal defense of slavery. The contributions to science made by colonial southerners were exceeded by those of southern scientists in the nineteenth century. No true scientific community existed in the South before 1860, but notable southerners did participate in the larger American and even European worlds of science. The most famous and popular southern scientist of his time was Matthew Fontaine Maury. Born in Virginia in 1806, Maury spent most of his life in the United States Navy. After a stagecoach accident in 1842, he found himself at a desk job in Washington. There he pursued his wide-ranging studies of winds and currents, which generally aided navigation and specifically enabled him to chart the course of the Gulf Stream.

Southerners did especially significant research in geology. Arguably the ablest scientist active in the South was William Barton Rogers, a native Pennsylvanian who as a teenager came to Virginia with his father, a science professor at William and Mary. In 1828, at twenty-four, William Rogers took over his deceased father's position at William and Mary; seven years later he moved to the University of Virginia. Rogers's work on the structure of the Appalachian Mountains gained him a national and an international reputation. Unhappy with the intellectual atmosphere at the university and with the state's support of his efforts. Rogers left Virginia in 1853 for his wife's New England, with the hope of establishing a polytechnic school. In 1862 he became the first president of the Massachusetts Institute of Technology.

Younger than Rogers and also exceptionally talented, Joseph LeConte taught in the 1850s first at the University of Georgia, his alma mater, and then at South Carolina College. Before entering upon his academic career in the South, LeConte studied at Harvard with the foremost American scientist of his day, Louis Agassiz. LeConte's first major publication, based on work begun on a research trip with Agassiz, discussed the formation of the keys and peninsula of Florida. LeConte was building his scientific reputation when the Union divided. He served the Confederacy as a scientist, but after 1865 he went west to the University of California at Berkeley, where he had a distinguished career.

Between 1820 and 1860 every southern state except Florida and Louisiana funded a geological survey. To conduct these surveys the legislators employed capable scientists, including William Rogers in Virginia. Legislators voted to spend money on such surveys because they anticipated economic advantages to result from them. They expected that agriculture would benefit from a better understanding of soils, and the identification of mineral deposits would aid mining and industry. Surely economic development would follow. Although the Panic of 1837 for a time curtailed financial support for these projects, they continued to the end of the antebellum era.

Edmund Ruffin, a Virginia planter who became a political radical during the sectional crisis, was one of the foremost agricultural reformers in America. Distressed about the declining fertility of his own and other tidewater plantations, Ruffin as early as 1818 began a series of experiments in an attempt to halt the debilitation of the land. From the study of soil chemistry he concluded that the acidic conditions in Virginia required neutralization before productivity could return. His own trials proved that marl, a fine shell deposit, would lower the acid content of the soil and make it productive once again. In his *Essay on Calcareous Manures*, published in 1833, and in an agricultural journal he founded, Ruffin pushed for agricultural reform. Although not all Virginia farmers and planters promptly followed his lead, he had a positive influence that extended beyond his state. North Carolina, South Carolina, and Georgia invited him to conduct agricultural surveys and advise on the renovation of worn-out lands.

Southerners made valuable contributions to other areas of science as well. When Dr. Josiah Nott was not writing his ethnological defenses of slavery, he was making detailed observations that increased the medical profession's knowledge about yellow fever and publishing widely on surgical techniques. Joseph Jones, a young Georgia physician with a bent for research, used his experiences as a Confederate surgeon to comment extensively on gangrene, the deadly scourge of the wounded, civilian as well as military. Dr. Jones also showed the potential of public health studies with his analyses of the sick and wounded in Confederate armies and of illness and mortality among Union prisoners of war. In Charleston, which had the finest museum of natural history in the South, the Lutheran clergyman John Bachman wrote substantively on the state's flora and fauna. Though no major centers of science appeared anywhere in the antebellum South, the men discussed here and their colleagues took part in investigations that added to the scientific knowledge of their day.

HISTORY AND BELLES LETTRES

The South also had an honorable tradition of history and belles lettres stretching from the Revolution to the Civil War. Early on southern writers became caught up in explaining their section and its mores. The first such work after the Revolution was Thomas Jefferson's *Notes on Virginia*, written in 1781–1782, then revised and published privately in France in 1785, and finally brought out two years later in England in what Jefferson regarded as the definitive version. *Notes* is at the same time a history, a geography, and a meditation. Originally intended to answer inquiries from France, the Revolutionary ally, *Notes* gave Jefferson the opportunity to comment on several topics of importance to him. Jefferson's concern about slavery and race—he considered the two to be inextricable—and his championship of the agrarian life pointed to the major themes of much of his later writing. *Notes* presented both agriculture and slavery as essential to the identity of Virginia and of the South.

In the half century following *Notes*, southerners made their most important literary efforts in history and biography. The first historian of the post-Revolutionary South was a transplanted Pennsylvanian. David Ramsay, a medical doctor, married a daughter of Henry Laurens, who gave him entrée to the elite of South Carolina. Ramsay believed that literature and the arts were "fixing their long and favorite abode in this new western world." Ramsay made his own contribution to literature with *A History of the Revolution in South Carolina* (1785), followed by a longer *History of the American Revolution* (1789). In the new century he published his *History of South Carolina* (1809). Although none of Ramsay's books broke a new literary path, his work does demonstrate the early determination of southerners to tell their story and to take literature seriously.

Southern writers who followed Ramsay continued to focus on the region's past. Probably the most notable was the Virginian William Wirt. A native of Maryland, Wirt at twenty headed for Virginia, where he did well. He served in both the legislative and judicial arms of the state government; he was attorney general in James Monroe's cabinet; and in 1832 he made an unsuccessful try for the presidency. All the while he thought of himself as a man of letters. Beginning with the anonymous publication of a series of essays in 1803, Wirt wrote chiefly about the society of his Virginia. He spent a dozen years on his major work, *Sketches of the Life and Character of Patrick Henry,* which appeared in 1817. His *Patrick Henry* reached far fewer readers than another biographical study that came out a few years earlier. Like Wirt, Mason Locke Weems was a Marylander who ended up in Virginia. A man of many occupations—he was at various times an itinerant book-seller and an Anglican clergyman—Weems published in 1805 his *Life of Washington,* probably the most popular biography in early nineteenth-century America. Embellished by tales of his own invention—we owe to Weems the legend that young Washington fessed up to cutting down his father's cherry tree—Weems's book went through forty editions before his death in 1825 and a multitude of others thereafter.

The writing of fiction in the South emerged in earnest with the work of John Pendleton Kennedy of Baltimore, who had an enormous influence on plantation fiction. Kennedy's first novel, *Swallow Barn,* published in 1832, described in charming and romantic terms a Virginia plantation of 1800 vintage. The planta-tion depicted by Kennedy could not be surpassed as a scene of warmth and high human values—hospitality, devotion to family, a sense of honor among the gen-try, kindly relations between masters and slaves. Although he found slavery morally indefensible, as a true son of the upper South he took the position that only southerners could deal with slavery; any interference by the North was ab-solutely unacceptable.

Kennedy spent much of his life in the larger world of business, and he also devoted time to the Whig party, which rewarded him with the post of secretary of the navy in President Millard Fillmore's cabinet. His literary focus, however, re-mained on the southern past. His *Horse-Shoe Robinson* (1835) and *Rob of the Bowl* (1838) deal with the pre-1800 South. Set in Virginia and South Carolina during the Revolution, *Horse-Shoe Robinson* focuses on the conflicts that raged between patri-ots and tories. *Rob of the Bowl* moves even further back in time, to seventeenth-century Maryland.

Two other writers who worked with southern themes approached their sub-ject from quite opposite political directions, though both were Virginians. Nathaniel Beverly Tucker, a patrician and half brother of John Randolph of Roanoke, studied law and moved to Missouri, where he served as a federal judge before returning to Virginia and a faculty appointment at the College of William and Mary. Deeply involved in sectional politics, Tucker in 1836 published his best-known novel, *The Partisan Leader: A Tale of the Future.* Purporting to describe events in 1849, Tucker discusses the evils of the tariff and the North and the joys of the master-slave relationship and the South. He even depicts the formation of a successful southern confederacy. William Alexander Caruthers, by contrast, dis-liked slavery and attempted to foster sectional goodwill. Hailing from the Vir-ginia uplands, not the tidewater, Caruthers devoted much of his work to more western regions. *The Kentuckians in New York* (1834) weaves a story out of the jour-neys of southerners and northerners to each other's homes; the plot of *Knights of the Horseshoe* (1845) hinges on a colonial expedition into the Shenandoah Valley. In *The Cavaliers of Virginia* (1834–1835), Caruthers tells a Gothic tale of Bacon's Rebel-lion.

None of those writers matched in importance the two men who stood far ahead of all their literary colleagues—Edgar Allan Poe and William Gilmore

Simms. Poe, a significant figure in the history of American writing, occupies a unique position in southern letters. Though born in Boston, he was reared in Virginia and identified himself with the South, whose institutions, including slavery, he defended. Although he did contribute substantial critical pieces to the *Southern Literary Messenger,* the section's leading magazine, in neither his poetry nor his fiction did Poe make significant use of southern subjects or materials. His characters and plots were not tightly connected to time or place. From a purely artistic viewpoint he surpassed all his southern contemporaries, but his work did not concentrate on the southern experience.

*W*ILLIAM GILMORE SIMMS

William Gilmore Simms, though no match for Poe as a literary artist, stood as the preeminent man of letters in the antebellum South. Born in Charleston in 1806, Simms remained a partisan of South Carolina, and though he traveled beyond its borders, he never lived anywhere else. His loyalty to his native state was the cornerstone of his powerful commitment to the South. Yet Simms was no provincial; as a young man he traveled to the North, and he was well known in the literary and publishing circles of New York City, where he found both lifelong friends and publishers for his books.

Simms began his literary career as a poet but gained his greatest renown as a

WILLIAM GILMORE SIMMS, THE LEADING MAN OF LETTERS IN THE ANTEBELLUM SOUTH (Courtesy South Caroliniana Library, University of South Carolina)

novelist. During his lifetime he published more than thirty novels—far too many, for the mediocrity of some of them still haunts his reputation; but in quality his best work approaches that of James Fenimore Cooper and Simms's great model, Sir Walter Scott. Simms wrote chiefly about the South, both the southwestern frontier and his own South Carolina. His interest in the Southwest stemmed from a youthful journey to Mississippi, where his father had moved. Simms rejected his father's advice to make his fortune in the West, but he did use the region as a setting for four border romances, most notable among them *Guy Rivers* (1834) and *Richard Hurdis* (1838).

After Simms's second marriage in 1836, to a plantation heiress, he settled at Woodlands Plantation, some seventy-five miles west of Charleston. Without question his best fiction dealt with his state. The Indian conflicts of the 1710s provided the background for *The Yemassee* (1835). His finest novels, such as *The Partisan* (1835) and *Woodcraft* (1852), treated the bitter strife between South Carolina's patriots and tories. Although Simms's work tended to be melodramatic, it had distinct strengths: superb descriptions of the landscape, development of memorable characters, an honest depiction of the Revolutionary conflict, careful attention to social class. In none of Simms's fiction, however, did he question the fundamental social institutions of his society.

Simms's devotion to the South prompted him to take up other literary tasks. Believing an appreciation of their past essential for South Carolinians—and by extension for all southerners—he published in 1840 a *History of South Carolina* and followed it three years later with a geography of his state. Simms also devoted considerable effort to biographical studies and published works on a founding colonist, John Smith (1840) and two Revolutionary heroes, Francis Marion (1844) and Nathanael Greene (1849). Although Simms's own writing consumed most of his time, he also strove to create a southern literary community by assisting and encouraging young writers and by working on literary journals, which he envisioned as highways connecting all southern literary endeavors with each other. From 1840 to 1860 he was either editing such journals or contributing to them, often both. Such periodicals tended to have short lives in the antebellum South. Only the *Southern Literary Messenger*, published in Richmond from 1834 to 1864, enjoyed a reasonably lengthy life span.

Although at one level Simms never achieved his goal, at another he knew hard-won success. The magazines never flourished as he hoped and southerners never became the serious literary consumers he wished, but Simms kept alive the ideal of a literary community in the South. And by 1860, thanks in large part to his efforts, Charleston was developing into the kind of literary center that he envisioned.

THE HUMORISTS

Although Simms's novel often had a strong comic dimension, he is not included among the writers known as humorists. In the antebellum era humor became a distinct genre, though it had origins in the colonial period. Humorous writing was not peculiar to the South; New England had its Down East comedy and other areas also had their humorists. The first major southern humorist set a high standard. Born in Augusta, Georgia, in 1790, Augustus Baldwin Longstreet had a varied career. A graduate of Yale and of Tapping Reeve's Law School in Litchfield, Connecticut—to both of which he followed his friend John C. Calhoun—Longstreet began as a lawyer, then became a newspaper editor. Later he was ordained as a Methodist minister, and that work led him into education. He served as president of four colleges—two small denominational institutions, the University of Mississippi, and South Carolina College. Even with this active life Longstreet became the Adam of antebellum humorists. His *Georgia Scenes,* published in 1835, was a collection of stories that had appeared earlier in two Georgia newspapers. This was a publishing route that would become familiar to other southern humorists. Longstreet's stories revolved around the everyday life of the common white people of Georgia—horse trading, market day, social occasions and festivities, fights. With dialect a prominent feature, these tales provide a marvelous sense of who these Georgians were and how they lived. In a real sense *Georgia Scenes* is a historical source as well as a collection of comic stories.

Among the best of Longstreet's numerous literary descendants were Johnson J. Hooper and Joseph G. Baldwin. Hooper was a North Carolinian who emigrated to Alabama, where he moved about to pursue several occupations in addition to writing stories. Collected as *The Adventures of Captain Simon Suggs . . . ,* Hooper's work came out in 1845. Unlike Longstreet, who invented a variety of leading characters, Hooper focused on only one. Through Simon Suggs, a wily trickster, Hooper satirized such serious subjects as political campaigns and camp meetings. Hooper found the comedy in everybody, the clever along with the gullible. Adopting a different approach, Joseph G. Baldwin used humor to describe a specific time and place. A Virginian who moved to the southwestern frontier in the hectic years just before the Panic of 1837, Baldwin wanted to convey the wide-open, turbulent society he entered. *The Flush Times of Alabama and Mississippi* (1853) recounts the essentially frontier character of a new area before settled ways and institutions took over. In humorous fashion Baldwin contrasts the Southwest, where nothing was nailed down, with his native Virginia, where everything was in place. Though *Flush Times* is fiction, it conveys a superb sense of those times.

The most original of all the southern humorists was George Washington Harris, a Pennsylvanian who migrated to eastern Tennessee. At various times he captained a steamboat, farmed, and engaged in other endeavors. In the 1850s he wrote stories about the most powerful comic figure created in the antebellum South, Sut Lovingood. Harris's *Sut Lovingood: Yarns Spun by a "Nat'ral Born Durn'd Fool,"* published in book form in 1867, describes the common whites of antebellum eastern Tennessee. Harris treats basically the same topics that most of his fellow humorists addressed, though he makes more pronounced use of the violence and crudity of primitive life. Social and religious occasions, superstitions, love and marriage, and sharp traders make up the bulk of Harris's plots. The heavy dialect in these stories discourages readers today, but the tales have a vitality and exuberance unmatched in antebellum southern fiction.

These four men and their numerous colleagues made two major contributions to southern history and letters. First, their works provide a description of the everyday life of the common white folk that is almost unique in its detail. They remained largely silent on the blacks. It is almost as if they lived and wrote in a slaveless world. For them and their society, slavery was a serious business; no one poked fun at it. A second and equally important contribution lies in the powerful legacy of their humor. In the late nineteenth and the twentieth centuries the great southern writers who made humor a central part of their works, most notably Mark Twain and William Faulkner, drew directly on the techniques and subjects of Longstreet, Harris, and their fellows.

For all its indisputable merits, the literary corpus of the antebellum South does not approach in distinction the literature produced in the North, chiefly in New England. These years have been said to represent the flowering of New England, and a galaxy of brilliant writers give substance to that claim. Herman Melville, Nathaniel Hawthorne, Ralph Waldo Emerson, Emily Dickinson—these writers had no equals in the slave states. Like their southern contemporaries, they were products of their region, but they brought to their art an intellectual detachment and a sense of irony about their own world which we do not find in the southerners. Those qualities are essential for literary achievement of the highest order. Caught up in defending their society, southern writers were unable to perceive the massive intellectual distance between irony and ridicule. They were too committed to their society, with its peculiar institution, to produce great literature. They could not distinguish detachment and criticism from hatred. The South would have to wait until another century for its literary flowering.

SCHOOLING

The story of education in the antebellum South reads very much like that of literature. Some of its parts had true merit, but the whole was not distinguished. Southern education moved into the nineteenth century without a secure foundation, for education was never a central concern in the colonial South.

During the antebellum era no statewide public school system existed. Southerners never heeded Thomas Jefferson's cry that the state ought to assume the responsibility of educating its young people. Even Jefferson's own Virginia rejected his proposals. By 1860 some states had made a respectable beginning while others were performing abysmally. In some cities, however, public schools made substantial headway. Charleston, Louisville, Mobile, and others had excellent schools, and without question the schools were better in the cities than in rural areas.

All too frequently a state made elaborate plans and then did nothing. A few states, however, went beyond planning to action. Kentucky and North Carolina made the best effort. In the 1830s the Kentucky legislature supported public schools by appropriating over half of the surplus revenue received from the federal government before the Panic of 1837 and by adopting a tax of 2 cents on all property in the state. In 1839 North Carolina permitted counties to levy taxes for schools, but the system remained decentralized until 1853, when the office of state superintendent of schools was created. Its first incumbent, Calvin H. Wiley, who for a score of years had been urging popular education, guided North Carolina to undisputed leadership in public education. By 1860 some 150,000 of the state's

220,000 white children were enrolled in more than 3,000 schools. No other state could match that record.

The southern states also had charity schools, a particular form of public school. In order to qualify their children for enrollment in these free schools, families had to declare themselves unable to pay for their children's education. Proud people—and southerners were surely proud—usually refused to make the necessary declarations of indigency. As a result, these schools were undersubscribed. In Alabama six years after the establishment of a charity system the state superintendent of education reported that nearly one-half of the eligible children did not attend.

Private academies, often called field schools, filled a crucial place in secondary education. In a basic sense they replaced the colonial system of educating children either with private tutors or by sending them to England. In the nineteenth century the South had more private secondary schools than any other section of the country. According to the 1850 census, the South had 2,700 academies to New England's 2,100 and the Middle West's 1,000. Many of these academies offered a vigorous and rigorous education that emphasized the classics and the Bible. Possibly the best known was headed by Moses Waddel, who held forth in Willington, South Carolina. A Presbyterian minister as well as teacher and headmaster, Waddel taught for six days and preached on Sundays. His curriculum focused on Greek, Latin, mathematics, religion, and public speaking. He counted among his alumni many notable southern leaders, but undoubtedly the most famous was John C. Calhoun.

The general failure of secondary education in the South is readily apparent in the figures on illiteracy. According to the 1850 census, 20.3 percent of southern whites were illiterate—a damning indictment of the educational system, or more precisely a dramatic indication of the lack of one. In the Middle States only 3 percent of the white population was illiterate, and in New England the comparable figure was less than 0.5 percent. Comparing the number of schools and teachers in South and North, the wide disparity in illiteracy is not surprising. The 1850 census indicates that the white population of the North was two and a half times larger than that of the South, but the number of both schools and teachers was three times greater in the North. Although the South added substantial numbers of schools and teachers in the final antebellum decade, the wide sectional gap remained.

The reasons for the lag in southern education were many. First, the population density in the southern states, even among the most populous, worked against a vigorous public school system. Virginia had only 14 white inhabitants per square mile and North Carolina but 12. Massachusetts, in contrast, had 127 inhabitants for each square mile. This pattern underscores the overwhelming rural character of the South. And in view of the state of communications, roads, and modes of travel in the first half of the nineteenth century, an effort to bring children together regularly over considerable distances would have faced formidable difficulties. In addition, neither wealthy planters nor middling farmers pressed southern legislatures to spend money on education. Neither group as a whole saw much benefit in public education for them or their children. Feeling no pressure, legislators did not rush into an area that many believed was a private matter, not a state function. Thus by the outbreak of the Civil War most public school systems in the South were rudimentary at best.

COLLEGES

The South had a much stronger record in higher education. Unlike the North, the post-Revolutionary South did not have a strong colonial base on which to build colleges. The College of William and Mary was really the only institution of higher learning in the southern colonies. The South witnessed no flurry of new private colleges after the Revolution, but a movement for public ones spread through the seaboard states. Pushed by the upper social order, public higher education became such a popular cause that the first state-supported colleges were established in the South. The debate still rages on which such school is the oldest. The University of Georgia (then known as Franklin College) received the first charter, in 1785, but it did not open until 1801. Although the University of North Carolina was not chartered until 1789, it welcomed students in 1795. South Carolina College was founded in 1801. Not until 1816, however, did the Virginia legislature give its blessing to the University of Virginia, and then only after the insistent advocacy of Thomas Jefferson. Undoubtedly the existence of William and Mary influenced the delayed entry of Virginia.

The desire for public institutions of higher learning did not remain restricted to the older states. The establishment of colleges became an integral part of the western march. The University of Tennessee, which was established in 1794 as East Tennessee College, received state assistance in 1807. Alabama founded its university in the very year it became a state, 1819. Mississippi and Louisiana waited for a time; the University of Mississippi dates from 1844; the University of Louisiana (which after the Civil War became Tulane University) came into being four years later. Before 1860 most southern states could boast of a state-supported college.

Some of these schools were quite good; they equaled first-rate institutions in the rest of the country. The best were probably the University of Virginia and South Carolina College. Without question the University of Virginia was the most influential. Jefferson, its founder, was both the political and intellectual father of the university. He not only urged the legislature to establish it but designed the campus and the buildings, planned the curriculum, and brought in the first faculty members, many from Europe. Jefferson's university had the first elective curriculum in the country and introduced the teaching of modern foreign languages. Its antebellum faculty included such academic stalwarts as the scientist William B. Rogers and the literary critic George Frederick Holmes. The University of Virginia was the only southern school that attracted many out-of-state students. South Carolina College became a strong institution under the presidency of Thomas Cooper, a Scottish chemist. Committed to a particular political philosophy as well as to academics, Cooper preached an extreme states-rights doctrine to a generation of Carolina leaders. Among its faculty South Carolina College could boast the most outstanding political scientist in the country, the German-born Francis

Lieber. Lieber left for Columbia University in 1857, however, after questions were raised about his fervor for slavery. The college also had the services of the youthful geologist Joseph LeConte.

Three states also supported military colleges. State leaders expected these institutions to train officers for state militias, but the academies had another purpose as well: their military discipline provided an acceptable means for governing and educating proud, unruly planters' sons who rejected all other efforts to regulate their behavior. The Virginia Military Institute (VMI), founded in 1839, is the oldest southern military school. Its most famous citizen was a professor who taught physics and artillery tactics to cadets and then later commanded many of them in battle, Thomas J. "Stonewall" Jackson. The Citadel, South Carolina's version of VMI, accepted its first students in 1842. The Citadel certainly succeeded with its military education, for during the Civil War some 90 percent of its living alumni became officers in the Confederate States Army. The last of the military schools to be established, Louisiana State Seminary of Learning and Military Academy (now Louisiana State University), opened its doors in 1860, with a former United States Army officer as superintendent. Although it had little time to educate students before the war broke out, it certainly had an impact on the conflict. With the onset of hostilities, all students and faculty joined the Confederate forces. The superintendent, however, went with the Union, where he served with considerable distinction; his name was William Tecumseh Sherman.

Public colleges did not, however, occupy the entire stage of higher education. Nonpublic institutions did exist, though prior to 1830 they were neither notable nor numerous; the one significant exception was Transylvania University, opened in Lexington, Kentucky, in 1789. By 1820 Transylvania was flourishing, with offerings in law and medicine as well as an undergraduate curriculum. When religious problems plagued the school in the mid-1820s, however, its light dimmed.

In the years between 1830 and 1860 religion became a major force in southern higher education. Spurred by the evangelical movement that surged throughout the South, the major denominations established colleges in almost every state. Many disappeared almost as quickly as they were founded; others were little more than high schools. Some not only survived but became well-known institutions. The Baptists started Wake Forest in North Carolina, Furman in South Carolina, and Baylor in Texas. The Methodists were responsible for Randolph-Macon in Virginia, Trinity (now Duke University) in North Carolina, and Emory in Georgia. The Presbyterians founded Hampden-Sydney in Virginia, Davidson in North Carolina, and Austin in Texas.

The church leaders whose efforts and determination ensured the success of this collegiate movement had two basic motives. One was clearly religious, or more precisely sectarian; the other had secular overtones. First, the churchmen became concerned that the public institutions either suffered from a lack of orthodoxy or failed to stress religion at all. These clerics and laymen wanted their young people educated in an environment where the doctrinal teachings of their particular denomination were emphasized. Second, a substantial portion of the religious educators believed that the public colleges had become too aristocratic as well as too worldly. As they saw it, their schools would not nurture displays of wealth and social position. To curtail snobbishness and preoccupation with wealth, some of them—Wake Forest was one—decreed that all students must engage in manual labor.

The last sectarian college established before the Civil War differed from the others in one important respect. When the Episcopalians founded the University of the South in Sewanee, Tennessee, in 1860, they certainly expected their school to inculcate Episcopalian values and doctrine; but they also wanted to educate young men as true southerners. Created as the sectional crisis deepened and southern self-consciousness heightened, Sewanee had a mission both sectarian and secular.

THE GROWTH OF EVANGELICAL RELIGION

The best estimates indicate that in 1800 only about 10 percent of white southerners belonged to a church. Some others attended a church occasionally. In the decade and a half before 1800 a network of evangelical churches had been created on both sides of the Appalachians, in the new western states as well as the old seaboard states, but they were the outposts of a faithful few. A New Englander who worked as a tutor in Richmond in the mid-1790s pictured the South as a religious wasteland. "Christianity is here breathing its last," he wrote home. "I cannot find a friend with whom I can even converse on religious subjects."

Yet only a few years later the South got religion. The spiritual fires that swept over that wasteland in the nineteenth century were sparked by a camp meeting in south-central Kentucky in the summer of 1800. A camp meeting was exactly what it sounds like. People from the surrounding area came together for a meeting. Expecting to stay a few days, they set up tents and lean-tos. In this environment, where people congregated to share a religious experience, the emotion that was generated among the faithful was contagious. The spiritual energy released during the Great Revival spread east, south, and west. A great interdenominational appeal, though clearly Protestant, swept across the South.

Properly understood, the Great Revival was the southern Great Awakening. In a fundamental sense, the revival never ended: religion assumed a permanently conspicuous place in the society. By 1860 the proportion of church members had more than doubled, and twice that many more—fully 40 percent of southern whites—actively participated in organized churches. The evangelical denominations both led and pushed this religious turnabout. Spearheaded by the Baptists and Methodists, who by 1860 claimed 80 percent of all southern church members, evangelical Protestantism captured the South.

Between the Great Revival and 1860 revivals became fixtures of southern life. The Methodists institutionalized the camp meeting, which became a key feature of the denomination. Essential to the success of Methodism were the circuit riders, the tireless ministers who served the isolated churches of the southern countryside. Each circuit rider served a number of churches spread over a considerable distance. On the frontier a circuit could encompass a hundred miles and twenty or more churches. The men who rode the circuits combined religious conviction with the courage of pioneers.

The experience of the Reverend William Redman, responsible for the White River Circuit in Arkansas, underscores the resoluteness of these mobile messengers. Because of the distance between his congregations, the Reverend Redman often slept alone on the ground with a saddlebag for a pillow. During one night he had just begun to drift off to sleep "when the sudden, terrific scream of a panther brought him to his feet." As he clung to his horse, which threatened to bolt, he feared "the blood-thirsty animal would rend him to pieces." But to Redman's great relief, the panther decided to look elsewhere for his nighttime meal. On the following morning Redman "paid his devotions to the God of Daniel, who had delivered him from so great a danger," then resumed his journey with "rejoicing." Only the dedication and zeal of itinerant preachers such as the Reverend Redman made possible the phenomenal growth of Methodism.

The other two evangelical denominations took a somewhat different tack. Both the Baptists and, to a lesser extent, the Presbyterians embraced the revival as central to their mission, but neither warmed to the camp meeting. The Baptists were particularly suited to capitalize on the changing role of religion in southern society. Because Baptists believed in the absolute independence of individual churches, no ecclesiastical hurdles hindered the organization of a Baptist church anywhere a group wanted one. And because Baptists were not concerned about the educational attainments of their clergymen, anyone who desired to do so and who could find a congregation could become a minister. Instant churches and preachers were commonplace.

The Presbyterians did not match their evangelical brethren in growth. Their governance precluded the instantaneous church, but an even greater impediment was their insistence on an educated clergy. Those two considerations, added to a theology more intellectual than emotional in character, ensured that the Presbyterians would never match the Baptists and Methodists in growth rate or numbers. The Presbyterians attracted a larger portion of the social and economic elite than their evangelical competitors, but here again they were overshadowed, for the spiritual home of the upper orders was the Episcopal or Anglican church, the smallest of the major denominations and the one least affected by evangelicalism.

Neither the Roman Catholics nor the Jews challenged the overwhelming cultural as well as religious domination of the Protestants. Jews, who constituted less than 1 percent of the southern population in the first half of the nineteenth century, had arrived in the South before 1750. Locating mostly in cities—Charleston, for example, had a significant Jewish community—Jews as a group exercised little influence. They generally adopted the mores and the outlook of the larger society. Roman Catholics were more numerous than Jews but were not more influential, except in Louisiana. With its Franco-Spanish heritage, Louisiana accounted for more than half of the Catholics in the antebellum South. Outside Louisiana most Catholics, like most Jews, lived in cities along the seaboard and on the border with the free states. They, too, became part of the social, political, and cultural world fashioned by the dominant Protestants.

In the nineteenth century the evangelicals stood at the center of southern society. Whereas evangelicals had been outsiders in the eighteenth century, they made up the southern establishment in the nineteenth. Their prominent laymen occupied central posts in the society and their leading ministers, a number of them

SALEM BLACK RIVER PRESBYTERIAN CHURCH (1846)
Sumter District, South Carolina. This structure emphasizes the influence of
religion in the countryside. (Courtesy of Patricia H. Cooper)

originally from the North, became molders of opinion and influential public
spokesmen. The churches exercised considerable moral authority in the South.
When such men as the South Carolina Baptist Richard Furman, the Mississippi
Methodist William Winans, the Presbyterians Benjamin Palmer of Louisiana and
James H. Thornwell of South Carolina, and James Otey, Episcopal bishop of Tennessee, chose to speak, they had an audience. In towns, in villages, and in individual congregations, local clergymen enjoyed similar status and influence.

The message

On major issues the clergy's blessing, or at least its support, was critical. The
churches and their teachings permeated southern society. The churches did not
attack slavery or any other institution central to the society. In the late eighteenth
century some clerics, especially among the Methodists of the upper South, questioned the morality of slavery, but the extent of such opposition can be exaggerated, and even those limited reservations disappeared in the nineteenth century.
Ministers placed their influence and the authority of God behind the organization
of southern society in general and behind slavery in particular. Religious southerners did not have to choose between the promptings of their political chieftains
and the exhortations of their spiritual guardians; they were not at odds. According to the gospel pronounced from numerous pulpits, even secession was ordained by the Almighty.

JAMES H. THORNWELL, PRESBYTERIAN MINISTER
AND EDUCATOR (South Caroliniana Library, University of
South Carolina)

The attention of southern Protestants focused chiefly on personal conversion
and the spiritual health of the individual soul. The southern clergy were not out to
remake the world. A pervasive Calvinism underscored the widespread belief that
imperfect people lived in an imperfect world. The concept of perfectionism,
which stimulated and fueled reform movements in the North, was largely absent
from the southern religious vocabulary. Southern clergy surely strove to uplift
their congregations, but they had no vision of a perfect society. Ministers in-
veighed against immoral behavior, and local churches, acting as keepers of morality, enforced a moral code that defined as sins such acts as adultery, fornication,
intoxication, and in the most solemn congregations even dancing. But always the
focus was on the individual.

The influential Presbyterian minister and theologian James H. Thornwell,
who also served as president of South Carolina College, captured the essence of
southern Protestantism when he wrote that too many people regarded the church
as "a moral institute of universal good, whose business it is to wage war upon
every form of human ill, whether social, civil, political or moral, and to patronize

every expedient which a romantic benevolence may suggest as likely to contribute to human comfort, or to mitigate the inconveniences of life." Nonsense!
proclaimed Thornwell. In his view, God did not intend that "all ill shall be banished from this sublunary state, and earth be converted into a paradise, or that the
proper end of the Church is the direct promotion of universal good." God was
sovereign, and "the power of the church . . . is only ministerial and declarative."
Cementing himself and his religion to a literal reading of God's word, Thornwell
asserted, "The Bible, and the Bible alone, is [the church's] rule of faith and practice. Beyond the Bible she can never go and apart from the Bible she can never
speak."

Yet southern Protestantism did have a distinct reform dimension. Ministers
were especially concerned about greed, or what one of them termed "a lust for
mammon"—in our language, the almighty dollar. Ministers saw greed as a vicious cancer eating away at the vitals of southern society. Unchecked, the preachers predicted, it would destroy any hope for a godly South. From their pulpits
ministers thundered against putting money and the desire for it ahead of the Bible
and God. Christian citizens, they asserted, must be educated in Christian principles. This Christian education would take place in schools and colleges as well as
churches. The perceived need for a Christian education to counter the tendency to
greed became a primary motive in the founding of denominational colleges, and
it spurred the extraordinary efforts made by ministers to keep academies going.

The sin of greed was a constant theme during the antebellum period, and it
probably received special attention in the 1850s, a decade of general prosperity. In
the ministers' view, southern society never purged itself of this transgression;
spiritual transformation never occurred. From this vantage point the preachers
launched their one major criticism of slavery. They urged slave owners to follow
the biblical precepts defining a truly patriarchal system. According to the clergymen, decisions by masters to work slaves unduly hard and to break up families
signaled greed, not Christian stewardship. Sermon after sermon urged slave owners
to focus on becoming Christian stewards of what God had placed in their trust.

The major denominations made every effort to carry their version of the
Christian message to slaves. Slave owners often invited ministers to their farms
and plantations to preach to slaves, an invitation the clergymen eagerly accepted.
In addition, numerous congregations of all denominations, notably the widespread Baptists, permitted slaves to worship with whites, to become fellow
church members. Although blacks usually sat in a separate part of the church, a
balcony or a lean-to, they participated in the same religious service. Preachers,
however, often directed admonitions about obedience directly to the slaves. Moreover, the blacks were generally subject to the same church discipline as white
members.

The leading denominations also engaged in a separate mission to slaves.
While seemingly directed solely at converting and ministering to slaves, this crusade also encouraged Christian slaveholding. This combination produced for the
ministers the twin blessings of slavery. Carrying the Gospel to slaves could result
in the salvation of souls otherwise lost and also could offer masters the opportunity to demonstrate their allegiance to Christian principles. The major purpose of
the mission to the slaves was to bring the institution more in line with the Bible's

teachings as the ministers saw them. Never did they set out to destroy slavery, and it is impossible to overestimate the importance of the clergy's support of slavery.

SECTIONAL STRIFE

The commitment of southern churches and their ministers to southern institutions was underscored in the sectional divisions of the largest denominations. In the mid-1840s both the Baptists and the Methodists in the South broke with their northern brethren in disputes directly connected with slavery. In 1844 the general conference of the Methodist church asked the Methodist bishop of Georgia to take a leave from his episcopal office until he had disposed of the slaves he had acquired along with his second wife. Incensed by this action, which in their minds was tantamount to declaring slaveholding unchristian, southern Methodists moved to set up their own church. The next year in Louisville, the Methodist Episcopal Church, South, came into being. In that same year Baptists in the South, meeting in Augusta, organized the Southern Baptist Convention and withdrew from the national organization because its foreign mission board refused to appoint slaveholding missionaries.

The remaining two major Protestant denominations escaped sectional division before 1861. In 1837, before the Baptists and Methodists split, the Presbyterians had been divided by questions that were chiefly theological, though they did have implications for the church's involvement in social reform. The conservative Old School predominated in the South; these southerners had no difficulty getting along with their fellow traditionalists in the North. The liberal New School, which was more strongly oriented toward social action, counted few adherents below the Mason-Dixon line. As a result, an organized southern Presbyterian church did not come into existence until 1861. It lasted as a separate entity until 1983, however. Episcopalians never really divided; in fact, the church remained remarkably free of sectional disputes. An Episcopal Church in the Confederate States was formed in 1861, but when the war ended, the Episcopalians quickly reunited.

The bulwark provided by the churches and the clergy enabled antebellum southerners to live secure in the conviction that their society and its major social institution had God's approval.

12
The Free Social Order

❖

Rich planters, poor whites, black slaves—this stereotype of an antebellum social order comprising only three groups has survived for a century and a half. In the generation before 1860 it was adopted and preached by the abolitionists; the Republicans also made it a staple of their propaganda. In our own time popular novelists and moviemakers have conveyed it to millions in bold portraits with no blurred images. This distorted picture has little connection with historical reality.

The reality was considerably more complex. That conclusion is not simply the assessment of modern scholars who have carefully studied antebellum society. In 1860 Daniel R. Hundley, a native Alabamian, divided white southerners into seven classes. It is certainly possible to quarrel with Hundley's categories, and it would surely be unprofitable to classify every individual in the antebellum South, but recognition of the region's social diversity and complexity is essential to an understanding of the social order.

PLANTERS

The vast majority of southern white males fell into one of two broad categories: planters and yeomen. To be sure, substantial differences were to be found among planters. The planter class ranged from grand seigneurs reigning over acres and slaves accumulated across several generations to hard-charging buccaneers driving newly acquired slaves to carve plantations from the virgin forests west of the Mississippi to plain, hard-working folk tilling a modest acreage with a modest slave force. And over time thousands of planters moved from one group to another.

The homes of the planters were as various as the lives they led. In the years after 1815 the stately Georgian mansion that housed the tidewater aristocracy of the colonial era still adorned the old seaboard states. The 1820s, however, witnessed the advent of the architectural style that would prevail in the antebellum South and eventually become both symbol and stereotype of the antebellum regime. Based on the design of the classical Greek temple, the Greek Revival style,

GAINESWOOD, DEMOPOLIS, ALABAMA (1843–1859), PROBABLY DESIGNED
BY THE OWNER, NATHAN B. WHITFIELD (Courtesy of Patricia H. Cooper)

with its imposing columns, originated in the upper South and spread quickly
throughout the region. Some houses—Andrew Jackson's Hermitage outside
Nashville, for instance—were quite simple behind their great columns. Others,
such as Gaineswood in Demopolis, Alabama, were complex and lavish structures.
In the Mississippi Valley the Greek Revival meshed with the Creole tradition in
such magnificent structures as Houmas House in Ascension Parish, Louisiana.

Although the Greek Revival mansions denoted success and status in every
slave state, by the 1850s new styles and new wealth led in new directions. The
Italianate style, borrowed from Italian villas, added semicircular arches and tow-
ers. It was popular for a time but never drove the Greek Revival from its pinnacle.
The enormous riches that sugar brought to some planters in the decade before
1860 resulted in houses of unprecedented size and opulence. Possibly the largest
residence constructed in the antebellum South still stands today beside the Mississippi in Iberville Parish, Louisiana. Built for John Hampden Randolph in 1859,
Nottoway, or the White Castle, a Greek Revival–Italianate mansion, contains 64
rooms, 200 windows, and 165 doors. Randolph wanted Nottoway to outshine a
wealthy neighbor's home, Belle Grove, a house of comparable magnificence
which no longer stands. The desire for conspicuous display which motivated the
construction of these two enormous houses did not die in 1861. Belle Grove and
Nottoway clearly point the way to the "cottages" of Newport.

Most planters did not live in splendid columned mansions, though few were
so unpretentious as the Mississippi slave owner who named his home Log Hall.
The most common plantation residence was a simple rectangular frame house of
two stories with a chimney at either end. Such homes usually had either two or
four rooms on each floor, divided by a central hall. They might or might not be
painted. A number of these plain farmhouses still stand in the southern countryside. Over time some of these houses were enlarged by rooms extended rearward
or by the addition of a wing or wings; these additions rarely provided any architectural distinction. A family that really prospered or that had social ambitions

HOUMAS, ASCENSION PARISH, LOUISIANA (1840s), CENTER OF THE
HAMPTON FAMILY SUGAR PLANTATION (Courtesy of Patricia H. Cooper)

might place a portico or columns, most often two, at the front of their house in an
effort to mimic the Greek Revival mansion.

A glimpse at the lives and activities of some of these planters affords insight
into their class. At the ancestral home called Shirley, on the James River in tidewater Virginia, Hill Carter, scion of one of the most notable families in the state,
lived in a manner his grandfather would have recognized and applauded. A guest
provided an eyewitness account of a dinner at Shirley in 1833. The event began at
3 P.M., when the host led the family and their guests, in pairs, to the dining room.
At one end of the table he carved a saddle of mutton while at the other his wife la-
dled soup. Two young slave boys served from platters brimming with ham, beef,
turkey, duck, eggs, greens, sweet potatoes, and hominy. After champagne was
served, the upper tablecloth was removed and desserts were brought in: plum
pudding, tarts, ice cream, and brandied peaches. After dessert the second tablecloth was removed and on the mahogany table were placed figs, raisins, almonds,
and, in front of Hill Carter, "2 or 3 bottles of wine—Madeira, Port, and a sweet
wine for the ladies. After the glasses are filled, the gentlemen pledge their services
to the ladies, and down goes the wine." After the second glass the ladies retired,
but "the gentlemen . . . circulate[d] the bottle pretty briskly." Any man who
wished to follow the women from the table, however, could do so at his leisure
without insulting his host. After music and conversation, the guests headed for
home.

John Palfrey never knew such ease or such bounty. Immigrating to Louisiana
from Massachusetts shortly after the Purchase, he went bankrupt both as a ship's
chandler and as a plantation manager. Finally he managed to obtain land west of

NOTTOWAY, IBERVILLE PARISH, LOUISIANA (1859), BUILT FOR JOHN HAMPDEN RANDOLPH (Courtesy Louisiana Office of Tourism)

New Orleans, where in 1811 he began to clear away trees and brush and put up crude buildings with the help of twenty-three slaves. Surveying his past as a bankrupt and a widower, he named his new plantation Forlorn Hope. For a decade and a half floods and disease kept prosperity at a distance. After 1830, when he turned to sugar cane, Palfrey's situation brightened, and he knew some good fortune until his death in 1843. But for thirty years Palfrey's life had been one of uncertainty and struggle.

The experience of the Wade Hampton family of South Carolina bore little relation to Palfrey's. Wade I came to prominence out of the South Carolina piedmont after notable military service during the Revolution. He established himself near Columbia and became one of the first successful planters of short-staple cotton in the state. Commissioned as a brigadier general in the United States Army, Hampton found himself in American Louisiana, where he put his business acumen to work. Purchasing substantial acreage in sugar country, Wade I added a sugar barony to his established cotton estate. With drive and entrepreneurial skill, Wade I built up an agricultural empire. After his death his son Wade II and his grandson Wade III ruled their imperial domain from their plantation palace outside Columbia. At its height the Hampton holdings included vast cotton plantations in Mississippi as well as in South Carolina and a major sugar plantation in Louisiana. Precisely how many slaves the family owned is uncertain, but in all probability the number exceeded 1,000 in the three states.

Richard Eppes never knew the grandeur of the Hamptons. Born into a good but not first-rank family in Virginia, Richard attended the University of Virginia and graduated in 1842. He had intended a medical career, but he abandoned that plan when he inherited the family plantation. Although Eppes built up his slave force and his landholdings, he remained basically a farmer. He often rose at 4:30

in the morning to supervise the work on the plantation. A scientific farmer, he eagerly read the works of the agricultural reformers, bought machinery, used fertilizers, and was active in the local agricultural society. With little time for or interest in cultural matters, Eppes enjoyed smoking "segars," entertaining visitors, and attending the local Episcopal church, where he served on the vestry. He believed strongly in the immortality of the soul and confided to his diary that he hoped to be reunited in heaven with his first wife.

Obviously, the individuals who made up the planter class varied enormously; at the same time, important similarities bound them together. Almost all were engaged in commercial agriculture, though the crops and the scale of production varied. Thus the economic course of agriculture, especially of cotton, was fundamental to their financial well-being. All of these planters owned slaves. Whether they owned twenty or two hundred slaves, a considerable portion of their wealth was tied up in human property. The issue of slavery and its future was central to their lives. Not surprisingly, agriculture and slavery formed the heart of public discussion in the South. The special concerns of the planters became central for the entire region.

Southern slave owners in the nineteenth century lived in a world dominated by the expansion of capitalism made possible by the Industrial Revolution. Slave owners had a unique relationship with this new, powerful economic order. They shared basic characteristics with capitalists: the profit motive, the view of land and slaves as investments, a willingness to relocate to take advantage of an opportunity, an interest in investing in such enterprises as banks, railroads, and manufacturing. At the same time, planters possessed slaves; in economic terms, they owned their labor. By the nineteenth century their system was economically anachronistic and at odds with a concept central to capitalism: free labor. In the capitalist system workers were free to offer their labor to the highest bidder. If the highest bid was less than they needed to stay above poverty or if the working conditions were brutal, they were theoretically free to take a better offer if they could find one. The concept of free labor, with its actual or implied contract, was the bedrock of the emerging capitalism. To the new capitalists, slavery was an outmoded and immoral economic arrangement; to most southerners it was economically viable and humane. These conflicting perspectives on slavery contributed significantly to the growing tension between the free and slave societies.

In sum, most slave owners were enmeshed in the capitalist world at the same time that they stood somewhat apart from it. They certainly did not perceive any inevitable conflict between slavery and sustained economic growth.

YEOMEN AND POOR WHITES

Although the planters receive the most attention, it was the yeoman farmers who occupied the central place in southern society. Neither rich nor poor, the yeomen were property-owning farmers who might or might not own slaves. Between 80 and 90 percent of all small farmers in the antebellum South owned their own land. These people were surely not a peasantry. Most yeomen did not own slaves. No great social distance separated a farmer who owned three or four slaves from

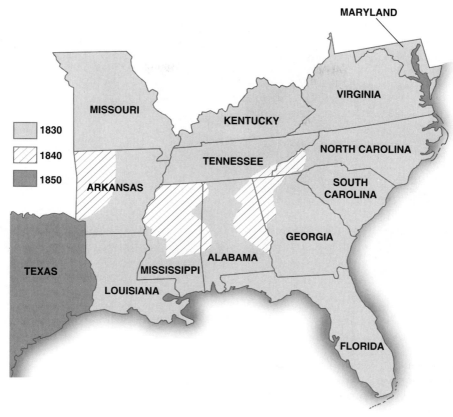

SPREAD OF SETTLEMENT IN THE SOUTH, 1830–1850

one who had none, though a person with a dozen or fifteen slaves stood considerably higher on the social scale than either. Just as the planter class covered a broad social and economic spectrum, so did the yeomanry.

Self-sufficiency and commitment to the market economy varied among them. As growers of tobacco, grain, livestock, and particularly cotton for money, most yeomen had at least some involvement in the market. They were neither pariahs nor ciphers in antebellum society. Property owners, they were also political citizens who could and did vote. Some families remained in a particular area over generations while others became part of the great westward movement. In addition, the economic and geographical expansion of the South permitted movement up the social ladder.

A glimpse at three very different families lends insight into the yeoman class. James F. Sloan made his home in the South Carolina upcountry. Born in Laurens District in 1819, Sloan started out as a tenant farmer, then became an overseer. In the early 1840s he bought land in bordering Spartanburg District and settled there with his wife and three children. In less than a year his wife died; two years later

EPPES HOUSE, AVOYELLES PARISH, LOUISIANA (1852), HOME OF A YEO-
MAN WHO OWNED A FEW SLAVES (Courtesy of Patricia H. Cooper)

he married again. Never owning any slaves, Sloan relied on himself and his family for labor, with assistance from neighbors at critical times. By the late 1850s
Sloan's sixty-acre farm was valued at $1,000. In addition to producing four to six
bales of cotton annually, he grew corn, oats, and wheat, and he also raised cattle,
hogs, and sheep.

Jacob Eaton and his family lived on a 160-acre farm in the North Carolina
piedmont. Jacob with his wife and their eight children lived in a three-room log
house with a loft where the boys slept. In 1860 they owned seven slaves, in all
probability one family. With their help the family raised crops and tended animals. Mrs. Eaton and her daughters spun their cotton into thread on spinning
wheels, wove the thread into cloth, and made their own clothing. The strong feeling of place and kinship within the family found expression in the family ceme-
tery, where generations were buried.

The family of Samuel Davis, in contrast, followed the moving frontier. As a
child Samuel moved with his parents from Philadelphia to colonial Georgia.
There he grew up and fought in the Revolution. As a reward for his military service, the state gave him land near Augusta, and he farmed it until 1793, when he
moved to Kentucky. There in Christian County he raised tobacco, corn, and
wheat. Early in the new century Samuel once again headed west; after a brief stop
in southern Louisiana he settled in Wilkinson County, Mississippi, where he commenced farming once again, this time with cotton as a market crop. Although he
had a few slaves, at various times ranging from two up to a dozen, he always
worked in his fields beside them. Throughout his peregrinations Samuel Davis

strove to better his circumstances, but upon his death in 1824 he was still the yeoman farmer he had always been. Although Samuel himself never moved up into the planter class, his son Jefferson surely did.

Below the yeomen on the social scale were the people designated as poor whites, both in the nineteenth century and by modern scholars. This group has also been called white trash, rednecks, crackers, and other names equally demeaning. Even the slaves joined in with their derisive "po' buckra." These poor whites lived largely on the margin of southern society. In the rural South they included owners of small plots of unproductive soil as well as tenants and agricultural laborers; the last two were not nearly so numerous as they were to become in the years after the Civil War and especially in the twentieth century. In some parts of the South, chiefly away from the main agricultural areas, trappers, hunters, and herders fit into this category. Unsuccessful artisans and laborers in towns and cities added to their number. In the antebellum years this lower class had little impact on the course of southern development. Impressive economic growth and massive geographical expansion offered sufficient opportunities for escape and mobility, both economic and social, to keep this lowest segment of the white social order small.

HARMONY OR DISHARMONY

Many scholars have pondered whether planters exploited such men as James Sloan, Jacob Eaton, and Samuel Davis or whether class conflict between the upper and lower orders characterized the antebellum South. This question is not at all new. Two southerners who wrote toward the end of the antebellum regime came down vigorously on opposite sides of the issue. Daniel Hundley, in his *Social Relations in Our Southern States* (1860), found unity and harmony among southern whites, and he thought the yeomen central to the society. The North Carolinian Hinton Helper, by contrast, argued in *The Impending Crisis of the South* (1857) that slave owners and the very system of slavery exploited the nonslaveholders by severely restricting the possibilities for economic advancement. Helper, however, did not at all challenge white supremacy. In fact, a virulent racism informs *The Impending Crisis*; Helper believed that blacks must leave the South. Although both industry and the general economy in the South were growing, the South certainly did not match the North. Just how severely slavery circumscribed southern economic growth and opportunity for southern farmers is difficult to say at this remove, but most scholars believe that Helper's basic point is correct. Few southerners of the 1850s shared that view, however. They believed, with good reason, that slavery powered an economic engine of considerable force. Suffice it to say here that the expansion of the southern economy provided sufficient wealth and opportunity to preclude any significant attacks on the regime for holding down the mass of its white citizens. Class antagonism and tension surely existed, and given the appropriate conditions, they could become powerful forces in southern society. The strains of wartime would bring some into the open, but before 1860 class conflict did not threaten the social order.

Of the many reasons for this basic social harmony, five stand out:

1. Race: An omnipotent racism convinced all whites that only bondage en-
    abled black and white to coexist without massive social trauma. This
    racism also made believable an ideology that placed all whites on an
    equal social and political level, despite sharp economic and social distinc-
    tions. John C. Calhoun articulated this view forcefully: "With us the two
    great divisions of society are not the rich and poor, but white and black;
    and all the former, the poor as well as the rich, belong to the upper class,
    and are respected and treated as equals, if honest and industrious."

2. Politics: By the Jacksonian era all white male adults had the right to vote,
    and they exercised it. Specific policies underscored the strength of the av-
    erage white southerner. Tax policy in the lower South, for example, pro-
    vides concrete evidence of their political standing. In those states the
    principal source of tax revenue was the tax on slaves—paid, of course, by
    slave owners. The land tax remained quite low; even when it rose some-
    what in the 1850s, it generally stayed below two mills on the dollar. In ad-
    dition, planters had to pay a luxury tax on race horses, pleasure carriages,
    private libraries, pianos, and similar property. This system was not at all
    like the ancien régime in prerevolutionary France, where the lower
    classes paid to support the upper classes.

3. Economic relations: Planters and yeomen, slaveholders and nonslave-
    holders quite often shared the same economic world. In only a very few
    areas, such as the sea islands, did planters operate in isolation from
    yeomen. Elsewhere the two groups provided essential services and mate-
    rials to each other. Planters with cotton gins ginned the cotton raised by
    yeomen. Yeomen sold livestock and grain to planters. Planters who
    needed additional labor at critical times often hired the slaves of yeomen,
    and even the yeomen themselves, whether or not they owned slaves.

4. Social mobility: Social mobility had always been a hallmark of southern
    society. Never, even in the colonial era, had the path to the top been
    blocked. The prosperity of the 1850s certainly did not encourage the belief
    that stagnation would ever completely close the path leading upward. It
    is true that the substantial increase in slave prices during that decade,
    which made it more difficult to become a first-time slave owner, worried
    some southerners; they feared increasing class conflict if prices should
    rise high enough to close off that option for good. That was indeed a legit-
    imate concern, but such a situation did not arise before 1860. No one can
    be sure what would have happened if the war had not come.

5. Kinship: The incredible geographic and economic growth of the South,
    along with the fluidity of social lines, guaranteed that members of indi-
    vidual families would range across the economic and social spectrum. Fa-
    thers, sons, brothers, mothers, daughters, sisters, not to mention collateral
    relatives, could find themselves significantly differentiated by wealth and
    social position. At times people who were successful turned their backs
    on kin who were less fortunate. It has always been so. But many others

proudly recognized family ties that spanned wide economic and social chasms.

THE PLACE OF WOMEN IN SOCIETY

Literary and historical mythology had tended to picture southern white women as spoiled belles idling away their time in languid conversation on their verandas, but few antebellum women would recognize themselves in that portrait. Of course, the advice literature of the time, widely read in the South as well as the North, portrayed the ideal woman as submissive, pure, and pious; domestic ideology thrived in countryside and city alike. In many ways southern families embodied the more general ideals and practices of Victorian America rather than those of a distinctively southern society. Some historians have argued that the subordination of women was critical to the security and ideology of a slave society, but in fact few southern intellectuals paid much attention to the place of women in their society.

Whether patriarchy was the official southern ideology is by no means clear. Some southern men often behaved like imperious lords of the manor, but so did many northern husbands. To be sure, southern writers urged women to cultivate a "quiet submission to the state of subordination ordained by heavenly wisdom." Louisa Cheves McCord, a remarkable South Carolinian who wrote forcefully and prolifically on political and economic questions, argued that women were "made for duty, not for fame." Yet in the South women were also expected to exert moral authority in the home; what has been called "domestic feminism" appeared as women assumed increasing control over the rearing, education, and religious instruction of their children. Southerners tended to place more emphasis on female virtue than northerners because any question raised about a woman's respectability would besmirch a family's honor—a most sensitive point in the South and an issue of such explosiveness that it sometimes led to duels.

The myth of the lazy belle notwithstanding, most southern women were too busy to worry about their place in southern ideology. Regardless of class, they worked at a wide variety of household and agricultural tasks. The advice literature and family documents alike portray women as scurrying about their kitchens and gardens, cooking for their families, sewing, and managing slaves. In their domestic routines their lives differed little from those of their northern counterparts, though there appears to have been somewhat less domestic discontent in the South and certainly less overt feminism than in the Northeast.

In many ways southern families were in transition between traditional and modern attitudes toward family life. "Companionate" marriage became increasingly the pattern in the South in the decades immediately preceding the Civil War: young people chose their own mates. Even parental influence on the selection of a spouse steadily declined. Both young people and their advisers placed more and more emphasis on romance and less and less on finance. Planters who still tried to arrange "good matches" for their daughters could not always get their way.

This greater freedom was also reflected in the decision of many women either to delay marriage or to stay single. Some young women expressed reluctance to give up their independence; because marriage greatly limited their property rights and means of escape were few, they feared making a bad choice. As one put it, "Liberty is sweeter to me than matrimony." The census data suggest that the rate of marriage in the southern states was about the same as that for the rest of the country.

The Place of Women in Marriage

Once married, the southern woman lost most of her legal rights. Some states had laws permitting husbands to punish their wives physically, and even after these abuses were outlawed in the 1840s and 1850s, juries seldom convicted wife-beaters, and judges handed down absurdly light sentences. Women trapped in bad marriages had few means of escape. If a woman left her husband, she also abandoned any property she had brought into the marriage and entered a world with few opportunities for single women, especially for those who had fallen into disgrace. And to leave one's husband was disgraceful.

Divorces were rare. Early in the nineteenth century divorce required the passage of a private bill in a state legislature, and most politicians set a high standard for acceptance of such a petition. Both men and women had difficulty obtaining divorces. As several states converted divorce into a judicial proceeding, the law shifted in favor of women. Every southern state except South Carolina, which had no divorce law, added adultery, cruelty, and desertion to the usual bigamy, impotence, and consanguinity as grounds for divorce. Lawmakers also gave courts wide discretion in defining "cruelty," and a number of judges would grant divorce on the grounds of mental cruelty. Of course some patriarchal elements survived. The woman had to prove her virtue beyond question and usually had to show that she had been a duly submissive wife. Yet southern judges, who tended to see themselves as paternalistic defenders of the weak, became increasingly generous in awarding property and child custody to women. Despite legal reforms and the growing number of divorces, the social stigma against divorce remained, and the antebellum divorce rate was minuscule.

Marriage and motherhood were still the destiny of most southern women. Women well understood that some men measured a woman's value by her fertility. Marriage began a lengthy round of pregnancies. The manuscript census for any southern county shows children spaced at intervals of two years or less; births only thirteen months apart were commonplace. After ten years of marriage, Elizabeth Perry of South Carolina had been pregnant ten times; these pregnancies had ended in four live births, two stillbirths, and four miscarriages. In St. Francisville, Louisiana, one thirty-seven-year-old woman had already borne sixteen children, and a neighbor ruefully remarked, "Her family may yet be much larger." Most women welcomed children, but the excitement soon wore off. "Babies to you are no novelty," one mother informed a friend, "and even to me the novelty is fast wearing away for I'm sometimes completely worn out in mind and body. Poor little girls I pity them all no matter whose they are."

Birth control techniques commonly used by educated northern women were only slowly adopted in the South. A mother of thirteen could only comment wearily: "I have so many little children and no prospect of ever stopping." Delayed weaning, abstinence, and coitus interruptus were evidently the only birth control techniques widely known and practiced in the South. Most southern states outlawed abortions performed after the quickening of the fetus, but no evidence suggests that abortions at any stage of pregnancy had ever been common in the South.

In addition to the burdens of child rearing, women faced seemingly endless rounds of household chores. Class differences appeared in the type and amount of housework done by women. On a typical day Jane Beale, a poor widow with nine children living in Fredericksburg, Virginia, put up pickles, cut out cloth, washed lamp chimneys, listened to her children recite their lessons, cleaned up the yard, whitewashed part of the house, cut up peaches, mended clothes, rid the bed of insects, and fed and milked the cow. After getting her youngsters to bed, she at last sat down to chat with her brother Sam—with, of course, knitting in her lap. For more comfortably situated women, the tasks were different but only slightly less demanding. Along with her mother and half sister in Marietta, Georgia, Mary Roberts worked hard to maintain a neat and respectable home. Rising early in the morning, she prepared breakfast and then hustled her nieces and nephews off to school. Then it was out to the yard to look after the ducks, turkeys, and chickens. She reserved the afternoon for reading, writing, sewing, and a walk outside. Visits from neighbors and friends might disrupt this routine. In the evening she read aloud to the family. Planters' wives, too, had their daily chores, and most ran their households carefully, but they had much more leisure than the typical farm woman. Ella Thomas sewed, cared for her children, worked in the garden, but still had time to read popular novels and the four magazines to which she subscribed.

THE LIFE OF THE FEMALE SPIRIT AND MIND

Although class differences certainly existed in southern society, evangelical religion sometimes helped women bridge these social distances. Like their menfolk, southern women tended to be Methodists or Baptists. Perhaps because church membership was one of the few public activities open to them, women flocked to the churches. Religion linked women to the world even as it led them to shun worldliness and materialism, but this connection did not threaten domestic ideology. Ministers argued that wives found it easier than their husbands to obey Christ because they had already learned the lessons of submission at home. Membership statistics are notoriously unreliable, but at least twice as many women as men joined southern churches, and the ratio may have been as high as 4 to 1. The reasons for this disparity are unclear, but contemporaries argued that women were more devout because they had more sorrows than men, a greater sense of dependence, and even a nervous system better suited to spiritual commitment. Perhaps women responded to the promise of a status in God's kingdom denied to them on earth.

Perhaps, too, they understood that religion increased women's influence in the home. The image of the pious mother and wife trying to convert her heathen-ish menfolk was not simply a product of the evangelical imagination. Accepting the ministers at their word, many southern women asserted their spiritual superiority by begging, prodding, and cajoling men into joining the church. And this proselytizing could easily move from the private to the public sphere. During the revivals that swept through the antebellum South, converts were far more numerous among women than among men. Bolder women gave their testimonies at prayer meetings, led prayers, and spoke in tongues, despite occasional criticism from nervous preachers anxious about preserving their own spiritual authority.

A short road led from churchwork to more secular forms of benevolence. The South lagged behind the rest of the country in benevolent organizations, but southern women held fairs, directed poor relief, and participated in many other activities that raised implicit questions about domestic ideology. As one wife told her husband in describing plans for a hospital benefit concert, it was silly for women to withdraw from community life simply because they married. Yet whatever the potential of such efforts, they hardly threatened male authority. "Ladies' societies" remained dependent on the support of ministers and church elders, and for the most part confined their efforts to safely conservative channels. In Charleston, for example, aristocratic women worked with poor women and orphans, not only to ease suffering but to convince the downtrodden that the local elite had their best interests at heart. The reformers' fondest hope was to turn these impoverished females into models of Victorian respectability. In a region that had few cities, women moved slowly and cautiously toward establishing reform societies outside the church. Some women engaged in poor relief, temperance work, and some agitation for educational reform, but most had more than enough to do with their own domestic duties. Numerous men praised southern women for staying at home with their families and cultivating genteel manners rather than following the busybody examples of their northern sisters.

Some southern intellectuals worried about the possible effects of northern feminism on southern women, but they need not have been concerned. Few southern women were either familiar with or sympathetic to the cause. Louisa McCord agreed with male conservatives that enfranchising women would "unsex" them. Even women who felt initially attracted to such radical ideas usually drew back from following their own reasoning to any logical conclusion. After thumbing through a French feminist novel, a young woman regretted doing so. "I do not like that kind of reading," she wrote, "it scares me of myself and makes me rebel against my lot." Therefore women as well as men kept the South "safe" from the women's rights movement.

One notable group of southern women conveyed their traditional view of women's place in the South to a wide audience. In dozens of books that sold tens of thousands of copies, the southern domestic novelists transmitted the vision of the South they prized. The genre known as domestic fiction, in which women wrote novels intended for female readers, originated in England, reached New England in the 1820s, and the South a decade later. The South during the last three antebellum decades produced five major domestic novelists—Augusta Evans, Caroline Gilman, Caroline Hentz, Maria McIntosh, and Mary Virginia Terhune.

These writers concentrated on defending the South and southern institutions, notably slavery, from all attacks. Acutely conscious of sectional differences, especially antislavery and antisouthern opinion in the North, they portrayed southern society as superior to northern. These women particularly praised what they saw in the South as a civilized, harmonious world guarded by a planter class imbued with *noblesse oblige*. Carrying no torch for women's rights, these five novelists advocated no radical change of any kind. Profoundly conservative, they wanted only to improve the South, the best society they knew. At its center they placed the plantation mistress who guarded southern values from outside threats. In their good society problems did exist, deriving chiefly from the excesses of the elite made possible by wealth and leisure. Yet all five writers were convinced that the heroic plantation mistress could and would ensure the triumph of their cherished social order.

Within the limits of social conservatism, however, the intellectual horizons of elite women expanded during the antebellum decades. Novels enjoyed great popularity, but well-to-do parents encouraged their daughters to read histories and classical literary works along with some Greek and Roman mythology. The great majority of southern women, though, probably read little or nothing during their lifetimes beyond a few schoolbooks, the Bible, and some devotional works, if they could read at all. In 1850 the adult female literacy rate ranged from a high of 86 percent in Mississippi to a low of 64 percent in North Carolina. Overall the literacy rate was 4 to 16 percentage points lower for southern women than for southern men. New England and the Middle Atlantic states, by contrast, generally had female literacy rates above 90 percent. Functional illiteracy was undoubtedly a greater problem than the available statistics suggest because many antebellum women read nothing. Nowhere were southern class differences more apparent than in the social distance between a planter's daughter thumbing through Shakespeare and a poor white woman who could not decipher a sales receipt or sign her name.

Many upper-class fathers took a keen interest in their daughters' education and worried about everything from their study habits to their social activities. These men hoped to encourage spirited and undisciplined adolescents to grow into intelligent and respectable young ladies. In other words, they stressed the type of education that would make their daughters into successful wives and mothers. The history of women's education in the nineteenth-century South therefore became a story of brave beginnings and limited achievements. Ideological barriers did as much as tight finances to slow improvements.

Advocates of improved education for women had to be cautious in making their case. Better schooling, they argued, would improve women without changing them; the educated woman would still be the "heart" of the home, whose "head" would still be the husband. Learning science, mathematics, or Latin would not exempt women from domestic chores.

For more ambitious parents and their daughters the multiplication of female academies during the antebellum decades seemed promising. But most of these schools enrolled fewer than a hundred students and experienced serious financial troubles. Yeoman families could not afford institutions where tuition alone ran to more than $100 a year. Only the elite enjoyed the luxury of sending their children to good boarding schools.

At least the new academies and female colleges did expand educational opportunities for the daughters of the planters. Southerners still doubted that girls needed to study advanced mathematics, Latin, or Greek, but reformers called for more history, philosophy, science, and mathematics in the curriculum. During the 1850s several schools added geometry and trigonometry to their course offerings. Such ornamental subjects as painting, drawing, needlework, and music declined in importance. Surprisingly few institutions emphasized the "domestic arts." By 1850 a southern girl of means could follow a curriculum in many ways comparable to that of her brothers. Yet for the most part, women's education remained conservative, haphazard, and woefully inadequate. Most so-called colleges were nothing more than glorified academies. Despite curricular reform, stringent budgets and reactionary attitudes hemmed in women on every side. The women of yeoman and poor white families had even fewer opportunities and faced the full force of social as well as sexual prejudice.

WOMEN IN THE ECONOMIC AND POLITICAL SYSTEMS

The subordination of women rested on a firm legal foundation. Despite some use of prenuptial agreements, most women gave up their property rights when they married. State legislatures slowly expanded women's property rights, but the purpose was more to protect estates from fortune hunters, and thus to safeguard the interests of women's male relatives, than to improve women's status.

Such legal disabilities made widows reluctant to remarry and even gave single women pause. Yet the road to financial independence was all but closed to unmarried women. The typical female head of household in the antebellum South owned little or no property, and for those who chose to remain unmarried, economic mobility remained a most elusive goal.

Avenues of opportunity were few. The 1860 census listed housekeeper, seamstress, and farmer as the most common female occupations, though census takers classified many women who managed farms or plantations as "housekeepers." Women who worked in their husbands' businesses were also often overlooked. But even when the undercounting is taken into account, it remains true that most women who worked outside the home labored at menial jobs. Women might supplement other family income by doing laundry or making clothes, but they could hardly make enough to support themselves or their children.

In the course of the Industrial Revolution many of the traditional female crafts, such as spinning and weaving, were transferred from the home to the factory. More and more women worked in the textile mills; by 1860 white women made up more than 10 percent of the labor force in five of the future Confederate states. On the eve of the Civil War, several thousand southern women worked in factories, but the general employment picture was hardly bright.

Educated women might teach school, if for no other reason than the respectability of the profession. But even when women overcame the expected objections of their male relatives, the classroom did not represent a golden opportunity. Some women offered private lessons in their homes, a practice that clearly tied their income to the number of pupils they could accommodate and hold. Teachers earned as little as $200 a year and seldom found the profession altogether satisfying. A handful of women wrote for a living, but with indifferent results, from both literary and financial standpoints.

Despite limited opportunities, women played an important role in the southern economy. In addition to their domestic activities, they ran farms and plantations. Although some women deplored slavery and a few even condemned the institution, historians have too often permitted this unrepresentative group to speak for a largely silent or proslavery majority. And even the appearance of antislavery sentiments could be deceiving. The famous diarist Mary Boykin Chesnut lived comfortably with both her antislavery sentiments and her slaves; she enjoyed the luxury of clean white sheets, fresh cream in her coffee, breakfast in bed, and more than enough leisure to denounce slavery in her diary. It would also be a mistake to confuse exasperation with slaves, often expressed in diaries and letters at the end of a long day, with abolitionism. Most women simply accepted slavery without thinking much about it.

A few women dealt with slaves in the most basic manner on plantations they operated. When Rachel O'Connor's husband died, probably between 1815 and 1820, she took over the management of the family plantation in West Feliciana Parish, Louisiana. Over the next quarter century Rachel O'Connor made a success of it by determination and hard work. Starting out with a single overseer for assistance, she produced as many as 150 bales of cotton annually along with corn, potatoes, and other essentials for the provisioning of her slaves and livestock. She took great pride in the care she gave her slaves, and evidently was both an effective and humane mistress. The record indicates neither runaways nor serious resistance to her authority.

Life as a slave-owning planter was never simple for Rachel O'Connor. At times she struggled to obtain vital credit, and at others she battled disease. At one point seventeen of her slaves and her overseer were down with cholera. During the 1830s she bought more land and increased the size of her operation. A confident and competent planter by the end of that decade, when her white overseer retired, she turned his job over to a young male slave. When age and illness slowed her down, a neighbor hired another white overseer to give overall direction. By Rachel O'Connor's death at age seventy-two in 1846, she had built up an estate of 1,000 acres of land and eighty-one slaves. Despite the resentment of some nearby male slave owners that a female planter lived among them, Rachel O'Connor made her way successfully in a tough, male-dominated world.

Widows and single women made up about 10 percent of the slaveholding class. The education of these mistresses began in early childhood, when they observed how slavery worked and, if the family was wealthy, were given personal servants. And though the vast majority of white women were not ultimately responsible for the work and welfare of a slave force, work with and on behalf of slaves made enormous demands on their time and energy.

In this complicated world of black and white families, white women became active and for the most part willing participants in the slave system. Although the prevalence of the "good mistress" has been greatly exaggerated, such persons did exist. A marvelously complex paternalism, in which most white women played their expected roles, developed out of an oppressive system. Devoted mistresses paid attention to the health and general well-being of each slave. They nursed the sick and held religious services in the quarters.

But an inevitable concomitant of paternalism is condescension. The housewife who slipped a slave child corn bread and sausage under the table was treating the child as one would a pet dog. Such "privileges" as riding in a carriage at the foot of the mistress and sleeping under her bed bespoke more degradation than status. Some mistresses relied on their slaves to do the smallest tasks. The thoughtless exploitation of black labor occurred daily in southern homes, but even white women with antislavery convictions seldom recognized its significance. In hot weather slaves fanned their mistresses to keep them cool. White women pleasantly remembered such scenes; slaves remembered falling asleep and getting whipped.

Despite the close bonds that occasionally developed between mistresses and their female slaves, race and class overcame sexual solidarity. Humane mistresses saw their duty as attempting to civilize the blacks on their place. Such considerations led to the famous scenes of tearful women protecting slaves from the lash or preventing sales that would break up slave families. Yet for every woman who tried to soften the harsher aspects of the institution, there were others who did not hesitate to order whippings and could themselves apply the lash with a will. Brutality and sadism were by no means a male monopoly. One angry mistress brutally pressed a recalcitrant slave girl's head under a rocking chair; another, in a fit of exasperation brought on by a poorly cooked potato, put out a slave's eye with a fork.

If women willingly participated in some of the most brutal acts, they were themselves victims of the system. Miscegenation, one of the great chinks in the slaveholders' moral armor, greatly troubled many white women. Yet rather than condemn slavery, most condemned black women for luring white men into sin. Rather than call into question their husbands' behavior, these women conveniently blamed the slaves. Even Mary Chesnut concluded her famous lament on miscegenation by denouncing the promiscuity of blacks. Whatever their doubts or possible feelings of guilt, busy women suppressed them and became absorbed by their many household duties. Most mistresses did far more to sustain slavery than to subvert it.

The mounting abolitionist crusade elicited a defensive response from southern women, much as it did from southern men. Women seldom discussed a defense of slavery in their diaries and letters, but many implicitly accepted the major tenets of the proslavery argument. Southern women novelists supported slavery; only Louisa McCord made any substantial contribution to proslavery literature. McCord's essays on political economy in general and slavery in particular demonstrated that women could be effective polemicists.

Women of course occupied a marginal position in southern political culture. As one writer put it, "one of [women's] highest privileges is to be politically merged in the existence of their husband[s]." But even in public life the fiction of marital unity sometimes broke down. Many women commented on public issues only in their private writings or in family discussions, but yeoman and upper-class women could be fierce partisans. The wives of politicians not only closely followed their husbands' careers but offered astute advice on politics. Ambitious and sophisticated women might display more drive than their husbands.

Of course women had few opportunities to express their opinions on a more public stage, but subtle changes took place in their relations with the masculine world of politics. Beginning with the 1840 presidential campaign, women marched in parades, attended rallies, and listened to speeches. A few even wrote to public officials to express their opinions on controversial issues.

As sectional tensions mounted during the 1850s, women became increasingly likely to comment on political questions. A smattering of comments on the issue of slavery in the territories became a flood after John Brown's raid, an event that became a powerful symbol of the threat posed by antislavery agitation to southern domestic life. The election of 1860 did not arouse much female interest, but the secession debates did. The dissolution of the Union and the firing on Fort Sumter made many women pay attention to public events for the first time in their lives. Perhaps even more than men, women weighed the question of secession to see how this step would affect family and local interests. And more than many men, they worried about the bloody consequences of disunion. Women took a more active part in family political discussions, and a few even broke with fathers and husbands during the crisis.

Secession also gave women expanded public roles. From sporting secession cockades to attending rallies for southern rights to sewing flags and uniforms, women became increasingly active. To be sure, conservative social values inhibited them. Women usually refused to speak at flag-presentation ceremonies; no one suggested they enter public life or fight for their country. The model for female courage remained largely passive—the Spartan mother sending her menfolk off to battle. During the secession crisis, women mouthed men's words: liberty, honor, southern rights, abolition fanatics. But they also glimpsed the human faces and future sufferings beneath the abstractions.

FREE BLACKS

Between the dominant white community and the slaves lived the free blacks. Before the Revolution they formed quite a tiny group. Statistics for the colonial era are largely unavailable and certainly imprecise, but they send a clear signal about the size of this group. Maryland in 1755 had 1,817 free blacks; as late as 1780 Virginia could count even fewer. Centered in the Chesapeake, these people had probably always been free. They or their forebears had come to the colonies as indentured servants or as laborers in some other capacity.

The Revolution had a major impact on the free black population in the Chesapeake. Without question their numbers shot up; by 1790 Maryland had 8,043 and Virginia 12,766. This substantial increase came from two sources. The lesser of the two was the freedom given slaves for military service by Maryland and Delaware. Although the number involved was small, it did add to the total, and this practice, though restricted, helped absorb runaway slaves into the growing free population. The major impetus to the growth of free blacks came from manumission. In 1782 Virginia passed a law enabling masters to free slaves by deed or by will;

within a decade Maryland, Delaware, and Kentucky followed suit. Influenced by the Revolutionary ideology of freedom and inalienable rights, hundreds of masters in these states of the upper South broke the chains of their slaves. These newly emancipated blacks generally remained in the countryside to work as agricultural laborers. This was certainly an auspicious beginning, though emancipation never moved into the lower South, and even in the upper South free blacks remained a small percentage of the black population.

In the portions of the old Southwest which had been under French and Spanish control a different pattern prevailed. Louisiana and such towns as Mobile and Pensacola had free black communities that originated in liaisons between white masters and their black slaves. With the support of the central governments back in Europe, white fathers often emancipated their illegitimate mulatto offspring. The number leaped from under 200 in 1769 to 2,000 in 1800. Unlike their counterparts in the American upper South, these free blacks congregated in urban areas. They also strove to make themselves indispensable to the whites. During the Revolution the free blacks fought in Louisiana and Florida with the Spanish against the British, and in 1815 they again did battle with the invading British, this time under American authority.

After 1800, however, the growth of the free black population slowed. The enormous geographic and economic expansion heralded by the purchase of Louisiana in 1803 and by the rise of cotton changed the economic calculus of slavery. Also as time passed the ideological influence of the Revolution, never deep or pervasive where slavery was concerned, waned. Virginia in 1806 drastically tightened the 1782 emancipation law by requiring that a manumitted slave leave the state within one year or face reenslavement. Tougher laws spanned the region. They became almost totally restrictive in Kentucky, where emancipation had no legal effect until the freed slave left the state, and in Mississippi, where each individual manumission required a special act of the legislature. The size of the free black population in 1860 shows clearly just how effective nineteenth-century legislation and practice had been. Only 261,918 free blacks lived in the slave states, 86 percent of them in their traditional home, the upper South. Since 1800 the number of slaves had more than quadrupled while the free blacks increased at a considerably lesser rate, some two and one-half times. The free blacks were surely not holding their own against the surge of slavery.

Free blacks found their legal situation tenuous at best. Whites systematically barred them from the rights and symbols associated with freedom, especially American freedom. Because the law presumed that all blacks were slaves, free blacks had to have documents proving their freedom. Several states restricted their movements, and all banned free blacks from certain occupations; blacks could not, for instance, enter the printing trade. They could not participate in politics or testify in court against whites. Owning guns was prohibited, and stiff criminal penalties were standard. In the public arena—in theaters, railroads, and steamboats, for example—segregation along with inferior facilities and accommodations prevailed.

In the nineteenth century free blacks remained on the economic margin. In the upper South most still lived in the countryside. Although a few became landowners—1,200 black Virginians enjoyed that status in 1860—the great majority (75 percent in North Carolina) found employment as rural laborers. Across the South free blacks generally fared much better in the urban areas, where most in the lower South lived. There the men worked at such skilled trades as carpentry, masonry, and tailoring. In the upper South quite a few were employed as factory hands. Some jobs seemed universal: men worked as waiters and women as domestics.

Free blacks did not form a phalanx; class differences surely existed among them, at times notably so. In the cities, especially in the lower South, a three-caste system grew up. A largely mulatto upper class that monopolized the best jobs available to free blacks made every effort to separate itself from the mass of poorer free blacks, few of whom had any white blood. This system was prevalent in the Caribbean but never became that strong in the South outside of older cities such as New Orleans and Charleston. Although this division was clear within the black community and to some whites, the powerful racism pervading the South ensured that the basic social lines were drawn along racial, not economic, lines. To the overwhelming majority of whites a black was a black, whether free or slave, whether mulatto or not. As a result, all free blacks teetered precariously on a precipice.

*B*LACK *MASTERS*

Despite the sharp and deep racial divide that characterized the antebellum South, a few free blacks became masters of black slaves. This group, never large, numbered some 3,600 in 1850. The great majority were artisans in such cities as Charleston, where in 1860 more than 70 percent of South Carolina's black masters resided. The slaves of most of these men were their own wives and children. A free person could purchase a spouse from a willing owner. If a free black husband owned his wife, their children were slaves, because status was inherited from the mother. When manumission statutes tightened, husbands and fathers could not easily free wives and children.

A handful of free blacks operated slave plantations just as their white counterparts did. The Metoyer family of Natchitoches Parish, Louisiana, in 1850 possessed thousands of acres and more than 400 slaves. The Metoyer clan, which traced its roots to a slave who was emancipated by her French master in the late eighteenth century, built a slave empire that rivaled all but the very largest. Most of the Metoyers married the mulatto sons and daughters of neighboring white planters, who accepted the Metoyers as fellow slaveholders, if not as equals. In their enclave, centered on the still-standing Melrose Plantation, the Metoyers constructed a Roman Catholic church, operated schools, and ran several businesses.

The South Carolinian William Ellison in 1816, at age twenty-six, gained his freedom from his owner, who was probably his father. As a slave Ellison learned several trades, including work on cotton gins, and cotton gins became his road to wealth. Upon being freed Ellison migrated to Sumter District, where he manufactured and sold his own gins. Prospering, Ellison began to buy land and slaves. By 1860 he owned fifty-nine slaves, who worked on his plantation and in his gin shop. The local planter elite permitted Ellison to join their Anglican church,

WISDOM HALL, STATEBURG, SOUTH CAROLINA (LATE EIGHTEENTH
CENTURY), HOME OF WILLIAM ELLISON (South Caroliniana Library, University
of South Carolina)

though the pew he was given was set apart from the others at the rear. Just like
the children of successful whites, who tended to marry the sons and daughters of
the tidewater aristocracy, Ellison's children married into the free black elite of
Charleston. His commitment to the slave regime was seemingly total. He sold
slaves, mostly children, and bought slaves, mostly adult males. William Ellison
died in 1861, but during the war the Ellison plantation, run now by his sons, produced foodstuffs for the Confederate army.

The Metoyers and the Ellisons were exceptions to the rule. Toward the end of
the 1850s the free blacks' position was shifting from precarious to perilous. Free
blacks just did not fit into the white South. And many whites, including those in
the legislatures, began to ask questions that posed great danger to all free blacks.
If, as the proslavery argument maintained and most whites believed, blacks were
specially suited for slavery, then why were not all blacks enslaved? If blacks possessed uniquely slavelike characteristics, why were any blacks at all not only free
but masters of slaves? Legislatures began to provide ominous answers. In 1859
the Arkansas legislature passed a law ordering all free blacks out of the state by
January 1, 1860. Any who remained after that date would have a choice: either
choose a master and voluntarily submit to servitude or be sold into slavery.
Arkansas was not an isolated case. In their final sessions before the war both Missouri and Florida lawmakers passed similar legislation. Mississippi was on the
verge of doing so. Debate in other states made it clear that the elimination of free
blacks from the slave states had become a possibility. Even the Ellisons and their
peers in South Carolina were not immune to the threat; they, too, feared what the
white majority might do. Without question the legal status of free blacks was
eroding rapidly and dangerously. The evidence strongly indicates that freedom

for any blacks was about to disappear in several states. But the onset of war riveted white attention on a different danger.

LIBERTY AND HONOR

The dominant whites who threatened the free blacks were surely a diverse lot. Vast differences in wealth, education, manners, diet, and outlook on life separated the squires of tidewater plantations from the hardscrabble farmers of the mountain ridges and piney woods. At the same time, southern whites shared certain fundamental values.

As the increasing difficulties faced by the free blacks underscored, all white southerners believed in the superiority of the white race, or in white supremacy. It is impossible to exaggerate the power of race. Without question it occupied a central position in the southern view of slavery; to southern whites it made both necessary and possible the solidarity of whites vis-à-vis the black slaves. Historians have shown, however, that similar views about white supremacy held in the North, and in western Europe as well. Thus while a general conviction about white superiority defined an essential portion of southern values, it surely did not make up the whole.

Critical to understanding the southern mentality is comprehending its passionate commitment to liberty. Liberty meant the opposite of slavery, and like their Revolutionary forefathers, southerners of the nineteenth century knew precisely what slavery entailed: loss of control over one's family, loss of control over one's future, loss of control over one's very person. To white southerners confronting this stark truth, their liberty was utterly crucial. They did not separate their devotion to liberty from their knowledge of slavery. Maintaining their liberty necessitated retaining dominion over their institution of slavery. From the perspective of southern whites, failure on that front would result in their own enslavement.

To white southerners loss of control over slavery threatened not only their liberty but their honor. In the white southern mind liberty and honor could not be pried apart. Welded together, they became the core of the southern psychology. A man who possessed liberty could call himself honorable; no free man would allow his reputation to be besmirched by dishonor. With honor gone, liberty became problematical. The absence of liberty and honor carried the awful connotation of the degraded slave. Thus for white southerners, escape from the dreaded status of slave required the maintenance of their liberty and honor, no matter the cost.

The great novelist William Faulkner dramatized the pervasiveness and power of southern honor in his story "An Odor of Verbena." Though the story takes place during the Reconstruction years, the values that influence the characters and actions are clearly antebellum. Young Bayard Sartoris, faced with avenging the killing of his father, feels the pressure of a solid wall of community conviction. Honor demands that he act. If he fails to act, Bayard's personal honor will be tarnished and he will be shamed before the community. Whites of both the upper and lower social orders, men and women, a former slave, even the killer of Bayard's father—all expect Bayard to observe the code that required a man to preserve his honor through action identifiable by the community as well as by himself. Bayard ultimately decides against killing, but still he must confront his father's killer in order to retain both his personal honor and his honor in the community. The two cannot be separated. The values of the individual and the community reinforce each other.

It is difficult to comprehend this southern sense of honor today, for in our time honor has little meaning, even as a civic virtue. But for antebellum southerners life itself was less precious than honor. Most agreed with Andrew Jackson, who condemned the slanderer as far worse than the murderer because the murderer took only life whereas the slanderer took honor. A man who permitted slander to go unchallenged was a man shamed and degraded before his community and in his own eyes. Community opinion and personal opinion merged. Just as the collective South had to protect its honor, individual southerners had to prove that no slavelike characteristics tarnished their honor. Duels still were fought in the South long after they had disappeared from the rest of the nation. That politicians and newspaper editors made up a disproportionate share of the duelers underscores the intimate connection between the determination to protect one's private honor and the public requirement that it be guarded. With public attention riveted on them, neither politicians nor editors could ever turn aside from a challenge. The duel both permitted and demanded protection of honor.

The duel came to America with class-conscious European officers who crossed the ocean to fight in the Revolution. British, French, and German officers brought the tradition of private warfare to vindicate the honor of gentlemen. The practice impressed Americans, and not just those who lived below the Mason-Dixon line, at least not in the aftermath of the Revolution. Undoubtedly the most famous duel in American history took place in 1804 in New Jersey when Aaron Burr killed Alexander Hamilton.

The duel, however, became increasingly associated with the South. Northerners condemned dueling, and it all but disappeared in the North, especially after the Burr-Hamilton contest. Officially the South took an identical stand. As early as 1802 North Carolina set the death penalty for dueling; ten years later South Carolina mandated a prison term and a substantial fine for everyone involved in a duel. All the other southern states passed similar legislation.

But the idea of the duel had penetrated to the essence of white southern society. Laws could not eradicate it. The roster of southern politicians who fought on the field of honor includes such notables as Andrew Jackson, Henry Clay, and John Randolph of Roanoke, as well as scores of individuals not so well known. These duels rarely replicated the romanticized contest of two swordsmen. Almost without exception the weapon of choice was a gun; the firearms used ranged from pistols to rifles, even shotguns. To escape legal prohibitions, duelists often slipped across state lines for their combat or met on islands in rivers separating states. Legislatures also exempted individual duelists from the penalties of antidueling laws just as readily as they passed such laws. A leading handbook on dueling illustrates the paradox of the attempt to outlaw an institution that embodied the fundamental values of southern society. Written in 1838 by John L. Wilson, a former governor of South Carolina, *The Code of Honor; or Rules for the Government of Principals and Seconds in Duelling* provided directions on such mechanics as the issuing of challenges and the duties of seconds; and it also had much to say about the high moral principles and social value of dueling.

One man's response to a duel in 1809 helps us to understand the powerful social force behind the practice. Upon hearing that Henry Clay had survived a duel, a close friend expressed delight. "Your firmness and courage is admited [*sic*] now by all parties," he wrote. Then Clay's companion came to the heart of the southern view of the duel. "I had rather heard of your Death," he informed Clay, "than to have heard of your backing in the smallest degree." But this was no apostle of dueling. On the contrary, he "disapprove[d] [*sic*] Dueling in general, but it seems absolutely necessary sometimes for a mans dignity." General disapprobation salved by the unquestioning acceptance of particular necessity seems to have been the guiding principle of most white southerners.

Although the duel affected chiefly the upper orders of society, worship of the two-headed god Liberty-Honor permeated the white social order. A Scottish traveler who gave special attention to working people was convinced that southern "men of business and mechanics" tended more than their northern counterparts to "consider themselves men of honor" and "more frequently resent any indignity shown them even at the expense of their life, or that of those who venture to insult them." Daniel R. Hundley, the Alabamian who lived in the North and an acute observer of southern mores, concluded that the men in the middle order of southern society possessed "the stoutest independence" and would never allow themselves to be humiliated by anyone. In his story "The Fight," Augustus Baldwin Longstreet captured precisely the place occupied by liberty and honor among them. After Billy Stallings insulted Bob Durham's wife, Bob felt his honor tarnished and in a ritual akin to the duel he demanded satisfaction from Billy. Admitting "I've said enough for a fight," Billy accepted the challenge. Thereupon with fists and teeth the two Georgians proceeded to defend their honor.

Though men took the action, the rest of the family formed important parts of the concept of southern honor. Women seldom wielded enough power to bring honor to a family, but they could certainly bring it dishonor, especially through sexual immorality. Yet women were responsible for upholding not only the morality but the piety of the home.

Upper-class women displayed intense pride in their families, chiefly in the accomplishments of their male relatives. But at the same time, women well understood the gap between the ideals of honor and daily behavior. In casual conversations, usually with other women, they often commented on the general helplessness of menfolk, especially around the house. They often seemed skeptical of male bravado and even joked about having to obey their "lord and master." They certainly knew about breaches of honor, if not in their own households, in those of their relatives and neighbors.

If southern women differed at all from southern men on the question of honor, they possibly took it somewhat less seriously; they particularly deplored the use of violence to avenge perceived insults. One would be hard-pressed to find a southern woman defending dueling or fighting. But their relative isolation from the rough-and-tumble masculine world prevented them from confronting the complexities in the notion of southern honor. Indeed, property and divorce laws were in large part designed to insulate women from the world of competition, the better to uphold patriarchal authority.

Therefore in most senses female honor remained a negative concept, defined by the absence of scandal rather than positive achievement. A man's honor did not exactly depend on his wife's fulfillment of her traditional role, but her failure to fulfill it would at least set tongues wagging and could raise more serious questions.

By the same token, the sexual double standard helped maintain the virtue of the white woman while reinforcing the macho image of the independent-minded southern man. Although miscegenation cast dishonor on the family as well as on the guilty man, such offenses were more often than not passed over in silence or dismissed as the more or less natural behavior of highly sexed men. Despite a few notable complaints about such polite hypocrisies, these questions hardly threatened either the stability of the social order or the conventional beliefs of antebellum southerners.

SLAVERY AS A SUBJECT OF DISCUSSION

Slavery's position as the bedrock of the southern god Liberty-Honor meant that the South neither could nor would permit anyone else, any outsider, to control it, or even to discuss its future. Not that all white southerners agreed on every aspect of slavery. It is impossible to know precisely how many southerners at any one time or over time thought slavery a good, a necessity, or an evil. Even so, the evidence will not support the case that very many whites ever opposed the institution or felt guilty about it. Whatever the opinion of individual southerners, the collective South stood as one with the thoughtful commentator who wrote in 1833: "So interwoven is [slavery] with our interest, our manners, our climate and our very being, that no change can ever possibly be effected without a civil commotion from which the heart of a patriot must turn with horror."

Because the white South was in such complete agreement with that view, substantial public discussions about the value of slavery were quite rare. Such conversations surely occurred during the Revolutionary period, but in the debates over whether or not to ratify the Constitution, both supporters and opponents focused on the need to protect slavery. Certainly the last major discussion—and it was the first in a half century—took place in the Virginia legislature during the winter of 1831–1832. The argument against slavery had added force at that time because of Nat Turner's revolt, which had occurred in August 1831 and terrified white Virginians. Some legislators called boldly for preparations to end the long association between Virginia and slavery. These men—most of them from the transmontane region of the state, where few slaves lived—argued that slavery was injurious to the economy of the state and to the mores of its white citizens. These enemies of slavery also believed that the demise of slavery must be accompanied by the emigration of blacks. They saw no way for free whites and large numbers of free blacks to live side by side. Other legislators emphasized the immense investment in slaves and praised the morality of the institution. They maintained that the vast sum needed to effect even gradual emancipation could not be raised. In 1830 Virginia had more than 470,000 slaves valued at around $100 million, at a time when the annual state budget totaled less than $500,000. Moreover, the supporters of slavery thought large-scale emigration utterly impractical. When the vote took place, slavery won comfortably. The questions raised about slavery had no more practical impact than they had had fifty years earlier.

The state and the legislature permitted this open questioning of slavery for two major reasons. First, at this moment Virginia and the South had not yet felt the full fury of the abolitionists' assault. Second, the questioners were not outsiders but Virginians who were upholding a Virginia tradition, though a distinctly minority one.

After the onslaught of abolition the debate was not repeated. From the southern viewpoint, any questioners aligned themselves with either abolitionists or free-soilers, both of whom southerners identified as groups who wanted to enslave the South. No white southerners who cherished liberty and honor wanted to be associated with such people; neither would the larger society permit any of its own to associate publicly with those it defined as endangering the South.

13

Political Parties and the Territorial Issue

❖

Wh+ hite southerners participated in a political world dominated by two great parties, the Democratic and the Whig. Across the South in the early 1840s, Democrats and Whigs battled over economic and financial policies. The bitter scrapping over these issues at both the national and state levels seemed to herald a return to old political ways. Earlier the Jeffersonian Republicans and the Federalists as well as the Democrats and the National Republicans had divided over questions of national economic power, including a national bank and the tariff. After 1840, Whigs and Democrats took opposite sides on that same basic issue. Partisan squabbling in the states over banking and related financial matters reinforced the division in national politics. The political parties appeared to have shoved aside slavery-related topics to concentrate on economics and finance.

As the presidential election of 1844 approached, Democrats and Whigs prepared to carry on the fight over finance which had characterized state contests and congressional debates. To lead them in their newfound cause southern Whigs joined their northern comrades in uniting behind Henry Clay. Support for Clay quickly turned into adulation. As new converts to the doctrine of national economic power—Clay's American System—southern Whigs were in an extravagant mood. One of them caught it perfectly: "Clay the high comb cock. The election begins and ends. Clay is the president and the nation redeemed." The Democrats, by contrast, were defensive and somewhat lethargic. Martin Van Buren apparently would win their presidential nomination for a third time. By the end of 1843 he had vanquished all competitors, including Calhoun, who had made his strongest bid for the presidency. Most southern leaders supported Van Buren, bud he had never generated much excitement among southern voters. They simply did not respond to him, even though on the slavery issue he had always done what southern Democrats had asked. Without much thought the Democrats prepared to combat Clay's nationalism with their time-honored theme of states rights.

THE POWER OF TEXAS

But it was not to be. President John Tyler enjoyed being president and wanted to remain in the White House. At the least he wanted to leave his mark. To achieve either goal he needed an issue, a dramatic one. Usually dismissed as an unimportant president, John Tyler was in fact of enormous importance. Between 1815 and 1860 only Andrew Jackson and John C. Calhoun had more influence on southern politics, and a legitimate argument can be made that Tyler ranked with the other two. A Virginian immersed in the political and plantation world of his native state, Tyler naturally thought about the South. As a veteran of Hugh White's campaign for the presidency in 1836, Tyler knew that no other issue so aroused southerners as a perceived outside threat to slavery, which, of course, jeopardized their conception of their liberty. If Tyler could succeed in stirring up the South, he might sweep past Van Buren to become the Democratic choice; if the Democrats rejected him, he might even initiate a third party based in the South.

The political hopes of John Tyler formed the background for the drive to annex Texas. After revolting from Mexico in 1836, Texas proclaimed itself an independent republic. Because American immigrants led the revolt and the new country, many people in Texas and in the United States wanted Texas to join the Union. But the existence of slavery in Texas made annexation a delicate issue. Such political considerations checked both Andrew Jackson and Martin Van Buren, because they worried about the possible effect of annexation on northern Democratic unity, but not John Tyler. Texas became his issue for arousing the South. Tyler and his advisers also convinced themselves that annexation was in the national interest. By the summer of 1843 they believed that Great Britain had designs on Texas, which included abolishing slavery and challenging the dominance of American cotton in the British market. The Tyler men, joined by Calhoun, who became secretary of state in February 1844, were confident that with Texas they could gain the attention and support of the South. They anticipated southern public opinion "boil[ing] and effervesc[ing] . . . more like a volcano than a cider Barrel."

Texas could cause such a thunderous reaction because it touched the raw nerve of southern politics. The threat of abolition on their border—Texas physically touched Arkansas and Louisiana—would arouse southerners. When somebody other than themselves talked about tampering with slavery on their own ground—and Texas was practically so—southerners heard only one sound, the clanking of the shackles that would end their freedom to control their own affairs.

The force of Texas first hit the southern Democrats. The Tyler men, including Calhoun, had close ties to the Democratic party, and they still hoped to thwart Van Buren. The Tyler-Calhoun combine could hope that Texas would "unsettle all calculations as to the future course of men and parties." And it surely did; the reaction among southern Democrats was volcanic. They reached for Texas as the drowning reach for lifelines. The southern Democrats thought they had an issue that could give even Van Buren popularity. They were savoring the possibility of victory when Van Buren let loose a bombshell: he announced his opposition to the immediate annexation of Texas. Dumbfounded, southerners searched for an ex-

planation. They never imagined that he would stand against them; always before
he had done what they asked on slavery-related matters. Van Buren's opposition
to Texas meant his political death in the South. Most important, he broke the party
compact as southerners interpreted it. By refusing to follow the South's lead on a
critical slavery-related issue, Van Buren, as one southern political observer understood, had violated "the *sanctum sanctorum.*"

In the Democratic national convention of 1844 the southerners led the successful fight to deny Van Buren the nomination. In his stead the convention chose
James K. Polk, a Tennessee Jacksonian who planted cotton and owned slaves. The
convention also adopted a pro-Texas platform. Southern Democrats were thrilled;
even Calhoun cheered. In the South the party had not known such exuberance
and unity since 1828.

While the southern Democrats were overjoyed, nervousness gripped the
southern Whigs, who feared the impact of Texas on their party because northern
Whigs were adamantly opposed to annexation. All worried that it might lead to
war, because Mexico still claimed Texas. Southern Whig senators joined with their
northern colleagues to kill Tyler's treaty of annexation, but still Texas would not
go away; it knocked the southern Whigs off balance. For the first time in presidential politics they felt the initiative slipping away. The Texas blitz exploded Whig
unity. Southern Whigs wanted to win with Clay and their economic program, but
Texas struck too deep. With *slavery* and *liberty* on everyone's lips, southerners of
all persuasions responded to the issue of Texas. Whigs began to talk more and
more about Texas and less and less about banks and tariffs. Not that they accepted
the Democrats' call for immediate annexation, but they tried to blur partisan lines.
The state convention of Georgia Whigs caught the party in motion: "We are in
favor of the annexation of Texas to the United States, at the earliest practicable period consistent with the honor and good faith of the nation." Whigs ranged across
the Texas landscape. Defection did occur, but it never became widespread. Many
Whigs argued for annexation, with various conditions. Some remained firmly opposed, Others stayed with their leaders, who tried to straddle Texas. Pressed by
northern Whigs not to deviate from his initial stand against Texas, Clay was buf-
feted by powerful southern winds. Hard-pressed southern Whigs implored Clay
to open the Texas door, at least a bit. Trapped in these political crosswinds, Clay
tried to make all happy. He published three public statements supposedly clarify-
ing his position on Texas, but none of them satisfied anyone. By no means did
Clay go all the way to the Democratic position, but he bent to the necessity of
southern politics.

Texas obliterated economics. The Texas issue proved again that in the South
nothing could withstand the force of a political issue closely connected with slavery and liberty. The politics of slavery made it impossible for economic nationalism to prevail over Texas as an issue. Although southern Whigs were never of one
mind on Texas, it shattered their unity. And the constant Democratic pressure
made its restoration impossible.

The election results confirmed the triumph of Texas. Clay carried only four
states; below the border he polled fewer votes than Harrison had won in 1840.
The almost 60,000 new voters cast Democratic ballots. Despite their backing away
from outright opposition to annexation, the southern Whigs managed to hold

only their committed vote. Because of the variety of Whig stances on Texas, from ardent championship to outright opposition, Clay and Polk did not offer the South a clear choice. A vote for Polk was surely an aye vote, but a vote for Clay could have been an aye, a nay, or a maybe.

Before Polk's inauguration in March 1845, Tyler achieved his goal of bringing Texas into the Union. A joint resolution of Congress, not a treaty, authorized his action, which he took literally in the last hours of his presidency. Texas as a political issue was over, but the force it unleashed became even more potent.

POLK AND THE MEXICAN WAR

When James K. Polk became president, he approved Tyler's last-minute action. With Texas in the Union, Polk could turn his full attention to his own presidential agenda, which contained two main objectives. He wanted economic reform that would bring down the Whig Tariff of 1842 and revive the Independent Treasury of Van Buren's time; and he wanted to ensure the continued westward expansion of the United States. In Polk's mind Texas was not the end but the beginning. He especially coveted California, which still belonged to Mexico.

Polk accomplished his economic goals. Congress, voting along partisan lines, recreated the Independent Treasury and passed the Tariff of 1846, which significantly decreased duties. This triumph of Democratic economic measures really ended the Democratic-Whig rivalry on that front, a rivalry that in the South had begun with the Panic of 1837 and increased with the rise of the Clay Whig party. In the South a national bank and the tariff largely disappeared as political issues.

With them went state financial issues. After 1845 the political rhetoric in the South no longer contained copious references to banks, specie payments, and allied subjects. In the mid-1840s the general upturn in the southern economy, led by rapidly increasing prices for cotton and slaves, dulled the cutting edge of financial weapons. Political resolution of such divisive topics as the chartering of new banks also helped alter the language of southern politics. By 1847 banking was no longer a rousing issue in any of the southern states.

As financial concerns receded, Polk's determination to expand the nation's borders created an issue of great power. His decision to send units of the United States Army under Major General Zachary Taylor to establish the Mexican-Texan, or Mexican-American, border on the Rio Grande and to reach out for California led to war between Mexico and the United States.

When Polk's drive westward brought on armed conflict with Mexico, Democrats, south and north, supported their president. The Democratic party had adopted western expansion as its own natural child. Democrats saw in the westward movement a magnificent opportunity to strengthen the nation and their party. They certainly envisioned no internal party problems from expansion. The declaration of war by Congress in May 1846 occasioned little disaffection. The one notable defector from the party was conspicuous by his loneliness. John C. Calhoun had been an enthusiastic supporter of Polk during the campaign and during the first year of his presidency. He was prepared to back Polk on a defensive posture toward Mexico, but he would not countenance what he called offensive moves. But Calhoun rallied almost no one to his standard. Southern Democratic politicians to a man, including most Calhounites, stood behind the war.

While the southern Democrats sang the praises of expansion and beat the drums of war, the southern Whigs knew little joy. For them Texas had been the worst kind of political medicine. Instead of invigorating the Whigs, it sickened them and their party. For southern Whigs, Texas represented more than the loss of a presidential election they had expected to win; it wounded the party by sundering northerners and southerners. While southern Whigs had divided minds about Texas, northern Whigs vehemently opposed it. While the politics of slavery forced southern Whigs to bend toward Texas, northern Whigs proudly proclaimed their adamant opposition. With Texas finally behind them, southern Whigs wanted no more divisive issues, and they rightly feared that an attempt to add more land to the Union would lead to nothing but disaster for them. They knew it would strain their party, perhaps this time to the breaking point. Besides, they feared that the South and the nation might also suffer, if expansion led to general sectional antagonism.

The outbreak of war between the United States and Mexico in May 1846 stirred great excitement. The general response across the South approached jubilation. The many newspapers that had clamored for war, especially those in the Mississippi Valley from St. Louis to New Orleans, were overjoyed. The government's call for volunteers to serve in Mexico resulted in an overwhelming turnout. Tennessee was asked to provide 3,000 troops, but nearly 30,000 came forward to join up. Kentucky filled its quota within two weeks after Congress declared war. In Baltimore it took only thirty-six hours to raise the allotted number of citizen soldiers. Many Mississippians complained bitterly that so few of them were called to put on the uniform and follow the flag. These were not isolated instances. In the first year of the war almost twice as many officers and enlisted men went into the ranks of the United States Army from the slave states as from the free states, roughly 45,000 to 24,000. Such prominent southern politicians as Gideon Pillow, a Tennessee associate of President Polk, and John A. Quitman, an important Mississippi planter and politician, became well-known political generals.

The war proceeded just as most Americans, northerners and southerners, assumed it would. After his initial victorious engagements in the Rio Grande Valley, General Taylor plunged into northern Mexico where he defeated the Mexican army in major battles at Monterrey in September 1846 and again at Buena Vista in February 1847. After those triumphs, which made the Louisiana resident a national hero, the war in the north subsided while the main action shifted southward. In the spring of 1847 an expeditionary force under Major General Winfield Scott captured Vera Cruz, on the eastern coast. After the fall of Vera Cruz, Scott, in a brilliant action, drove inland toward Mexico City, which fell to the Americans in September. The capture of Mexico City basically ended the fighting. The United States had won a great military victory, and the South had surely had a part in it. Of the combat casualties, which totaled some 1,800 killed and wounded, over half came from the slave states.

During the course of the war the South's fervor for it declined somewhat. Among the Democrats, Calhoun never reconciled himself to what was happening. Most Whigs were never happy with either the expansionist policy that brought on the confrontation with Mexico or the declaration of war itself. As the war wore one, they increased their criticism of Polk and his handling of the conflict, but they were careful never to criticize the army. The southern Whigs in Congress believed it their patriotic duty to support the military effort as long as Americans were in combat. The Whigs also remembered what had happened to the last party to oppose a war; after the War of 1812 the Federalist party had disappeared. At the same time they worried about the political and national difficulties that would result from the expected American victory. In view of their uneasiness about the war, the southern Whigs found themselves in a somewhat uncomfortable position as they celebrated American victories and cheered the winning generals, Scott and especially Taylor.

THE RISE AND FORCE OF THE TERRITORIAL ISSUE

The major postwar problem crystallized before the end of hostilities. If the American victory that all assumed would take place did in fact occur and brought with it the additional territory that Polk went to war to obtain, then the political battle lines were clearly drawn. In fact, they had been staked out early on. When Zachary Taylor first sent his soldiers splashing across the Rio Grande into Mexico, an obscure Democratic congressman from Pennsylvania introduced a measure that would put his name in the history books. On August 8, 1846, as Congress considered an appropriations bill to provide money for negotiations on territorial adjustments with Mexico, David Wilmot proposed an amendment that would forever prohibit slavery in any territory won from Mexico. The immediate response was not partisan but sectional—the South no, the North yes. Still in the summer of 1846 no one was quite sure what the Wilmot Proviso meant. Some thought it simply a sniping attack on President Polk from disaffected Democrats who would soon quiet down. Others feared that the proviso could be a harbinger of a vicious fight over the handling of all future territories. Some thought it terrible and some considered it wonderful. Some wished the proviso would just fade away, but it was not about to do so. The Wilmot Proviso embodied too much that was fundamental about the United States.

The locking of the door to expansion by an antislave or free-soil majority had massive implications. For southerners the Wilmot Proviso carried one ominous message: the South could no longer control its own affairs; the South had lost the power to direct its own destiny. The North would have the South bound by the same shackles that the white South clamped on its black slaves.

For white southerners territorial expansion was not just another political issue that they might win or lose. Expansion had been central in southern history since the colonial era. For two centuries new land had offered southerners the traditional avenue to wealth and position, whether in the piedmont, across the Appalachians, in the Southwest, or beyond the Mississippi. Southerners of every economic and social position had taken advantage of the opportunity provided by plentiful, cheap land. Those who aspired to yeoman and planter status as well as those who had already made it saw the West as the place to make it even bigger.

For the last antebellum generation neither this attitude toward new land nor the reality of its rewards had diminished. The West was still a magic kingdom drawing southerners with its promises.

The issue of territorial expansion involved more than social mobility and economic opportunity. In an expanding nation the South had always recognized that the extension of southern boundaries was vital for the maintenance of the political power the South must have if it was to protect its interests and guarantee its liberty. In the morning of the Constitution southern leaders believed that the chief benefits of territorial expansion would accrue to their section and permit it to dominate the new nation. Long before the 1840s, however, the southern leadership recognized that continued expansion would not bring domination but still was necessary to keep the South abreast of a North booming in population and wealth. Through the Missouri crisis and into the 1840s the South managed to maintain its political leverage, though it was falling behind in population and total wealth. When both Texas and Florida were admitted to the Union as slave states in 1845, the slave South demonstrated that it had not fallen off the pace. At the end of the decade there were fifteen free and fifteen slave states.

In the southern view, that parity was critical, for political power formed a basic prerequisite for the liberty of a free people. As the South viewed political reality, the closing of the territories to slavery foretold a dismal political fate. New states carved from the territories closed to slavery could only augment the political might of the anti-South forces that had imposed the proviso. Then a people who had not been able to prevent the proviso might become powerless over their own slaves. An increasingly mighty anti-South majority could decree the destruction of slavery itself. Such a catastrophe, if it was to come at all, probably lay far in the future, but temporal distance made the possibility no less real to white southerners. In the late 1840s the South faced the distinct possibility of its first defeat ever on a major slavery question. Never since the Constitutional Convention of 1787, when the South clearly drew the line, had it been vanquished on a momentous slavery issue.

The proviso touched even more than the political power that the South had grown accustomed to and expected. A formal ban on slavery in the territories insulted southerners as individuals and as a community. The proviso's adoption by the rest of the nation, acting through the Congress, stigmatized the South as unclean, as dishonorable. With the proviso as the law of the land, the South would become the American Ishmael, denied full participation in a great national undertaking because it had an un-American social system and held un-American values. White southerners prided themselves on their patriotism and cherished their honor, and the thought of such banishment outraged them. Just as individual southerners unhesitatingly protected their own honor, the collective South struck back at the proviso and all that it implied. The southerners exclaimed that they would never allow anyone to pin a badge of degradation on them. In the southern mind, free-soilers or provisoists became as vile as abolitionists. Most southerners never separated the two groups, because both desecrated the South's image of itself, challenged the right of the South to govern its own destiny, and ultimately threatened the South with destruction of its liberty. Talk of severing the Union should the proviso pass became commonplace.

Whether the insistence of the southerners on their right to take their slaves into the territories meant that they wanted or expected to do so remains a vexing question. Throughout the history of expansion white southerners who responded to the attraction of the West had been accompanied by black slaves. Never had white southerners thought of expansion apart from their institution of slavery. In the southern experience, the two had always converged. In the late 1840s southerners spoke both negatively and positively about carrying slaves beyond Texas, and it is impossible to enumerate precisely the numbers in each camp. The possibility of actually taking slaves into the territories, however, was not the crucial issue in the national debate—at least, not between the introduction of the Wilmot Proviso in 1846 and the passage of the Kansas-Nebraska Act in 1854. During those eight years southerners fought to establish the right to take slaves into the new territories, or at least to prevent the denial of that right. Honor demanded and liberty required not only the struggle but victory. Calhoun expressed the mind and heart of every southerner in 1849:

> What then do we insist on is, not to extend slavery, but that we shall not be prohibited from immigrating with our property, into the Territories of the United States, because we are slaveholders; or, in other words, we shall not on that account be disenfranchised of a privilege possessed by all others, citizens and foreigners, without discrimination as to character, profession, or color. All, whether savage, barbarian, or civilized, may freely enter and remain, we only being excluded.

Eventually, of course, the political motive so much a part of the southern battle against the proviso would necessitate new slave states. Even if the South secured affirmation of its rights in the territories, the South could not sit quietly by and watch all the common territory turned into free states. When the opportunity arose in the late 1850s to create a slave state in Kansas, the South employed all its political power in an attempt to do so.

THE PARTISAN RESPONSE

By 1847 the Wilmot Proviso held indisputable title as the chief public topic in the South. It occupied first place on the list of concerns for both Democrats and Whigs, neither of whom lost any time in attacking the proviso. A Democratic governor proclaimed "our unalterable purpose of maintaining our rights, at all hazards and to the last extremity." Not to be outdone, a leading Whig newspaper editorialized: "We shall indulge in no bluster or bravado on the [proviso]. Of this, however, the North may be assured, that, whenever the South shall be called upon to *act*, it will present an undivided, stern, inflexible front to its fanatical assailants."

At the same time that the two sides denounced the proviso, each sought some way to keep the national party intact. Party integrity could be maintained if southerners could get their northern colleagues to bypass the proviso or at least meet it obliquely. If not, then the party would cease to serve its major function, guarding southern liberty. Such an outcome guaranteed a political death certificate for the afflicted party.

Along with that danger, the proviso crisis offered a genuine opportunity to southern partisans. If either the Democrats or the Whigs could resolve their intra-party difficulties in a manner clearly advantageous to the South, then they could place their southern opponents in an extremely perilous political position. From the 1790s the first commandment of a successful party in the South had been to protect southern liberty. The politics of slavery only intensified that fundamental law of southern politics. Southern Democrats and southern Whigs strove to place each other on the political chopping block.

The proviso posed immediate problems for southern Democrats. Because it came from certified Democrats, southern Whigs had a ready-made weapon, which they promptly used. Charging that the Democratic party harbored the orig-inators of the proviso, southern Whigs attacked southern Democrats for coddling enemies of the South and for caring less about the safety of the South than about winning place and reward. The hard-pressed Democrats knew exactly the re-sponse required by the politics of slavery. Not only did they have to assert un-equivocally their loyalty to the South, they also had to prove they were not in the clutches of the provisoists. As they searched for a solution to the proviso problem, the southern Democrats met head-on the influence of Calhoun, whose followers, with close ties to Democrats in several states, worked to get the southern Demo-crats to give their northern brethren an ultimatum.

The final Calhounite–southern Democratic position rested on two pillars. First, they publicly pledged "determined resistance" against the proviso "at all hazards and to the last extremity." Next, they announced that southern Demo-crats would support no presidential candidate "who does not unconditionally, clearly, and unequivocally declare his opposition to the principles and provisions of the Wilmot Proviso." These two pledges merged to become the dogma of southern Democrats down to the upheaval of 1860.

The southern Democrats hoped for an accommodation with their northern colleagues both because tangible political rewards were associated with national political power and because they still believed that the party provided the surest vehicle for southern safety. Most major northern leaders desired a settlement on the proviso just as fervently as the southerners. As a result, they kept the provi-soist minority huddled against the shore, away from the full current. The north-erners recognized the potential political dynamite of the proviso, but they also believed that their constituents would stay with them if an acceptable alternative to the proviso could be devised.

Searching for a way around the proviso, the Democrats came up with popular sovereignty. Presented by northerners eager to retain their southern connection, popular sovereignty became the formula that won the allegiance of Democrats in both sections. Based on the supreme Democratic principle that the people were sovereign, popular sovereignty first declared the Wilmot Proviso unconstitutional and then insisted that the settlers in a territory, not the Congress or anyone else, should make the decision on slavery in their territory.

Popular sovereignty added to its political allure by leaving the time frame for the crucial decision on slavery conveniently vague. Although popular sovereignty implied that settlers could accept or reject slavery during the territorial stage, its advocates did not talk about territorial legislatures. The doctrine also asserted that all settlers had to abide by the basic principles of the Constitution. Northerners who took the implication as the chief thrust could argue that popular sovereignty allowed the first territorial legislature to ban slavery if it chose to do so. But southerners who stressed the constitutional-principles theme asserted that a decision on slavery had to await statehood, for territories lacked the authority to decide so fundamental a question as slavery. Only a state had that authority. For southern Democrats, popular sovereignty thus became an extension of their traditional doctrine of states rights. The obvious inconsistency and vagueness inherent in popular sovereignty provided much of its political beauty. Professing loyalty to popular sovereignty, albeit in different versions, both northern and southern Democrats could banish the Wilmot Proviso from their political vocabulary.

Popular sovereignty clearly delighted the vast majority of southern Democrats. Only the Calhounites dissented. Calhoun correctly defined popular sovereignty as an ingenious political construct designed to avoid the sectional confrontation he lusted for and believed the proviso would provide. But few southerners shared his desire for confrontation. To them popular sovereignty seemed a perfect doctrine—liberty without confrontation. Southern Democrats believed they could defend it as a guarantee for the South; it also enabled them to represent their northern comrades as denouncing the hated proviso. When the national party, in convention in 1848, placed its imprimatur on popular sovereignty, the southerners cheered. As they saw it, the Democratic party had shunted aside the threat to southern liberty posed by the Wilmot Proviso. To the South, southern Democrats shouted that only they had a foolproof way to guarantee southern liberty, the doctrine of popular sovereignty.

Southern Whigs found themselves perched on the same political precipice occupied by their Democratic opponents. Although they could and did blame the Democrats for giving birth to the proviso, they also had to contend with political reality—every northern Whig in Congress had voted for it. The Wilmot Proviso hit the Whig party even harder than Texas. Northern Whigs supported the proviso just as vigorously as southern Whigs opposed it. Despite this clear sectional division, the national Whig party had not taken an official stand on the proviso. Until it did, southern Whigs had no reason to give up their party. If, like southern Democrats, they could neutralize the proviso, then the Whig party would remain the source of political reward and the guardian of the South it had been since birth. But with the northern leadership more eager to make the proviso its issue than to placate the South, it was most unlikely that the party could reach agreement on a stated formula such as popular sovereignty.

The gods of politics favored the southern Whigs, or so it seemed. The war in Mexico that the party had opposed created several heroes, one of them very special. Major General Zachary Taylor, who had commanded the successful American forces in the early engagements along the Rio Grande and during the invasion of northern Mexico, vaulted from obscurity to instant fame. A legitimate military hero, Taylor possessed other characteristics immensely attractive to southern Whigs. A professional soldier, he called Baton Rouge, Louisiana, home; moreover, he owned a cotton plantation in Mississippi and more than a hundred slaves. The likes of Taylor had not been seen in the South since Andrew Jackson—an authentic military hero who was a slaveholding cotton planter. Southern Whigs had never before come close to possessing such a political property. For them Taylor was a godsend, and they quickly made him their champion. That Taylor had no political experience, really no political past of any kind, bothered the southern Whigs not at all. They looked to the future and saw it dominated by the slave-owning hero Zachary Taylor, resplendent in his new Whig uniform.

Zachary Taylor caught on like wildfire. With Taylor as the party nominee, southern Whigs would not need a public party pronouncement against the proviso. They could bring their cause to southern voters in the form of Zachary Taylor, whose name, home, occupation, and possessions were all identified with the South. All by himself Taylor would prove conclusively where the Whig party stood on the proviso; neither he nor the Whig party had to say a thing.

If this political magic was to work, the northern Whigs would also have to accept Taylor. Although the extreme antislavery men refused to back a slaveholder, many northern Whigs, remembering the voters' liking for victorious generals, found Taylor attractive. Besides, they were fumbling for issues; the economic catastrophe they had predicted under Polk had not occurred. Placing the party on record against the proviso and pushing full steam against it would win votes in the North but fracture the party. Moreover, attractive candidates were scarce. If they ran Taylor as a national hero and as a good Whig who as president would surely not veto a congressionally approved proviso, the northern Whigs thought they could win.

The Whig factions made their peace by uniting behind a warrior. The convention that nominated Taylor adopted no platform and thus kept its silence on the proviso. The southerners were thrilled. To persuade southern voters of their party's ability to defend the South in this moment of crisis they could offer no doctrine, but to their minds they had something vastly superior—a southern hero.

CRISIS AND COMPROMISE

In 1848 the parties in the South asked for votes in return for trust and protection; the Democrats offered a platform, the Whigs a man. The man triumphed. Although each party held its loyalists, Taylor attracted some Democrats and a large share of new voters. He won more than 51 percent of the popular vote and carried states all the way from the Mason-Dixon line to Louisiana. With an energetic dedication to the politics of slavery, the southern Whigs saw themselves standing where the Democrats had stood twenty years earlier—in a position to dominate the South.

They were confident that their southern chieftain would guide them into the political promised land. Under Taylor's leadership they expected to solve the territorial problem that consumed the South, and in a way that would benefit the South and the Whig party. If this vision was to become reality, Zachary Taylor had to act like a good southerner and pull the northern Whigs along with him. The southern Whigs had no doubts.

The Mexican War ended in the spring of 1848, when Mexico ceded to the United States more than 500,000 square miles of its territory, including California and the bulk of the modern Southwest. This outcome translated the Wilmot Proviso from theoretical possibility into hard reality. Events gave neither the nation

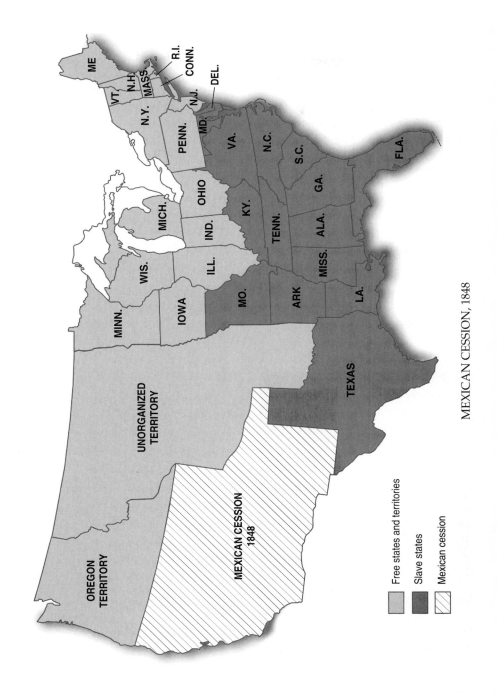

MEXICAN CESSION, 1848

Free states and territories
Slave states
Mexican cession

nor its political leaders time to absorb the implications of the cession before they had to make critical decisions regarding its governance and the status of slavery in it. The gold rush to California in 1849, which excited everyone, mandated prompt governmental action.

The question of California brought about the crisis of Zachary Taylor's presidency. Taylor wanted to bring in California as a state immediately, to be followed promptly by the rest of the Mexican Cession as a second state, New Mexico. Everyone realized that immediate statehood meant free states, because not enough time had elapsed since the end of the war for more than a handful of slaves to be carried into the area. As a result, the South would be completely shut out of the cession. Southern Whigs cried out in anguish. Although before Taylor's inauguration a number of them had pushed for statehood as a way to solve the terrible problem of the territories, they had backed away. Southern Democrats' definition of Taylor's proposal as an executive proviso and a strong shift in southern public opinion made it impossible for southern Whigs to defend their president's policy. Shocked and bewildered, they implored Taylor to recognize their political plight. But the old general was steadfast; he refused. With leading southern Whigs and Taylor at loggerheads, shouts about impeachment and military force reverberated as far as the White House. Taylor told the beleaguered southerners that his policy would not change, and if they did not like it, he did not care. Southerners, the president made clear, could march with him or he would surely march without them.

TYLER, POLK, AND TAYLOR: THREE SOUTHERN PRESIDENTS WHO POWERFULLY INFLUENCED THE COURSE OF SOUTHERN AND NATIONAL POLITICS

John Tyler (Virginia State Library)

James K. Polk (Brady Collection, National Archives)

Zachary Taylor (National Portrait Gallery, Smithsonian Institution, Washington, D.C., Gift of Barry Bingham, Sr.)

Precisely why Zachary Taylor took such an uncompromising position on the territories is exceedingly difficult to understand. Early in his administration, northern Whigs, including proviso stalwarts, became dominant; Whigs below the border had no strong voice among Taylor's advisers. The reasons for that situation are not at all clear. What is clear, however, is that the southerners assumed too much, and while they assumed, others acted. Some historians have argued that Taylor set out to build a new party. More likely his stance was heavily influenced by his view of the West and by his own army career of some forty years. Taylor did not believe that slavery could prosper in the West, and he saw the territorial issue as nationally divisive. When he decided on his policy, he viewed it as in the national interest, and with the habit of command cultivated by four decades as an army officer he announced that his way was the only way, no matter the pleas and needs of southern Whigs. Thus Taylor was an unusual southerner—a large slave-holder who staunchly defended slavery in the states but just as adamantly opposed giving southerners even the right to carry their slaves into the territories.

Taylor's statehood policy and his absolute refusal to consider any alternatives led to a national crisis. To many southerners the president's program eliminated them from national territory paid for in no small part by their blood and treasure.

And in fact soldiers from the slave states suffered more battle-related casualties in Mexico than their comrades from the free states. Prodded by Calhoun, who seized what he perceived as an opportunity for his sought-after confrontation, bipartisan groups of southerners called for a meeting in Nashville in the spring of 1850 to consider ultimatums to be presented to the North. Talk of disunion moved out into the open. Out of the crisis came the first serious emergence of fire-eaters, as secessionists were sometimes called. For the fire-eaters the Union could never furnish safety for the South, because to them the Union aimed to destroy southern liberty. Rejecting Calhoun's desire to ensure southern safety in the Union, they strove to break up the Union, the ultimate act of independence.

Into this political whirlwind stepped Henry Clay. Back in the Senate for the first time since his defeat for the presidency, Clay reported that "the feeling of disunion" and sectional animosity "is stronger than I had hoped or supposed it could be." Convinced that Taylor's insistence on a free California and a free New Mexico might tear the country apart if nothing were done to mollify angry southerners, Clay proposed a broad-based compromise. For the North he would admit California as a free state and halt the slave trade in the District of Columbia. For the South he would organize the remainder of the Mexican Cession into two territories, New Mexico and Utah, with no mention of slavery, and enact a tough fugitive slave law that would give the federal government responsibility for apprehending and returning slaves who had escaped to the free states. Clay completed his compromise proposals by providing for a settlement of the troublesome Texas–New Mexico boundary dispute.

Clay's compromise deranged parties in the South. Believing that the proposed compromise offered them a haven from the storm caused by Taylor's policy—after all, the fugitive slave bill would affirm the legitimacy of slavery and the territorial measures would shunt aside the hated proviso—the southern Whigs leaped to support it. That leap did not restore party unity, however, for most northern Whigs remained with President Taylor, who opposed the compromise. Great irony resulted—antislavery northern Whigs were supporting a southern slaveholding president while southern Whigs fought him desperately. The Democratic response was exactly the opposite. Searching for a way out of the crisis, the northern Democrats considered Clay's package reasonable and backed it. Southern Democrats, heavily influenced by the Calhounites, charged that Clay's compromise sold out the South. The key was California, and to a prompt admission of a free California they cried never.

The strain showed within the South as well as in the national party alliances. Although the great majority of southern Whigs stood behind Clay, a number of leading Democrats who felt that Calhoun had led their comrades astray made common cause with their former Whig opponents. In the three Deep South states of Alabama, Georgia, and Mississippi, party lines broke down completely. There a Democratic minority joined a Whig majority to form Union parties, while a few Whigs combined with most Democrats to form Southern Rights parties. These new combinations had two basic results. In the short term both traditional parties disappeared; in the long term the Whig party never reappeared.

From the winter all the way into the summer of 1850 the public mood was tense. The compromise seemed stalled in Congress. President Taylor remained

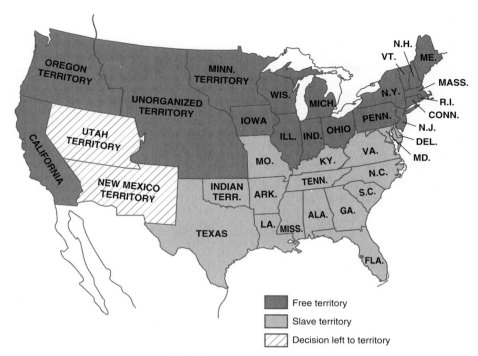

THE COMPROMISE OF 1850

unswerving in his determination to bring California in as a free state without concession to the South. When his opponents accused him of endangering the Union, he talked of using military force. Then, in July, the sudden death of Zachary Taylor eliminated an immense obstacle to compromise. A new parliamentary strategy in Congress enabled the compromise to pass: each of its parts was made into a separate bill. When each bill reached the desk of the new president, Millard Fillmore of New York—never a Taylor confidant—he signed every one into law. The Compromise of 1850 was a fact. Across the country the decreasing tension was audible; most Americans, North and South, rejoiced.

Without question an immense crisis had passed. With Congress stalemated and President Taylor unbending, the foundation for a ferocious confrontation was in place, but a legitimate secession crisis could have occurred only without the compromise and with Taylor. Without Taylor and with the compromise, the nation could relax. The overwhelming majority of southerners considered themselves good Americans. They had no desire to leave the Union provided their prized liberty remained secure. The organization of New Mexico and Utah did not overtly deny southern rights in the common territory. And extremely important, the Fugitive Slave Act affirmed the Americanism of the South's peculiar institution. No wedge had been driven between southern and American.

THE ILLNESS AND DEATH OF THE WHIGS

Southerners fell in line behind the compromise, though some did so reluctantly. At every turn southern voters overwhelmingly cast their ballots for candidates and parties that endorsed the compromise. Politicians who had spoken vigorously against it banked their rhetorical fires. The success of the compromise doomed the Southern Rights parties in the Deep South, which had staked their political careers on their opposition to it. The fire-eaters wandered into the wilderness, where they would languish until the end of the decade. Still, southerners were emphatic that their acceptance of the compromise did not at all mean that they valued the Union above all else. The famous Georgia Platform, written by adherents of the compromise in Georgia, affirmed the strong southern accent with which support for the settlement was expressed. The platform proclaimed that Georgia—read the South—would resist even unto secession, if necessary, should Congress prohibit slavery in either New Mexico or Utah, or weaken or repeal the Fugitive Slave Law, or refuse to admit a new slave state, or act against slavery on federal property in a manner "incompatible with the safety, and domestic tranquility, the rights and the honor of the slaveholding states." For southern Americans the Union provided no safe harbor unless it explicitly protected southern interests and honor.

The presidential contest of 1852 underscored the triumph of the compromise. In the South both parties announced their support for it. Southern Democrats who had fought the compromise made peace with those who had supported it, and the reunited party presented a solid front to southern voters. Nationally all Democrats rallied around Franklin Pierce of New Hampshire, who made clear his respect and support for southern institutions as well as his backing of the compromise. Southern Whigs had more problems because many of their northern counterparts still refused to fall in line behind the compromise. In an attempt to mask this serious internal division, the Whig party once again turned to an old general, Winfield Scott, like Taylor a hero of the Mexican War. But the recent experience with Taylor muted many southern Whigs' enthusiasm for Scott. The turmoil in Whig ranks pointed to the possibility of an electoral disaster, which is precisely what occurred. In both popular and electoral votes Pierce crushed Scott, who could not even hold the border. Scott carried only Tennessee and Kentucky; Pierce took everything else, with a larger percentage of the popular vote than any other Democrat had won since Andrew Jackson. No other Whig presidential nominee had ever done so poorly in the slave states as Scott.

This disaster compounded the immense political difficulties the southern Whigs faced. Since the late 1840s they had found it more and more difficult to maintain their political position in the states, even those that had been party strongholds. In state elections in 1852 and 1853 the Democrats devastated the Whigs. Below the border southern politicians vied for eleven governorships, eleven senates, and eleven houses; after 1853 the Whigs controlled only two, the houses in North Carolina and Tennessee. Congressional elections for the Thirty-third Congress, which convened in December 1853, only added to the Whigs' misery. The states below the border elected sixty-five representatives, but no more than fourteen were Whig. In state after state Whig leaders lamented the "decisive breaking up of our party," and almost all of them blamed the ascendancy of anti-slavery northern Whigs for the calamity.

With the Whigs reeling, the Democrats seemed to be moving again toward dominance of southern politics when yet another mighty shock struck the South and the nation. The compromise had barely become national policy when the territorial issue flared up again. This time it had to do with part of the Louisiana Purchase, the Nebraska Territory (basically the present states of Nebraska and Kansas). The trouble began innocently enough. The march westward brought the need for governmental organization in Nebraska, and such expansionist politicians as Senator Stephen A. Douglas of Illinois, Democratic chairman of the Senate Committee on Territories, pushed for congressional action. That should have posed no problem, certainly no sectional problem, for Nebraska was clearly above the Missouri Compromise line that supposedly settled the slavery question in the Louisiana Purchase. Certainly Douglas started out in 1853 with that view. But a number of southerners believed that if popular sovereignty had been good enough for New Mexico and Utah and had become the stated policy of the Democratic party, it should also govern the organization of Nebraska. Then southern Whigs, in almost their last thrust with the politics of slavery, proposed the specific repeal of the Missouri restriction against slavery. After much discussion, including a talk with President Pierce at the White House, Senator Douglas agreed to modify his bill by declaring the Missouri Compromise prohibition null and void and by creating a second territory, Kansas, as well as Nebraska. The Kansas-Nebraska Act easily got through the Senate in March 1854, but the House took another ten weeks while a bitter struggle took its toll on both parties. The northern Democrats divided; many went with Pierce and Douglas, but an equally substantial number refused to sanction what they perceived as a breach of the Missouri Compromise. Party unity took a substantial blow, and the repercussions were still evident in 1860. The northern Whigs in Congress to a man voted against Kansas-Nebraska, and to make matters even worse for the southerners, the northerners clamored to make their opposition to repeal of the Missouri Compromise line a partisan issue against the Democrats.

For the South, Kansas-Nebraska was a Pyrrhic victory. The passage of the Kansas-Nebraska Act contributed enormously to the growing anti-South feeling in the North and to a political realignment already under way. In the North, free-soil forces, nativism, and anti-Catholicism were pushing toward party reorganization. Kansas-Nebraska propelled that shift. It led directly to the death of the Whig party, which opened the political doors for a new anti-Democratic party. In the North two major contenders, the Know-Nothings (or the Americans) and the Republicans, competed to succeed the Whigs. Nativism in all its manifestations was the prime concern of the Know-Nothings, while the Republicans emphasized free soil and its corollary, antisouthern attitudes.

By the end of 1854 the proud, once powerful Whig party had disappeared as an effective political force in the South. Continued defeats in state elections underscored the party's pathetic condition—"floored, routed, battered, bruised, and whipped," as one loyalist described it with dismal accuracy. And the key reason for that plight was the stiffening antisouthern stance of northern Whiggery.

Through its activities between 1849 and 1854 northern Whiggery had demonstrated that it had little sense of southern rights and honor as the South understood them. The impossibility of representing the party as a guardian of the South weakened the commitment of the party faithful and resulted in an avalanche of defeats at the ballot box. Southern Whigs who had always demanded that northern Whigs follow their direction on slavery-related issues had no intention of reversing roles. A prominent spokesman captured the essence of the southern Whigs' predicament: "The Southern Whig cannot stand on a northern platform."

Just as national issues had given birth to the Whig party, so they presided over its death. Local financial issues and intrastate sectionalism could not provide the keystone for the Democratic-Whig system. At both birth and death national issues with particular southern meanings and manifestations were in the ascendancy. The southern Whigs drew the flaming sword of sectional politics to gain their political identity, and they died by that same sword. Party legitimacy in the South derived solely from the ability to protect southern liberty, a power southern Whigs could no longer claim for their party. A party stalwart spoke truthfully when he lamented that the Kansas-Nebraska Act "put an extinguisher upon the Whig party."

THE KNOW-NOTHING EPISODE

The disintegration of the Whig party did not return the South to 1800 or to 1828, when one dominant party claimed the allegiance of almost every politically active southerner. The intense partisanship stemming from two decades of Democratic-Whig rivalry could not and did not disappear. After all, southern Whigs believed that they had left their party because it first left them. There was no mad rush to join the Democrats, though some Whigs did make the shift. Most, however, yearned for a new political home in a new party that would offer them political sustenance while it honored southern rights.

Almost immediately this hope was fulfilled. As the Whig party disintegrated, the Know-Nothing party spread across the South. It spread so rapidly that it almost seemed fully grown at birth. The adherence of numerous Whigs and major Whig newspapers made it possible for the Know-Nothings to mount campaigns against the Democrats in every slave state in 1855.

The Know-Nothing party arose in the Northeast out of nativist sentiments. It articulated the powerful antagonism many native-born Americans felt toward the immigrants, chiefly Irish, who poured into the seaboard cities in the late 1840s and early 1850s. The Roman Catholicism of most of the newcomers added a religious bias to nativist thinking. The name Know-Nothing signified the successful nativist appeal to working-class men who perceived their jobs and status endangered by the new immigrants. Many of these people believed the Irish were engaged in a conspiracy engineered by the Roman Catholic church to undermine the American republic. They responded in like fashion; clandestine meetings, esoteric rituals, and pervasive secrecy heightened the party's appeal and gave meaning to its name: when questioned about its activities, its members to a man claimed to know nothing about it. Know-Nothings claimed that only they cared seriously about the plight and future of the average working American.

In the South party ideology was not so crucial. With neither large-scale immigration nor a substantial Roman Catholic population, except in Louisiana and the border state of Maryland, southerners cared much less about the ideological tenets of the new party. Even in Louisiana political reality tempered its impact, for the heavily Roman Catholic sugar-planting area, which had been a Whig bastion, became a center of Know-Nothing activity. Southern Know-Nothings wanted most of all a national party with which they could confront the Democrats. The party's northern wing would have to be controlled by conservatives who would make it a citadel against free-soil sentiment. The entire party, then, would have to stand for popular sovereignty in all territories and for the Fugitive Slave Act. Otherwise, the Democrats would destroy the Know-Nothings in the South. Southern Know-Nothings strove to get the national party to meet its needs. The contest over a slavery plank wracked the party's national conventions in 1855 and 1856. In 1855 the southerners got a declaration they approved, but in so doing antagonized many northerners. Then in 1856 the northerners won out. Northern and southern Know-Nothings could not unite on a slavery position that could survive in the politics of slavery.

The southern Democrats constantly slammed them as being unreliable friends of the South. Know-Nothings had no doubt about the political effectiveness of the "battering ram" of slavery used against them. The Know-Nothing party had a short, unhappy life in southern politics. In the state elections of 1855 its candidates were soundly whipped, except along the border. When the presidential election of 1856 came along, they fared no better. The Democrats, with James Buchanan of Pennsylvania, the last in a long line of northern Democrats with southern ties and proclivities, smashed the Know-Nothings, even though they had as a candidate the former president Millard Fillmore, once championed by southern Whigs. Carrying every state but Maryland and winning almost 60 percent of the popular vote, the Democrats sent the Know-Nothings reeling. After the debacle of 1856 the Know-Nothing party was finished as a major contender. It could not survive exposure to the politics of slavery.

After the rapid demise of the Know-Nothings, no new party arose in the South to take its place. The fleeting career of the Know-Nothings indicated that the northern connection so critical for southerners in a national party no longer existed, at least not outside the Democratic party. Aside from northern Democrats, no substantial number of northerners seemed available to participate in a national party dedicated to preserving the southern view of parties. Even so, not all southerners identified themselves as Democrats, though more and more former Whigs and Know-Nothings moved into the party. Those who refused to shift expressed their opposition in a variety of local parties, often called simply the Opposition party. Although they did use local as well as national issues to plague the Demo-crats occasionally, they never made a national connection. They were not even unified in the South. Certainly they posed no major threat to the dominant Democrats. The Democrats, however, had trouble enough outside the South. The emerging Republican party, a northern phenomenon, which in 1856 had bested the Know-Nothings in the free states, challenged the orientation and power of the Democrats. Within the Democracy itself the smoldering discontent over sectional policy threatened to become a conflagration. The flash point was Kansas.

14

The Crisis of the Union

❖

*I*n the South the disintegration of Whiggery heralded a return to an older version of southern politics, one-party domination. In the North, however, the demise of the Whig party resulted in a new kind of politics—a completely new party that exploded the traditional politics of national parties. The Republican party was strictly a northern party that made no effort to hide its regional identity. Never before had a major party been so thoroughly northern in its orientation and approach to politics. Starting out in opposition to the Kansas-Nebraska Act, the Republican party called on the North to assert its strength or forever be ground down by what it called "the slave power." By late 1856, when it ran its first presidential race, the Republican party had become the chief competition for the Democrats in the free states. Though it lost the election, the Republican party showed impressive strength across the North. Almost overnight it had become a potent political force.

SOUTHERN REACTION TO THE REPUBLICAN PARTY

Southerners of all persuasions were horrified by the emergence of the Republican party. The party platform of 1856, which emphasized the virtues of the Wilmot Proviso while condemning slavery as a "relic of barbarism," reinforced the southern perception that the new party made its stand on an "avowed and unrelenting hostility to the domestic institutions and the equal constitutional rights of the Southern States." To southern ears Republican orators "poured forth a foul stream of vituperation upon the southern people," and "left no means, however wicked, untried to excite irreconcilable hatred of them in the minds of the people of the North." Even the possibility of a Republican president terrified most southerners.

The rise of the Republican party so traumatized southerners because its electoral success destroyed the traditional arrangements that to southerners had secured their liberty. No southerners, except for a few in the border states, either ran for office as Republicans or helped formulate party policy. Moreover, with their appeal aimed solely at the North, the Republicans' strategy for political victory needed the South not at all, even to win the presidency. No major party had ever so completely repudiated the South. Although neither the Federalists nor the National Republicans enjoyed a strong southern base, each counted prominent southerners among its adherents and each tried to win southern votes. From the southern perspective the Republican party loomed like a giant tidal wave ready to obliterate the political world finely crafted by three generations of southern politicians. A Republican victory in a national election would mock the essence of liberty, local control. Accordingly, southern eyes saw in a potential Republican triumph a mortal threat.

For southerners the Republicans compounded their sinfulness by not only threatening southern liberty but by hurling insults in the process. When Republicans claimed that slavery violated the American creed, they made white southerners pariahs in their own land. But southerners proudly identified themselves as Americans; they wore their American heritage as a badge of honor. This casting of doubt on their tribal credentials southerners viewed as an unforgivable slander. With their good name slandered, southerners believed their liberty already jeopardized, for in the South good name and integrity of reputation were the personal hallmarks of free and honorable men. Facing what they could characterize only as an outrageous and unprincipled assault on their institutions, their values, their patriotism, and their liberty, the collective South denounced the Republican party.

The existence of the Republican party stiffened commitment to the basic mission that had always given legitimacy and nobility of purpose to political parties in the South—protection of southern interests and liberty in the nation. Now southern politicians confronted a major political foe with the publicly avowed mission of shackling southern power. Proclaiming that it intended to force the South to conform to its vision of the nation, the Republican party announced that its primary aim was to curb the illegitimate power of the South. Never before had southern politicians faced such an ominous challenge.

That challenge reinforced the general mission of defense and protection. Opposition parties immediately began to question Democratic stewardship of southern interests. The politics of slavery had not died with the organized Whig party; the forces it expressed were too fundamental. Every opposing political group slashed at the Democrats for losing sight of their sacred duty—to protect the South. As they had been doing for decades, the Democrats countered vigorously. Even though their opponents were but pale shadows of the once formidable Whigs, the Democrats went after them for betraying the South—betrayal because they preferred to win office and snipe at the Democrats rather than join forces to present a united front to the new determined enemy. According to the Democratic script, the Opposition parties really aided the Republicans. But the Democrats could not simply attack; they also had to defend their unwavering commitment to southern liberty. Kansas provided the opportunity and the requirement.

THE TRAUMA OF KANSAS

After the passage of the Kansas-Nebraska Act, the Territory of Kansas opened for settlement. As in most other such areas, the majority of settlers who poured into

Kansas were not interested in the sectional conflict. They wanted land of their own and a better living. But ardent partisans, northerners and southerners, saw Kansas as critical for the future. Each group wanted Kansas to end up on its side, either free or slave. As a result, zeal squeezed out moderation; moderates were unable to manage events or politics in Kansas. Groups of marauders burned, pillaged, and murdered in the name of a larger good. They turned the territory into what many called Bleeding Kansas, a violent microcosm of the sectional crisis. A free Kansas formed a major rallying cry of the Republican party. For many southerners, especially southern Democrats, Kansas became a contest with the hated Republicans.

Confrontations occurred in Washington as well as in Kansas. In May 1856, Senator Charles Sumner, Republican of Massachusetts, delivered in the Senate a long, angry speech titled "The Crime against Kansas." The crime, according to Sumner, was the South's effort to bring slavery to Kansas—in his terms, the "rape" of Kansas. As he lashed out at the South, Sumner also made abusive references to the senior senator from South Carolina, Andrew P. Butler. Butler's cousin, Representative Preston Brooks, took offense at Sumner's remarks and determined that Butler's honor had to be protected. And because Butler was in South Carolina, Brooks decided that he would stand for his kinsman. Two days after the speech Brooks entered the Senate chamber, walked up to Sumner at his desk, and announced that he would punish Sumner for insulting his cousin. Thereupon he proceeded to beat Sumner over the head with his gutta-percha cane. With blows raining upon him and blood spilling about his face, Sumner bolted up, wrenching the desk from the floor, stumbled about, and collapsed. Brooks continued to pound Sumner until others pulled him away. Immediately Sumner became a Republican martyr to the barbaric slave power while the delighted Brooks won the plaudits of southern zealots and his constituents, who reelected him unanimously and gave him a new cane with the inscription "Use Knock-Down Arguments."

In Kansas territorial politics became so inflamed that proslavery and free-soil camps refused to participate in the same political process. From this bitterness emerged the Lecompton Constitution. In 1857, when proslavery forces decided to hold a constitutional convention in preparation for statehood, free-soilers boycotted it. Meeting in Lecompton, this convention adopted a proslavery constitution. Aware that antislavery men significantly outnumbered them, the proslavery men did not submit the issue of slavery to a general referendum, in which it would surely have been defeated. They allowed only a partial referendum; Kansans could vote on the future admission of slaves into the territory, but they could not express an opinion on the slaves already there. Holding true to Kansas form, the free-soilers did not vote. These facts were as well known in Washington as in Kansas.

For southern Democrats the Lecompton Constitution required a major decision. As Democrats they recognized it as the alleged fruit of popular sovereignty, the gospel of their party. But popular sovereignty meant the wishes of the majority, and the southern Democratic leadership knew full well that no majority in Kansas desired the Lecompton Constitution. They also knew that in a fair vote Kansans would repudiate it. These tainted credentials made acceptance of the Lecompton Constitution extremely difficult for many northern Democrats. Having staked their political future on popular sovereignty, most northern Democrats were prepared to persevere with it despite Republican cries for free soil. But the political potency of those cries made it impossible for the bulk of the northern Democrats to accept the handiwork of Lecompton, a mockery of popular sovereignty. If the southern Democrats made an all-out effort for Lecompton, the ensuing struggle would threaten party unity.

On the other hand, southern Democrats realized that the Lecompton Constitution provided an opportunity to add a slave state to the Union without further ado. The South had not had such an opportunity since 1845. Many southerners felt that if they lost on Kansas, they might never have so good a chance again. Kansas did border on slave territory; it abutted Missouri and was just northwest of Arkansas.

Southerners also believed that if a slave Kansas were refused admission, the great battles over constitutional rights would have been fought in vain. This was especially true because of the southern victory in the Dred Scott case. Handed down by the United States Supreme Court in March 1857, the Dred Scott decision gave constitutional sanction to the southern position on slavery and the territories. The majority decision was written by Chief Justice Roger B. Taney, a Marylander placed on the Court by Andrew Jackson. Although Taney prepared the decision for the seven-man majority, the other six wrote concurring opinions. The two dissenters also filed opinions. Thus all nine members of the Court went on record, confusing the issue more than they clarified it. Still the basic conclusions reached by Chief Justice Taney were clear enough, though scholars have questioned his arguments. Two of them were most crucial: (1) blacks, even free blacks in free states, were not and could not be citizens because the Constitution did not consider them so; (2) the Missouri Compromise was unconstitutional because Congress had no power to exclude slavery from any territory.

Partisan politics also influenced southern Democrats' stance on the issue of Kansas. Their opponents had been attacking them for not caring enough about the South. The interests of the South, according to the Opposition script, aroused little concern among southern Democrats angling for reward and place in the corrupt administration of James Buchanan. If the southern Democrats allowed a new slave state to slip through their grasp, they would hand their opponents a golden political issue. In this atmosphere, party stalwarts in the states pressed the leaders in Washington to act.

Thus both ideology and politics propelled the southern Democrats to demand acceptance of Lecompton and the admission of Kansas as a slave state. When they moved to make these demands party policy, President Buchanan and his administration wheeled into line, but the southerners could not nudge their northern comrades into a united stand. The ablest and most popular northern Democrat, Senator Stephen A. Douglas of Illinois, had made popular sovereignty his political creed ever since Kansas-Nebraska; he had stumped the North for it. And he could not accept the mockery Lecompton made of his doctrine, certainly not with the Republicans mounting a major campaign for his Senate seat. In his march away from Lecompton and the southerners, Douglas led a sizable number of northern Democrats.

Douglas's defection was a grave matter for southern Democrats. His opposition not only decreased the chance that Congress would admit Kansas under the Lecompton Constitution; it also represented the disloyalty of a man southerners had thought a staunch friend. Moreover, Douglas's action challenged the southern conception of the party and its rules. For the first time since Van Buren's rejection of Texas in 1844, a major northern Democratic leader had refused to accept the South's demands on a key slavery issue. But whereas the southerners had overpowered Van Buren, they could not move Douglas.

Despite vigorous efforts, the southerners failed to obtain congressional approval for Lecompton. In control of the Senate, they and the administration stalwarts did win on Lecompton there, even though Douglas opposed it; but they were unable to gain passage in the House, in no small part because of the Douglas Democrats. To camouflage their embarrassing defeat, they managed to have the Lecompton Constitution returned to Kansas for a popular referendum. Although Lecompton was dead, the southerners were able to claim that Congress had not summarily dismissed their policy.

The southern Democrats needed that face-saving device. The Oppositionists savaged them over Douglas's apostasy, over party defections in the House, over the defeat of Lecompton. They kept asking what had happened to the vaunted prosouthern Democratic party. Even the compromise provided ammunition to be used against them. Now they were blasted for betraying principle for lucre: "How harshly does the word [compromise] grate upon the Southern ear. With what unctuous sweetness does it roll from the lips of aspirants for federal position."

The experience of Lecompton devastated the southern Democrats. Although they claimed the party still belonged to them and it did have control of the Senate as well as the administration, the party had been tattered. With Douglas as outcast, a glaring gap cut through the party's northern front. And southern rage only widened the gap. Furious with Douglas and eager to make an example of him, the southerners set out to destroy him. The party was more fractured than it had been since Jackson's second term, when massive defections helped create the Whig party. Battered and fragmented, the Democratic party limped toward 1860.

ECONOMIC AND INDUSTRIAL GROWTH

While the southern Democrats were suffering political setbacks, the economy of the South was growing and prospering, even booming. The dominant agricultural sector knew real prosperity. Production of cotton, sugar cane, and tobacco increased significantly, and prices either stayed firm or advanced. By 1860 the value of southern agricultural products reached beyond $525 million. In the 1850s southern farmers and planters experienced the best of all possible agricultural worlds—increasing production with stable or rising prices.

Not surprisingly, a general optimism governed the mood of the agricultural South. A significant reason for this positive outlook was the widespread conviction that ample, productive land lay yet uncultivated within the borders of the 1850 South. Most southerners believed that they already had within reach the additional land necessary to sustain growth in the agricultural economy and to ensure continuity in the broad landholding pattern, which guaranteed opportunity both for an increasing population and for those squeezed out in other areas. Not only politicians trumpeted the good times; sober-minded agricultural journals also expressed general optimism about the South's economy. Most writers for the journals predicted an exceedingly bright future for southern agriculture.

Without question agriculture dominated the southern economy, but in the last two antebellum decades significant industrial growth occurred. This growth was initially spurred by the Panic of 1837, which severely depressed cotton prices until the mid-1840s. From just over $53 million in 1840, capital invested in manufacturing jumped to $93.6 million in 1850 and then leaped to $163.7 million in 1860. During the 1850s the value of manufacturing output shot up 79 percent, to $186.9 million. This development, however, was not evenly distributed. Industry had become an important part of the economy in Virginia and Kentucky, but it was barely visible in Arkansas and Florida. On the whole, the border states and the upper South had a more substantial industrial plant than the lower South. Even so, the cotton South registered impressive relative gains, though the absolute numbers remained small.

In comparison with the rest of the country, however, the South lagged far behind in industrial growth. In 1860 the slave states accounted for 15 percent of the value of manufactured goods produced in the United States; the eleven states that were to form the Confederacy contributed but 10 percent. In that same year the per capita value of New England's manufacturing output was $149.47, in the middle states $96.28, in the Northwest $37.33, and in the South only $17.09.

The South's relative underdevelopment does not negate its significant and increasingly visible gains. Industrialization had made a strong beginning and a variety of industries were prospering in the South. The bellwether of nineteenth-century industrialization, the railroads, had certainly advanced into the South. In the early days of railroading the South could boast the longest road in the world—the South Carolina Railroad, which in 1833 covered the 136 miles between Charleston and Hamburg, a village on the Savannah River opposite Augusta, Georgia. In the 1830s attempts were also made to connect Charleston with the Ohio Valley by crossing the Appalachians. Conflicting political pressures hindered that effort, and the Panic of 1837 struck its death blow. In fact, the panic hampered all railroad construction.

By the 1850s, however, railroads were beginning to cover much of the South, especially east of the Mississippi. Alabama provides a superb example of what was happening in the South. In 1850 the state had only 100 miles of railroad, costing around $2 million. Between 1850 and 1860 the mileage leaped to 610 at a cost of $15 million, raised chiefly from public and private sources within the state. Alabama was a microcosm of the railroad boom sweeping the South. In 1860 more than 10,000 miles of railroad, five times more than in 1850, tracked across the future Confederacy. These railroads were no match for the trunk lines between the Atlantic seaboard and the Northwest, which were reshaping national transportation patterns, but one of these lines, the Baltimore and Ohio, had its eastern terminus in the border-state city of Baltimore. Most of the southern routes went from port cities back into farming country. On the eve of secession a major intersectional artery was being completed, the Illinois Central, which linked New Orleans with Chicago and the Northwest. By the end of the antebellum era few east-west

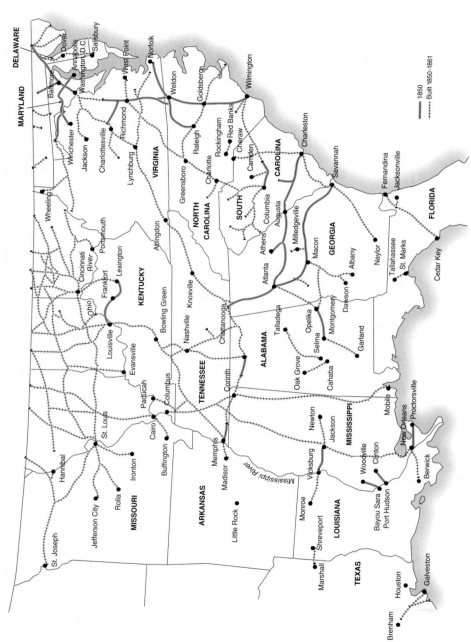

RAILROADS IN THE SOUTH, 1850–1860

1850
Built 1850-1861

roads existed. Charleston and Savannah were connected with Memphis via Chattanooga and Atlanta, and from Memphis a road ran through Chattanooga and Knoxville on to Richmond. But in both instances several lines, not a single trunk line, made these connections possible.

The massive growth of railroads demonstrates not only southern economic development but also the South's commitment to the industrial component of its economy. Without substantial assistance from state and local governments, this burst of railroad building would not have occurred. Legislatures and localities provided enormous sums for railroad projects. To 1860, the state of Virginia had put up $24 million and Tennessee $17 million. The westernmost southern state, Texas, was also deeply involved in helping railroads; by 1861 the legislature had contributed 5 million acres of land and authorized $1.8 million in state bonds. In one notable instance a state actually went into the railroad business. Although Georgia was surely friendly to private railroads, it built and operated the Western and Atlantic, which connected Atlanta and Chattanooga. Completed in 1851, the Western and Atlantic earned between $800,000 and $900,000 annually during the next decade, and more than half of the money was profit. Across the South (exclusive of Maryland and Missouri) the states invested over $81 million in railroad construction and support while counties and municipalities invested a total of approximately $55 million. These numbers leave no doubt that southerners believed iron rails essential for their economic future.

Other prominent southern industries included ironworks, tobacco processing, and textiles. The iron industry in the South dated back to the eighteenth century. Its colonial capital was Virginia, which retained that title throughout the antebellum decades. As the industry grew larger and more sophisticated, Richmond became the most important iron-manufacturing center in the slave states. Although Virginia's production soared by almost 200 percent in the 1850s, it remained far behind that of Pennsylvania, the national leader.

Virginia and North Carolina dominated the tobacco industry. In 1860 their factories turned out more than $14.5 million worth of processed tobacco. Fully 60 percent of all plug and smoking tobacco produced in the United States came from these factories. Cigars were made chiefly in the North, and cigarettes did not appear until after the Civil War. Plug or chewing tobacco stood first among tobacco products. Its use was so ubiquitous that spittoons were provided even on the floor of the United States Senate. Favorite brands had hordes of loyal chewers; one of them, Wedding Cake, was shipped from Virginia to England and Germany as well as to American distribution centers such as Baltimore and New York.

The southern textile industry originated early in the nineteenth century, but substantial development did not take place until the 1840s. When cotton prices collapsed following the Panic of 1837, investors turned from cotton fields to cotton mills. In North Carolina alone thirty-two mills were founded during that decade. By 1860 textile mills dotted the fall line from Virginia through the Carolinas and Georgia down to Alabama. The fall line provided most advantageous locations for textile mills, as it provided the water power that ran them. Although southern textile mills did not begin to outproduce the New England mills until late in the century, by 1860 between one-fifth and one-fourth of the national output was accounted for by the slave states.

The South also provided a home to numerous other industrial enterprises. Several involved the processing of southern agricultural products. Rice mills and sugar mills were found mostly in South Carolina, Georgia, and Louisiana, the center of rice and sugar cane farming. The milling of wheat and corn ranked among the leading southern industries. While small mills spanned the region, Baltimore and Richmond were the leaders; Richmond claimed one of the largest grain mills in the world. At ropewalks in Kentucky and Missouri the hemp crop was transformed into rope. Sawmilling and the naval stores industry exploited one of the region's most widespread and valuable resources, its forests. The mining of gold in Georgia, of coal in Virginia, and of salt chiefly in Virginia and Kentucky added another dimension to the southern industrial scene. In one area of manufacturing the South had a national monopoly: the building of cotton gins. Remarkable individuals led the southern industrial effort; among the most notable were William Gregg, Joseph Reid Anderson, and Daniel Pratt.

*I*NDUSTRIAL LEADERS AND SUPPORT FOR INDUSTRY

William Gregg was a vigorous apostle of southern industrialism. Born in Virginia in 1800, Gregg moved around until 1824, when he settled in South Carolina. He became a highly successful jeweler in Charleston and Columbia. After a tour of New England in 1844, he returned to South Carolina convinced of the virtues of industry and determined to build up the textile industry. In a pamphlet called *Essays on Domestic Industry*, published in 1845, he advocated the development of manufacturing in the South by the employment of the poor whites in the countryside. Gregg argued that in their current occupations, mostly marginal farming, these people were not making a positive contribution to the economy, but as factory workers they could have a significant effect on the growth of southern industry. He also believed that industrial employment would improve their moral and social condition. Factory work, Gregg thought, should be for whites only; in his judgment, slaves should remain in the fields.

Gregg did more than advocate; he also acted. In order to demonstrate the validity of his ideas he opened a mill in Graniteville, South Carolina, just east of Augusta, in 1846. At Graniteville he replicated the New England mill village. He constructed eighty-five cottages to house his workers. He built a school and instructed a compulsory attendance policy; Gregg himself occasionally acted as truant officer. He promulgated rules for the morality of the village and what he saw as the uplift of the inhabitants. Dancing and drinking were prohibited; churchgoing was encouraged; picnics and lectures on personal improvement were featured. The village at Graniteville provided homes for some 300 local employees, who worked under a superintendent and foremen brought down from the North. These workers produced chiefly cheaper grades of cloth, which had a substantial southern market, and some finer goods, which were sold in both the South and the North. Gregg's Graniteville turned out to be a profitable cotton mill; it paid dividends ranging from 7 to 18 percent every year until the Civil War.

Just as Gregg was the most prominent individual in textiles, Joseph Reid

WILLIAM GREGG, TEXTILE
ENTREPRENEUR (Courtesy
South Caroliniana Library, Univer-
sity of South Carolina)

Anderson dominated the iron industry. A Virginian educated at West Point, the twenty-eight-year-old Anderson went to work for Tredegar Iron Works in Richmond in 1841. Seven years later Anderson became the president of Tredegar. Under Anderson's leadership Tredegar grew from a small foundry into one of the largest and best-equipped ironworks in the nation. The company manufactured steam engines for sugar mills and for numerous other enterprises. Securing federal contracts to provide cannon for the United States Navy, Tredegar by 1860 had produced and sold 1,300 of them. Railroads were large customers; Tredegar supplied them with spikes, rails, and even locomotives.

In the 1850s Tredegar employed 800 workers, a figure topped by only three other ironworks in the country. Anderson's decisions about his labor force were important not only for his company but for the whole of southern industry. Unlike Gregg, he had no reservations about using slaves. He made extensive use of them, buying some and hiring others. When white workers went on strike, Anderson fired them and brought in more slaves, who were trained by white foremen. A number of white southerners had claimed that slaves could never be trained to work in an iron mill or any other sophisticated industrial plant. Anderson proved those naysayers wrong. By 1848 slaves held most of the jobs, both skilled and unskilled, in the rolling mills. Twelve years later one-third of the slaves were paddlers, heaters, and rollers; others worked as blacksmiths, strikers, teamsters, and common laborers. Performing effectively, slaves at Tredegar held back neither technological improvements nor profits.

GREGG'S TEXTILE MILL, GRANITEVILLE, SOUTH CAROLINA (Courtesy of
South Caroliniana Library, University of South Carolina)

Daniel Pratt, unlike Anderson and Gregg, was not a native southerner. Born
in 1799 into a New Hampshire farm family, Pratt learned the carpentry trade as a
youth. At twenty he journeyed to Georgia, where he worked first as a carpenter
and then for a company that made cotton gins. After a dozen years he moved to
Alabama, where in 1838 he founded Prattville, just north of Montgomery. At
Prattville, Daniel Pratt presided over an industrial village very much like those he
had left behind in New England. In his new village Pratt established several enterprises, including a gristmill, a lumber mill, a textile mill, and a carriage factory,
but it was for the manufacture of cotton gins that the village and its founder became famous. As early as 1851 the 200 laborers Pratt employed to make cotton
gins produced some 600 gins annually. Pratt accounted for fully 25 percent of the
total production of cotton gins. On the eve of the Civil War his property at
Prattville was capitalized at more than $500,000.

Gregg, Anderson, and Pratt did not preach the gospel of industrialism to an
empty church. As the investment in railroads makes clear, most southerners were
eager to back industrial development. An enthusiasm quite like the boosterism
usually associated with later years pervaded the South. The principled apprehension that had led the Jeffersonians to oppose the growth of industry and cities was
relegated to a minority of ideologues. Even the Democratic party generally
adopted the industrial course, though that decision did prompt grumbling and
occasionally outright opposition from some of the party faithful. Neither the anti-
industry ideologues nor the unhappy Democratic partisans could blunt the thrust
of industrial development. The southerners who cheered the railroads and the
factories had not turned their backs on agriculture. Most of them repeatedly acknowledged the supremacy of agriculture in the South. A substantial portion of
the capital invested in industry came from planters, who had no intention of leaving their plantations or of becoming economic and social vassals to anyone.
Spokesmen for industrial growth asserted that industry would buttress agricul-

DANIEL PRATT, SOUTHERN INDUSTRIALIST
(*De Bow's Review*)

ture and would increase prosperity. Noting the political contest with the North, proindustry southerners insisted that industrialization also promoted the interests of the South.

No one boosted southern industrial growth more vigorously or more effectively than James D. B. De Bow. Born in Charleston in 1820, De Bow graduated from the College of Charleston and practiced law for a few years before he found his real calling. After attending a commercial convention De Bow decided he wanted to publish a commercial journal in a place with a more vigorous economy and enterprising spirit than his home city. He chose New Orleans, and in January 1846 he brought out the first issue of *De Bow's Review*. Although in the beginning De Bow and his *Review* struggled, by the end of the decade both had become rousing successes. By 1850 *De Bow's Review*, with almost 5,000 subscribers, had one of the largest circulations of the magazines published in the South. The *Review* concentrated on improving and developing the southern economy. De Bow insisted that industry and agriculture complemented each other. To his mind, the South would need vigor and growth in both sectors if it were to reach its economic potential. An energetic champion of slavery and southern rights, De Bow did not be-

PRATTVILLE, ALABAMA, DANIEL PRATT'S INDUSTRIAL VILLAGE IN 1851
(*De Bow's Review*)

lieve that industry threatened either. On the contrary, he argued that only significant industrial development would guarantee the preservation of southern rights
and institutions. As a promoter of southern industrialism De Bow had no peers in
his time.

De Bow strove successfully to create an organization that would work to implement his vision of a diversified, dynamic southern economy. As early as the
1830s commercially oriented southerners met at various sites to address trade and
transportation issues. Finally in 1852, with De Bow and his *Review* trumpeting the
cause, the Southern Commercial Convention was founded in Baltimore. Thereafter the Southern Commercial Convention met at least annually until 1859 in
cities across the region. Literally thousands of southerners attended these con-
claves to share ideas and advocate southern economic progress and diversification. They never attempted to sabotage the centrality of slavery in the South or to
challenge the supremacy of commercial agriculture. They vigorously supported
both. At the same time the delegates urged industrial growth, and they championed financial assistance from both the state and federal governments. For them
industrial development and governmental aid would complement agriculture in
a growing and prosperous South.

Despite a healthy career during most of the 1850s, the Southern Commercial
Convention by the end of the decade became a victim of heightened sectional tension, captured by sectional zealots. With their particular political agenda they
shoved aside economic matters and drove away traditional delegates. At the last
convention in 1859, when the chief topic was reopening the African slave trade,
attendance was abysmal, less than 10 percent what it had been two years earlier.

COMMERCIAL AND URBAN DEVELOPMENT

Banks have an important role in any expanding economy. According to the conventional wisdom, the few banks in the South were poor and dominated by
planters hostile to industrial growth. Current scholarship, however, casts consid-

erable doubt on that traditional interpretation. Southern banks grew at healthy and respectable rates. Between 1840 and 1860 the South matched the rest of the country in growth rates of the number of new banks and in increases in deposits and circulating notes, though it lagged somewhat behind the other sections in the values of its loans. These banks supplied an adequate medium of exchange and financed a wide range of projects, chiefly agricultural but industrial as well.

Southern banks were not monoliths. The South had branches of the Bank of the United States during its lifetime, state banks, and private banks, both chartered and unchartered. The banks' chief problem in assisting economic development came in such states as Alabama and Tennessee, where politics heavily influenced their operations. Certainly no sectionwide planter elite worked to prevent banks from participating in commercial and industrial activities. And southern banks surely participated in them.

Thoughts of industry and banks usually bring cities to mind. The South before 1860 has not generally been considered fertile ground for cities. Without question the South was overwhelmingly rural, but so was the North, though it had a larger urban population than the South. Although the South could not match the North in large urban areas, still southern cities occupied an important position in the region. The most notable cities included older ones, such as Charleston and New Orleans, as well as St. Louis, which seemed to spring up almost instantaneously in the 1840s. Between 1800 and 1850 the South outpaced the North in the growth rate of the urban population as compared with the growth rate of the entire population. In 1850 the slave states claimed six of the fifteen largest cities in the country; in 1860, five.

These urban areas were not distributed evenly across the region. The border states claimed the largest, Baltimore, along with three others in the top half dozen. New Orleans provided the single member of that group located in the lower South, but half of those in the first ten were in states that seceded. At the same time five states lacked a town with more than 10,000 people—North Carolina, Florida, Mississippi, Arkansas, and Texas. Of the ten largest cities, all but two— Richmond and Washington—were either seaports or river ports. So were most of the major northern cities. Until mid-century water afforded the chief mode of transportation, but when railroads began to challenge steamboats, the inland towns and cities began to assume more importance.

In the 1850s a second tier of towns and cities rose toward prominence. Several served as seats of state government. Just as important, they became crossroads of the rails spreading across the region. Among these cities were Columbia, Montgomery, Jackson, Chattanooga, and Atlanta.

The economic base of southern cities was commerce; banking and trade were significant activities. Originally waterborne commerce, both river traffic and ocean shipping, formed the heart of the trade that gave vibrancy to the cities. The arrival of the railroads had no adverse effect on the coastal and river ports; in most instances, railroads either complemented or supplemented shipments that had previously moved by water. Railroads did, however, influence the types of goods the cities handled. The opening of trunk lines between the Atlantic seaboard and the Northwest, for example, greatly reduced the grain traffic on the Mississippi, and that change had a considerable impact on New Orleans. Still the

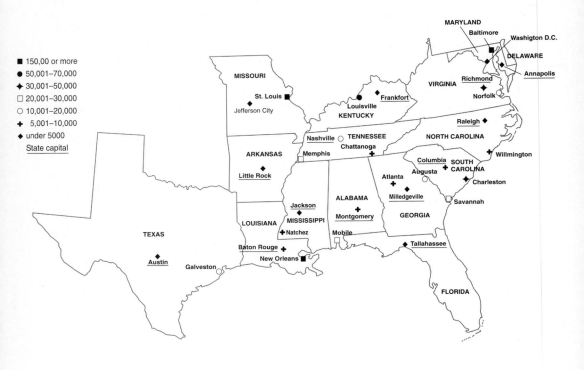

■ 150,00 or more
● 50,001–70,000
✦ 30,001–50,000
☐ 20,001–30,000
○ 10,001–20,000
✚ 5,001–10,000
◆ under 5000
State capital

STATE CAPITALS AND MAJOR CITIES, 1860

massive increase of the cotton crop kept both the quantity and the value of trade in New Orleans on the rise.

The activities and problems of southern cities were similar to those in the North. Southern city dwellers organized professional associations and benevolent societies. They joined literary societies and fraternal organizations. Theater, which in the older cities dated back to the colonial era, flourished. Civic pride often helped build and always gloried in first-class hotels, such as the St. Charles in New Orleans. Issues of public safety, fire protection, sanitation, and disease concerned city folk everywhere in the country. Because of the South's warm, humid climate, the link between poor sanitation and the spread of disease posed a particular threat to southern cities, especially those in the lower South. Yellow fever and cholera epidemics terrified all residents of coastal cities; 10 percent of the population of New Orleans died when yellow fever struck in 1853. Ignorance about the close tie between the lack of sanitation and the prevalence of disease ensured serious problems, which would remain until the germ theory of disease triumphed after the Civil War.

One notable factor differentiated southern cities from those in the North: the presence of slaves. Some historians have argued that urban anonymity and the inability of masters to exercise tight control over their bondspeople in heavily populated areas undermined the institution. Little evidence supports such a conclusion, however. It is true that on the whole, urban slaves enjoyed more freedom from their masters' authority than their country counterparts did, mainly because the work of artisans and domestics often took them away from their masters' premises. But the fact of the slaves' blackness and the presumption that all blacks were slaves sharply restricted their activities. Urban slavery in the 1850s was certainly not dying. Though the slave population declined in some Atlantic seaboard cities, it increased in many interior ones. The best explanation seems to be the level of the need for slaves in the countryside. Good times in agriculture increased the demand for slaves, and owners either transferred them from urban occupations to agricultural operations or sold them.

One of the most important functions of towns and cities has gone largely unnoticed by historians. It was there that the planters conferred with the bankers, industrialists, lawyers, merchants, and factors who made up the rest of the southern elite. Nowhere else could these seemingly diverse groups come together to discuss the business, financial, and political matters that concerned them all. Thus in a real sense towns and cities helped unify the diverse elements of the antebellum South.

CONFIDENCE AND ANXIETY

No matter where observers of the southern economy looked in the late 1850s, they viewed a scene painted in bold, bright colors: thriving agriculture and prosperous industry, profitable banking, and cities sharing in the prosperity. It was a heady time for southerners. Their slave-based economy appeared strong and solid.

Most scholars claim that the southern economy would have faltered eventually because of an inherent incompatibility between industry and slavery. Some contemporaries had the same thought. These people argued that slavery should remain confined to farms and plantations, for only there could it flourish. To their way of thinking, slaves in factories would erode the southern system they cherished. Not surprisingly, this bleak forecast usually came from the same men who were filled with foreboding about industrial growth. Theirs was a small group, largely unheard and unheeded.

Most southerners of the 1850s envisioned no inevitable conflict between slavery and industry, and there was no good reason for them to foresee such a clash. Until the end of the antebellum period slavery and industry cooperated fully. Most industrialists certainly did not oppose slave labor in their factories. The closest student of industry and slavery concluded that probably 5 percent of the slave population toiled in southern industrial plants. These people worked in every kind of enterprise, from small lumber mills to such large factories as the ironworks in Tennessee controlled by the Whig leader John Bell, in which 365 slaves labored. The books and ledgers of industrial enterprises that employed slaves reveal a widespread prosperity that demonstrates the effectiveness of that labor. The use of slaves in industry also led to innovative business practices. Industrial accidents could be very costly to the factory and mill owners who bought or hired slaves, so some businessmen began to insure the lives of their slaves.

By every economic measure southerners of 1860 were confident, even over-confident. The Panic of 1857, which hit the northern economy hard, struck only a glancing blow at the South; agriculture barely felt it. That experience, after the devastation wreaked by the panics in 1819 and 1837, provided what southerners considered a clear measure of their economic strength. When James H. Hammond, United States senator from South Carolina, proclaimed in 1858, "Cotton is king," most southerners chorused agreement: their cotton ruled the economic world. Grandiose rhetoric aside, a keen student of the antebellum southern economy has concluded that southerners had concrete reasons for their optimism: "Before the war, the South was wealthy, prosperous, expanding geographically, and growing economically at rates that compared favorably to the rest of the country."

This booming economy contributed to a swelling pride, but simultaneously southerners worried about the erosion of their power in the nation. In a fundamental way, the two apparently separate phenomena were closely connected. The same boom that underlay prosperity in the South generated a powerful economic surge in the free states. During the 1850s the North began to stride firmly toward the industrial and financial might that would characterize its economy in the last quarter of the nineteenth century. This expanding economy had a political counterpart, the Republican party. And the Republicans challenged the traditional political role of the South in the nation at the very moment when impressive prosperity and growth marked the southern economy.

THE ELECTION OF 1860

Thus a proud but anxious South both anticipated and dreaded the presidential election of 1860. The once vigorous political champion of southern liberty, now tattered, would either mend or tear itself further in Charleston, the site of the eighth Democratic national convention, which began on April 23, 1860. A love feast it was not. Vindictive southerners were determined to deny Stephen Douglas the party nomination, though he was clearly the most popular Democrat in the North, and some of those states the party had to carry to win the election. In addition the southerners demanded a platform containing a provision for federal protection of slavery in the territories, which they claimed the Dred Scott decision mandated. They knew that Douglas could never accept such a plank; he knew that if the party accepted it, Republicans would destroy Democrats in the North. Neither the southerners nor Douglas would back down. When the convention rejected the southerners' demands, delegates from the lower South walked out. Efforts to reunify the convention failed. Adjournment and a call for reconvening was the best the party could do. The debacle at Charleston provided indisputable proof of the party's disunity.

The public spectacle of a feuding Democratic party was repeated in Baltimore in late June. Baltimore had been the site of every Democratic convention between 1832 and 1852. Many party loyalists hoped that in Baltimore some of the unity of an earlier time would somehow reappear in 1860. But it was not to be; the wrangling was as bitter as ever. Once again the Democratic convention failed to mend itself. In Baltimore party disarray became public dismemberment when each of the two dominant groups called itself the Democratic party and nominated a presidential candidate. The Douglas loyalists gave their nomination to their hero; the breakaway southerners placed their imprimatur on John C. Breckinridge of Kentucky, vice president of the United States. For the first time since its creation, the Democratic party could settle on neither a standard-bearer nor a platform.

Failure to maintain party unity fractured the Democratic effort in the South. A divided Democracy made it extremely difficult for southern loyalists to claim convincingly that their party remained the impenetrable shield of the South. Despite the difficulties, they made their traditional case for their party, but the Democratic troubles brought another force into the southern presidential field. It was composed of Opposition men, former Whigs, and former Know-Nothings. Although this new group called its new political home the Constitutional Union party, it was not a party at all, but an ad hoc reaction to special circumstances. The almost simultaneous occurrence of the disruption of the Democratic party, the threat of the Republicans, and the presidential election caused all anti-Democrats to coalesce into a unit. That only powerful national issues in conjunction with an approaching presidential election could effect this unification, even if temporary, reconfirmed the primacy of national issues in southern politics. Between the collapse of the Know-Nothings and 1860, the numerous anti-Democrats across the South had not been able to arrange themselves into a single force to confront the Democrats. Such unity was impossible because no overriding national issue appeared and because no northern connection existed for a second national party in the South.

But the immediate demands of 1860 led some conservative northerners, opposed to the Republican and Democratic parties alike, to look to Constitutional Unionism as a solution to their problem. Coming together in Baltimore in May, these men called for allegiance to the Constitution and for patriotism and forbearance as the watchwords of all Americans. By awarding their nominations to old-line, conservative Whigs—John Bell of Tennessee for president and Edward Everett of Massachusetts for vice president—the Constitutional Unionists emphasized both their political ancestry and their hopes for the political future. The crisis of 1860 led southern Constitutional Unionists to hope that their temporary northern friends would become permanent allies.

During the election campaign, however, the Constitutional Unionists did not stake out a new direction for southern politics. Leaping to the attack, they condemned the Democrats for failing to secure the South. According to the Constitutional Unionists, the southern Democrats had neglected their sacred mission—to protect southern liberty. Instead the southern Democrats grasped for place and reward while the Republican horde prepared to devour southern liberty. In such dire times, the Constitutional Unionists asserted, southern voters could not put their trust in the faithless Democratic party. The Constitutional Unionist script ended with the obvious conclusion: southerners could count only on the new party.

With the politics of slavery in full bloom, the South voted. No sure champion had arisen to turn back the Republican challenge. With no hero to rally round, southerners divided their votes. Although the southern Democratic candidate, John C. Breckinridge, carried eleven of fifteen slave states, he won a popular majority in only seven. Despite an attempt to persuade southerners that Douglas would protect their interests, the northern Democratic candidate generally received less than 15 percent of the popular vote, and in several states less than 10 percent. He fared little better along the border, except in Missouri, which he carried with just over one-third of the vote. The Constitutional Union party was much stronger. It won the electoral vote of one border state and two in the upper South, and also took 40 percent of the popular vote in the states that would soon form the Confederacy. By every usual measurement the southern Democrats retained their supremacy. Still, Lecompton and the party breakup hurt. More than four of every ten voting southerners cast their ballots for a temporary party—a party that had no history, only claims, and thin ones, that it could guarantee southern liberty, and only the barest hope that it could win the presidential election or even become a force in Congress.

The campaign and election of 1860 dramatized the disintegration of the traditional order in southern politics. For more than three decades the Democratic party had claimed a unique role in protecting southern interests and liberty; on that very issue it had eliminated the Whigs and wrecked the Know-Nothings. Now it was in disarray. The Constitutional Union party was little more than an improvised response to a special political situation. Even though it had no record and campaigned chiefly on hope, it did win the votes of tens of thousands of southerners. That performance signaled the rampant disorder in southern politics. Though these facts were unsettling, southerners were much more distressed by yet another. The hated and feared Republican party won the presidential election. Though the Republican candidate, Abraham Lincoln of Illinois, garnered only a minority of the national popular vote, just 40 percent, he carried every free state save New Jersey, which he divided with Douglas, and won a clear majority in the electoral college, 180 to 123. Now the Republican party, with its antisouthern platform and with no southerners in its inner councils, would control the national administration. In the history of the nation this was absolutely unprecedented.

THE FIRE-EATERS

What this Republican triumph heralded many southerners feared they had glimpsed back in October 1859. Then the avenging angel of abolition, John Brown, a bloody veteran of Bleeding Kansas, had aimed his fury against slavery at Harper's Ferry, Virginia. An apostle of violence, Brown acted out his favorite biblical passage, "Without the shedding of blood there is no remission of sins." Claiming the role of a prophet charged by God Almighty to root out the evil of slavery, Brown led his band in an assault on the federal arsenal at Harper's Ferry. His professed goal was to foment and lead a slave uprising that would spread southward and sound the death knell of the bondage he hated. Brown's raid failed utterly. Federal troops smashed his attack and captured or killed most of his followers. Brown himself was captured, tried by the state of Virginia for treason, and on December 2 hanged. Although major Republican leaders repudiated Brown's violent tactics, he became almost a saint in northern antislavery circles. Southerners were appalled; countless thousands saw Brown and his crusade as a direct manifestation of Republicanism.

When the despised Lincoln won the election of 1860, southerners saw the slave collar about to be clamped on their own necks. Major Republican leaders had made clear their intention "to take the Government out of unjust and unfaithful hands, and commit it to those which will be just and faithful." This kind of declaration southerners read as the proclamation of conquerors. From their own viewpoint, southerners had been faithful stewards of the Constitution; now their enemies seemed ready to treat them as a vanquished people who had no claim on liberty. By definition absence of liberty meant the presence of slavery. And slavery, southerners equated with degradation. In this gloomy vision the white South would become enslaved to tyrannical Republicanism.

This outlook explains why so many southerners framed the overriding issue of 1860 and 1861 as a matter of submission. Slaves submitted; no honorable white person would do so. Although few southerners saw civil war as inevitable, many believed that "even that, *if it must come,* would be preferable to submission to Black Republicans, involving as it would all that is horrible, degrading, and ruinous." Many southerners preferred death "to liv[ing] a slave to Black Republicanism." In the words of one, "I would be an equal, or a corpse." Millions shared that sentiment.

With traditional political patterns unraveled and southern liberty facing an epic crisis, the fire-eaters surged into significance. A new and potent force in southern politics, the fire-eaters had sprouted in the crisis of 1850, then with widespread acceptance of the great compromise became dormant during most of the decade, only to blossom at its end. While Democrats and Constitutional Unionists struggled over who could better protect the South in the Union, the fire-eaters aimed to destroy the Union, which they pictured as a dagger poised to plunge into the heart of the South.

The fire-eaters were a small band. The three states where they were most prominent were South Carolina, which had the largest concentration of slaves, 57 percent of the population; Mississippi, second only to South Carolina with 55 percent; and Alabama, with 45 percent of its population slave. Fire-eaters operated on a smaller scale but with impact in Florida, Georgia, Texas, and Virginia. They were scarce elsewhere.

Fire-eaters were not simply large slaveholders. Much of their local leadership seems to have come from relatively young town dwellers in plantation counties. Undoubtedly the intimate relationship between the possession of slaves and the passion for liberty helps explain the citadels of fire-eating. When whites in the centers of black slavery perceived the destruction of slavery at hand, the possibilities assumed terrifying proportions because that destruction would necessarily include, according to the southern calculus, the extermination of their liberty. In 1860 the fire-eaters had no doubt that the future of slavery was at stake. To them Republican domination of the national government meant at once the extinction of black slavery and the imposition of white slavery.

The leading fire-eaters were a diverse lot. The dean of the group was Robert

Robert Barnwell·Rhett (Courtesy of South
Caroliniana Library, University of South
Carolina)

Edmund Ruffin (Brady Collection,
National Archives)

TWO FIRE-EATERS

Barnwell Rhett of South Carolina. Sixty years old in 1860, Rhett claimed long adherence to the cause of disunion; he had been a secessionist since the early 1830s. Active in the public world, he served in the Congress from the late 1830s to the early 1850s. In 1852 he resigned his seat as a United States senator in disgust after his state formally refused to oppose the Compromise of 1850. But public office did not provide Rhett's chief platform. He and his son controlled the Charleston *Mercury*, the most prominent fire-eating newspaper in the South. Under the guidance of the Rhetts, it broadcast the message of southern radicalism across the South. Fourteen years younger than Rhett, William Lowndes Yancey of Alabama was the orator of secession. Born in South Carolina, reared in the North in the household of an abolitionist foster father, Yancey came back to the South as a young man and finally settled in Alabama, where he became a major figure among the more radical Democrats. In a time and place where political speaking was a cultivated art, none ranked higher than Yancey. Thousands thronged to hear him cry out, "It is the right to save ourselves from despotism and destruction."

　　Rhett and Yancey had less politically visible but no less dedicated comrades. None was more interesting than the venerable Edmund Ruffin. Born into a notable Virginia family in 1794, Ruffin was one of the nation's foremost proponents of scientific agriculture. After an unhappy term in the Virginia legislature, he shunned direct involvement in politics, but he wrote numerous secessionist essays. As he was convinced that only blows from the outside could invigorate the "sluggish blood" of his fellow southerners, he cheered John Brown's raid. During the campaign of 1860 he sent to the governor of each slave state a pike he had obtained from Brown's cache of weapons; on each pike Ruffin had affixed a label: "SAMPLE OF THE FAVORS DESIGNED FOR US BY OUR NORTHERN BRETHREN." Lincoln's election seemed to be God's answer to his prayers.

In addition to proclaiming the gospel of secession, the fire-eaters are rightly associated with two other campaigns that stirred the South in the late 1850s: the call to reopen the African slave trade and filibustering. Since 1808 it had been illegal to import slaves from outside the United States. While smuggling did occur, few were brought in, though the number was possibly increasing a bit in the late 1850s. Restarting the African trade became a cry of radical southerners, including prominent fire-eaters like Yancey and Ruffin. Supporters of a renewed international commerce in slaves argued that because slavery was salutary for blacks, bringing in new Africans could not be wrong. "If it is right to buy slaves in Virginia and carry them to New Orleans," Yancey asked, "why is it not right to buy them in Africa and carry them there?" Most southerners, however, shied away from the issue. Because the trade had been gone for so long, they had no knowledge of how it would work. Moreover, they could not reconcile their image of their paternal world of slavery with hauling Africans across the Atlantic Ocean. There were also concerns about the great trouble that pushing the reopening issue would cause with the North. Despite shrill rhetoric, very little actually happened. In 1858 the Louisiana House of Representatives authorized the importation of African "apprentices" (a subterfuge for slaves), but the state Senate did not concur. The next year the rump Southern Commercial Convention meeting in Vicksburg passed a resolution favoring repeal of the prohibition. Neither action had any concrete repercussions.

Likewise, filibustering, the name given to forceful efforts to overthrow regimes in Central America and the Caribbean, chiefly Cuba, failed to arouse widespread support in the South. Fire-eaters, however, often praised filibusters, and some, notably John A. Quitman of Mississippi, participated in filibustering enterprises. In the 1850s many southerners eagerly sought Spanish-owned Cuba, where slavery still flourished. Heavily influenced by southern politicians, the administration of Franklin Pierce made an unsuccessful attempt to wrest Cuba from Spain with diplomacy and dollars. Filibusters, however, were not content with diplomatic activities. They were willing to use force, and in doing so to violate neutrality laws that prohibited military expeditions from United States soil to foreign countries. Twice they mounted invasions of Cuba that ended disastrously. While purchase or annexation commanded considerable attention among southerners, interest in illegal military action was scant.

Even fewer southerners were excited by the Central American enterprises. In Central America, however, filibusters succeeded, temporarily. In 1856 the mysterious William Walker, the "gray-eyed man of destiny," took control of Nicaragua. A native Tennessean who had migrated to California in 1850, Walker had led earlier, failed forays into northwestern Mexico and lower California. Finally triumphing in Nicaragua, Walker was distressed by the lack of American support. He reinstituted slavery in Nicaragua in a desperate attempt to obtain backing in the South. It did not work. With both the American and British governments against him, Walker could not even maintain himself, much less implement his grand scheme of taking over all of Central America. His filibustering career concluded with his execution in 1860 in Honduras.

Few southerners ever seriously supported either filibustering or reopening the African slave trade. The activities of the zealots who sustained either or both did have one tangible result, however. Their rhetoric and their actions aided those in the North who proclaimed that the South was embarked on a reckless course of expanding slavery.

THE LOWER SOUTH SECEDES

Because the fire-eaters' demand for secession was drastic and unprecedented, their success depended in no small part on outside events. Most southerners considered themselves patriotic Americans. They were far from eager to destroy what their grandfathers had helped create, their fathers had helped nurture, and they helped guide. Secession required a great leap into the political unknown, and most southerners were unlikely to heed the fire-eaters' call unless outside events made it especially attractive. Thus John Brown's raid, the breakup of the Democratic party, and particularly Lincoln's election were bountiful gifts to the fire-eaters from the gods of politics.

The election of Abraham Lincoln was the essential catalyst that enabled the fire-eaters to precipitate the revolution they craved. The Republican victory undermined the major pledge of the southern Democrats that they and their party guaranteed the liberty and safety of the South in the Union. Southerners generally viewed the Republican triumph not as a one-time happening but as the culmination of a decade and more of anti-South politics. Southerners of almost every political persuasion agreed when a sober-minded editor depicted Lincoln's triumph as "incontrovertible proof of a diseased and dangerous public opinion all over the North, and a certain forerunner of further and a more atrocious aggression." In short, practically every white southerner looked upon a future Republican administration with combined apprehension and anger. Now, one political unknown, the fire-eaters' secession, was matched by another, Republicans in power.

In the lower South the reaction to Lincoln's election was immediate. Governors called legislatures into session, and legislatures called for prompt elections of delegates to convene in December 1860 and January 1861 to consider appropriate actions. Nothing predestined the decision of these conventions. Ultimately the decision for secession was massively influenced by the tactics of the fire-eaters, who understood the opportunity Lincoln's victory provided and with boldness and shrewdness hurried to apply the pressure that would explode the Union.

For the fire-eaters timing was crucial. If they could accomplish secession in any one state, then the basic question would be changed: the other states would then be deciding not simply whether to secede or not, but whether to join or oppose a sister slave state. Recognizing the importance of immediate action, the fire-eaters moved smartly in the state where they had the greatest influence. On December 20, 1860, the South Carolina convention voted unanimously to secede, to break all ties to the old Union. Fire-eaters everywhere rejoiced. An Alabamian was thrilled: "At this point the accumulated aggression of a third of a century fell like shackles at her feet, and free, disenthralled, regenerated, she stood before her devoted people like the genius of liberty, beckoning them on to the performance of their duty."

The relationship between the fire-eaters and the process of secession raises the question of popular support for secession and the unity behind it. Secession was a public issue; no closed-door conspiracy broke up the Union. In every state speeches, editorials, and campaigns engaged the voting South. Initially the fire-eaters led the crusade, with Lincoln's election giving them multitudes of followers; then the traditional political leadership, especially the Democrats, took charge. People who questioned the wisdom of a pell-mell rush to immediate secession, most of whom called themselves cooperationists, lived chiefly in areas and counties with few slaves. In South Carolina, Florida, Mississippi, and Texas a substantial to overwhelming majority of the white population favored immediate secession, and the outcome was never in serious doubt, though only Texas held a popular referendum on the convention's decision.

In the other three states of the lower South—Georgia, Alabama, and Louisiana—the contest was seemingly considerably closer because of the strength of the cooperationists. The popular vote for delegates to the conventions and the early convention votes themselves revealed substantial public backing for the cooperationist position. But too great a distinction can be drawn between immediatists and cooperationists. The cooperationists opposed immediate secession, not secession at any time. Thus the debate in campaigns and conventions focused on tactics rather than on the fundamental issue. Not even all cooperationists belonged to the same camp: for some, cooperation meant a southern convention; for others, a joint statement by two or more states; for still others, simply the secession of another state. In the end, almost every cooperationist in every state quickly and wholeheartedly signed the ordinance of secession. One of their major newspapers warned, "It may prove a fatal, an unretrievably fatal error," if their stance should "be misconstrued into *submission,* or a delay designed eventually to lead to submission."

In the furor of the winter of 1860–1861 the cooperationists could have said nothing else. They agreed that the South had to guard the liberty now jeopardized by Lincoln's victory. Thus to mount an effective opposition to the immediatists they would have had to offer a credible alternative to secession. They had none, at least none that more than a few could agree on. The most striking characteristic of the cooperationists in the crisis was confusion. They could not decide whether to campaign and could not agree on a political goal to articulate if they did. Perhaps in the depths of their being they thought the immediatists were right.

By the first of February 1861 all the states of the lower South had left the Union—South Carolina, December 20, 1860; Mississippi, January 9; Florida, Janu-

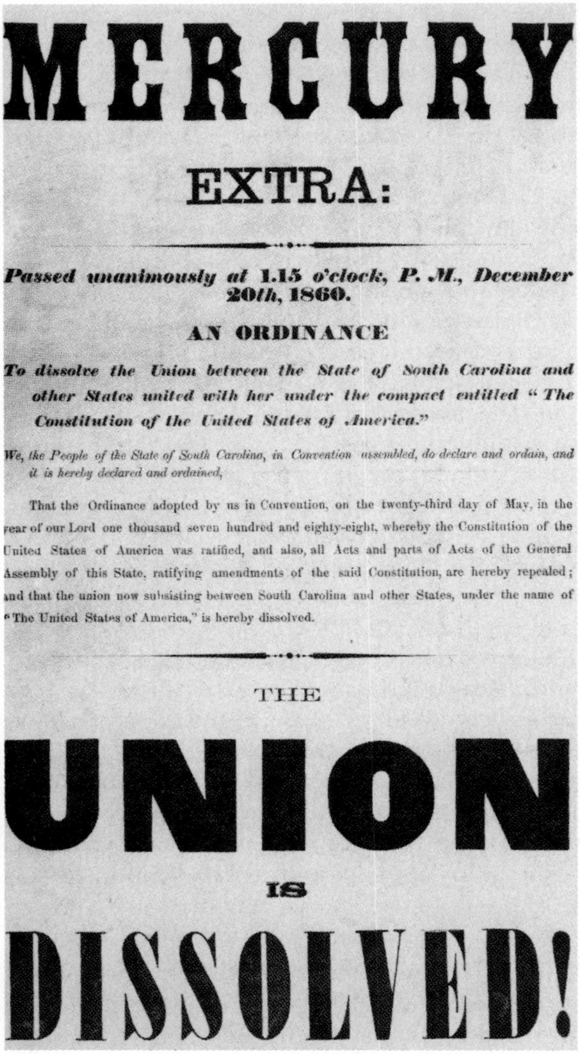

MERCURY

EXTRA:

Passed unanimously at 1.15 o'clock, P. M., December 20th, 1860.

AN ORDINANCE

To dissolve the Union between the State of South Carolina and other States united with her under the compact entitled "The Constitution of the United States of America."

We, the People of the State of South Carolina, in Convention assembled, do declare and ordain, and it is hereby declared and ordained,

That the Ordinance adopted by us in Convention, on the twenty-third day of May, in the year of our Lord one thousand seven hundred and eighty-eight, whereby the Constitution of the United States of America was ratified, and also, all Acts and parts of Acts of the General Assembly of this State, ratifying amendments of the said Constitution, are hereby repealed; and that the union now subsisting between South Carolina and other States, under the name of "The United States of America," is hereby dissolved.

THE

UNION

IS

DISSOLVED!

SECESSION ANNOUNCE-
MENT BY THE CHARLESTON
MERCURY (New York Public
Library)

ary 10; Alabama, January 11; Georgia, January 19; Louisiana, January 26; Texas, February 1.

THE UPPER SOUTH AND THE BORDER STATES

With eight states in the upper South and on the border still in the Union, the hopes of the fire-eaters still had not been realized. The upper South, which stretched more than a thousand miles from Virginia to Arkansas, did not secede upon Lincoln's election, not even upon his inauguration as president on March 4. The paucity of fire-eaters everywhere and their absence in many places relaxed the political pressure for secession. In the one state where the fire-eaters did have a noticeable voice, Virginia, their influence was offset by the vigorously antisecessionist transmontane region, most of which became West Virginia during the war. That the upper South did not secede along with the lower South did not signify that it looked upon the rise of the Republican party and Lincoln's election as normal occurrences. The rhetoric in these states matched that in their more southerly neighbors. This rhetoric, however, did not propel the upper South into rapid secession, because the political equation lacked the crucial multiplier, the fire-eaters. Leaders in the upper South asserted that Lincoln's triumph had surely challenged southern liberty, but it remained unvanquished in the absence of some overt act such as adoption of the Wilmot Proviso or interference with the interstate slave trade.

At the same time, the upper South did not have a free political hand; it could not escape the politics of slavery. The fact of seven secessions and the formation in February of the Confederate States of America had a massive impact on the upper South. At this juncture states and a combination of states replaced political parties and groups as the motivating force behind the politics of slavery. That politics fundamentally influenced the decision of the upper South, even though in those four states a majority of voters joined in a new Union party to oppose secession.

With the lower South out of the Union, the question facing people in the upper South was not simply whether to secede but whether to aid their brothers farther south. If in any way the new Confederacy and the old Union came into confrontation, then the upper South would come face to face with its ultimate decision. Its hand would be forced, and the antisecessionists did not at all relish the thought that their future might be controlled by the states that had broken up the Union. Perched perilously between the Union and the Confederacy, the upper South no longer had complete freedom of decision. Confrontation between the Union and the Confederacy, or even a single seceded state, meant for the upper South the choice between freedom and slavery. In the vocabulary of southern politics, coercion by the federal government entailed enslavement of the coerced states and destruction of their citizens' liberty. An antisecessionist Virginia editor spoke bluntly:

> An issue has been made. The subjection of South Carolina or any seceding state, in consequence of their determination not to submit to the policy of the Republicans, is a blow at the entire South—subjection to all. We are, thenceforth, humiliated. We are conquered. We could not hold up our heads in that Union any more.

Thus when the guns roared at Fort Sumter and President Lincoln called for troops to put down the rebellion, the upper South said no. Virginia (April 7), Arkansas (May 6), Tennessee (May 7), and North Carolina (May 20) all seceded.

A distinctly different situation prevailed in the four border states. A small slave population made three of these states "slave" chiefly in a technical and legal sense. Only Kentucky, where slaves accounted for 20 percent of the population, can realistically be said to be a slave state in the social, economic, and political senses. Slaves accounted for only 13 percent of the population in Maryland, 10 percent in Missouri, and less than 2 percent in Delaware. The number of slave owners was correspondingly small—just a fraction over 2 percent of the population in both Maryland and Missouri and no more than one-half of 1 percent in Delaware. Moreover, the percentages of both slaves and slave owners had declined markedly during the 1850s. In them unconditional Unionist sentiment flourished and fire-eaters were rare. This political reality, coupled with an antisecessionist governor in Maryland and the political and military moves of the federal government, made secession impossible.

The percentage of slaves in Kentucky approached that of Arkansas and Tennessee, yet they seceded and Kentucky did not. Geography and political tradition help to explain the behavior of Kentucky. Its northern frontier marked the boundary between freedom and slavery. This proximity to the free states had two important consequences. First, as in the other border states, a powerful, unconditional Unionist sentiment flourished in Kentucky. Second, many Kentuckians wanted to avoid taking sides because they could envision their homeland becoming a major battleground.

The political heritage of Kentucky buttressed this desire to steer clear of overt partisanship. Even after Fort Sumter, Kentucky declared neutrality in any conflict between the United States and the Confederate States. Well aware that their great statesman, Henry Clay, had gained fame as the compromiser in earlier sectional crises, Kentuckians strove to follow his example. In a conscious attempt to emulate Clay, United States Senator John J. Crittenden led the major effort to avert secession and conflict. The compromise he proposed to the Senate in December 1860 was to solve the territorial problem by resurrecting the Missouri Compromise line and extending it all the way to the Pacific Ocean. To legitimize this extension, Crittenden advocated a constitutional amendment that would overcome the Dred Scott ruling against congressional prohibition of slavery in any territory. But neither Republicans nor southern Democrats gave Crittenden much encouragement or support. His failure presaged the failure of his state's hopes for neutrality. Within months both Confederate and Union armies entered the state, and the Union's military superiority settled Kentucky's fate.

THE FORMATION OF THE CONFEDERACY

The Confederate States of America was taking shape even before secession had run its course. On February 4, 1861, delegates from six states of the lower South met in Montgomery, Alabama, to create a new government; later they were joined by a delegation from Texas. Thus seven states initially made up the Confederate States of America. The men in Montgomery acted in more diverse capacities than any other such group in American history.

In their capacity as delegates to a constitutional convention, they went about their deliberations with great unity of purpose. For the mass of southerners in 1861, the Confederate States of America replicated the United States of America, the country they had loved before it had, in their minds, been distorted beyond recognition by the Republicans. The builders of the Confederate States set out to construct a government that would protect the liberty they held so dear. Like their ancestors, they felt compelled to have a written constitution, and they borrowed heavily from the one they knew and admired. The Constitution of the Confederate States adopted the separation of powers, created a federal system, and in general provided the same structure of government that guided the United States.

There were notable differences, however. In an attempt to avoid the political corruption the delegates associated with presidential reelection maneuvers, the Confederate Constitution prescribed a single six-year term for president. Other major changes underscored the great themes that had dominated southern politics since the Revolution. In Article I black slavery was specifically recognized and given explicit constitutional sanction and protection: "No bill of attainder, *ex post facto* law, or law denying or impairing the right of property in negro slaves shall be passed." Likewise the Constitution affirmed the legitimacy of slavery in any territory the new nation might acquire. One section of the document prohibited a protective tariff. And the concept of states rights was elevated to a first principle: the preamble declared that the Confederacy derived from "each State acting in its sovereign and independent character."

With the drafting of a constitution completed, the delegates transformed themselves into an electoral college. Again they decided to follow the practice of the United States and elect the president and vice president by state. This first time each state would have one vote. After discussing various possibilities, the delegates unanimously chose Jefferson Davis of Mississippi as president of the Confederate States of America and Alexander Stephens of Georgia as vice president. Both had been notable figures in southern politics. A Mississippi planter and a Democrat, the fifty-two-year-old Davis had been educated at West Point and had served with distinction in the Mexican War and as Franklin Pierce's secretary of war. Before and after his stint in Pierce's cabinet, Davis had been a major figure in the United States Senate. Though a stalwart southern-rights man, Davis was not a fire-eater. The choice of Alexander Stephens, formerly a leading Whig and in 1860–1861 a cooperationist, was dictated in part by the drive for unity: it would underscore the single-mindedness of the new Confederates. Stephens was a graduate of the University of Georgia and a lawyer who for a decade and a half had been a major Whig spokesman in the United States House of Representatives. The delegates correctly believed they had selected two eminently qualified, reasonable men to lead their new nation. Of course they had no intention of denying the people of the Confederacy the ultimate right to choose their own leaders. The crisis required immediate action, but the designation of Davis and Stephens was declared to be provisional until a general election could be held. The election was scheduled for November; the permanent president and vice president would be inaugurated in February 1862.

After Davis and Stephens took office, they worked with the delegations, now acting as Congress, to create an administrative structure and a body of laws that would breathe life into the Confederate States of America. In doing so they were mindful that eight slave states remained in the Union. Every effort would be made to secure their partnership in the new country. The infant Confederate government also had to devote attention to its immediate neighbor, the United States. Such matters as the proper political relationship and trading policy had to be settled, but an even more pressing issue was the military posts within the Confederacy still occupied by the United States Army. As states had left the Union, most federal military installations in them either had been captured or had surrendered. In neither instance had any blood been shed. Two major posts, Fort Pickens at Pensacola, Florida, and Fort Sumter in Charleston Harbor, still remained in Union hands. As the Confederate government saw it, a foreign power stood uninvited on its soil. Many Confederates believed that theirs could not be a truly independent country until the Confederate flag flew over every military post within the Confederate States of America.

Map Essay

The Geography of the Civil War

---❖---

These maps emphasize the critical events leading up to the Civil War and outline the most important military engagements of the conflict. The first two focus on the two crucial political events of 1860 and 1861: the presidential election and secession. The former delineates the sectionalism that dominated the presidential contest while the latter illustrates the range of reactions in the slave states to the outcome of that election. The third map depicts the harbor of Charleston, South Carolina, where the first shots of the war were fired. The final five maps are designed to help clarify the campaigns of the war. They identify the key army movements and specify the locations of the major battles in both the eastern and western theaters.

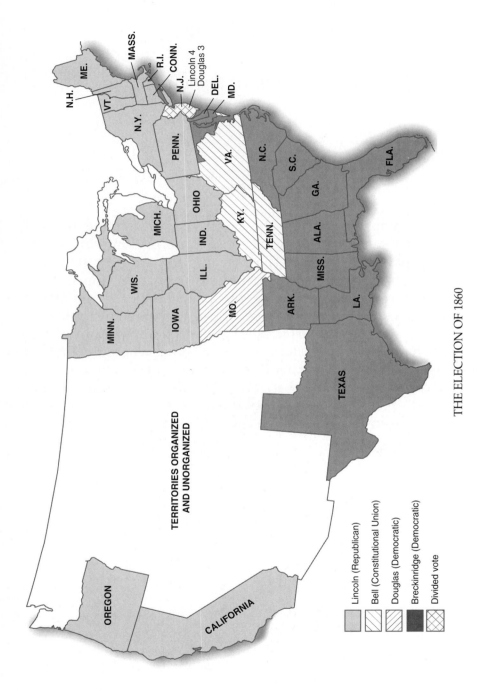

THE ELECTION OF 1860

Lincoln (Republican)

Bell (Constitutional Union)

Douglas (Democratic)

Breckinridge (Democratic)

Divided vote

TERRITORIES ORGANIZED
AND UNORGANIZED

OREGON

CALIFORNIA

MINN.

WIS.

IOWA

ILL.

IND.

MICH.

OHIO

PENN.

N.Y.

VT

N.H.

ME.

MASS.

R.I.

CONN.

N.J.

Lincoln 4
Douglas 3

DEL.

MD.

VA.

KY.

TENN.

N.C.

S.C.

GA.

ALA.

MISS.

ARK.

LA.

TEXAS

FLA.

MO.

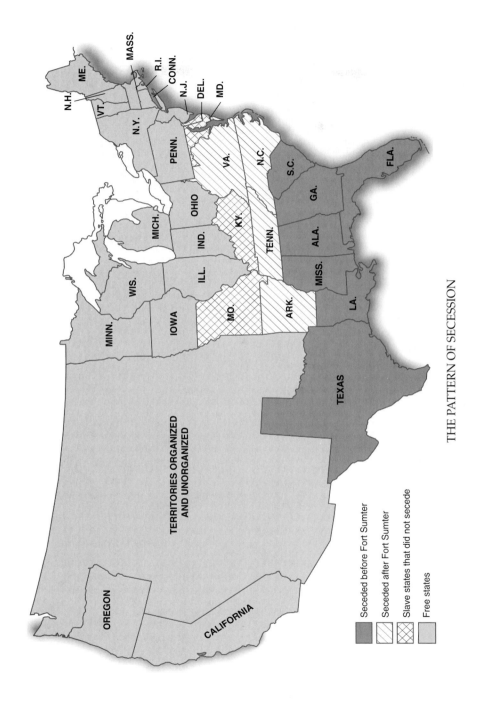

THE PATTERN OF SECESSION

Seceded before Fort Sumter

Seceded after Fort Sumter

Slave states that did not secede

Free states

Confederate batteries

Charleston

Cooper River

Ashley River

Fort Moultrie

Fort Sumter

ATLANTIC OCEAN

CHARLESTON HARBOR, 1861

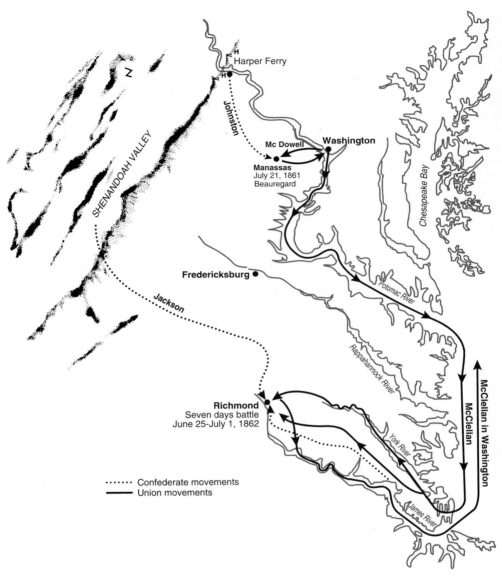

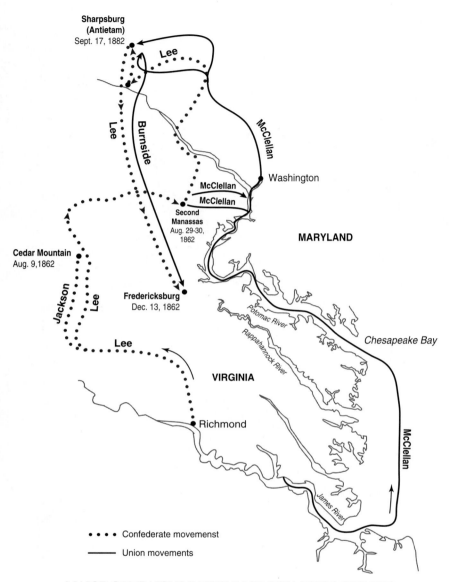

Sharpsburg
(Antietam)
Sept. 17, 1882

Lee

Lee

Burnside

McClellan

Washington

McClellan

McClellan

Second
Manassas
Aug. 29-30,
1862

MARYLAND

Cedar Mountain
Aug. 9,1862

Jackson

Lee

Fredericksburg
Dec. 13, 1862

Lee

VIRGINIA

Richmond

Potomac River

Rappahannock River

Chesapeake Bay

McClellan

James River

• • • Confederate movemenst

——— Union movements

MAJOR CAMPAIGNS IN THE EAST, JULY–DECEMBER 1862

334

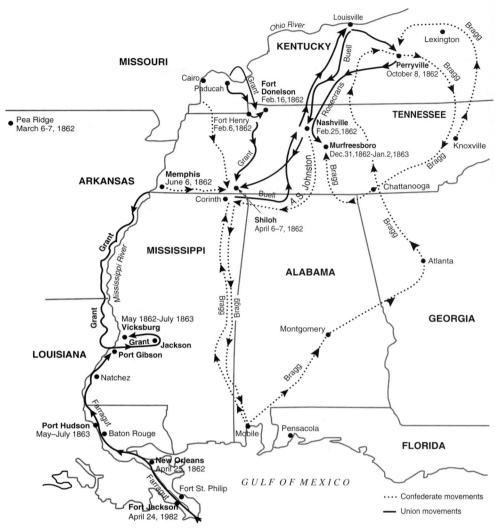

Ohio River

MISSOURI

Cairo
Paducah

Fort Donelson
Feb.16,1862

Fort Henry
Feb.6,1862

Pea Ridge
March 6-7, 1862

ARKANSAS

Memphis
June 6, 1862

Corinth

Shiloh
April 6–7, 1862

MISSISSIPPI

Mississippi River

Grant

May 1862-July 1863
Vicksburg

Grant ● **Jackson**

LOUISIANA

● **Port Gibson**

● Natchez

Port Hudson
May–July 1863

● Baton Rouge

New Orleans
April 25, 1862

Fort St. Philip

Fort Jackson
April 24, 1982

GULF OF MEXICO

Louisville

KENTUCKY

Lexington

Buell

Perryville
October 8, 1862

Bragg

Rosecrans

TENNESSEE

Nashville
Feb.25,1862

Murfreesboro
Dec.31,1862-Jan.2, 1863

Knoxville

A.S. Johnston

Bragg

Buell

Chattanooga

Bragg

ALABAMA

● Atlanta

Montgomery

Bragg

GEORGIA

Mobile

Pensacola

FLORIDA

Farragut

Farragut

······ Confederate movements
——— Union movements

MAJOR CAMPAIGNS IN THE WEST, 1861–SUMMER 1863

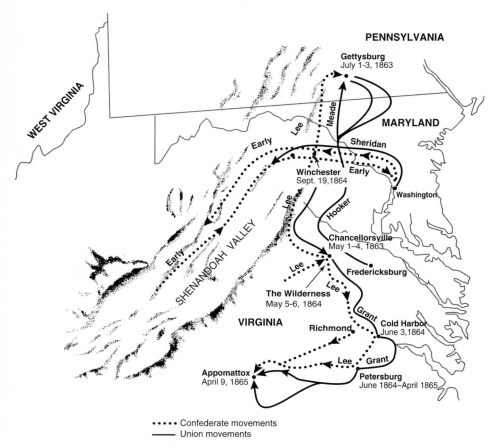

Gettysburg
July 1-3, 1863

PENNSYLVANIA

WEST VIRGINIA

MARYLAND

Meade

Lee

Early

Sheridan

Early

Winchester
Sept. 19,1864

Washington

Hooker

Lee

SHENANDOAH VALLEY

Early

Chancellorsville
May 1–4, 1863

Lee

Lee

Fredericksburg

The Wilderness
May 5-6, 1864

Lee

Grant

VIRGINIA

Richmond

Cold Harbor
June 3,1864

Lee

Grant

Appomattox
April 9, 1865

Petersburg
June 1864–April 1865

•••• Confederate movements
—— Union movements

MAJOR CAMPAIGNS IN THE EAST, MAY–1863–APRIL 1865

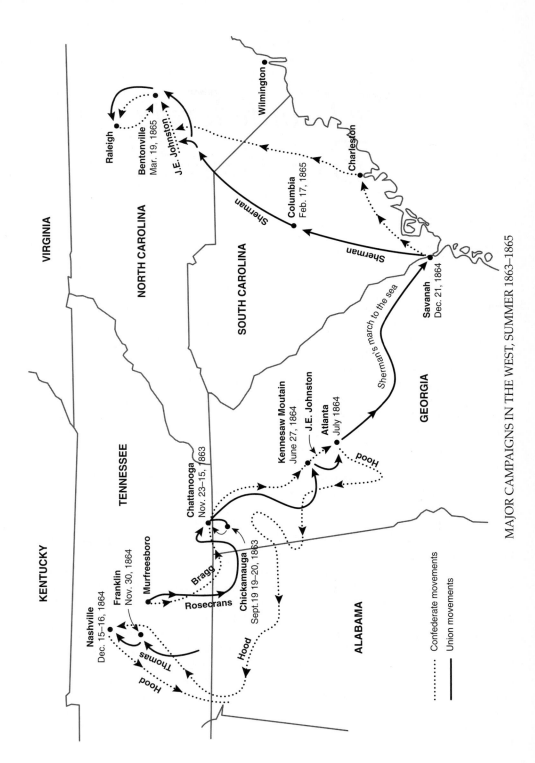

MAJOR CAMPAIGNS IN THE WEST, SUMMER 1863–1865

KENTUCKY

VIRGINIA

TENNESSEE

NORTH CAROLINA

SOUTH CAROLINA

GEORGIA

ALABAMA

Nashville
Dec. 15–16, 1864

Franklin
Nov. 30, 1864

Murfreesboro

Chattanooga
Nov. 23–15, 1863

Chickamauga
Sept. 19 19–20, 1863

Kennesaw Moutain
June 27, 1864

J.E. Johnston

Atlanta
July 1864

Savanah
Dec. 21, 1864

Columbia
Feb. 17, 1865

Charleston

Wilmington

Raleigh

Bentonville
Mar. 19, 1865

J.E. Johnston

Sherman

Sherman

Sherman's march to the sea

Hood

Hood

Thomas

Bragg

Rosecrans

Hood

.... Confederate movements

——— Union movements

337

15

The Confederate Experience

---------❖---------

Fort Sumter stands three miles from Charleston, at the point where the harbor meets the Atlantic Ocean. Construction on it had begun in the late 1820s, as part of a plan devised after the War of 1812 by Secretary of War John C. Calhoun to defend the nation's seacoast from attack. Still unfinished in the spring of 1861, Fort Sumter had become the most visible symbol of the divided nation. Even though the fort lay entirely within the borders of South Carolina, and thus of the Confederate States of America, the Stars and Stripes still flew over the masonry structure. Manned by eighty-five men under the command of Major Robert Anderson, Fort Sumter gave force to President Abraham Lincoln's cry that the Union remained inviolable while it challenged the Confederacy's claim to independence.

Fort Sumter became the prize in the first great contest between the Union and Abraham Lincoln and the Confederacy and Jefferson Davis. The stakes were more political than military, for the Sumter garrison, massively outnumbered and outgunned by Confederate troops and artillery, could not hope to win a fight. On the political front, however, the potential rewards and dangers were much greater. Some of Lincoln's advisers, including military leaders, recommended withdrawal from Fort Sumter, but the president rejected their advice. To his mind, to pull out was to concede the Confederacy's independence and possibly to end his cherished dream of keeping the Union whole. Even so, Lincoln realized that a straightforward military reinforcement not only would require a Confederate counteraction but might push both the upper South and the border states into the Confederacy, which would then have fifteen states instead of the seven Deep South states it now had. To double the Confederacy's base was to court disaster for the Union. Rejecting reinforcement as well as withdrawal, Lincoln decided on a master stroke. He announced that he would resupply Fort Sumter. He would send in no new soldiers or guns, only food and medicine for the troops already there. This action, Lincoln proclaimed, would leave unchanged the calculus of power in Charleston Harbor. This masterful maneuver provided a clear sign of the political genius that would make Lincoln such a great president and war leader.

While Lincoln made his momentous decision, President Jefferson Davis and his advisers also pondered the problem of Fort Sumter. Powerful arguments supported the contention that the Confederates should take the fort. The first was that the Union's occupation of Fort Sumter mocked the Confederacy's independence. According to this thinking, the Confederate States of America could not stand as an independent nation so long as another power maintained an uninvited military force within the Confederacy's borders. Second, some Confederates feared, with justification, that hotheads in South Carolina might strike against the fort on their own initiative. Any such action would undermine the authority of the Confederate government and commit it to a course it had not decided upon. Some Confederate leaders also maintained that a Confederate move against Fort Sumter would mobilize the citizenry behind the government and, equally important, bring the upper South within the Confederate fold. Those who opposed direct action stressed the harm that could come from a first strike. Such an attack, they argued, would lose the Confederacy numerous friends in the North and at the same time strengthen Lincoln's hand. But these arguments did not prevail. President Davis decided to demand the surrender of Sumter, and if it were not forthcoming, he would attack.

From Montgomery orders went to General Pierre G. T. Beauregard of Louisiana, in command of all Confederate forces at Charleston, to demand the

CONFEDERATE PRESIDENT JEFFERSON DAVIS (Mississippi Department of Archives and History)

surrender of Fort Sumter. If Major Anderson refused, Beauregard was to take the fort. Presented with this alternative, Anderson told the Confederates that he would have to evacuate the fort unless new supplies reached him. Beauregard, aware of the criticalness of the situation in Charleston Harbor, informed his government in Montgomery of Anderson's response. The new directive issued to Beauregard gave him some latitude. If Anderson would provide a specific date for his evacuation, Beauregard was not to open fire. Once again Beauregard contacted Anderson, who did specify a date for withdrawal but added a qualification: he would evacuate Fort Sumter unless controlling instructions from his government directed a different course of action. Beauregard now knew he had no choice; his orders had been explicit. At 4:30 A.M. on Sunday, April 12, the Confederate batteries aimed at Fort Sumter opened fire. After thirty-three hours of bombardment Anderson surrendered. War had begun.

PLANS AND POLICY FOR WAR

With the onset of hostilities, the Confederate government suddenly found itself a war government. Thus almost from its birth the chief mission of the Confederate government became the fighting of a great war.

Jefferson Davis and his advisers faced a formidable task. They led a country that had just been created. This new country had no armed forces, no treasury, no economic or fiscal policy, no foreign policy or diplomatic missions. It did not even have that most popular scourge of all governments, a bureaucracy. The Confederate leaders had to confront problems in all of these areas simultaneously. They could not address one, solve it, then move to the next. All had to be coped with at once, for all were crucial; none could be postponed. Moreover, all interacted with one another.

The Confederate government began its operations in Montgomery, Alabama. In the center of the Deep South, Montgomery was a logical place for the convening of the delegates from the states that created the Confederate States of America, wrote the Constitution, and selected the first president and vice president. But after Fort Sumter and the secession of Virginia, a movement commenced to move the capital from Montgomery to Richmond. Numerous reasons prompted this pressure. A small town, Montgomery had neither the facilities nor the services to house conveniently either the apparatus or the personnel of the government. Richmond, though no metropolis, offered considerably more. In addition, Richmond was the most important industrial center in the Confederacy. To guarantee its protection, some Confederates argued, it should be made the capital.

Motives other than size and industry also worked in favor of Richmond. Confederates were thrilled when Virginia, the ancient mother and leader of the South, finally sided with them. Many of them believed it only appropriate that their capital be located in the native state of George Washington and other founders who had led the colonies to victory in the American Revolution. In his inaugural address in Montgomery, President Jefferson Davis proudly equated the Confederates of 1861 with their Revolutionary War ancestors. Southerners, in Davis's mind, "labored to preserve the government of our fathers in its spirit." Accordingly, in May 1861 the entire Confederate government was transferred to Richmond, which remained the capital of the Confederate States of America for the new nation's lifetime.

After April 12 all of the tasks confronting the Confederate leadership coalesced into one immense undertaking—the conduct of war. An army had to be raised. Even before Fort Sumter the Confederate Congress had authorized the recruitment of 100,000 volunteers for the Confederate States Army. In May the Congress provided for 400,000 more; by July 1861 the Confederacy, with a white population only one-quarter the size of the Union's, had nearly two-thirds as many men under arms. Although southerners did respond enthusiastically to the colors, the Confederate War Department had difficulty arming them. Some 150,000 muskets were available from captured United States arsenals in the seceded states, but most were obsolete. The first Confederates who joined up brought their own firearms—hunting rifles, shotguns, even ancient flintlock muskets. In 1861 each regiment in the Confederate Army wore its own uniform. Although the government designated the famous cadet gray as the official color, in fact an enormous variety of outfits colored Confederate units. Never did all Confederate soldiers wear a regulation uniform.

At the same time that Confederate authorities strove to find ways to equip their fighting men with the tools of war, they had to make critical decisions about the methods of financing the war. With an overwhelmingly agricultural economy and a tradition of low taxes, the South was not financially ready for a major modern war. Southern leaders believed that the economic power of their cotton would force France and especially Great Britain to intervene on their behalf. No one was quite sure what form such intervention would take, but most envisioned a variety of measures, including financial assistance. With that utterly erroneous faith in European aid and with a massive hostility to taxation, the Confederate Congress at the outset rebuffed the argument of Secretary of the Treasury Christopher Memminger that secure financial support for the war required a levy of taxes.

Denied tax revenue, the Confederate government turned to borrowing. Early in 1861 the government issued $15 million in bonds, which took up most of the available specie in the Confederate states. Then in May a produce loan authorized farmers and planters to pledge a portion of their crop income in return for bonds equal in value to the market price of their pledge. This tactic produced little revenue, as the income from the pledged crops never kept up with the depreciation of Confederate currency. Efforts to raise money in Europe met with no more success, though in late 1862 a loan was negotiated with a French banking house. The Erlanger loan, so called after the banking house, eventually provided between $6 million and $8.5 million to the Confederacy for the purchase of war goods and the repayment of old debts. It was far from enough.

The chief source of revenue was the treasury notes issued by the Confederate government. The introduction into the Confederate economy of large amounts of paper money backed by nothing but hope set off an inflationary spark that soon became a conflagration. In 1864, after three years of this avalanche of paper money, it took $46 to buy what $1 had bought in 1861. From a base of 100 at the beginning of 1861 the price index shot upward to 762 by 1865. This inflationary surge, the result of a reckless fiscal policy, wrecked the economy. Inflation grew so intolerable that popular pressure pushed Congress to enact taxes in an effort to curb it. In 1863 Congress responded by instituting a variety of taxes—excise taxes, license taxes, a 5 percent tax on land and slaves, even an income tax. But the package was too little too late. Lax enforcement and active evasion combined to make the new laws largely ineffective.

Misplaced faith in the omnipotence of cotton governed Confederate diplomatic strategy as well. The Davis administration set one overriding diplomatic goal: to win recognition from the European powers, chiefly France and Great Britain. In cotton the Confederate government thought it had the lever that would force Great Britain to recognize the Confederacy as an independent nation and possibly even intervene in the war on the Confederate side. And when Great Britain adopted a pro-Confederate stance, France would not be far behind.

Confederate authorities might have built up credits in Europe by exporting as much cotton as possible. Instead, to make sure that Great Britain would follow the path they intended, they embargoed all the cotton remaining within their borders. In their view, the British economy could not withstand the absence of Confederate cotton. They made a grave miscalculation. In the first place, cotton was not so central to the British economy as they assumed. Then, to undermine their plans even further, the great crop of 1859 had enabled British merchants and manufacturers to stockpile huge quantities of cotton. Finally, Great Britain had two other sources of cotton within its own empire: Egypt and India. Cotton never forced Great Britain or anyone else to recognize the Confederacy. In short, the cotton the Confederates considered their ace turned out to be a joker.

Even so, the act of a zealous Union naval officer made it appear, at least momentarily, that the Confederacy might get its wish. In November 1861 a Union warship stopped and boarded a British mail packet, the *Trent,* which carried two Confederate diplomats: the Virginian James Mason, traveling to London, and John Slidell of Louisiana, bound for Paris. Mason and Slidell were removed from the *Trent* and taken to a prison in Boston. Huzzahs greeted the news in the North, but London was enraged by the lack of respect shown to the British flag. Tension grew between the two governments, but cool heads and moderation prevailed. The British demanded an apology and the release of the diplomats, and the French sent a supporting note. The Lincoln administration replied that the action had occurred without authorization and ordered the diplomats released. Britain accepted that explanation. Mason and Slidell went on to their posts in Europe; neither succeeded in gaining recognition for the Confederacy.

At home the Confederate leaders had to wrestle with the problems of fighting a war. The Davis administration never developed any written war plans. In a fundamental sense, Davis and his advisers settled on a basic strategy that under the circumstances appeared both logical and reasonable. They had one chief goal, to be let alone. Thus they decided not to go on the strategic offensive; they would not try to secure their independence by attacking the North. This decision resulted in large part from a realistic appraisal of the Confederacy's resources. President Davis wanted to strike at the North, but he realized that he just did not have the means to do so. To a friend he wrote in 1862, "My early . . . hope was to feed upon the enemy and teach them the blessings of peace by making them feel in its most tangible form the evils of war. The time and place for invasion has been a question not of will but of power." And though in three instances Davis was able to carry the war into enemy territory, he never commanded the sustained power for an offensive strategy.

Instead his troops would stand on the defensive and guard their own territory. From Virginia in the east to the Mississippi River and beyond, the Confederate frontier covered more than 1,000 miles. And the coastline stretching from Virginia on the Atlantic around Florida and across the Gulf of Mexico all the way to the Rio Grande was much longer. If the Union was to subdue the Confederacy, it would have to attack this immense domain. When the Union forces moved into various portions of their territory, the Confederates would strike them at points of opportunity. Thus the Confederates would combine selected offensives with their basic defensive posture. This strategy also included an unstated or undeveloped intention—to wear down the enemy. By luring the Union armies to invade their land—an operation that would require huge numbers of troops and enormous sums to maintain them, and one that was bound to result in substantial casualties—the Confederates hoped to make the North pay a higher price in men, money, and matériel than it could afford. In this view, the Union had neither the will nor the substance to pay the terrible cost necessary to subjugate the Confederacy.

To manage the war the Confederacy had no general staff in the modern sense, with overall command responsibility. Early on the Confederates implemented a departmental command structure: the country was divided into various departments, the commander of each department reporting to the War Department in Richmond. This structure, which seemed rational but worked against cooperation and concentration, remained in place until almost the end of the war. President Davis had a military adviser, but the adviser had no command responsibility. The president acted not only as the constitutional commander in chief but also often as a general in chief, transmitting his orders through the secretary of war. If the numerous departments were to be coordinated in any way, he would have to do the coordinating. To command the major departments Davis assigned the senior generals of the Confederate States Army, most of whom had been professionals in the prewar United States Army. When their states had seceded and formed the Confederacy, they had resigned their commissions in one army to become officers in another.

The Naval War

On the water the Confederates found a different problem. The Confederacy had an immense seacoast and a vast river system, but no navy at all. President Davis gave the task of creating one to former United States Senator Stephen Mallory of Florida. Mallory's job as secretary of the navy was complicated by the Union's decision to impose a blockade on the entire coast for the purpose of impeding both exports such as cotton and imports of war matériel. While Mallory pondered how best to deal with the blockade, he also had to think about protecting the rivers that provided avenues of invasion into the Confederate interior.

Mallory and other officials knew that they could never match the United

States Navy ship for ship. To counter the Union's overwhelming numerical superiority, the Confederates turned to technology. As early as May 1861 Secretary
Mallory began talking about building a navy of ironclads that could destroy the
blockade. Upon investigation, however, Mallory found that because of technological deficiencies and the production of other war matériel, Confederate ironworks
could not provide the necessary iron sheeting. To obtain the desired vessels the
Confederates entered into contracts with European companies, but Union diplomacy and financial difficulties impeded deliveries. Though the Confederates
managed to get some ironclads in the water, their fleet of oceangoing ironclads
never materialized.

Their first serious effort resulted in naval history. In 1861 and early 1862 Confederates at Norfolk, Virginia, overhauled the captured Union ship *Merrimac*, clad
it in iron, and renamed it the *Virginia*. With this armored vessel, equipped with
guns mounted on all sides, the Confederates aimed to smash the blockade. On
March 2, 1862, the *Virginia* steamed to the mouth of the Chesapeake Bay to challenge blockading Union ships. The first day was a rousing success. As the *Virginia*
sank two ships and forced three others aground, the shots from the Union navy
just bounced off its iron coat. On the second day, however, the *Virginia* was met
not by wooden ships but by another ironclad. The Union's *Monitor* did not look at
all like its southern opponent. A revolving turret with two guns sat on a hull low
in the water; observers called the ship "a tin can on a shingle." On March 9 the
first battle in history between two ironclads took place. After three hours of hard
fighting, neither had substantially damaged the other. But that draw ended the
Confederates' dream that ironclads could end the blockade. As for the *Virginia*,
when Union forces captured Norfolk in May 1862, the Confederates wrecked the
ship. The North went on to build dozens of ironclads based on the design of the
Monitor.

Because the *Virginia* could not overcome the *Monitor*, the Confederate navy
never seriously challenged the Union navy on the high seas. Instead the Confederates sent raiders or cruisers to disrupt Union commerce, a strategy that proved
quite successful. Confederate raiders or cruisers captured or destroyed more than
250 merchant ships flying the Stars and Stripes. The most famous of all the
raiders, the *Alabama*, built in England and commanded by Captain Raphael
Semmes, sank sixty-two merchant vessels and one warship between its commis-
sioning in 1862 and its destruction by the United States Navy in 1864, off the coast
of France.

Although Mallory never realized his dream of defeating the blockade with
ironclads, the Confederates did construct other iron-coated vessels. Generally
smaller than the *Virginia*, they were designed to stop Union gunboats on southern
rivers. Despite enormous technical and manufacturing difficulties, the Confederate navy managed to place ironclads on the Mississippi and at other strategic
spots, such as Mobile Bay. Yet technological shortcomings hampered the effective
use of these vessels. Maneuverability on the narrow waterways was always a
problem. Most of these ships had short careers. Mechanical shortcomings, chiefly
engine failure, caused as many casualties among the ironclads as enemy shot.
Many ended up scuttled by their own crews.

THE EASTERN THEATER, 1861–1862

On the ground serious military conflict began in the summer of 1861. The first major battle took place in Virginia, between Richmond and Washington, the corridor that would provide more battlefields than anywhere else during the war. When the Confederate capital was moved to Richmond, a clamor arose in Washington for Union troops to march on the city. Many Washingtonians seemed to regard the coming confrontation as an opportunity for a holiday outing. Confederates, for their part, were confident that they could block any Union advance. Many Confederates, in fact, believed that the South's manliness and fighting skills were so superior that any Confederate force could whip a considerably larger Yankee force.

Americans commenced killing and maiming each other in significant numbers on July 21, 1861, no more than twenty-five miles south of Washington, along a small stream called Bull Run. The First Battle of Manassas, the name given the carnage by the Confederates, provided a foretaste of what this war would be like. First Manassas was no holiday. The congressmen and other picnickers who followed the Union army to watch the gala affair were to have no counterparts at later contests. At First Manassas the roughly 70,000 men in the two armies, fairly evenly divided, demonstrated that both sides could fight and that each would demand a heavy price in suffering and blood from the other. More than 2,700 Union troops were killed, wounded, or missing; the Confederates lost almost 2,000.

First Manassas introduced commanders to real battle. General Pierre G. T. Beauregard, the conqueror of Fort Sumter, found the direction of thousands of soldiers in the turmoil of battle considerably more complicated than aiming artillery at a fixed position. His colleague General Joseph E. Johnston, whose army from the Shenandoah Valley joined Beauregard's on the battlefield, proved that the new mobility provided by the railroad would enable commanders to concentrate troops rapidly at critical points. But for the movement of Johnston's 12,000 men from fifty miles away to reinforce Beauregard, the Union army under Brigadier General Irvin McDowell would probably have claimed the first victory. But the combination of Beauregard and Johnston overwhelmed the Federals. On the field many Confederate officers who later had important roles in the war gained their first experience commanding soldiers in battle. They included Jubal A. Early, Edmund Kirby-Smith, and Thomas J. Jackson, who received his famous nickname, Stonewall, for a stalwart stand against charging Union units.

The Confederate victory at Manassas taught a hard lesson. Though the Confederates won on that hot July day, their army was too bloodied and too exhausted to take full advantage of its tactical triumph. Those who called for the victorious Confederates to hurry to Washington and end the war had little understanding of the hard blow the battle had dealt the Confederate army. Beauregard and Johnston had blunted the Union advance, but they could neither destroy their enemy nor promptly take the offensive. A similar pattern would appear often over the next four years, on both sides.

After First Manassas the two armies, almost as if suffering from shock, went into practically permanent quarters facing each other. Not until the beginning of 1862 did they begin to stir. A new commander of the Union army fresh from early victories in western Virginia, Major General George B. McClellan, took charge. McClellan planned to use the Union's superiority on the water to move his army from the environs of Washington around the Confederate army to a point below Richmond, on the peninsula between the York and James rivers, where Virginia had first been settled and where George Washington had defeated the British at Yorktown. With the advent of McClellan the main Union army in the East, which became known as the Army of the Potomac, swelled massively, to some 100,000 men.

In the face of this threat, the Confederates struck back with the audacity and imagination that were to be their trademarks in the Virginia theater. Both of these characteristics were intimately associated with two men who became captains of the first rank. General Robert E. Lee, fifty-five years old and serving that spring as military adviser to President Davis, had been born into one of the great Virginia families. But the Lees had lost their economic and political leadership by the time Robert came to maturity. Now that the Lees were no longer great planters, Robert took another road. After graduating from West Point in 1829, he served as a professional soldier. During his more than thirty years as an army officer Lee distinguished himself in the Mexican War and enjoyed a sterling reputation among senior officers. A colonel in 1861, he refused the offer to command the Union field army and, upon the secession of Virginia, resigned his commission. When Virginia joined the Confederacy, he became a full general in its army. In the spring of 1862 Lee was still an unproven general; in fact, in his first combat assignment, in western Virginia, he had lost to George McClellan. Major General Thomas J. "Stonewall" Jackson, only thirty-eight years old, was also a Virginian, but from the transmontane region of the state, not the tidewater. Although he lacked Lee's pedigree, Jackson, too, had graduated from West Point, had been in the regular army, and had participated in the Mexican War. But he had given up his army career, and the 1850s found him on the faculty of the Virginia Military Institute in Lexington.

Together Lee and Jackson derailed McClellan's plan. In order to make Lincoln and his advisers divert units intended for McClellan, Lee urged Jackson stationed in the Shenandoah Valley to advance down the valley toward the Potomac River. In a series of dazzling marches and attacks, the stern, taciturn Jackson confused and defeated several Union generals in the Shenandoah. Jackson's victories worked precisely as Lee had hoped. Because of Jackson's success, the Federals were not able to concentrate as many troops below Richmond as McClellan had hoped.

Because Joseph Johnston had been wounded, Lee now commanded the major Confederate field army, the Army of Northern Virginia. He ordered Jackson to move rapidly and secretly from the Shenandoah Valley to Richmond. When Jackson joined him, Lee intended to take the offensive and destroy McClellan. During the last week in June, in a series of bitter fights known as the Seven Days Battle, Lee did stop McClellan's advance on Richmond, but at a terrible price. During the week's fighting the Federals suffered almost 16,000 casualties out of 100,000 in their army. The Confederates, usually on the attack, took even heavier casual-

ROBERT E. LEE, THE GREAT
CONFEDERATE WARRIOR
(Cook Collection, Valentine
Museum, Richmond, Va.)

ties—more than 20,000, practically one-fourth of their army. These casualty figures meant that with Lee in command ferocity would have to be added to audacity and imagination.

Lee and other Confederate leaders had little time to savor the turning back of
McClellan. When information arrived that a new force had started south from
Washington, Lee dispatched Stonewall Jackson to counter it. Then, convinced that
Jackson was facing a major threat, Lee hurried north from Richmond to join forces
with his subordinate. In a daring move that sent Jackson around and deep in the
rear of the Federal army, commanded by Major General John Pope, Lee struck and

punished the Federals on the same ground where the first great battle had been fought. With the success of the Second Battle of Manassas, Lee and the Confederates had the initiative and the power of decision.

Lee and President Davis decided to go north, to carry the war out of the Confederacy into the Union. Various motives prompted this decision. Without question the general and the president wanted to relieve the pressure on Virginia. They thought of the food available in Maryland and anticipated new recruits for the Army of Northern Virginia. And they hoped that the presence of a major Confederate army in the eastern states, especially a victorious one, would convince the North that the South could not be defeated. When Lee crossed the Potomac, the Confederates had one eye cocked toward England. A triumph on enemy soil might just persuade the British to intervene on behalf of the Confederacy.

But events turned out otherwise. Marylanders did not flock to the Confederate colors. Even more important, a set of Lee's confidential orders fell into the hands of McClellan, once again leading the Army of the Potomac against the Confederates. With that information McClellan moved more rapidly than Lee expected. Confronting this new development, Lee altered his plan of rapid movement through Maryland toward Pennsylvania in favor of regrouping to face McClellan. The two old foes joined battle again along Antietam Creek at Sharpsburg, Maryland. By attacking the Confederates piecemeal instead of in sustained fashion, McClellan frittered away his substantial numerical advantage of 35,000 men. Even though Lee's thin lines held and the Confederates could claim that the Federals had not driven them from the field, Sharpsburg smashed the Confederates' great expectations for this advance into enemy country. McClellan suffered

THE PRICE OF BATTLE: CONFEDERATE DEAD AT SHARPSBURG (Library of Congress)

more than 11,000 casualties, but Lee sustained almost 12,000. The combined casualties—about four times as many as the Americans suffered on D-Day in World
War II—made this the single bloodiest day of the war. Lee had no choice but to retreat into Virginia. Strategically the Union won a decisive victory at Sharpsburg.

THE WAR IN THE WEST, 1861–1862

While cries of "On to Richmond!" reverberated in the East, critical developments
took place in the West. The initial crucial question involved the fate of Kentucky.
Of the border states it had the greatest percentage of slaves and the largest number of Confederate sympathizers. The Confederacy hoped that Kentucky would
secede and join the new nation, but many Kentuckians remained loyal to the
Union. For Kentucky any North-South conflict would literally become a war of
brother against brother. That deep division can be seen in the family of Senator
John J. Crittenden, whose attempt at compromise failed in the winter of 1860–
1861. One of his sons became a general in the Confederate army, the other a general in the Union army. To escape that horror, Kentucky attempted to remain neutral. Despite an official state proclamation of neutrality, both sides pressed Kentucky, and both took recruits and supplies. For several months, however, neither
sent organized forces across the Kentucky border. But in September 1861, to
thwart an expected Federal advance, Confederate soldiers entered the state. Technically the Confederacy was the first to violate neutral borders, but Union troops
crossed the Ohio River promptly thereafter. Thus the Confederates, commanded
by General Albert Sidney Johnston, a stalwart of the prewar United States Army
who had a glowing though unproven reputation as a great soldier, occupied a line
stretching from east to west through the center of the state. With both sides there
in force, the state threatened to become the first great western battleground.

Confederates and Yankees did not, however, fight a major battle for Kentucky.
Because of the insight and determination of an unimpressive-looking Union general who chewed on cigars, the Confederates had to pull out of Kentucky without
much fighting at all. At the beginning of 1862, Ulysses S. Grant was still a relatively obscure officer, but he would not remain unknown much longer. Grant recognized that the two rivers flowing northward through Tennessee and Kentucky
into the Ohio offered an opportunity both to flush Johnston out of Kentucky and
to invade the Confederate heartland. The Cumberland River went to Nashville;
the Tennessee River cut through the entire state whose name it bore. Grant
planned to send a combined navy-army force up the rivers to blast the Confederates by sea and land.

The Confederates were also aware that the Cumberland and the Tennessee
provided a watery highway into their interior. To block any Union advance, the
Confederates constructed two forts on the Kentucky-Tennessee border where
only fifteen miles separated the two rivers. Fort Henry, on the eastern bank of the
Tennessee, and Fort Donelson, on the western bank of the Cumberland, guarded
the water routes. They proved no match, however, for Grant's land-sea attack.
Poorly situated, Fort Henry had to contend with the rising waters of the Tennessee as well as the advancing Federals. It did neither successfully and fell on

February 6. Ten days later Fort Donelson, plagued by command problems, capitulated to Grant's infantry.

Grant's victory meant disaster for the Confederacy. With his Kentucky line fatally breached and a Federal army in his rear, Johnston pulled out of Kentucky. With Grant astride the two rivers, Tennessee offered no haven, so Johnston retreated southwestward across the state. Not only Kentucky came under Union control; so did central Tennessee, with its important supply point at Nashville and the ironworks of the Cumberland River valley.

Grant did not rest on his laurels. He pushed on up the Tennessee with the goal of inflicting a crippling blow on the Confederate war effort in the West. Flung back across hundreds of miles and two states, Johnston stopped to regroup in northeastern Mississippi. At some point he had to stand and fight, and Albert Johnston decided the time was now. His army had been strengthened by bringing in every available soldier; he even got General Beauregard as second in command. Moreover, his opponents had temporarily divided their forces. Grant was coming up the Tennessee with the main body, but Federal units sent to Nashville had not yet rejoined him. Grant's army of around 40,000 was encamped on the western bank of the Tennessee just inside the state at Pittsburg Landing, near a small country place of worship called Shiloh Church.

Johnston and Beauregard planned to drive Grant into the Tennessee River before any reinforcements could reach him. At daylight on April 6 the Confederates, 40,000 strong, stormed out of the woods into a generally surprised Union army. Neither Grant nor his generals had expected an attack. During the day the soldiers in gray and blue fought with a ferociousness never before seen on the continent. The bloodletting was appalling. Among the casualties was General Johnston, mortally wounded while urging his men forward. For a time a Confederate victory seemed inevitable, but vigorous stands by individual Federal units kept Grant's line intact. Nightfall found the Confederates short of their goal, and Grant prepared to take the offensive the next day with the reinforcements that arrived during the night. When Beauregard was unable to hold Grant back, he withdrew into Mississippi. The casualties shocked everyone; each side suffered more than 1,700 killed and 8,000 wounded. Though at terrible cost, the Confederates served notice at Shiloh that the western war had not yet ended.

The frightful carnage on Civil War battlefields resulted in large part from technological improvements in weaponry. Chief among these advances was the rifling—the cutting of spiral grooves within barrels—of both infantry and artillery weapons. Rifling imparted a spin to a bullet which greatly increased the range and accuracy of a weapon. The effective range of the basic infantry musket went from 100 yards to 300 or 400 yards. In the face of this enhanced firepower, the traditional infantry charge, widely relied on by most commanders, usually led to disaster. A participant in a Confederate charge described the attack as the "work of death." "Volley after volley of musket balls sweep through the line and mow us down like wheat before the scythe." Witnessing such devastation, a junior officer wailed, "Down! down! go the boys."

After the shooting stopped, grisly sights surrounded the survivors. A Confederate veteran of Chancellorsville described the dead everywhere, some with their heads shot off, some with their brains oozing out, some pierced through the head with musket balls, some with their noses shot away, some with their mouths smashed, some wounded in the neck, some with broken arms or legs, some shot through the breast and some cut in two with shells.

Being killed outright, however, was often preferable to being wounded. Because both medical knowledge and sanitary conditions were primitive, many of the wounded eventually died or survived severely maimed. Military hospitals were appalling places. A Confederate soldier observed:

> The sorriest sights . . . are in those dreadful field-hospitals, established in barns, under large tents, and in houses. The screams and groans of the poor fellows undergoing amputation are sometimes dreadful—and then the sight of arms and legs surrounding those places, as they are thrown into great piles is something one that has seen the results of battle can never forget.

Farther west, beyond the Mississippi, the conflict also raged. In 1861 both sides struggled over control of Missouri, like Kentucky a slave state that had not seceded. For a time in mid-year the Confederates controlled most of the southern half of the state, but by early 1862 Confederate forces had been pushed back into Arkansas. In March 1862 a key battle took place in northwestern Arkansas, at Pea Ridge, where a decisive Union victory ended any serious Confederate threat to Missouri. The remainder of the war in this vast area, including Arkansas, northern Louisiana, and Texas—the Confederacy's Trans-Mississippi Department— was not of primary importance. Few troops, long distances, and poor transportation made military operations difficult. Trans-Mississippi's chief contribution to the war effort was as a supplier of such critical items as horses. When Union victories in 1863 closed the Mississippi, eastward traffic slowed and the entire Trans-Mississippi came under military command. With the closure of the great river, President Davis gave the departmental commander, General Edmund Kirby-Smith, the right to exercise civil as well as military authority. Kirby-Smith remained in charge of the Trans-Mississippi for the duration of the war.

The bloodbath at Shiloh had not paralyzed the Confederate leadership. On the contrary, standing and fighting seemed to rejuvenate the Confederates. The shocking loss of New Orleans, the major port of the Confederacy and the guardian of the lower Mississippi, had somehow to be overcome. Only three weeks after Shiloh, New Orleans had fallen to a Union naval task force under David G. Farragut, which had run past the downriver forts defending the city. Determined to turn events around, President Davis replaced Beauregard, who had fallen back deeper into Mississippi, with General Braxton Bragg, an organizer and a disciplinarian. Initially this seemed a wise move, for Bragg determined to take the offensive. By a roundabout rail route he took the bulk of his army to Chattanooga to assist the Confederates defending eastern Tennessee. But once he arrived there, Davis ordered Bragg to invade Kentucky with the combined force of around 50,000 troops.

Such an advance offered enormous potential for the Confederates. With their major western field army in Kentucky, much of the territory lost since Forts Henry and Donelson would seem once again to be within their grasp. Nashville and central Tennessee were still in Federal hands, but the Union forces would evacuate them if the Confederates prevailed in Kentucky. The Confederates hoped not only to recruit Kentucky volunteers and replenish their supplies but to add Kentucky to the roster of Confederate states—a major political triumph. Then the front line would be the Ohio River, not the Tennessee. Strategically, politically, and psychologically the Confederates could gain enormously. But of course this outcome depended on the Confederates' success on the battlefield.

Bragg, who took his army from Mississippi to Kentucky with confidence and decisiveness, lost those characteristics in Kentucky. Once in the state, he did not promptly effect the concentration of all Confederate troops in order to fight the Union forces on ground favorable to him. Nor could he decide on priorities between an aggressive political policy aimed at inaugurating a Confederate governor and a military plan designed to end in Confederate triumph. The campaign that began with such anticipation ended in a muddle. The political goals went nowhere, and the major fight on October 8, 1862, at Perryville in the central part of the state, found Bragg outnumbered by Federal forces commanded by Major General Don Carlos Buell. With less than half of his army on the field, he pulled away after a day of fighting. His hopes shattered, Bragg retreated to Tennessee.

A CHANGING WAR

Decisive military victories in Maryland and Kentucky could have put the Confederate States of America in an almost unassailable position. Such triumphs would have put immense pressure on Lincoln to work out some plan for peace. But Lincoln never felt that pressure; it was Jefferson Davis who had to contend with fundamentally altered circumstances.

The strategic reverses suffered by the Confederates in the autumn of 1862 settled the basic international question. Defeat in Kentucky and especially in Maryland exploded the Confederates' dream that Great Britain and perhaps other European powers would intervene on their behalf. Because of Britain's naval power, no one else in Europe would act unless Great Britain led the way. And serious discussions had occurred in England about the proper policy toward the United States and the Confederate States. A weakened United States would certainly be in Britain's interest. And though cotton from Egypt and India had made the loss of the South's cotton less serious than it would have been otherwise, a guaranteed supply from the South would boost Britain's textile industry and general economy. But the foreign policy of the Lincoln administration made clear to the British government that any action to benefit the Confederacy would probably mean war with the United States. Thus England was not going to get involved unless the evidence clearly pointed toward a Confederate victory. And after Sharpsburg and Perryville, the signs indicated confusion at best and the South's defeat at worst. So if the Confederacy were to prevail, it would have to do so without help from England.

The Confederate retreat from Maryland also provided an opportunity for Lincoln to claim the moral high ground. At the outset the Confederacy established independence as its chief war aim, while Lincoln claimed he fought to preserve the Union. As for slavery, Lincoln stated, he would take any stand that would aid preservation of the Union. But after Sharpsburg, Lincoln issued his Emancipation Proclamation, and the elimination of slavery became a second major goal of the war. The proclamation made a decision to help the South even more difficult for England and France because both opposed slavery. Even though the Emancipation Proclamation could not and did not even attempt to free all slaves, it was a significant document. Claiming that his war powers gave him the required authority, Lincoln announced that all slaves held in states still in rebellion on January 1, 1863, would become free. The proclamation did not free slaves in the states of the Union or in those areas of the Confederacy occupied by Union forces. Despite its limitations, it did alter in a basic way the moral calculus of the war.

The Confederates reacted angrily. In a message to the Confederate Congress, President Davis denounced the proclamation as "the most execrable measure in the history of guilty man." He even threatened to treat captured Federal officers as "criminals engaged in inciting servile insurrection." The Union's warning that it would hold Confederate officers for similar treatment guaranteed that Davis's threat would never be carried out. Despite the outcries of the Confederate leaders, many of them recognized that the Emancipation Proclamation put them on the moral as well as the military defensive.

Although disappointed by the refusal of the European powers to intervene and outraged by the Emancipation Proclamation, the Confederate government moved forthrightly to strengthen its ability to carry on the war. The first necessity was manpower. Even before Shiloh and the Seven Days, Confederate authorities recognized that volunteers alone could never meet the requirements for soldiers. On April 1, 1862, the Confederate Congress enacted the first conscription law in American history; it made all white men between the ages of eighteen and thirty-five eligible for military service, though it permitted substitutes and exempted the clergy and men in critical occupations, such as ironworkers, teachers, and state employees. In the fall Congress extended the upper age limit to forty-five and established an exemption for owners and overseers of twenty or more slaves. As troop requirements grew more desperate, Congress continued to respond. In February 1864 it broadened the age brackets to include ages seventeen to fifty and curtailed exemptions.

Though conscription was not popular, it helped to fill Confederate ranks. Some state officials opposed conscription as an invasion of local and states rights by the central government. The provision permitting owners and overseers of more than twenty slaves to escape the draft brought forth cries that this was a rich man's war and a poor man's fight. Despite the problems, the statistics demonstrate the overall effectiveness of the various conscription bills. The Confederate population included approximately 1 million white males between seventeen and forty-five; some 750,000 served in the Confederate military. When the men who worked in vital civilian positions are taken into account, it becomes clear that most of those million men directly aided the Confederate war effort. With the help of conscription the Confederate government kept sizable armies in the field until the final months of the war.

Fighting men could accomplish nothing, however, without the materials of war. At the commencement of hostilities the Confederate government had no ready supply of arms; its inventory consisted solely of armaments captured from federal arsenals. But because of the efforts of one of the true geniuses of the Confederacy, Confederate soldiers usually had weapons and ammunition. In April 1861 an obscure captain in the old United States Army accepted a commission as major and assignment as chief of the Confederate Ordnance Department. A native Pennsylvanian, a graduate of West Point, and the son-in-law of a former governor of Alabama, Josiah Gorgas set about arming the defenders of the Confederacy. With immense organizational gifts and astonishing enterprise, Gorgas turned plowshares into swords. At the outset he sent an agent to Europe to buy arms and ammunition, which entered the Confederacy through the blockade. Then Gorgas created a munitions industry. He built powder mills; the largest, at Augusta, produced 1 million pounds of gunpowder in 1863 alone. To obtain the essential ingredient, potassium nitrate, or niter, Gorgas mined saltpeter in caves, created niter beds from carcasses of dead animals, and collected the contents of chamber pots. The Tredegar ironworks in Richmond made a wide variety of essential items, such as propeller shafts and plate for ironclads. New foundries to cast cannon were established at Augusta, Columbus, and Macon, in Georgia; a naval gunworks was built at Selma, Alabama. Looking back from the spring of 1864, Gorgas accurately observed in his diary: "Where three years ago we were not making a gun, a pistol nor a sabre, no shot nor shell (except at the Tredegar Works)—a pound of powder—we now make all these in quantities to meet the demands of our large armies." While many men were promoted to high rank because of their performance on the battlefield, Gorgas advanced only to brigadier general, but without him the combat generals would never have been able to lead armies in battle for four years.

The government agencies in charge of procuring and supplying food and clothing had no Josiah Gorgas. Armies often drew from the areas in which they operated for clothing and especially for food. Most soldiers provided most of what they wore, and it was never abundant. Footwear was particularly shoddy and in short supply, though by 1864 shoe factories in Richmond were turning out 800 pairs a day. To feed its troops the government called on planters and farmers to shift from cotton to foodstuffs. The production of cotton declined dramatically, from just under 4 million bales in 1860 to around 300,000 in 1864. The spread of the territory occupied by Union troops surely accounted for some of this decrease, as did the difficulty of marketing the crop; but just as certainly support for the government's efforts contributed significantly. Corn and wheat shipments from farms and plantations to armies crisscrossed the South. Most field armies used nearby food sources as much as possible; the Shenandoah Valley, for example, served as the granary for Lee's Army of Northern Virginia.

HOPE BECOMES DESPAIR

After the Confederate setbacks in Maryland and Kentucky, the war returned southward for the winter. But in neither East nor West did hibernation set in. In

Tennessee, at Murfreesboro or Stones River, and in Virginia, at Fredericksburg, armies fought bloody December battles, neither of which had any significant strategic importance. In mid-December at Fredericksburg, Lee pummeled a new opponent, Major General Ambrose Burnside, from a strong defensive position. At the end of the month, in an uncoordinated attack, Bragg failed in an effort to defeat the Federal army commanded by Major General William S. Rosecrans and to open the road to Nashville, only thirty miles beyond Murfreesboro. After these two inconclusive fights the armies waited for spring.

The spring and summer of 1863 brought two great offensives. In the East Robert E. Lee mounted his second campaign north of the Potomac, while in the West Ulysses Grant struck vigorously at the great Confederate stronghold on the Mississippi, Vicksburg. In May at Chancellorsville, just west of Fredericksburg, Lee in a brilliant battle whipped Major General Joseph Hooker and turned back another Union drive for Richmond. Although Chancellorsville stood as a notable Confederate victory, it demanded a high price. Wounded by fire from his own men, Stonewall Jackson contracted pneumonia and died on May 10. Despite that blow, Lee retained enormous confidence in his officers and men. Having reorganized the Army of Northern Virginia, he once again aimed it at the North. Although Confederate officials no longer seriously contemplated European intervention, President Davis and Lee wanted the war in enemy country. The food, fodder, and other supplies available in Maryland and Pennsylvania would lessen the demand on Virginia. But also the Confederate leadership wanted northerners to experience the presence of armies, troops, and battle. A resounding victory on Union territory could put enormous pressure on Lincoln to recognize the Confederacy and negotiate with the Davis administration. It was not to be, however. Lee's offensive ended in early July in a small Pennsylvania town, Gettysburg. There, after three days of desperate fighting, Lee failed to overcome a Union army commanded by Major General George G. Meade. Having lost more than 25,000 men—over one-third of his troops—Lee once again led his bleeding army back into Virginia.

While Lee was marching northward toward his fateful rendezvous at Gettysburg, Grant was menacing Vicksburg. Vicksburg was of critical importance to the Confederates because along with Port Hudson, just over a hundred miles to the south in Louisiana, it kept the Mississippi open for communication with the Trans-Mississippi area, which provided horses and other critical items. Jefferson Davis ordered the commander at Vicksburg, Lieutenant General John C. Pemberton, a northerner who had sided with the Confederacy, to hold at all costs. After failing to capture Vicksburg from the North, Grant conducted one of the most brilliant campaigns of the war. On the western bank of the Mississippi he moved his army overland; south of Vicksburg he transported his troops to the eastern bank. Then he moved rapidly northeastward toward Jackson before turning back to the west and driving toward Vicksburg. Knocked off balance by Grant's daring and his rapid movements, the Confederates responded ineffectively. By late May, Grant had Pemberton cooped up in Vicksburg; the siege lasted some six weeks. On July 4, 1863, one day after Lee's defeat at Gettysburg, Vicksburg capitulated. With Port Hudson falling to the Union on July 8, the entire length of the Mississippi came under Federal control.

The losses at Gettysburg and Vicksburg were major blows. In the East the Union forces inflicted heavy casualties on the main Confederate field army and forced it to retreat into Virginia. In the West President Lincoln finally realized a major strategic goal, command of the Mississippi. The bagging of the 30,000 troops in the Vicksburg garrison did nothing to help the Confederate war effort, either. In the Washington-Richmond corridor as well as the Mississippi Valley the Federals had the upper hand and the initiative.

Despite the Confederate disaster at Vicksburg, Bragg's Army of Tennessee remained whole and in the field, though after Murfreesboro he had eventually retreated all the way to Georgia. In September, however, Bragg struck the Union army under Rosecrans in a bitter contest known as the Battle of Chickamauga. Reinforced by 12,000 men from Lee's army, transported by rail to northern Georgia, Bragg overwhelmed his foes and drove them back into Chattanooga. Bragg occupied the heights surrounding the city and attempted to force a surrender, but Chattanooga was still holding out in October, when Grant arrived to take command of the besieged Union forces. Immediately he reopened the Union supply line as a prelude to breaking Bragg's hold on the city. In late November he launched attacks that broke through Bragg's lines; once again the Confederates withdrew into Georgia.

The year 1864 opened with the Confederates on the defensive across the South. In Virginia, on ground just west of his triumphs at Fredericksburg and Chancellorsville, Lee awaited still another march on Richmond. This time his antagonist would be Grant, the conqueror of Vicksburg and Chattanooga, now a lieutenant general in command of all Union armies. While Grant prepared to hurl his troops against Lee, his chief subordinate in the West, Major General William T. Sherman, moved out of Chattanooga and pointed his divisions toward Atlanta and the Army of Tennessee, now under Joseph Johnston, who had replaced the oft-defeated and oft-criticized Bragg.

Grant and Sherman gave Lee and Johnston more than they could handle. The two Confederate generals waged quite different campaigns. From the moment Grant crossed his front in early May, Lee assaulted him on every possible occasion. In a series of bloody engagements—the Wilderness, Spotsylvania Courthouse, the North Anna—Lee delivered fierce blows that would have stopped and probably turned back his previous foes, but Grant kept driving ahead, despite horrendous losses. Finally on June 3 at Cold Harbor, only ten miles from Richmond, Grant launched a frontal assault that resulted in 7,000 Union soldiers killed or wounded, most in the first few minutes. In a month of bitter fighting Lee had inflicted on the Union army casualties about equal to the 60,000 men with whom he started the campaign. And still Grant remained in his front. Lee despaired of what would happen if Grant pinned him in a static position where he could not maneuver. To one of his commanders he predicted with terrible accuracy that if the contest between him and Grant ever "bec[a]me a siege, . . . then it [would] be a mere question of time."

Joe Johnston in Georgia never attacked Sherman. By superb handling of his troops in a succession of flanking moves, Sherman thoroughly confused Johnston, who did not seem to understand what his canny opponent was about. After six weeks Sherman had maneuvered Johnston out of mountainous north Georgia to the banks of the Chattahoochee River, with Atlanta in sight and the plains of central and south Georgia beyond. An understandably upset Jefferson Davis could get no plan from Johnston, who informed the president that Sherman's actions would determine his own. Believing he had no choice, Davis relieved Johnston and replaced him with General John B. Hood, a ferocious combat leader who had had an arm maimed at Gettysburg and a leg amputated at Chickamauga but was untested as an army commander. Hood did his president's bidding and fought vigorously, albeit unsuccessfully, for Atlanta. After six weeks and several hard fights, the city fell to Sherman on September 1.

In the fall of 1864 the Confederates faced a bleak military situation. Lee found himself in trenches at Petersburg with overextended lines and his maneuverability gone. Even so, he tried to recreate the circumstances of 1862 by using the Shenandoah Valley to alarm Washington and lessen the pressure on his beleaguered army. Back in the summer he had dispatched Lieutenant General Jubal A. Early with 10,000 troops he could not really spare to stop a Federal incursion in the Shenandoah. After doing so, Early headed down the valley toward the Potomac. He crossed the Potomac and in mid-July came up to the fortifications guarding the northwestern approach to Washington. Lee's hopes were realized when Grant sent an entire corps, more than 15,000 men, up from Petersburg to counter Early. But 1864 was not 1862; the numerical disparity was too great. Even without that corps, Grant maintained inexorable pressure on Lee. At the same time superior Federal numbers forced Early back into Virginia. There he could not contend with the Federal force under Major General Philip Sheridan. By October Sheridan had both decimated Early's little army and laid waste to the Shenandoah. In the trenches at Petersburg, as Grant kept moving southward, Lee could only watch the thin gray line of defenders becoming thinner.

In the West, General Hood received permission from President Davis to strike at Sherman's rear and his supply lines. As a result, the two major armies marched away from each other. While Hood headed for Tennessee with visions of a dazzling victory, Sherman started for Savannah and the sea with his veteran army and without substantive opposition. Christmas brought vastly different tidings to the two sides. Hood made it to Tennessee, but his gross tactical errors and the Union's numerical superiority wrecked the Army of Tennessee. Battles at Franklin and Nashville claimed more than half of his infantry. After a superior Union army under Major General George H. Thomas smashed the Confederates at Nashville, a battered Army of Tennessee limped back into Mississippi, where for all practical purposes it ceased to exist. Simultaneously Sherman was cutting a wide swath through central and south Georgia on his march to the sea. He gave President Lincoln a special Christmas present, the city of Savannah.

THE IMPACT OF THE WAR

The Confederate military effort did not take place in a vacuum. As the battlefield contests began consistently to go against the gray armies, other areas also experienced severe dislocations and setbacks. The economy went out of control. Inflation, inevitable in the absence of a realistic fiscal policy, seemed propelled by gunpowder. Between mid-summer and the early fall of 1863 prices rose by 58 percent. Between October 1863 and February 1864 the cost of a barrel of flour in Richmond leaped from $70 to $250. The tightening blockade made any item from abroad difficult to obtain and therefore precious. As advancing Union armies overran more and more Confederate territory, less and less was available to produce foodstuffs for fighting men and civilians alike.

The fate of coffee, a favorite drink of southerners regardless of social standing, indicates the deprivations caused by the war and how southerners attempted to cope with them. Few southerners could contemplate a world without coffee. But by 1862 real coffee practically disappeared for all but the wealthiest, and even they could not count on obtaining it. Southerners never quit struggling to concoct a replacement. Almost every imaginable item was substituted for the unavailable coffee bean. Parched corn, rye, wheat, okra seed, sweet potatoes, and blends of them all ended up in Confederates' coffee cups. No one mistook any of these concoctions for real coffee, however.

Confederate reverses also affected politics. Confederate politics became chiefly the politics of personality. In the spring of 1861 southerners had united behind a cause and a president to lead them. Past political loyalties and divisions over secession dissolved in the cheering moment of the birth of the Confederate States of America. Old parties did not survive as identifiable entities, and no new ones were created. Involvement with parties would somehow have seemed unpatriotic. Because the government was not identified with a party, its opponents could not band together in a party of loyal opposition. When natural and normal opposition to administration policies arose, it had no institutional outlet. Without such a forum, opposition to the Davis administration, as well as support of it, became a matter of vituperation.

Consumed by the cause of the Confederacy and determined to take any step he believed necessary to gain its independence, Jefferson Davis neither envisioned nor developed the political dimension of his presidency. He did, after all, face a monumental task. Like George Washington, he had to create a nation where none had existed, but unlike Washington, he did not have the shared experience of a successful revolution as a foundation for his building. Davis's revolution consisted of current events. When Davis supported conscription and other measures that increased the power of the central government, he knew that he was going against the South's tradition of limited government and local power. But to Davis ultimate victory, in his mind the only legitimate goal, required such measures. And anyone who opposed one of his policies, including Vice President Alexander Stephens and strong-minded governors, became not just a political opponent on that issue but an enemy of the cause. In a similar manner Confederates who honestly feared a powerful central government condemned the president as a power-mad despot who did not care about the principles on which the Confederacy was founded. As personal attacks, even vendettas, became commonplace, the Confederate Congress often resembled little more than a shouting hall.

Davis as war leader was unquestionably committed to securing independence for the Confederate States of America. He tried valiantly to rouse the people to carry on the fight. In both 1863 and 1864 he traveled into the Deep South to call on citizens for sacrifice, courage, and determination. His overall view of the Confederate war effort was certainly reasonable, but he permitted personal squabbles to influence command and professional decisions. His bitter conflict with both Joe Johnston and Beauregard made him unwilling to make the best and fullest use of either general. Although both of them must share the blame for their bad relations with the president, he did not rise above their pettiness. His commitment to Braxton Bragg, by contrast, lasted long after Bragg, who had lost the confidence of senior commanders, could function effectively as commanding general of the Army of Tennessee. It is easy to criticize Davis's management of the war, but he confronted an increasingly horrendous situation.

Southern society also felt the impact of war. At the outset whites expressed great enthusiasm for the Confederate enterprise. They saw themselves as the true sons and daughters of the American Revolution and as the only faithful constitutionalists. Moreover, their ministers proclaimed the Confederate enterprise as blessed by God and under His care. From pulpits across the Confederacy the message boomed loud and clear: God was on the side of the South; the Confederates were His chosen people. Cheers supported the political leadership; volunteers populated the military. But the seemingly unstoppable Union advances and the hardships of total war eroded both unity and enthusiasm. Class antagonism surfaced when rich men were permitted to hire substitutes to do their duty for them, and the exemption from conscription for owners and overseers of twenty or more slaves especially rankled. Increasing numbers of men began to avoid military service; desertion came to occupy the attention of almost every Confederate commander. Most deserters did not come from the upper orders of society. Some scholars have argued that desertion did at least as much as battle casualties to undermine the strength of Confederate armies. That claim is extreme, though undoubtedly desertion hurt and hurt severely.

Avoidance of service and desertion had concrete causes. Most Confederate men had gone into the military to defend their homes and their families from invasion. They wanted to protect their liberty. But the tide of the war, particularly after 1863, raised questions of how best to carry out what most Confederate soldiers considered their most sacred mission. By 1864 Union armies were pouring into almost every state. The invading bluecoats were threatening the social organization the Confederacy was formed to preserve. To some men, defense of home and family required them to return to protect their loved ones and property. Confederate defeats spurred desertion. As the situation on the battle lines and the home front became increasingly desperate, the cries of home became louder and louder.

The cries underscored the plight of people on the home front. Trying to obtain his son's release from the army, a father informed the War Department, "If you dount send him home I am bound to louse my crop and cum to suffer. I am eiaghty one years of adge." In her effort to bring her husband back a desperate wife made a forceful case. "Thare is no use," she declared, "in keeping a man thare to kill him and leave widows and poore little orphen children to suffer. . . . My poor children have no home nor no Father." Many soldiers could have but one response to such pleas. One Confederate civilian went straight to the heart of the issue: "What man is there that would stay in the armey and no that his family is sufring at home?" By the last winter of the war thousands of soldiers disappeared from the ranks. To their minds their fundamental duty lay at home, not in the army.

Four years of war did affect the status of southern women. When so many men from every social and economic class went off to fight, women had to assume many of their duties. In far greater numbers than before 1861 women began to manage farms, plantations, and slaves. The wounding and killing of fathers, husbands, brothers, and sons often turned temporary management into what seemed like a permanent condition. Women worked in factories, engaged in charitable activities, and even commented on political matters. Those endeavors surely differed sharply from the experience of the vast majority of women during the prewar years. Even so, very few tried to make any fundamental alterations in their position in southern society. Most were too busy trying to survive to view their activities as somehow threatening conventional definitions of female propriety. As a result, what appeared to be a striking transformation in the economic and social roles of southern women had mostly short-term effects. When the war ended, most women resumed their traditional roles, and old definitions of the proper relations between the sexes prevailed once more. The war did not create a new southern woman.

THE WAR AND SLAVERY

Although the war did not transform the place of women, it had a momentous impact on black southerners. The South's black slaves contributed immensely to the Confederate war effort. On farms and plantations they produced the food that fed the soldiers. Their labor enabled tens of thousands of whites to enter the ranks. An Alabama newspaper underscored this relationship when it observed that slavery permitted the South "to place in the field a force so much larger in proportion to her white population than the North."

Slaves did a lot more, however, than toil in fields. They made up a substantial percentage of the industrial labor force in mines, ironworks, ordnance plants, and other enterprises. Blacks also helped on specific military projects, such as fortifications—work that their owners did not always volunteer. From the beginning the Confederate government recognized the enormous value of slaves. Accordingly, Congress passed legislation permitting the impressment of slaves for military necessity.

Though most slaves remained faithful to their masters through most of the war, new circumstances strained the old relationship and eventually broke it down. When masters marched off to war they left ultimate control of slaves with others, usually overseers or other family members. Then impressment carried slaves off farms and plantations and put them under the control of government officials. Though disruptive, neither of these situations endangered the system. The advance of Union armies, however, did pose a mortal threat to it. Many slaves took the first opportunity that presented itself to escape to Union lines. To prevent such occurrences, numerous owners transferred their slaves to remote locations in the hope of evading Union forces. Even slaves who had been loyal to masters or the surrogates of masters were moved at the approach of blue-clad soldiers, for loyalty to a master stopped when a realistic chance for freedom presented itself.

Developments at Brokenburn Plantation in northeastern Louisiana illustrate just what the war did to slaves and slaveholders. In the spring of 1861 the men went to war with body servants and the public blessings of the house servants and the field hands. In that initial summer Kate Stone, twenty-year-old daughter of the plantation mistress, confided to her diary that "the house servants have been giving a lot of trouble lately—lazy and disobedient. . . . I suppose the excitement in the air has infected them." When the Yankees moved against Vicksburg, just to the east of Brokenburn, during the summer of 1862, Kate worried that they would come and take the family's slaves. Her mother told all the male slaves to hide from the Yankee soldiers. "We think they will," she consoled herself. But in early July, Kate admitted, "Generally when told to run away from the soldiers, they go right to them." In the spring of 1863: "All the Negroes are running away now." By this time many of the Brokenburn slaves had been moved to rented property in the western part of the state. During the summer the remaining whites and blacks headed west. Brokenburn had become a casualty of the war.

By the spring of 1865 the Confederate States of America itself was succumbing. The hungry, ragged veterans in Lee's army and the broken corporal's guard that remained from the Army of Tennessee could no longer hold against the powerful armies of Grant and Sherman. From the trenches at Petersburg, Lee told Davis that he would soon be forced to give up Petersburg, and that move would require the evacuation of Richmond. Called back to command the skeleton of the Army of Tennessee in North Carolina, Joe Johnston could hardly even slow down Sherman, who in the winter had laid waste to South Carolina on his way from Savannah to link up with Grant in Virginia.

Jefferson Davis did not want to contemplate surrender. In a last desperate effort to gain Confederate independence he severed the powerful cultural forces that had given the antebellum South its basic identity and had brought about the creation of the Confederate States of America. At least since the Revolution white southerners had been unable to separate their liberty from their institution of black slavery. Slavery governed the definition of liberty. But in that final, anguished winter Davis split what previously had been unsplittable; he separated liberty from slavery. He reluctantly concluded that to secure liberty the Confederacy must jettison slavery. In this last lunge Davis reached in two directions at once. He dispatched a confidential agent to Europe with instructions to offer Britain and France emancipation in turn for their recognition of the Confederacy. England said never. It was too late. To arrest the disintegration of his armies, Davis simultaneously advocated the enlistment of slaves as soldiers. When one of his generals had broached the idea a year earlier, he had rebuffed it. But in March, with Lee's support, Davis prevailed on a reluctant Congress to enact a law that would permit black slaves to don gray uniforms. The bill did not, however, offer emancipation in exchange for military service. Whether or not slaves would have fought for their masters will never be known. The war ended before the formation of any black regiments.

*T*HE END

The end came in April and May. On April 9, 1865, Palm Sunday, at Appomattox Courthouse, eighty-five miles southwest of Richmond, Lee surrendered the Army

COLUMBIA DESTROYED (Kean Archives, Philadelphia)

of Northern Virginia to Grant. Some two weeks later, just outside Durham, North Carolina, Joe Johnston capitulated to Sherman. By May 4 all Confederate forces east of the Mississippi had surrendered. Still President Davis refused to give up. Calling for continued resistance, he retreated through the Carolinas in the hope of getting to the Trans-Mississippi and carrying on the war from there. But in south Georgia on May 10 a Union cavalry detachment captured Davis and his party. Finally on May 26 General Edmund Kirby-Smith surrendered his Trans-Mississippi army. The Confederate States of America ceased to exist.

Although arguments about whether or not the Confederacy could win abound, its defeat was not foreordained. At least three possibilities offered a chance for a different result. The first two would have involved European intervention. Help could have come at the very beginning of the war if Great Britain had refused to permit the Union to blockade Confederate ports. More likely, Great Britain would have acted in the autumn of 1862 had the Confederates won on the battlefield in Kentucky and Maryland. Had Lee triumphed at Antietam, Great Britain might have moved in such a way as to impel Lincoln to make peace with an independent Confederacy. The third chance occurred in the hot, bloody summer of 1864. If Grant had concluded that enough Union blood had soaked the Virginia ground and had followed his predecessors in retreat, or if Sherman had been stopped before Atlanta, then a political shift could easily have occurred in the North which would have forced Lincoln out of office in favor of a peace government. That none of those possibilities turned out to favor the Confederacy does not mean they did not exist. The proper conclusion to draw is that the results on specific battlefields and the character and ability of particular generals and leaders had an enormous impact on the outcome.

RICHMOND IN RUINS (Library of Congress)

Many reasons explain the Union victory and the Confederate defeat. The North enjoyed a substantial advantage in two critical areas—a significantly larger population and a vastly more powerful industrial machine. Neither of them, not even both together, guarantees military success or failure. During both the American Revolution and the Vietnam war the greater power lost. In the 1770s and 1780s America prevailed over Great Britain, then the leading military and industrial power in the world. Almost 200 years later in the 1960s and 1970s the United States, with almost unlimited military and industrial strength, failed to subdue North Vietnam. The critical difference in war is not material superiority alone but the will to use that superiority. In neither the American Revolution nor the Vietnam war did the stronger side throw all of its might against the weaker with absolute determination to win. But that is precisely what Abraham Lincoln did. He never wavered; he would never relent or hold back. He was willing to use his advantage to the fullest. And he stayed in the fight until he found commanders who had a resoluteness that matched his own. With that kind of leadership the side with the stronger battalions and the larger factories prevailed.

Defeated in open battle, the Confederates did not try to keep their cause alive through guerilla warfare. Having experienced the brute force of the Union military juggernaut, which had blasted their armies and destroyed their land, they believed they had made their stand and had nothing left to prove. Moreover, they thought guerilla activities might very well lead to anarchy and the social disintegration of their homeland. Without question racial considerations were critical in this assessment. Although no one knew where the elimination of slavery might lead race relations, anxiety about the racial situation worked mightily against any cause that could end in lawless marauding in the South.

The South in the spring of 1865 was a broken land. The Confederate experience had cost the South dearly. Slavery and the hundreds of millions of dollars invested in it disappeared with the Confederacy. Physical destruction marred the southern landscape like an ugly scar. Two-thirds of the railroads, the bulk of the industrial plant, countless bridges and buildings, thousands of homes, a huge quantity of livestock—all were destroyed during the war. The human price staggers the imagination. With 260,000 men killed and at least that many more wounded, few white families did not know the grief of a dead or maimed father, husband, brother, or son. Confederate casualties accounted for almost 9 percent of the southern white population. Though the Union suffered 360,000 dead, its casualties did not quite reach 3 percent of the population. In World War II American casualties amounted to only a fraction over one-half of 1 percent of the population. Trying to cope with an uncharted racial course and with massive physical and human devastation, southerners, black and white, faced an uncertain future.

$\mathcal{B}$iographies

❖

Biographies of notable individuals provide much information and have considerable value. The following is an alphabetical listing (by subject) of biographies of many of the major figures in southern history. In appropriate instances more than one biography is cited. Published diaries, memoirs, and collections of letters are covered in the Bibliographical Essay.

Joseph R. Anderson
Charles R. Dew, *Ironmaker to the Confederacy: Joseph R. Anderson and the Tredegar Ironworks* (New Haven, Conn., 1966).

Pierre G. T. Beauregard
T. Harry Williams, *P. G. T. Beauregard: Napoleon in Gray* (Baton Rouge, La., 1955).

John Bell
Joseph H. Parks, *John Bell of Tennessee* (Baton Rouge, La., 1950).

Daniel Boone
John M. Faragher, *Daniel Boone: The Life and Legend of an American Pioneer* (New York, 1992).

Braxton Bragg
Grady McWhiney and Judith L. Hallock, *Braxton Bragg and Confederate Defeat*, 2 vols. (New York and Tuscaloosa, Ala., 1969, 1991).

John C. Breckinridge
William C. Davis, *Breckinridge: Statesman, Soldier, Symbol* (Baton Rouge, La., 1974).

William Byrd II
Kenneth A. Lockridge, *The Diary, and Life, of William Byrd II of Virginia* (Chapel Hill, N.C., 1987).
Pierre Marambaud, *William Byrd of Westover, 1674–1744* (Charlottesville, Va., 1971).

John C. Calhoun
Irving H. Bartlett, *John C. Calhoun: A Biography* (New York, 1993).
John Niven, *John C. Calhoun and the Price of Union: A Biography* (Baton Rouge, La., 1988).
Charles M. Wiltse, *John C. Calhoun*, 3 vols. (Indianapolis, Ind., 1944–1951).

Robert Carter
Louis Morton, *Robert Carter of Nomini Hall: A Virginia Tobacco Planter of the Eighteenth Century* (Williamsburg, Va., 1945).

William A. Caruthers
Curtis C. Davis, *Chronicler of the Cavaliers; A Life of the Virginia Novelist, Dr. William A. Caruthers* (Richmond, Va., 1953).

Mary Boykin Chesnut
    Elisabeth Muhlenfeld, *Mary Boykin Chesnut: A Biography* (Baton Rouge, La., 1981).
Henry Clay
    Robert V. Remini, *Henry Clay: Statesman for the Union* (New York, 1991).
Thomas Cooper
    Dumas Malone, *The Public Life of Thomas Cooper* (New Haven, Conn., 1926).
William H. Crawford
    Chase C. Mooney, *William H. Crawford, 1772–1834* (Lexington, Ky., 1974).
John J. Crittenden
    Albert D. Kirwan, *John J. Crittenden: The Struggle for the Union* (Lexington, Ky., 1962).
Jefferson Davis
    William C. Davis, *Jefferson Davis: The Man and His Hour* (New York, 1991).
Joseph Davis
    Janet S. Hermann, *Joseph E. Davis: Pioneer Patriarch* (Jackson, Miss., 1990).
James D. B. De Bow
    Otis C. Skipper, *J. D. B. De Bow, Magazinist of the Old South* (Athens, Ga., 1958).
Stephen A. Douglas
    Robert W. Johannsen, *Stephen A. Douglas* (New York, 1973).
Frederick Douglass
    William S. McFeely, *Frederick Douglass* (New York, 1990).
    Dickson J. Preston, *Young Frederick Douglass: The Maryland Years* (Baltimore, 1980).
George Fitzhugh
    Harvey Wish, *George Fitzhugh: Propagandist of the Old South* (Baton Rouge, La., 1943).
Issac Franklin
    Wendell H. Stephenson, *Issac Franklin: Slave Trader and Planter of the Old South* (Baton Rouge, La., 1938).
Christopher Gadsden
    E. Stanly Godbold, Jr., and Robert H. Woody, *Christopher Gadsden and the American Revolution* (Knoxville, Tenn., 1982).
Bernardo de Gálvez
    Jack D. L. Holmes, *Galvez* (Birmingham, Ala., 1980).
Josiah Gorgas
    Frank E. Vandiver, *Ploughshares into Swords: Josiah Gorgas and Confederate Ordnance* (Austin, Tex. , 1952).
Nathanael Greene
    Theodore Thayer, *Nathanael Greene: Strategist of the American Revolution* (New York, 1960).
William Gregg
    Broadus Mitchell, *William Gregg: Factory Master of the Old South* (Chapel Hill, N.C., 1928).
James H. Hammond
    Drew G. Faust, *James Henry Hammond and the Old South: A Design for Mastery* (Baton Rouge, La., 1982).
George Washington Harris
    Milton H. Rickels, *George Washington Harris* (New York, 1965).
Patrick Henry
    Richard R. Beeman, *Patrick Henry: A Biography* (New York, 1974).
George F. Holmes
    Neal C. Gillispie, *The Collapse of Orthodoxy: The Intellectual Ordeal of George Frederick Holmes* (Charlottesville, Va., 1972).

John B. Hood
>   Richard M. McMurry, *John Bell Hood and the War for Southern Independence* (Lexington, Ky., 1982).

Johnson J. Hooper
>   William S. Hoole, *Alias Simon Suggs: The Life and Times of Johnson Jones Hooper* (University, Ala., 1952).

Andrew Jackson
>   James C. Curtis, *Andrew Jackson and the Search for Vindication* (Boston, 1976).
>   Robert V. Remini, *Andrew Jackson,* 3 vols. (New York, 1977–1984).

Thomas J. "Stonewall" Jackson
>   Lenoir Chambers, *Stonewall Jackson,* 2 vols. (New York, 1959).

Thomas Jefferson
>   Noble E. Cunningham, *In Pursuit of Reason: The Life of Thomas Jefferson* (Baton Rouge, La., 1987).
>   Dumas Malone, *Jefferson and His Time,* 6 vols. (Boston, 1948–1981).
>   Merrill Peterson, *Thomas Jefferson and the New Nation: A Biography* (New York, 1970).

Andrew Johnson
>   Hans Trefousse, *Andrew Johnson: A Biography* (New York, 1989).

Albert S. Johnston
>   Charles P. Roland, *Albert Sidney Johnston: Soldier of Three Republics* (Austin, Tex., 1964).

Joseph E. Johnston
>   Craig L. Symonds, *Joseph E. Johnston: A Civil War Biography* (New York, 1992).

Joseph Jones
>   James O. Breeden, *Joseph Jones, M.D.* (Lexington, Ky., 1975).

John P. Kennedy
>   J. V. Ridgely, *John Pendleton Kennedy* (New York, 1966).

Edmund Kirby-Smith
>   Joseph H. Parks, *General Edmund Kirby Smith, C.S.A.* (Baton Rouge, La., 1954).

Henry Laurens
>   David D. Wallace, *The Life of Henry Laurens* (New York, 1915).

Joseph LeConte
>   Lester D. Stephens, *Joseph LeConte: Gentle Prophet of Evolution* (Baton Rouge, La., 1982).

Robert E. Lee
>   Thomas L. Connelly, *The Marble Man: Robert E. Lee and His Image in American Society* (New York, 1977).
>   Douglas S. Freeman, *R. E. Lee,* 4 vols. (New York, 1934–1935).
>   Emory M. Thomas, *Robert E. Lee: A Biography* (New York, 1995).

Francis Lieber
>   Frank Freidel, *Francis Lieber: Nineteenth-Century Liberal* (Baton Rouge, La., 1947).

Abraham Lincoln
>   David Herbert Donald, *Lincoln* (New York, 1995).

Augustus B. Longstreet
>   John D. Wade, *Augustus Baldwin Longstreet: A Study in the Development of Culture in the South* (New York, 1924).

Rawlins Lowndes
>   Carl J. Vipperman, *The Rise of Rawlins Lowndes, 1721–1800* (Columbia, S.C., 1978).

Lachlan McIntosh
>   Harvey H. Jackson, *Lachlan McIntosh and the Politics of Revolutionary Georgia* (Athens, Ga., 1979).

Nathaniel Macon
    William E. Dodd, *The Life of Nathaniel Macon* (Raleigh, N.C., 1903).
James Madison
    Irving Brant, *James Madison,* 6 vols. (Indianapolis, Ind., 1941–1961).
    Ralph Ketcham, *James Madison: A Biography* (New York, 1971).
    Jack N. Rakove, *James Madison and the Creation of the American Republic* (Glenview, Ill., 1990).
Stephen R. Mallory
    Joseph T. Durkin, *Stephen R. Mallory: Confederate Navy Chief* (Chapel Hill, N.C., 1954).
John Marshall
    Albert Beveridge, *The Life of John Marshall,* 4 vols. (Boston and New York, 1916–1919).
    Francis N. Stites, *John Marshall: Defender of the Constitution* (Boston, 1987).
George Mason
    Helen H. Miller, *George Mason: Gentleman Revolutionary* (Chapel Hill, N.C., 1975).
James Monroe
    Harry Ammon, *James Monroe: The Quest for National Identity* (New York, 1971).
Daniel Morgan
    Don Higginbotham, *Daniel Morgan, Revolutionary Rifleman* (Chapel Hill, N.C., 1961).
Josiah Nott
    Reginald Horsman, *Josiah Nott of Mobile: Southerner, Physician, and Racial Theorist* (Baton Rouge, La., 1987).
James Oglethorpe
    Phinizy Spalding, *Oglethorpe in America* (Chicago, 1977).
Charles Cotesworth Pinckney
    Marvin R. Zahniser, *Charles Cotesworth Pinckney: Founding Father* (Chapel Hill, N.C., 1967).
James K. Polk
    Charles G. Sellers, Jr., *James K. Polk,* 2 vols. (Princeton, N.J., 1957–1966).
John A. Quitman
    Robert E. May, *John A. Quitman: Old South Crusader* (Baton Rouge, La., 1985).
John Randolph of Roanoke
    Robert Dawidoff, *The Education of John Randolph* (New York, 1979).
Robert Barnwell Rhett
    Laura A. White, *Robert Barnwell Rhett, Father of Secession* (New York, 1931).
Thomas Ritchie
    Charles H. Ambler, *Thomas Ritchie: A Study in Virginia Politics* (Richmond, Va., 1913).
Edmund Ruffin
    David F. Allmendinger, *Ruffin: Family and Reform in the Old South* (New York, 1989).
    William Mathew, *Edmund Ruffin and the Crisis of Slavery in the South: The Failure of Agricultural Reform* (Athens, Ga., 1988).
Winfield Scott
    Charles W. Elliott, *Winfield Scott: The Soldier and the Man* (New York, 1937).
William Gilmore Simms
    John C. Guilds, *Simms: A Literary Life* (Fayetteville, Ark., 1992).
John Smith
    Philip L. Barbour, *The Three Worlds of Captain John Smith* (New York, 1964).
    Alden T. Vaughan, *American Genesis: Captain John Smith and the Founding of Virginia* (Boston, 1975).

Alexander H. Stephens

Thomas E. Schott, *Alexander H. Stephens of Georgia: A Biography* (Baton Rouge, La., 1988).

Roger B. Taney

Carl B. Swisher, *Roger B. Taney* (New York, 1935).

John Taylor of Caroline

Robert E. Shalhope, *John Taylor of Caroline: Pastoral Republican* (Columbia, S.C., 1980).

Zachary Taylor

K. Jack Bauer, *Zachary Taylor: Soldier, Planter, Statesman of the Old Southwest* (Baton Rouge, La., 1985).

Holman Hamilton, *Zachary Taylor,* 2 vols. (Indianapolis, Ind., 1941–1951).

James H. Thornwell

James O. Farmer, Jr., *The Metaphysical Confederacy: James Henley Thornwell and the Synthesis of Southern Values* (Macon, Ga., 1986).

Nathaniel Beverly Tucker

Robert J. Brugger, *Beverly Tucker: Heart over Mind in the Old South* (Baltimore, 1978).

John Tyler

Robert Seager II, *And Tyler Too: A Biography of John and Julia Gardiner Tyler* (New York, 1963).

Martin Van Buren

John Niven, *Martin Van Buren and the Romantic Age of American Politics* (New York, 1983).

George Washington

John R. Alden, *George Washington: A Biography* (Baton Rouge, La., 1984).

James T. Flexner, *George Washington: A Biography,* 4 vols. (Boston, 1965–1972).

Douglas S. Freeman, *George Washington: A Biography,* 7 vols. (completed by John A. Carroll and Mary W. Ashworth; New York, 1948–1957).

Eli Whitney

Constance M. Green, *Eli Whitney and the Birth of American Technology* (Boston, 1956).

Bibliographical Essay

❖

GENERAL

No full bibliography of southern history exists. For the period between 1820 and 1860, however, Fletcher M. Green and J. Isaac Copeland, *The Old South* (Arlington Heights, Ill., 1980), is fairly comprehensive, though the scholarship it incorporates obviously stops some years ago. In this essay we make no claim for inclusiveness; at least another volume of equal length would be required to discuss thoroughly the vast body of writing on southern history. Our goal here is to provide a guide to the major literature on the history of the South. The biographies of notable individuals already listed will be cited in brief form again only where they are especially relevant.

For any student of the South several basic reference works provide indispensable assistance. David C. Roller and Robert W. Twyman, eds., *The Encyclopedia of Southern History* (Baton Rouge, La., 1979), in almost 1,400 pages, treats an incredible number and variety of topics. Charles R. Wilson and William Ferris, eds., *Encyclopedia of Southern Culture* (Chapel Hill, N.C., 1989), in more than 1,500 pages, reflects an extraordinarily broad definition of culture, with entries ranging from "architecture" to "wrestling." For scholarly assessments of the historical literature, both Arthur S. Link and Rembert W. Patrick, eds., *Writing Southern History: Essays in Historiography in Honor of Fletcher M. Green* (Baton Rouge, La., 1967), and John B. Boles and Evelyn Thomas Nolen, eds., *Interpreting Southern History: Historiographical Essays in Honor of Sanford W. Higginbotham* (Baton Rouge, La., 1987), are essential. For superb coverage of southern literary history from the colonial era forward, consult the older Jay B. Hubbell, *The South in American Literature, 1607–1900* (Durham, N.C., 1954), and the more modern Louis D. Rubin, Jr., et al., eds., *The History of Southern Literature* (Baton Rouge, La., 1985). *Historical Statistics of the United States: Colonial Times to 1970,* 2 vols. (Washington, D.C., 1975), and Donald B. Dodd and Wynelle S. Dodd, comps., *Historical Statistics of the South, 1790–1970* (University, Ala., 1973), provide ready access to statistical data taken overwhelmingly from United States censuses. At least one of these titles is relevant to every subject discussed in this book.

THE COLONIES AND THE REVOLUTION

The best general study of the early British colonial South is still Wesley Frank Craven, *The Southern Colonies in the Seventeenth Century, 1670–1689* (Baton Rouge, La., 1949). No comparable book is yet available for the eighteenth century. Two books with valuable perspectives on the southern colonies focus on cultural transformation and development: Jack P. Greene, *Pursuits of Happiness: The Social Development of Early British Colonies and the Formation of American Culture* (Chapel Hill, N.C., 1988), and David Hackett Fischer, *Albion's Seed: Four British Folkways in America* (New York, 1989). T. H. Breen, ed., *Shaping Southern Society: The Colonial Experience* (New York, 1976), brings together notable articles on the colonial South. Excellent introductions to the individual colonies can be found in a modern series covering all of the original British colonies. The volumes dealing with the South include Warren W. Billings et al., *Colonial Virginia: A History* (White Plains, N.Y., 1986); Kenneth Coleman, *Colonial Georgia: A History* (New York, 1976); Aubrey C. Land, *Colonial Maryland: A History* (Millwood, N.Y., 1981); Hugh T. Lefler and William S. Powell, *Colonial North Carolina: A History* (New York, 1973); and Robert M. Weir, *Colonial South Carolina: A History* (Millwood, N.Y., 1983).

The number of studies on the environment and on the first Americans is growing. On ecological history in general, see Albert E. Cowdrey, *The Land, This South: An Environmental History* (Lexington, Ky., 1983). Timothy Silver also addresses ecological history in *A New Face in the Countryside: Indians, Colonists, and Slaves in South Atlantic Forests, 1500–1800* (Cambridge, Eng., and New York, 1990). On the Indians, see Tom Hatley, *The Dividing Paths: Cherokees and South Carolinians through the Era of Revolution* (New York, 1993); Charles M. Hudson's massive *Southeastern Indians* (Knoxville, Tenn., 1976); James H. Merrell, *The Indians' New World: Catawbas and Their Neighbors from European Contact through the Era of Removal* (Chapel Hill, N.C., 1989); Peter H. Wood et al., eds., *Powhatan's Mantle: Indians in the Colonial Southeast* (Lincoln, Neb., 1989), which contains particularly informative essays; J. Leitch Wright, Jr., *The Only Land They Knew: The Tragic Story of the American Indians in the Old South* (New York, 1981), which concentrates heavily on the colonial period and also makes controversial claims for Indian populations. In three books that cover all the colonies, not just the southern ones, James Axtell has argued for the centrality of the interaction between the Europeans and the natives: *The European and the Indian: Essays in the Ethnohistory of Colonial North America* (New York, 1981); *The Invasion Within: The Contest of Cultures in Colonial North America* (New York, 1985); and *After Columbus: Essays in the Ethnohistory of Colonial North America* (New York, 1988).

Exploration has commanded the attention of several historians. Samuel Eliot Morison, *The European Discovery of America: The Northern Voyages, A.D. 500–1600* (New York, 1971), is wonderful on Spanish and French exploration as well as on English efforts before 1600. Paul E. Hoffman focuses on the earliest Spanish forays in *A New Andalucia and a Way to the Orient: The American Southeast during the Sixteenth Century* (Baton Rouge, La., 1990). On the first serious English attempt at colonization, see David B. Quinn, *Set Fair for Roanoke: Voyages and Colonies, 1584–1606* (Chapel Hill, N.C., 1985). Still useful is Verner W. Crane, *The Southern Frontier, 1670–1732* (Ann Arbor, Mich., 1929); also see Alan V. Briceland, *Westward from Virginia: The Exploration of the Virginia-Carolina Frontier, 1650–1710* (Charlottesville, Va., 1987).

Several books illuminate developments in the French and Spanish colonies. David J. Weber, *The Spanish Frontier in North America* (New Haven, Conn., 1992), is thorough on Florida and deals with Spanish Louisiana. Two recent books have opened new avenues in the study of colonial Louisiana: Gwendolyn M. Hall, *Africans in Colonial Louisiana: The De-*

velopment of Afro-Creole Culture in the Eighteenth Century (Baton Rouge, La., 1992), the product of remarkable research, and Daniel H. Usner, Jr., *Indians, Settlers, and Slaves in a Frontier Exchange Economy: The Lower Mississippi Valley before 1783* (Chapel Hill, N.C., 1992), which emphasizes interaction among the three groups. Also helpful are John G. Clark, *New Orleans, 1718–1812: An Economic History* (Baton Rouge, La., 1970); John P. Moore, *Revolt in Louisiana: The Spanish Occupation, 1766–1770* (Baton Rouge, La., 1976); and Charles E. O'Neill, *Church and State in French Colonial Louisiana: Policy and Politics to 1732* (New Haven, Conn., 1966). Three volumes of Marcel Giraud's detailed five-volume study *A History of French Louisiana* have thus far been translated into English: Vol. 1, *The Reign of Louis XIV, 1698–1715* (Baton Rouge, La., 1974); Vol. 2, *Years of Transition, 1715–1717* (Baton Rouge, La., 1993); and Vol. 5, *The Company of the Indies, 1723–1731* (Baton Rouge, La., 1991).

John J. McCusker and Russell R. Menard, *The Economy of British North America, 1607–1789* (Chapel Hill, N.C., 1985), is the best treatment of the colonial economy. Joyce E. Chaplin, *An Anxious Pursuit: Agricultural Innovation and Modernity in the Lower South, 1730–1815* (Chapel Hill, N.C., 1993), argues for the dominance of commercialism. Ronald Hoffman et al., eds., *The Economy of Early America: The Revolutionary Period, 1763–1790* (Charlottesville, Va., 1988), collects helpful articles. On economic matters in specific colonies, see Paul G. E. Clemens, *The Atlantic Economy and Colonial Maryland's Eastern Shore: From Tobacco to Grain* (Ithaca, N.Y., 1980); Converse D. Clowse, *Economic Beginnings in Colonial South Carolina, 1670–1730* (Columbia, S.C., 1971); Peter A. Coclanis, *The Shadow of a Dream: Economic Life and Death in the South Carolina Low Country, 1670–1920* (New York, 1989), a superb book; John C. Rainbolt, *From Prescription to Persuasion: Manipulation of Eighteenth [Seventeenth] Century Virginia Economy* (Port Washington, N.Y., 1974).

Social, cultural, and intellectual life has drawn considerable recent attention. On intellectual matters, a good beginning is Richard Beale Davis's encyclopedic *Intellectual Life in the Colonial South, 1585–1763*, 3 vols. (Knoxville, Tenn., 1978). Sumptuously illustrated, Jessie Poesch, *The Art of the Old South: Painting, Sculpture, Architecture, and the Products of Craftsmen* (New York, 1983), covers an important area. Mills Lane's magnificent *Architecture of the Old South* (New York, 1993) treats the colonial era as well as the antebellum period. Although, as the following paragraphs show, much recent and innovative work has been done on the social history of the southern colonies, Carl Bridenbaugh, *Myths and Realities: Societies of the Colonial South* (Baton Rouge, La., 1952), is still the only general study. Likewise Julia C. Spruill, *Women's Life and Work in the Southern Colonies* (Chapel Hill, N.C., 1938), remains the only overall account, though many of the titles discussed below address the role of women in southern society. Also see Winthrop D. Jordan and Sheila L. Skemp, eds., *Race and Family in the Colonial South* (Jackson, Miss., 1987).

Studies that focus on specific colonies have great value. Edmund S. Morgan, *American Slavery, American Freedom: The Ordeal of Colonial Virginia* (New York, 1975), at the same time the best study of seventeenth-century Virginia and a brilliant investigation of the origins of slavery, and Rhys Isaac, *The Transformation of Virginia, 1740–1790* (Chapel Hill, N.C., 1982), which uses the perspective and methodology of cultural anthropology, have been exceptionally influential. Others that merit attention include Richard R. Beeman, *The Evolution of the Southern Backcountry: A Case Study of Lunenberg County, Virginia, 1746–1832* (Philadelphia, 1984); T. H. Breen, *Tobacco Culture: The Mentality of the Great Tidewater Planters on the Eve of Revolution* (Princeton, N.J., 1985); Lois G. Carr et al., *Robert Cole's World: Agriculture and Society in Early Maryland* (Chapel Hill, N.C., 1991); Wesley Craven, *White, Red, and Black: The Seventeenth-Century Virginian* (Charlottesville, Va., 1971); Harold E. Davis, *The Fledgling Province: Social and Cultural Life in Colonial Georgia, 1733–1776* (Chapel Hill, N.C., 1976); Richard Davis, *Literature and Society in Early Virginia, 1608–1840* (Baton Rouge, La., 1973); Alan Gallay, *The Formation of a Planter Elite: Jonathan Bryan and the Southern Colonial Frontier* (Athens, Ga., 1989); Wesley M. Gewehr, *The Great Awakening in Virginia, 1740–1790*

(Durham, N.C., 1930); Harvey H. Jackson and Phinizy Spalding, eds., *Forty Years of Diversity: Essays on Colonial Georgia* (Athens, Ga., 1984); Rachel N. Klein, *Unification of a Slave State: The Rise of the Planter Class in the South Carolina Backcountry, 1760–1808* (Chapel Hill, N.C., 1990); Aubrey Land et al., eds., *Law, Society, and Politics in Early Maryland* (Baltimore, 1977); Gloria Main, *Tobacco Colony: Life in Early Maryland, 1650–1720* (Princeton, N.J., 1983); James R. Perry, *The Formation of a Society on Virginia's Eastern Shore, 1615–1655* (Chapel Hill, N.C., 1990); George C. Rogers, Jr., *Charleston in the Age of the Pinckneys* (Norman, Okla., 1969); Darrett B. Rutman and Anita H. Rutman, *A Place in Time: Middlesex County, Virginia, 1650–1750* (New York, 1984); Aaron M. Shatzman, *Servants into Planters: The Origins of an American Image—Land Acquisition and Status Mobility in Seventeenth-Century South Carolina* (New York, 1989); Thad W. Tate and David L. Ammerman, eds., *The Chesapeake in the Seventeenth Century: Essays on Anglo-American Society* (Chapel Hill, N.C., 1979); Albert H. Tillson, Jr., *Gentry and Common Folk: Political Culture on a Virginia Frontier, 1740–1789* (Lexington, Ky., 1991); Stephen S. Webb, *1676: The End of American Independence* (New York, 1984), which has considerable material on seventeenth-century Virginia as part of a full, though controversial, treatment of Bacon's Rebellion; and Louis B. Wright, *The First Gentlemen of Virginia: Intellectual Qualities of the Early Colonial Ruling Class* (San Marino, Calif., 1940). Additionally, the first three volumes of Douglas Freeman's mammoth *George Washington* contain an enormous amount of material on social, economic, and political matters in eighteenth-century Virginia.

Studies of slavery deal with the social and cultural life of whites as well as blacks. Three of them have special significance: David Brion Davis, *The Problem of Slavery in the Age of Revolution, 1770–1823* (Ithaca, N.Y., 1975), a probing analysis of the question of slavery in the midst of revolution for liberty; Winthrop Jordan, *White over Black: American Attitudes toward the Negro, 1550–1812* (Chapel Hill, N.C., 1968), an impressive study of racial perceptions; and Edmund Morgan, *American Slavery, American Freedom*. Other worthy and informative books include Ira Berlin and Ronald Hoffman, eds., *Slavery and Freedom in the Age of the American Revolution* (Charlottesville, Va., 1983), a valuable collection of essays; Sylvia R. Frey, *Water from the Rock: Black Resistance in a Revolutionary Age* (Princeton, N.J., 1992), which illuminates the slave world; Gwendolyn Hall, *Africans in Colonial Louisiana*; Allan Kulikoff, *Tobacco and Slaves: The Development of Southern Cultures in the Chesapeake* (Chapel Hill, N.C., 1986); Daniel C. Littlefield, *Rice and Slaves: Ethnicity and the Slave Trade in Colonial South Carolina* (Baton Rouge, La., 1981); Duncan J. MacLeod, *Slavery, Race, and the American Revolution* (Cambridge, Eng., 1974); Gerald W. Mullin, *Flight and Rebellion: Slave Resistance in Eighteenth-Century Virginia* (New York, 1972); Mechal Sobel, *The World They Made Together: Black and White Values in Eighteenth-Century Virginia* (Princeton, N.J., 1987), which stresses the impact of each race and culture on the other; Betty Wood, *Slavery in Colonial Georgia, 1730–1775* (Athens, Ga., 1984); and Peter Wood, *Black Majority: Negroes in Colonial South Carolina from 1670 through the Stono Rebellion* (New York, 1974), which emphasizes the contribution of the slaves to the colony's economic success.

On African slavery, consult Paul E. Lovejoy, *Transformation in Slavery: A History of Slavery in Africa* (New York, 1983); Suzanne Miers and Igor Kopytoff, eds., *Slavery in Africa: Historical and Anthropological Perspectives* (Madison, Wis., 1977); and John Thornton, *Africa and Africans in the Making of the Atlantic World, 1400–1680* (Cambridge, Eng., 1992). Philip D. Curtin's *Atlantic Slave Trade: A Census* (Madison, Wis., 1969) revolutionized the quantitative dimension of the slave trade, while James A. Rawley, *The Trans-Atlantic Slave Trade* (New York, 1981), contains a full, descriptive account of that trade.

Political subjects are treated in numerous books. In *Liberty and Slavery: Southern Politics to 1860* (New York, 1983), William J. Cooper, Jr., presents an interpretive analysis. Jack Greene, *The Quest for Power: The Lower Houses of Assembly in the Southern Royal Colonies, 1689–1776* (Chapel Hill, N.C., 1963), provides superb treatment of a major theme. See also

William W. Abbott, *The Royal Governors of Georgia, 1754–1775* (Chapel Hill, N.C., 1959); Richard M. Brown, *The South Carolina Regulators* (Cambridge, Mass., 1963); A. Roger Ekrich, *"Poor Carolina": Politics and Society in Colonial North Carolina, 1729–1776* (Chapel Hill, N.C., 1981); David W. Jordan, *Foundations of Representative Government in Maryland, 1632–1715* (Cambridge, Eng., 1987); Eugene Sirmans, *Colonial South Carolina: A Political History* (Chapel Hill, N.C., 1966); and Charles S. Sydnor, *American Revolutionaries in the Making: Political Practices in Washington's Virginia* (New York, 1965), a sparkling account of political culture in one state.

For the Revolutionary era one must always recognize that the southern colonies acted in conjunction with the northern colonies. Thus major works on the period contain much of value on the southern experience. Bernard Bailyn, *The Ideological Origins of the American Revolution* (Cambridge, Mass., 1967) and *The Origins of American Politics* (New York, 1968), along with Gordon S. Wood, *The Creation of the American Republic, 1776–1789* (Chapel Hill, N.C., 1969) and *The Radicalism of the American Revolution* (New York, 1992), discuss fundamental questions of ideology and politics. Edmund Morgan and Helen M. Morgan, *The Stamp Act Crisis: Prologue to Revolution* (Chapel Hill, N.C., 1953), is the standard account. Edmund Morgan's *Inventing the People: The Rise of Popular Sovereignty in England and America* (New York, 1988) illuminates the origins of what became a basic principle of the Revolution; in addition, see his engaging and enlightening *Meaning of Independence: John Adams, George Washington, and Thomas Jefferson* (Charlottesville, Va., 1976). Also helpful are Robert A. Becker, *Revolution, Reform, and the Politics of American Taxation, 1763–1783* (Baton Rouge, La., 1980); Richard Beeman et al., eds., *Beyond Confederation: Origins of the Constitution and American National Identity* (Chapel Hill, N.C., 1987), a first-rate collection of essays; H. James Henderson, *Party Politics in the Continental Congress* (New York, 1974); Alice H. Jones, *Wealth of a Nation to Be: The American Colonies on the Eve of the Revolution* (New York, 1980), an investigation of wealth in Revolutionary America; Forrest McDonald, *Novus Ordo Seclorum: The Intellectual Origins of the Constitution* (Lawrence, Kans., 1985); Pauline S. Maier, *The Old Revolutionaries: Political Lives in the Age of Samuel Adams* (New York, 1980); Jackson T. Main, *The Social Structure of Revolutionary America* (Princeton, N.J., 1965); Peter Onuf, *Statehood and Union: A History of the Northwest Ordinance* (Bloomington, Ind., 1987); J. G. A. Pocock, *The Machiavellian Moment: Florentine Political Thought and the Atlantic Republican Tradition* (Princeton, N.J., 1975); Jack N. Rakove, *The Beginnings of National Politics: An Interpretive History of the Continental Congress* (New York, 1979); and Garry Wills, *Inventing America: Jefferson's Declaration of Independence* (New York, 1978). There is no good study of southern loyalists or Tories, though Robert S. Lambert, *South Carolina Loyalists in the American Revolution* (Columbia, S.C., 1987), covers one state. Paul H. Smith, *Loyalists and Redcoats: A Study in British Revolutionary Policy* (Chapel Hill, N.C., 1964), discusses the importance the British placed on the Loyalists. Staughton Lynd, *Class Conflict, Slavery, and the United States Constitution: Ten Essays* (Indianapolis, Ind., 1968), and Donald Robinson, *Slavery in the Structure of American Politics, 1765–1820* (New York, 1979), make often exaggerated claims for the centrality of slavery. They find it in every crevice of national affairs.

On the South specifically, see John Alden, *The South in the American Revolution, 1763–1789* (Baton Rouge, La., 1957) and *The First South* (Baton Rouge, La., 1961), which addresses the intriguing question of the beginnings of southern distinctiveness. Jeffrey J. Crow and Larry E. Tise, eds., *The Southern Experience in the American Revolution* (Chapel Hill, N.C., 1978), contains helpful articles on diverse topics. Ronald Hoffman et al., eds., *An Uncivil War: The Southern Backcountry during the American Revolution* (Charlottesville, Va., 1985), and Edward J. Cashin, *The King's Ranger: Thomas Brown and the American Revolution on the Southern Frontier* (Athens, Ga., 1989), highlight a noteworthy subject. State studies have value: Kenneth Coleman, *The American Revolution in Georgia, 1763–1789* (Athens, Ga., 1958); Ronald Hoffman, *A Spirit of Dissension: Economics, Politics, and the Revolution in Mary-*

land (Baltimore, 1973); Jerome J. Nadlehaft, *The Disorders of War: The Revolution in South Carolina* (Orono, Me., 1981); John E. Selby, *The Revolution in Virginia, 1775–1783* (Charlottesville, Va., 1988). James R. Morrill, *The Practice and Politics of Fiat Finance: North Carolina in the Confederation, 1783–1789* (Chapel Hill, N.C., 1969), and Charles G. Singer, *South Carolina in the Confederation* (Philadelphia, 1941), analyze events in two states during the Confederation period.

On the military conflict in the South, Don Higginbotham, *The War of American Independence: Military Attitudes, Policies, and Practice, 1763–1789* (New York, 1971); Charles Royster, *A Revolutionary People at War: The Continental Army and American Character, 1775–1783* (Chapel Hill, N.C., 1979); John Shy, *A People Numerous and Armed: Reflections on the Military Struggle for American Independence* (New York, 1976); and Christopher Ward, *The War of the Revolution,* 2 vols. (New York, 1952), supply a full background and a rich context. On key actions, see John S. Pancake, *This Destructive War: The British Campaign in the Carolinas, 1780–1782* (University, Ala., 1985); M. F. Treacy, *Prelude to Yorktown: The Southern Campaigns of Nathanael Greene* (Chapel Hill, N.C., 1963); and Russell F. Weigley, *The Partisan War: The South Carolina Campaign of 1780–1782* (Columbia, S.C., 1970). Vol. 5 of Douglas Freeman's *George Washington* is thorough on Yorktown; and J. Barton Starr, *Tories, Dons, and Rebels: The American Revolution in British West Florida* (Gainesville, Fla., 1976), covers the westernmost campaigns.

Primary documents, including the letters, diaries, speeches, and travel accounts of contemporaries, have no match for imparting the flavor of a particular time. Especially notable published collections for the colonial and Revolutionary South include William Abbott et al., eds., *The Papers of George Washington: Colonial Series,* 9 vols. (Charlottesville, Va., 1983–1994); *Revolutionary War Series,* 5 vols. to date (Charlottesville, Va., 1985–   ); *Confederation Series,* 2 vols. to date (Charlottesville, Va., 1992–   ); *Presidential Series,* 4 vols. to date (Charlottesville, Va., 1987–   ); James C. Ballagh, ed., *The Letters of Richard Henry Lee,* 2 vols. (New York, 1912–1914); Philip L. Barbour, ed., *The Complete Works of Captain John Smith, 1580–1631,* 3 vols. (Chapel Hill, N.C., 1986); Warren Billings, ed., *The Old Dominion in the Seventeenth Century: A Documentary History of Virginia, 1606–1689* (Chapel Hill, N.C., 1975); Julian P. Boyd et al., eds., *The Papers of Thomas Jefferson,* 28 vols. to date (Princeton, N.J., 1950–   ); Edmund C. Burnett, ed., *Letters of Members of the Continental Congress,* 8 vols. (Washington, D.C., 1921–1936); Thomas D. Clark, ed., *Travels in the Old South: A Bibliography,* 3 vols. (Norman, Okla., 1956–1959), a superior guide to travel accounts; Elizabeth Donnan, ed., *Documents Illustrative of the Slave Trade to America,* 4 vols. (Washington, D.C., 1930–1935); Jonathan Elliot, ed., *The Debates in the Several State Conventions on the Adoption of the Constitution . . . ,* 5 vols. (Philadelphia, 1907); Hunter D. Farish, ed., *Journal and Letters of Philip Vickers Fithian, 1773–1774: A Plantation Tutor of the Old Dominion* (Williamsburg, Va., 1943); John C. Fitzpatrick, ed., *The Writings of George Washington from the Original Manuscript Sources, 1745–1799,* 37 vols. (Washington, D.C., 1931–1944); Worthington Ford et al., eds., *Journal of the Continental Congress, 1774–1789,* 34 vols. (Washington, D.C., 1904–1937); Jack Green, ed., *The Diary of Colonel Landon Carter of Sabine Hall, 1752–1778,* 2 vols. (Charlottesville, Va., 1965); Philip M. Hamer et al., eds., *The Papers of Henry Laurens,* 14 vols. to date (Columbia, S.C., 1968–   ); Don Higginbotham, ed., *The Papers of James Iredell,* 2 vols. (Raleigh, N.C., 1976); Richard J. Hooker, ed., *The Carolina Backcountry on the Eve of the Revolution: The Journal and Other Writings of Charles Woodmason, Anglican Itinerant* (Chapel Hill, N.C., 1953); William T. Hutchinson et al., eds., *The Papers of James Madison,* 17 vols. to date (Chicago and Charlottesville, Va., 1962–   ); Donald Jackson and Dorothy Twohig, eds., *The Diaries of George Washington,* 6 vols. (Charlottesville, Va., 1976–1979); Merrill Jensen et al., eds., *The Documentary History of the Ratification of the Constitution,* 10 vols. to date (Madison, Wis., 1976–   ), superior to Elliots's edition but not yet complete; Aubrey Land, ed., *Bases of Plantation Society* (New York, 1969); Elsie Pinckney and Marvin Zahnisner, eds., *The Letter-*

book of Eliza Lucas Pinckney, 1739–1762 (Chapel Hill, N.C., 1972); Robert A. Rutland, ed., *The Papers of George Mason, 1725–1792*, 3 vols. (Chapel Hill, N.C., 1970); Richard K. Showman et al., *The Papers of Nathanael Greene*, 7 vols. to date (Chapel Hill, N.C., 1976–　); Paul H. Smith et al., eds., *Letters of Delegates to Congress, 1774–1789*, 19 vols. to date (Washington, D.C., 1976–　), superior to Burnett's edition but not yet complete; Charles C. Tansill, ed., *Documents Illustrative of the Formation of the Union of the American States* (Washington, D.C., 1927), a convenient source for numerous documents related to the Constitutional Convention; Marion Tinling, ed., *The Correspondence of the Three William Byrds of Westover, Virginia, 1684–1776*, 2 vols. (Charlottesville, Va., 1977); Richard Walsh, ed., *The Writings of Christopher Gadsden, 1746–1805* (Columbia, S.C., 1966); Maude H. Woodfin and Marion Tinling, eds., *Another Secret Diary of William Byrd of Westover, 1696–1726* (Richmond, Va., 1942); Louis Wright, ed., *The Prose Works of William Byrd of Westover: Narratives of a Colonial Virginian* (Cambridge, Mass., 1966); and Louis Wright and Marion Tinling, eds., *The Secret Diary of William Byrd of Westover, 1709–1712* (Richmond, Va., 1941).

FROM THE CONSTITUTION TO THE 1840S

No single book covers in detail southern affairs from the 1780s to the 1840s. William Cooper, *Liberty and Slavery*, offers an interpretive analysis of politics in the period. Thomas P. Abernethy, *The South in the New Nation, 1789–1819* (Baton Rouge, La., 1961), goes over the chronological ground of thirty crucial years, albeit in uneven fashion. Strong on geographical expansion and Indian relations, it slights ideology and politics and contains practically nothing on slavery. Charles S. Sydnor, *The Development of Southern Sectionalism, 1819–1848* (Baton Rouge, La., 1948), is strongest on the 1820s and weakest on the 1840s. William W. Freehling's *The Road to Disunion: Secessionists at Bay, 1776–1854* (New York, 1990) offers a wide-ranging discussion that emphasizes differences within the region. Robert F. Durden's argument in *The Self-Inflicted Wound: Southern Politics in the Nineteenth Century* (Lexington, Ky., 1985) that the South moved in the 1820s from liberal and optimistic to conservative and defensive overlooks the fundamental commitment made to slavery during the Revolution. Durden's interpretation follows that of William E. Dodd in two old but obviously influential books: *Statesmen of the Old South, or From Radicalism to Conservative Revolt* (New York, 1911), and *The Cotton Kingdom* (New Haven, Conn., 1920). Stanley Elkins and Eric McKitrick in their massive and impressive *The Age of Federalism: The Early American Republic, 1788–1800* (New York, 1993) discuss numerous topics central to southern developments. Henry Adams's classic *History of the United States during the Administrations of Jefferson and Madison*, 9 vols. (New York, 1889–1891), still has enormous value, and because of their intimate involvement in the nation, southerners occupy a major place in his story. Merrill Peterson's *Great Triumvirate: Webster, Clay, Calhoun* (New York, 1987) uses the lives of these three individuals as avenues to approach American history between the War of 1812 and 1850; here, as in Adams, southerners and the South play leading roles. James S. Young, *The Washington Community, 1800–1828* (New York, 1966), makes an intriguing argument on how the capital city's rude character and living arrangements affected politics.

On the party that dominated the South in the early national period, Noble Cunningham has two basic volumes, *The Jeffersonian Republicans: The Formation of Party Organization, 1789–1801* (Chapel Hill, N.C., 1957) and *The Jeffersonian Republicans in Power: Party Operations, 1801–1809* (Chapel Hill, N.C., 1963). Three especially valuable studies emphasizing ideology are Joyce Appleby, *Capitalism and a New Social Order: The Republican Vision of the 1790s* (New York, 1984); Lance Banning, *The Jeffersonian Persuasion: Evolution of a Party Ideology* (Ithaca, N.Y., 1978); and Drew R. McCoy, *The Elusive Republic: Political Economy in Jeffersonian America* (Chapel Hill, N.C., 1980). In his *Last of the Fathers: James Madison and the Re-*

publican Legacy (New York, 1989) McCoy brilliantly analyzes Madison's thought while he probes the meaning of the constitutional Union. For detailed treatment of the southern Republicans who refused to follow party shifts, see Norman K. Risjord, *The Old Republicans: Southern Conservatism in the Age of Jefferson* (New York, 1965). Alexander DeConde, *This Affair of Louisiana* (New York, 1976), illuminates a primary event of the Jefferson years.

For the history of southern Federalists, three books are required reading: George Rogers, *Evolution of a Federalist: William Loughton Smith of Charleston, 1758–1812* (Columbia, S.C., 1962), absolutely first-rate; Lisle A. Rose, *Prologue to Democracy: The Federalists in the South, 1789–1800* (Lexington, Ky., 1968); and James H. Broussard, *The Southern Federalists, 1800–1816* (Baton Rouge, La., 1978). Also see Joseph W. Cox, *Champion of Southern Federalism: Robert Goodloe Harper of South Carolina* (Port Washington, N.Y., 1972). Although it has little on the South, Linda Kerber, *Federalists in Dissent: Imagery and Ideology in Jeffersonian America* (Ithaca, N.Y., 1970), is revealing on why the Federalists had so much trouble in the South. Also the South did not share equally in the party's renewed vigor sparked by younger Federalists claimed by David Fischer, *The Revolution of American Conservatism: The Federalist Party in the Era of Jeffersonian Democracy* (New York, 1965).

Monographs on activities in individual states during this time are Richard Beeman, *The Old Dominion and the New Nation, 1788–1801* (Lexington, Ky., 1972); Joan Wells Coward, *Kentucky in the New Republic: The Process of Constitution Making* (Lexington, Ky., 1972); Delbert H. Gilpatrick, *Jeffersonian Democracy in North Carolina, 1789–1816* (New York, 1931); Rachel Klein, *Unification of a Slave State*; George R. Lamplugh, *Politics on the Periphery: Factions and Parties in Georgia, 1783–1806* (Newark, Del., 1986); Norman Risjord, *Chesapeake Politics, 1781–1800* (New York, 1978), the best of these books; and John H. Wolfe, *Jeffersonian Democracy in South Carolina* (Chapel Hill, N.C., 1940).

On the dynamic relationship between slavery and politics, David Brion Davis, *Slavery in the Age of Revolution,* and Winthrop Jordan, *White over Black,* remain pertinent. See also Robert McColley, *Slavery and Jeffersonian Virginia* (Urbana, Ill., 1973), and John C. Miller, *The Wolf by the Ears: Thomas Jefferson and Slavery* (New York, 1977).

Superb coverage of the War of 1812 can be found in J. C. A. Stagg's substantial *Mr. Madison's War: Politics, Diplomacy, and Warfare in the Early American Republic, 1783–1830* (Princeton, N.J., 1983), which concentrates on the war. On the southern front, specifically the Indian campaigns and the contest for New Orleans, the first volume of Robert Remini's *Andrew Jackson* tells the story in detail. Also see Frank L. Owsley, Jr., *Struggle for the Gulf Borderlands: The Creek War and the Battle of New Orleans, 1812–1815* (Gainesville, Fla., 1981).

Historians have not avidly pursued the important issues reflected in the disintegration of the Jeffersonian Republican party. This theme does, however, form a part of George Dangerfield's lively *Era of Good Feelings* (New York, 1952), which does not slight southern developments. No good monographs analyze the South and such central topics as the tariff, internal improvements, the second Bank of the United States, the Panic of 1819, and the critical election of 1824, though Albert R. Newsome, *The Presidential Election of 1824 in North Carolina* (Chapel Hill, N.C., 1939), looks at one state. The Missouri crisis receives thorough treatment in Glover Moore, *The Missouri Controversy, 1819–1821* (Lexington, Ky., 1953). Missouri is also the initial crisis discussed by Don E. Fehrenbacher, *The South and Three Sectional Crises* (Baton Rouge, La., 1980). Fehrenbacher looks at constitutional matters in *Constitutions and Constitutionalism in the Slaveholding South* (Athens, Ga., 1989). Fletcher M. Green, *Constitutional Development in the South Atlantic States, 1776–1860* (Chapel Hill, N.C., 1930), first called attention to the democratization of southern politics.

Jacksonianism has occupied the talents of a legion of historians. The fullest study of the party in the South is William Cooper, *The South and the Politics of Slavery, 1828–1856* (Baton Rouge, La., 1978). Other books that have particular pertinence for students of southern history include William Freehling, *Road to Disunion*; Richard P. McCormick, *The Second*

American Party System: Party Formation in the Jacksonian Era (Chapel Hill, N.C., 1966); Marvin Meyers, *The Jacksonian Persuasion: Politics and Belief* (Stanford, Calif., 1960); Robert Remini, *The Legacy of Andrew Jackson: Essays on Democracy, Indian Removal, and Slavery* (Baton Rouge, La., 1988); Arthur M. Schlesinger, Jr., *The Age of Jackson* (Boston, 1945); Charles Sellers, *The Market Revolution: Jacksonian America, 1815–1846* (New York, 1992); John William Ward, *Andrew Jackson: Symbol for an Age* (New York, 1955); and Harry L. Watson, *Liberty and Power: The Politics of Jacksonian America* (New York, 1990), the best modern synthesis. On the key issues of the Jackson presidency, see Donald Cole, *The Presidency of Andrew Jackson* (Lawrence, Kans., 1993); Richard E. Ellis, *The Union at Risk: Jacksonian Democracy, States' Rights, and the Nullification Crisis* (New York, 1987); William Freehling, *Prelude to Civil War: The Nullification Controversy in South Carolina, 1816–1836* (New York, 1966); Richard B. Latner, *The Presidency of Andrew Jackson: White House Politics, 1829–1837* (Athens, Ga., 1979); William G. McLoughlin, *Cherokee Renascence in the New Republic* (Princeton, N.J., 1986); Merrill Peterson, *Olive Branch and Sword: The Compromise of 1833* (Baton Rouge, La., 1982); Robert Remini, *Andrew Jackson and the Bank War* (New York, 1967); and Ronald N. Satz, *American Indian Policy in the Jacksonian Era* (Lincoln, Neb., 1975).

For the growth of the Whig opposition and the resulting Whig party, see William Cooper, *Politics of Slavery;* William Freehling, *Road to Disunion;* and Richard McCormick, *Second American Party System,* along with Thomas Brown, *Politics and Statesmanship: Essays on the American Whig Party* (New York, 1985); George R. Poage, *Henry Clay and the Whig Party* (Chapel Hill, N.C., 1936); and Arthur C. Cole's older *Whig Party in the South* (Washington, D.C., 1913). In his *Political Culture of the American Whigs* (Chicago, 1979), Daniel W. Howe underestimates the special characteristics of southern Whiggery. Two statistical analyses of congressional voting emphasize the existence of party loyalty: Thomas B. Alexander, *Sectional Stress and Party Strength: A Computer Analysis of Roll-Call Voting Patterns in the United States House of Representatives, 1836–1860* (Nashville, Tenn., 1967), and Joel H. Silbey, *The Shrine of Party: Congressional Voting Behavior, 1841–1852* (Pittsburgh, 1967).

A number of substantial state and local studies illuminate both the Democratic-Whig competition and the southern political world between the 1820s and 1860. The best of them are Lacy K. Ford, Jr., *Origins of Southern Radicalism: The South Carolina Upcountry, 1800–1860* (New York, 1988), and J. Mills Thornton III, *Politics and Power in a Slave Society: Alabama, 1800–1860* (Baton Rouge, La., 1978). Other worthy titles include William H. Adams, *The Whig Party of Louisiana* (Lafayette, La., 1973); Charles H. Ambler, *Sectionalism in Virginia from 1776 to 1861* (Chicago, 1910); Paul H. Bergeron, *Antebellum Politics in Tennessee* (Lexington, Ky., 1982); Daniel W. Crofts, *Old Southampton: Politics and Society in a Virginia County, 1834–1869* (Charlottesville, Va., 1992); Herbert J. Doherty, Jr., *The Whigs of Florida, 1845–1854* (Gainesville, Fla., 1959); William S. Hoffman, *Andrew Jackson and North Carolina Politics* (Chapel Hill, N.C., 1958); Thomas E. Jeffrey, *State Parties and National Politics: North Carolina, 1815–1861* (Athens, Ga., 1989); Marc W. Kruman, *Parties and Politics in North Carolina, 1836–1865* (Baton Rouge, La., 1983); John V. Mering, *The Whig Party in Missouri* (Columbia, Mo., 1967); Edwin A. Miles, *Jacksonian Democracy in Mississippi* (Chapel Hill, N.C., 1960); Horace Montgomery, *Cracker Parties* (Baton Rouge, La., 1950); Paul Murray, *The Whig Party in Georgia, 1825–1853* (Chapel Hill, N.C., 1948); Ulrich B. Phillips, *Georgia and State Rights* (Washington, D.C., 1902); Arthur W. Thompson, *Jacksonian Democracy on the Florida Frontier* (Gainesville, Fla., 1961); and Harry Watson, *Jacksonian Politics and Community Conflict: The Emergence of the Second Party System in Cumberland County, North Carolina* (Baton Rouge, La., 1981). A clear, modern vantage point for Virginia politics is Craig M. Simpson's *A Good Southerner: The Life of Henry A. Wise of Virginia* (Chapel Hill, N.C., 1985). On the structure of politics, see also two books by Ralph A. Wooster, *Politicians, Planters, and Plain Folks: Court-*

house and Statehouse in the Upper South, 1850–1860 (Knoxville, Tenn., 1975) and *The People in Power: Courthouse and Statehouse in the Lower South, 1850–1860* (Knoxville, Tenn., 1969).

Published primary materials especially relevant for this period include *Annals of Congress* (1789–1824), *Register of Debates in Congress* (1825–1837), *Congressional Globe* (1833–1861), for congressional debates; William Abbott et al., *Papers of Washington: Presidential Series;* John S. Bassett, ed., *Correspondence of Andrew Jackson,* 7 vols. (Washington, D.C., 1926–1935); Chauncey S. Boucher and Robert P. Brooks, eds., *Correspondence Addressed to John C. Calhoun, 1837–1849* (Washington, D.C., 1930); Julian Boyd et al., eds., *Papers of Jefferson;* Thomas Clark, ed., *Travels in the Old South,* the guide to travel accounts; Noble Cunningham, ed., *Circular Letters of Congressmen to Their Constituents, 1789–1829,* 3 vols. (Chapel Hill, N.C., 1978); John Fitzpatrick, ed., *Writings of Washington;* Paul L. Ford, ed., *The Writings of Thomas Jefferson,* 10 vols. (New York, 1892–1899); William Freehling, ed., *The Nullification Era: A Documentary Record* (New York, 1967); William Hutchinson et al., eds., *Papers of Madison;* James F. Hopkins et al., eds., *The Papers of Henry Clay,* 10 vols. and supp. (Lexington, Ky., 1959–1992); J. Franklin Jameson, ed., *Correspondence of John C. Calhoun* (Washington, D.C., 1900); Herbert A. Johnson et al., eds., *The Papers of John Marshall,* 6 vols. to date (Chapel Hill, N.C., 1974–   ); Robert L. Meriwether et al., eds., *The Papers of John C. Calhoun,* 21 vols. to date (Columbia, S.C., 1959–   ); Harold D. Moser et al., eds., *The Papers of Andrew Jackson,* 4 vols. to date (Knoxville, Tenn., 1980–   ); Milo M. Quaife, ed., *The Diary of James K. Polk: During His Presidency, 1845–1849,* 4 vols. (Chicago, 1910); Herbert Weaver et al., eds., *The Correspondence of James K. Polk,* 8 vols. to date (Nashville, Tenn., 1969–   ).

*F*ARMS AND PLANTATIONS, MASTERS AND SLAVES

Lewis C. Gray published the standard history of antebellum southern agriculture more than sixty years ago. With thorough treatments of cultivation, processing, and marketing, *History of Agriculture in the Southern United States,* 2 vols. (Washington, D.C., 1933), remains a remarkable achievement and an invaluable aid. Complementing Gray, Sam B. Hilliard, *Atlas of Antebellum Southern Agriculture* (Baton Rouge, La., 1984), provides marvelous cartographic treatment of the subject. Other noteworthy volumes include Hilliard, *Hog Meat and Hoecake: Food Supply in the Old South, 1840–1860* (Carbondale, Ill., 1972), which focuses on both the food supply and internal trade patterns; Harold D. Woodman, *King Cotton and His Retainers: Financing and Marketing the Cotton Crop of the South, 1800–1925* (Lexington, Ky., 1968), which details marketing processes; and Gavin Wright, *The Political Economy of the Cotton South: Households, Markets, and Wealth in the Nineteenth Century* (New York, 1978), the best analysis of the cotton economy in the prewar South.

Other basic crops have also had their historians: Henry C. Dethloff, *A History of the American Rice Industry, 1685–1985* (College Station, Tex., 1988); James Hopkins, *A History of the Hemp Industry in Kentucky* (Lexington, Ky., 1957); Joseph C. Robert, *The Tobacco Kingdom: Plantation, Market, and Factory in Virginia and North Carolina, 1800–1860* (Durham, N.C., 1938); and J. Carlyle Sitterson, *Sugar Country: The Cane Sugar Industry in the South, 1753–1950* (Lexington, Ky., 1953).

For agricultural developments in specific states, see, in addition, James C. Bonner, *A History of Georgia Agriculture, 1732–1860* (Athens, Ga., 1964); Cornelius O. Cathey, *Agricultural Developments in North Carolina* (Chapel Hill, N.C., 1956); Peter Coclanis, *Shadow of a Dream;* R. Douglas Hurt, *Agriculture and Slavery in Missouri's Little Dixie* (Columbia, Mo., 1992); Richard G. Lowe and Randolph B. Campbell, *Planters and Plain Folk: Agriculture in*

Antebellum Texas (Dallas, 1987); John H. Moore, *The Emergence of the Cotton Kingdom in the Old Southwest: Mississippi, 1770–1860* (Baton Rouge, La., 1988); Alfred G. Smith, Jr., *Economic Readjustment of an Old Cotton State: South Carolina, 1820–1860* (Columbia, S.C., 1958).

No subject in southern history has attracted more attention or drawn a more talented group of scholars than slavery. Peter J. Parish's, *Slavery: History and Historians* (New York, 1989) offers an instructive guide to this literature, up to its date of publication. The initial classic, Ulrich Phillips, *American Negro Slavery* (New York, 1918), explored virgin territory but was marred by the racial outlook of the author and his time. Replacing Phillips, Kenneth M. Stampp, *The Peculiar Institution: Slavery in the Ante-Bellum South* (New York, 1956), combined massive archival research with a modern view of race. In an early emphasis on the human beings who were slaves, Melville J. Herskovits argued for the significance of their African cultural background in *The Myth of the Negro Past* (New York, 1941). For our time Stanley Elkins, *Slavery: A Problem in American Institutional and Intellectual Life* (Chicago, 1959), has probably had more influence than any other single book. This slim volume directed attention to the slaves and their behavior rather than to the institution. That perspective, along with the civil rights movement, shifted the chief approach of slavery scholarship to an effort to understand slaves in their bondage.

To date, the major result of this inquiry has been Eugene D. Genoves, *Roll, Jordan, Roll: The World the Slaves Made* (New York, 1974), an impressively researched study that places the slaves in the forefront as it probes their world. Two other books also deserve special mention: Herbert G. Gutman, *The Black Family in Slavery and Freedom, 1750–1925* (New York, 1976), which focuses on the family as critical in slave life, and Lawrence W. Levine, *Black Culture and Black Consciousness: Afro-American Folk Thought from Slavery to Freedom* (New York, 1977), which illuminates the cultural world of the slaves.

Studies that cast light on other important areas of slavery include John Blassingame, *The Slave Community: Plantation Life in the Antebellum South* (New York, 1979), and George P. Rawick, *From Sundown to Sunup: The Making of the Black Community* (Westport, Conn., 1972), which emphasize the positive characteristics of the slave community; Janet D. Cornelius, *When I Can Read My Title Clear: Literacy, Slavery, and Religion in the Antebellum South* (Columbia, S.C., 1991); Charles B. Dew, *Bond of Iron: Masters and Slaves at Buffalo Forge* (New York, 1994), an excellent case study of industrial slavery; Paul D. Escott, *Slavery Remembered: A Record of Twentieth-Century Slave Narratives* (Chapel Hill, N.C., 1979); Jacqueline Jones, *Labor of Love, Labor of Sorrow: Black Women, Work, and the Family from Slavery to the Present* (New York, 1985); Ronald L. Lewis, *Coal, Iron, and Slaves: Industrial Slavery in Maryland and Virginia, 1715–1865* (Westport, Conn., 1979); Leslie H. Owens, *This Species of Property: Slave Life and Culture in the Old South* (New York, 1976); Albert J. Raboteau, *Slave Religion: The "Invisible" Institution in the South* (New York, 1978); Todd L. Savitt, *Medicine and Slavery: The Diseases and Health Care of Blacks in Antebellum Virginia* (Urbana, Ill., 1978), a model for further investigation of this crucial subject; Robert S. Starobin, *Industrial Slavery in the Old South* (New York, 1970), a pathbreaking book; Sterling Stuckey, *Slave Culture: National Theory and the Foundations of Black America* (New York, 1988); Michael Tadman, *Speculators and Slaves: Masters, Traders, and Slaves in the Old South* (Madison, Wis., 1989), an excellent treatment of a critical topic; William L. Van Deburg, *The Slave Driver: Black Agricultural Labor Supervisors in the Antebellum South* (Westport, Conn., 1979); Richard C. Wade, *Slavery in the Cities: The South, 1820–1860* (New York, 1964), a valuable study, though it exaggerates the incompatibility between cities and slavery; Thomas L. Webber, *Deep like the River: Education in the Slave Community* (New York, 1978); and Deborah G. White, *Ar'n't I a Woman? Female Slaves in the Plantation South* (New York, 1985).

During the past decade a number of books have clarified the legal dimensions of slavery. Paul Finkelman has been in the forefront of this effort: *An Imperfect Union: Slavery, Federalism, and Comity* (Chapel Hill, N.C., 1981), which concentrates on slavery's meaning for the federal system; *Slavery in the Courtroom: An Annotated Bibliography of American Cases* (Washington, D.C., 1988); and *The Law of Freedom and Bondage: A Casebook* (New York, 1986). In *The American Law of Slavery, 1810–1860: Considerations of Humanity and Interest* (Princeton, N.J., 1981), Mark V. Tushnet maintains that slavery forced the creation of a distinctive southern legal system. Three studies focus on developments in the states: Michael S. Hindus, *Prison and Plantation: Crime, Justice, and Authority in Massachusetts and South Carolina, 1767-1868* (Chapel Hill, N.C., 1980); Judith K. Schafer, *Slavery, the Civil Law, and the Supreme Court of Louisiana* (Baton Rouge, La., 1994); and Philip J. Schwarz, *Twice Condemned: Slaves and the Criminal Laws of Virginia, 1705–1865* (Baton Rouge, La., 1988). Also see the notable collection of articles in Kermit L. Hall, ed., *The Law of American Slavery: Major Interpretations* (New York, 1987).

Eugene Genovese, *From Rebellion to Revolution: Afro-American Slave Revolts in the Making of the Modern World* (Baton Rouge, La., 1979), places the southern story in a hemispheric context, albeit within a Marxist framework. Herbert Aptheker, *American Negro Slave Revolts* (New York, 1963), covers all the major revolts, though it greatly overestimates the number of organized attacks on the system. For discussions of the major revolts (except the one in Louisiana in 1811, which has not been thoroughly studied), see Peter Wood, *Black Majority,* on the Stono Rebellion; Gwendolyn Hall, *Africans in Colonial Louisiana,* for the Pointe Coupee conspiracy; Douglas R. Egerton, *Gabriel's Rebellion: The Virginia Slave Conspiracies of 1800 and 1802* (Chapel Hill, N.C., 1993), especially, and Gerald Mullin, *Flight and Rebellion,* on Gabriel's conspiracy; William Freehling, *Prelude to Civil War,* and John Lofton, *Denmark Vesey's Revolt: The Slave Plot That Lit a Fuse to Fort Sumter* (Kent, Ohio, 1983), on the Vesey conspiracy; and Stephen B. Oates, *The Fires of Jubilee: Nat Turner's Fierce Rebellion* (New York, 1975), on the most famous revolt.

Published to wide acclaim as the culmination of quantitative research on slavery, Robert W. Fogel and Stanley L. Engerman, *Time on the Cross,* 2 vols. (Boston, 1974), soon came under withering attack for methodological flaws. For a sweeping critique, consult Paul A. David et al., *Reckoning with Slavery: A Critical Study in the Quantitative History of American Negro Slavery* (New York, 1976). Fogel and Engerman, however, did push a point made by earlier scholars, that slavery was economically vibrant and generally profitable. Eugene Genovese, by contrast, in *The Political Economy of Slavery: Studies in the Economy and Society of the Slave South* (New York, 1965), argued for the backwardness and lack of profitability in the system.

A number of state and local studies have value. Those written before the revolution in the historiography of slavery focus on the institution, not on the slaves. They include J. Winston Coleman, *Slavery Times in Kentucky* (Chapel Hill, N.C., 1940); Chase Mooney, *Slavery in Tennessee* (Bloomington, Ind., 1957); James B. Sellers, *Slavery in Alabama* (University, Ala., 1950); Charles Sydnor, *Slavery in Mississippi* (New York, 1933); Joe Gray Taylor, *Negro Slavery in Louisiana* (Baton Rouge, La., 1963); and Orville W. Taylor, *Negro Slavery in Arkansas* (Durham, N.C., 1958). More modern studies include Randolph Campbell, *An Empire for Slavery: The Peculiar Institution in Texas, 1821–1865* (Baton Rouge, La., 1989); Margaret W. Creel, *"A Peculiar People": Slave Religion and Community-Culture among the Gullahs* (New York, 1988); Barbara J. Fields, *Slavery and Freedom on the Middle Ground: Maryland during the Nineteenth Century* (New Haven, Conn., 1985); Norrece T. Jones, Jr., *Born a Child of Freedom yet a Slave: Mechanisms of Control and Strategies of Resistance in Antebellum South Carolina* (Hanover, N.H., 1990); Charles Joyner, *Down by the Riverside: A South Carolina Slave Community* (Urbana, Ill., 1984); Ann P. Malone, *Sweet Chariot: Slave Family and Household Structure in Nineteenth-Century Louisiana* (Chapel Hill, N.C., 1992); Julia F. Smith, *Slavery and Plantation Growth in Antebellum Florida, 1821–1860* (Gainesville, Fla., 1973) and *Slavery and Rice Culture in Low Country Georgia, 1750–1860* (Knoxville, Tenn., 1985). For a superior synthesis of recent scholarship, see Peter Kolchin, *American Slavery, 1619–1877* (New York,

1993). John B. Boles, *Black Southerners, 1619–1869* (Lexington, Ky., 1983), remains useful. For brief introductions to a wide variety of subjects, Randall M. Miller and John Davis Smith, eds., *Dictionary of Afro-American Slavery* (New York, 1988), is helpful.

Investigations of planters and plantation management help immensely to understand the slave plantation. Drew Faust's brilliant *James Henry Hammond* explores with insight and imagination the activities of a larger planter and slave owner. See also Malcolm Bell, Jr., *Major Butler's Legacy: Five Generations of a Slaveholding Family* (Athens, Ga., 1987); Avery O. Craven, *Rachel of Old Louisiana* (Baton Rouge, La., 1975); Weymouth T. Jordan, *Hugh Davis and His Alabama Plantation* (University, Ala., 1948); and Theodore Rosengarten, *Tombee: Portrait of a Cotton Planter* (New York, 1986). John S. Otto, *Cannon's Point Plantation, 1794–1860: Living Conditions and Status Patterns in the Old South* (Orlando, Fla., 1984), presents the results of an extensive archaeological investigation. John M. Vlach, *Back of the Big House: The Architecture of Plantation Slavery* (Chapel Hill, N.C., 1993), charts the locations of buildings. William K. Scarborough, *The Overseer: Plantation Management in the Old South* (Baton Rouge, La., 1966), discusses that crucial position. Ulrich Phillips, *Life and Labor in the Old South* (Boston, 1929), is still worthwhile on the texture of rural life.

Comparative studies provide a broader perspective for comprehending slavery in the American South. The first comparison was with other slave societies in the New World. Pertinent titles include Ira Berlin and Philip D. Morgan, eds., *Cultivation and Culture: Labor and the Shaping of Slave Life in the Americas* (Charlottesville, Va., 1993); Carl M. Degler, *Neither Black nor White: Slavery and Race Relations in Brazil and the United States* (New York, 1971); Laura Foner and Eugene Genovese, eds., *Slavery in the New World: A Reader in Comparative History* (Englewood Cliffs, N.J., 1969); Herbert S. Klein, *Slavery in the Americas: A Comparative Study of Virginia and Cuba* (Chicago, 1967); Roderick A. McDonald, *The Economy and Material Culture of Slaves: Goods and Chattels on the Sugar Plantations of Jamaica and Louisiana* (Baton Rouge, La., 1993). Other unfree systems have also been analyzed; two especially notable books are Peter Kolchin, *Unfree Labor: American Slavery and Russian Serfdom* (Cambridge, Mass., 1987), with its different angle on slavery in the South, and Orlando Patterson, *Slavery and Social Death: A Comparative Study* (Cambridge, Mass., 1982), an ambitious attempt to devise an all-inclusive theory of slavery. Also see Shearer D. Bowman, *Masters and Lords: Mid-19th Century U.S. Planters and Prussian Junkers* (New York, 1993).

Numerous superb publications of primary materials contribute to an understanding of agriculture, slavery, and slave owners. The best and most helpful among them include John S. Bassett, ed., *The Southern Plantation Overseer as Revealed in His Letters* (Northampton, Mass., 1925); John Blassingame, ed., *Slave Testimony: Two Centuries of Letters, Speeches, Interviews, and Autobiographies* (Baton Rouge, La., 1977); Carol Bleser, ed., *Secret and Sacred: The Diaries of James Henry Hammond, a Southern Slaveholder* (New York, 1988); James Breeden, ed., *Advice among Masters: The Ideal in Slave Management in the Old South* (Westport, Conn., 1980); Helen T. Catterall, ed., *Judicial Cases concerning American Slavery and the Negro,* 5 vols. (Washington, D.C., 1926–1937); James M. Clifton, ed., *Life and Labor on Argyle Plantation: Letters and Documents of a Savannah River Plantation, 1833–1867* (Savannah, Ga., 1978); Edwin A. Davis, ed., *Plantation Life in the Florida Parishes of Louisiana, 1836–1846, as Reflected in the Diary of Bennett H. Barrow* (New York, 1943); Edmund L. Drago, ed., *Broke by the War: Letters of a Slave Trader* (Columbia, S.C., 1991); J. H. Easterby, ed., *The South Carolina Rice Plantation As Revealed in the Papers of Robert F. W. Allston* (Chicago, 1945); Frances Anne Kemble, *Journal of a Residence on a Georgian Plantation in 1838–1839,* ed. John A. Scott (Athens, Ga., 1984), an account by the English wife of a sea island planter; Michael Meyer, ed., *Frederick Douglass: The Narrative and Selected Writings* (New York, 1984), an excellent collection including the autobiography and other writings of the famous former slave who became an abolitionist; Robert M. Myers, ed., *The Children of Pride: A True Story of Georgia and the Civil War* (New Haven, Conn., 1972), the correspondence of a slave-owning family;

Solomon Northup, *Twelve Years a Slave,* ed. Sue Eakin and Joseph Logsdon (Baton Rouge, La., 1968), a fascinating autobiography of a slave; Charles L. Perdue et al., eds., *Weevils in the Wheat: Interviews with Virginia Ex-Slaves* (Charlottesville, Va., 1976); Frederick Law Olmsted, *The Cotton Kingdom: A Travellers's Observations on Cotton and Slavery in the American Slave States,* ed. Arthur M. Schlesinger, Sr. (New York, 1984), an excellent edition of the writings of the man who wrote the most thorough accounts of travel in the slave states; George Rawick, ed., *The American Slave: A Composite Autobiography,* 41 vols. (Westport, Conn., 1972–1979), the fullest documentary record of the slave experience based on interviews conducted in the twentieth century with former slaves; Willie Lee Rose, ed., *A Documentary History of Slavery in North America* (New York, 1976); Robert Starobin, ed., *Blacks in Bondage: Letters of American Slaves* (New York, 1974) and *Denmark Vesey: The Slave Conspiracy of 1822* (Englewood Cliffs, N.J., 1970), a collection of documents; Henry I. Traigle, *The Southampton Slave Revolt of 1831: A Compilation of Source Material Including the Full Text of the "Confessions" of Nat Turner* (Amherst, Mass., 1971), also a collection of documents.

LIFE OF THE MIND, EDUCATION, AND RELIGION

Lewis P. Simpson in four books, *Mind and the American Civil War: A Meditation on Lost Causes* (Baton Rouge, La., 1989), *The Brazen Face of History: Studies in the Literary Consciousness in America* (Baton Rouge, La., 1980), *The Dispossessed Garden: Pastoral and History in Southern Literature* (Athens, Ga., 1975), and *The Fable of Southern Writers* (Baton Rouge, La., 1994), places the intellectual history of the antebellum South in the context of American and western European development. Drew Faust, *A Sacred Circle: The Dilemma of the Intellectual in the Old South, 1840–1860* (Baltimore, 1977), took southern intellectuals and their endeavors seriously while showing that they did also. Michael O'Brien and David Moltke-Hansen, eds., *Intellectual Life in Antebellum Charleston* (Knoxville, Tenn., 1986), illustrates the variety and the complexity in one of the region's chief centers of intellectual activity. Louis Rubin, *The Edge of the Swamp: A Study in Literature and Society of the Old South* (Baton Rouge, La., 1989), emphasizes the impact of slavery on southern writers. On the leading literary figure, also consult John Guilds, ed., *"Long Years of Neglect": The Work and Reputation of William Gilmore Simms* (Fayetteville, Ark., 1988); Mary C. Simms Oliphant et al., eds., *The Letters of William Gilmore Simms,* 6 vols. (Columbia, S.C., 1952–1982); Jon L. Wakelyn, *The Politics of a Literary Man: William Gilmore Simms* (Westport, Conn., 1973); and Mary Ann Wimsatt, *The Major Fiction of William Gilmore Simms: Cultural Traditions and Literary Form* (Baton Rouge, La., 1989). Three studies focus on the Virginia debate around 1830 over the nature and future of the state and the place of slavery in it: Dickson D. Bruce, Jr., *The Rhetoric of Conservatism: The Virginia Convention of 1829–30 and the Conservative Tradition in the South* (San Marino, Calif., 1982); Alison G. Freehling, *Drift toward Dissolution: The Virginia Slavery Debate of 1831–1832* (Baton Rouge, La., 1982); and John Robert, *The Road from Monticello: A Study of the Virginia Slavery Debate of 1832* (Durham, N.C., 1941). In *The Freedom-of-Thought Struggle in the Old South* (New York, 1964), Clement Eaton stressed the closing of the southern mind on the subject of slavery. Two other books by Eaton, *The Growth of Southern Civilization, 1790–1860* (New York, 1961) and *The Mind of the Old South* (Baton Rouge, La., 1967), provide general descriptions of a diversity of topics.

Other meritorious works on various subjects include Jesse T. Carpenter, *The South as a Conscious Minority, 1789–1861: A Study in Political Thought* (New York, 1930); James X. Corgan, ed., *The Geological Sciences in the Antebellum South* (University, Ala., 1982); Richard Davis, *Intellectual Life in Jefferson's Virginia, 1790–1830* (Chapel Hill, N.C., 1964); C. Hugh Holman, *The Roots of Southern Writing: Essays on the Literature of the American South* (Athens, Ga., 1972); Ronald L. Numbers and Todd Savitt, eds., *Science and Medicine in the Old South*

(Baton Rouge, La., 1989); Michael O'Brien, *A Character of Hugh Legare* (Knoxville, Tenn., 1985) and ed., *All Clever Men Who Make Their Way: Critical Discourse in the Old South* (Fayetteville, Ark., 1982); J. V. Ridgely, *Nineteenth-Century Southern Literature* (Lexington, Ky., 1980); and Kenneth Stevens, *Charleston: Antebellum Architecture and Civic Destiny* (Knoxville, Tenn., 1988). Waldo W. Braden, ed., *Oratory in the Old South, 1828–1860* (Baton Rouge, La., 1970), provides an introduction to what many southerners considered the premier art form.

On the proslavery argument specifically, five books command attention: George M. Fredrickson, *The Black Image in the White Mind: The Debate on Afro-American Character and Destiny, 1817–1914* (New York, 1971); Eugene Genovese, *The World the Slaveholders Made: Two Essays in Interpretation* (New York, 1969), which has an important discussion of George Fitzhugh; Reginald Horsman, *Josiah Nott*; William S. Jenkins, *Pro-Slavery Thought in the Old South* (Chapel Hill, N.C., 1935), the first and still the only general survey; and Larry Tise, *Proslavery: A History of the Defense of Slavery in America, 1701–1840* (Athens, Ga., 1987), a not entirely successful effort to redefine the conventional chronological framework and to place the proslavery stance at the center of the conservative tradition. The best modern compilation of proslavery writings is Drew Faust, ed., *The Ideology of Slavery: Proslavery Thought in the Antebellum South* (Baton Rouge, La., 1981).

On religion three titles are essential: John Boles, *The Great Revival, 1787–1805* (Lexington, Ky., 1972); Anne C. Loveland, *Southern Evangelicals and the Social Order, 1820–1860* (Baton Rouge, La., 1980); and Donald G. Mathews, *Religion in the Old South* (Chicago, 1977). Additional items meriting serious attention are David Bailey, *Shadow on the Church: Southwestern Evangelical Religion and the Issue of Slavery, 1783–1860* (Ithaca, N.Y., 1985); John Boles, ed., *Masters and Slaves in the House of the Lord: Race and Religion in the American South, 1740–1870* (Lexington, Ky., 1988) and *Religion in Antebellum Kentucky* (Lexington, Ky., 1976); Jon Butler, *Awash in a Sea of Faith: Christianizing the American People* (Cambridge, Mass., 1990), which offers valuable commentary on southern developments; C. C. Goen, *Broken Churches, Broken Nation: Denominational Schism and the Coming of the Civil War* (Macon, Ga., 1985); Samuel S. Hill, Jr., *The South and the North in American Religion* (Athens, Ga., 1980); E. Brooks Holifield, *The Gentlemen Theologians: American Theology in Southern Culture, 1795–1860* (Durham, N.C., 1978); John W. Kuykendall, *Southern Enterprise: The Work of National Evangelical Societies in the Antebellum South* (Westport, Conn., 1982); Donald Mathews, *Slavery and Methodism: A Chapter in American Morality, 1780–1845* (Princeton, N.J., 1965); and Mitchell Snay, *Gospel of Disunion: Religion and Separatism in the Antebellum South* (New York, 1993). The strongest denominational histories are David E. Harrell, Jr., *Quest for a Christian America: The Disciples of Christ and American Society to 1866* (Nashville, Tenn., 1966), and Ernest T. Thompson, *Presbyterians in the South, 1607–1861* (Richmond, Va., 1963). See also three books by Walter B. Posey: *The Development of Methodism in the Old Southwest, 1783–1824* (Tuscaloosa, Ala., 1933), *The Presbyterian Church in the Old Southwest, 1778–1838* (Richmond, Va., 1952), and *The Baptist Church in the Lower Mississippi Valley, 1776–1845* (Lexington, Ky., 1957); and Leonard Dinnerstein and Mary D. Palsson, eds., *Jews in the South* (Baton Rouge, La., 1973). Samuel Hill, ed., *Encyclopedia of Religion in the South* ([Macon, Ga.], 1984) offers brief introductions to a multiplicity of topics.

The history of education, both precollegiate and collegiate, in the antebellum South has not yet received the attention it deserves. Clement Eaton, *Growth of Southern Civilization*, probably still has the best survey, though a thin one. As of now, the story must be pieced together from various books on religion and intellectual life; many of the titles cited on pages 383–384 touch on education. For the precollege level there are really no substantive monographs. The best studies of institutions of higher learning are Thomas G. Dyer, *The University of Georgia: A Bicentennial History* (Athens, Ga., 1985); Daniel W. Hollis, *South Carolina College* (Columbia, S.C., 1951); David G. Sansing, *Making Haste Slowly: The Troubled*

History of Higher Education in Mississippi (Jackson, Miss., 1990), which discusses the antebellum University of Mississippi; and William D. Snider, *Light on the Hill: A History of the University of North Carolina at Chapel Hill* (Chapel Hill, N.C., 1992). E. Merton Coulter wrote a delightful account of student life at the University of Georgia in his *College Life in the Old South* (Athens, Ga., 1951). See also Nora C. Chaffin, *Trinity College, 1830–1892: The Beginnings of Duke University* (Durham, N.C., 1950), and Albea Godbold, *The Church College in the Old South* (Durham, N.C., 1944).

THE FREE SOCIETY

The ideology and social dynamics of the antebellum South remain lively topics of debate among historians. In several extremely influential works Eugene Genovese has depicted the antebellum South as a premodern culture dominated by slaveholding planters who had a strong antipathy to both capitalism and democracy. See three of his books already cited, *Political Economy; Roll, Jordan, Roll;* and *World the Slaveholders Made.* In his recent *The Slaveholders' Dilemma: Freedom and Progress in Southern Conservative Thought, 1820–1860* (Columbia, S.C., 1992), Genovese emphasizes the intellectual strength of the defenders of slavery and southern society and argues for their distinctiveness. William Cooper, *Politics of Slavery* and *Liberty and Slavery;* Lacey Ford, *Origins of Southern Radicalism;* and Mills Thornton, *Politics and Power* present a different view of the southern political world, though they certainly do not agree on all issues. Thornton and Ford also have superb discussions of the white social world, and both conclude that unity prevailed over disunity. James Oakes, *The Ruling Race: A History of American Slaveholders* (New York, 1982), places the planters fully in the capitalist world and disagrees fundamentally with Genovese on their world view. More recently Oakes has argued for the impact of liberal capitalism on the southern view of freedom, *Slavery and Freedom: An Interpretation of the Old South* (New York, 1990). See also Randolph Campbell and Richard G. Lowe, *Wealth and Power in Antebellum Texas* (College Station, Tex., 1977); Bruce Collins, *White Society in the Antebellum South* (New York, 1985); Paul Escott, *Power and Privilege in North Carolina, 1850–1900* (Chapel Hill, N.C., 1985); Kenneth S. Greenberg, *Masters and Statesmen: The Political Culture of American Slavery* (Baltimore, 1985); John C. Inscoe, *Mountain Masters, Slavery, and the Sectional Crisis in Western North Carolina* (Knoxville, Tenn., 1989); and Raimondo Luraghi, *The Rise and Fall of the Plantation South* (New York, 1978), a Marxist interpretation considerably less powerful and subtle than Genovese's.

On the yeomen, an older study that should not be forgotten is Frank L. Owsley, *Plain Folk in the Old South* (Baton Rouge, La., 1949). Also see Everett Dick, *The Dixie Frontier: A Social History of the Southern Frontier from the First Transmontane Beginnings to the Civil War* (New York, 1948); Grady McWhiney's controversial *Cracker Culture: Celtic Ways in the Old South* (Tuscaloosa, Ala., 1988); Charles C. Bolton, *Poor Whites of the Antebellum South: Tenants and Laborers in Central North Carolina and Northeast Mississippi* (Durham, N.C., 1994), which makes grand claims on limited evidence; and Edward Magdol and Jon Wakelyn, eds., *The Southern Common People: Studies in Nineteenth-Century Social History* (Westport, Conn., 1980), a collection of informative articles. In his first-rate *Plain Folk and Gentry in a Slave Society: White Liberty and Black Slavery in Augusta's Hinterlands* (Middletown, Conn., 1985), J. William Harris found unity dominant, as did Bill Cecil-Fronsman, *Common Whites: Class and Culture in Antebellum North Carolina* (Lexington, Ky., 1992). No student of the antebellum South should overlook two books by southerners of the era: Hinton R. Helper, *The Impending Crisis of the South: How to Meet It,* ed. George Fredrickson (Cambridge, Mass., 1968), condemned the regime, while Daniel R. Hundley, *Social Relations in Our Southern*

States, ed. William Cooper (Baton Rouge, La., 1979), presented it in a positive fashion. Mills Lane's *Architecture of the Antebellum South* and Jessie Poesch's *Art of the Old South* contribute to an understanding of the architectural environment.

Important books that probe critical dimensions of southern society include W. J. Cash's unique and remarkable *Mind of the South* (New York, 1941); Fred Hobson's intriguing *Tell about the South: The Southern Rage to Explain* (Baton Rouge, La., 1983); John M. McCardell's suggestive *Idea of a Southern Nation: Southern Nationalists and Southern Nationalism, 1830–1860* (New York, 1979); William R. Taylor's imaginative *Cavalier and Yankee: The Old South and American National Character* (New York, 1961); and Bertram Wyatt-Brown's provocative *Southern Honor: Ethics and Behavior in the Old South* (New York, 1982).

Many other books contribute to an understanding of southern society. The most worthy of them include Barbara L. Bellows, *Benevolence among Slaveholders: Assisting the Poor in Charleston, 1670–1860* (Baton Rouge, La., 1993), which considers a woefully neglected topic; Dickson Bruce, *Violence and Culture in the Antebellum South* (Austin, Tex., 1979); John Hope Franklin, *A Southern Odyssey: Travelers in the Antebellum North* (Baton Rouge, La., 1976), a study of southern travelers reacting to the North, and *The Militant South, 1800–1861* (Cambridge, Mass., 1956); Guion G. Johnson, *Antebellum North Carolina: A Social History* (Chapel Hill, N.C., 1937); Rollin G. Osterweis, *Romanticism and Nationalism in the Old South* (New Haven, Conn., 1949); Rosser H. Taylor, *Antebellum South Carolina: A Social and Cultural History* (Chapel Hill, N.C., 1942); and Jack K. Williams, *Dueling in the Old South: Vignettes of Social History* (College Station, Tex., 1980).

Women have not until recently begun to receive the scholarly attention they deserve. The starting point for consideration of women is Anne F. Scott, *The Southern Lady: From Pedestal to Politics, 1830–1930* (Chicago, 1970), the first modern treatment. Since then a number of historians have been mining the substantial archival materials on women in the antebellum South. Catherine Clinton, *The Plantation Mistress: Woman's World in the Old South* (New York, 1982), concentrates entirely on the mistresses of large plantations along the seaboard. A local study is Suzanne Lebsock, *The Free Women of Petersburg: Status and Culture in a Southern Town, 1784–1860* (New York, 1984). Bertram Wyatt-Brown's *Southern Honor* discusses insightfully the place and role of women in antebellum southern society. Elizabeth Fox-Genovese, *Within the Plantation Household: Black and White Women of the Old South* (Chapel Hill, N.C., 1988), with a strong theoretical dimension, and George C. Rable, *Civil Wars: Women in the Crisis of Southern Nationalism* (Urbana, Ill., 1989), provide superb in-depth coverage.

Historians continue to investigate largely unexplored areas. Such studies include: Victoria E. Bynum, *Unruly Women: The Politics of Sexual and Social Control in the Old South* (Chapel Hill, N.C., 1992), with a somewhat misleading title, for it is really about three North Carolina counties; Christie A. Farnham, *The Education of the Southern Belle: Higher Education and Student Socialization in the Antebellum South* (New York, 1994); Sally G. McMillen, *Motherhood in the Old South: Pregnancy, Childbirth, and Infant Rearing* (Baton Rouge, La., 1990); Elizabeth Moss, *Domestic Novelists in the Old South: Defenders of Southern Culture* (Baton Rouge, La., 1992).

Other books that emphasize the family are Carol Bleser, ed., *In Joy and Sorrow: Women, Family and Marriage in the Victorian South, 1830–1900* (New York, 1991), a collection focusing on individual marriages; Orville V. Burton, *In My Father's House Are Many Mansions: Family and Community in Edgefield, South Carolina* (Chapel Hill, N.C., 1985); Joan E. Cashin, *A Family Venture: Men and Women on the Southern Frontier* (New York, 1991); Jane T. Censer, *North Carolina Planters and Their Children, 1800–1860* (Baton Rouge, La., 1984); Robert C. Kenzer, *Kinship and Neighborhood in a Southern Community: Orange County, North Carolina, 1849–1881* (Knoxville, Tenn., 1987); Jan Lewis, *The Pursuit of Happiness: Family and Values in Jefferson's Virginia* (New York, 1983); and Steven M. Stowe, *Intimacy and Power in the Old South: Ritual in the Lives of the Planters* (Baltimore, 1987). Sally McMillen has a succinct synthesis of current scholarship in *Southern Women: Black and White in the Old South* (Arlington Heights, Ill., 1992).

On free blacks, Ira Berlin, *Slaves without Masters: The Free Negro in the Antebellum South* (New York, 1974), is an excellent general treatment. Two meritorious books on unusual individuals illuminate the complex, precarious world of the free black: Michael P. Johnson and James L. Roark, *Black Masters: A Free Family of Color in the Old South* (New York, 1984), and Gary B. Mills, *The Forgotten People: Cane River's Creoles of Color* (Baton Rouge, La., 1977). Also see Letitia W. Brown, *Free Negroes in the District of Columbia, 1790–1846* (New York, 1972); Edwin Davis and William R. Hogan, *The Barber of Natchez* (Baton Rouge, La., 1954); John Hope Franklin, *The Free Negro in North Carolina, 1790–1860* (Chapel Hill, N.C., 1943); Luther P. Jackson, *Free Negro Labor and Property Holding in Virginia, 1830–1860* (New York, 1942); Larry Koger, *Black Slaveowners: Free Black Masters in South Carolina, 1790–1860*, rpt. ed. (Columbia, S.C., 1995); Loren Schweninger, *Black Property Owners in the South, 1790–1915* (Urbana, Ill., 1990); Herbert E. Sterkx, *The Free Negro in Antebellum Louisiana* (Rutherford, N.J., 1972); and Marina Wikramanayake, *A World in Shadow: The Free Black in Antebellum South Carolina* (Columbia, S.C., 1973).

Published source materials provide invaluable assistance in assessing the free people in southern society. Many of the items listed in the section "Farms and Plantations, Masters and Slaves" are certainly appropriate here. For other helpful titles consult William Hogan and Edwin Davis, eds., *William Johnson's Natchez: The Ante-Bellum Diary of a Free Negro* (Baton Rouge, La., 1951); Michael Johnson and James Roark, eds., *No Chariot Let Down: Charleston's Free People of Color on the Eve of the Civil War* (Chapel Hill, N.C., 1984); Philip N. Racine, ed., *Piedmont Farmer: The Journals of David Golightly Harris, 1855–1870* (Knoxville, Tenn., 1990); Allie B. W. Webb, ed., *Mistress of Evergreen Plantation: Rachel O'Connor's Legacy of Letters, 1823–1845* (Albany, N.Y., 1983).

*T*HE SECTIONAL CRISIS AND THE CONFEDERACY

On the southern economy Gavin Wright's *Political Economy of the Cotton South* is helpful. Although much work remains to be done, several important books investigate the industrial sector of that economy and analyze public policy. See Fred Bateman and Thomas Weiss, *A Deplorable Scarcity: The Failure of Industrialization in the Slave Economy* (Chapel Hill, N.C., 1981), and Laurence Shore, *Southern Capitalists: The Ideological Leadership of an Elite, 1832–1885* (Chapel Hill, N.C., 1986). In his *Banking in the American South from the Age of Jackson to Reconstruction* (Baton Rouge, La., 1987), Larry Schweikart argues that southern banks assisted economic development and growth. Vicki V. Johnson, *The Men and the Vision of the Southern Commercial Conventions, 1845–1871* (Columbia, Mo., 1992), addresses a surprisingly neglected subject. Worthy state studies include George D. Green, *Finance and Economic Development in the Old South: Louisiana Banking, 1804–1861* (Stanford, Calif., 1972); Milton S. Heath, *Constructive Liberalism: The Role of the State in Economic Development in Georgia to 1860* (Cambridge, Mass., 1954); Alfred Smith, *Economic Readjustment of an Old Cotton State;* and Peter Wallenstein, *From Slave South to New South: Public Policy in Nineteenth-Century Georgia* (Chapel Hill, N.C., 1987).

For individual industries and industrialists, consult James P. Baughman, *Charles Morgan and the Development of Southern Transportation* (Nashville, Tenn., 1968); Kathleen Bruce, *Virginia Iron Manufacture in the Slave Era* (New York, 1932); Ernest M. Lander, Jr., *The Textile Industry in Antebellum South Carolina* (Baton Rouge, La., 1969); Randall M. Miller, *The Cotton Mill Movement in Antebellum Alabama* (New York, 1978); John Moore, *Andrew Brown and Cypress Lumbering in the Old Southwest* (Baton Rouge, La., 1967); Merl E. Reed, *New Orleans and*

the Railroads: The Struggle for Commercial Empire (Baton Rouge, La., 1966); and Allen W. Tre-
lease, *The North Carolina Railroad, 1849–1871 and the Modernization of North Carolina* (Chapel
Hill, N.C., 1991).

Four useful titles on cities are Blaine A. Brownell and David R. Goldfield, eds., *The City
in Southern History: The Growth of Urban Civilization in the South* (Port Washington, N.Y.,
1977), a collection of helpful articles; David Goldfield, *Urban Growth in the Age of Sectionalism: Virginia, 1847–1861* (Baton Rouge, La., 1977) and *Cotton Fields and Skyscrapers: Southern
City and Region, 1607–1980,* rev. ed. (Baltimore, 1989); and Lawrence H. Larsen, *The Rise of
the Urban South* (Lexington, Ky., 1985). For specific locations, consult Harriet E. Amos, *Cotton City: Urban Development in Antebellum Mobile* (University, Ala., 1985); D. Clayton James,
Antebellum Natchez (Baton Rouge, La., 1968); James M. Russell, *Atlanta, 1847–1890: City
Building in the Old South and the New* (Baton Rouge, La., 1988); and Kenneth W. Wheeler, *To
Wear a City's Crown: The Beginnings of Urban Growth in Texas, 1836–1865* (Cambridge, Mass.,
1966).

The sectional conflict between 1845 and 1861 has stimulated a number of major studies
in which southern developments occupy a prominent place. Consult Allan Nevin's magnificent *Ordeal of the Union,* 2 vols. (New York, 1947) and *The Emergence of Lincoln,* 2 vols.
(New York, 1950); Roy F. Nichols's impressive *Disruption of American Democracy* (New York,
1948); and David M. Potter's superlative *Impending Crisis, 1848–1861,* completed by Don
Fehrenbacher (New York, 1976). Michael F. Holt takes a bold and imaginative look at the
final antebellum decade in *The Political Crisis of the 1850s* (New York, 1978). A straightforward, now-dated account focusing on southern opinion, especially newspaper opinion, is
Avery O. Craven, *The Growth of Southern Nationalism, 1848–1861* (Baton Rouge, La., 1953).
Recent brief surveys are Roger L. Ransom, *Conflict and Compromise: The Political Economy of
Slavery, Emancipation, and the Civil War* (New York, 1989), with emphasis on economics
broadly viewed, and Richard W. Sewell, *A House Divided: Sectionalism and Civil War,
1848–1865* (Baltimore, 1988).

Best on the Mexican War is K. Jack Bauer, *The Mexican War, 1846–1848* (New York,
1974). Robert Johannsen, *To the Halls of Montezuma: The Mexican War in the American Imagination* (New York, 1985), analyzes the American, including southern, reaction to Mexico. In
a tidy little book, *Reluctant Imperialists: Calhoun, the South Carolinians, and the Mexican War*
(Baton Rouge, La., 1980), Ernest Lander discovered a dearth of enthusiasm for war in the
state supposedly the most hot-blooded.

The great question of slavery and the territories has been a central theme. William
Cooper, *Politics of Slavery,* provides a thorough treatment that relates ideological founda-
tions to political manifestations. In addition to the books already cited on the 1845–1861 pe-
riod, see also Don Fehrenbacher, *South and Three Sectional Crises;* William Freehling, *Road to
Disunion;* Eugene Genovese, *Political Economy of Slavery;* Holman Hamilton, *The Crisis and
Compromise of 1850* (Lexington, Ky., 1964); Frederick Merk, *Slavery and the Annexation of
Texas* (New York, 1972); Chaplain Morrison, *Democratic Politics and Sectionalism: The Wilmot
Proviso Controversy* (Chapel Hill, N.C., 1967); James Oakes, *Ruling Race* and *Slavery and Free-
dom;* Gerald W. Wolff, *The Kansas-Nebraska Bill: Party, Section, and the Coming of the Civil War*
(New York, 1977). Don Fehrenbacher has a superb discussion of the legal and constitu-
tional issues in *The Dred Scott Case: Its Significance in American Law and Politics* (New York,
1978). On key events during the crisis of 1850, consult John Barnwell, *Love of Order: South
Carolina's First Secession Crisis* (Chapel Hill, N.C., 1982), and Thelma N. Jennings, *The
Nashville Convention: Southern Movement for Unity, 1848–1851* (Memphis, Tenn., 1980). Details on Kansas can be found in James Rawley, *Race and Politics: "Bleeding Kansas" and the
Coming of the Civil War* (Philadelphia, 1969), and Kenneth Stampp, *America in 1857: A Nation
on the Brink* (New York, 1990), which has considerable detail on Lecompton.

On the individual states, consult the state studies cited above on page 378. W. Darrel

Overdyke, *The Know-Nothing Party in the South* (Baton Rouge, La., 1950), though dated, is the only general study of that phenomenon. Local studies are not plentiful, but see Jean H. Baker, *Ambivalent Americans: The Know-Nothing Party in Maryland* (Baltimore, 1975), and Leon C. Soule, *The Know-Nothing Party in New Orleans* (Baton Rouge, La., 1961).

Several studies emphasize the minority of southerners who were determined to expand the South's boundaries in a southerly direction and those few who agitated for a renewal of the international slave trade: Charles A. Brown, *Agents of Manifest Destiny: The Lives and Times of the Filibusters* (Chapel Hill, N.C., 1980); Robert May, *The Southern Dream of a Caribbean Empire, 1854–1861* (Baton Rouge, La., 1973); and Ronald T. Takaki, *A Pro-Slavery Crusade: The Agitation to Reopen the African Slave Trade* (New York, 1971).

Secession remains a most vexing question. Although scholars have been scrutinizing secession for many years, no general treatment has yet replaced Dwight L. Dumond's still useful *The Secession Movement, 1860–1861* (New York, 1931), but see William L. Barney, *The Road to Secession: A New Perspective on the Old South* (New York, 1972). Ralph Wooster, *The Secession Conventions of the South* (Princeton, N.J., 1962), charts convention membership. The two most recent overviews present conflicting interpretations: William Cooper, *Liberty and Slavery,* and Michael Holt, *Political Crisis.* An important book on the upper South is Daniel Crofts, *Reluctant Confederates: Upper South Unionists in the Secession Crisis* (Chapel Hill, N.C., 1989). The best of the state studies once again are Lacey Ford, *Origins of Southern Radicalism* and Mills Thornton, *Politics and Power.* Eric Walther, *The Fire-Eaters* (Baton Rouge, La., 1992), is an excellent commentary on the sectional radicals. Other worthy monographs are Jean Baker, *The Politics of Continuity: Maryland Political Parties from 1858 to 1870* (Baltimore, 1973); William Barney, *The Secessionist Impulse: Alabama and Mississippi in 1860* (Princeton, N.J., 1974); Walter L. Buenger, *Secession and the Union in Texas* (Austin, Tex., 1984); Steven Channing, *Crisis of Fear: Secession in South Carolina* (New York, 1970); William J. Evitts, *A Matter of Allegiances: Maryland, 1850–1861* (Baltimore, 1974); Thomas Jeffrey, *State Parties and National Politics;* Michael Johnson, *Toward a Patriarchal Republic: The Secession of Georgia* (Baton Rouge, La., 1977); Marc Kruman, *Parties and Politics in North Carolina;* Harold S. Schultz, *Nationalism and Sectionalism in South Carolina, 1852–1860: A Study of the Movement for Southern Independence* (Durham, N.C., 1950); Joseph Sitterson, *The Secession Movement in North Carolina* (Chapel Hill, N.C., 1939); and James M. Woods, *Rebellion and Realignment: Arkansas's Road to Secession* (Fayetteville, Ark., 1987).

For understanding the party that most of the white South perceived as the great enemy, these volumes are essential: Eric Foner, *Free Soil, Free Labor, Free Men: The Ideology of the Republican Party before the Civil War* (New York, 1970), on ideology; William W. Gienapp, *The Origins of the Republican Party, 1852–1856* (New York, 1987), on party formation; David Potter, *Lincoln and His Party in the Secession Crisis* (New Haven, Conn., 1962) and Kenneth Stampp, *And the War Came: The North and Secession Crisis, 1860–1861* (Baton Rouge, La., 1950), on the secession crisis.

Books on the Civil War and the Confederacy are legion. Richard N. Current et al., eds., *Encyclopedia of the Confederacy,* 4 vols. (New York, 1993), provides brief introductions to an immense number of topics. Allan Nevins's *War for the Union,* 4 vols. (New York, 1959–1971), is history in the grand manner. For a superb but much briefer account, see James M. McPherson, *Battle Cry of Freedom: The Civil War Era* (New York, 1988), which concentrates on the war years. Charles Royster, *The Destructive War: William Tecumseh Sherman, Stonewall Jackson, and the Americans* (New York, 1991), powerfully probes the question of why Americans pursued such a violent course against each other. On the Confederacy, two general studies provide good starting points: E. Merton Coulter's detailed *Confederate States of America, 1861–1865* (Baton Rouge, La., 1950), and Emory M. Thomas's more interpretive *Confederate Nation, 1861–1865* (New York, 1979). Shelby Foote's magnificent *The Civil War: A Narrative,* 3 vols. (New York, 1958–1974), is a beautifully written narrative with a broad sweep. Drew Faust, *The Creation of Confederate Nationalism: Ideology and Identity in the Civil War South* (Baton Rouge, La., 1988), is an intelligent inquiry into a difficult subject.

The political history of the Confederacy has not generally been well served by historians. Two notable exceptions are Kenneth C. Martis's invaluable *The Historical Atlas of the Congresses of the Confederate States of America: 1861–1865* (New York, 1994) and George Rable's pathbreaking *Confederate Republic: A Revolution against Politics* (Chapel Hill, N.C., 1994). Additional worthy studies are Thomas Alexander and Richard E. Beringer's meticulous *Anatomy of the Confederate Congress: A Study of the Influence of Member Characteristics on Legislative Voting Behavior, 1861–1865* (Nashville, Tenn., 1972); William Davis, *"A Government of Our Own": The Making of the Confederacy* (New York, 1994), which details the crucial early months in Montgomery; and Paul Escott's suggestive *After Secession: Jefferson Davis and the Failure of Confederate Nationalism* (Baton Rouge, La., 1978). Also see Douglas B. Ball, *Financial Failure and Confederate Defeat* (Urbana, Ill., 1991); Albert B. Moore, *Conscription and Conflict in the Confederacy* (New York, 1924); Frank Owsley, *State Rights in the Confederacy* (Chicago, 1925); Rembert W. Patrick, *Jefferson Davis and His Cabinet* (Baton Rouge, La., 1944); May S. Ringold, *The Role of the State Legislatures in the Confederacy* (Athens, Ga., 1966); William M. Robinson, Jr., *Justice in Grey: A History of the Judicial System of the Confederate States of America* (Cambridge, Mass., 1941); and Richard C. Todd, *Confederate Finance* (Athens, Ga., 1954). John C. Schwab's *Confederate States of America, 1861–1865: A Financial and Industrial History of the South during the Civil War* (New York, 1901) has still not been completely replaced.

On Confederate diplomacy, the standard work is Frank Owsley, *King Cotton Diplomacy: Foreign Relations of the Confederate States of America* (Chicago, 1959); see also Lynn M. Case and Warren F. Spencer, *The United States and France: Civil War Diplomacy* (Philadelphia, 1970); D. P. Crook, *Diplomacy during the American Civil War* (New York, 1975); and Howard Jones, *Union in Peril: The Crisis over British Intervention in the Civil War* (Chapel Hill, N.C., 1992).

On the civilian front, Charles W. Ramsdell, *Behind the Lines in the Southern Confederacy* (Baton Rouge, La., 1944), is still valuable. Other worthy titles are Mary A. DeCredico, *Patriotism for Profit: Georgia's Urban Entrepreneurs and the Confederate War Effort* (Chapel Hill, N.C., 1990); Wayne K. Durrill, *War of Another Kind: A Southern Community in the Great Rebellion* (New York, 1990); Gardiner H. Shattuck, Jr., *A Shield and Hiding Place: The Religious Life of Civil War Armies* (Macon, Ga., 1987); James W. Silver, *Confederate Morale and Church Propaganda* (Tuscaloosa, Ala., 1957); and Bell I. Wiley, *The Road to Appomattox* (New York, 1968). For the story of women, George Rable, *Civil Wars,* is best; also see Mary Elizabeth Massey, *Bonnet Brigades* (New York, 1966), and Bell Wiley, *Confederate Women* (Westport, Conn., 1975).

Books on individual states usually address economic, political, and social as well as military topics. They include John G. Barrett, *The Civil War in North Carolina* (Chapel Hill, N.C., 1963); John K. Bettersworth, *Confederate Mississippi: The People and Policies of a Cotton State in Wartime* (Baton Rouge, La., 1943); T. Conn Bryan, *Confederate Georgia* (Athens, Ga., 1953); Charles E. Cauthen, *South Carolina Goes to War, 1861–1865* (Chapel Hill, N.C., 1950); John E. Johns, *Florida during the Civil War* (Gainesville, Fla., 1963); and John D. Winters, *The Civil War in Louisiana* (Baton Rouge, La., 1963).

Several interesting books discuss the questions the war raised for masters and slaves. Bell Wiley, *Southern Negroes, 1861–1865* (New Haven, Conn., 1938), was for many years the standard account and still has great value. Robert Durden, *The Gray and the Black: The Confederate Debate on Emancipation* (Baton Rouge, La., 1972), focuses on the emancipation issue. Leon F. Litwack, *Been in the Storm So Long: The Aftermath of Slavery* (New York, 1979), tells the story of the slaves' response to freedom, while James Roark, *Masters without Slaves: Southern Planters in the Civil War and Reconstruction* (New York, 1977), delineates the slave owners' response to emancipation. For the story in four locations, see John Cimprich, *Slavery's End in Tennessee, 1861–1865* (University, Ala., 1985); Clarence L. Mohr, *On the Threshold of Freedom: Masters and Slaves in Civil War Georgia* (Athens, Ga., 1986); Janet Hermann, *The Pursuit of a Dream* (New York, 1981); and Willie Lee Rose's masterful *Rehearsal for Reconstruction: The Port Royal Experiment* (Indianapolis, Ind., 1964). Winthrop Jordan has an intriguing investigation of a possible slave conspiracy, *Tumult and Silence at Second Creek: An Inquiry into a Civil War Slave Conspiracy* (Baton Rouge, La., 1991).

On the military history of the Confederacy the books have no end. Here we will point only to those that deal with major topics. On the war in the east, Douglas Freeman's *R. E. Lee* and his superlative history of the Army of Northern Virginia, *Lee's Lieutenants: A Study in Command,* 3 vols. (New York, 1942–1944), are the best overall. On the western war, Thomas L. Connelly has two excellent volumes on the Army of Tennessee: *Army of the Heartland: The Army of Tennessee, 1861–1862* (Baton Rouge, La., 1967) and *Autumn of Glory: The Army of Tennessee, 1862–1865* (Baton Rouge, La., 1971). For the often-forgotten Trans-Mississippi theater, consult Albert Castel, *General Sterling Price and the Civil War in the West* (Baton Rouge, La., 1968); Alvin M. Josephy, Jr., *The Civil War in the American West* (New York, 1991); and Robert L. Kerby, *Kirby-Smith's Confederacy: The Trans-Mississippi South, 1863–1865* (New York, 1972). Michael Fellman, *Inside War: The Guerrilla Conflict in Missouri during the American Civil War* (New York, 1989), looks at a brutal struggle. Richard M. McMurry, *Two Great Rebel Armies: An Essay in Confederate Military History* (Chapel Hill, N.C., 1989), compares the two most significant Confederate field armies.

On Confederate command and strategy, see Thomas Connelly and Archer Jones, *The Politics of Command: Factions and Ideas in Confederate Strategy* (Baton Rouge, La., 1973); Archer Jones, *Civil War Command and Strategy: The Process of Victory and Defeat* (New York, 1992) and *Confederate Strategy from Shiloh to Vicksburg* (Baton Rouge, La., 1961); Alan T. Nolan, *Lee Considered: General Robert E. Lee and Civil War History* (Chapel Hill, N.C., 1991); Frank Vandiver, *Rebel Brass: The Confederate Command System* (Baton Rouge, La., 1956); Steven E. Woodworth, *Jefferson Davis and His Generals: The Failure of Confederate Command in the West* (Lawrence, Kans., 1990). Bell Wiley's classic *Life of Johnny Reb: The Common Soldier of the Confederacy* (Indianapolis, Ind., 1943) tells the story of the private soldier, as does James I. Robertson's *Soldiers Blue and Gray* (Columbia, S.C., 1988). James McPherson, *What They Fought For, 1861–1865* (Baton Rouge, La., 1994), concentrates on the reasons soldiers gave for fighting. For the revolution in weaponry and the reality of combat, see Gerald F. Linderman, *Embattled Courage: The Experience of Combat in the American Civil War* (New York, 1987); Grady McWhiney and Perry D. Jamieson, *Attack and Die: Civil War Military Tactics and the Southern Heritage* (University, Ala., 1982); and Reid Mitchell, *Civil War Soldiers* (New York, 1988). Virgil C. Jones has written the fullest account of the naval war, *The Civil War at Sea,* 3 vols. (New York, 1960–1962). On the epochal *Monitor-Virginia* battle, see William Davis, *Duel between the First Ironclads* (New York, 1975). A recent attempt to explain the defeat of the Confederacy, Richard Beringer et al., *Why the South Lost the Civil War* (Athens, Ga., 1986), is not convincing. That same issue is probed without agreement by several historians in Gabor Boritt, ed., *Why the Confederacy Lost* (New York, 1992).

Published primary materials are extraordinarily rich for the late antebellum and Confederate years. The chief works include John Q. Anderson, ed., *Brokenburn: The Journal of Kate Stone, 1861–1868* (Baton Rouge, La., 1972); Ira Berlin et al., eds., *Freedom: A Documentary History of Emancipation, 1861–1867. . .,* 4 vols. to date (New York, 1982–   ); *Congressional Globe,* for congressional debates; Lynda L. Crist et al., eds., *The Papers of Jefferson Davis,* 8 vols. to date (Baton Rouge, La., 1971–   ); E. Merton Coulter, *Travels in the Confederate States: A Bibliography* (Norman, Okla., 1948), the guide to travel accounts; Clifford Dowdey, ed., *The Wartime Papers of R. E. Lee* (Boston, 1961); Dwight Dumond, ed., *Southern Editorials on Secession* (New York, 1931); Charles East, ed., *The Civil War Diary of Sarah Morgan* (Athens,

Ga., 1991); Le Roy P. Graf et al., *The Papers of Andrew Johnson*, 11 vols. to date (Knoxville, Tenn., 1967–   ); Robert U. Johnson and Clarence C. Buel, eds., *Battles and Leaders of the Civil War*, 4 vols. (New York, 1888), the finest compilation of accounts by participants; J. B. Jones, *A Rebel War Clerk's Diary at the Confederate States Capital*, 2 vols. (Philadelphia, 1866); *Journal of the Congress of the Confederate States of America, 1861–1865*, 7 vols. (Washington, D.C., 1904–1905), which contains a record of legislative activities but no speeches; Albert Kirwan, ed., *The Confederacy* (Cleveland, Ohio, 1959), a convenient collection of documents on diverse subjects; John F. Marszalek, ed., *The Diary of Miss Emma Holmes, 1861–1866* (Baton Rouge, La., 1979); Robert Myers, ed., *The Children of Pride; Official Records of the Union and Confederate Navies in the War of the Rebellion*, 30 vols. (Washington, D.C., 1894–1922), the basic published documentary record of the naval war; Ulrich Phillips, ed., *Correspondence of Robert Toombs, Alexander Stephens, and Howell Cobb* (Washington, D.C., 1913); James D. Richardson, ed., *A Compilation of the Messages and Papers of the Confederacy, Including the Diplomatic Correspondence, 1861–1865*, 2 vols. (Nashville, Tenn., 1906); Dunbar Rowland, ed., *Jefferson Davis, Constitutionalist: His Letters, Papers, and Speeches*, 10 vols. (Jackson, Miss., 1923); William Scarborough, ed., *The Diary of Edmund Ruffin*, 3 vols. (Baton Rouge, La., 1972–1989); *War of the Rebellion: A Compilation of the Official Records of the Union and Confederate Armies*, 128 vols. (Washington, D.C., 1880–1901), the basic published documentary record of the land war; C. Vann Woodward, ed., *Mary Chesnut's Civil War* (New Haven, Conn., 1981) and Woodward and Elisabeth Muhlenfeld, eds., *The Private Mary Chesnut: The Unpublished Civil War Diaries* (New York, 1984).

Index

Index